State and Local Government

State and Local Government

SECOND EDITION

Ann O'M. Bowman

University of South Carolina

Richard C. Kearney

University of Connecticut

Houghton Mifflin Company   Boston   Toronto

Dallas   Geneva, Illinois   Palo Alto   Princeton, New Jersey

To those who do, from those who teach.
And especially for Rachel, Roxanne, and Joel.

Sponsoring Editor: Margaret H. Seawell
Senior Development Editor: Frances Gay
Project Editor: Christina Horn
Senior Production/Design Coordinator: Renée Le Verrier
Senior Manufacturing Coordinator: Priscilla Bailey
Marketing Manager: Karen Natale

Cover photograph: Illinois State Capitol, Springfield.
                      The Image Bank/Tim Biever
Cover design: Ron Kosciak

(Illustration credits continue on page R-28.)

Printed in the U.S.A.

Library of Congress Catalog Card Number: 92-72368

ISBN:
Student text: 0-395-63845-3
Examination text: 0-395-66385-7

23456789-DH-96 95 94 93

Contents

Preface

S
tate and local government is a fascinating and exciting subject to study and teach. In spite of the "Great Recession" of 1990–1992, and even as the national government confronts massive budget deficits, the vitality and problem-solving capacity of state and local governments continues to grow. The states and localities of this country represent the best hope for the United States to remain a world economic power and an example of democracy.

Ironically, the troubles in Washington, D.C., seriously threaten the resurgence in state and local government. With less financial aid and leadership from the federal government, "fend for yourself federalism" has become more than a catch phrase. And, meanwhile, seemingly intractable problems plague government decision makers at all levels—ineffectual schools, drug-related crime and health problems, prison overcrowding, and environmental degradation, to name just a few.

In the second edition of this text we attempt to capture the immediacy and vitality of state and local governments as they courageously attack the problems of the 1990s. A major goal is to foster a continuing student interest and involvement in state and local politics and policy. We know that many of the students who read this book will work in state or local government in some capacity. We want them to know that it is a place where one person can still make a difference, and serve a cause rather than a corporation. For those who go on to graduate study in political science or public administration, it is a fertile field for study and research.

The Theme of State and Local Government

The book revolves around a central theme: the increased capacity of state and local governments to function effectively in the years ahead. From one end of the country to the other, state and local governments have restructured their institutions, increased their accessibility to citizens, and developed innovative strategies for tackling tough public problems. These are the same levels of government routinely dismissed as outmoded and ineffective a mere two decades ago.

Our confidence in these governments does not blind us, however, to the varying capabilities of the fifty states and the more than 84,000 units of local government. Some are better equipped to function effectively than others. Some state and local governments benefit from talented leadership, enjoy a healthy economy, and are populated by an active citizenry. Others do not fare so well. The important point is that, as a group, state and local governments have moved to a higher plane. Even those states and communities perennially clustered at the lower end of various scales have made quantum leaps in their capability.

....

Changes in the Second Edition

The political landscape of state and local government is changing rapidly. Throughout the second edition we have incorporated new topics and emerging issues while maintaining the basic themes and chapter arrangement. For this edition, we have focused the central theme of the book even more on the increased pressures on state and local government in difficult economic times and the creative ways that they are responding to these challenges.

New "Problem Solving" boxes give examples of many solutions to problems faced by state and local governments around the country. The box in Chapter 2 discusses the initiatives taken by state and local governments to promote foreign trade. In Chapter 3, one of the boxes describes Oregon's approach to controlling medical costs. The box in Chapter 6 describes local efforts to reform negative campaign advertising. One of the boxes in Chapter 7 discusses approaches governors have used to deal with fiscal problems. The boxes in Chapter 8 on Total Quality Management and Enterprise Management describe techniques to improve the efficiency and productivity of state and local bureaucracies. The box in Chapter 12 presents new reform efforts to promote entrepreneurial government that is innovative and market oriented. And a box in Chapter 14 describes efforts to cool off overheated growth without stifling it. These are just a few of the examples of innovative solutions presented in these boxes.

In addition, all chapters have been thoroughly updated. In Chapter 1, "New Directions in State and Local Government," for example, we include population shifts across the country from 1980 to 1990. As in the first edition, this book provides thorough coverage of state and local institutions, processes, and policies. For example, federalism's central importance is recognized in two chapters. Chapter 2 traces the development of the federal system, and Chapter 3 links contemporary intergovernmental relations with higher education and social welfare policy, giving practical application to theoretical concepts. In Chapter 3, we have included a new section on Bush's approach to federalism and a new section on congressional mandates, pre-emptions, and set-asides in legislation dealing with state governments. The chapter also discusses the issue of increased Medicaid and health care costs and ways states have tried to deal with them.

In Chapter 5, "Participation and Interest Groups," the section on initiatives has been updated and new research on interest groups included. New uses of technology in polling are also described. Chapter 6, "Political Parties, Campaigns, and Elections," has been reorganized and updated, and it includes state elections from 1988 to the 1990s.

The text examines the three branches of state government—the executive, legislative, and judicial—with an eye on their performance. In Chapter 8, "The

Bureaucracy,'' downsizing, rightsizing, and new ways of delivering services are included, and the section on sexual harassment has been updated. Chapter 9, on state legislatures, discusses the movement for term limitations and the challenges of redistricting in accordance with the 1990 census.

Local governments, although creatures of the state in many ways, are not treated as afterthoughts. Two chapters concentrate on localities—Chapter 11 is devoted to the types and structures of local government and Chapter 12 to leadership. We have included a new section on land use and zoning to Chapter 11 and added more material on women and blacks in local government to Chapter 12. State-local relations are the subject of two other chapters, and localities are also brought in when appropriate throughout the book. We have reversed the order of Chapters 13 and 14 for this edition, so that "State-Local Relations" now comes first, followed by "State and Local Finance." The fiscal stress of 1990–1992 is a major theme of Chapter 14, and a minor undercurrent running throughout the book.

Four policy chapters illustrate the theme of increased state and local government capacity. In preparing for the second edition, we considered whether to change any or all of the policy issues we covered in the first edition—education, economic development, criminal justice, and environmental issues. We ultimately decided, however, that these are still by far the most salient policy issues facing state and local governments today, and so we stayed with them.

Two of the policy topics, education and criminal justice, have offered challenges to state and local governments for more than two hundred years. In the 1990s, states and school districts are experimenting with a variety of educational innovations such as voucher systems and magnet schools. For this edition, we have also included new material on the involvement of the business community in public schools. In criminal justice, the privatization of prisons and new strategies for sentencing and releasing criminals enliven the policy arena. The chapter also includes new material on community policing.

The other two policy chapters, economic development and environmental policy, present powerful and compelling issues for the future. The significance of economic development to nonnational governments is evident as governors embark on international trade missions and as local officials offer lucrative incentive packages to entice new industry. This chapter has been revised for this edition. It includes a revised section on approaches to economic development and new sections on the promotion of travel and tourism, the arts, and sports. And although the national government often dominates environmental policymaking, state and local governments are leaving their indelible marks in this field as well. In this chapter, we have included new decentralized solutions to environmental problems.

Features of the Text

Several features make the book accessible to the reader. Each chapter opens with an outline and closes with a summary. A future-oriented conclusion focuses on the theme of government capacity. In addition to the Problem Solving boxes, some chapters have Profile boxes that focus on a particular group or jurisdiction. For example, in Chapter 11, a Profile box relates how and why Florida made Disney World a special district. Photographs and cartoons help bring the world of state and local government to life for students. Maps, tables, and figures provide up-to-date information in an engaging format.

A glossary of key terms is located in the margins of the text. In addition, a very helpful *Instructor's Resource Manual with Test Items,* written by Professor Harold B. Birch, is available to the instructor. The manual, which is classroom tested by Professor Birch, features learning objectives, an overview of each chapter, suggested lecture topics and readings, multiple-choice questions, terms for identification, and essay questions.

....

Acknowledgments

The book has benefited from the reactions and recommendations of helpful reviewers who, from their vantage points around the country, often reminded us that not all states and localities operate similarly. We thank the following:

Thad Beyle, University of North Carolina at Chapel Hill
Alan R. Carter, Schenectady County Community College
Richard T. Conboy, Lake Superior State University
Eugene P. Dvorin, California State University, Los Angeles
Michael P. Federici, Concord College
James R. Forrester, West Liberty State College
Gary Halter, Texas A&M University
Thomas M. Holbrook, University of Wisconsin, Milwaukee
Steven G. Koven, Iowa State University
Martin P. Sutton, Bucks County Community College
Clive S. Thomas, University of Alaska, Juneau

A great many people helped bring the second edition of *State and Local Government* into print. At Houghton Mifflin, Margaret Seawell, Frances Gay, and Celena Sun deserve special thanks, and Christina Horn, who has worked on both editions, warrants extra special thanks. Research assistance was provided by Jeff Greene and John Cavanaugh at The University of South Carolina and by Kelly McInerney and Stacia Smith at The University of Connecticut. Rick Kearney appreciates word processing assistance by Eppie Azzaretto. Both of us would like to thank Chuck Kegley, who contributed professional advice and counseling for both editions of the text. Finally, Carson, Joel, and Kathy contributed in special ways to the final product.

A.O'M.B.
R.C.K.

State and Local Government

New Directions for State and Local Government

Fifty states—it has a nice round-number ring to it. Of course, after New Mexico and Arizona were admitted to the Union in 1912, the number of states was a decidedly non-round forty-eight. It wasn't until 1959, with the addition of Alaska and Hawaii, that the number of states reached fifty. But why stop there? Some people in the District of Columbia believe that it should become a state, which would bring the total to fifty-one. Similar thinking extends to the commonwealth of Puerto Rico—a possible number fifty-two. And while we're at it, why not subdivide some of the existing states and create new ones? Take Kansas, for example. Voters in nine southwestern Kansas counties recently approved measures to secede from the state. Although the voting was unofficial, representatives from twenty-two Kansas counties called for a constitutional convention to be held in September 1992.[1] The intent of the convention was to draft a document that would establish the boundaries and fundamental laws of a new state. Discussions were underway regarding the possible inclusion of discontented residents of panhandle counties in Oklahoma and Texas, and even a Colorado county or two. The interest in secession has grown out of the perception of inequitable tax burdens and a corresponding lack of political clout. To the disaffected in these states, a new state ("Heartland"?), seems just the solution.

States and their communities are dynamic entities. Even something as fundamental as the composition of the United States and the boundaries of the individual units can change. A **federal system** such as ours, characterized by multiple centers of power (see Chapter 2), places a premium on politics. The politics of America's states and communities is the subject of this book.

Places and Images

Each place has its own image. Say *Chicago* and an image immediately springs to mind. *California* inspires a different but distinct mental picture. Images are of all kinds. Some states call to mind terrain and climatic images: Minnesota's freshly fallen snow, Oregon's rugged coastline and rain forests, Florida's balmy climate and beaches, Pennsylvania's rolling countryside, Arizona's desert beauty. Others conjure up economic images: West Virginia and coal mining, Nevada and gambling, Michigan and automobile manufacturing, Iowa and agriculture, Montana and ranching, Hawaii and tourism, Massachusetts and high technology.

A community's identity is wrapped up in images and symbols, too. Consider the National Basketball Association team nicknames. Of course the Houston team would be the Rockets; Philadelphia, the 76ers; Miami, the Heat. But the Los Angeles Lakers or the Utah Jazz? You say that you have been to Los Angeles and you do not remember a lake-dotted city, or that you have visited Utah and do not recall the sounds of saxophones wafting through the air. Well, the L.A. franchise originated in Minneapolis, which has an abundance of lakes, and the

In 1956, Georgia changed its flag from the one shown on the right to the one on the left, incorporating the Confederate battle flag in its design. Seeking an image more appropriate for the 1996 Olympics to be held in Atlanta, Georgia's governor has advocated a return to the earlier version.

Jazz were in New Orleans before they headed west. These images are strong. In a strange and sad case, violent crime soared in the late 1980s in the nation's capital, home of the NBA's appropriately named Washington Bullets.

Images are not trivial. They matter because they project and reflect public perceptions, which can be both accurate and inaccurate. They offer a shorthand understanding of a place, a slice of the whole. States and communities have become much more conscious of their images in recent years, and many have launched promotional campaigns to change undesirable perceptions: "Say yes to Michigan" and "Houston Proud" are examples.

One of the most vivid demonstrations of the importance of image occurred in North Dakota in 1989, when legislators gave serious consideration to a resolution that would have dropped the word *North* from the state's name.[2] Supporters of the resolution argued that the change in name would have a significant impact on the state's image to outsiders. The name *North Dakota* was said to summon images of "snowstorms, howling winds, and frigid temperatures."[3] Focus-group sessions conducted by the state's director of tourism reported that participants' most common impressions of North Dakota were "cold" and "flat." Even residents of the state were reported to suffer from a kind of mass inferiority complex because of North Dakota's location. The geographical designation *North* was thought to be the problem. Simply going with *Dakota*, a word that means "friend" or "ally" in the Sioux language, would project a warmer image of the state, supporters claimed. (One wag countered that if a warmer image was wanted, the new name ought to be *Palm Dakota*.) Ultimately, however, lawmakers were unmoved by the arguments of the proponents. Opponents of the measure cited everything from tradition to identity to cost, and in March 1989 the state Senate defeated the resolution by a 36-to-15 margin. North Dakota remains North Dakota. But this kind of concern with image indicates the importance of identity to state and local governments.

....

The People: Designers and Consumers of Government

A book on state and local government is not only about places and governments; it is also about people—the public and assorted officeholders—and the institutions they create, the processes in which they engage, and the policies they adopt. Thus this volume contains chapters on institutions, such as legislatures; processes, such as elections; and policies, such as those pertaining to education. But in each case, people are the ultimate focus. A legislature is composed of legislators and staff members who deal with constituents; elections involve candidates, campaign workers, and voters (as well as nonvoters); and education essentially involves students, teachers, administrators, parents, and taxpayers. Thus the word *people* encompasses an array of individuals and roles in the political system.

Ethnic-Racial Composition

More than 249 million people live in this country. Some Americans can trace their heritage back to the *Mayflower,* whereas others look back only as far as a recent naturalization ceremony. Very few can claim indigenous (native) American ancestry. Instead, most Americans owe their nationality to some forebear who came here in search of a better life—or, in the case of a significant minority, the descendants of slaves, to ancestors who made the journey to this country not out of choice but because of physical coercion. The appeal of the United States to economic and political refugees from other countries continues, with Central Americans, Indochinese, and Soviet Jews among the most recent arrivals. News photographs of Haitians crowded aboard rickety boats in a desperate attempt to gain asylum in the United States remind us of the strength of the attraction.

The United States is a nation of immigrants. This means ethnic richness and cultural diversity. Large cities, in which immigrants have found economic opportunity, often have distinct ethnic enclaves—Greektown, Little Italy, Koreatown. Some people continue to think of themselves in a hyphenated way, as Polish-Americans or Irish-Americans. In fact, by 1988, some prominent black leaders, the Reverend Jesse Jackson among them, were calling for use of the term *African-American* as a recognition of the cultural heritage of blacks. Ethnicity and culture still matter, despite the melting pot. The rioting that erupted in multi-ethnic South Central Los Angeles after the verdict in the Rodney

King–police brutality case confirms their significance. Ethnicity and culture affect state and local government.

Population Growth and Migration

The 1990 Census figures reflect substantial population shifts across the country. During the 1980s, California added 5.6 million people, 3 million more people called Florida home, and Texas grew by 2.6 million.[4] In percentage terms, the four fastest-growing states were Nevada, which registered a phenomenal 50 percent increase, and Alaska (37 percent), Arizona (35 percent), and Florida (33 percent). Yet as the populations of these states exploded, other states lost population. West Virginia shrank by 8 percent, with population losses of 4.7 percent recorded by Iowa, 3.4 percent by Wyoming, and 2.1 percent by North Dakota. The population changes in the states reflect both migration and natural growth (births and deaths). For example, California estimated that during 1990, about one-quarter of its new residents had immigrated from other countries and another one-quarter had come from other states, with the remaining increase a function of natural growth. In large measure, the population shifts during the 1980s were a continuation of the Frostbelt-to-Sunbelt migration patterns of the 1970s, when growth in the southern and western regions of the country far outpaced that of the Northeast and Midwest. Figure 1.1 offers a view of the United States based on state population size rather than square miles.

Over the next decade, the U.S. Bureau of the Census expects a national growth rate of 7.2 percent.[5] Arizona, Nevada, New Mexico, and Florida are projected to increase by more than 20 percent. At the other end of the scale are Iowa and West Virginia, for which population losses exceeding 7 percent are projected. Other expected nongrowth states during the 1990s include North Dakota (−4.7 percent), Pennsylvania (−2.7 percent), Wyoming (−2.6 percent), and Nebraska (−2.0 percent).

Keep in mind that these Census Bureau projections are based on the continuation of existing trends. Unexpected economic conditions or environmental events could upset the anticipated patterns. For example, the Census Bureau had earlier estimated that the population of the District of Columbia would drop from its 1980 level of 638,000 to 376,500 by the year 2000. But now that the rate of migration from the District has slowed, the Census Bureau estimates a 2000 population of 634,000.[6] Population growth and migration carry economic and political consequences for state and local governments. As a general rule, power and influence follow population. A state's representation in the U.S. Congress and its votes in the electoral college are at stake.

Political Culture

One of the phrases that a new arrival in town hears from long-time residents is "We don't do things that way here." When applied to government, the concept

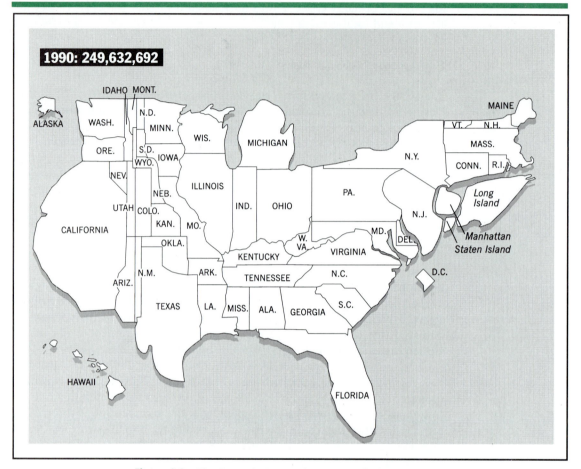

1990: 249,632,692

Figure 1.1   The States in Proportion to Population, 1990

The Great Plains and the Rocky Mountains may cover a lot of territory, but there aren't many people living there, as this population-based map shows.

Source: Map by Richard Furno. © 1991 The Washington Post.

political culture

The attitudes, values, and beliefs that people hold toward government.

behind this statement is **political culture**—the attitudes, values, and beliefs that people hold toward government.[7] As developed by political scientist Daniel Elazar in the 1960s, the term refers to the way in which people think about their government and the manner in which the political system operates. Although easy to define, political culture is difficult to measure.

According to Elazar, the United States is an amalgam of three major political cultures, each of which has distinctive characteristics. In an *individualistic political culture*, politics is a kind of open marketplace in which people participate because of essentially private motivations. In a *moralistic political culture*, politics is an effort to establish a good and just society. Citizens are expected to be active in public affairs. In a *traditionalistic political culture,* politics functions to maintain the existing order, and political participation is confined to social elites. These differing conceptions about the purpose of government and the role of politics lead to different behaviors. Confronted with similar conditions, officials in an individualistic community would resist initiating a program unless public opinion demanded it; leaders in moralistic areas would adopt the new program, even without pressure, if they believed it to be in the public interest; and traditionalistic rulers would initiate the program only if they thought it would serve the interests of the governing elite.

Few states are characterized by pure forms of these cultures. Instead, cultural erosion and synthesis have produced hybrid versions, as illustrated by the map in Figure 1.2. Because of historical migratory and settlement patterns, seventeen states are predominantly individualistic, seventeen tend toward moralistic cultures, and sixteen have traditionalistic cultures. Generally, traditionalistic cultures have characterized the South, individualistic cultures have developed in the middle and southwestern sections of the country, and moralistic cultures have predominated in the far north, the northwest, and the Pacific Coast. California is an interesting case because its northern sections attracted central state migrants with an individualistic orientation to politics, whereas Yankees and their Midwestern descendants took a moralistic political culture to southern California. On the map, a hybridized culture has a two-letter designation. The first letter refers to the dominant culture in the state, the second to the secondary culture. Florida (TI), for example, is dominated by a traditionalistic culture, although pockets of individualistic culture exist. Elazar's pioneering work has been extended to the community level by researchers such as Joel Lieske who use race, ethnicity, and religion to identify subcultures.[8] With counties as the building blocks, Lieske constructed ten cultural regions that are relatively homogenous and contiguous. He gives the regional clusters names like "Rurban," "Blackbelt," "Border," and "Germanic."

Political culture is a factor in the differences (and similarities) among states. One study, for example, found that political culture influenced the accessibility of state government structures and political processes to the public.[9] Other research has linked political culture to policy outcomes; for instance, moralistic states demonstrate the greatest tendency toward innovativeness, whereas traditionalistic states exhibit the least.[10]

Political culture is not the only explanation for why states do what they do, however. Socioeconomic characteristics (income and education levels, for example) and political structural factors (the amount of competition between political parties) also contribute to states' and communities' identities. In fact, sorting out the cause-and-effect relationships among these variables is a daunting job.[11] Suffice it to say that political culture, socioeconomic characteristics, and political structure combine to produce government behavior. For example, the most innovative states typically have nontraditional political cultures, high levels of wealth and education, and active two-party politics.

Figure 1.2   Dominant Political Cultures
The political cultures of states reflect population flows and settlement patterns. Recent years have seen an increase in the number of states dominated by an individualistic culture.

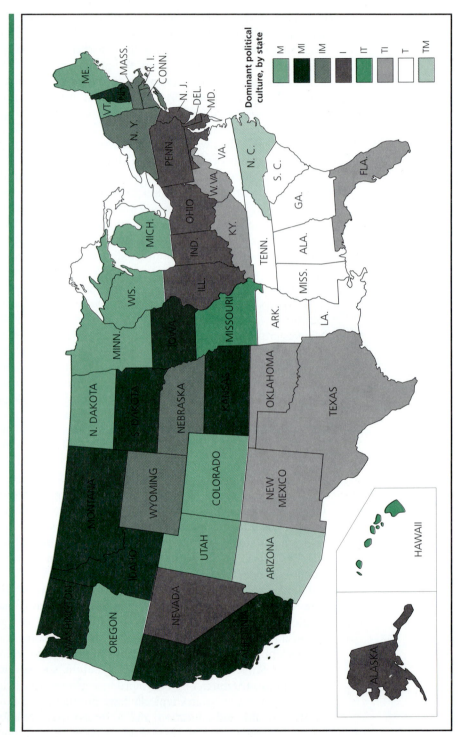

Dominant political culture, by state

- M
- MI
- IM
- I
- IT
- TI
- T
- TM

ME.
VT.
N.H.
MASS.
R. I.
CONN.
N. Y.
N. J.
DEL.
MD.
PENN.
W.VA.
VA.
N. C.
S. C.
GA.
FLA.
OHIO
IND.
KY.
TENN.
ALA.
MISS.
MICH.
ILL.
MISSOURI
ARK.
LA.
WIS.
MINN.
IOWA
N. DAKOTA
S. DAKOTA
NEBRASKA
KANSAS
OKLAHOMA
TEXAS
NEW MEXICO
MONTANA
WYOMING
COLORADO
IDAHO
UTAH
ARIZONA
WASHINGTON
OREGON
NEVADA
CALIFORNIA
HAWAII
ALASKA

Source: Daniel J. Elazar, *American Federalism: A View from the States,* 3d ed. (New York: Harper & Row, 1984), p. 135. Copyright © 1984 by Harper & Row, Publishers, Inc. Reprinted by permission of HarperCollins Publishers.

The Study of State and Local Government

The study of state and local government has typically received short shrift in the survey of American politics.[12] Scholars and journalists tend to focus on glamorous and imperial presidents, a rancorous Congress, and a rightward shifting and powerful Supreme Court. National issues capture the lion's share of media attention. Even people who are fierce partisans of nonnational (that is, state and local) governments frequently feel that the action takes place away from center stage. Yet state and local politics are fascinating theater, precisely because of their involvement in our day-to-day lives. Instead of international battles over the trade imbalance or the debt owed U.S. banks by Third World nations, we have disputes between New York and New Jersey over business exodus and commuter taxes. Instead of record-setting national budget deficits, we have **jurisdictions** that engage in inventive actions to live within their financial means. And rather than deciding which weapons systems will protect the nation from the attacks of evil empires, local governments are charged with providing for the immediate safety and well-being of citizens—in our homes, on the streets, at the workplace.

jurisdiction
The territorial limit under a government authority.

The concerns of state and local governments are fundamental, the real concerns of the American public. Perhaps they lack style—admittedly, efficient garbage collection and effective regulation of funeral homes do not make for riveting drama. Yet these are the issues that affect all of us.

From Sewers to Science: The Functions of State and Local Governments

State and local governments are busy. They exist, in large measure, to provide services to the public. This is no easy task. Nonnational governments must offer services efficiently, effectively, and fairly, and they must do so with limited financial resources. The high costs of inefficient government lead to higher taxes and thus to greater citizen displeasure with government, which in turn can lead to tax revolts and taxpayer exodus. A government performs effectively if it accomplishes what it sets out to do. Another expectation is that government function fairly—that its services be delivered in an equitable manner. It is no wonder, then, that state and local governments constantly experiment with new programs and new systems for delivering services, all the while seeking efficiency, effectiveness, and equity. For instance, the massive restructuring of Wyoming's state government begun in 1989 was intended, according to the governor, to produce "a better method of delivering services from the state government to the citizens."[13]

Each year, the Ford Foundation sponsors "Innovations in State and Local Government" awards to recognize the creativity that abounds in governments throughout the nation. Ten jurisdictions are selected for the prestigious and

By forming support groups, Fresno County, California's K–Six Early Intervention Partnership program is able to reach at-risk students before their problems overwhelm them. The program won an innovation award in 1991.

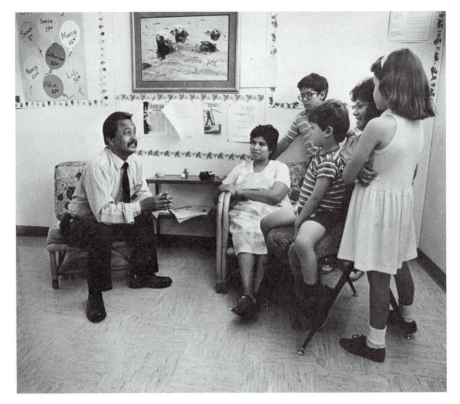

lucrative ($100,000) prize. The criterion for the awards is that the government's innovation be successful and easily replicated by other jurisdictions. After reviewing the applications of almost 2,000 contenders, the 1991 winners and their innovations included

- Maryland's statewide system of family support centers
- Massachusetts's "prevent pollution before it happens" project
- New Jersey's school-based service centers for at-risk youth
- Philadelphia's antigraffiti network
- San Diego County's trauma intervention programs
- Seattle's matching fund for neighborhood self-help projects[14]

Although some of the winning innovations are internal to government operations and carry the promise of increased efficiency, others have a policy goal, such as educational improvement or a stronger economy. The unifying characteristic of the group is the willingness to try something new.

Our Approach

The argument of this book is that state and local governments are resurgent, and that they have a greater capacity to play central roles in the American federal

capacity

The ability of govern-
ment to respond effec-
tively to change, to
make decisions effi-
ciently and respon-
sively, and to manage
conflict.

system than ever before. **Capacity** refers to a government's ability to respond effectively to change, make decisions efficiently and responsively, and manage conflict.[15]

In looking at capacity and resurgence, we find that it sometimes makes sense to measure the states against one another. In many instances, however, it is more meaningful to chart a government's performance from one time period to another. Even states that perennially cluster at the bottom of fifty-state rankings have made tremendous strides over the past two decades. Their relative ranking may not have changed substantially, but the improvement in the performance of their governments over time is in many cases noteworthy.

Our stance is tempered by the reality of federalism, by the overlapping spheres of authority of the national and state governments. There are clear instances in which national government intervention in the affairs of a state or local government is defensible. For example, the environmental problems of the 1960s and 1970s exceeded state and local governments' ability to handle them (see Chapter 18), and so corrective action by the national government was generally welcomed. Our approach takes into account intergovernmental relations (that is, the relationships among the three levels of government)—particularly the possibilities for cooperation and conflict. Jurisdictions (national, state, or local) possess policymaking authority over an identifiable chunk of territory. Yet they confront innumerable situations in which they must work together to accomplish an objective. Indeed, the characteristics of cooperation and conflict define the American federal system.

....

State and Local Government Capacity

Discussions of American government typically proceed from an explicitly national perspective. They examine national actions and assess their impact on lower-level governments. But it is important to remember that the discussion can proceed in the opposite direction as well. That is, we can focus on state and local governments and evaluate their contribution to evolving intergovernmental relations.

This section takes a distinctly nonnational approach. Its underlying premise is that the Reagan administration's "New Federalism," the effort to give many national government powers to the states and cities, was made easier by the existence of increasingly capable state and local governments. Republican presidents as far back as Eisenhower had attempted to restore powers to nonnational governments; they met with little success, however, primarily because state and local governments were unprepared to handle new responsibilities.[16] With notable exceptions, states and their local governments in the 1950s and 1960s were havens of traditionalism and inactivity.

Those days are as outmoded as a black-and-white television set. Consequently, the Reagan administration encountered state governments able, if not always willing, to assume additional functions. But federalism in the 1980s meant more than the national government's delegation of unwanted activities. Very important is the fact that states and their local governments have designed and implemented "an explosion of innovations and initiatives."[17] Whether New Federalism will be long lasting or short-lived depends in great measure on the performance of nonnational governments. (New Federalism is discussed in detail in Chapter 3.)

The blossoming of state governments in the 1980s—their transformation from the weak link in the federal chain to viable and progressive political units—resulted from a number of actions and circumstances.[18] In turn, the resurgence of state governments has generated a number of positive outcomes, including increased capacity in local governments. State and local governments will need every bit of their capacity to address the challenges that await.

How States and Localities Increased Their Capacity

The national government has shown itself to be increasingly unwilling to confront many of the problems facing our complex society. Admittedly, it has been occupied with concern over the country's global competitiveness. The worsening national debt and the increasing trade imbalance have provided little relief. And these problems have come on the heels of two decades of foreign and domestic policy failures, such as the Vietnam War, the War on Poverty, and Watergate. Moreover, the widespread belief that there is too much power in Washington and that it has been discharged irresponsibly has grown among the public.[19] At the same time, however, states have been demonstrating the capacity to act in a positive manner in policy fields that are of interest and importance to them.

In the 1980s, states also began rethinking their treatment of local governments. Greater realization that local government problems meant state government problems signaled a new era in state-local relations. As states loosened the reins on local governments, allowing them to function more effectively, local capacity increased. As a result, local governments today can better handle the problems they encounter, because they have greater authority to do so. In addition, state governments have increased the financial aid that flows to local governments. Admittedly, a fine line separates state assistance from state interference in local affairs, and state governments continue to struggle to find the optimal balance. (The relationship of states to their local governments is fully examined in Chapters 13 and 14.)

State Reform   While Washington has stumbled, state governments have been quietly and methodically reforming themselves. They have modernized their constitutions and restructured their institutions. During the past twenty years, more than three-quarters of the states have ratified new constitutions or substantially amended existing ones. Formerly thought of as the "drag anchors of state programs" and as "protectors of special interests,"[20] these documents have been streamlined and made more workable. Even in states without wide-scale constitutional reform, tinkering with constitutions is almost never-ending through the amendment process. Virtually every state general election finds constitutional issues on the ballot. (State constitutions are discussed in Chapter 4.)

States have also undertaken a variety of internal adjustments intended to improve the operations of state government.[21] Modernized constitutions and statutory changes have strengthened the powers of governors by increasing appointment and removal powers and by allowing longer terms, consecutive succession, larger staffs, enhanced budget authority, and the power to reorganize the executive branch.[22] State bureaucracies are staffed by more professional administrators,[23] and the bureaucracy is more and more demographically representative of the public.[24] Annual rather than biennial sessions, more efficient rules and procedures, additional staff, and higher salaries have played a part in making reapportioned state legislatures more professional, capable, and effective.[25] State judicial systems have been the targets of reform as well; examples include the establishment of unified court systems, the hiring of court administrators, and the creation of additional layers of courts.[26] (State institutions—the governor, state agencies, legislatures, and the courts—are addressed in Chapters 7 through 10.)

The State and Local Presence in Washington, D.C.   Nonnational governments have energized their lobbying efforts in the nation's capital. The National Governors' Association, the National Conference of State Legislatures, and the Council of State Governments are the three major state-level organizations; the National League of Cities, the National Association of Counties, the U.S. Conference of Mayors, and the International City Management Association are major players for local governments. Beyond the "Big Seven," as they are known in Washington, D.C., are myriad others representing a variety of state and local officials—for example, the Association of State Highway and Transportation Officials and the National Association of State Development Agencies. In addition, most states and a few of the largest cities have their own liaison offices in Washington.[27]

The intergovernmental lobbies serve an important function in watching out for the interests of their members in the nation's capital. Congress regularly solicits these organizations for information and advice on proposed legislation; and through the State and Local Legal Center, nonnational governments are increasing their potential impact on the federal judiciary. Beyond lobbying, these groups provide a forum in which jurisdictions can learn from one another.

What Increased Capacity Has Meant

In combination, the forces discussed in the preceding section have enhanced state and local government capacity and led to a resurgence that has generated a variety of positive outcomes. These outcomes work to reinforce the performance of nonnational governments; that is, they are building on their successes. In effect, capacity breeds more capacity.

Improved Revenue Systems The recession of the early 1980s and the wave of popularly sponsored taxation and expenditure limitations at state and local levels caused states to implement new revenue-raising strategies in order to maintain existing service levels. States also granted local governments more flexibility in their revenue systems. Texas, for example, now allows cities the option of providing property-tax relief to residents while increasing the local sales tax.

State governments over the past decade have first increased user charges, gasoline taxes, and so-called sin taxes on alcohol and tobacco, and then only reluctantly raised sales and income taxes. Revenue structures have been redesigned to make them more diversified and more equitable. State "rainy day funds," legalized gambling through state-run lotteries and pari-mutuels, and extension of the sales tax to services are examples of diversification strategies. Exemptions of food and medicine from consumer sales taxes and the enactment of property-tax breaks for poor and elderly people characterize efforts at tax equity. States constantly tinker with their revenue-raising schemes. For instance, in 1991, Minnesota entertained the idea of a Nintendo-accessible state lottery.[28] Public outcry over the conversion of a children's toy into an instrument for state-approved gambling in the home eventually killed the plan. As this example shows, recession-wracked states have become even more creative in redesigning their revenue systems. (The issue of state and local finances is taken up in Chapter 14.)

Expanding the Scope of State Operations Unlike the national government, which is shedding functions like unwanted pounds, state governments are adding functions. In some instances, states are filling in the gap left by the national government's de-emphasis of an activity. State-sponsored low-income housing programs are a good example of this behavior; increased state regulation of the trucking industry is another.[29] When the U.S. Congress failed to enact family-leave legislation giving workers unpaid leave to care for newborn babies and ailing relatives, states responded.[30] California, Hawaii, and Oregon were among the states enacting family-leave measures in 1991. In other cases, states have taken the initiative in ongoing intergovernmental programs by creatively utilizing programmatic authority and resources. In health care, for instance, states are involved in designing and maintaining the mechanisms such as managed-care plans that channel services to those in need.[31] Many governors now travel overseas to pitch their states' exports and suitability for foreign investment. States are taking on the role of policy innovators and experimenters in the U.S. federal system; and in so doing, they are creating a climate for local government creativity and inventiveness.

Faster Diffusion of Innovations Among states, there have always been leaders and followers. The same is true for local governments. Now that these governments are doing more policymaking, they are looking more frequently to their neighbors for advice, information, and models. For example, if a state is trying to control the spread of acquired immune deficiency syndrome (AIDS), it is likely to look to New York, California, and Massachusetts, the early leaders in the field. In 1983, New York became the first state to take legislative action, creating a multifunctional AIDS Institute;[32] California and Massachusetts quickly followed suit. These states were the first to address tough problems such as testing for the disease, providing counseling to high-risk groups, and seeking new anti-AIDS drugs. By the end of 1985, more than half of the states had created an AIDS task force of some form or another.

Local-level innovations spread quickly, too. In 1987, attention turned to Rochester, New York, when that city overhauled its educational system in hopes of reversing the forces of social disarray in the community.[33] The new plan boosted teacher salaries to the highest in the nation (outside Alaska); in exchange, teachers were asked to take on the additional role of social worker. Miami, San Diego, Pittsburgh, and Toledo have adopted parts of the Rochester plan in their public schools. In 1991, attention shifted to Dade County, Florida, where, in a controversial experiment, a *private* company was hired to run a *public* elementary school.[34] If the experiment succeeds, other school districts are likely to follow suit.

State and local governments learn from each other. Communication links are increasingly varied and frequently used. A state might turn to nearby states when searching for policy solutions. Regional consultation and emulation is logical: Similar problems beset jurisdictions in the same region; a program used in a neighboring state is politically more acceptable than one from a distant state; and organizational affiliations bring state and local administrators together with their colleagues from nearby areas.

Interjurisdictional Cooperation   Accompanying the quickening flow of innovations has been an increase in interjurisdictional cooperation. States are choosing to confront and resolve their immediate problems jointly. Many local governments have forged regional organizations to develop areawide solutions to pressing problems. Such collaboration takes many forms, including informal consultations and agreements, interstate committees, legal contracts, reciprocal legislation, and interstate compacts. Eight northeastern states, anxious to improve air quality in their region, entered into an anti-smog pact in 1992. Environmental commissioners in the affected states formed an organization called the Northeast States for Coordinated Air Use Management. Informal cooperation was involved when thirteen southern states united to hold a regional presidential primary in 1988. Super Tuesday, as the primary became known, was designed to strengthen the influence of the South in the nomination process. States agreed to participate because they could see some benefit from cooperation.

Increased jurisdictional cooperation fosters a healthy climate for joint problem solving. In addition, when state and local governments solve their own problems, they protect their power and authority within the federal system.

Increased National-State Conflict   An inevitable by-product of more capable state and local governments is intensified conflict with the national government. One source of this trouble has been federal laws and grant requirements that supersede state policy; another is the movement of states onto the national government's turf. National-state conflict is primarily a cyclical phenomenon, but contention has increased in recent years. In fact, it has reached such a pitch that an "intergovernmental regulatory relief act" has been proposed in Congress.[35] If passed, this act would require the national government to reimburse the states and local governments for the costs of complying with expensive federal *mandates* (requirements). In addition, two Midwestern senators introduced legislation in 1991 to clarify and limit federal preemption of state and local government powers.

Conflict characterizes a variety of policy areas: the removal of the exemption of local governments from federal antitrust laws (laws against business monopolies); disagreement over energy and water resources; the minimum drinking age; the speed limit on interstate highways; air and water quality standards; interstate trucking; severance taxes (fees imposed on the extraction of mineral resources from the earth); registration and taxation of state and municipal bonds; offshore oil drilling; land management and reclamation; and the storage and disposal of hazardous chemical wastes. Even something as basic as agriculture can be a battleground, as the Texas commissioner of agriculture discovered when he unveiled his plan to bypass the U.S. Department of Agriculture and sell beef directly to the European Community.[36]

National-state conflicts are resolved (and sometimes made worse) by the federal judicial system. Cases dealing with alleged violations of the U.S. Constitution by state and local governments are heard in national courts and decided by national judges. Sometimes the rulings take the federal government into spheres long considered the purview of state and local governments. In Kansas City, Missouri, for instance, a federal district judge forced the local school board to increase taxes to pay for a court-ordered magnet plan.[37]

According to a recent study, the U.S. Supreme Court under Chief Justice Warren Burger (1969–1986) tended to side with the states in national-state conflicts.[38] The decisions of the Rehnquist Court (from 1986), however, have been mixed. For example, in a 1988 decision, the Court overturned a century-old precedent and ruled that Congress can tax all interest on state and local government bonds.[39] But in *Webster* v. *Reproductive Health Services* (1989) and *Planned Parenthood* v. *Casey* (1992)—the most important abortion cases to reach the Court since *Roe* v. *Wade*—the Court gave states greater latitude in regulating abortion.[40] However, the Court upheld presidential authority to call up a state National Guard for overseas training, regardless of gubernatorial objection.[41] Thus a judicial victory for states in one area is often countered by a defeat in another. Some observers anticipate that as the Court becomes dominated increasingly by Reagan- and Bush-era appointees, it will be more receptive to states' interests in intergovernmental disputes.[42]

Problems Facing State and Local Governments

Increased capacity does not mean that all state and local problems have been solved. Two tough challenges face nonnational governments today.

Financial Distress   One of the most intractable problems involves money. In the late 1970s and early 1980s, states got a taste of the havoc that can be wreaked by financial problems. The nationwide recession caused state tax revenues to decline; the national government cut back its financial assistance to state and local governments; and taxpayers, most vividly in California's Proposition 13, indicated their readiness to revolt. By 1983, many states were facing budget deficits for the first time since the Great Depression. States and their local governments were forced to choose between two relatively unappetizing options: reducing service expenditures or raising revenues. Most states responded by combining the least painful varieties of both. Programs were cut, activities that could be deferred were deferred, and hiring freezes were imposed in government agencies. States increased taxes and turned to user fees and lotteries as revenue-raising devices. In the end, national economic recovery eventually lessened the fiscal difficulties of the states. But cyclical peaks and troughs in the national economy as well as fundamental changes in public finance mean that state and local financial challenges will not disappear.

As the 1990s dawned, ominous clouds once again hovered over the financial horizon. Policymakers in affected states searched furiously for solutions in an effort that one pundit labeled "a new kind of big game hunt for state budget entrepreneurs."[43] New York faced a budget shortfall of close to $1 billion; California, a whopping $9 billion. By fall 1991, thirty-one states had raised taxes by a combined $16.2 billion and twenty-nine states had cut spending by $7.5 billion.[44] The situation was severe enough that some Floridians and Texans swallowed hard and began talking about the imposition of a personal income tax in their states. And in Connecticut, where the governor and legislature spent much of 1991 embroiled in a battle over the state's new income tax, the 1992 revenue projections showed another, albeit smaller, budget gap.

As states become the center of innovative programs and take on more responsibilities, spending pressures will grow. For example, in 1985, the Medicaid program consumed, on average, about 10 percent of a state's expenditures. By 1991, additional federal mandates had pushed state program costs to 14 percent of state expenditures, with projections of 22 percent by 1995.[45] Capable state and local governments do operate efficiently, but they still require dollars, especially as the national government shifts funding burdens to them. Where to find those dollars is the proverbial $64,000 question.

Increased Interjurisdictional Conflict   Conflict is inherent in a federal system, because each of the entities has its own set of interests along with a share of the national interest. When one state's pursuit of its interests negatively affects another state, conflict occurs. And such conflict can become destructive, threatening the continuation of state resurgence. In effect, states end up wasting their energies and resources on counterproductive battles among themselves.

Interjurisdictional conflict particularly develops in two policy areas very dear to state and local governments: natural resources and economic development. States rich in natural resources want to use them in a manner that will yield the greatest return. Oil-producing states, for instance, levy severance taxes that raise the price of oil. And states with abundant water supplies resist efforts by arid states to tap into the supply. In both of these examples, the essential question revolves around a state's right to control a resource that occurs naturally and is highly desired by other states. Resource-poor states argue that resources are in fact national and should rightfully be shared among states. The result is a series of seemingly endless battles played out in the federal courts.

In economic development, the conflict is extensive because all jurisdictions want healthy economies. To achieve this end, states try to make themselves attractive to business and industry through tax breaks and regulatory relaxation. The conflict arises when they get involved in bidding wars—that is, when an enterprise is so highly valued that actions taken by one state are matched and exceeded by another. Suppose, for example, that an automobile manufacturer is considering shutting down an existing facility and relocating. States hungry for manufacturing activity will assemble a package of incentives such as below-cost land, tax concessions, and subsidized job training in an attempt to attract the manufacturer. The state that wants to keep that manufacturer will try to match these inducements. In the long run, economic activity is simply relocated from one state to another. The big winner is the manufacturer.

This scenario is played out at the local level as well. For instance, when the American Cancer Society decided to leave New York City after three-quarters of a century, Atlanta, Baltimore, Dallas, Denver, Houston, Indianapolis, and Memphis were among the eager suitors. Atlanta's bid—$15 million in tax-free financing from the city, a free parcel of land valued at $2.5 million, and $1 million for moving expenses—secured the prize.[46]

....

Is Capacity Enough?

Whether state and local governments can become the new heroes of American federalism depends on their ability to solve pressing problems. The interaction of three unique characteristics of our fifty-state system—diversity, competitiveness, and resiliency—suggests that they can.[47] Consider the diversity of the United States. States and their communities have different fiscal capacities (some are rich, some are poor) and different voter preferences for public services and taxes (some are liberal, some are conservative). Along with the national government's reluctance to equalize intergovernmental fiscal disparities, these differences perpetuate diversity. As a result, citizens and businesses are offered real choices in taxation and expenditure policies across different jurisdictions.

Diversity is tempered, however, by the natural competitiveness of a federal system. No state can afford to be too far out of line with the prevailing thinking on appropriate levels of taxes and expenditures. During the 1970s, a high-tax state, Massachusetts, was labeled "Taxachusetts," and poor-service states like Mississippi were castigated for backwardness. Neither state could flourish by being at the extreme end of the scale. States with lower taxes became more attractive than Massachusetts; states with better services became more inviting than Mississippi. Citizens and businesses usually have the option of relocating. Eventually, the workings of government, through an attentive public and enlightened opinion leaders, brought Massachusetts's tax levels and Mississippi's service levels back into line with prevailing thinking. Such competition over taxes and expenditures stabilizes the federal system.

The third characteristic, resiliency, reflects the ability of state governments to recover from adversity. The number of curves thrown at state governments in the form of global economic shifts, national policy redirection, and citizen demands would confound even the most proficient of batters. State governments have shown a remarkable ability to hit the curve ball—perhaps not effortlessly, but certainly consistently. States are survivors. For example, to find the innovative proposals for welfare reform these days, look at the state level, which has witnessed a veritable burst of activism in policy initiatives.[48] Resiliency is the key.

It is unlikely that the days of unchallenged national dominance will return. The national government is mired in its own problems, such as the unrelenting national debt and mounting trade deficits. Given the increased capacity of state and local governments, it is far more likely that the action will occur beyond the Beltway encircling Washington, D.C. The most talked about topics in gubernatorial state-of-the-state messages as the 1990s began were economic development, education, drugs and crime, and the environment.[49] However, at the same time that demands on state government are increasing, the recession is forcing states to **downsize**—that is, to reduce the size and cost of government.[50] Little wonder, then, that state leaders throughout the nation are turning to an inspirational book entitled *Reinventing Government*[51] for guidance. The decade will certainly test the capacity of diverse, competitive, and resilient states.

downsize

To reduce the size and cost of government.

Summary

State and local governments are moving in new directions. Their progress is facilitated by the coalescing of two developments: a national government intent on limiting its role in domestic programs, and nonnational governments committed to expanding their capacity to function effectively.

Places and people set the context for the operation of state and local governments. The past decade and a half have seen the improvement of state revenue systems, the expansion of the scope of state operations, a faster diffusion of innovations, increased interjurisdictional cooperation, and increased national-state conflict. Two serious challenges await revitalized state and local governments: financial distress and interjurisdictional conflict.

Key Terms

federalism
political culture
jurisdiction

capacity
downsize

2

The Evolution of Federalism

21

The men who met in Philadelphia during the hot summer of 1787 to draw up the Constitution were not wild-eyed optimists, nor were they revolutionaries. In fact, they were consummate pragmatists. The Framers held to the belief of English political philosopher Thomas Hobbes that human beings are contentious and selfish, and some of them openly disdained the masses. For example, Gouverneur Morris of New York declared of the American people: "The mob begin to think and reason. Poor reptiles! . . . They bask in the sun, and ere noon they will bite, depend upon it."[1]   Most of the Framers agreed that their goal in Philadelphia was to find a means of controlling lower forms of human behavior while still allowing citizens to have a voice in making the laws they were compelled to obey. The "philosopher of the Constitution," James Madison, formulated the problem in terms of **factions**, groups that pursue their own interests without concern for the interests of society as a whole. Political differences and self-interest, Madison felt, led to the formation of factions, and the Framers' duty was to identify "constitutional devices that would force various interests to check and control one another."[2]

faction

Any group of citizens or interests united in a cause or action that threatens the rights or interests of the larger community.

Three practical devices to control factions were placed in the U.S. Constitution. The first was a system of representative government in which citizens would elect individuals who would filter and refine the views of the masses. The second was the division of government into three branches (executive, legislative, judicial). The legislative body was divided into two houses, each with a check on the activities of the other. Equal in power would be a strong chief executive with the authority to veto legislative acts, and an independent judiciary. Finally, the government was structured as a federal system, in which the most dangerous faction of all—a majority—would be controlled by the sovereign states. Insurrection in one state would be put down by the others, acting through the national government.[3] Madison's ultimate hope, according to federalism scholar Richard H. Leach, was that the new Constitution would "check interest with interest, class with class, faction with faction, and one branch of government with another in a harmonious system of mutual frustration."[4]

Sometimes today there appears to be more frustration than harmony, but Madison's dream came true. The American federal system is the longest-lived constitutional government on earth. Its dimensions and activities are vastly different from what the Framers envisioned, but it remains a dynamic, adaptable, and usually effective system for conducting the affairs of government.

This chapter explains the historical, legal, and constitutional evolution of American federalism, from the Articles of Confederation to the 1990s. Chapter 3 shows how the sometimes esoteric principle of federalism works in practice.

Unitary, Confederate, and Federal Systems

Powers and responsibilities can be divided among different levels of government in three ways: through a unitary government, a confederacy, or a federal system.

Increased federal fund-
ing for urban mass
transit is expected to
encourage new sys-
tems like Atlanta's
MARTA.

In order to understand our federal system, we must know how it differs from the other forms of government.

The great majority of countries (more than 90 percent) have a **unitary government**, in which most if not all legal power is located in the central government. The central government may create or abolish regional or local governments as it sees fit. These subgovernments can exercise only those powers and responsibilities granted to them by the central government. In France, the United Kingdom, Argentina, Egypt, and the many other countries with unitary systems, the central government is very strong and the regional or local jurisdictions are very weak.

unitary government

One in which all authority is derived from a central authority.

confederacy

A league of sovereign states in which a limited central government exercises few independent powers.

A **confederacy** is the opposite of a unitary system. In a confederacy, the central government is very weak and regional governments are powerful. The regional jurisdictions establish a central government to deal with areas of mutual concern, such as national defense and currency production, but they severely restrict the central government's authority in other areas. If they see fit, they may change or even abolish the central government. The United States began as a confederacy, and the southern states formed one following secession in 1860. The former Soviet Union is experimenting with a confederacy today as it attempts to move away from a highly centralized unitary model. On an international level, however, the United Nations and other cross-national organizations are confederacies.

A federal system falls somewhere between the unitary and confederate forms in the method in which it divides powers among levels of government. It has a minimum of two governmental levels, each of which derives its power directly from the people and each of which can act directly on the people within its jurisdiction without permission from any other authority. Each level of government is supreme in the powers assigned to it, and each is protected by a constitution from being destroyed by the other.[5] Thus federalism is a means of dividing the power and functions of government between a central government and a specified number of geographically defined regional jurisdictions. In effect, people hold dual citizenship, in the national government and in their regional government.

In the U.S. federal system, the regional governments are called states. In others, such as that of Canada, they are known as provinces. Altogether there are approximately twenty federal systems in the world.

The Move Toward Federalism

The drive for independence by the thirteen American colonies was in large measure a reaction to "a history of repeated injuries and usurpations" (according to the Declaration of Independence) under a unitary system of government. The Declaration of Independence proudly proclaimed the colonies' liberation from the "absolute tyranny" exercised over them by the English Crown.

The struggle for independence dominated political debate in the colonies, and there was little time to develop a consensus on the form of government best suited to the future needs of American society. Hence, the move toward federalism was gradual. It is interesting that the first independent government established in America was a confederacy; thus Americans tested two types of government— unitary and confederate—before deciding permanently on the third.

The Articles of Confederation

During the War for Independence, the colonies, now called states, agreed to establish a confederation. A *unicameral* (one-house) Congress was created to exercise the authority of the new national government. Its powers were limited to the authority to wage war, make peace, enter into treaties and alliances, appoint and receive ambassadors, regulate Indian affairs, and create a postal system. The states held all powers not expressly granted to the Congress. The governing document, the Articles of Confederation, was effective from 1776 to 1787, and was officially ratified by the new Congress in 1781.

The inherent weaknesses of the confederacy quickly became apparent. The central government was unable to carry out its basic responsibilities, such as paying pensions to war veterans or staffing military garrisons in the western territories, because it did not have the power to force the states to pay their share of the bill. The central government had to rely on the good will of the states for all of its revenues and, therefore, often could not honor its financial obligations to private individuals, firms, or foreign governments. Bankruptcy was a chronic concern. Furthermore, the lack of national authority to regulate either domestic or international commerce led to discriminatory trade practices by the states, particularly through the use of protective tariffs. National laws were unenforceable in state courts. These and many other defects were important concerns. But the key event that brought together representatives of the states to draft a constitution for a new type of government was Shays's Rebellion. Daniel Shays, a Revolutionary War officer, led an armed revolt of New England farmers over debt and taxes. The weak central government had difficulty putting down the rebellion.

The Constitutional Convention

How did the Framers create a long-lasting and successful system of government that seems to have the best features of both unitary and confederate forms? It would be nice to say that they carefully integrated the best theories of various political philosophers into a grand plan for government. Truly the Framers were learned men, well schooled in the theories of politics, and most of them did believe in designing a government that would serve the people and ensure justice. But above all they were pragmatists; they developed a practical compromise on the key issues of the day, including the proper role of the national government and the states. The reconciliation of the interests and powers of the states with the need for a strong national government, what Madison called a "middle ground," was an American invention. Today, the United States stands as the prototypical federal system.

The Constitutional Convention turned on the self-interest of large states and small states. The large states supported the Virginia Plan, introduced by Edmund Randolph, which proposed a strong central government spearheaded by a powerful two-house Congress. Because representation in both chambers was to be based on population, larger states would be favored. The smaller states countered with the New Jersey Plan, which put forward a one-house legislature composed of an equal number of representatives from each state. There were other differences between the two plans (for example, the Virginia Plan had a single chief executive, whereas the New Jersey Plan had a multimember executive), but the issue of state representation was paramount.

The New Jersey Plan was defeated by a vote of 7 to 3, but the smaller states refused to give in. Finally, Connecticut moved that the lower house (the House of Representatives) be based on the population of each state and the upper house (the Senate) on equal state membership. This Great Compromise was approved, and it ensured that a faction of large states would not dominate the small ones.

The Framers reached another important compromise by specifying the powers of the new central government. Those seventeen powers, to be exercised through Congress, included taxation, regulation of commerce, operation of post offices, establishment of a national court system, declaration of war, conduct of foreign affairs, and administration of military forces.

A third key compromise reached by the Framers concerned the question of who should resolve disputes between the national government and the states: Congress, the state courts, or the Supreme Court? The importance of the decision that the Supreme Court would be the final arbiter was understood only years later, when the Court established the supremacy of the national government over the states through several critical rulings. As we shall see, the Court seemingly relinquished this role in the 1980s, turning the refereeing responsibility over to Congress.

The Evolution of American Federalism

nation-centered federalism

Theory in which the national government is dominant over the states.

Despite the fact that the new Constitution made the national government much stronger than it had been under the Articles of Confederation, the power of the states was still important. As James Madison wrote, "The powers delegated by the proposed Constitution to the federal government are few and defined. Those which are to remain in the State governments are numerous and infinite . . . the powers reserved to the several States will extend to all the objects which, in the ordinary course of affairs, concern the lives, liberties, and properties of the people, and the internal order, improvement, and prosperity of the State."[6]

state-centered federalism

Theory in which the national government represents a voluntary compact or agreement between the states, which retain a dominant position.

State-centered Federalism

The first decades under the new Constitution witnessed a clash between profoundly different views on governing. George Washington, John Adams, and their fellow "Federalists" favored national supremacy, or **nation-centered federalism.** Opposed to them were Thomas Jefferson and the Republicans, who preferred **state-centered federalism.** Much of the debate then, as today, concerned the meaning of the **reserved powers** clause of the **Tenth Amendment** to the Constitution. Ratified in 1791, the Tenth Amendment gave support to the states by openly acknowledging that "the powers not delegated to the United States by the Constitution, nor prohibited by it to the States, are reserved to the states respectively, or to the people." But in fact, the Tenth

reserved powers

Those powers residing with the states by virtue of the Tenth Amendment.

Tenth Amendment

The amendment to the Constitution, ratified in 1791, reserving powers to the states.

Amendment was an early omen of the eventual triumph of nation-centered federalism. As pointed out by constitutional scholar Walter Berns, if the states were intended to be the dominant federal actors, they would not have needed the Tenth Amendment to remind them.[7]

Those who defended the power of the states under the Constitution—that is, state-centered federalism—expressed their view in terms of three concepts. First, the Constitution was a *compact*, an agreement, among the sovereign states, which maintained their sovereignty, or the right of self-governance. Second, the powers of the national government listed in the Constitution—the **enumerated (delegated) powers**—were to be interpreted narrowly. Third, the national government did not have the exclusive right to determine the scope of its own powers, and the states were obliged to resist any unconstitutional efforts by the national government to extend its authority.[8]

enumerated (delegated) powers

Those expressly given to the national government in Article I, Section 8 of the Constitution.

This **compact theory** of federalism became the foundation for states' rights arguments. In particular, it became central to the fight of the southern states against what they considered discrimination by the North. During the 1820s, a national tariff that hurt the agricultural economy of the southern states became an issue. The economy of the South had already begun a protracted period of decline while the North prospered. The tariff, which placed high taxes on imported manufactured goods from Europe, hit the South hard, for the South produced few manufactured goods. Rightly or wrongly, the southerners blamed the "tariff of abominations" for many of their economic problems.

compact theory

A theory of federalism that became the foundation for states' rights arguments.

In 1828, Vice President John C. Calhoun provided the theoretical foundation for his home state of South Carolina to attack the tariff and other "insults." In Calhoun's view, the United States was composed of sovereign states united in a central government through a compact. The powers of the national government had been entrusted to it by the states, not permanently handed over. Calhoun claimed that the states thus had complete authority to reinterpret the validity of the compact at any time.

Calhoun proposed that if a state found a national law to be in violation of the Constitution, the state had the right to **nullify** or veto the law, making it invalid within that state's borders. This action became known as **interposition.** The federal law in question could then be submitted to the delegates of a national convention for approval or put to a vote in the state legislatures. Most important, Calhoun declared that if a large majority of the states sided with the national government, the nullifying state had the right to *secede*, or withdraw from the Union.

nullification

The refusal or failure of a state to recognize or enforce a U.S. law within its boundaries.

Calhoun's full remedy for righting wrongs against the states was complex and is little more than an interesting historical curiosity today. But in 1832 his theory had considerable impact. That year, after an additional tariff was enacted by the national government, South Carolina nullified it. President Andrew Jackson and the Congress threatened military action to force the state to comply with the law, and Jackson even threatened to hang Calhoun, who by this time had resigned from the vice presidency.[9]

interposition

The action of a state to nullify an act of Congress within its own borders.

Ultimately, eleven southern states (led by South Carolina) did secede from the Union, and formed the Confederate States of America. The long conflict between state sovereignty and national supremacy was definitively resolved by five years of bloodshed and the eventual readmittance of the renegade states to the Union. The Civil War, often referred to in the South as The War Between the States, remains the single most violent episode in American history, resulting in more than 620,000 deaths (more than in all our other wars combined) and countless civilian tragedies.

The Growth of National Power Through the Constitution and the Judiciary

Although the compact theory of federalism was a factor until the mid-nineteenth century, a *nation-centered* concept of federalism has dominated since then. For the most part, the national government has been the primary force, with the states and localities generally following its lead. Many times the national government has been best positioned to deal with the major problems of governing the nation, and it has been supported by the Supreme Court's interpretations of key sections of the Constitution.

The National Supremacy Clause   The Judiciary Act of 1789, passed by the first Congress, established the U.S. Supreme Court and various lower courts. It also stated that the U.S. Supreme Court would have jurisdiction over state supreme courts when they hold a national law to be unconstitutional, support a state law over the U.S. Constitution, or rule against a right or privilege claimed under national law or the Constitution. The Judiciary Act of 1789 thus established the supremacy of national law and the Constitution, and made the U.S. Supreme Court the final arbiter of any legal disputes between the national government and the states. This act was constitutionally grounded in the **national supremacy clause** (Article VI, Section 2), which provides that national laws and the Constitution are the supreme laws of the land.

national supremacy clause

Article VI of the Constitution, which makes national laws superior to state laws.

The Necessary and Proper Clause   The fourth chief justice of the United States, John Marshall, was the architect of the federal judiciary during his thirty-four years on the bench. Almost single-handedly, he made it a coequal branch of government. Several of his rulings laid the groundwork for the expansion of national governmental power. In the case of *McCulloch* v. *Maryland* (1819), two issues were before the bench: the right of the national government to establish a national bank, and the right of the state of Maryland to tax that bank, once it was established.[12] The secretary of the treasury, Alexander Hamilton, had proposed a bill that would allow Congress to charter such a bank for depositing national revenues and facilitating the borrowing of funds. Those who wanted to limit the power of the national government, such as James Madison and Thomas Jefferson, argued that the Constitution did not provide the government with the specific authority to charter and operate a national bank.

necessary and proper clause

Portion of Article I, Section 8 of the Constitution that authorizes Congress to enact all laws "necessary and proper" to carry out its responsibilities.

The crux of the issue was how to interpret the **necessary and proper clause**. The final power delegated to Congress under Article I, Section 8 is the power "to make all laws which shall be *necessary and proper* for carrying into execution the foregoing powers, and all other powers vested by this Constitution in the Government of the United States" (emphasis added). Jefferson argued that *necessary* meant "indispensable," while Hamilton asserted that it meant merely "convenient." Hamilton argued that in addition to the enumerated powers, Congress possessed **implied powers**. In the case of the national bank, valid congressional action was implied through the powers of taxation, borrowing, and currency found in Article I, Section 8.

implied powers

Those that are not expressly granted by the Constitution but that are inferred from the enumerated powers.

Meanwhile, the state of Maryland levied a tax on the new national bank, which had been located within its borders, and the bank had refused to pay. Maryland also claimed that the congressional act creating the national bank was unconstitutional, because it did not accord with Congress's delegated powers, and that the bank was not "indispensable" for the execution of delegated powers.

The bank dispute was eventually heard by Supreme Court Chief Justice Marshall. Marshall was persuaded by the Hamiltonian point of view. He pointed out that the Constitution nowhere stipulates that the only powers that may be carried out are those expressly described in Article I, Section 8. Thus he ruled that Congress had the implied power to establish the bank, and that Maryland had no right to tax it. Significantly, *McCulloch* v. *Maryland* meant that the national government had an almost unlimited right to decide how to exercise its delegated powers. Over the years, Congress has enacted a great many laws that are only vaguely, if at all, associated with the enumerated powers, and that stretch the phrase *necessary and proper* beyond its logical limits.

The Commerce Clause   Another important ruling of the Marshall Court extended national power through an expansive interpretation of the **commerce clause** of Article I, Section 8. The commerce clause gives Congress the power "to regulate commerce with foreign nations, and among the several states, and with the Indian tribes." In *Gibbons* v. *Ogden* (1824),[11] two important questions were addressed by Marshall: What *is* commerce? And how broadly should Congress's power to regulate commerce be interpreted?

commerce clause

Article I, Section 8 of the U.S. Constitution, which permits Congress to regulate trade with foreign countries and among the states.

The United States was just developing a national economy as the industrial revolution expanded. National oversight was needed, along with regulation of emerging transportation networks and of state activities related to the passage of goods across state lines (interstate commerce). Marshall defined commerce very broadly, and held that Congress's power to regulate commerce applied not only to traffic across state boundaries but, in some cases, also to traffic of goods, merchandise, and people *within* a state.

Gibbons v. *Ogden* was an important ruling because it expanded national power across state lines and opened up the prospects for trade by eliminating the constraints of state-created monopolies and other barriers. For example, steamboat navigation and railroads flourished, thus tremendously aiding the economic development of the United States. The full implications of Marshall's rulings were not realized until many years later, and they remain a strong point of contention between state governments and the national government today. What *is* widely accepted is the contention that the Marshall Court was a primary cause of the expansion of national government authority and its eventual supremacy over the states.

There have been two additional constitutional bases for the federal judiciary's furtherance of national government power: the general welfare clause and the Fourteenth Amendment.

general welfare clause

The portion of Article I, Section 8 of the Constitution that provides for the general welfare of the United States.

The General Welfare Clause   The **general welfare clause** of Article I, Section 8, states that "the Congress shall have power to lay and collect taxes, duties, imposts, and excises to pay the debts and provide for the common defense and *general welfare* of the United States" (emphasis added). This clause was interpreted very narrowly before the Great Depression of the 1930s. The early position on the role of the national government in aiding the poor was established by President Franklin Pierce in 1854, in a veto of a bill that would have provided national assistance to insane people who were indigent. Pierce claimed that if Congress provided for these people, it would open the door to those paupers who were not insane. And as a result, the states would eventually turn to the national government for funds to assist the poor.[12] Pierce and most other government officials of the time believed that poor people were responsible for their own plight and that it was up to private charity and state and local governments to provide limited assistance.

The Great Depression inflicted massive unemployment and poverty throughout the country, and made necessary a major change in the national government's attitude. Despite their best efforts, the states and localities were staggered by the tremendous loss of tax revenues and by the need to help poor and displaced persons obtain food and shelter. Pierce's worst fears were realized as state officials came to Washington, hats in hand. Franklin D. Roosevelt, who won the presidency in 1932, set in motion numerous programs that completely redefined federal responsibility for the general welfare.

Roosevelt's "New Deal" included a massive Federal Emergency Relief Act, establishment of the Tennessee Valley Authority, the National Industrial Recovery Act, the Agricultural Adjustment Act, the National Labor Relations Act, the Wealth Tax Act, the Banking Act of 1935, the Social Security Act, and other statutes that collectively propelled the national government into a position of dominance within the federal system. For instance, the Social Security Act of 1935 allowed the national government to assist the poor and jobless through old-age insurance, unemployment insurance, welfare programs, and health services. It was twice challenged as an unconstitutionally broad interpretation of the general welfare clause, but the Supreme Court on both occasions upheld the use of federal tax revenues to aid the aged, poor, and unemployed. Thus the national role was extended into fields previously within the province of the states, the localities, and the private sector.

Fourteenth Amendment

Enacted in 1868 to protect the rights of freed slaves, this amendment contains due process and equal rights provisions that now apply to all citizens.

The Fourteenth Amendment   Ratified by the states in 1868, the **Fourteenth Amendment** gave former slaves official status as citizens of the United States and of the state in which they lived. It included two other very important principles as well: *due process* and *equal protection* of the laws. "No state shall make or enforce any law which shall abridge the privileges or immunities of the citizens of the United States; nor shall any state deprive any person of life, liberty, or property, without due process of law; nor deny to any person within its jurisdiction the equal protection of the laws." The Fourteenth Amendment has been utilized by the federal courts to increase national power over the states in several critical fields, especially civil rights, criminal law, and election practices.

For example, black residents of the United States were guaranteed citizenship but otherwise profited very little from the Fourteenth Amendment until the 1954 Supreme Court decision in *Brown* v. *Board of Education*. Up to that time the Court had interpreted the amendment very narrowly with respect to civil rights, permitting, for example, a "separate but equal" approach for public schools that perpetuated segregation. In *Brown* v. *Board of Education*, however, it held that segregation in the public schools implied unequal treatment of the races and therefore violated the Fourteenth Amendment. Public schools throughout the country were ordered to desegregate "with all deliberate speed."[13]

The judiciary's application of the Fourteenth Amendment to state and local governments is illustrated by many contemporary cases that have, for example, established the rights of a person accused of a crime (*Miranda* v. *Arizona*), forced states to reapportion their legislature (*Baker* v. *Carr, Reynolds* v. *Sims*), ordered local officials to hike property taxes to pay for school desegregation (*Missouri* v. *Jenkins*), required formal hearings for welfare recipients before benefits are terminated (*Goldberg* v. *Kelly*), and declared state laws that prohibit abortion unconstitutional (*Roe* v. *Wade*). (As mentioned in Chapter 1, the Court adjusted its position on abortion rights in *Webster* v. *Reproductive Health Services* (1989) and *Planned Parenthood* v. *Casey* (1992), by affirming states' rights to restrict access to abortion.) The national judiciary still exerts a major influence on the affairs of state and local governments. During the past few years, more than half of all cases decided by the U.S. Supreme Court have involved state and local governments.

The Growth of National Power Through Congress

The U.S. Supreme Court has not been the only force behind nation-centered federalism; Congress has worked hand in hand with the judiciary. The commerce clause represents a good example. Given the simple authority to control or eliminate state barriers to trade across state lines, Congress now regulates commercial activities within a state's boundaries as well, as long as these activities have substantial national consequences. The states have made literally hundreds of legal challenges to such exercise of the commerce power, but almost all of these have been resolved by the U.S. Supreme Court in favor of the national government.

As the U.S. economy became increasingly complex and the states more and more interdependent, the national government's role in promoting and regulating commerce expanded. Following the Civil War, the national government granted money and land to corporations for the construction of canals and railroads. It also began regulating some of the excesses of business, which non-national governments were unable to do because they could not pursue a culpable firm across state borders. Congress has also used the authority of the Commerce Clause to expand national power into fields only vaguely related to commerce, such as civil rights.[14]

Taxing and Spending Power

Sixteenth Amendment

Enacted in 1913, this amendment grants the national government the power to levy income taxes.

Taxing and Spending Power   Other factors have conspired with the nationalization of the U.S. economy to promote the growth of national power, including two world wars and the bitter experiences of the Korean and Vietnam wars. But probably the most controversial source of the rise in national power in recent years has been the use of the *taxing and spending power* by Congress to extend its influence over the state and local governments. Under Article I, Section 8, Congress holds the power to tax and spend to provide for the common defense and general welfare. But the **Sixteenth Amendment**, which grants Congress the power to tax the income of individuals and corporations, moved the center of financial power from the states to Washington, D.C. Through the income tax, the national government raises huge amounts of money, most of which is spent in the states. Congress has insisted on some sort of accountability in how state and local governments spend these funds.

grant-in-aid

An intergovernmental transfer of funds or other assets, subject to conditions.

The Grant-in-Aid   The **grant-in-aid**, which transfers funds for a particular purpose from one level of government to another, is the primary means for distributing national revenues to the states and localities. Attached to federal grants are a variety of conditions to which the recipients must adhere if they are to receive the money. These include requirements for recipient governments to match national contributions in accordance with some sort of ratio (the interstate highway program requires one state dollar for every ten federal dollars) and regulations directly related to the purposes of the individual grant, such as meeting national standards for the quality of drinking water under the Safe Drinking Water Act. (The staggering growth in national grants-in-aid during the 1960s and 1970s and the strings attached to them receive a full discussion in Chapter 3.)

federal pre-emption

The principle that national laws take precedence over state laws.

Federal Pre-emption   The national government has also seized power through the process known as **federal pre-emption**. The legal basis for pre-emption is Article VI of the Constitution, the national supremacy clause. Whenever a state law conflicts with a national law, the national law is dominant.

  Some federal pre-emption concerns the requirements attached to grants. The minimum drinking age is a case in point; any state failing to enforce a minimum drinking age of twenty-one risks losing substantial sums of federal highway funds. Congressional passage of a national law that supersedes state legislation is directly pre-emptive. An example is the Air Quality Act, which replaced state standards on permissible levels of air pollutants with minimum national standards. An extreme case of pre-emption is the Voting Rights Act of 1965, which enables the U.S. Justice Department to exercise an advance veto over changes in election procedures and jurisdictions in specified states and localities, and to substitute national voting registrars for local ones where abuses in voting rights have occurred. Congress also pre-empts state law when it passes legislation that gives national administrators the power to veto programs, plans, and policies developed by state and local officials. Federal courts may also contribute to pre-emption through their interpretations of the history and objectives of federal laws that "occupy the field" in certain policy areas, such as high-level radioactive waste management.

Gutting of the Tenth Amendment   Actions by the Congress and the federal courts have gradually undermined the Tenth Amendment, which reserves to the states all powers not specifically granted to the national government or prohibited to the states. In fact, it is very difficult to identify any field of state activity not intruded on by the national government today. Although the Tenth Amendment is a declaration of the original division of powers between nation and states under the Constitution, it bears little relevance to the configuration of American federalism in the 1990s and has held little importance in the minds of most Supreme Court justices.[15] It has become "but a truism that all is retained which has not been surrendered,"[16] and the states have unwillingly surrendered more and more of their erstwhile rights and privileges.

The one event that temporarily revived the Tenth Amendment in recent years was the decision of the U.S. Supreme Court in *National League of Cities* v. *Usery* (1976). At issue were the 1974 amendments to the Fair Labor Standards Act (FLSA), which extended federal minimum wage and maximum hour requirements to state and local employees. In a surprising turnaround that contradicted the previous forty years of case law, the Supreme Court ruled in favor of the states and localities, saying that Congress did not have the constitutional right to impose wage and hour requirements on employees carrying out their basic—or integral—functions, such as law enforcement and firefighting.[17]

Following a spate of litigation in the lower courts aimed at determining just which state and local activities were "integral," and a series of Supreme Court rulings that appeared to refute the decision in *Usery*, the Supreme Court in 1985 heard the case of *Garcia* v. *San Antonio Metropolitan Transit Authority*. In *Garcia* the Court expressly reversed its findings in *Usery* and once again applied federal wage and hour laws to nonnational governments—in this specific instance, to a mass transit system run by the city of San Antonio. The 5-to-4 Court majority found the *Usery* decision to be "not only unworkable but inconsistent with established principles of federalism."[18]

The *Garcia* case was met with a hail of criticism. The Court had excused itself from future controversies involving state claims against congressional power exercised under the commerce clause. Now Congress alone, with little or no judicial oversight, would be allowed to determine, through the political process, how extensively it would intrude on what had been state and local prerogatives. One dissenting Supreme Court justice wrote that "all that stands between the remaining essentials of state sovereignty and Congress is the latter's underdeveloped capacity for self-restraint."[19] Congress was thus unshackled from the last chain that restrained it from exercising complete national power in the field of commerce. In the view of some critics, the states were relegated to the status of any other special interest group. In short, the Tenth Amendment appeared to be irrelevant.

Powers Remaining with the States

Has judicial and congressional intervention in the affairs of state and local governments rendered them mere administrative appendages of the national government? Is state sovereignty a relic of the past? Is federalism obsolete in the 1990s? The answer to each of these questions is a resounding no. While the idea of state-centered federalism was effectively quashed by the Civil War, and states' rights are quite limited in the Constitution and in practice, the states do retain considerable power.

The states are explicitly mentioned or directly referred to fifty times in the U.S. Constitution. They are specifically guaranteed territorial integrity, the power to maintain a militia (the National Guard), and various powers related to commerce, taxation, and the administration of justice. States participate in national governance by electing their residents as representatives in Congress. All have two members in the Senate and at least one in the House of Representatives. States also determine the time, place, and manner of holding elections for congressional seats. They participate in presidential elections through the electoral college, in which each state is allotted presidential votes based on its total number of senators and representatives in Congress. Finally, amendments to the U.S. Constitution must be ratified by three-fourths of the states.

The most direct influence of the states, and their primary importance, stems from the actions they take (or choose not to take) that affect the lives of those who live within their borders. The states provide a broad spectrum of services, from higher education to corrections. They tax us, spend money on us, and employ us. Our state government touches our lives in some way every day.

Models of Federalism

Perceptions of the role of the states in the federal system have shifted from time to time throughout our history. Those who study the federal system have attempted to describe these perceptions through various models, which attempt to present something complex in a form that is readily understandable. These models have been used both to enhance understanding and to pursue ideological and partisan objectives. One complete inventory uncovered 326 models of federalism,[20] but only the best-known ones are reviewed here, to demonstrate that the American federal system and people's perceptions of it change.

Dual Federalism (1787–ca 1932)

dual federalism

Theory in which the responsibilities and activities of the national and state governments are separate and distinct.

The model of **dual federalism** holds that the national and state governments are sovereign and equal within their respective spheres of authority as set forth in the Constitution. The national government exercises those powers specifically designated to it, and the remainder are reserved for the states. The nation and the states are viewed as primarily competitive, not cooperative, in their relationships with one another.

Figure 2.1 shows two ways to conceptualize dual federalism. "Layer cake" federalism[21] is represented in the left half of the figure, and the "coordinate authority" model[22] is on the right. Both demonstrate the separation of national and state authority. In layer cake federalism, the local government is implicitly subsumed by state authority; in the coordinate authority model, this relationship is explicit.

Dual federalism, which has its roots in the compact theory (see p. 27), was dominant for the first 145 years of American federalism, although the Civil War and other events led to substantial modifications of the model during the early 1900s.[23] Until 1860, the functions of the national government remained largely restricted to the delegated powers. Federal financial assistance to the states was very limited. The states had the dominant influence on the everyday lives of their citizens, acting almost unilaterally in such areas as elections, education, economic development, labor relations, and criminal and family law.[24] After the Civil War shattered the doctrines of interposition, nullification, and secession, and dealt the compact theory of state-centered federalism a severe blow, the nation-centered view became paramount. Intergovernmental finance emerged, with the introduction of the federal grant-in-aid. By the end of the era of dual federalism, fifteen grant programs were operational in education, highways,

Figure 2.1

Dual Federalism

In dual federalism, local governments are implicitly (in the layer cake model) or explicitly (in the coordinate authority model) located within the realm of state authority.

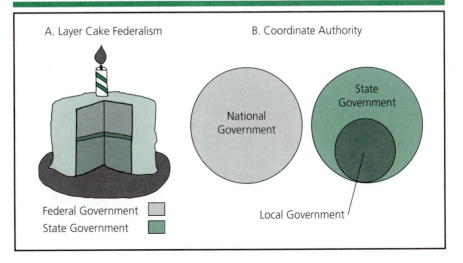

A. Layer Cake Federalism   B. Coordinate Authority

National Government

State Government

Federal Government

State Government

Local Government

welfare, and other fields. The national government was dominant in banking, economic regulation, and military power.

The national government's new activities, however, did not take away the states' traditional functions. They retained responsibility for their historical functions and even enlarged their activities in many fields, such as taxation and regulatory policy. For the most part, national and state governance continued to be carried out separately.

Cooperative Federalism (ca 1933–ca 1964)

cooperative federalism

A model of federalism that stresses the linkages and joint arrangements among the three levels of government.

The selection of a specific date for the demise of dual federalism is rather subjective, but 1933, when Franklin Roosevelt became president, is as good a date as any. Roosevelt's New Deal buried dual federalism by expanding national authority over commerce, taxation, and the economy.

Cooperative federalism has been called the "marble cake model,"[25] in recognition of the increased sharing of responsibilities and financing by all levels of government. It has also been referred to as the "overlapping authority model" (see Figure 2.2).[26] Beginning with the Great Depression, the national government increasingly cooperated with states and localities to provide jobs and social welfare, to develop the nation's infrastructure, and to promote economic development.

The cooperative aspects of this era were evident in governmental finances. The national government spent huge amounts of money to alleviate the ravages of the Depression and to get the American economic machinery back into gear. Total federal expenditures rose from 2.5 percent of the gross national product (GNP) in 1929 to 18.7 percent just thirty years later, far surpassing the growth

Figure 2.2

Cooperative Federalism

The marble cake and overlapping authority variants of cooperative federalism show that government responsibilities are shared.

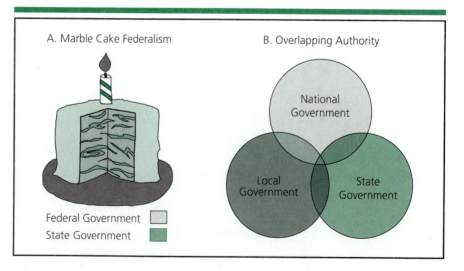

A. Marble Cake Federalism

B. Overlapping Authority

National Government

Local Government

State Government

Federal Government

State Government

in state and local spending during the same period. The number of federal grants-in-aid rose from twelve in 1932, with a value of $193 million, to twenty-six in 1937, with a value of $2.66 billion. By 1960, there were 132 separate grant programs. A substantial amount of the federal aid was sent directly to local governments, particularly counties and school districts. The variety of grant programs exploded. By 1939, there were grants for maternal and child health, old-age assistance, aid to the blind, fire control, treatment of venereal disease, public housing, road and bridge construction, and wildlife conservation. Before the era of cooperative federalism ended in 1964, programs in airport construction, cancer research, fish restocking, school milk, water pollution, waste treatment, and many other areas had been added.

Contemporary Variations on Cooperative Federalism (ca 1964 to the Present)

There have been many recent variations on the broad theme of cooperative federalism. All of them stress intergovernmental sharing.[27] Among these variations are creative federalism, picket fence federalism, and New Federalism.

creative federalism

A model of cooperative federalism in which many new grants-in-aid, including direct national-local financial arrangements, were made.

Creative Federalism   **Creative federalism** was devised by President Lyndon B. Johnson to promote his dream of a "Great Society." Johnson sought to build the Great Society through a massive national government attack on the most serious problems facing the nation: poverty, crime, poor health care, and inadequate education, among others. The vehicle for the attack was the federal grant-in-aid. More than two hundred new grants were put into place during the five years of Johnson's presidency. The major "creativity" in Johnson's policy of vast government spending involved bypassing the states in distributing funds for some seventy of the new programs. Federal disbursements went directly to cities and counties rather than through the states. Understandably, the states did not appreciate the loss of influence over how localities could spend their national dollars.

picket fence federalism

A model that portrays program specialists in national, state, and local bureaucracies as major policy and administrative actors.

Picket Fence Federalism   **Picket fence federalism** (see Figure 2.3) is a model offered by former North Carolina governor and present U.S. Senator Terry Sanford that illustrates the important role of national, state, and local administrators within functional programs.[28] Officials specializing in a single program area, such as public welfare, have closer attachments to their functional (program) counterparts at all levels of government than to various mayors, governors, and legislators. For example, welfare officials in the federal Department of Health and Human Services share professional training, education, goals, and values with state, county, and municipal social welfare employees. They tend to be more responsive to these associates than to the president, governor, mayor, county executive, or various legislative bodies. As a consequence, coordination and implementation of social welfare policies are likely to be influenced more by functional specialists than by elected, "generalist" officials.

Figure 2.3

Picket Fence Federalism

The horizontal and vertical "boards" on this fence indicate the common interests of functional program specialists at all three levels of government.

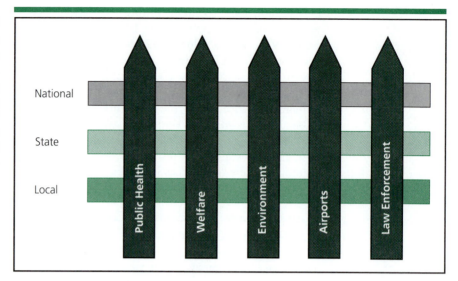

The picket fence model describes many aspects of American federalism from the mid-1960s to the mid-1970s. However, it is overdrawn today, since it fails to account for competing programs (for example, health services for children or for the aged) and for different professions (such as psychiatrists and social workers) in the same field (such as human services) who battle over program goals. The model also fails to appreciate the success of government interest groups such as the National Governors' Association and the National League of Cities in challenging program professionals and reasserting executive leadership over programmatic agencies.[29]

New Federalism

A model that represents a return of powers and responsibilities to the states.

New Federalism   **New Federalism** is a model that has been employed with separate but closely related meanings by two different presidents. The New Federalism of Richard Nixon called for a fundamental reordering of national-state-local relations. Partly in reaction to the centralizing excesses of creative federalism, New Federalism was intended to restore power to the states and localities and to improve intergovernmental arrangements for delivering services. Among the major policy changes brought about by the Nixon administration were the establishment of ten regional councils to coordinate national program administration across the country, and the simplification and streamlining of federal regulations that apply to state and local government. States and localities were also given greater flexibility in program spending and decision making through revenue sharing, in which the national government distributed billions of dollars to the states and localities with few strings attached.

Ronald Reagan's brand of New Federalism is discussed in detail in Chapter 3. Like Nixon's version, it sought to give more power and program authority to states and localities, at least in theory. However, Reagan's main goal—to shrink the size of the national government—soon became obvious.

....

The Advantages and Disadvantages of Federalism

Federalism, as it has evolved in the United States, is a reasonably effective system of government. That it is not perfect, or well suited to the circumstances of most other nations, is demonstrated by the fact that it exists in only a small number of countries. Federalism offers certain advantages and disadvantages that deserve consideration.

The Advantages

There are five major arguments in favor of a federal system of government.

1. *A federal system facilitates the management of social and political conflict.* First, it broadly disperses political power among governments. The American federal system includes a national government with a *bicameral* (two-chamber) legislative branch. The U.S. Senate represents the geographical diversity of the states, with two senators for each territorial unit, and the House of Representatives is apportioned on the basis of population. This system enables general as well as regional concerns to reach the central government. Local interests are expressed in state capitols through state legislatures and, of course, in city and county councils and other local legislative bodies. Ideally, this arrangement allows government to deal with problems before they reach the crisis stage. Many potential centers exist for resolving conflicts. In addition, citizens may express loyalty to more than one government: A person might consider herself an Atlantan, a Georgian, *and* an American.

Second, a federal system provides numerous bases from which political parties can express interests and ideas, thus helping to maintain a balanced party system. The Democrats may have little influence in the state government of New Hampshire, but they dominate the politics of Arkansas. Republicans may have held the White House for most of the last twenty-five years, but a majority of governors are Democrats. The point is that the federal system helps strengthen the political parties by providing a wellspring for continual rebirth and rebuilding.

Finally, federalism achieves unity through diversity. The United States has an increasingly diverse population that varies in ethnicity, color, religious preference, and many other factors. These differences are not distributed randomly in the population; rather, people who share certain traits tend to cluster together. And state and local governments represent such groups. For example, the large and growing Hispanic population of Texas is increasingly gaining representation in the state legislature and in mayoral and city council offices.

2. *Federalism promotes administrative efficiency.* The transfer of responsibility from the national government to states and localities, in order to provide the wide variety of services that citizens demand, helps deliver those services more efficiently. From public elementary education to garbage collection, the government closest to the problem seems to work best in adapting public programs to local needs.

Problem Solving 2.1

Telecommuting for Clean Air

The Problem: Maricopa County, Arizona (which includes Phoenix), has an increasingly serious air pollution problem largely attributable to vehicular traffic. The rapidly growing metropolitan motoring population was driving an average daily total of 50 million miles and emitting around a thousand tons of air pollutants each day. A 1988 state law mandated a 5 percent annual reduction in worker travel for all major county employers.

The Solution: Telecommuting. As the major Maricopa County employer, the state government decided to experiment with telecommuting, which permits employees to work at home. Communication with the office takes place by telephone, modem and personal computer, and fax machine.

An initial total of 189 volunteers from four state agencies were trained in telecommuting procedures. The typical participant had driven about 31 miles per day (round trip) to work and spent $86.00 monthly on travel. After six months, a comparison of telecommuters with a sample of non-telecommuters found that the volunteers avoided a total of 97,078 driving miles and 3,705 hours of stressful driving time over the period. They saved some $10,372 in combined driving expenses. Most important, the telecommuters kept an estimated 1.9 tons of pollutants from being emitted into the Arizona air.

Some positive spillover effects were also noted. Telecommuters reported that they were able to work more efficiently and effectively while meeting job objectives. Morale improved, and retention of employees was enhanced. State officials were recommending in 1991 that the program be extended to other state agencies.

Source: Adapted from M. J. Richter, "Telecommuting in Arizona: Compounded Benefits," *Governing* 4 (July 1991): 67. Used by permission.

Certainly there are advantages to operating on a large scale in some areas, such as national defense and environmental protection. Problems that do not respect jurisdictional lines are more efficiently addressed by a central government. But a centralized bureaucracy in Washington, D.C., is ill-prepared and probably incapable of designing and implementing services whose scale and dimensions vary from place to place. It is difficult to imagine the local office of the national government in Idaho or Nevada overseeing garbage collection; unit costs would soar. The enormous task of providing mundane public services to the 250 million people living across this vast land calls for a decentralized system. Federalism helps keep the national government from collapsing under its own weight.

3. *Federalism encourages innovation.* A tremendous variety of approaches for solving problems exists in the American federal system. States and localities can customize their policies to the diversity of their residents' demands and needs, and heterogeneity flourishes. New policies are constantly being tested by the more than 84,000 government "laboratories." (See Problem Solving 2.1 for a recent example.) More and more, state and local governments exchange information on policy approaches, thus further encouraging experimentation and flexibility across the country. Interestingly, virtually all national government programs have been tested initially at the state or local level. Examples include

unemployment compensation, income assistance, and job health and safety programs. On occasion, state and local governments effectively carry out responsibilities conventionally relegated to the national government. International trade is one interesting example, as explained in Problem Solving 2.2.

4. *A federal system maximizes political participation in government.* Citizens have opportunities to participate at all three levels of government through elections, public hearings, and other means. The local and state governments serve as political training camps for aspiring leaders, who can test the waters in a school board or county council election and, if successful, move on to bigger electoral prizes in the state or national arena. The great majority of presidents and U.S. senators and representatives got their start in state or local politics. In all, almost one million offices are regularly filled through elections. These opportunities for public participation mean that government is accessible to the people. Citizens can have a meaningful say in decisions that affect their lives. Furthermore, access increases accountability in government, thereby helping to ensure that citizens' demands are taken into consideration during policy formation.

5. *A federal system helps protect individual freedom.* A major reason that the Framers chose a federal system of government was that it provides numerous potential points of opposition to national government policies and political ideology. The fear expressed in eloquent detail by Madison was that a strong central government unchecked by the sovereign states would encourage a tyranny of the majority. Madison argued that the numerous checks inherent in a federal system would control the effects of faction, making "it less probable that a majority of the whole will have a common motive to invade the rights of other citizens; or if such a common motive exists, . . . more difficult for all who feel it to discover their own strength and to act in unison."[30] From Madison's perspective, the states serve as defenders of democracy by ensuring that no national ideological juggernaut can sweep over the entire nation, menacing the rights of individual citizens.

The Disadvantages

Federalism has performed admirably in the United States, but it is not without flaws. Ironically, its weaknesses are closely related to its strengths.

1. *Federalism may facilitate the management of conflict in some settings, but in others it makes conflict more dangerous.* This has occurred in federal experiments in Nigeria, Canada, and Yugoslavia. In Nigeria, the formal recognition of tribally based regions helped to spawn a devastating civil war in the 1960s. In Canada, recognition by the national government of the ethnically French province of Quebec helped fuel a secessionist movement during the 1970s that has yet to burn out. The civil war in the former Yugoslavia that began in 1991 is the most recent example of the failure of federalism. The lesson seems to be that a unitary government may be more appropriate for a country marked by strong ethnic, racial, linguistic, or religious divisions.

2. *Although providing services through governments that are close to the people can promote efficiency, federalism can also hinder progress.* It is extraordinarily

Problem Solving 2.2

Promoting Foreign Trade

The Problem: Beginning in the 1970s and continuing through the 1980s, the United States lost ground as a world economic power. Massive federal budget deficits and growing trade deficits wounded the national economy during an era of fundamental change in the nature of American production of goods and services. Increasing foreign competition from European and Asian countries resulted in a loss of U.S. markets at home and abroad. The federal government appeared unable to mount an effective foreign trade policy and largely overlooked the potential contributions of states and localities.

The Solution: State and local governments take the initiative in promoting foreign trade. Following the pioneering lead of Virginia, which was the first to post state employees overseas to assist with economic development, forty-three states today maintain foreign offices—Minnesota alone has eight. In fact, "more states have offices in Japan than in Washington, DC."[1] States also sponsor trade shows and conferences, publish international newsletters, advertise heavily in foreign publications, and frequently send official delegations abroad on trade missions to facilitate state economic development activities. In the words of President Bush, governors "are becoming our economic envoys . . . restoring American international competitiveness and expanding world markets for American goods and services."[2]

Early efforts concentrated on convincing foreign firms to invest and relocate in the states, making the states the most important factor in shaping foreign investment policy.[3] Gradually the priority shifted to developing overseas markets for American-made goods. State leadership has opened up countless new markets and developed many new and valuable trade relationships. Recently, states and localities aggressively embarked on programs to attract foreign tourists.

The future of the United States depends on a healthy domestic economy closely linked to the global marketplace. Trade and economic development initiatives of the state and local governments are a good illustration of how federalism promotes innovative and effective coping behavior.

---

1. "A View from the Commission," *Intergovernmental Perspective* 16 (Spring, 1990): 2.
2. Blaine Liner, "States and Localities in the Global Marketplace," *Intergovernmental Perspective* 16 (Spring, 1990): 14.
3. Susan Tolchin and Martin Tolchin, *Buying into America* (New York: Times Books, 1988).

---

difficult, if not impossible, to coordinate the efforts of all state and local governments to combat social and economic problems. Picture trying to get 84,000 squawking and flapping chickens to move in the same direction at once. Business interests level this criticism when they encounter government regulations on products and services that vary widely across the United States.

3. *Not surprisingly, so many governments lead to duplication and confusion.* Fifty-one separate and independent court systems bring about a great deal of confusion. A complex federal system like our own is a lawyer's sweet dream. A good example is the legal snarl that developed over the will of the multimillionaire Howard Hughes. Born and raised in Texas, Hughes spent much of his life and made the bulk of his fortune in California and Nevada. He died in an airplane, without a will. It took many years, the involvement of the U.S. Supreme Court, and millions of dollars in attorneys' fees taken from the estate before Hughes's business affairs and inheritance were settled. Along with hordes

of lawyers, five different state court systems were involved, each with its own unique set of rules and precedents.[31]

4. *Federalism may promote state and local innovation, but it can also hinder national programs and priorities.* The many points of involvement for state and local government can encourage obstruction and delay and result in an ineffective national government. An obvious example is the successful opposition of the southern states to voting rights for African-Americans for more than a hundred years. Federal laws and the U.S. Constitution set forth the right of black Americans to vote, but some states systematically denied them this right until implementation of the national Voting Rights Act of 1965.

5. *Broad opportunity for political participation is highly desirable in a democracy, but it may encourage local biases that damage the national interest.* Hazardous, radioactive, and solid wastes must be disposed of somewhere, but local officials and citizens are quick to scream, "Not in my back yard!" Another example involves smoking and chewing tobacco, which are major causes of illness and high health care costs; representatives from the tobacco-growing states typically defend the industry from regulation, taxation, or abolition.

····································

Local Governments in American Federalism

In a formal sense, local governments in the American federal system operate under a unitary system. Municipalities, counties, towns, townships, school districts, and other local governments are created by the states. Their powers depend on what the states decide to let them do. This was a conscious decision on the part of the Framers, who rarely mentioned the role of local governments in their debates on federalism. Local governments are nowhere named in the U.S. Constitution.

Dillon's Rule

Dillon's Rule

A rule that limits the powers of local government to those expressly granted by the state, or those closely linked to expressed powers.

Local government powers are derived primarily from the state constitutions. Federal and state courts have consistently upheld the dependency of localities on the state since Iowa Judge John F. Dillon first laid down **Dillon's Rule** in 1868. Dillon's Rule established that local governments may exercise only those powers explicitly granted to them by the state, those clearly implied by these explicit powers, and those absolutely essential to the declared objectives and purposes of the local government. When there is doubt regarding the legality of any specific local government power, the courts will resolve it in favor of the state.[32]

The result of Dillon's Rule is that local governments have relatively little discretionary power. When local officials want to take on a new responsibility or provide a new service, they must first ask the state legislature or the governor for the appropriate authority. This rule applies even to such mundane matters as opening a city skating rink or operating a concession stand at a municipal ballpark.

Home Rule

home rule

The legal ability of a local government to run its own affairs, subject to state oversight.

Thus, in theory and in constitutional law, local governments are cloistered within the walls built by the state. However, most state constitutions have partially opened the doors for at least some types of local governments through home rule. **Home rule** is a legal arrangement by which the state issues local governments a charter that allows discretion and flexibility in carrying out their activities. In effect, it recognizes a form of dual federalism *within* states by formally delegating certain powers to local government.[33] Because the courts have excluded any local powers other than those specifically enumerated, this grant of local authority may be rather limited. Approximately half the states have carried home rule a step further, by granting localities a general range of powers to perform their duties. In these states the localities do not have to make special requests before taking care of traditional city business.

Home rule has resulted in some autonomy for municipalities, counties, and towns (but it does not usually apply to special-purpose forms of local government such as school districts or water and sewer districts). Although it has broadened their scope of authority beyond Dillon's Rule, many localities remain highly dependent on the state. A controversial decision handed down by the U.S. Supreme Court in 1982 reaffirmed the dependency of local governments and restricted broad grants of authority under home rule. In *Community Communications Co.* v. *City of Boulder*, the Court held that local governments do not have immunity from antitrust suits filed under the Sherman Antitrust Act, unless specifically granted by the states.[34] (An antitrust suit seeks to break up a monopoly on some good or service.) Prior to the *Boulder* decision it was widely assumed that local governments, like the states, could not be sued for conduct alleged to have anticompetitive effects on a firm. The *Boulder* case, which involved a city monopoly on cable TV, spawned more than two hundred lawsuits in areas ranging from ambulance service and taxicabs to garbage collection. Because of this, Congress passed a law in 1984 limiting the damages to be paid by localities found to be violating antitrust law. The importance of *Boulder*, which was modified by subsequent Supreme Court decisions,[35] is that local governments continue to be held to the standards of Dillon's Rule. They have only those powers and immunities specifically granted to them by the states or clearly related to their delegated powers. Immunity from antitrust suits is not within the realm of specified or implied powers under home rule.

....

Interstate Cooperation

The states often cooperate formally or informally in dealing with common problems. This is known as *horizontal federalism*. Formal methods for cooperation are grounded in the U.S. Constitution. Informal ones have evolved from day-to-day interactions.

Cooperation Under the Constitution

There are four formal provisions for interstate cooperation.

1. *The full faith and credit clause* of the Constitution binds every citizen of every state to the laws and policies of other states. This means, among other things, that a person who has a legitimate debt in North Dakota will be made to pay even if he moves to Montana. Crossing a state boundary does not alter a legal obligation. The courts have interpreted full faith and credit to apply to contracts, wills, divorces, and many other legalities. The clause does not, however, extend to criminal judgments.

2. *The interstate rendition clause* begins where full faith and credit leaves off, covering those convicted of criminal violations. Governors are required to extradite (return) fugitives to the state in which they were found guilty or are under indictment (although in certain cases they may refuse.)

3. *The privileges and immunities clause* states that "the citizens of each state shall be entitled to all privileges and immunities of citizens in the several states." This clause was intended by the Framers to prevent any state from discriminating against the citizens of another state who happen to be traveling or temporarily dwelling outside their own state's borders. Of course, states do discriminate against nonresidents in such matters as out-of-state tuition, hunting and fishing license fees, and residency requirements for voting. The Supreme Court has upheld these and other minor discrepancies, so long as the "fundamental rights" of nonresidents are not violated. Such rights include the right to conduct business, to have access to state courts, and to travel freely across state borders. Floridians cannot keep New Yorkers from settling and working in Tampa any more than Californians could prevent refugees from the Dust Bowl from moving to the Golden State during the Depression.

4. Finally, the *interstate compact clause* authorizes the states to negotiate compacts. Early interstate compacts were used to settle boundary disputes. More than 120 are in effect today in a wide variety of areas, including shared water resources, pest control, and education.

The interstate compact is an effective means of resolving complex problems between states. It has the force of law, is highly flexible, and is adaptable to some of the toughest problems confronting the states. The compact has also become an active vehicle for change. Its usefulness is readily apparent in some of its most recent applications. For example, the Western Regional Education Compact allows a fifteen-state region to share higher-education resources. Instead of each state building and operating its own medical, dental, veterinary, and other professional schools, regional programs permit out-of-state students to pay in-state tuition.

Informal Cooperation Among the States

Interstate cooperation can be facilitated through a variety of informal methods. Examples include regional interstate commissions, such as the Appalachian

Regional Commission (ARC),[36] which was created by national legislation in 1965 to attack poverty in the states of Appalachia. The ARC coordinates federal aid programs in the region and allocates its own funds for improvements in public health, transportation, and other areas. Another example is found in the Mississippi Delta region, where several states in 1990 adopted a ten-year economic development plan to help pull the area out of its own circle of poverty.

States also develop uniform laws to help manage common problems. The National Conference of Commissioners on Uniform State Laws has met regularly since 1892 to develop comparable model statutes on approximately 150 topics ranging from child support to welfare cheating. States may voluntarily adopt the uniform laws proposed by the conference.

Interstate cooperation increasingly occurs through information sharing among elected and appointed officials and the organizations to which they belong. The National Governors' Association, the National Conference of State Legislatures, the Council of State Governments, and many other organizations meet each year to share information. They also publish professional journals, newsletters, and research reports.

The scope and number of cooperative mechanisms have expanded substantially in response to the gradual shift of federal responsibilities to the states and the new and more complex problems facing them. Increasing interstate cooperation is also a product of the resurgence of the states as innovative, effective, and responsive actors within the American federal system. Of course, interstate relations do not always go well; occasionally, the states get into serious (and not so serious) conflicts and disagreements. Those that the states cannot settle themselves are taken directly to the U.S. Supreme Court for resolution.

An Enduring Issue of Federalism

A single broad issue in American federalism transcends all others: what is the proper balance of power and responsibility between the national government and the states? The debate over this profound question first arose in preconstitutional days, as Adams, Jefferson, Madison, Hamilton, and others put forward their views. The Constitution represents a compromise between the most knowledgeable figures of the times, who decided that both levels of government would be sovereign and strong.

In recent times the balance of power and responsibility undeniably has shifted toward the national government. But not all the growth in national governmental power and responsibility has occurred at the expense of the states and localities. They too have increased their respective scope of activities in the social and economic lives of their citizens. Government has grown at all levels. The states are determined to oppose further federal pre-emptions of their powers and responsibilities. They have fought to protect the health, safety, and physical environment of their citizens, often with standards and commitment that far exceed those of the federal government. They have continued to serve as political laboratories for experiments in service delivery and other fields, in spite of severe reductions in federal financial support and expensive government spending requirements. As the burdens of governing 250 million Americans have grown, the limitations of the national government have become evident. The states have stepped forward as vigorous and progressive partners in federalism. Dual federalism is a vestige of earlier, simpler times. Effective federalism in the United States today demands a cooperative partnership among nation, states, and localities.

The question of the balance of power and responsibility in American federalism is no less important now than it was two hundred years ago. The focus of the debate has shifted, however, to a pragmatic interest in how the responsibilities of governing should be sorted out among the three levels of government. As pointed out by Samuel H. Beer, an insightful observer of American government, "The American federal system has never been static. It has changed radically over the years, as tides of centralization and decentralization have altered the balance of power and the allocation of functions among the different levels of government."[37] The pendulum marking the balance has swung to and fro over the two centuries of American federalism. Today it swings in the direction of the state and local governments.

....

Summary

The evolution of American federalism continues in the 1990s. From the early experiment with a confederation of states, to state-centered (compact) federalism, to nation-centered federalism, the trend has generally been in the direction of stronger national government. The states, however, remain very important political actors. The power relationships among the three levels of government are described by various models, including dual federalism, picket fence federalism, and cooperative federalism. Cooperative federalism is the operative model today, under the variant known as New Federalism.

Federalism has certain advantages and disadvantages. Among the advantages are managing conflict and promoting efficiency, innovation, participation, and individual freedom. But federalism can also exacerbate conflict, hinder progress, lead to duplication, obstruct national programs, and encourage local bias. Two special concerns in American federalism are the role of local governments and methods for permitting interstate cooperation.

Key Terms

factions	Tenth Amendment
unitary government	enumerated (delegated) powers
confederacy	compact theory
nation-centered federalism	nullification
state-centered federalism	interposition
reserved powers	national supremacy clause

necessary and proper clause
implied powers
commerce clause
general welfare clause
Fourteenth Amendment
Sixteenth Amendment
grant-in-aid
federal pre-emption

dual federalism
cooperative federalism
creative federalism
picket fence federalism
New Federalism
Dillon's Rule
home rule

3

Federalism and Public Policy

A mong the many points made in the preceding chapter, two stand out: the American federal system is constantly evolving, and it is remarkably complex. Federalism is a matter of power, authority, and—of course—money. The change and complexity that characterize it have been both legal and financial. Federalism is a question not only of which level of government will do what but of which level will pay for it. Often, the correct answer is "all levels." Most national domestic programs are implemented through an intricate intergovernmental partnership.

This chapter discusses intergovernmental relations of the Reagan and Bush periods and the implications for the remainder of the decade. In the process, it focuses on the importance of federalism in *public policy*, which involves actions by governments to solve problems or pursue a particular course to improve society. When in 1980 Republican Ronald Reagan defeated the incumbent president, Democrat Jimmy Carter, a new era in American federalism began. Since then, intergovernmental financial relations have changed, the responsibilities of each level of government have been altered, and states and their local governments have become sources of innovation and creative problem solving. We have entered a period that some have called "fend-for-yourself federalism."[1]

Intergovernmental Financial Relations

"Give me money, that's what I want. . . ." So goes the refrain of an old blues tune that is not about government but might have been. Money has always been important to government, although the word *money* is seldom used. Instead, the talk is of revenues and expenditures. **Revenues** are the funds that governments have at their disposal. They are derived from taxes, fees and charges, and transfers from other levels of government. **Expenditures** are the ways in which the governmental revenues are disbursed. Governments spend money to operate programs, to build public facilities, and to pay off debts. The twentieth century has seen steady increases in both revenues and expenditures at all levels of government.

revenues

Monies raised by governments from taxes, fees, enterprises, and payments from other levels of government.

expenditures

Allocations of government monies.

The Grant-in-Aid

By the 1980s, the grant-in-aid (see Chapter 2) had become the primary mechanism for transferring money from the national to the state and local governments.[2] The national government makes grants available for a number of reasons: to redistribute wealth, to establish minimum policy standards, and to achieve national goals. But grants are primarily designed to meet the needs of state and local governments, including natural resource and environmental protection, transportation, community and regional development, education, and health care.

Discretion of Recipients   There are two major variations in grants: the amount of discretion (independence) the recipient has in determining how to spend the money, and the conditions under which the grant is awarded. Imagine a spectrum running from maximum discretion to minimum discretion. The grant labels that correspond to these end points are **revenue sharing** and **categorical grants,** respectively. Under revenue sharing, states and communities are allocated funds that they may use for any purpose. A categorical grant, in contrast, can be used by the recipient government only for a narrowly defined purpose, such as removing asbestos from school buildings, acquiring land for outdoor recreation, training managers of bus systems, or constructing waste disposal systems.

Located between revenue sharing and categorical grants on the discretion spectrum are block grants. **Block grants** are *broad-based grants;* that is, they can be used anywhere within a functional area, such as elementary and secondary education, transportation, or training and employment. The difference between categorical and block grants is that the recipient government decides how block grants will be spent. For instance, a local school system can decide whether getting rid of the asbestos in school buildings is more important than buying microscopes for the science laboratory; but the school system cannot spend those block grant dollars outside the functional area of education.

Block grants and revenue sharing give nonnational governments considerable flexibility in responding to pressing needs and preferred goals. These grant mechanisms assume that state and local governments can make rational choices among competing claims.

Conditions for Grants   Grants also vary in the manner in which they are awarded. A **formula grant** makes funding available automatically, based on state and local conditions such as poverty level or unemployment rate. A **project grant** is awarded to selected applicants, based on administrative assessments of the strength of competing proposals. Block grants are distributed on a formula basis; categorical grants can be either formula- or project-based; approximately one-third are formula and two-thirds are project grants.[3] Formula grants offer more discretion to the recipient government than project grants do. (This is not the case for the national government, however. Project grants give the granting agency wide latitude in determining which projects will be funded.)[4]

These two characteristics, the amount of discretion enjoyed by the recipient jurisdiction and the manner in which the grant is awarded, are important for understanding the grant system. Another, less prominent factor also affects intergovernmental financial relations: the existence of *matching requirements.* Some federal grants require that the recipient government use its own resources to pay a certain percentage of program costs. This arrangement is designed to stimulate state and local spending and to discourage nonnational governments from participating in a program simply because money is available. For example, if a state government wants funding through the Boating Safety Financial Assistance program administered by the U.S. Department of Transportation, it must

---

revenue sharing

A "no-strings" form of financial aid from one level of government to another.

categorical grant

A form of financial aid from one level of government to another to be used for a narrowly defined purpose.

block grant

A form of financial aid from one level of government to another for use in a functional area.

formula grant

A funding mechanism that automatically allocates monies based on conditions in the recipient government.

project grant

A funding mechanism that awards monies based on the strength of an applicant government's proposal.

contribute 50 percent itself. For a local government to participate in the U.S. Interior Department's Urban Parks program, it must provide from 15 percent to 50 percent of the costs. In each case, the recipient government's commitment to boating safety or urban parks is likely to be higher because of the joint funding. Most categorical grants carry a matching requirement.[5] Major exceptions to the trend toward matching grants, however, are in elementary, secondary, and vocational education and in health care programs.

Recent Changes in National Expenditures

During the 1980s, the flow of dollars from the national government to state and local governments slowed down. Although the $136.9 billion in federal grants flowing to states and localities in 1990 appears massive, federal aid as a share of state and local government expenditures had actually shrunk by one-third since its 1978 peak. Table 3.1 provides a historical look at national grant-in-aid expenditures. It is important to remember that the figures in the table have not been adjusted for inflation; the $24.1 billion spent in 1970 was worth vastly more than it would be today. Furthermore, the amounts do not take into account the increase in population since 1970. The second column of figures in Table 3.1 documents the decreasing proportion of national dollars in the expenditures of state and local governments in the 1980s. The final column reflects the fact that aid to states and localities consumes an increasingly smaller share of the federal government's budget.

The End of General Revenue Sharing   A principal factor in the decline of national aid to state and local governments during the 1980s was the termination of revenue sharing. Called *General Revenue Sharing* (GRS) when enacted

Table 3.1

Historical Trends in Federal Grant-in-Aid Outlays

Year	Total Grant-in-aid Outlays (in billions of dollars)	Federal Grants as a Percentage of State and Local Expenditures	Federal Grants as a Percentage of Federal Outlays
1970	$ 24.1	19.2%	12.3%
1975	49.8	22.7	15.0
1980	91.5	25.8	15.5
1985	105.9	20.9	11.2
1990	136.9	18.0	10.9

Note: Years are fiscal years. Dollar figures are not adjusted for inflation or population growth.

Source: U.S. Office of Management and Budget, *The Budget of the United States Government, Fiscal Year 1992, Historical Tables* (Washington, D.C.: U.S. Government Printing Office, 1991), p. 132.

during the Nixon administration, this program was immensely popular with state and local officials. GRS provided funds, with no strings attached, to state and general-purpose local governments (cities, counties, towns, townships). GRS fell out of favor with Congress in 1986 mostly because of tax effort: In the eyes of Congress, the availability of GRS funds allowed local governments to keep taxes unnaturally low, since they could use GRS funds to pay bills. If national dollars were going to be used in this way, Congress wanted more control over them. Moreover, the Reagan administration wanted to discontinue GRS because of the mounting national budget deficit. Accordingly, federal funds to localities through GRS fell from $6.8 billion in 1980 to zero in 1988.[6]

The Continuing Importance of National Funds   Although the Washington-funded portion of state and local government expenditures has hovered around 18 percent since 1987, it remains an important source of revenue for non-national governments. The data in Table 3.2 provide an indication of the magnitude of the fiscal flow in states and regions. Grants to state and local governments averaged approximately $525 per person in fiscal year 1990. However, the funds were not spread evenly across the country. As the first column of figures in Table 3.2 shows, Wyoming and Alaska, where people are few and far between, received the most per capita. Federal grants poured into these states at the rate of more than $1,200 per person. At the bottom of the list are Florida and Virginia, where federal grant monies averaged just over $350 per person. States battle over their share of grant allocations in Congress. For example, during 1991 reauthorization hearings for a five-year, $105 billion surface transportation bill, "donor" states, which pay more out in federal gasoline taxes than they receive in grants, fought with those states that are net beneficiaries (e.g., California receives 89¢ on the gasoline tax dollar, while Alaska gets $7.80). It should be noted that national expenditures in nongrant forms affect state and local economies substantially. In the nongrant category are payments to individuals, notably through the social security system; purchases by the national government; and wages and salaries of federal workers.

The Impact of National Cuts   Cutting grant funds carries a human price. Items excised from the national budget translate into a loss of benefits for the public. The Reagan administration cuts hit poor people particularly hard.[7] For example, public service jobs for the poor were eliminated, funding for low-income students was reduced, unemployed Americans could no longer receive a stipend while enrolled in job training, and rents for public housing increased while the number of new subsidized housing units declined. Governmental actions in Washington, D.C., can translate into real anguish in Gary, Indiana, or Pine Bluff, Arkansas, or in any other community across the United States.

Complicating intergovernmental financial relations was the 1985 Balanced Budget and Emergency Deficit Control Act (the Gramm-Rudman-Hollings bill), which was aimed at reducing the federal budget deficit. This law mandated that the national budget deficit be reduced to preset levels each year, with the goal of a balanced budget by 1991. The failure of Gramm-Rudman, as it was called, to put a dent in the deficit led Congress to enact the Budget Enforcement

State and Region	Per Capita Grants to State and Local Governments	Per Capita State Rank
U.S. Average	$525	—
New England	619	—
Connecticut	600	15
Maine	621	12
Massachusetts	641	9
New Hampshire	385	47
Rhode Island	770	4
Vermont	670	8
Middle Atlantic	663	—
Delaware	470	36
Maryland	491	33
New Jersey	514	28
New York	876	3
Pennsylvania	515	27
Great Lakes	485	—
Illinois	462	39
Indiana	437	42
Michigan	511	29
Ohio	497	31
Wisconsin	519	26
Plains	488	—
Iowa	464	38
Kansas	412	45
Minnesota	541	21
Missouri	425	44
Nebraska	494	32
North Dakota	737	6
South Dakota	734	7

[a]Among the largest programs in this category (federal expenditures only) are Medicaid, Aid to Families with Dependent Children (AFDC), and highway programs.

Table 3.2
(cont.)

State and Region	Per Capita Grants to State and Local Governments	Per Capita State Rank
Southeast	$ 475	—
Alabama	520	25
Arkansas	532	23
Florida	354	50
Georgia	484	35
Kentucky	555	19
Louisiana	630	11
Mississippi	620	13
North Carolina	444	40
South Carolina	542	20
Tennessee	557	18
Virginia	361	49
West Virginia	562	17
Southwest	436	—
Arizona	442	41
New Mexico	633	10
Oklahoma	498	30
Texas	406	46
Rocky Mountain	549	—
Colorado	434	43
Idaho	565	16
Montana	740	5
Utah	487	34
Wyoming	1,253	2
Far West[b]	482	—
Alaska	1,303	1
California	468	37
Hawaii	540	22
Nevada	368	48
Oregon	601	14
Washington	528	24

[b]Alaska and Hawaii are excluded from the Far West regional total but are included in the U.S. total.

Source: U.S. Advisory Commission on Intergovernmental Relations, *Significant Features of Fiscal Federalism, 1991*, Vol. 2 (Washington, D.C.: ACIR, 1991): 52, 53.

Problem Solving 3.1

Managing Federalism Through Intergovernmental Bodies

The Problem: Local governments are directly responsible for many important aspects of social service delivery systems. But within a single metropolitan area there are numerous local governments and private providers that share social service responsibilities without any formal coordinating mechanisms. Funds and mandates from various national and state agencies sometimes seem to work at cross-purposes and against local needs. How can local communities set their own priorities and coordinate social service delivery systems in the face of almost overwhelming complexity and confusion?

The Solution: Set priorities and coordinate services through the creation of intergovernmental bodies (IGBs). IGBs are established voluntarily by elected and appointed officials from local governments and private funding organizations (such as foundations or the United Way.) A local perspective on human ser-

vice issues is developed to reflect special problems of the metropolitan area and its various communities.

The most successful IGBs select one or two critical problems at a time and focus their energies on them. Among the activities they pursue are needs assessment, fund raising, cross-agency management, and advocacy of local interests to state, federal, and private funding entities. Examples include the Human Resources Steering Committee of Roanoke, Virginia, which offers projects directed toward the homeless and teen pregnancy; the Metropolitan Human Services Commission of Tulsa, Oklahoma, which conducts social service needs studies and maintains an extensive countywide data base to facilitate planning and service delivery; and the Coalition for Human Services Planning of Indianapolis–Marion County, Indiana, which operates a transportation program for the handicapped, a foster care plan, and various neighborhood improvement projects.

Source: Adapted from Robert Agranoff, "Managing Federalism Through Metropolitan Human Services Intergovernmental Bodies," *Publius: The Journal of Federalism* 20 (Winter 1990): 1–21.

Act (BEA) in 1990. BEA set spending ceilings for domestic programs that, if exceeded, must be counteracted by spending cuts in other domestic programs. The law extends the Gramm-Rudman deficit targets to 1996. An additional complication from the perspective of state and local officials was passage of the Tax Reform Act (TRA) in 1986, which immediately affected state tax collections and financing options for economic development.[8] All in all, the late 1980s brought tremendous insecurity to intergovernmental financial relations. Problem Solving 3.1 explains one way local governments have learned to cope with the confusion.

Reagan's New Federalism

Ronald Reagan made his feelings about federalism quite clear in his 1982 State of the Union message.

This administration has faith in state and local governments and the constitutional balance envisioned by the founding fathers. Together, after fifty years of taking power away from the hands of the people in their states and local communities, we have started returning power and resources to them.[9]

With this sentiment, the Reagan administration set out on an ambitious quest to devolve power and authority—that is, to turn back a variety of programs to state and local governments. In speaking to the National Conference of State Legislatures, President Reagan used a construction analogy to convey his message. He compared the federal system to a masonry wall composed of bricks (the states) and mortar (the national government). By 1980, the wall, in his view, had become more mortar than bricks.[10] His solution was to chip away at the mortar and let the bricks carry more weight.

A New "New Federalism"

The motivation for Reagan's New Federalism was not only decentralization but, more important, budget cutting. One scholar termed it "a radical departure in intergovernmental fiscal relations characterized by devolution, disengagement, and decremental budgeting."[11] State and local governments were given more freedom to spend an ever-declining amount of federal funds. The strings were cut with a double-edged sword. In other words, state and local governments were forced to assume greater financial responsibility for an array of programs. In effect, the national government said to the states and localities, "If these programs are so important to you, then fund them yourselves." Unfortunately, many state and local governments were not in a position to pay up.

Reagan's Proposals The first actions under Reagan's New Federalism involved specific proposals to combine existing categorical grants into comprehensive block grants. Reagan was successful in winning congressional approval to merge fifty-seven categorical grants into nine new block grants and to eliminate another sixty categorical grants in 1981.[12] The merger resulted in four health-related block grants: Child and Maternal Health Services; Preventive Health and Health Services; Primary Care; and Alcohol, Drug Abuse and Mental Health. The remaining five block grants were Social Services, Low-Income Home Energy Assistance, Community Services, Community Development for Small Cities, and Elementary and Secondary Education. The funding for the new block grants represented an almost 25 percent decrease from the previous year's allocation for the separate categorical grants.[13] The Reagan administration contended that state and local governments would need less money because the block grants would reduce paperwork. In addition, state governments were to enjoy new freedom in administering the block grants.

Buoyed by his successful grant consolidation effort, President Reagan next proposed a swap of programs between the national and state governments. This proposal, known as the "turnback," was intended to be the centerpiece of New

Federalism. The states were to assume financial and administrative responsibility for two massive programs, Aid to Families with Dependent Children (AFDC) and the food stamp program, and forty smaller ones such as child nutrition and education for the handicapped, in exchange for a national takeover of the Medicaid program. Although national funds would have eased state assumption of the programs initially, the plan called for total state funding of the turned-back programs by 1991. Concern that these arrangements would financially strap all but the wealthiest states effectively stalled the proposal.

After being turned down on turnbacks, the Reagan administration switched tactics. Instead of grand restructuring proposals, the president chose to chip steadily away at existing grant programs. Congress, with an eye on deficit reduction, was generally receptive to the Reagan-proposed funding reductions. Typically, Congress responded by making smaller-than-requested cuts in many of the aid programs.

The final salvo in Reagan's New Federalism came in the form of an *executive order*—a presidential action that has the effect of law. Executive Order 12612, issued by President Reagan in October 1987, called for a strict interpretation of the Constitution regarding the distribution of responsibilities between states and the national government.[14] According to Executive Order 12612, the national government should not take action unless a vital national interest is involved. The order set new standards for resolving conflicts between national statutes and state laws, restricting a federal agency's ability to rule that a federal statute pre-empts state law. It also required federal agencies to prepare federalism assessments to accompany their proposed policies. These assessments were intended to gauge the financial, administrative, and legal impact of national action on the states.

In Retrospect

These actions may not have constituted the "Reagan Revolution" that some people predicted. As two observers noted, "Reagan could not succeed in a grand-scale dismantling of the whole constellation of grants to local and state governments."[15] But there has certainly been a redirection of financial responsibility.

The full force of Reagan's impact was deflected by a number of factors. One was the organization of certain interests in American society. The findings of researchers examining programmatic changes during the Reagan era make this point quite convincingly.[16] Political scientists Paul E. Peterson, Barry G. Rabe, and Kenneth K. Wong found that Reagan-sponsored efforts at decentralization were most effectively resisted in programs such as health care, where well-organized beneficiaries and policy professionals were established. Federal health care programs such as Medicare have become institutionalized and are thus fairly resistant to threats. But in federal housing programs, the administration was able to achieve more of its objectives because professional and constituent support was limited, and so there is now a substantially reduced national role in housing.

Federal budget cuts during the 1980s had deleterious effects on public housing projects. Some experts believe that the deteriorated condition of many public housing complexes has contributed to the problem of homelessness.

The degree of the Reagan administration's success depended on the organization of interests and their relative power.

Another factor limiting Reagan's success was internal to the administration. Administration proposals betrayed a basic ambivalence regarding intent. The administration's New Federalism, in all its manifestations, was held together by the unifying theme of reduced spending; but beyond that organizing principle, the actions were "inconsistent and incoherent," according to some.[17]

The Bush Approach to Federalism

The Reagan legacy lived on with George Bush in the White House. Although the style has been different—in the view of many state and local officials, the Bush administration has been more sympathetic—the substance remains the same.[18] For example, President Bush has reaffirmed his administration's support for Executive Order 12612. In two policy areas, transportation and education, Bush has emphasized the sorting out of national, state, and local responsibilities. Under the Intermodal Surface Transportation Efficiency Act of 1991, state and local governments will increase their share of costs for 700,000 miles of federally assisted highways in return for greater flexibility in project selection and funding. And in the area of education, the president called the nation's governors together for a summit (the first in fifty years) to exhort the states to take a leading role in achieving a series of educational performance goals. Further evidence of the devolutionary emphasis can be found in the budgets that President Bush has submitted to Congress. They contain a section entitled "Encouraging Experimentation" that highlighted innovative programs undertaken by states and localities.

In his 1991 State of the Union message, President Bush proposed $22 billion in "turnovers," federal programs that would be shifted to the states. Among the programs initially targeted for turnover were $5.9 billion in state administrative expenses for Medicaid, Aid to Families with Dependent Children, and food stamps as well as $3.1 billion in Community Development Block Grants (CDBG), the last significant monetary link between the federal government and cities.[19] Other programs slated for the states were $5.5 billion in public and subsidized housing programs, $2.1 billion in Environmental Protection Agency (EPA) construction grants, and $1.8 billion in assorted educational programs.

The nation's mayors reacted negatively to this turnover proposal, primarily because they did not want to see their CDBG funds under the control of state government. State officials, however, supported the turnover concept. The National Governors' Association (NGA) responded with its own $15.2 billion turnover proposal consolidating fifty-three categorical grant and loan programs into a block grant with eight functional components. (The NGA proposal excluded the contentious CDBG turnover.) The National Conference of State Legislatures endorsed a $21.3 billion package that would merge eighty-five programs into twelve block grants. Congressional debate over the merits of the various plans continues. It is clear, however, that in a federal system defined by huge national budget deficits, the spending ceilings in the Budget Enforcement Act, and the spiraling costs of the savings and loan bailout, new national program initiatives are unlikely. As the realignment of national-state-local relations continues, the role of the states intensifies.

The Curious Reintrusion of the Feds

Although the White House is saying "let the states and localities do it," Congress continues to impose mandates and pre-empt the states. In addition, Congress has begun to include set-asides in block grants. To state and local governments, the refrain is beginning to sound uncomfortably like "you do it, but do it our way."

federal mandate

A requirement that a state or local government undertake a specific activity or provide a particular service.

Mandates are especially burdensome when they are unfunded—that is, when the national government requires the states and localities to take action and does not provide any funding. Who pays? The states and localities do. Consider the Americans with Disablilities Act (ADA) passed by Congress in 1990. It mandates that all fixed-route public transportation systems be made accessible to the handicapped. This will require the purchase of new buses with wheelchair lifts, modification of the existing fleet, and provision of paratransit services through customized vehicles and specialized routes. The Congressional Budget Office estimates that the new equipment and modifications will cost operators of public transportation systems (primarily local governments) somewhere between $35 million and $45 million annually. Making subway stations and other transit facilities accessible is expected to cost several hundred million dollars over the next thirty years.[20] Yet federal funding represents only a fraction of the total costs that state and local governments will bear in implementing the ADA. Other recent federal legislation with costly mandate provisions includes the 1990 Clean Air Act Amendments and the 1991 Medicaid provisions.

Pre-emption represents another intrusion of the national government into the state sphere. It takes two forms: *total* pre-emption, whereby the national government removes all regulatory authority for a given function from states and localities; and *partial* pre-emption, whereby the national government establishes minimum national standards for state-implemented programs. While president, Reagan signed into law a total of ninety-two pre-emptive statutes.[21] Although ten of these bills provided regulatory relief to states and localities from earlier judicial and congressional pre-emptions, eighty-two were truly pre-emptive. Examples of totally pre-emptive actions include the Safe Drinking Water Act of 1986, the Prescriptive Drug Marketing Act of 1987, and the Ocean Dumping Ban Act of 1988. And among the partially pre-emptive statutes are the Product Liability Risk Retention Act of 1981, the Cable Communications Policy Act of 1984, and the National Appliance Energy Conservation Act of 1987. Thus, when mandates and pre-emption are taken into consideration, a different picture of intergovernmental relations emerges. As one analyst concluded in 1991, "The past decade was characterized by increasing regulatory burdens imposed on states and localities, punctuated by occasional examples of regulatory relief and deferral."[22] Another termed the period a shift from cooperative federalism to coercive federalism.[23]

set-asides

Requirements in block grants that assign a certain percentage expenditure for a particular activity.

Set-asides offer an alternative mechanism through which policymakers in Washington, D.C., can influence the behavior of distant governments. Set-asides are provisions in block grants that designate a certain percentage expenditure on a particular activity. For example, the Alcohol, Drug Abuse and Mental Health Block Grant of 1988 contains requirements that states spend 50 percent of the funds on services to intravenous (IV) drug users.[24] The Congress reasoned that the sharing of hypodermic needles among addicts was contributing to the spread of the AIDS virus, and that states were not doing enough to address the problem. But state leaders, while admitting that AIDS was a national priority, argued that the problem was not uniformly spread around the country. Why should Montana spend the same proportion of its funds on IV drug users as New York? Perhaps Montana should spend its drug abuse funds on adolescent alcohol abusers. In any case, the issue is clear: Who should decide how federal funds are to be spent—the government allocating the funds or the government implementing the program?

State and local officials see set-asides as the reattachment of strings that twenty years of "New Federalism" had cut. Along with mandates and pre-emptions, set-asides are ways in which a national government constrained by harsh budgetary realities can continue a modicum of policy activism. Will increased financial burdens for states and localities struggling with the aftermath of the 1990–1992 economic recession trigger innovation and creativity? One observer responds, "The best answer right now is 'surely' in some places, 'maybe' in many others."[25] In those "maybe" states, some officials have begun to talk wistfully of "turnups"—that is, having the national government assume greater financial responsibility for mandated programs.[26]

In sum, the Reagan and Bush years muddied the waters of federalism more than they clarified them. The remainder of this chapter seeks to make the concept of federalism more tangible by examining two distinctive policy fields. The first, social welfare policy, has been dominated and directed by the national government. It is a highly complex and often confusing area, characterized by shifting goals and strident ideological and partisan debates. In fact, it was conflict over social welfare policies that ultimately sank Reagan's New Federalism. The second policy area, higher education, has been dominated and directed by the states. It is relatively simple to comprehend and exhibits fairly broad agreement on goals and objectives.

Although in many respects social welfare and higher education appear at opposite ends of the policy spectrum, they share at least one very important trait. Like almost all public policy fields in American federalism, they involve key contributions by all three levels of government—national, state, and local. Intergovernmental sharing of policymaking and program implementation is central to federalism.

Social Welfare Policy and Federalism

Social welfare policy is intended to assist those people who, for various reasons, need help in coping with poverty or other burdens that afflict them either temporarily or permanently. Aid to the poor and disadvantaged is the classic redistributive policy, whereby income is transferred from those in the upper and middle economic strata to those in the lower. It is an accepted principle today that government should provide a safety net for those at the economic margins of society.

The recipients of government assistance are diverse, including such people as an unemployed Haitian immigrant in a Miami slum whose English is poor and whose prospects for a good job are even poorer, a Vietnamese immigrant living with an extended family in San Francisco while working during the day and studying at night, a fifteen-year-old unwed mother in Cleveland who has little formal education and no job skills, a high school graduate in Detroit who was paralyzed because of an automobile accident and will probably never be able to earn a living, a Massachusetts family that has moved to North Carolina to look for work because both wage earners were laid off, and an eighty-year-old widow in Phoenix trying to make ends meet on her monthly social security check. These images are stereotypes, but they reflect some of the many faces of poverty in America. Some poor people do not receive any welfare benefits but choose to fight their battles by themselves; some need temporary help until they get back on their feet again; and some are likely to be dependent on government assistance for the rest of their lives. Many of the poor work forty-hour jobs at low wages; others have never drawn a paycheck.

The Meaning of Poverty

There are very few cases of absolute deprivation in this country. The necessities of life—food, clothing, housing—are widely available to all through government programs (the homeless represent a perplexing exception). The extreme, life-threatening poverty found in Ethiopia or rural Bolivia simply does not occur here. Instead, poverty in the United States consists of relative deprivation: Some people are relatively poor when their wealth and income are compared to those of the middle class.

The national government uses a statistic called the *poverty line* to define poverty in quantitative terms. It is set at three times the amount of income necessary to purchase essential food. The official poverty line changes each year as the cost of food rises (or, very rarely, falls). In 1989, it was pegged at $12,675 for a nonfarm family of four and at $6,311 for an individual.[27] The poverty line is important because it helps determine who qualifies for various forms of public assistance.

Poverty in America was once associated largely with old age, but this is no longer true. As the population has grown older and senior citizens have organized as a formidable interest group, higher social security benefits, federal programs such as Medicare, and age-based preferences in local property and state income taxes have eased elderly people's financial burdens. Today the most alarming poverty victims are children. One of every four children is born into poverty, and that rate has been rising every year since 1970. Children are now more than twice as likely as the elderly to be poor.

Childhood poverty is related to a host of factors, the most obvious of which is the "feminization of poverty." This term refers to the startling growth of female-headed households over the past three decades. Single mothers of young children may choose to stay at home and take care of the children, in which case they may have to depend entirely on support from public assistance programs. If they find work, they must somehow contend with the serious shortage and high cost of day-care facilities. Their children often suffer from an unstable environment and deprivation. Poor children are at high risk for criminal behavior and drug abuse.

As we shall see, child poverty is being met with innovative responses by state and local governments. Unfortunately, limited governmental resources are leading inevitably to a generational reckoning, when society will have to decide how to allocate its resources between the old and the young.

Social Welfare and Ideology

Intense debates over political ideology and values have always stormed over the social welfare policy landscape, resulting in confused policy goals, a faulty patchwork of programs, and perpetual crisis. Until recently, conservatives and liberals propounded starkly opposing points of view on the causes of poverty and the appropriate government response.

Conservatives, who generally believe in a restricted role for government, have tended to accept a modern version of the nineteenth-century view that "the giving of relief is a violation of natural law."[28] According to this viewpoint, the poor are victims of their own deficiencies. If they are to rise above poverty, they must hoist themselves up by their own bootstraps. From this perspective, the poor get what they deserve. Charles Murray, in his book *Losing Ground,* lays out the conservatives' classic beliefs on government aid to the poor.[29] He attacks the social welfare system for interfering with the free market, discouraging more productive allocations of public funds, undermining the work ethic, encouraging immoral behavior, and creating a permanent "underclass" of dependent welfare recipients.

For liberals, who generally believe in a broad and active role for government, poverty is a structural problem. People fall into poverty because of factors essentially beyond their control, such as inadequate schooling, poor parents, lack of job training opportunities, a shortage of job openings, various forms of discrimination, and the up-and-down cycles of a capitalistic economy. According to this view, people cannot help being poor; and so it becomes the responsibility of government not only to relieve their poverty through public assistance programs but also to provide the poor with the appropriate skills and physical environment to enable them to become self-sufficient.

The Origins of Social Welfare Policy   Our flawed and fragmented social welfare policy today is a reflection of shifting conservative and liberal control over the Congress and the presidency. The basic foundations of the welfare system were laid by the liberal Democratic administration of Franklin D. Roosevelt in response to the Great Depression of the 1930s. Private charity and state and local relief programs were completely inadequate for combating a 25 percent unemployment rate and a collapsed national economy. The national government responded with massive programs designed to provide temporary relief through public assistance payments, job creation, and social security.

Since the 1930s, competing political parties and ideologies have sewn together a patchwork of programs to help the poor and unfortunate. The most generous contributor was President Lyndon B. Johnson's War on Poverty during the 1960s. Johnson greatly expanded the budgets of existing welfare programs and initiated new, expensive efforts to attack poverty, such as the Economic Opportunity Act of 1965, which included Head Start (an educational program for disadvantaged children), the Job Corps, and community action programs. Some of the War on Poverty programs seemed to work, and others clearly did not. Generally, however, the Roosevelt and Johnson policies improved the lot of the poor.[30]

The Republican approach to social welfare policy has consisted mostly of a conservative, minimalist posture. President Richard M. Nixon was an exception. His proposed Family Assistance Plan would have established a federally funded minimum subsistence level for all Americans through direct cash payments to the poor. Most existing welfare programs would have been scrapped in favor of the income maintenance proposal, but Nixon's plan was unable to win congressional approval. Democratic President Jimmy Carter sought to resurrect the idea during the late 1970s, but again it failed to capture congressional favor. The conservative President Reagan sought to simplify social welfare policy by turning over control of certain programs to the states and localities, but the major impact of this approach was to halt temporarily some of the escalating welfare costs by cutting back on national funding. Reagan's actions led to an alarming increase in the number of families below the poverty line, even while the national economy registered moderately high growth. When Reagan took office in 1981, approximately 13 percent of all Americans were living in poverty; by 1983 that rate had risen to 15.2 percent. And in 1989, following six years of economic growth, the rate was again 13 percent. This figure included 10.1 percent of whites, 31.3 percent of blacks, and 26.2 percent of Hispanics.[31] Altogether, nearly 32 million Americans had fallen below the official poverty line.

A Social Welfare Consensus   Interestingly, a social welfare consensus brought together conservatives and liberals into a new coalition for reform in the late 1980s.[32] Conservatives admitted the responsibility of government to help the truly needy and economically vulnerable, and liberals saw the need to attach certain obligations to welfare checks and to address the "behavioral dependency" of the underclass. Behavioral dependency, which means that poor people become dependent on society for their economic well-being through their own choices, is a serious problem for this country's underclass, which is disproportionately young, male, black, and urban. Many of these people are school and societal dropouts—borderline illiterates with no job skills. A disproportionate number become involved in drugs and crime.[33]

The new consensus may reflect a common view of poverty, but there is less agreement on how to solve the problem. There *is* an understanding that different types of poverty should be treated distinctively. For example, children, seniors, single parents, working adults, and nonworking adults all have different needs. There is also agreement that government should help those who can climb out of poverty through job training and placement, and that able-bodied welfare recipients have an obligation to seek a job or perform public work.

Beyond these basic elements, the new consensus tends to unravel. Conservatives seek "better" behavior from the poor, admonishing them to complete high school, find employment (even at low wages), and either get married and stay married or not have babies. Liberals are more willing to utilize social programs to transfer government resources to the poor.[34] Despite these differences, the social welfare consensus was broad enough to enable congressional passage of the Family Support Act of 1988. This law incorporated conservative principles of personal responsibility along with liberal principles of poverty relief. Certainly there is no magic solution to the perennial problem of poverty, however. It will, indeed, always be with us.

Figure 3.1

Social Welfare Expenditures by Level of Government

The national government is still dominant in social welfare spending. The uncontrollable growth of such institutionalized programs as social security and Medicaid has boosted the national government's percentage of total welfare funding.

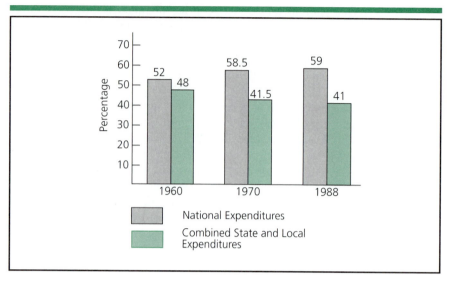

Source: U.S. Bureau of the Census, *Statistical Abstract of the United States, 1991* (Washington, D.C.: U.S. Government Printing Office), p. 357.

Current Social Welfare Policy

After the Great Depression, social welfare policy became primarily the responsibility of the national government, with very limited roles reserved to the states and localities. Today the U.S. government continues to dominate the field by legislating and regulating social welfare programs and by providing the bulk of the money to pay for them (see Figure 3.1). The states, however, have brought the federal programs into action, administered them, and drawn up rules to determine who is eligible for benefits. (The states have also designed their own programs.) Cities and counties have been involved in program implementation to a lesser extent.

The trend today is toward more state and local participation in designing and carrying out social welfare policies. As is the case in most public policy fields, the nonnational governments are the vanguard of innovation and program experimentation. Nevertheless, the money still comes overwhelmingly from Washington, D.C. About 59 percent of social welfare spending comes from the national government today.

There are dramatic variations among the states in levels of social welfare spending. In the largest program, Aid to Families with Dependent Children, California spends $620 and Alaska spends $619 per recipient each month. At the bottom of the AFDC list are Alabama and Mississippi, which pay only $114 and $118, respectively.[35] States controlled by the Democratic party tend to be more generous than Republican states, and strong party competition drives up benefit levels. Political culture has an impact as well. Moralistic political culture is conducive to high benefit levels, whereas traditionalistic political culture depresses aid to the poor. Individualistic states fall in between the two extremes. The relationship between a dominant liberal or conservative ideology and state welfare spending should be obvious.

Types of Social Welfare Programs

The only way to get even a loose mental grip on complex intergovernmental social welfare policies is to examine the most significant ones individually. Programs fall into three categories: direct cash transfers, in-kind benefits, and social insurance (see Table 3.3). Almost all are entitlement programs that pay benefits to any individual who meets legal eligibility requirements (for example, below poverty level, or sixty-five or older).

direct cash transfer

The transfer of cash, such as in the form of a social security check, from one level of government to an individual, citizen beneficiary.

Direct Cash Transfers   **Direct cash transfers** are welfare programs that directly convey money, in the form of government checks, to qualifying recipients. Administrative arrangements vary by type of program.

1. *Aid to Families with Dependent Children* was included in the Social Security Act of 1935 to furnish financial aid to poor children whose fathers had died. Today, however, AFDC payments go almost entirely (90 percent) to single-parent families in which the living father is divorced or separated from or has never married the mother.[36] A father who heads a family can also qualify.

   AFDC is the most costly and most controversial social welfare program in the United States. Critics claim that it causes marriages to break up or to be consciously avoided; encourages young, nonworking, unwed women to get pregnant; promotes migration of the poor to states paying higher AFDC benefits; and perpetuates dependency into future generations. No one professes fondness for AFDC, not even the recipients. This circumstance helps account for the 13 percent reduction in benefits from 1970 to 1988.[37] During the 1990–1992 recession, forty states either cut or froze AFDC payments.

   AFDC is jointly funded by national and state governments, and programs are administered at the state and local levels. Eligibility standards and payment amounts, set by the states, vary widely (the average monthly check in 1989 was $383).

2. *Supplemental Security Income* (SSI) is entirely financed and operated by the national government. Created in 1974, SSI combined three existing programs—Old Age Assistance, Aid to the Blind, and Aid to the Disabled. Its recipients are people who are unable to work because of old age or physical or mental disabilities.

3. *General assistance* is a state and local program intended to help poor people who do not qualify for AFDC or SSI, such as the nonworking but physically able poor. State benefit levels vary greatly. Fifteen states do not offer the

Table 3.3

Major Social Welfare
and Social Insurance
Programs, 1989

Program Category and Name	Number of Recipients (in millions)	Who Funds	Who Administers	Total Expenditures (in billions)
Direct Cash Transfer				
AFDC	11.2	National, state	State, local	$ 17.4
SSI	4.6	National	National	14.6
General assistance	1.4	State, local	State, local	43.2
In-kind Program				
Food stamps	19.0	National	State, local	11.7
Medicaid	23.5	National, state	State, local	54.5
Social Insurance				
Social Security	39.1	National	National	230.8
Medicare	33.6	National, state	National, state	98.3
Unemployment compensation	7.3	State, private	State	14.3
Worker's compensation	94.0	State, private	State	30.8

Source: U.S. Bureau of the Census, *Statistical Abstract of the United States, 1991* (Washington, D.C.: U.S. Government Printing Office, 1991).

program at all, and several others cut back severely on general assistance funding during the recession of 1990–1992. Michigan discontinued the program in 1991.

in-kind program

The payment of a noncash social welfare benefit, such as food stamps or clothing, to an individual recipient.

In-Kind Programs   **In-kind programs** provide benefits "in kind" rather than in cash, in order to address problems of poverty, hunger, and illness.

1. *Food stamps* are coupons that can be used to purchase food. They are paid for by the national government, which also carries half of the administrative expenses. The program was established in 1964, and benefit levels are uniform throughout the United States. Both the working and nonworking poor can qualify.

2. *Medicaid* is a health care assistance program for the poor (AFDC and SSI recipients automatically qualify). It is jointly funded by the national and state governments and is enormously expensive ($72.5 billion in 1990). The Medicaid program provides free health care to uninsured poor people and is the principal source of assistance for long-term institutional care for the physically and mentally disabled and the elderly. It must be distinguished from Medicare, which grants health-care assistance to the aged (see below). Since its inception in 1965, Medicaid has been racked with scandals; and doctors, pharmacists, dentists, and other professionals have been charged with everything from performing unnecessary surgery and inflating fees to filing reimbursements for imaginary patients. Medicaid has also placed an increasingly onerous burden on state budgets, as discussed below.

3. *Housing programs* exist in several forms today. The earliest program to provide public housing units was established in 1937, when federal subsidies were given to local governments for the construction of low-rent public housing. Since 1974, the Housing and Community Development Act has given rent subsidies directly to the poor, who apply them to private rental units.

4. *Other in-kind programs* include numerous types of public assistance, such as the national school lunch program, Head Start, energy assistance for low-income families, legal services, supplemental food programs, employment assistance, family planning, foster care, and services for the mentally retarded. National, state, and local participation depends on the specific program in question. The diversity of in-kind programs is compelling evidence of the complexity of the poverty problem.

social insurance

A benefit program made available by a government to citizens in need, as a right of those citizens.

Social Insurance   **Social insurance** is distinguished from social welfare programs by the fact that recipients contribute financially through the Social Insurance Trust Fund, established by the Social Security Act of 1935. These are not true welfare programs, inasmuch as participants pay in advance for their future well-being. However, they do help in the broad effort to relieve poverty. Contributions to social insurance come from social security payments by individual workers and by their employers.

1. *Social security* (officially known as Old Age, Survivors, Disability, and Health Insurance) is entirely paid for and run by the national government. Monthly payments (averaging $567 in 1989) are mailed to retired people, to the disabled, and to the spouses and dependent children of workers who retire, die, or become disabled.

2. *Medicare* provides federal health care benefits for people over the age of sixty-five in exchange for a monthly premium and modest copayments of medical expenses. It was created in 1965 through an amendment to the Social Security Act. Medicare costs have escalated rapidly as a result of the growing number of senior citizens and ballooning health care bills. The program was expanded by Congress in 1988 to furnish unlimited coverage for catastrophic illness upon payment of a deductible.

Head Start programs, such as this one in the Washington, D.C., area, have been a generally successful example of in-kind programs.

3. *Unemployment compensation* was mandated by the Social Security Act of 1935. It requires employers and employees to contribute to a trust fund administered by individual states. Those who lose their jobs through lay-offs or dismissals draw unemployment benefits for as long as forty-six weeks.

4. *Worker's compensation* is also a part of the Social Security Act. Financed by employers and administered by the states, it establishes insurance for workers and their dependents to cover job-related accidents or illnesses that result in death or disability. Its cost, which is closely associated with the price of health care, has been escalating rapidly in recent years.

Social welfare policy clearly exhibits the interdependent nature of the federal system. The national government pays for and operates some programs on its own—social security is one example. State and local governments take care of general assistance. Approximately three of every four social welfare dollars come from Washington, D.C., but the states and localities perform key administrative roles in most public assistance efforts. The private and nonprofit sectors also contribute through charities like the United Way and institutions such as hospitals and clinics.

State Innovations in Social Welfare

The consensus on social welfare policy has two critical goals. One pertains to the well-being of children and, of necessity, the American family. The other aims to help people replace welfare checks with paychecks. The respective roles of national, state, and local governments in these two policy initiatives are still being sorted out. Undeniably, however, the states and localities are the prime innovators in social welfare policy today.

Saving the Children   There are several important reasons for the sad plight of children. AFDC benefits have declined in terms of noninflationary dollars since 1978. In addition, AFDC has not provided incentives for welfare parents to seek and maintain jobs. Another reason is that more and more children live with a single parent because of high divorce rates, illegitimate births, and irresponsible fathers who refuse to support their offspring. Even if single mothers have the necessary education or skills to secure employment, in the absence of family or friends their children often must be placed in the care of older siblings or left on their own. Few opportunities for affordable, subsidized, or free day care exist. Finally, too many children are being born not only into poverty but into sickness as well. Because of inadequate diets, lack of health insurance, ignorance about prenatal care, drug abuse, and the spread of AIDs, many mothers give birth to premature, underweight, and sickly children. Some simply cannot survive.

A line has been drawn in the sandbox as children's issues have risen to the top of national and state policy agendas. Historically, the national government has addressed such problems, and it continues to do so today through programs like Head Start. However, the states and some local governments have their own agendas. Some of the successful program experiments under way today are likely to be adopted into national law in the future. As more resources are devoted to children, welfare expenditures for adults and the elderly are likely to decline.

The Family Support Act of 1988 requires most AFDC recipients to participate in state-run jobs, training, or education programs, among other things. Congress also boosted the income of low-income working parents by eliminating their federal income tax obligations under the Tax Reform Act of 1986 and expanding their tax credits under the Child Care Act of 1990.

To deal with the growing problem of absentee fathers, the Family Support Act of 1988 requires the states to withhold court-ordered child support payments from the wages of absent parents, even if the parent has not fallen behind in payments. States are also required to establish paternity for children born out of wedlock, through blood tests and other laboratory techniques. The result is that more fathers are being held financially responsible for their offspring. The states now have additional authority to speed judicial and administrative procedures for obtaining paternal support, to establish guidelines for judges to determine the appropriate size of child support awards, and to monitor support payments.

The Family Support Act of 1988 borrowed heavily from state experience and innovations and was effectively promoted by the governors. Wisconsin blazed the trail with its Child Support Assurance System, under which any parent not living with his or her minor children is legally obligated to share a portion of the income that parent has earned; the rate rises with the number of children. Payments may be withheld from the parent's paycheck or from income tax refunds. In addition to ensuring that absentee parents meet their legal obligations, the Wisconsin plan is expected to relieve AFDC caseloads by 20 percent.[38]

The issue of day care for children of working and single parents has also received a great deal of attention from the state and local governments, while the national government has struggled in vain to produce child-care legislation. State and local governments are subsidizing day care programs through tax breaks and are experimenting with various child-care arrangements. In Virginia, a state agency has been created to provide day care for young children from poor and single-parent families. States are also taking the lead in improved prenatal care, in an effort to reduce the nation's shameful infant mortality rate of ten deaths for every thousand live births (which exceeds the rate of sixteen industrialized nations).[39] South Carolina reduced its infant mortality rate from 18.5 in 1978 to 13.2 in 1986 through health care programs for young and economically deprived mothers and mothers-to-be. Certainly it is less costly to invest at the front end of a person's life than to try to correct medical and other ailments later.

Workfare: Turning Welfare Checks into Paychecks   The AFDC program helps support 4.4 million families with 8 million children. In the past, money has been handed over to recipients by the national and state governments, and little has been required in return. The idea behind workfare is to help these parents find jobs. Jobs should produce more household income than AFDC, improved self-images and self-reliance for recipients, and financial savings for taxpayers and the national government.

Workfare is not a new idea. The Nixon administration's Work Incentive (WIN) program required employable AFDC recipients to register for work, or for education and training courses aimed at making them more employable. But WIN was a failure. Few recipients actually participated through doing public work (such as cleaning parks or painting government buildings). Some did get jobs, but they tended to be the most easily employable recipients anyway, and most jobs were low-wage, with few opportunities for advancement.[40] In 1981, Congress converted WIN into something resembling a block grant by permitting the states to restructure the program and implement their own workfare variations.

Workfare was the centerpiece of the 1988 Family Support Act. Under this legislation, the first major overhaul of welfare policy in over fifty years, each state was to implement a Job Opportunities and Basic Skills (JOBS) program. JOBS seeks to combine job-related education, training, and services with a requirement that welfare parents obtain employment. Eventually, all able-bodied AFDC parents of children over age three must participate or risk having their benefits reduced. States help them with child-care and transportation costs. In two-parent welfare families, one adult must contribute sixteen hours of work per week to the state if the search for a job fails. States are permitted to fashion their own approach to JOBS, and must match national government funds with a specified proportion of their own, ranging from 10 to 50 percent.

At first blush, the Family Support Act might appear to represent continued national government dominance of welfare policy. But, in fact, the major elements of the act originated and developed in the states and were adopted at the national level at the insistence of the governors.[41] The states had conducted a number of workfare experiments on their own during the 1980s. California's GAIN (Greater Avenues for Independence) has been one of the most widely praised programs. It contains several phases and options for recipients. If an initial job search leads to nothing, the AFDC recipient is formally assessed and brought into a contractual arrangement that stipulates the obligations of the recipient and of the county administering the program. Education, training, and additional job searches typically follow. If a job is still not to be had, the recipient must work for one year in a public or nonprofit position designated by the county, in order to earn the AFDC check. Some of the workfare jobs lead to regular jobs; others are mindless busywork.[42] Program successes have been modest in most states, although projected AFDC savings are expected to exceed program costs within two to five years.[43] The severe economic recession of 1990–1992 boosted unemployment and welfare rolls and made it difficult to place JOBS participants in jobs. States struggled to find matching funds as tax revenues declined. Still, some promising welfare-to-work experiments are taking place, including family support centers, early childhood education programs, school-based programs, and the development of novel partnerships among state, local, private, and nonprofit organizations.[44]

Wisconsin is experimenting with Learnfare. Under this program, AFDC parents are penalized monetarily if their teenagers pile up an unacceptable number of unexcused school absences. AFDC parents who themselves are under the age of twenty must attend school or a vocational education program or risk the loss of AFDC payments and their driver's license. Thus, school attendance is made equivalent to adult work. By mid-1992, at least thirteen other states had adopted or introduced Learnfare legislation.[45]

Social Welfare and Federalism

Enormous social welfare challenges confront national, state, and local governments. The pivotal issue in terms of federalism is which level of government should have primary responsibility for the poor and unfortunate. Historically, the national government has done so. But it is testimony to the dynamism of the federal system that the answer is no longer so certain.

State and local officials are caught in a dilemma. On the one hand, they are physically and emotionally close to the problems of the poor, and attentive to the demands of these constituents. On the other hand, they do not have the financial resources necessary to alleviate poverty within their boundaries. It would help if poverty and related problems were clearly definable and solvable, but they are not. It would also help if the national government were in better financial shape, but it is hamstrung by its enormous debt.

Federal fiscal problems afflict the states, too, as the Congress pushes spending and program responsibilities on the state and local governments. Medicaid is an excellent example. State expenditures on health care for the poor have exploded from $12.5 billion in 1970 to an estimated $66 billion in 1995. Every year since 1984 (Medicaid was created in 1965), the Congress has enacted at least one new law expanding Medicaid eligibility and, as a consequence, state spending requirements. By 1991, Medicaid was not only the second largest spending program in most states but also the fastest growing, consuming 14 percent of total expenditures.[46] Accordingly, states were forced to either raise taxes or reduce funding for other programs.

In 1991, forty-nine governors formally asked Congress to impose a two-year moratorium on new Medicaid spending mandates. Decrying the burgeoning Medicaid costs in his state of Missouri, Republican Governor John Ashcroft observed that if the states were to continue serving as policy laboratories, the national government "needs to stop pilfering our laboratory equipment."[47]

Some states released their creative juices to raise their portion of Medicaid dollars (the federal government pays 50 percent of the cost of most Medicaid services). To gain federal matching payments, states established "voluntary contribution" programs in which hospitals and other health care providers "donated" money to the state. Once matching funds were received, the donations were paid back to the contributors. Another ploy was the "provider tax." Here, the state levied a special tax on health care providers, used the revenues to match federal money, then paid it back. Such strategies were attacked by federal officials, who labeled them "scams." In November 1991, an agreement between the Bush administration and the National Governors' Association disallowed the "donation" scheme and capped the provider tax at 25 percent of a state's Medicaid expenditures.[48]

Two states, Hawaii and Massachusetts, tired of awaiting national health care legislation, have passed universal health care coverage laws themselves. Massachusetts postponed implementing its 1988 program due to a serious budget crisis, but in Hawaii the plan, originally enacted in 1974, has been expanded and is working surprisingly well. Nearly 100 percent of Hawaii's citizens are insured (compared to 78 percent nationally), and the Aloha State enjoys one of the lowest infant mortality and chronic disease death rates in the country.[49] Such state experiments appear to be pushing the national government inexorably toward a national health care plan. Problem Solving 3.2 describes a highly controversial health care innovation in Oregon.

Poverty is a very complex economic, social, and behavioral phenomenon that demands multiple, intergovernmental responses. Because state and local governments cannot manage social welfare policy by themselves, they must tap the revenue-raising capacity of the national government for what is, after all, a national problem. Indeed, this is one policy area in which some degree of standardization and centralization is called for. Poor people in New Mexico should not be treated worse than their counterparts in New Jersey. Standard-

Problem Solving 3.2

The Rising Cost of Medical Care for the Poor

The Problem: Oregon, like the other states, is struggling to pay the rapidly rising costs of Medicaid. Congressional mandates expanding Medicaid coverage, the inflation of health care costs, and changing demographics (with respect to higher numbers of poor children and elderly and disabled people who require nursing home care) have drained state budgets.

The Solution: Whereas most states have cut Medicaid expenses by reducing reimbursements for health care providers (for example, doctors' fees, hospital costs, pharmaceuticals) or tightening eligibility standards (and thereby leaving more people without any form of insurance), Oregon has taken a new path: rationing health care. A 1989 Oregon law extended Medicaid coverage to an additional 120,000 individuals but set up a system for ranking 709 medical conditions—some would be covered by Medicaid, others would not. Top priority is given to potentially fatal but curable ailments such as appendectomies and bronchial pneumonia. Preventive care (for example, child immunization, birth control, maternity care) receives high priority. Last come conditions in which treatment cannot cure or improve the quality of life (such as the terminal stage of AIDS or the common cold). The list was drawn up by a statewide committee of laypersons and medical experts. The extent of state Medicaid funding would determine where the line would be drawn. For fiscal year 1992, it was drawn at item 587. Coverage for the 122 conditions below the line would thus be denied.

Ironically, Oregon's plan met with a storm of criticism from members of Congress, whose very actions and inactions have provoked the Medicaid crisis. The plan cannot be executed without federal approval, and such was considered unlikely as of mid-1992. However, Oregon's pioneering effort to devise a rational means of Medicaid cost control could spur the federal government to take the steps necessary to overhaul the floundering national health care system.

Sources: Julie Rovner, "Oregon Plan Sparks Emotional Debate Over Rationing Health Care," *Congressional Quarterly* (May 18, 1991): 1278–1284; Penelope Lemov, "Climbing Out of the Medicaid Trap," *Governing* 5 (October 1991): 49–53.

ization of some benefits and centralization of policymaking by the national government tend to diminish inequities in state and local funding of social welfare programs.[50] The states and localities are best at policy experimentation, innovation, and administration within their own jurisdictions. They contribute meaningfully to social welfare policy, but they cannot solve the problems of the poor and disadvantaged on a national level.

However, state and local innovation and experimentation cannot flourish in the face of stifling and obstructive federal rules, regulations, and mandates. For instance, while the Family Support Act of 1988 has many strong points and has helped laggard states improve their social welfare program results, it has hindered some of the most ambitious state welfare-to-work efforts. A federal mandate that workfare participants must spend, and have documented, 20 hours a week in classes or job training has caused "welfare workers and teachers to spend more time keeping track of clients' whereabouts and less time trying to help them."[51] In other states the 20-hour requirement is met through nonproductive "supervised study halls." States bristle at such overregulation by the federal government, insisting that whether workfare programs last 15 hours or 25 hours should be determined by those closest to the clients—not faraway federal bureaucrats.

....

Higher Education Policy and Federalism

The goals of higher education policy have changed in response to the needs of American society, but they remain clear in contrast to social welfare policy goals. To be sure, controversy arises in the area of higher education policy, but never has it taken on the intensity and partisan rancor of social welfare policy arguments. This is mostly because higher education goals are clear and understandable, and the means to achieve them are widely agreed upon. Higher education policy strives to embrace learning, to promote social and economic mobility, to instill cultural and moral values, and, most recently, to assist the states in economic development. The last goal springs from the continuing need to upgrade and retool the work force, and from the growing recognition that universities, through research and development, foster economic innovation and growth.[52]

Unlike social welfare policy, which was developed and funded initially at the national level, higher education was first the responsibility of the private sector, states, and localities. Colleges and universities developed initially as private institutions available to the socioeconomic elite. A major landmark in the popularization of higher education was the Morrill Act of 1862, in which the national government established the public land-grant college system in order to teach agriculture and "mechanical arts." These colleges, largely vocational in nature, were aimed at increasing the levels of knowledge and efficiency on the farms and in the factories. Private colleges such as Yale, Harvard, and Columbia remained the premier institutions for education in the classics for some time, but gradually the land-grant institutions began to expand the scope of their curricula, and eventually achieved a level of education equal to and in some cases better than that of the best private colleges. Any list of the United States' most prestigious universities today will have at the top such land-grant institutions as Penn State, Cornell, and the universities of Wisconsin, Minnesota, and California.

Today there are approximately 3,690 institutions of higher education in the United States, not counting the numerous two-year (junior college) and vocational (technical) schools. Enrollment exceeds 12.2 million students. State-supported colleges and universities predominate. More than 78 percent of students are enrolled at public institutions today, compared to only 49 percent in 1947.[53]

Intergovernmental Roles

Public higher education is predominantly a state government responsibility. Its recognized significance to state economic well-being means that state involvement will continue in the years ahead. Some state government activities, such as increased commitment of resources, would be welcomed. Others, such as bureaucratic, political, and ideological intrusions, are uninvited and unwanted by professional educators.

The national government's presence in higher education policymaking is probably more pronounced than most people realize. The Morrill Act donated national lands for state schools. Various G.I. bills have entitled returning war veterans to a college education at government expense and helped fuel tremendous expansion in higher education facilities for a burgeoning student population. Financial aid to veterans was severely curtailed after President Nixon terminated the military draft, but other programs provide students with grants and loans (the most important being the National Defense Education Act, the Basic Educational Opportunity Grant, and guaranteed student loans). Although the Reagan administration substantially cut back funding of these programs, they still sustain tens of thousands of college students. The national government also supports higher education with research grants that help develop new programs, support faculty and graduate students, pay indirect costs, and purchase research materials and laboratory equipment. Finally, although the national government does not operate a national university (as in the case with most governments around the world), the Defense Department provides huge sums of money for professional training, military officer training, correspondence courses, and the military service academies.

In 1987, the national government spent $17 billion on its assorted programs in higher education. However, this made up only 12.8 percent of all expenditures, a decline from 16.6 percent in 1970 (see Figure 3.2). The state share was 30 percent. Other sources of money for higher education are tuition, endowments, private gifts, and grants and contracts.

Given the national government's limited financial support, it is little wonder that its policy impacts are mostly indirect. Research grants can affect the disposition of institutional resources through matching requirements and other conditions, but national influence on decision making within colleges and universities is otherwise quite limited. Public higher education remains primarily a state government undertaking dominated by state and university officials.

Actors in Higher Education Policy

The president of a university is the chief spokesperson and fund raiser for that institution, and is often the most influential lobbyist for university causes both in the legislature and in the business world. But he or she must share influence over the university with many other people. The president is usually appointed by, and responsible to, a university governing board called the *regents* or *trustees*. Some states select the members of these boards through popular elections, but most provide for appointment by the governor and/or legislature. Seats on the governing board are typically filled with prominent university supporters from government and business. Private institutions, though recipients of state char-

Figure 3.2

National, State, and Local Expenditures for Higher Education

The national government's share of support for higher education has been declining over the past twenty years, forcing universities to look more to state and local governments, and particularly to private sources.

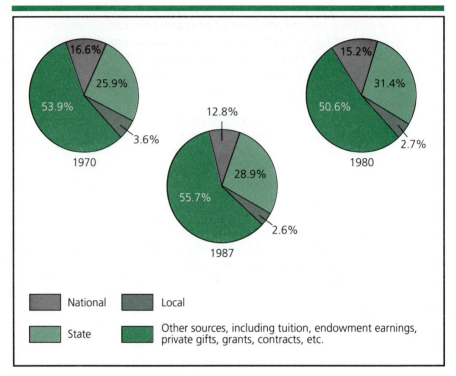

National

State

Local

Other sources, including tuition, endowment earnings, private gifts, grants, contracts, etc.

Source: U.S. Bureau of the Census, *Statistical Abstract of the United States, 1991* (Washington, D.C.: U.S. Government Printing Office, 1991), p. 134.

ters and various amounts of state financial aid, operate with a greater amount of autonomy.

A few states still administer higher education policy through individual governing boards for each public college and university, but most look to an umbrella agency for development of broad policy directions and coordination of curricular and other relations among the various higher education institutions.[54] Usually referred to as the *state commission on higher education,* this statewide governing board is appointed by the governor in almost all states. Its members must simultaneously advocate higher education policy and spending and represent the governor's own higher education preferences. Twenty-two states have eliminated the governing boards for individual institutions by consolidating their functions into a statewide board.

Legislatures have elevated their policy role in higher education, primarily through expenditure decisions. Universities are certain to find faithful friends and strong supporters among the legislators who represent the district in which the campus is situated and among their graduates in legislative seats. But college officials are seldom given a blank check, as legislative committees are taking more seriously their responsibility to ensure that higher education, like other activities of state government, strives for greater efficiency, effectiveness, and accountability.

The governors have become the most important policy actors in higher education. As we have mentioned, they appoint governing board members in most states, and in some cases they sit on these boards as *ex officio* members (appointed by virtue of their office). The chief executive also exercises direct influence over university affairs through the budgetary process. Gubernatorial support for increased appropriations or a new building on campus usually counts heavily in the legislature.

The increased scope of gubernatorial interest in higher education issues has been widely noted. A Carnegie Foundation study found that "the Governor, in many states, is now the one dominant figure in higher education."[55] In some instances gubernatorial involvement has gone beyond the bounds of propriety. In well-known cases, governors have brazenly attempted to dismiss members of governing boards and university presidents. Others have fired football or basketball coaches or the athletic director. Usually, however, the governor's involvement is positive, and clearly in the best interest of higher education. To many chief executives, the union between campus and state economic development is a marriage made in heaven.[56]

Problems in Higher Education and What the States Are Doing

Public attention remains concentrated on primary and secondary school reform, which is well under way, but more attention has shifted to the United States' institutions of higher learning. Pressures for change are building, and an agenda is developing for future policy actions at all levels of government. Five major policy problems can be identified.

Quantity   The quantity issue has to do with how states should coordinate and administer their complex systems of higher education. In some states, individual institutions are the norm. In others, particularly the territorially large ones, a main "flagship" campus has numerous sister campuses spread about the state. In some states the "little sisters" have far outgrown the original campus in size and quality.

Academic, administrative, political, and "turf" conflicts, among others, plague higher education. Two-year schools want to become four-year colleges, which themselves aspire to become full-fledged graduate universities. Regional institutions fight for their share of the higher education budget. Duplication of graduate degree programs unnecessarily strains budgets, as do superfluous and debt-ridden small regional campuses. States must decide how to coordinate and manage such issues and what organizational arrangements to employ. Diverse responses have ensued. Most states have created statewide governing boards for centralized planning and budgeting, program evaluation, and policy recommendations. There is a long and highly valued history of institutional autonomy in higher education, but obvious benefits can be derived from some administrative centralization and control. In states where individual governing boards continue to exist, they are becoming more the active agents in policy matters and less the pawns of the university president. Special coordinating mechanisms are being utilized in some states. For example, at least nine states have created new boards to organize university-based activities in high technology.

Quality   A second and increasingly important policy problem is quality—how to make and keep higher education relevant to society and capable of significant contributions to the state's quality of life. Higher education will always be elitist in the sense that those who derive direct benefits from it are largely students from middle- and upper-income families. Even students from lower socioeconomic backgrounds who attend college are elite, since they must have the intellect and ambition necessary to secure scholarships and other forms of financial aid. However, higher education offers benefits to the society at large beyond the immediate confines of the campus. An important question is how colleges and universities should be linked to society, and which objectives should be paramount.

During the 1960s and early 1970s, higher education institutions were criticized for selling their souls to the defense industry and to business interests. Such allegations are much rarer today, when universities are widely accepted as resources for attracting new investments and promoting economic development. As one education expert explains, "Having a first-class university is essential. A state that lacks one is putting itself out of business as far as economic development goes. . . . In a world of growing economic competition and social complexity, it is the university to which the state turns for assistance."[57]

The dilemma is how to graduate well-educated students with a sense of public ethics while working with government and business to promote economic growth. Universities need businesses for grant and contract revenues and for opportunities to test research and theory in applied settings. And businesses need universities for fresh ideas and talented human resources. Cooperation strongly benefits both parties and furthers state economic development. The models for this kind of relationship are California's Silicon Valley and North Carolina's Research Triangle, but almost every state has some formal means to promote partnerships in technology and business innovation. Nonetheless, institutions of higher education must refrain from seeking capitalistic relevance at the price of failing to transmit historical, social, and cultural knowledge. Profits and productivity are important, but they should not define a society.

Faculty   A third higher education policy problem is how to recruit and keep outstanding faculty, especially in mathematics and science, given the tradition of low salaries in academe. The lack of qualified math and science instructors in colleges is related to the curriculum choices of students. Between 1975 and 1984, the proportion of freshmen choosing to pursue a science or math major fell from 13 percent to 8 percent.[58] The percentage is only slightly higher today.

Foreign graduate students predominate in many of the sciences as well as in engineering, raising the question of whether the United States is training its future economic competitors.

The problem of recruiting and retaining qualified faculty can be solved by offering higher salaries to professors and financial incentives to graduate students. More research and teaching fellowships and larger graduate student stipends would make for a useful start. This is an area where some federal financial assistance would have tangible results. Of course, it is primarily up to the states to see that professors and promising graduate students receive the necessary financial inducements. And, with respect to science and engineering, student interest must be spawned as early as primary school.

Politicization   A fourth policy problem is the politicization of higher education. As in primary and secondary education (see Chapter 15), conflict has moved beyond the confines of the professional community (faculty, administrators, and governing boards) and into the legislative and gubernatorial arenas. The trend toward greater politicization in college and university funding and policy decisions is largely a function of economic considerations, ranging from the challenge of keeping institutions operating during hard times to that of fostering economic development. Universities are perceived by political leaders as state resources that should be utilized efficiently to promote growth and prosperity. The "ivory tower" has become more like a corporate boardroom, with legislators and the governor constituting the board of directors.

State intrusion into the previously sacrosanct affairs of colleges and universities can be harmful. Bureaucratic interference in the form of unnecessary or unworkable rules, regulations, and controls can obstruct effective university operations. Politicians may attempt to influence hiring decisions or facility locations, and community groups or individual politicians may try to influence internal institutional matters such as what subject matter is or is not taught or which guest speakers should or should not be invited to campus. Such intrusions often cause academicians to hoist the banner of academic freedom to defend themselves.[59]

The politicization of higher education is apt to persist as long as the game has such high stakes for political and business leaders. The worst kind of counterproductive intervention can be eliminated if university presidents and governing boards educate potential intervenors about their proper role in higher education and the need to maintain academic freedom and institutional integrity.

Student Costs   Finally, higher education confronts the problem of spiraling student costs. College costs have risen much faster than inflation since 1980. In 1990, for instance, the average expenses for room, board, and tuition totaled more than $41,000 for four years. That figure is expected to rise to $100,000 by the year 2000 if present rates of increase continue. The leap in college costs has been particularly evident in private universities, which are now well out of the financial reach of most prospective students. Combined with the national government's cutbacks on grants and low-interest loans to children of low-income families, rising education costs mean that a college education is becoming unfeasible for more and more young people.

Higher education fell into hard times as the decade of the '90s began. The economic recession forced nearly every state and many universities to cut higher education budgets, to raise tuition and fees, or, in many instances, to do both. Legislative and popular interest focused on higher education as a government subsidy program, as indeed it is. In 1990, tuition covered an average of only 26 percent of the actual costs of educating a student—in contrast to about 45 percent in the mid-1950s. In the years ahead, students and their parents will likely have to pick up a growing share of their education expenses. In fact, several state legislatures and boards of regents have recently discussed turning their leading public universities into semiprivate institutions by hiking tuition and fees close to the average level in private colleges ($10,017 per year in 1991). Examples include Minnesota, Wisconsin, California, and Virginia.[60]

The potential harm of higher tuition is, of course, the prospect that more students will be priced out of a college degree. The American value of an open system of higher education may be diminished, along with the value of upward mobility.

Just as Socrates urged students of all ages to examine their own lives in order to be truly knowledgeable, so must our colleges and universities undergo a perpetual process of self-examination to cope with ever-present political and economic pressures. Both types of pressure are certain to grow. How they are dealt with will be a key determinant of the quality of life in the year 2000 and beyond.

....

Federalism's Evolving Nature

Social welfare and higher education are very different in terms of historical development, goals and objectives, and level of government control. The national government, however uncomfortably, dominates social welfare policy. Suggested swaps and turnbacks to the state and local governments reflect this discomfort. The vitality of the nonnational governments can be seen in their growing willingness to accept greater responsibility for the social welfare of their citizens. Reductions in federal funding and greater state autonomy have made social welfare a fast-evolving policy field. It will take time to determine whether decentralization of poverty policy ultimately shortchanges the poor. Time will also tell whether the states and localities can meet what might be their most difficult challenge in federalism.

Higher education policy is also evolving, but much more slowly and with little tension between levels of government. The national, state, and local governments are basically comfortable with their respective roles. Certainly more federal money would be welcomed, but not at the expense of policy autonomy. Control over higher education policy is crucial to the states, because universities are key factors in state economic development and other important values.

Together, the two policy fields examined in this chapter illustrate the necessity for intergovernmental sharing of the burdens of governance in a highly diverse and complex society. Federalism permits numerous possibilities for conflict and cooperation in the exercise of power.[61] But in the end, all 84,000 American governments are in the same situation. As President John F. Kennedy observed many years ago, state, local, and national governments are "allies under the Constitution [and] must work closely together . . . for the benefit of our country, which all of us seek to serve."[62]

....

Summary

A recent analysis of intergovernmental relations concluded that "federalism is under siege."[63] The Reagan years left an indelible mark on American federalism, because of the administration's emphasis on shifting responsibility out of Washington and into state capitals. The fundamental ideas of New Federalism have essentially been maintained under the Bush administration.[64] For the states, the next decade offers both challenges and opportunities as their relationship with the national government continues to evolve. As the Hawaii universal health insurance plan aptly demonstrates, the states do not lack good ideas. But what they frequently need is more money. As the trend toward reduced national expenditures continues, state capacity will be sorely tested.

Social welfare and higher education policy are two important illustrations of federalism in practice. Although these two policy fields differ in many respects, both involve key contributions from all three levels of government. This intergovernmental sharing of responsibilities is central to federalism.

Key Terms

revenues   project grant
expenditures   federal mandate
revenue sharing   set-asides
categorical grant   direct cash transfer
block grant   in-kind program
formula grant   social insurance

4

State Constitutions

The Evolution of State Constitutions

The First State Constitutions | Legislative Supremacy |
The Growth of Executive Power

Weaknesses of Constitutions

The Trouble with Long Constitutions | Substantive Problems

Contemporary Constitutional Reform

The Essential State Constitution | Constitutions Today

Methods for Constitutional Change

Informal Constitutional Change | Formal Constitutional Change

State Resurgence and Constitutional Reform

D oes a citizen have the right to freedom of expression in a private shopping mall? Specifically, does a citizen have the constitutionally protected right to collect shoppers' signatures on a petition opposing a United Nations resolution against Zionism, even if the shopping center owners object? The U.S. Supreme Court has said no on two occasions.[1] But in 1979, the supreme court of California ruled that citizens do have the right to petition in private shopping centers as part of their protected right to free speech.[2] The owners of the Prune Yard Shopping Center appealed to the U.S. Supreme Court, hoping for a reversal of the California decision, but the decision was upheld. The Court based its ruling on the principle that state constitutions can create broader rights of free speech than those guaranteed in the federal constitution.

The *Prune Yard* case illustrates the new *judicial federalism*, whereby state supreme courts are increasingly grounding their rulings on the language of their state—rather than the national—constitution. It also reflects the fact that state constitutions are once again becoming the guardians of civil liberties, as they were throughout the early history of the United States.

All state constitutions serve as instruments of political power. They set forth the basic framework and operating rules for government, distribute power to the three branches, limit the scope of governmental authority, and protect individual rights. Constitutions represent the *fundamental law* of a state, superior to statutory law. They provide a set of rules for the game of state government, and those who master the regulations and procedures have a strong advantage over novices. Everything that a state government does and represents is rooted in its constitution. Only the federal constitution and federal statutes take priority over it. This is why the constitution is called the fundamental law.

To most people, however, constitutional law still means the federal document. State constitutions are often neglected in secondary school and college courses in history and political science. Astonishingly, a 1988 national survey discovered that 51 percent of Americans were not aware that their state had its own constitution.[3]

In the American system of *dual constitutionalism*, in which there are both national and state constitutions, the national government is supreme within the spheres of authority specifically delegated to it in the U.S. Constitution. Powers granted to the national government are denied to the states. But the national constitution is incomplete. It leaves many key constitutional issues to the states, including local finance, public education, and the organization of state and local government.[4] In theory, state constitutions are supreme for all matters not expressly within the jurisdiction of the national government or forbidden by federal constitutional or statutory law. In practice, however, congressional and federal court interpretations have expanded the powers of the national government and, in some fields, eroded the powers of the states.

The earliest state constitutions were simple documents reflecting an agrarian economy, single-owner businesses, and horse-and-buggy transportation. As American society and the economy changed, it became necessary to alter the rules of state government. Constitutional reform has been a regular theme throughout the American experiment in federalism. It has occurred in several waves, the first beginning around 1800. Some reforms have reflected changing political fortunes; newly powerful groups have pressed to revise the state constitution to reflect their interests, or one or another political party has gained control of state government and sought to solidify its power. Constitutional reforms have promoted different views of politics and the public interest, as when Progressive reformers rallied for honest and efficient government in the late nineteenth and early twentieth centuries.[5] Since the 1960s, constitutional revisions have concentrated power in the governor's office, unified court systems, and generally sought to make state government more efficient, effective, responsive, and capable of adapting to changing social and economic forces.

The Evolution of State Constitutions

When the states won their independence from Great Britain more than two hundred years ago, there was no precedent for writing constitutions. The thirteen colonial charters provided the foundation for the new state constitutions. The thirteen original colonial charters were brief documents (around five pages each) that the Crown had granted to trading companies and individuals for governance of settlements in the new territories. As the settlements became full colonies, these charters were expanded to incorporate the "rights of Englishmen"—political and civil rights first enumerated by the Magna Carta in 1215. They also laid down some basic principles of colonial government.[6]

The First State Constitutions

Following the War of Independence, the former colonies drafted their first constitutions in special revolutionary conventions or in legislative assemblies first brought together during the war. With the exception of Massachusetts, the new states put their constitutions into effect immediately, without popular ratification.

In content, most of these documents simply extended the colonial charters, removing references to the king and inserting a bill of rights. The constitutions of Connecticut and Rhode Island, for example, differed only slightly from those states' colonial charters. All the documents incorporated the principles of limited government: a weak executive branch, the separation of powers, checks and balances, a bill of rights to protect the people and their property from arbitrary government actions, and (except for Pennsylvania) a bicameral legislature.[7] The earliest constitutions were not progressive. Essentially, they called for government by an aristocracy. Officeholding and voting, for instance, were restricted to white males of wealth and property.[8]

Only one of the thirteen original state constitutions, that of Massachusetts, survives (although it has been amended 116 times). It is the oldest active

A painting showing the signing of the Massachusetts state constitution, which is the oldest active constitution in the world.

constitution in the world. Its longevity can be attributed in large part to the foresight of its drafter, John Adams, who grounded the document in extensive research of governments that took him all the way back to the Magna Carta. Even after many amendments, the Massachusetts constitution reflects a composite of the wisdom of the foremost political philosophers of the eighteenth century: John Locke, Jean-Jacques Rousseau, and the Baron de Montesquieu.[9]

Legislative Supremacy

The first state constitutions reflected the framers' fear and distrust of the executive, a result of their experiences with the colonial governors. The governors were not all tyrants; but because they represented the British Crown and Parliament, they became a symbol of oppression to the colonists. As a result, the guiding principle of the new constitutional governments was **legislative supremacy**, and the legislatures were given overwhelming power at the expense of governors. Most governors were to be elected by the legislature, not the people, and were restricted to a single term of office. (In Pennsylvania, executive power was exercised through a multimember board.) State judiciaries also were limited in authorized powers; and judges, like governors, were to be elected by the legislature. The pre-eminence of legislative power was so great that an English

legislative supremacy

The legislature's dominance of the other two branches of government.

observer, Lord James Bryce, was moved to remark: "The legislature . . . is so much the strongest force in the several states that we may almost call it the government and ignore all other authorities."[10]

The Growth of Executive Power

Disillusionment with the legislatures soon developed, spreading rapidly through the states during the early 1800s. There were many reasons for disenchantment, including the legislatures' failure to meet the new demands caused by rapid population growth and the Industrial Revolution; the growing amount of legislation that favored private interests; and a mounting load of state indebtedness, which led nine states to default on their bonds in a single two-year period.

Gradually the executive branch began to accumulate more power and stature through constitutional amendments that provided for popular election of governors, who were given longer terms and the authority to veto legislative bills. The constitutions of states admitted to the Union during the early 1800s established stronger executive powers at the outset. This trend toward centralization of power in the executive branch continued during the 1830s and 1840s, the so-called Jacksonian era; however, the Jacksonian principle of popular elections to fill most government offices resulted in a fragmented state executive branch. The governor now had to share authority with a lieutenant governor, an attorney general, a treasurer, and other popularly elected officials, and with numerous agency heads appointed by the legislature. Although the growth of the governor's powers continues today, the divided nature of the executive branch still makes it difficult for an individual to exercise those powers.

As executive power grew, levels of public confidence in state legislatures continued to erode. This circumstance was reflected in the process of constitutional revision. One delegate at Kentucky's 1890 constitutional convention proclaimed that "the principal, if not the sole purpose of this constitution which we are here to frame, is to restrain the legislature's will and restrict its authority."[11] Also affecting constitutional change were broader social and economic forces in the United States, such as the extension of suffrage and popular participation in government, the rise of a corporate economy, the Civil War and Reconstruction, the growth of industry and commerce, the process of urbanization, and a growing movement for government reform. States rapidly replaced and amended their constitutions from the early 1800s to 1920 in response to these and other forces. The decade immediately after the Civil War saw the highest level of constitutional activity in American history, much of it in the southern states; between 1860 and 1870, twenty-seven constitutions were supplanted or thoroughly revised as Confederate states ratified new documents after secession, then redrew the documents after Union victory to incorporate certain conditions of readmission to the United States.

Constitutional change after Reconstruction was driven by the Populist and Progressive reform movements. During the late 1800s, the Populists championed the causes of the "little man," including farmers and laborers. They sought to open up the political process to the people through such constitutional devices as the initiative, the referendum, and recall (see Chapter 5). The Progressives, who made their mark during the 1890–1920 period, were kindred spirits whose favorite targets were concentrated wealth, machine politics, and boss rule in the cities. They focused on corruption at the state level as well, particularly in New York, Wisconsin, and California. In these and other states, reformers successfully promoted constitutional revisions such as regulation of campaign spending, party activities, and conflicts of interest; replacement of party conventions with direct primary elections; and selection of judges through nonpartisan elections.

Weaknesses of Constitutions

In spite of the numerous constitutional amendments and replacements enacted during the nineteenth and twentieth centuries, by 1950 the states were buffeted by a rising chorus of criticism of their fundamental laws. Ironically, many states were victims of past constitutional change, which left them with documents that were excessively long, frustratingly inflexible, and distressingly detailed. In general, state constitutions still provided for a feeble executive branch, because they granted limited administrative authority to the governor, permitted the popular election of numerous other executive branch officials, and organized the executive into a hodgepodge of semiautonomous agencies, boards, and commissions. State judiciaries remained uncoordinated and overly complex, while legislatures suffered from archaic structures and procedures. Statutory detail, out-of-date language, local amendments (those that apply only to designated local governments), and other problems contaminated the documents and straitjacketed state government.

The Trouble with Long Constitutions

From the first constitutions, which averaged 5,000 words, state documents expanded into enormous tracts of verbiage averaging 27,000 words by 1967. (The U.S. Constitution has 8,700 words.) Some of this growth resulted from increasing social and economic complexity, and from a perceived need to be very specific about what the legislatures could and could not do. The states did have to delineate their residual powers (those not delegated to the national government), identify the scope of their responsibility, and define the powers of local governments. And state constitutions are much easier to amend than the federal constitution. But some constitutions went too far. Louisiana's exceeded 253,000 words. Georgia's contained around 583,500 words, if local provisions were counted, surpassing Tolstoy's *War and Peace* in length. Even today the constitution of South Carolina limits local government indebtedness but lists seventeen pages of exceptions. Maryland's constitution devotes an article to off-street parking in Baltimore. Oklahoma's sets the flash point for kerosene at

115 degrees for purposes of illumination,[12] and California's deals with a compelling issue of our time—the length of wrestling matches.

Not surprisingly, lengthy state constitutions tend to be plagued by contradictions and meaningless clauses. Article II, Section 13 of Pennsylvania's constitution states that "the sessions of each House and of committees of the whole shall be open, unless when the business is such as ought to be kept secret." Other constitutions suffer from superfluous formality, legal jargon, redundancy, and poor grammar. Some constitutions address problems that are no longer with us, like the regulation of steamboats[13] or the need to teach livestock feeding in Oklahoma public schools.

Verbose constitutions fail to distinguish between the fundamental law and issues that properly should be decided by the state legislature.[14] Excessive detail leads to litigation, as the courts must rule on conflicting provisions and challenges to constitutionality; hence the courts are often unnecessarily burdened with decisions that should be made by the legislature. Once incorporated into a constitution, a decision becomes as close to permanent as anything can be in politics. Unlike a statute, which can be changed by a simple legislative majority, constitutional change requires an extraordinary majority, usually two-thirds or three-fourths of the legislature. This requirement hampers the legislature's ability to confront problems quickly and makes policy change more difficult. Too many amendments may also deprive local governments of needed flexibility to cope with their own problems. Too much detail generates confusion, not only for legislatures and courts but also for the general public. It encourages political subterfuge to get around archaic or irrelevant provisions, and breeds disrespect or even contempt for government.

Many detailed provisions are intended to favor or protect special interests, such as public utilities, farmers, timber companies, religious groups, and many others. A 1966 study by Lewis Froman found that the longest constitutions are in those states with the strongest interest groups.[15] A more recent study by David Nice, however, discovered no statistical relationship between interest group strength and long, detailed constitutions.[16] Rather, Nice found long constitutions in states with little competition between political parties. He suggests that one-party states are characterized by intraparty dissension and unstable political coalitions that produce unpredictable legislative outcomes. As a result of these conditions, interest groups often try to insulate their pet agencies and programs from uncertainty by placing protective provisions for them in the constitution. Such efforts are less likely to occur where a strong opposition party exists "to serve as watchdog, critic, and disciplinary force."[17]

Substantive Problems

In addition to contradictions, anachronisms, wordiness, and grants of special privilege, the *substance* of state constitutions has drawn criticism. Specific concerns voiced by reformers include the following:

- *The long ballot.* As elected executive branch officials are not beholden to the governor for their jobs, the governor has little or no formal influence on their decisions and activities. Reformers who seek to strengthen the governor's powers wish to restrict the executive branch to a maximum of two elected leaders: the governor and the lieutenant governor.

- *A glut of boards and commissions.* This reform of the Jacksonian period was intended to expand opportunities for public participation in state government and to limit the powers of the governor. In the late twentieth century, it leads to fragmentation and a lack of policy coordination in the executive branch.
- *A swamp of local governments.* There are more than 84,000 municipalities, counties, and special-purpose districts in the states. Sometimes they work at cross purposes, and nearly always they suffer from overlapping responsibilities and absence of coordination.
- *Restrictions on local government authority.* Localities in some states have to obtain explicit permission from the state legislature before providing a new service, tapping a new source of revenue, or exercising any other authority not specifically granted them by the state.
- *Unequal treatment of racial minorities and women.* Constitutional language sometimes discriminates against African-Americans, Latinos, and women by denying them certain rights guaranteed to white males. (Arizona's constitutional provision requiring statewide executive officers to be male had to be deleted in 1988 when Rose Mofford became governor.)
- *Long delays in the administration of justice.* Court systems are in a condition of anarchy in some states, where no one seems to have control over case management, judicial interactions, or administration. The result is lengthy delays in the disposition of cases.

Contemporary Constitutional Reform

Shortly after World War II, these problems began to generate increasing commentary on the sorry condition of state constitutions. One of the most influential voices came in 1955 from the Commission on Intergovernmental Relations, popularly known as the Kestnbaum Commission. In its final report to the president, the commission stated that

> the Constitution prepared by the Founding Fathers, with its broad grants of authority and avoidance of legislative detail, has withstood the test of time far better than the constitutions later adopted by the States. . . . The Commission believes that most states would benefit from a fundamental review of their constitution to make sure that they provide for vigorous and responsible government, not forbid it.[18]

Model State Constitution

The experts' ideal of the structure and contents of a state constitution.

Another important voice for constitutional reform was the National Municipal League, which developed a **Model State Constitution** in 1921 that is now in its sixth version.[19]

Thomas Jefferson believed that each generation has the right to choose for itself its own form of government. He suggested that a new constitution every nineteen or twenty years would be appropriate. Given the large number of constitutional changes since 1960, it would appear that the states have taken his remarks to heart. Every state has altered its fundamental law in some respect during this period, and new or substantially revised constitutions have been put into operation in more than half the states. During the 1970s alone, ten states held conventions to consider changing or replacing their constitution. One of these was Louisiana, which set a record by adopting its eleventh constitution; Georgia is in second place with nine. Table 4.1 provides a summary of state constitutions today.

Extensive constitutional revision is continuing in the 1990s. It has brought many documents closer to conformity with the National Municipal League's Model State Constitution, which serves as an ideal to strive for. The authors of the Model State Constitution recognized that in fact no document can be suitable for all the states, because they differ too much in history, society, economics, and political culture. But there are certain basic principles that reformers believe should be found in a sound constitution. These may change over time, as indicated by the several revisions of the model constitution itself. A good constitution strikes a balance between the need for stability and the requirement for enough flexibility to deal with emerging problems. It is brief, readable, and simple enough for the average citizen to understand. It is logical, as well as devoid of the unnecessary obscurity and jargon associated with the legal profession. Where possible, familiar language is used in place of technical and legal terms.[20]

The Essential State Constitution

The Model State Constitution has twelve basic articles, which are embodied to a greater or lesser extent in the various state constitutions today. The following list provides a brief description of each article and the ways in which its contents are changing.

Bill of Rights   Individual rights and liberties were first protected in state constitutions. They closely resemble, and in some cases are identical to, those delineated in the first eight amendments to the U.S. Constitution. For example, all state constitutions protect citizens from deprivation of life, liberty, and property without "due process of law." Originally, the national Bill of Rights protected citizens only from actions by the U.S. government. State constitutions and courts were the principal guardians of civil liberties until 1868, when the adoption of the Fourteenth Amendment extended the protective umbrella of the national courts over the states.[21] U.S. Supreme Court rulings also applied the U.S. Bill of Rights to the states, especially during the Warren Court beginning in 1953. By implication, some states had failed to uphold their trust.

In the 1980s, however, activist states began to reassert guarantees of individual rights under state constitutions. At a minimum, state constitutions must protect and guarantee those rights found in the U.S. Bill of Rights. But state constitutional provisions may guarantee additional or more extensive rights to citizens. Seventeen states now have equal rights amendments that guarantee sexual equality and prohibit sex-based discrimination. The U.S. Constitution

Table 4.1 State Constitutions

State	Number of Constitutions*	Effective Date of Present Constitution	Estimated Length (number of words)	Number of Amendments Submitted to Voters	Number of Amendments Adopted
Alabama	6	Nov. 28, 1901	174,000	726	513
Alaska	1	Jan. 3, 1959	13,000	31	22
Arizona	1	Feb. 14, 1912	28,876	198	109
Arkansas	5	Oct. 30, 1874	40,720	164	76
California	2	July 4, 1879	33,350	781	471
Colorado	1	Aug. 1, 1876	45,679	239	115
Connecticut	4	Dec. 30, 1965	9,564	26	25
Delaware	4	June 10, 1897	19,000	—	119
Florida	6	Jan. 7, 1969	25,100	79	53
Georgia	10	July 1, 1983	25,000	35	24
Hawaii	1	Aug. 21, 1959	17,453	93	82
Idaho	1	July 3, 1890	21,500	187	107
Illinois	4	July 1, 1971	13,200	11	6
Indiana	2	Nov. 1, 1851	9,377	70	38
Iowa	2	Sept. 3, 1857	12,500	51	48
Kansas	1	Jan. 29, 1861	11,865	115	87
Kentucky	4	Sept. 28, 1891	23,500	58	29
Louisiana	11	Jan. 1, 1975	51,448	51	27
Maine	1	March 15, 1820	13,500	186	157
Maryland	4	Oct. 5, 1867	41,349	233	200
Massachusetts	1	Oct. 25, 1780	36,690	143	116
Michigan	4	Jan. 1, 1964	20,000	47	16
Minnesota	1	May 11, 1858	9,500	206	112
Mississippi	4	Nov. 1, 1890	24,000	133	102

State				
Missouri	4	March 30, 1945	42,000	115	74
Montana	2	July 1, 1973	11,866	25	15
Nebraska	2	Oct. 12, 1875	20,048	283	189
Nevada	1	Oct. 31, 1864	20,770	175	108
New Hampshire	2	June 2, 1784	9,200	274	142
New Jersey	3	Jan. 1, 1948	17,086	52	39
New Mexico	1	Jan. 6, 1912	27,200	231	120
New York	4	Jan. 1, 1895	80,000	274	207
North Carolina	3	July 1, 1971	11,000	34	27
North Dakota	1	Nov. 2, 1889	20,564	222	125
Ohio	2	Sept. 1, 1851	36,900	245	145
Oklahoma	1	Nov. 16, 1907	68,800	274	133
Oregon	1	Feb. 14, 1859	26,090	367	188
Pennsylvania	5	1968	21,675	25	19
Rhode Island	2	May 2, 1843	19,026	99	53
South Carolina	7	Jan. 1, 1896	22,500	647	463
South Dakota	1	Nov. 2, 1889	23,300	185	97
Tennessee	3	Feb. 23, 1870	15,300	55	32
Texas	5	Feb. 15, 1876	62,000	483	326
Utah	1	Jan. 4, 1896	11,000	126	77
Vermont	3	July 9, 1793	6,600	208	50
Virginia	6	July 1, 1971	18,500	23	20
Washington	1	Nov. 11, 1889	29,400	153	86
West Virginia	2	April 9, 1872	25,600	107	62
Wisconsin	1	May 29, 1848	13,500	168	124
Wyoming	1	July 10, 1890	31,800	97	57

* All information is through January 1, 1990. The constitutions referred to in this table include those Civil War documents customarily listed by the individual states.

Source: "General Information on State Constitutions," Table 1.1, in *The Book of the States, 1990–91* (Lexington, Ky.: Council of State Governments, 1990), pp. 40–41. © 1990 The Council of State Governments. Reprinted with permission.

does not guarantee a right of privacy, but ten states do. Four states in 1989 gave constitutional rights to crime victims (Florida, Michigan, Texas, and Washington). Californians enjoy the right to fish, and residents of New Hampshire hold the right to revolution. Pure water is a right guaranteed to all Pennsylvanians, while Californians have a right to safe schools.

The major reason for the rebirth of state activism in protecting civil liberties and rights has been the conservatism (relative to the Warren Court) of the U.S. Supreme Court since 1969, when Warren Burger became chief justice. One commentator accused the Supreme Court of having abdicated its role as "keeper of the nation's conscience."[22] As we have noted, the states' power to write and interpret their constitutions more aggressively than the U.S. Constitution in protecting civil rights and liberties has been upheld by the Supreme Court, as long as the state provisions have "adequate and independent" grounds.[23] Increasingly, civil rights and liberties cases are being filed by plaintiffs in state rather than federal courts, based on state bill of rights protections.

Two cases from California illustrate how states can interpret their constitutional protections differently from principles that have issued from the U.S. Supreme Court. In *People* v. *Anderson* (1972), the California Supreme Court declared the state's death penalty to be unconstitutional, even though the death penalty is permissible under certain conditions according to the U.S. Supreme Court. At issue in this case was constitutional language. The U.S. Bill of Rights prohibits "cruel *and* unusual punishment," whereas California's bans "cruel *or* unusual punishment."[24] Thus California's provision was more restrictive. The Golden State's electorate reacted to this ruling by amending the state constitution to permit the death penalty.[25]) The second case involved identical national and state constitutional language concerning search and seizure of evidence. In 1973, California's high court held that the U.S. Supreme Court had inaccurately interpreted the Fourth Amendment. The identical state provision was interpreted to afford greater protection from illegal search and seizure than the U.S. Supreme Court had granted (in *U.S.* v. *Robinson*).[26] Problem Solving 4.1 provides another example of more extensive protection under a state constitution.

Power of the State   This very brief article simply says that the powers enumerated in the constitution are not the only ones held by the state—that the state indeed has all powers not denied to it by the state or national constitution.

Suffrage and Elections   This article provides for the legal registration of voters and for election procedures. Recent extensions of voting rights and alterations in election procedures have been made in response to U.S. Supreme Court decisions and to national constitutional and statutory changes. Generally, states have improved election administration, liberalized registration, voting, and officeholding requirements, and shortened residency requirements. The voting age is eighteen years in all states; and the age for holding legislative office is typically twenty-one, although it varies depending on the office. Some states have amended this article to require the disclosure of campaign expenditures.

Problem Solving 4.1

How Personal (and Private) Is Your Garbage?

The Problem: In the 1988 case of *California* v. *Greenwood,* the U.S. Supreme Court ruled that police search and seizure of garbage placed on the streetside for collection does not violate the Fourth Amendment of the U.S. Constitution, even if the police do not have a search warrant. A remarkably similar case was heard two years later by the New Jersey state supreme court (*State* v. *Hempele* [1990]). Should the justices of the state supreme court defer to the U.S. Supreme Court by upholding the legality of police searches of garbage for evidence of drug use?

The Solution: New Jersey's court based its decision on the Fourth Amendment–type protection of the state constitution. It decided that one's trash is personal, even if deposited on the curb for pickup, as it reveals information about the private life and personal habits of its owners. New Jersey Justice Robert L. Cliffort proclaimed that a "free and civilized society should comport itself with more decency" than to allow "vestiges of a person's most private affairs" to be exposed and meddled with.

Thus, New Jersey protects a person's privacy—and garbage—more expansively than does the federal government.

Source: Adapted from Stanley H. Friedelbaum, "Supreme Courts in Conflict: The Drama of Disagreement," *Intergovernmental Perspective* 17 (Fall 1991): 27–29.

Others have imposed campaign contribution and spending limitations, and a few have provided for partial public financing of election campaigns.

The Legislative Branch This article sets forth the powers, procedures, and organizing principles of the legislature. In a pair of decisions in the 1960s, the U.S. Supreme Court ordered that state legislatures be apportioned on the basis of one person, one vote. That is, legislators must represent approximately the same number of constituents—House members the same as other House members and senators the same as other senators. District lines must be redrawn every ten years, after the national census has revealed population changes.

States have taken numerous actions in this article to approach greater conformity with the Model State Constitution, including increasing the length and frequency of legislative sessions, streamlining rules and procedures, and authorizing special sessions. Instead of stipulating specific dollar amounts for legislators' pay and fringe benefits (which are soon rendered inappropriate by inflation), most state constitutions now establish a procedure to determine and occasionally adjust the compensation of legislators. Specific pay levels are implemented through statute.

Interestingly, the model constitution for many years recommended a unicameral legislature as a means to overcome complexity, delay, and confusion. In the most recent revision of its book, the National Municipal League tacitly recognized the refusal of the states to follow this suggestion (only Nebraska has a single-house general assembly) by providing recommendations appropriate for a bicameral body.

The Executive Branch   The powers and organization of the executive branch, which are outlined in this article, have seen many notable modifications. Essentially, executive power continues to be centralized in the office of the governor. Governors have won longer terms and the right to run for re-election. Line item vetos, shorter ballots, the authority to make appointments within the executive branch, and the ability to reorganize the state bureaucracy have also increased gubernatorial powers (see Chapter 7). Several states have opted for team election of the governor and lieutenant governor. Some have lowered the minimum age for the top two officers from thirty to twenty-five years.

The Judicial Branch   All states have substantially revised court organization and procedures as well as election of judges. Moreover, a large majority have unified their court systems under a single authority, usually the state supreme court. Court procedures have been modernized under the office of the court administrator. Many states now select judges through a merit plan rather than by gubernatorial appointment, legislative election, or popular election (see Chapter 10). The states have also established commissions to investigate charges against judges and to recommend discipline or removal from the bench when necessary.

Finance   This article consists of provisions relating to taxation, debt, and expenditures for state and local government. A wave of tax and expenditure limitations swept across the states during the late 1970s and early 1980s, and tax relief has been granted to senior citizens, veterans, and handicapped people in many states.

Local Government   Here, the authority of municipalities, counties, and other local governments is granted. Most states have increased local authority through home rule provisions, which give localities more discretion in providing services. Local taxing authority has also been extended. Mechanisms for improved intergovernmental cooperation, such as consolidated city and county governments and regional districts to provide services, have been created.

Public Education   In this article the states provide for the establishment and maintenance of free public schools for all children. Higher-education institutions, including technical schools, colleges, and universities, are commonly established in this section. Some states have constitutional provisions for other functions, such as highways and transportation, health care, housing, and law enforcement.

Civil Service   The Model State Constitution sets forth a *merit system* of personnel administration for state government, under which civil servants are to be hired, promoted, paid, evaluated, and retained on the basis of competence, fitness, and performance instead of political party affiliation or other such criteria. All states must include certain public workers in merit systems, as mandated by federal law, but there is a great deal of variability in how states deal with other employees (see Chapter 8).

Intergovernmental Relations   Some states stipulate, as recommended by the Model State Constitution, specific devices for cooperation among various state entities, among local jurisdictions, or between the state and its localities. They may detail methods for sharing in the provision of certain services, or they may list cost-sharing mechanisms such as local option sales taxes. As the need for intergovernmental cooperation has grown, some states have substantially expanded the length of this article.

Constitutional Revision   In this article the methods for revising, amending, and replacing the constitution are described. Generally, the trend has been to make it easier for the voters, the legislature, or both to change the constitution. For example, several states have enabled voters to implement revisions through citizen initiative petitions (see Chapter 5). All states except Delaware ensure citizen participation in the constitutional amendment process through initiatives or by requiring voter ratification of all changes.

Constitutions Today

In general, state constitutions in the 1990s conform more closely to the Model State Constitution than those of the past did. They are shorter, more concise, and simpler, and they contain fewer errors, anachronisms, and contradictions. They give the state legislatures more responsibility for determining public policy through statute, rather than through constitutional amendment. The two newest states, Alaska and Hawaii, have documents that follow the model constitution quite closely.

However, much work remains to be done. Some state constitutions are still riddled with unnecessary detail because new amendments have continually been added to the old documents, and obsolete provisions and other relics can still be found. But there are more important deficiencies as well, which demand the attention of legislators and citizens in states whose constitutions inhibit the operations of state government and obstruct the ability to adapt to change. In some jurisdictions, the governor's formal powers remain weak; a plethora of boards and commissions makes any thought of executive management and coordination a pipe dream; local governments chafe under the tight leash of state authority; and many other problems persist. Constitutional revision must be an ongoing process if the states are to be able to cope with the changing contours of American society.

The case of Mississippi is instructive. For several years a growing coalition of reformers has sought to rewrite the Magnolia State's archaic fundamental law. The document was written in 1890 and has been amended 102 times. Some discriminatory provisions are still included (a ban against interracial marriages was finally removed in 1989). Mississippi's constitution is widely accused of hobbling gubernatorial authority, sustaining an unwieldy state bureaucracy, and restricting local governments. In 1985, Governor Bill Allain established a constitutional study commission, which recommended sweeping changes that were supported by the next governor, Ray Mabus. However, entrenched senior leaders in the House and Senate stifled Mabus's efforts to call a constitutional convention and to let the voters decide on proposed amendments through a referendum. Critics contend that without far-reaching government reform, Mississippi will remain at the bottom of the list of states in terms of capability, accomplishments, and quality of life.[27]

Methods for Constitutional Change

There are only two methods for altering the U.S. Constitution. The first is the *constitutional convention*, at which delegates representing the states assemble to consider modifying or replacing the Constitution. Despite periodic calls for a national constitutional convention, only one has taken place—in Philadelphia, more than two hundred years ago. However, the states fell just two votes short of calling a convention during the mid-1980s over a proposal to require the national government to balance its budget. Two-thirds of the states must agree to call a convention; three-fourths are required to ratify any changes in the constitution.

The second means of amending the U.S. Constitution is through congressional initiative, wherein Congress, by a two-thirds vote of both houses, agrees to send one or more proposed changes to the states. Again, three-fourths of the states must ratify the proposals. Since 1787, more than one thousand amendments have been submitted to the states by Congress. Only twenty-seven have been approved (the most recent in 1992), and the first ten of these were appended to the Constitution as a condition by several states for ratification. Note that neither method for amending the U.S. Constitution provides for popular participation by voters, in stark contrast to the citizen participation requirements for state constitutional change, as we shall see later in this chapter.

interpretation

An informal means of revising constitutions whereby members of the executive, legislative, or judicial branch apply constitutional principles and law to the everyday affairs of governing.

A possible scenario for popular participation in amending the U.S. Constitution would be a proposed referendum for Puerto Ricans to decide their own status. Problem Solving 4.2 explains the situation.

Informal Constitutional Change

One informal and four formal methods for amending state constitutions exist. The informal route is **interpretation** of constitutional meaning by the state

Problem Solving 4.2

Should Puerto Rico Become the Fifty-first State?

The Problem: The Caribbean island of Puerto Rico is a commonwealth of the United States. Its odd status—neither a nation nor a state—has always been a consuming policy issue on the island and a recurring point of debate in Congress.

The Solution: Let Puerto Ricans decide their own status through a plebiscite.

Puerto Rico became a possession of the United States in 1898 following the Spanish-American War. About the size of Connecticut, Puerto Rico has a population of about 3.5 million people. Its residents have one of the highest per capita incomes in the Caribbean, largely because of significant tax subsidies for U.S. firms operating on the island under Section 936 of the Internal Revenue Code. Yet unemployment runs about 20 percent, and approximately 60 percent of the people receive food stamps. Total U.S. aid is $5 billion per year.

Puerto Ricans are U.S. citizens and enjoy unrestricted emigration to the mainland. They pay social security taxes but not federal income taxes. In terms of politics, an elected governor and legislature govern, subject to U.S. congressional oversight. Puerto Rico does not have voting representatives in Congress, although presidential primaries are held (Bill Clinton won handily in 1992).

A small but vocal segment of Puerto Ricans have sought full independence for many years. In 1950, *independistas* attempted to assassinate President Truman, and in 1954 they wounded five representatives in an armed attack on Congress. The FALN, an independence-seeking terrorist organization, has engaged in bombings and other attacks on the mainland.

Those favoring independence (approximately 5 percent of the population according to recent polls) argue that the Spanish culture and language of the island would be sacrificed by statehood. Statehood advocates believe that full social welfare benefits would help alleviate poverty on the island, and that having two U.S. senators and up to six representatives in Congress would be of great benefit.

The implications of a change in status, whether independence or statehood, are complex. Independence would mean an end to U.S. welfare payments and would probably increase poverty and privation. If independence becomes inevitable, a massive emigration of Puerto Ricans to the mainland would likely precede the status change (an estimated 1.7 million native Puerto Ricans already live in the U.S.). Independence or statehood would terminate the Section 936 tax advantages, which save U.S. corporations on the island more than $2 billion per year (much to the chagrin of U.S. communities that have lost runaway corporations, especially pharmaceuticals, to the island). Another interesting twist is that statehood would possibly lead to reverse migration to Puerto Rico, as mainlanders returned to their cultural home.

Plebescites on independence were held in 1951 and 1967, and the votes were 3 to 1 for commonwealth status both times (statehood was not an option on the ballots). A new plebiscite on statehood, independence, or commonwealth status was to be held in 1991, and again in 1992, but both efforts were killed in Congress. Even in organizing and counting the vote, difficult questions emerge. For example, should mainland Puerto Ricans be permitted to cast ballots? What if the vote is split between the three options and none receives a majority?

The issues of Puerto Rico's status cannot be settled until these and other questions are answered satisfactorily.

Sources: Nicholas Lemann, "The Other Underclass," *The Atlantic* (December 1991): 96–110; "Pain Relief," *U.S. News & World Report* (July 1, 1991): 16; "Puerto Rico Bill Killed in Senate," *Congressional Quarterly Weekly Report,* June 15, 1991, p. 1588.

legislature, executive branch, or courts, or through usage and custom. The force of habit can be a powerful influence, specific constitutional provisions notwithstanding.

State supreme courts play the most direct role in changing constitutions through interpretation. In large measure, a constitution is what the judges say it is in their decisions from the bench. The power of the state supreme courts to review executive actions, legislative actions, and decisions of lower courts is known as **judicial review.** This power evolved in the states much as it did on the national level—through the courts' own insistence that they hold this authority. During recent years, as the U.S. Supreme Court has become more conservative and less activist in its interpretations of the law, some state courts have moved in the opposite direction.

We have already noted that state supreme courts have the authority to interpret and apply state guarantees of civil rights and liberties more broadly than the U.S. Supreme Court's interpretation of the Bill of Rights in the U.S. Constitution. The U.S. Supreme Court does not review state court decisions that rest on "adequate and independent" state grounds—that is, decisions clearly and properly based on state constitutional provisions.[28] In practice, state supreme courts are often guided by constitutional rulings of the U.S. Supreme Court and high courts in other states. Because courts apply similar constitutional language to many common issues, it is natural for them to share their experiences in legal problem solving.[29] Interaction and the sharing of legal precedents between state and national courts have existed since the earliest days of our federal system. Of course, the national courts are supreme under the U.S. Constitution and will strike down any serious constitutional contradictions between the nation and the states, but since the advent of the Burger Court, the U.S. Supreme Court has shown "a studied deference to the work of the state judiciaries."[30]

Several states, including California, Connecticut, New York, and Washington, have recently earned reputations as judicial activists. However, it is safe to say that the majority of state supreme courts continue to base their rulings on national precedents and decisions. Some state justices are simply too set in their ways to embark on a new legal voyage. Others fear national court reversal of their rulings, or perhaps feel that judicial activism would sit poorly with the voters, who could turn them out of office.[31]

Formal Constitutional Change

ratification

The formal approval of a constitution or constitutional amendment by a majority of the voters of a state.

The four formal procedures for constitutional change are legislative proposal, initiative, constitutional convention, and constitutional commission. All of them involve two basic steps, *initiation* and **ratification**. The state legislature, or in some cases the voters, propose (initiate) a constitutional change. Then, in all states but one, the proposed amendment is submitted to the voters for approval

judicial review

The power of the U.S. Supreme Court or state supreme courts to declare unconstitutional not only actions of the executive and legislative branches but also decisions of lower courts.

(ratification). The exception is Delaware, where the legislature can implement a constitutional revision without a vote of the people.

Legislative Proposal Historically, this is the most common road taken to revision; more than 90 percent of all changes in state constitutions have come through **legislative proposal**, which is permitted in all fifty states (see Table 4.2). Since 1970, around 70 percent of legislatively proposed constitutional changes have been ratified by the voters.

legislative proposal

The most common means of amending a state constitution, wherein the legislature proposes a revision, usually by a two-thirds majority.

The specifics of legislative proposal techniques vary, but most states require either two-thirds or three-fifths of the members of each house to approve a proposal before it is sent to the voters for ratification. Twelve states require two consecutive legislative sessions to consider and pass a proposed amendment. The procedure can become quite complicated. Connecticut's constitution, for example, states that modification can come only after a three-fourths vote in each house during one session *or* after a majority vote in each house for two consecutive sessions between which an election was held. South Carolina's legislative proposal must be passed by two-thirds of the members of each house; then it is sent to the people during the next general election. If a majority of voters show approval, the proposal returns to the next legislative session, in which a majority of legislators have to concur.

Almost all states accept a simple majority for voter ratification of a proposed revision. In New Hampshire, however, two-thirds of the voters must approve of the proposal. Hawaii, Illinois, Louisiana, Nebraska, New Mexico, and Tennessee also apply some restrictions to simple majority rule. Tennessee, for instance, requires approval by a majority of the citizens casting a vote for governor, and New Mexico mandates a three-fourths vote for amendments concerning suffrage and education matters.

Legislative proposal is probably best suited to revisions that are relatively narrow in scope. However, some legislatures, such as South Carolina's, have presented a series of proposals to the voters over a period of years and thereby have significantly revised the document. The disadvantage to such a strategy is that it tends to result in a patchwork of amendments that can conflict or overlap with other constitutional provisions. This spawns additional revisions, which lead to increased litigation in the state supreme court. Thus, if the legislative proposal is used too frequently, it complicates and lengthens the constitution.

initiative

Proposed law or constitutional amendment that is placed on the ballot by citizen petition.

Initiative Seventeen states permit their citizens to initiate and ratify changes in the constitution on their own, bypassing the legislature (see Table 4.3). Oregon was the first to use this method, in 1902. Only four of these states are east of the Mississippi River, thus reflecting the fact that the **initiative** was a product of the Progressive reform movement of the early 1900s. Most of the territories admitted as states during this period chose to

Table 4.2

State Constitutional Changes and Methods of Initiation, Selected Years

Method	1970–71	1974–75	1978–79	1982–83	1986–87	1988–89
Total Proposals						
All methods	403	352	395	345	275	267
Legislative proposal	392	332	319	330	243	246
Initiative	5	13	17	15	18	21
Constitutional convention	6	7	51	0	14	0
Constitutional commission	0	0	8	0	0	0
Total Adopted						
All methods	224	256	277	258	204	199
Legislative proposal	222	244	223	255	191	188
Initiative	1	8	6	3	5	11
Constitutional convention	1	4	48	0	8	0
Constitutional commission	0	0	0	0	0	0
Percent Adopted						
All methods	56	73	70	75	74	74
Legislative proposal	57	74	70	77	78	76
Initiative	20	62	35	20	28	55
Constitutional convention	17	57	94	—	57	—
Constitutional commission	—	—	0	—	—	—

Source: Data for each year from same year's edition of *The Book of the States* (Lexington, Ky.: Council of State Governments). Reprinted with permission. Copyright by The Council of State Governments.

permit the initiative (known as constitutional initiative in some states). Twenty-three states also authorize the initiative for enacting the statutory change (see Chapter 5).

The initiative is used much less frequently than legislative proposal in amending constitutions (see Table 4.2), although it was used the most since the 1930s during the decade of the 1980s, when 89 amendments were proposed and 33 adopted.[32] It is also less successful in terms of the percentage of amendments that are adopted by the voters. On average, from 1970 to 1989, only about 37 percent of the initiatives were written into state constitutions. Perhaps the most famous initiative is California's Proposition 13, enacted in 1978, which unleashed a wave of tax and expenditure limitations across the states.

State	Number of Signatures Required on Initiative Petition
Arizona	15% of total votes cast for all candidates for governor in last election
Arkansas	10% of voters for governor in last election
California	8% of total voters for all candidates for governor in last election
Colorado	5% of total legal votes for all candidates for secretary of state in last general election
Florida	8% of total votes cast in the state in the last election for presidential electors
Illinois*	8% of total votes cast for candidates for governor in last election
Massachusetts	3% of total votes cast for governor in preceding biennial state election (not fewer than 25,000 qualified voters)
Michigan	10% of total voters for all candidates in last gubernatorial election
Missouri	8% of legal voters for all candidates for governor in last election
Montana	10% of qualified electors, the number of qualified electors to be determined by number of votes cast for governor in preceding general election
Nebraska	10% of total votes for governor in last election
Nevada	10% of voters who voted in entire state in last general election
North Dakota	4% of population of the state
Ohio	10% of total number of electors who voted for governor in last election
Oklahoma	15% of legal voters for state office receiving highest number of voters in last general state election
Oregon	8% of total votes for all candidates for governor in last election at which governor was elected for four-year term
South Dakota	10% of total votes for governor in last election

* Only Article 6, "The Legislature," may be amended by initiative petition.

Source: Adapted from "Constitutional Amendment Procedure: By Initiative," Table 1.3, in *The Book of the States, 1990–91* (Lexington, Ky.: Council of State Governments, 1990). Reprinted with permission. Copyright by The Council of State Governments.

The initiative requires that a proposed constitutional amendment receive a certain percentage or number of signatures by registered voters before it can be placed on a statewide ballot for a ratification vote. Oklahoma requires 15 percent of the votes cast in the race for the statewide office that received the highest number of votes in the last general election. Eight states specify that the petition signatures must be collected widely throughout the state, as a means of ensuring that an initiative that favors one region does not become embodied in the constitution. In Montana, 10 percent of the petition signatures must come from two-fifths of the state's legislative districts.

In general, a petition for constitutional amendment is sent to the office of the secretary of state for verification that the required number of registered voters have signed their names. Then the question is placed on a statewide ballot in the next general election. Ratification requires a majority vote of the people in most states, although four have further requirements for approval. For instance, Nevada mandates a majority popular vote on an amendment in two consecutive general elections.

It is usually easy enough to collect the required number of signatures to place a proposed amendment on statewide ballot. But it is much more difficult to pass the initiative, once it receives a close public examination and opposing interests are activated.

direct initiative

A procedure by which the voters of a jurisdiction propose the passage of constitutional amendments, state laws, or local ordinances, bypassing the legislative body.

If the legislature is circumvented altogether and propositions are placed directly on the general election ballot by citizens, the procedure is called a **direct initiative**. If a legislature participates by voting on the citizen proposal, as it does in Massachusetts, or if it otherwise contributes substantively to the amendment process, the procedure is known as an **indirect initiative.** Eight states allow indirect initiatives.

The initiative is useful in making limited changes to the state constitution and, in recent years, has addressed some controversial issues that state legislatures have been loath to confront. Colorado voters, for example, adopted an initiative to prohibit the use of public funds for abortions. Other controversial proposals in the 1980s and early 1990s included those for legalized gambling, a unilateral nuclear arms freeze, gun control, and prayer in the public schools.

indirect initiative

Similar to the direct initiative, except that the voter-initiated proposal must be submitted to the legislature before going on the ballot for voter approval.

A major advantage of the initiative is that it permits the people's will to counter a despotic or inertia-ridden legislature. For instance, Illinois voters in 1978 reduced the size of the House of Representatives from 177 to 118 after the legislature voted itself a huge pay raise during a period of economic hardship. Another advantage is that this method appears to enhance citizen interest and participation in government. However, the initiative can be abused by special interests with selfish motives who seek to gain privileges, and under crisis conditions it can result in ill-conceived, radical changes to the constitution. The initiative can also result in just the kind of excessive detail and poorly drafted verbiage that is so widely condemned by constitutional scholars and reformers.[33]

Constitutional Convention Legislative proposals and initiatives are quite specific about the type of constitutional change that is sought. Only those questions

constitutional convention

An assembly of delegates chosen by popular election or appointed by the legislature or the governor to revise an existing constitution or to create a new one.

that actually appear on the ballot are considered. In contrast, a **constitutional convention** assembles delegates who suggest revisions or even an entirely new document, then submit the proposed changes to the voters for ratification. The convention is especially well suited to consider far-reaching constitutional changes or a new fundamental law. Convention proposals are less likely to be ratified by the people than legislative proposals are, but they have higher success rates than initiatives.

The states have held more than 230 constitutional conventions during their history. The convention is the oldest method for constitutional change in the states and is available in all fifty of them. The process begins when the electorate or the legislature decides to call for a constitutional convention. No state permits a convention to be called through the petition process; the legislature must either call a convention unilaterally or place the issue before the people on the general election ballot. A third possibility exists in fourteen states, where the question of calling a convention must be regularly voted on by the electorate, as Thomas Jefferson once proposed. Alaskans and Iowans consider a constitutional convention every ten years; in New York and Maryland, the convention issue is submitted to the voters every twenty years. In all states, the legislature can decide on its own to submit to the voters the question of whether to hold a constitutional convention; and in some, including Virginia and Maine, the legislature may call a convention without asking for voter concurrence. Except in Delaware, proposals emerging from the convention must be ratified by the voters before they become part of the constitution.

Delegates to a convention are usually elected by the voters from state House or Senate districts. The total number of delegates has varied from 40 in Virginia to 481 in New Hampshire, but it averages 170. Recently, most delegates have been elected on a nonpartisan basis, although some states provide for partisan ballots. Generally, partisan election selects delegates with more years of experience in politics, whereas nonpartisan selection is associated with fewer professional politicians.[34]

Conventions are usually dominated by middle-aged and elderly white males with high levels of formal education.[35] Many are professionals; the percentage of lawyers alone typically ranges from 25 to 50 percent. There is normally a substantial number of educators and businesspeople and a smattering of homemakers.[36] This delegate composition is not surprising, since convention calls are strongly supported by higher socioeconomic groups in urban areas.[37] Recent conventions have been more representative of state population characteristics, however. Hawaii's 1978 convention, for instance, comprised more ethnic, female, and occupationally diverse members than did the delegate pool in the 1968 convention.

The characteristics of a delegate pool are important for several reasons. First, the delegates need knowledge of and experience in state government and politics if they are to contribute meaningfully to the debate and drafting of proposed amendments. It is usually not too difficult to attract qualified people for service; the experience is important, unique, and a privilege, and it is not as time-consuming as running for and serving in the legislature. Second, the delegates should represent a cross-section of the state's population insofar as possible. If the delegate pool does not reflect gender, racial, regional, ethnic, and other salient characteristics of the population, the fruit of its labor may lack legitimacy in the eyes of substantial numbers of voters. Finally, partisanship should be avoided where possible. Partisan differences can wreck consensus on major issues and destroy the prospects for voter ratification of suggested amendments that emerge from the convention, as experiences in Michigan, Illinois, and New York have aptly demonstrated.[38] Of course, delegates elected on a partisan ticket are more likely to divide along party lines than are those selected through nonpartisan election.

All conventions experience some divisions, partisan or not. The basic conflict is frequently between those who favor comprehensive constitutional change—reformers—and supporters and protectors of the status quo. Splits can also develop between urban and rural interests, regional interests, and blacks and whites. One study of constitutional conventions in six states found that a large majority of delegates began the convention with an idealized view that the debates and decisions would be above party politics and generally statesman-like.[39] Most delegates kept that perspective throughout their respective conventions, with the exception of those attending the highly politicized Illinois and New York assemblies, who tended to emerge with more cynical views.

Voter approval of convention proposals is problematic. If partisan, racial, regional, or other disagreements dominate media reports on the convention, voter approval is difficult to obtain. People naturally tend to regard suggestions for sweeping changes in the basic structures and procedures of government with skepticism. And, if they have not been regularly involved with and informed of the progress of the convention, they may be reluctant to give their approval to the recommendations.

Delegates usually understand these dynamics and are sensitive to how their proposed changes may affect the general public. They must, for example, carefully consider how to present the proposed amendments for ratification. There are two choices: the all-or-nothing strategy of consolidating all changes in a single vote, and the piecemeal strategy, which presents each proposal as a separate ballot decision. In recent years, voters have tended to reject inclusive packages. Each suggested change is certain to offend some minority, and when all the offended minorities coalesce, they may well constitute a majority of voters.[40] In 1968, for example, Maryland voters soundly rejected a new constitution, but separate amendments later submitted to the people were approved.

However, separate proposals do not ensure victory. Texas's eight constitutional amendments each met defeat in 1975 for several reasons, including conflicts among the delegates, popular discontent with the legislature (which had formulated the proposals and organized *itself* as the convention), and a general perception that since the state had a large budget surplus and low taxes, there was no pressing need for change. The Texas convention proposed a new constitution of only 17,500 words, to replace a badly written, scrambled 63,000-word document with more than 200 amendments. Amazingly, after spending some $4 million and many months in debate, the Texas convention became the first in history to reject its own creation. Under virulent public criticism and pressure, the legislature the next year reorganized the rejected document into eight constitutional amendments and submitted them to the voters in the general election. All were voted down by margins of 2.5 to 1 or more.[41] Florida's voters rejected a series of eight proposed amendments in 1978, largely because the proposals were so complex that people could not understand them.[42]

constitutional commission

A meeting of delegates appointed by the governor or legislature to study constitutional problems and propose solutions.

Constitutional Commission   Often called a *study commission,* the **constitutional commission** is usually established to study the existing document and to recommend changes to the legislature. It may be created by statute, legislative resolution, or executive order of the governor in all states, but not by initiative. Little or no citizen participation is associated with this method of constitutional change. Depending on the mandate, the study commission may examine the entire constitution with a view toward replacement or change, it may focus on one or more specific articles or provisions, or it may be given the freedom to decide its own scope of activity. Commission recommendations to the legislature and/or governor are only advisory, thus helping to account for this method's popularity with elected officials, who sometimes prefer to study a problem to death rather than engage it head on. Some or all of the recommendations may be submitted to the voters; others may be completely ignored. Only in Florida can a commission send its proposals directly to the voters.[43]

Some constitutional commissions, called *preparatory commissions,* are created to do the groundwork for a forthcoming constitutional convention. Typically, they arrange for convention staff, lay out a schedule, and in some cases submit suggestions for constitutional change to the convention.

Commission size averages twenty members, either private citizens or public officials who are usually appointed by the governor or by the governor and the legislature. Selection may reflect such factors as geography, political party, and occupation. Meetings are normally held over a period of about one and one-half years, typically in the state capital.

Only twenty-four commissions have operated since 1970. Service on a constitutional commission can be a thankless task, as legislators sometimes ignore the commission's recommendations or employ them as a symbolic device for relieving political pressure. For example, Kentucky's 1987–1988 Revision Commission recommended seventy-seven changes to the constitution, but only one was referred by the legislature to the voters as a proposed amendment.[44] When used properly, however, commissions can furnish high-quality research inexpensively and relatively quickly.

State Resurgence and Constitutional Reform

Constitutions are designed specifically to meet the needs of each state. The rich political culture, history, economics, values, and ideals of the state community are reflected in its constitutional language. Through their constitutions the states experiment with different governmental institutions and processes. As super patriot Thomas Paine observed more than two hundred years ago, "It is in the interest of all the states, that the constitution of each should be somewhat diversified from each other. We are a people founded upon experiments, and . . . have the happy opportunity of trying variety in order to discover the best."[45]

State constitutions were the original guardians of individual rights and liberties, with their own bills of rights preceding those of the U.S. Constitution by many years. They are reassuming their rightful position in American government today and will become increasingly important as counterweights to the conservative U.S. Supreme Court of the 1990s as independent state constitutional law develops further.

Few tasks in government are more difficult than modernizing a constitution. The process requires "sustained, dedicated, organized effort; vigorous, aggressive and imaginative leadership; bipartisan political support; education of the electorate on the issues; judicious selection of the means; and seemingly endless patience."[46] In the words of constitutional scholar W. Brooke Graves, "The advocate of constitutional reform in an American state should be endowed with the patience of Job and the sense of time of a geologist."[47] The solemn duty of framing the original state constitutions, which was so effectively discharged by our predecessors, must be matched by the continuous oversight of present and future generations. Changes are necessary to adjust state governments to the vagaries of life in the 1990s and beyond.

The constitutional changes enacted in the states during the three decades since the Kestnbaum Commission report have generally resulted in documents that "are shorter, more clearly written, modernized, less encumbered with restrictions, more basic in content and have more reasonable amending processes. They also establish improved governmental structures and contain substantive provisions assuring greater openness, accountability and equity."[48] The states have made a great deal of progress in modernizing their governments. As state constitutional scholar Richard Leach has put it, "There are not many constitutional horrors left."[49]

Terry Sanford, former governor of North Carolina and currently U.S. senator, has referred to old-style constitutions as "the drag anchors of state programs, and permanent cloaks for the protection of special interests and points of view."[50] These constitutions held back progress and delayed the states' resurgence as lead players in the drama of American federalism. Recent constitutional amendments have reflected, and indeed caused, profound changes in state government and politics. Since the genesis of modern reform in the mid-1960s, some forty states have adopted new constitutions or substantially amended existing ones. Problems persist, and future constitutional tinkering and replacements will be necessary. But in most states, the constitutional landscape is much cleaner and more functional than it was twenty-five years ago.

....

Summary

As instruments of political power, constitutions establish the basic structure and operating rules for state government. Most states have modernized their constitutions during the past twenty-five years, thereby bringing them closer to the Model State Constitution, by among other things strengthening executive power and making the documents clearer and more concise. Many constitutions, however, remain outdated and in need of reform. Constitutions can be revised through legislative proposal, initiative, or constitutional convention. All methods require voter approval.

Key Terms

legislative supremacy
Model State Constitution
interpretation
judicial review
ratification
legislative proposal

initiative
direct initiative
indirect initiative
constitutional convention
constitutional commission

Participation and Interest Groups

A larmed by the growing disengagement of citizens from their governments, two communities recently took actions to reverse the trend. In
Phoenix, Arizona, a "futures forum" was designed to develop a
"destiny-changing vision" for the community through diverse, widespread citizen participation.[1] And in Charlotte, North Carolina, a citizens forum launched
an ambitious self-evaluation and strategic planning process.[2] In both communities, the effort was intended to reinvigorate the citizen-government relationship. Although the process was time-consuming, each community emerged
from the exercise with a clearer vision of where it wanted to go and how it was
going to get there. Most important, that vision was determined by the *citizens.*

Participation

participation

*Actions through which
ordinary members of
a political system at-
tempt to influence
outcomes.*

Democracy assumes citizen **participation**—taking action to influence government. There is persistent evidence that citizens are not much interested in
participation. We have grown accustomed to reports of low voter turnout and
public hearings that no public attends. On the surface, government works just
fine with limited participation: The interests of the active become translated into
public policy, and those who are inactive can be safely ignored, because they do
not vote. If, however, some traditional nonvoters (such as low-income, less-
educated citizens) went to the polls, then vote-seeking candidates might be
forced to pay more attention to their interests, and public policy might be
nudged in a different direction. In this light, it is important to understand both
why many people do participate and why others do not.

Why and How People Participate

In a representative democracy, voting is the most common form of participation. For many citizens, it is a matter of civic responsibility. It is a fundamental
facet of citizenship—after all, it is called "the right to vote." Citizens go to the
polls to elect the officials who will govern them. But there are other methods of
participation. Consider the citizen who is unhappy because the property taxes
on her home have increased substantially from one year to the next. What
options are available to her besides voting against incumbent officeholders at the
next election? As shown in Figure 5.1, she can be either active or passive and her
actions either constructive or destructive. Basically, she has four potential responses: loyalty, voice, exit, and neglect.[3]

According to this formulation, voting is an example of *loyalty,* a passive but
constructive response to government action. It shows the irate taxpayer's underlying support for her community despite her displeasure with specific tax
policies. An active constructive response is *voice:* The aggrieved property owner
could contact officials, work in the campaign of a candidate who promises to
lower tax assessments, or (assuming that others in the community share her
sentiments) participate in antitax groups and organize demonstrations.

Figure 5.1

Possible Responses
to Dissatisfaction in
the Community

Each of these participa-
tory options affects
public policy decisions
in a community. Citi-
zens who choose the
voice option frequently
find themselves in the
thick of things.

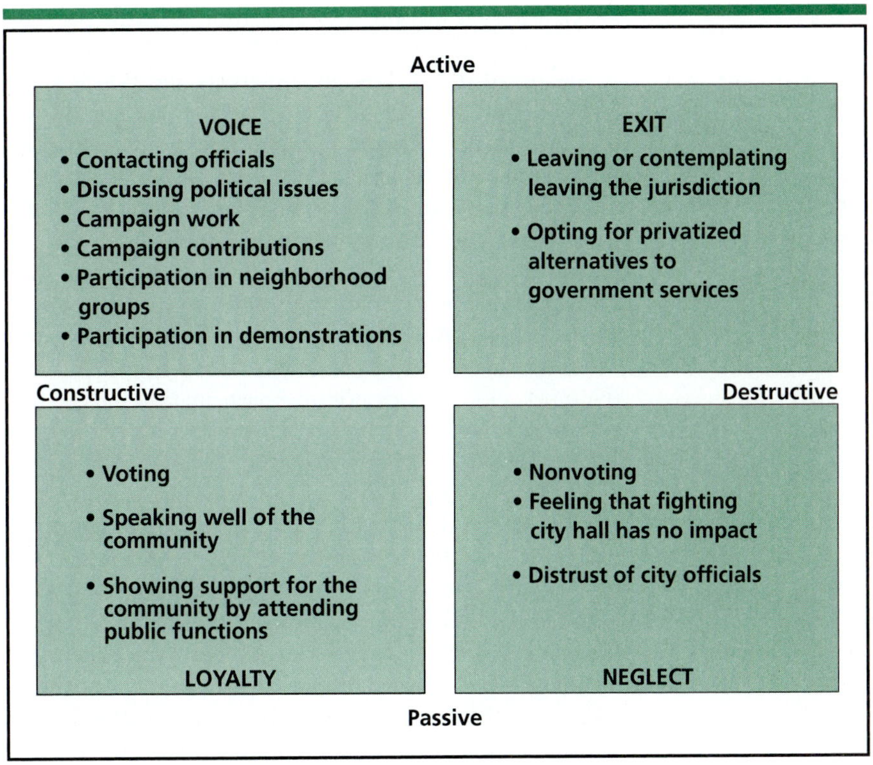

Active

VOICE
- Contacting officials
- Discussing political issues
- Campaign work
- Campaign contributions
- Participation in neighborhood groups
- Participation in demonstrations

EXIT
- Leaving or contemplating leaving the jurisdiction
- Opting for privatized alternatives to government services

Constructive									Destructive

- Voting
- Speaking well of the community
- Showing support for the community by attending public functions

- Nonvoting
- Feeling that fighting city hall has no impact
- Distrust of city officials

LOYALTY							**NEGLECT**

Passive

Source: William E. Lyons and David Lowery, "The Organization of Political Space and Citizen Responses to Dissatisfaction in Urban Communities: An Integrative Model," *Journal of Politics* 49 (May 1986): 331. Reprinted by permission of the authors and the University of Texas Press.

Destructive responses (those that undermine the citizen-government relationship) are similarly passive or active. If the citizen simply shrugs and concludes that "you can't fight city hall," she is exhibiting a response termed neglect. She has virtually given up on the community and does not participate. A more active version of giving up is to *exit*—that is, to leave the community altogether (this is often referred to as "voting with your feet"). The unhappy citizen will relocate in a community that is more in line with her tax preferences.

Every citizen confronts these participatory options. It is much healthier for the political system if citizens engage in the constructive responses, but some individuals are likely to conclude that constructive participation is of little value to them and opt for neglect or, in more extreme cases, exit.

Nonparticipation

What explains the citizens who choose neglect as their best option? One explanation for nonparticipation in politics is socioeconomic status. Individuals with lower levels of income and education tend to participate less than wealthier, more educated individuals do.[4] Tied closely to income and education levels is occupational status. Unskilled workers and hourly wage earners do not participate in politics to the same degree that white-collar workers and professionals do. Individuals of lower socioeconomic status may have neither the interest nor the resources to become actively involved in politics.

Other explanations for nonparticipation have included age (younger people have participated less than middle-aged individuals), race (blacks have participated less than whites), and gender (women have participated less than men). However, of these factors, only age continued to affect political activity in the 1980s. African-American political participation actually surpasses that of whites when socioeconomic status is taken into consideration,[5] and the gender gap in the types and levels of political participation has virtually disappeared.[6]

The explanation for nonparticipation does not rest solely with the individual. Institutional features—that is, the way the political system is designed—may suppress participation. For example, local governments that have instituted nonpartisan elections, in which candidates run without party affiliation, have removed an important mobilizing factor for voters. Voter turnout tends to be lower in these elections than in partisan contests. Moreover, some state governments still have not modernized their voter registration procedures to make the process quick and easy, thus discouraging potential registrants. City council meetings scheduled at 10:00 A.M. put a tremendous strain on workers who must take time off from their jobs if they want to attend; consequently, attendance is low. And local governments in which it is difficult for citizens to contact the appropriate official with a service request or complaint are not doing much to facilitate participation. Features like these play an often unrecognized role in dampening participation.

The Struggle for the Right to Vote

State constitutions in the eighteenth and early nineteenth centuries entrusted only propertied white males with the vote. They did not encourage public involvement in government, and the eventual softening of restrictions on suffrage did not occur without a struggle. Restrictions on property ownership and wealth were eventually dropped, but women and blacks were still denied the right to vote.

In an effort to attract women to its rugged territory, Wyoming enfranchised women in 1869. The suffragists—women who were actively fighting for the right to vote—scored a victory when Colorado extended the vote to women in 1893. Gradually, other states began enfranchising women and in 1920 the Twentieth Amendment to the U.S. Constitution, forbidding states to deny the right to vote "on account of sex," was ratified.

Even after the Fifteenth Amendment (1870) extended the vote to blacks, some southern states clung defiantly to traditional ways that denied blacks and poor people their rights. Poll taxes and literacy tests kept the poor and uneducated, regardless of race, from voting. Furthermore, southern Democrats designed the "white primary" to limit black political influence. In the one-party South, the Democratic primary elections, in which candidates for the general election were chosen, were the scene of the important contests. Thus blacks were still barred from effective participation, because they could not vote in the primaries. The general election amounted to little more than ratification of the party's choices, because so few elections were contested by the Republicans. In *Smith* v. *Allwright* (1944), the U.S. Supreme Court ruled that since primaries were part of the machinery that chose officials, they were subject to the same nondiscriminatory standards as general elections, and the days of the white primary came to an end.

Segregationists in the South continued their battle against the pressures of modernization and fairness.[7] Although the number of black voters increased steadily during the mid-twentieth century, substantial discrimination remained. The outlawing of the white primary forced racists to resort to more informal methods of keeping blacks from the polls—including physical intimidation. Blacks gained access to the polls primarily through national enactments such as the Civil Rights Act of 1964 and the Twenty-fourth Amendment (1964), which made poll taxes unconstitutional.

Voting Rights Act of 1965

The law that effectively enfranchised racial minorities by giving the national government the power to decide whether individuals are qualified to vote and to intercede in state and local electoral operations when necessary.

The **Voting Rights Act of 1965** finally broke the back of the segregationists' efforts. Under its provisions, federal poll watchers and registrars were dispatched to particular counties to investigate voter discrimination. To this day, counties covered under the Voting Rights Act (all of nine southern states and parts of seven other states) must submit to the U.S. Department of Justice any changes in election laws, such as new precinct lines or new polling places.

Over time, judicial interpretations, congressional actions, and Justice Department rules have modified the Voting Rights Act. One of the most important modifications has been to substitute an "effects" test for the original "intent" test. In other words, if a governmental action has the effect of discouraging minority voting, whether intentionally or not, the action must be rejected. Civil rights activists welcomed this change, because proving the intent of an action is much more difficult than simply demonstrating its effect.

Voting Patterns

Figure 5.2 demonstrates the fact that voter turnout has been steadily declining for a number of years. Note, however, that the data show voter turnout as a percentage of the voting-age population. Not all people who have reached the age of eighteen are in fact eligible to vote (for example, convicted felons who have not had their civil rights restored are ineligible), and the percentages in Figure 5.2 tend to understate the percentage of eligible voters who show up at the polls. Nevertheless, it is true that twenty and thirty years ago, more than 60 percent of the voting-age population customarily turned out for a presidential election. Since 1972, when eighteen-year-olds were given the right to vote, the proportion has dropped to under 55 percent. And in off-year elections, when

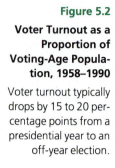

Figure 5.2

Voter Turnout as a Proportion of Voting-Age Population, 1958–1990

Voter turnout typically drops by 15 to 20 percentage points from a presidential year to an off-year election.

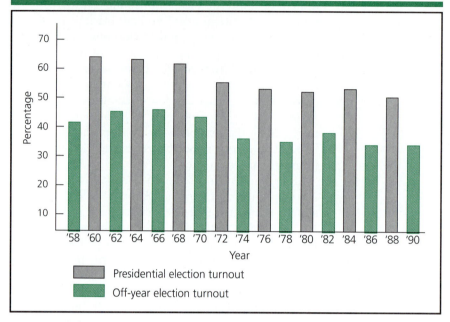

Source: Data from U.S. Bureau of the Census, *Statistical Abstract of the United States* (Washington, D.C.: U.S. Government Printing Office, 1964, 1976, 1988, 1990).

there is no presidential race, voter turnout has declined from the mid–40 percent range to the mid–30s.

Voter turnout is affected by several factors. First, it varies according to the type of election. A presidential race usually attracts a higher proportion of eligible voters than a local election does. Turnout for elections is higher when a presidential contest is on the ballot than in off-years, when many state races occur. Second, attractive candidates running a close race seem to increase voter interest. When each candidate has a chance to win, voters sense that their vote will matter more than in a race with a sure winner. Voter turnout in mayoral elections in eight cities is reported in Table 5.1. In only two cities did voter turnout, as a percentage of registered voters, exceed 50 percent.

There are noteworthy differences among states in proportions of both voting-age population registered and voter turnout. Nationally, 66.3 percent of the voting-age population was registered to vote in the late 1980s. But when we look at the figures for individual states, wide variation appears. Compare two states with very similar voting-age populations: Oklahoma, with 2.4 million, and South Carolina, with 2.5 million. Eighty-three percent of the voting-age population in Oklahoma were registered; in South Carolina, the comparable figure was 52.6 percent.[8]

States can also be differentiated according to voter turnout rates. States with moralistic political cultures typically experience higher voter turnout than do

City	Mayoral Candidate	Candidate Total	Voter Turnout
Baltimore	Kurt SCHMOKE (D)	66,969	28.30%
	Samuel Culotta (R)	25,859	
Boston*	Raymond FLYNN	63,582	40.50%
	Edward Doherty	21,659	
	All others	12	
Dallas*	Steve Bartlett	84,834	36.20%
	Kathryn Cain	41,990	
	Forrest Smith	20,895	
Houston*	Bob Lanier	152,792	33.59%
	Sylvester Turner	135,173	
Indianapolis	Steve Goldsmith (R)	110,545	47.00%
	Louis Mahern (D)	79,817	
	All others	5,903	
Philadelphia	Edward Rendell (D)	288,467	60.80%
	Joe Egan (R)	132,811	
	All others	27,752	
Salt Lake City*	Deedee Corradini	20,417	45.39%
	David Buhler	16,453	
San Francisco*	Frank Jordan	104,098	50.70%
	Art AGNOS	97,726	

Note: Capital letters denote an incumbent.
 * denotes a nonpartisan race.

states with traditionalistic political cultures. For example, Utah voters have historically turned out for state elections at about twice the rate of Georgia voters. States with competitive political parties tend to turn out a higher proportion of voters; each party needs to mobilize individuals who identify with it in order to win. Finally, the states can affect turnout by the way in which they administer the elections. People who are registered tend to vote. Making registration as easy as it is in Wisconsin, where voters can register at the polls on election day, is one way to bolster turnout.

Should Nonvoting Be a Concern?

Many people are staying home on election day, watching "America's Funniest Home Videos" instead of voting. When asked why they did not vote, these citizens offer responses ranging from "It was too much trouble" to "I didn't like either of the candidates" to "My vote won't change the system." To them, voting simply was not in their interest. In the U.S. political system, this is a choice that individuals can make.

Many other citizens are concerned about the extent of nonvoting, as shown by the drive to increase voter turnout, which takes two principal forms: (1) public relations efforts, such as public service advertisements in which celebrities tell us why they vote, and (2) procedures that make registration and absentee voting easier. Over half (twenty-nine) of the states have adopted a system whereby voters can register by mail.[9] In more than twenty states, individuals can register to vote when they apply for a driver's license or register their automobile.[10] (This is known as motor-voter registration.) And some states have moved the closing date for registration nearer to the actual date of the election, giving potential voters more time to register. This is important, because campaigns tend to heighten the public's interest in the election. A potential voter is not encouraged to participate when he or she is told at the registration office that "the books have closed" for next week's election. Most states now close their registration books fewer than thirty days before an election, and Wisconsin, Maine, Minnesota, and Wyoming allow registration on election day.[11] North Dakota is the only state in the nation that does not require voter registration.

Absentee balloting has also been made easier than it was in the past. Most states still require a voter applying for an absentee ballot to supply an acceptable reason, such as being away on business or in school, but some have lifted these restrictions and allow any voter to vote in absentia. These states include Alaska, California, Iowa, Kansas, Oregon, and Washington.[12] Voting by mail is likely to increase. Although turned down by their respective legislatures, the secretaries of state in Hawaii and Minnesota proposed conducting the 1992 presidential primaries in their states with mail ballots.[13]

Ironically, the effects of nonvoting are not always clear. First of all, higher turnout might not affect election results. An analysis of the 1988 presidential election indicated that if nonvoters had voted, the outcome would not have changed.[14] In a similar vein, recent research suggests that as a group, nonvoters and voters do not hold significantly different policy preferences.[15] Second, as Figure 5.1 shows, the potential participant has other options. Although voting is declining, people are engaging in alternative forms of participation.

Election-Day Lawmaking

What happens when the government does not respond to the messages that the people are sending? More and more, the answer is to transform the messages into ballot propositions and let the citizens make their own laws. As explained in Chapter 4, *initiatives* are proposed laws or constitutional amendments that are placed on the ballot by citizen petition, to be approved or rejected by popular vote. An initiative lets citizens enact their own laws, bypassing the state legislature. This mechanism for legislation by popular vote was one of several reforms of the Progressive era, roughly 1890 to 1920. Other Progressive reforms included the popular referendum and the recall. The **popular referendum** allows citizens to petition to vote on actions taken by legislative bodies.[16] It provides a means by which the public can overturn a legislative enactment. (A popular referendum is different from a general **referendum**—a proposition that requires voter approval before it can take effect. Constitutional amendments and bond issues are examples of general referenda.) The **recall** election requires elected officials to stand for a vote on their removal, before their term has expired. Recall provides the public with an opportunity to force an official out of office.

> **popular referendum**
>
> *A special type of referenda whereby citizens can petition to vote on actions taken by legislative bodies.*

> **referendum**
>
> *A procedure whereby a governing body submits proposed laws, constitutional amendments, or bond issues to the voters for ratification.*

> **recall**
>
> *A procedure that allows citizens to vote elected officials out of office before their term has expired.*

The key characteristic shared by initiative, popular referendum, and recall is that they are actions begun by citizens. The Progressives advocated these mechanisms to expand the role of citizens and to restrict the power of intermediary institutions such as legislatures, political parties, and elected officials.[17] Their efforts were particularly successful in the western part of the United States (see Figure 5.3), probably because of the difficulty of amending existing state constitutions in the East and an elitist fear of the working class (the industrialized immigrants in the Northeast and the rural black sharecroppers in the South). The newer western states, in contrast, were quite open, both procedurally and socially. In 1898, South Dakota became the first state to adopt the initiative process. And the initiative was actually used for the first time in Oregon in 1902, when citizens successfully petitioned for ballot questions on mandatory political party primaries and local-option liquor sales. Both of the initiatives were approved.

Today, twenty-three states allow the initiative. A few use the indirect initiative, which gives the legislature an opportunity to consider the proposed measure. If the legislature fails to act, or if it rejects the measure, the proposal is put before the voters at the next election. But most states use the direct initiative. Popular referendum is provided for in twenty-five states, and recall of state officials in fifteen. These figures understate the use of these mechanisms throughout the country, however, because many states without statewide initiative, popular referendum, and recall allow their use at the local government level.[18]

The Initiative

The first step in the initiative process is the petition. A draft of the proposed law (or constitutional amendment) is circulated along with a petition, which citizens must sign. The petition signature requirement varies by state but usually falls between 5 and 10 percent of the number of votes cast in the preceding statewide

Figure 5.3 State Use of the Initiative
In the past fifty years, only Wyoming (1968) and Florida (1978) have joined the ranks of initiative states.

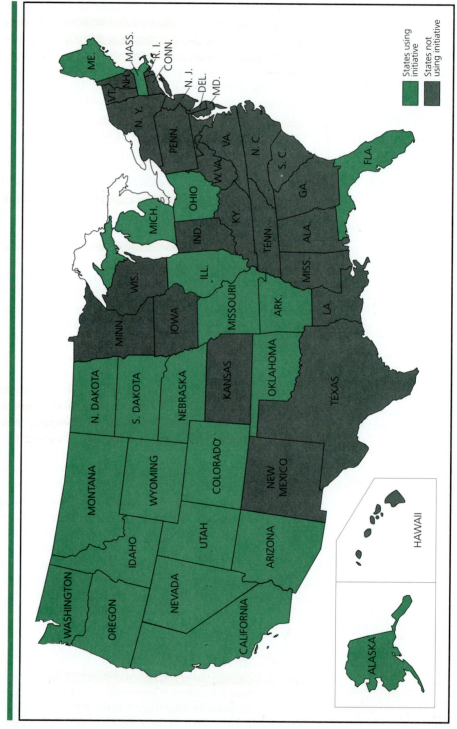

States using initiative

States not using initiative

Source: Ann O'M. Bowman and Richard C. Kearney, *The Resurgence of the States* (Englewood Cliffs, N.J.: Prentice-Hall, 1986), p. 115. Reprinted by permission of Prentice-Hall, Inc., Englewood Cliffs, N.J.

election. For example, if the requirement is 7 percent and 1 million people voted in the last governor's race, a petitions needs 70,000 signatures to be valid. In California, more than 600,000 registered voters' signatures are needed for a measure to make a statewide ballot. To ensure that a matter is of statewide concern and that signatures have been gathered beyond a single area, some states set geographic distributional requirements. In Montana, for example, signature requirements must be met in at least one-third of the legislative districts; in Nebraska, in two-fifths of the counties.

California, which has been referred to as "the world's largest direct democracy," has transformed the signature-gathering process into a science.[19] Its first innovation was to replace standard door-to-door canvassing with an operation based in shopping malls, whereby proponents buttonhole shoppers to explain the initiative and ask them to sign the petitions. California's most recent contribution to the signature-gathering process has been to use direct mail: Petition forms are simply mailed to a preselected, computer-generated list of likely signers. This is a costly but simple way of collecting signatures.

The Return of Initiatives   The 1950s and 1960s saw little use of the initiative process, but the grassroots fervor of three kinds of groups reactivated the process in the 1970s: environmental activists, consumer advocates, and tax limitation organizations. In 1976, for example, measures to restrict nuclear power were on the ballot in seven states. The propositions were defeated in every instance. Yet the environmental groups' pioneering efforts eventually bore fruit: Antinuclear measures have been much more successful in recent years, as demonstrated in the 1989 vote to shut down a nuclear power plant outside Sacramento, California. The most influential modern initiative was California's Proposition 13 (1978), which rolled back property taxes in the state and spawned an immediate wave of tax reduction propositions across the land.

Other factors have contributed to the increased popularity of initiatives. Some observers believe that wavering public confidence in government, shaken by political chicanery, among other things, has led citizens to take matters into their own hands. Historically, the initiative process has been used more during times of economic strain such as during the late 1970s and early 1980s. In addition, new methods of signature collection have brought the initiative process within the reach of virtually any well-financed group with a grievance or concern. These factors combine to make the current climate ripe for election-day lawmaking.

Recent Initiatives   If ballot questions are an indication of the public's mood, then the public had quite an attitude in 1990. Five different types of issues found citizens collecting signatures on petitions: the environment, taxing and spending, abortion, education, and term limits. Once on the ballot, however, many of the measures went down to defeat.[20] Uneasy Californians defeated the "Big Green" initiative (see Profile 5.1) as well as a forest preservation measure. Also suffering voter rejection were a stream protection referendum in Missouri, a land-use planning proposal in Washington, and a recycling measure in Ore-

Profile 5.1

Big Green Goes Down to a Big Defeat

Voters in California, a state on the cutting edge of environmentalism, shocked the rest of the country when they overwhelmingly rejected Proposition 128, the California Environmental Protection Act, in 1990. Known as "Big Green," the initiative would have protected just about everything from the oceans to the ozone layer. California's regulatory laws, ranging from pesticide contamination of food and timber harvesting to offshore oil drilling and global warming, would have been rewritten. In retrospect, the comprehensive nature of the measure contributed to its defeat. Opponents of Big Green used their $11 million war chest to promote their slogan, "It does too much, it costs too much." With opponents outspending supporters at the rate of approximately 2 to 1, Big Green suffered an electoral loss of similar proportions.

Big Green grew out of environmentalists' frustration with the state legislature and the governor, who had gutted or killed a series of environmental protection bills. Taking policymaking into their own hands, conservationists cobbled together Big Green. To bolster their chances, organizers enlisted a celebrity cast that included Chevy Chase, Jane Fonda, Cybill Shep-

herd, and Bruce Willis to appear in a thirty-minute television commercial. Resembling an MTV video, the commercial was composed of a series of modular pieces that, in the words of one director, "keep the facts coming at you in a very fast, hip, modern look." The commercial also included a telephone number (1-900-BE GREEN) that, when called, allowed people to contribute $5 to the campaign automatically.

Borrowing a page from the environmentalists' book, opponents of Big Green developed an alternative measure for the 1990 ballot. Dubbed "Big Brown" by conservationists, this business-sponsored measure contained much more modest protections for the environment. In addition, it included a "poison pill" that would invalidate a successful Big Green, if the business-backed bill passed by a greater margin.

In the end, Big Green opponents did not have much to worry about. The fall of 1990 was an unsettling period, with the Persian Gulf crisis in full swing and the effects of the recession beginning to be felt. California voters, worried about the potential costs of Big Green, voted no.

Sources: William Greider, "California's Big Green Brings the Law to Earth," *Rolling Stone,* August 23, 1990, pp. 53, 56; James A. Barnes, "A Heady Mix of Politics, Show Biz . . . Pushing for 'Big Green' Initiative," *National Journal* 22 (September 1990): 2050–2051; Paul Rauber, "Flying False Colors," *Sierra* (September/October 1990): 20–24; Paul Rauber, "Losing the Initiative?" *Sierra* (May/June 1991): 20, 22, 24.

gon. Voters across the country reacted negatively to a variety of tax cuts and limits on government spending. In Massachusetts, voters defeated a multifaceted proposal that would have decreased the state income tax rate, reduced fees charged by state agencies, and forced a cutback in social welfare services. Nebraskans turned back a constitutional amendment limiting increases in state and local government spending to 2 percent per year. Voters in California and Colorado also rejected measures that would have hampered state and local officials' abilities to raise taxes. Tax-weary Oregon voters, bucked the trend, however, and approved a proposition that imposed limits on property taxes.

Two Oregon initiatives that would have restricted access to abortion were defeated, whereas a Nebraska proposal guaranteeing the right to an abortion was approved. These two states also had education measures on their ballots.

Nebraskans voted to retain their finance plan, which would reduce disparities between rich and poor school districts, while Oregonians rejected a proposal to provide a personal income tax credit to parents who choose home schooling or private education for their children. One topic that met with unqualified success in the three states in which it appeared on the 1990 ballot was term limits. Voters in Oklahoma and then in California and Colorado imposed limits on the tenure of their elected officials. (This topic is discussed in detail in Chapter 9.)

Because so few states hold elections in odd-numbered years, the initiative process tends to be cyclical. In those "off-years," initiative proponents spend their time laying the groundwork for the next campaign. Washington, which holds elections in odd-numbered years, is an exception. And it was there that a 1991 ballot initiative captured the nation's attention. No, not term limits, although that was on the ballot and went down to a somewhat unexpected defeat. Something more personal: the right to die. Initiative 119 asked voters whether doctors should be allowed to kill terminally ill patients who have made a written request to die.[21] Known as physician-assisted suicide, the measure touched off emotional public debate. Supporters in California, Florida, and Oregon began their own petition drives in hopes of qualifying the issue for their 1992 ballots. With the eyes of the nation on them, 70 percent of Washington's registered voters turned out on election day and defeated the initiative by a 54 to 46 percent margin.

Possible Overuse of Initiatives   In the 1988 elections, there were 238 ballot questions (including initiatives and referenda) in forty-one states. California led the way, with twenty-nine statewide issues on the ballot, along with a bewildering array of local questions. The California situation raises troubling questions about the use of initiatives in particular and the wisdom of direct democracy more generally. By resorting to initiatives, citizens can bypass (or, in the case of indirect initiatives, prod) an obstructive legislature. And initiatives can be positive or negative; that is, they can be used in the absence of legislative action or they can be used to repudiate actions taken by the legislature. But is the initiative process appropriate for resolving tough public problems? Seldom are issues so simple that a yes-or-no ballot question can adequately reflect appropriate options and alternatives. A legislative setting, in contrast, fosters the negotiation and compromise that produce workable solutions. Legislatures are deliberative bodies, not instant problem solvers.

Related to this concern is the question of whether the public is too ill-informed to make intelligent choices or whether it falls prey to emotional appeals. Well-financed business and religious groups have used the initiative process to their advantage. The executive director of the publication *Initiative Quarterly* argues that the initiative is no longer "the people's tool but a special interest process—pure and simple." For example, Scientific Games Inc., a major lottery ticket maker, spent $1.5 million in California and Oregon to promote the petitions for a lottery in those states.[22] The firm virtually bankrolled the signature collection process. California's experience with reforming the automobile insurance system through initiative is instructive. In 1988, five competing automobile insurance initiatives appeared on the ballot. Approximately $75 million was spent on their behalf, and voters had to sort their way through a maze of conflicting information and exaggerations from all sides. One analysis concluded, "Democracy never looked so ugly."[23] Claiming that the public is being hoodwinked, some initiative reformers are calling for clear identification of financial sponsors.

Taken to its extreme, the initiative process can become electronic democracy. Honolulu has conducted experimental "electronic town meetings" in which the pros and cons of particular issues are presented on television. Voters then either mail in ballots or record their opinion with a telephone call.[24] The advantages offered by specially targeted direct-mail appeals and instantaneous voting are not lost on legislators. The Alaska legislature, for instance, has pioneered the use of a teleconferencing system that allows its committees to receive audio and computer messages as testimony from citizens around the state.[25]

Legislators are of two minds when it comes to direct citizen involvement in policymaking. On the one hand, having the public decide a controversial issue such as abortion or school prayer helps legislators out of tight spots. On the other hand, increased citizen lawmaking intrudes on the central function of the legislature. The National Conference of State Legislatures, lawmakers' primary interest group, is seeking ways "to prevent usurpation of lawmakers' prerogatives" in the states that allow initiatives.[26] Given the popularity of initiatives, legislators must proceed cautiously with actions that would make them more difficult to use. So far, efforts to increase the signature requirements or to limit the kinds of topics an initiative may address have been unsuccessful. A citizenry accustomed to the initiative process does not look kindly on its dismantling.

The Recall

Recalls, too, were once a little-used mechanism in state and local governments. Only fifteen states provide for recall of state officials; and in six of these, judicial officers are exempt. City and county government charters, even in states without recall provisions, typically include mechanisms for recall of local elected officials. In fact, the first known recall was aimed at a Los Angeles city council member in 1904.[27] Recalls have a much higher petition signature requirement than initiatives do; it is common to require a signature minimum of 25 percent of the votes cast in the last election for the office of the official sought to be recalled. (Kansas, for example, requires a 40 percent minimum.)

Recall efforts usually involve a public perception of official misconduct. When a judge in Madison, Wisconsin, during a hearing in a juvenile sexual assault case in 1977, said from the bench, "Given the way women dress, rape is a normal reaction," outraged citizens organized a group to promote his recall.[28] The group, the Committee to Recall Judge Archie Simonson, was composed of individuals who were already members of groups such as the National Organization for Women and the Women's International League for Peace and Freedom. Their coalition launched a hard-fought campaign that resulted in the recall of the judge.

Figure 5.4

Sample Recall Ballot

Omaha voters recalled their mayor, Michael Boyle, in 1987 with this ballot. Former mayor Boyle resurfaced in 1989 in a race for mayor but was defeated.

OFFICIAL BALLOT

A **X** CITY OF OMAHA	B **X** SPECIAL ELECTION	C **X** JANUARY 13, 1987

**OFFICIAL BALLOT
SPECIAL CITY ELECTION
HELD JANUARY 13, 1987**

Shall Michael Boyle be removed
from the Office of Mayor by recall?

☐ **FOR** THE RECALL
OF MICHAEL BOYLE

☐ **AGAINST** THE RECALL
OF MICHAEL BOYLE

Source: Office of the Election Commissioner, Omaha, Nebraska.

Once enough signatures have been collected and verified, a recall election is held. In some states, the ballot contains wording such as "Should Official X be recalled on the following charges?" (A brief statement of the charges would follow.) A majority vote is required to remove an official, and the vacancy created by a successful recall is filled by a subsequent special election or by appointment. In other states, the recall ballot is more like an election ballot. There is no simple yes-or-no vote on the official; instead, his or her name appears on a ballot along with those of challengers. To continue in office, the subject of the recall must receive the most votes. The ballot used to recall the mayor of Omaha, Nebraska in 1987 appears in Figure 5.4.

The number of recalls grew in the 1980s, the most notable being the ouster of Arizona governor Evan Mecham in 1987. Mecham's case was particularly interesting because it involved a number of possibilities: Mecham simultaneously faced recall, impeachment (formal charges by the House of Representatives), and a criminal indictment for violating campaign finance laws.[29] Even the threat of recall can be an effective weapon: Mecham was removed from office in 1988 following his conviction by the Arizona Senate in an impeachment trial.

The rationale for the recall process is straightforward: Public officials should be subject to continuous voter control.[30] As the organizer of the successful campaign to recall the mayor of Omaha stated, "We've shown you can fight city hall."[31] Whether it is used or not, the power to recall public officials is valued by the public. A recent national survey indicated that two-thirds of those polled favored amending the U.S. Constitution to permit the recall of members of Congress.[32] Perhaps the public, rather than being uninterested in politics, is in

fact quite interested and would like mechanisms that make it easier to participate.

Initiatives and recalls have helped open up state and local government to the
public. Yet ironically, increased citizen participation can also jam up the machinery of government, thus making its operation more cumbersome. Advocates
of greater citizen activism, however, would gladly trade a little efficiency to
achieve their goal. In the long run, citizen participation makes for government
vitality.

Interest Groups

interest group

An organized body of individuals with shared goals and a desire to influence government.

Interest groups offer another participatory venue for Americans. Joining a
group is a way for individuals to communicate their preferences—their interests—to government. Interest groups attempt to influence governmental decisions and actions by pressuring decision-making bodies to put more guidance
counselors in public elementary schools, to clamp restrictions on coastal development, to keep a proposed new prison out of a neighborhood, or to strengthen
state regulations on the licensing of family therapists. Success is defined in terms
of getting the group's preferences enacted. As we shall see, some groups are
more successful than others. In certain states, interest groups actually dominate
the policymaking process.

In considering the role of groups in the political system, we must remember
that people join groups for reasons other than politics. For instance, a teacher
may be a member of a politically active state education association because the
group offers a tangible benefit such as low-cost life insurance, but he may
disagree with some of the political positions taken by the organization. In
general, then, motivations for group membership are individually determined.[33]
This point was confirmed in recent research on Farm Bureau membership in five
midwestern states.[34] Farm Bureaus provide services and material benefits to
members, and they represent agricultural interests in the state capital. In this
case, no single all-encompassing explanation for fluctuations in membership
levels across the five states could be determined.

Types of Interest Groups

Interest groups come in all types and sizes. If you were to visit the lobby of the
state capitol when the legislature was in session, you might find the director of
the state school boards association conversing with the chairperson of the education committee, or the lobbyist hired by the state hotel-motel association
exchanging notes with the representative of the state's restaurateurs. If a legislator were to venture into the lobby, she would probably receive at least a
friendly greeting from the lobbyists and at most a serious heart-to-heart talk
about the merits of a bill. You would be witnessing efforts to influence public

policy. Interest groups want state government to enact policies that are in their interest or, conversely, not to enact policies at odds with their interest. And although the primary target of the groups' pressure is the legislature, state agencies, because of their rulemaking function, also receive their share of attention. For example, interest groups use the rule review process (in which a legislative committee reviews agency rules) as a point of possible influence.[35]

The interests represented in the capitol lobby are as varied as the states themselves. One that is well represented and powerful is business. Whether a lobbyist represents a single large corporation or a consortium of businesses, when he or she talks, state legislators listen. From the perspective of business groups (and other economically oriented groups), legislative actions can cost or save their members money. Therefore, the Chamber of Commerce, industry groups, trade associations, financial institutions, and regulated utilities maintain a visible presence in the state capitol during the legislative session. Table 5.2 documents the influential nature of business interests at the state level. Of course, business interests are not monolithic; occasionally they even find themselves on opposite sides of a bill.

Other interests converge on the capitol. Representatives of labor, both of established AFL-CIO unions and of professional associations such as the state optometrists' group or sheriffs' association, frequent the hallways and committee meeting rooms. They, too, are there to see that the legislature makes the "right" decision on the bills before it. For example, if a legislature were considering a bill to change the licensing procedures for optometrists, you could expect to find the optometrists' interest group immersed in the debate. Another workers' group, schoolteachers, has banded together to form one of the most effective state-level groups. In fact, as Table 5.2 indicates, schoolteachers' organizations are ranked among the most influential interest groups in more states than any other group. In forty-three states, they are among the top groups; in five states, they operate amid a second tier of influential groups. (The two states in which schoolteachers' organizations are not considered effective are Maryland and South Dakota.)[36]

Many other interest groups are active in state government, and a large number of them are ideological in nature. In other words, their political activity is oriented toward some higher good, such as clean air or fairer tax systems or consumer protection. Members of these groups do not have a direct economic or professional interest in the outcome of a legislative decision. Instead, their lobbyists argue that the public as a whole benefits from their involvement in the legislative process.

Interest Groups in the States

The actual interest group environment is different from one state to another. There is variation not only in the composition of the involved groups but also in the degree of influence they exert. Research by political scientists Ronald Hrebenar and Clive Thomas, and a team of researchers throughout the country,

Table 5.2

Ranking of the
Fifteen Most Influential Business
Interests in the Fifty
States

	Number of States in Which Interest Was Ranked Among . . .	
	Most Effective	Second Level of Effectiveness
1. School teachers' organizations (predominantly NEA)	43	5
2. General business organizations (Chambers of Commerce, etc.)	31	17
3. Bankers' associations (including Savings and Loan associations)	28	14
4. Manufacturers (companies and associations)	23	15
5. Traditional labor associations (predominantly the AFL-CIO)	23	13
6. Utility companies and associations (electric, gas, telephone, water)	20	17
7. Individual banks and financial institutions	20	12
8. Lawyers (predominantly state bar associations and trial lawyers)	15	15
9. General local government organizations (municipal leagues, county organizations, etc.)	15	18
10. General farm organizations (mainly state Farm Bureaus)	11	23
11. Doctors	14	16
12. State and local government employees (other than teachers)	16	11
13. Insurance (companies and associations)	13	14
14. Realtors' associations	12	8
15. Individual traditional labor unions	13	3

Source: Adapted from Clive S. Thomas and Ronald J. Hrebenar, "Interest Groups in the States," in Virginia Gray, Herbert Jacob, and Robert B. Albritton, eds., *Politics in the American States,* 5th ed. (Glenview, Ill.: Scott, Foresman/Little, Brown, 1990), p. 144. Copyright © 1990 by Virginia Gray, Herbert Jacob, and Robert B. Albritton. Reprinted by permission of HarperCollins Publishers.

Table 5.3

Interest Group
Impact

	States in Which the Overall Impact of Interest Groups Is:			
Dominant (9)	Dominant/ Complementary (18)	Complementary (18)	Complementary/ Dominant (5)	Subordinate (0)
Alabama	Arizona	Colorado	Connecticut	
Alaska	Arkansas	Illinois	Delaware	
Florida	California	Indiana	Minnesota	
Louisiana	Hawaii	Iowa	Rhode Island	
Mississippi	Georgia	Kansas	Vermont	
New Mexico	Idaho	Maine		
South Carolina	Kentucky	Maryland		
Tennessee	Montana	Massachusetts		
West Virginia	Nebraska	Michigan		
	Nevada	Missouri		
	Ohio	New Jersey		
	Oklahoma	New Hampshire		
	Oregon	New York		
	Texas	North Carolina		
	Utah	North Dakota		
	Virginia	Pennsylvania		
	Washington	South Dakota		
	Wyoming	Wisconsin		

Source: Clive S. Thomas and Ronald J. Hrebenar, "Interest Groups in the States," in Virginia Gray, Herbert Jacob, and Robert B. Albritton, eds., *Politics in the American States,* 5th ed. (Glenview, Ill.: Scott, Foresman/Little, Brown, 1990), p. 147. Copyright © 1990 by Virginia Gray, Herbert Jacob, and Robert B. Albritton. Reprinted by permission of HarperCollins Publishers.

provides fresh insights into the interest group scene. Table 5.3 classifies states according to the strength of interest groups vis-à-vis other political institutions in the policymaking process. Groups can dominate other political institutions such as political parties, they can complement them, or they can be subordinate to them.[37] As the listing in Table 5.3 shows, there are nine states in which interest groups are dominant—that is, in which they wield an overwhelming and consistent influence on policymaking. At the other end of the spectrum, however, there are no states in which interest groups are completely subordinate. Interest groups enjoy complementary relationships with other political institutions in eighteen states, whereas in twenty-three others, the complementary pattern is less stable.

For the most part, interest group politics is defined by its state context.[38] First of all, an inverse relationship exists between interest groups and political parties. In states where political parties are strong, interest groups tend to be weak; in states characterized by weak political parties, interest groups tend to be strong.[39] Strong parties provide leadership in the policymaking process, and interest groups function through them. In the absence of party leadership and organization, interest groups fill the void, becoming important recruiters of candidates and financiers of campaigns; accordingly, they exert tremendous influence in policymaking. Although the inverse relationship between parties and groups generally holds true, politics in states like New York and Michigan offers an interesting variation. In these states, groups are active and can be influential, but they work with the established party system in a kind of symbiotic relationship.[40]

A second, related truth adds a developmental angle to interest group politics. As states diversify economically, their politics are less likely to be dominated by a single interest.[41] Thus the interest group environment is becoming more cluttered, resulting in *hyperpluralism,* or a multiplicity of groups.

Kansas, which is undergoing economic diversification and urbanization, is also experiencing a change in the representation of interests.[42] Thirty years ago, the influential economic interests in Kansas policymaking were primarily banks, utilities, pipeline companies, railroads, and farm groups. The interest group universe has expanded significantly since then. Now, visitors to the state capitol in Topeka are likely to encounter lobbyists for the health care industry, education, local governments, insurance, telecommunications, and social services as well as the traditional interests. In addition, there are an increasing number of "single-interest" groups, such as Kansans for Pari-Mutuel (a group promoting dog racing), Kansans for Life (anti-abortion activists), and Traffic Safety Now. However, the increase in the number of groups and types of interests represented in Topeka does not necessarily signal a decline in the influence enjoyed by the dominant interests. Surveys of both legislators and lobbyists identify the constellation of interests surrounding banking, agriculture, education, business, utilities, the legal profession, and medical and health interests as the "consistently influential" forces in Kansas politics.[43] But now there are more groups clamoring for a piece of the action.

Kansas is not unique. Interest group politics in many states is becoming more pluralistic. As states increasingly become the arena in which important social and economic policy decisions are made, more and more groups will go to statehouses, hoping to find a receptive audience.

Techniques Used by Interest Groups

Interest groups want to have a good public image. It helps a group when its preferences can be equated with what is "good for the state" (or the community). Organizations use slogans like "What's good for the timber industry is good for Oregon" or "Schoolteachers have the interests of New York City at heart." Some groups have taken on the label "public interest groups" to designate their main interest as that of the public at large. Groups, then, invest resources in creating a good image.

Being successful in the state capitol or at city hall involves more than a good public image, however. For example, interest groups have become effective at organizing grassroots networks that exert pressure on legislators. If a teacher pay-raise bill is in jeopardy in the senate, for instance, schoolteachers throughout the state may be asked by the education association to contact their senators to urge them to vote favorably on the legislation. To maximize their strength, groups with common interests often establish coalitions. For example, eighteen environmental groups in Arkansas formed an umbrella organization, the Environmental Congress of Arkansas, to get their message out. Interest groups also hire representatives who can effectively promote their cause. To ensure that legislators will be receptive to their pressures, groups try to influence the outcome of elections by supporting candidates who reflect their interests.

A number of factors affect the relative power of an interest group. In their work, Hrebenar and Thomas identified ten characteristics that give some groups more political clout than others:

- The degree of necessity of group services and resources to public officials.
- Whether the group's lobbying focus is primarily defensive or offensive.
- The extent and strength of group opposition.
- Potential for the group to enter into coalitions.
- Group financial resources.
- Size and geographical distribution of group membership.
- Political cohesiveness of the membership.
- Political, organizational, and managerial skills of group leaders.
- Timing and the political climate.
- Lobbyist-policymaker relations.[44]

No single interest group is on the "high end" of all ten of these characteristics all of the time. However, returning to Table 5.2 for a moment, we find that the first six groups listed, influential in two-thirds of the states, possess quite a few of these factors. An indispensable group armed with ample resources, a cohesive membership, and skilled leaders, when the timing is right, can wield enormous influence in the state capitol. This is especially true when the group has taken a defensive posture—that is, when it wants to block proposed legislation. On the other hand, to a group lacking these characteristics, especially in the presence of potent opposition, victory comes less easily.

lobbying

The process by which groups and individuals attempt to influence policymakers.

Lobbying   Lobbying is the attempt to influence government decision makers. States have developed official definitions to determine who is a lobbyist and who is not. A common definition is "anyone receiving compensation to influence legislative action."[45] A few states, such as Nevada, North Dakota, and Washington, require everyone who attempts to influence legislation to register as a lobbyist (even those who are not being paid), but most exclude public officials, members of the media, and people who speak only before committees or boards from their definition. Counting lobbyists is a tricky endeavor, but a recent survey put Arizona and New Hampshire at opposite ends of the "average number of lobbyists per legislator" spectrum.[46] On average, Arizona has twenty-eight lobbyists per legislator; New Hampshire's ratio is less than one lobbyist per legislator.

In most states, lobbyists are required to file reports indicating how and on

whom they spent money. Concern that lobbyists would exert undue influence on the legislative process spurred states to enact new reporting requirements and impose tougher penalties for their violation. By 1992, the only states that did not require lobbyists to file reports on expenditures were Georgia, South Dakota, and Wyoming.[47] At the other extreme, Idaho and Nebraska required lobbyists to report their sources of income, total and categorized expenditures, the names of the individual officials who received their monies or gifts, and the legislation they supported or opposed.

To influence legislators in their decision making, lobbyists need access, so they cultivate good relationships with lawmakers. A study of interest group activity in North Dakota identified two primary functions of lobbyists: to provide testimony and to help legislators understand issues.[48] In Michigan, legislators and lobbyists alike agreed that providing information was "a strong source of power to lobbyists."[49] Legislators want to know how a proposed bill might affect the different interests in the state and their legislative districts, and what it is expected to achieve. Social lobbying—wining and dining legislators—still goes on, but it is being supplemented by the provision of information. A study of western states revealed a new breed of lobbyists trained as attorneys and public relations specialists, skilled in media presentation and information packaging.[50]

The influence of lobbyists specifically and of interest groups generally is a subject of much debate. The popular image is one of a mythical lobbyist whose very presence in a committee hearing room can spell the fate of a bill. But, in fact, his will is done because the interests he represents are widely considered vital to the state, because he has assiduously laid the groundwork, and because legislators respect the forces he can mobilize if necessary. Few lobbyists cast this long a shadow, however, and their interaction with legislators is seldom this mechanical. Much contemporary interest group research suggests that patterns of influence are somewhat unpredictable and highly dependent on the state context.[51]

political action committee (PAC)

An organization that raises and distributes campaign funds to candidates for elective office.

Political Action Committees **Political action committees** (PACs) made extensive inroads into state politics in the 1980s. Narrowly focused subsets of interest groups, PACs are political organizations that collect funds and distribute them to candidates. (Their electoral influence is discussed in Chapter 6.) PACs serve as the campaign financing arm of corporations, labor unions, trade associations, and even political parties. They grew out of long-standing laws that made it illegal for corporations and labor unions to contribute directly to a candidate. Barred from direct contributions, these organizations set up "political action" subsidiaries to allow them legal entry into campaign finance.

Recent research on interest groups in Iowa offers insights into PACs.[52] The categories of PACs and their relative share of the total number are business (45 percent), employee (26 percent), noneconomic (14 percent), professional (12 percent), and agriculture (3 percent). About one-half of the business PACs were established by finance or insurance interests and utilities or telecommunications groups. Health care specialists dominate the professional PACs. The noneconomic committees are composed largely of single-issue organizations, such as anti-abortion or antigambling PACs. The most noteworthy aspect of PACs is how important a source of campaign funds they have become. In 1984, PACs (excluding those affiliated with political parties) contributed 51 percent of the $1.6 million raised by candidates for the Iowa legislature.[53] The impact of PACs on state politics is just beginning to become clear. Some Michigan legislators, for example, consider PACs a potentially dangerous influence in state politics, because their money "buys a lot of access that others can't get."[54] One very likely possibility is that an independent interstate network of groups with money to spend could emerge as a real threat to political parties as recruiters of candidates and financiers of campaigns. This concern has led to calls for stricter state regulation of PACs in the years to come.

Local-Level Interest Groups

Interest groups function at the local level as well. Because so much of local government involves the delivery of services, local interest groups devote a great deal of their attention to administrative agencies and departments. Groups are involved in local elections and in community issues, to be sure, but their major focus is on the *actions* of government: policy implementation and service delivery.[55]

National surveys of local officials have indicated that although interest groups

1. Business-oriented groups (e.g., Chamber of Commerce, businesspersons' associations)
2. Neighborhood groups
3. Political parties
4. Civic groups (e.g., League of Women Voters, service clubs)
5. Professional organizations (e.g., bar association)
6. City service groups (e.g., transit, health, housing, education)
7. Labor unions
8. Civil rights groups (e.g., NAACP, Urban League)
9. Ethnic groups (nonblack, Hispanic)
10. Environmental groups
11. Women's political groups
12. Ideological nonparty groups (e.g., Moral Majority, ACLU)
13. Gay/lesbian political groups

Source: Howard A. Faye, Allan Cigler, and Paul Schumaker, ''The Municipal Group Universe: Changes in Agency Penetration by Political Groups, 1975–1986,'' paper presented at the annual meeting of the American Political Science Association, Washington, D.C., 1986. Reprinted by permission of the authors.

are influential in local decision making, they do not dominate the process.[56] The kinds of groups that appear on the local scene and their relative influence, according to local officials, are listed in Table 5.4. As is true at the state level, business groups are considered to be the most influential. Business-related interests, such as the local Chamber of Commerce or a downtown merchants' association, appear to wield power in the community. A very different yet increasingly influential group at the local level is the neighborhood-based organization. Groups that might not have been on the list twenty years ago include women's organizations, ideological groups (such as the Moral Majority), and homosexual rights groups. Thus far, these groups have not achieved the degree of influence accorded business and neighborhood groups.

Neighborhood organizations deserve a closer look. Some have arisen out of issues that directly affect neighborhood residents—a local school that is scheduled to close, a wave of violent crime, a proposed freeway route that will destroy homes and businesses. Others have been formed by government itself as a way of channeling citizen participation. For example, in 1974, the city council in Birmingham, Alabama, divided the city into ninety-three neighborhood associations. These groups provide a formal mechanism whereby residents can voice their concerns about the quality and quantity of municipal services.[57] One result has been to give voice to neighborhoods that were previously underrepresented.

Neighborhood groups, as well as others lacking a bankroll but possessing enthusiasm and dedication, may resort to tactics such as **direct action,** which includes protest marches at the county courthouse or standing in front of bulldozers in an effort to block their progress. Direct action is usually designed to attract attention to a cause, and it tends to be a last resort, a tactic employed

direct action

A form of participation designed to draw attention to a cause.

Profile 5.2

Taking It to the Streets: Anti-Abortion and Abortion-Rights Groups Battle in Buffalo

The city of Wichita, Kansas, came to a virtual standstill in the long hot summer of 1991 as Operation Rescue, the militant anti-abortion group, spent forty-six days blockading abortion clinics. Kneeling in prayer, singing hymns, and offering aggressive "sidewalk counseling" to abortion clinic patients, the Rescuers sought to persuade pregnant women to forgo abortions. Intensifying their efforts, some Rescuers chained themselves to clinic doors and to each other. Even as court orders restricted their access to abortion clinic property, the Rescuers continued their vigils. Some clinics shut down to avoid the controversy. By the time the Rescue caravans pulled out of Wichita, 2,600 people had been arrested. Now the American public was keenly aware that the battle over abortion was not confined to courtrooms and legislative chambers.

In the spring of 1992, the Operation Rescue turned its attention to Buffalo, New York, after the city's mayor virtually invited the group to his community. Vowing to shut down clinics to "rescue" women and their unborn babies, more than five hundred Rescuers descended upon Buffalo. However, when the Rescuers arrived in the city, they were greeted by organized opposition from abortion-rights activists. Not only had their confrontational behavior in Wichita attracted national attention; it had the unintended consequence of mobilizing abortion-rights supporters. The Pro-Choice Network of Western New York, Buffalo United for Choice, the Feminist Majority Foundation, and the National Women's Rights Organizing Coalition rallied to counter Operation Rescue's demonstrations. Carrying signs reading "Boot 'em Out of Buffalo" and "You're Not in Kansas Anymore," 1,500 abortion-rights advocates formed human barricades to keep the Rescuers away from the facilities. In addition, abortion-rights forces provided protection, usually in the form of escorts, to allow pregnant women access to the clinics.

Five days after the onset of demonstrations and protests outside the four targeted clinics in Buffalo, 350 arrests had been made. Most of those arrested were anti-abortion demonstrators who had defied police barricades. Clearly, Operation Rescue had met its match. Suddenly on the defensive, Operation Rescue regrouped and turned its sights on Syracuse and Rochester. Like a moving chess game, abortion rights activists vowed to follow them if they set up camp in another city.

Sources: Don Terry, "City Tires of Spotlight Drawn by Abortion Protests," *New York Times,* August 24, 1991, p. 11; Catherine S. Manegold, "Abortion Protesters Gather as a Fight Builds in Buffalo," *New York Times,* April 20, 1992, p. A11; "Temporary Jail Fills Up in Buffalo," *The State,* April 26, 1992, p. 3A; Mary B. Tabor, "Abortion Foes in Buffalo Regrouping," *New York Times,* April 27, 1992, p. A8.

---

when other efforts at influencing government policy have failed. The nation witnessed a stunning example of extreme direct action when riots broke out in poor, predominantly black and Hispanic sections of Los Angeles in May 1992. In this instance, as in Miami and Tampa in the 1980s, allegations of police brutality triggered violent upheaval, and in each case the eventual uneasy calm that settled over the neighborhood brought with it promises of increased government assistance. And, as Profile 5.2 details, when both sides of an issue engage in direct action, tensions often explode.

....

Citizen Access to Government

Citizens have opportunities to participate in government in ways that do not involve voting or joining organizations. Because state and local governments have undertaken extensive measures to open themselves to public scrutiny and stimulate public input, citizen access to government has been increased. Many of these measures are directly connected with the policymaking process. At the very least, they enable government and the citizenry to exchange information, and thus they contribute to the growing capacity of state and local governments. At most, they may alter political power patterns and resource allocations.[58]

Types of Official Access

Many of the accessibility measures adopted by state and local governments are the direct result of public demands that government be more accountable. These measures reflect citizens' rejection of "policymaking behind closed doors" and "government by announcement," whereby the public is removed from the process and hears about it only after a decision has been made. Other accessibility measures have resulted from an official effort to involve the public in the ongoing work of government.

Open Meeting Laws   Florida's 1967 "sunshine law" is credited with sparking a surge of interest in openness in government, and today **open meeting laws** are on the books in all fifty states. These laws do just what the name implies: They open meetings of government bodies to the public. Open meeting laws apply to both the state and local levels and affect the executive branch as well as the legislative branch. They are taken rather seriously, especially by the press.

open meeting laws

Statutes that open the meetings of government bodies to the public.

Basic open meeting laws have been supplemented by additional requirements in many states. More than forty states require advance public notice of meetings, thirty-seven insist that minutes be taken, thirty-five levy penalties against officials who violate the law, and thirty-one void actions taken in meetings held contrary to sunshine provisions.[59] These "brighter sunshine" laws make a difference. Whether a meeting is open or closed is irrelevant if citizens are unaware that it is occurring. If no penalties are assessed for violation, then there is less incentive for officials to comply.

Open Records Laws   In the same spirit as open meetings are provisions for open records. After the enactment of an open records law in Wisconsin in the nineteenth century, states gradually began to facilitate public access to government documents. All states now have some form of an open records law.

open records laws

Statutes that facilitate public access to government documents.

Open records laws are frequently called freedom-of-information acts. They are designed to make it easier for the public to obtain public records, although documents that are damaging to the public interest can be withheld. The trick is to determine just what is damaging and what is not. The courts are often called upon to make that determination when the press has requested information and a government agency has refused to provide it, as in the case of lists of contributors to state university foundations. Other exemptions to the open records requirement are documents dealing with individual matters such as juveniles, adoptions, paroles, and medical and mental health.

Administrative Procedure Acts After state legislation is passed or a local ordinance is adopted, an administrative agency typically is responsible for implementation. This process involves the establishment of rules and regulations and, hence, constitutes a powerful responsibility. In practice, agencies often have wide latitude in translating legislative intent into action. For example, if a new state law creates annual automobile safety inspections, it is the responsibility of the state's Department of Motor Vehicles to make it work. Bureaucrats might determine the items to be covered in the safety inspection, the number and location of inspection stations, and the fee to be charged. These items are just as important as the original enactment.

administrative procedure acts

Acts that standardize administrative agency operations as a means of safeguarding clients and the general public.

To ensure public access to this critical rule-making process, states have adopted **administrative procedure acts,** which usually require public notice of the proposed rule and an opportunity for citizen comment. Virtually all states provide for this "notification and comment" process, as it is known. In addition, some states give citizens the right to petition an administrative agency for an adjustment in the rules.

advisory committee

An organization created by government to involve members of the public in studying and recommending solutions to public problems.

Advisory Committees Another form of citizen participation that is popular in state and especially local governments is the **advisory committee,** in the form of citizen task forces, commissions, and panels. Regardless of name, these organizations are designed to study a problem and to offer advice, usually in the form of recommendations. People chosen to serve on an advisory committee tend to have expertise as well as interest in the issue and, in most cases, political connections. But not always. In 1991, Oregon's governor Barbara Roberts invited a random cross-section of Oregonians to attend interactive, televised meetings at one of thirty sites. The governor went live (on cable television) to each of the sites to ask citizens to assess the performance of their governments. She got an earful. But she also received invaluable input.[60]

Citizen advisory committees are useful because they provide a formal arena for citizen input. For example, New York City is divided into fifty-nine community boards that offer advice on planning.[61] Rather than leaving the growth and development of their community to chance or market forces or the desires of monied interests, citizens have an opportunity to offer their views on the preferable future. If officials heed public preferences, citizen advice can become the basis for public policy. Citizen advisory organizations also provide the governor, the legislature, or local officials with a "safe" course of action. In other words, in a politically explosive situation, a governor can say, "I've appointed a citizen's task force to study the issue and report back to me with recommendations for action." This buys time, with the hope that the issue will gradually cool down. Another benefit of these organizations is that they ease citizen acceptance of subsequent policy decisions, since the governor can note that an action "was recommended by an impartial panel of citizens." This is not to suggest that citizen advisory committees are merely tools for manipulation by politicians, but they do have uses beyond citizen participation.

Citizen Surveys One effective way of determining what is on the public's mind is to ask people, and this can be done in a systematic manner through citizen surveys. By sampling the population, government officials can obtain a reading of the public's policy preferences and its evaluation of governmental performance. Technological advances such as "computer-aided telephone interviewing" make it easier to scientifically sample public opinion in a state. Amid a budget crunch, Texas installed a toll-free hotline so that citizens could call in with money-saving suggestions. The telephone rang off the hook—more than 4000 calls were received in the first 20 days.

For local governments, citizen surveys have provided information on the effectiveness and quality of public services.[62] This procedure is far more systematic than simply relying on complaints as a means of identifying problems. For cities on the cutting edge of technology, surveys can be conducted through computer-based information systems such as Santa Monica, California's Public Electronic Network (PEN). Through PEN, Santa Monicans can convey their preferences to city government (and other residents) and participate in discussions of community issues. For citizens without access to personal computers and modems, the city has set up a series of public terminals.[63]

An important feature of citizen surveys is that they can counteract some of the bias that clouds most avenues of participation. As noted in the beginning of this chapter, political participation is generally an activity undertaken by those of middle to upper socioeconomic status. Nonparticipants seldom transmit their opinions to government. In a carefully designed citizen survey, one that gives all residents an opportunity to participate, those whose opinions are often muted have a better opportunity to be heard.

The Impact of Citizen Access

But the impact of citizen access is not always as much as hoped for. The federal General Revenue Sharing Act of 1972 required jurisdictions to create citizen advisory committees to help elected officials decide how the funds should be allocated in the community. Citizen input was intended to help determine whether the jurisdiction used its revenue-sharing money to purchase police cars, to rehabilitate low-income housing, or whatever. But most studies have found that these committees had a minor impact, at best, on allocation decisions.[64] They were less than full partners in the process.

This is a troublesome aspect of citizen participation. The system has been opened up, making government more accessible than ever before. Citizens have increased opportunities for participation, but their influence may be difficult to discern. A critical factor in the fate of citizen access programs is the commitment of government officials to the concept. Sincere encouragement and promotion of citizen access is likely to produce an outcome different from the sort of cosmetic treatment designed to satisfy the conditions of a grant.

Volunteerism

volunteerism

A form of participation in which individuals or groups donate time or money to a public purpose.

Voluntary action is participatory activity unrelated to the ballot box, groups, and access. People and organizations donate their time and talents to supplement or even replace government activity. **Volunteerism** is a means of bringing fresh ideas and energy, whether physical or financial, into government while relieving some of the service burden. One highly visible example of volunteerism is the "Adopt a Highway" program. Over the past five years, the number of local businesses and civic clubs willing to pick up litter along designated stretches of state highways has skyrocketed. You have probably noticed the "Adopt a Highway" signs with the names of the volunteering groups listed underneath. The state saves money, the roadsides stay cleaner, and the volunteering groups have good feelings and free advertising to go along with their sore backs. Washington created the first statewide volunteerism office in 1969, and by the mid-1980s forty other states had followed suit. One of the most ambitious efforts is "Volunteer for Minnesota," which assists local communities in the design of a program, including the actual recruitment, training, and placement of volunteers.[65]

Local governments use volunteers in a variety of ways. Generally, volunteerism is most successful when citizens can develop the required job skills quickly or participate in activities they enjoy, such as library work, recreation programs, or fire protection.[66] In addition to helping provide services to others, volunteers can be utilized for "self-help"; that is, they can engage in activities in which they are the primary beneficiaries. For example, some New York City neighborhoods take responsibility for the security and maintenance of nearby parks. Residential crime-watch programs are another variety of self-help. In both these instances, the volunteers and their neighborhoods benefit. Overall, studies show, volunteerism is especially successful in rural areas and small towns.[67]

Nongovernmental volunteerism can be an important supplement to government programs. For instance, an energetic new volunteerism campaign is under way in the Denver area. Unaffiliated with government, Metropolitan Denver GIVES is attempting to increase the amount of charitable giving and personal volunteering in the region.[68] Its effort is expected to be the prototype for similar campaigns in other metropolitan areas, such as Cleveland, Baltimore, and San Francisco. Voluntary organizations have multiplied and their involvement in local government has increased. This has given rise to speculation that voluntary organizations may eventually take on the role played by local political parties.

Volunteers turned out by the thousands to help clean up Los Angeles in the wake of the 1992 riots.

···

The Effects of Citizen Participation

Consider again the four quadrants of Figure 5.1. Constructive participatory behaviors, whether active or passive, invigorate government. The capacity of state and local governments depends on a number of factors, one of which is citizen participation. Underlying this argument is the implicit but strongly held belief shared by most observers of democracies that an accessible, responsive government is a legitimate government.

An example makes the point. In 1986, the Florida legislature enacted Visions 2000 to encourage community goal setting. Funding was made available by the state so that citizens could engage in debate and consider a number of scenarios for their community's future.[69] Researchers studying eight Florida communities discovered that without widespread citizen involvement, the goal-setting process can easily become a vehicle for special interests. When that occurs, the public is not likely to feel any loyalty to the resulting plan. And they are not likely to accord much legitimacy to the government that endorsed the process. This could lead to the destructive behaviors displayed in Figure 5.1: neglect or exit.

A mobilized public can generate systemwide change. From the perspective of government officials and institutions, citizen participation can be a nuisance because it may disrupt established routines. The challenge is to incorporate citizen participation into ongoing operations. The successful experiences of the Charlotte-Mecklenburg Citizens Forum in North Carolina and the Phoenix Futures Forum in Arizona offer hope.[70] Citizen involvement may not be easy or efficient, but in a democracy, it is the ultimate test of the legitimacy of that government. State and local governments, more often than not, pass that test.

Summary

Citizen participation affects the vitality of American state and local governments. Whether through voting or signing initiative petitions or marching in a demonstration, the power of the people is a force to be reckoned with. One of the ironies of the political system is that increased citizen activism may not make government run more smoothly. In fact, citizen participation may make government messy, increasing delays and conflict. The dramatic upsurge in election-day lawmaking, for example, has led some observers to question the wisdom of direct democracy in the United States of today.

As this chapter demonstrates, an array of participatory options is available to the citizen. Constructive actions include voting, signing petitions, joining groups, and attending meetings. One point to keep in mind is that many but not all citizens participate in the political system. Paying some attention to the reasons for nonparticipation and designing corrective measures may in the long run sustain government capacity.

Key Terms

participation
Voting Rights Act of 1965
popular referendum
referendum
recall
interest group
lobbying

political action committee (PAC)
direct action
open meeting laws
open records laws
administrative procedure acts
advisory committee
volunteerism

Political Parties, Campaigns, and Elections

When Bud Clark won re-election as mayor of Portland, Oregon, he faced more than the standard array of city problems. His campaign to retain the mayor's job had been expensive and he began his second term with a campaign debt of $60,000. As a joke, a local newspaper columnist suggested a ''Bucks for Bud'' campaign, encouraging the public to send the mayor a dollar bill to help retire his campaign deficit. To everyone's surprise, including the Mayor's, the idea took off. By 1992, nearly $30,000 had been sent to Bud.[1]

Political parties, campaigns, and elections are the stuff of representative democracy. On election day, the Democratic and Republican parties offer us slates of candidates to lead us. Candidates campaign hard for the glamorous jobs of governor, state legislator, mayor, and a variety of other state and local positions. In some states, even candidates for judicial positions compete in partisan races. But party involvement in our system of government does not end on election day—the institutions of government themselves have a partisan tone. Legislatures are organized along party lines; governors offer Republican or Democratic agendas for their states; county commissioners of different ideological stripes fight over the best way to provide services to local residents. Through the actions of their elected officials, political parties play a major role in the operation of government.

··

Political Parties

Lately the condition of contemporary American political parties has been described with words such as *decline, decay,* and *demise.* A more precise description would use the word *transformation,* which reflects the change that parties are experiencing but stops short of an epitaph. Even the experts are unsure of what lies ahead for political parties. One 1987 book on the subject, *The Party's Just Begun,* lays out a blueprint for party renewal.[2] And although we will stop short of similar words—*rejuvenation, revitalization*—we acknowledge that political parties are still evolving.

Political Parties in Theory and in Reality

responsible party model

A theoretical ideal in which political parties are issue-oriented, candidates toe the party line, and voters respond accordingly.

One ideal against which political party systems can be measured is called the **responsible party model,** which has several basic principles:

1. Parties should present clear and coherent programs to voters.
2. Voters should choose candidates according to the party programs.
3. The winning party should carry out its program once in office.
4. At the next election, voters should hold the governing party responsible for executing its program.[3]

According to this model, political parties carve out identifiable issue positions, base their campaign appeals on them, and endeavor to enact them upon taking office. Voters select candidates who represent their preferences and hold office-holders accountable for their performance.

But even a casual observer of the American scene would recognize that U.S. political parties fall somewhat short of the responsible party mark. For example, American political parties stand for different things in different places, so a single, coherent program is unworkable. Although Democratic politicians tend to be more liberal than their Republican counterparts, it would be difficult to find an abundance of liberals in a Democrat-controlled southern state legislature. Furthermore, voters display a remarkable penchant for **ticket-splitting**—that is, voting for a Democrat for one office and a Republican for another in the same election. Many voters are fond of saying that they "vote for the person, not the party."

ticket-splitting

*Voting for candidates
of different political
parties in a general
election.*

Parties in the United States function as umbrella organizations that shelter loose coalitions of relatively like-minded individuals. A general image for each party is discernible: The Republicans typically have been considered the party of big business, the Democrats the party of workers. But even though many people identify with the party of their parents, they hold that identification increasingly lightly. In what used to be called "the solid South," a label that indicated the region's historically overwhelming support for the Democratic party, one finds fewer and fewer "yellow dog Democrats"—people who would vote for the Democratic nominee "even if he was a yellow dog." And Republicans, once regarded as oddities in the region, have become respectable. One classic South Carolina tale recalls an election in 1924 in which the Republican candidate received 1,100 of the 50,000 votes cast for president. A leading Democratic politician reportedly commented that he was "astonished to know that they were cast and shocked to know that they were counted."[4] Now the Republican party considers the South a good source of partisan support.

Party Organization

Political parties are decentralized organizations. There are fifty state Republican parties and fifty state Democratic parties. Each state also has local party organizations, most typically at the county level. Although they interact, each of these units is autonomous, a situation that is good for independence but not so helpful to party discipline. Specialized partisan groups, including the College Democrats, the Young Republicans, Democratic Women's Clubs, Black Republican Councils, and so on, have been accorded official recognition.[5] Party organizations are further decentralized into precinct-level clusters, which bear the ultimate responsibility for turning out the party's voters on election day. Figure 6.1 shows a typical state party organization.

State Parties   Each state party has a charter or by-laws to govern its operation. The decision-making body is the state committee, sometimes called a central committee, which is headed by a chairperson and composed of members elected in party primaries or at state party conventions. State parties, officially at least,

Figure 6.1

Typical Political Party Organization

Most political party organizations look something like this. Party workers at the bottom of the chart are direct links to voters.

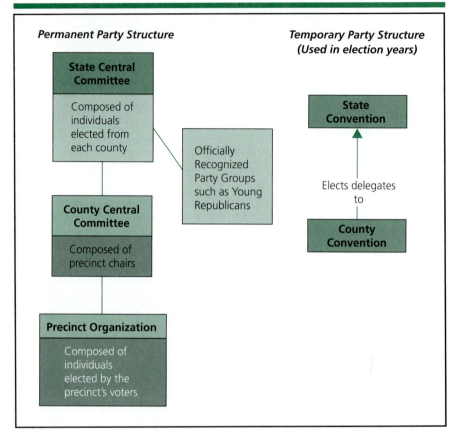

head their party's push to capture statewide elected offices. But despite their attempts to formulate platforms and develop a party-centered fund-raising appeal, they do not play a leading role in campaigns. Instead, their efforts are aimed at promoting good feelings about the party and protecting it from partisan attacks by the other party.

State party organizations vary widely in their organizational vitality and resources. Approximately one-quarter of them employ salaried chairpersons, and most have staffs numbering between three and ten people, and annual budgets in the $250,000 to $500,000 range.[6] Republican organizations generally outstrip Democratic ones in these measures of organizational strength.

Local Parties County party organizations are composed of committee members chosen at the precinct level. These workers are volunteers whose primary reward is the satisfaction of being involved in politics. But the work is rarely glamorous. Party workers are the people who conduct voter registration drives, who drop off the lawn signs for residents' front yards, organize candidate forums, and stand at the polls and remind voters to "Vote Democratic" or "Vote Republican." A recent survey of local party organizations shows that, come

Table 6.1

Percentage of Local
Parties Performing
Electoral Activity

Activity	Percentage
Distributed literature	98.0
Conducted telephone campaign	94.7
Provided lawn signs	93.5
Coordinated county-level campaigns	86.0
Contributed money to candidates	85.2
Conducted voter registration drives	82.9
Ran newspaper advertisements	82.0
Purchased billboard advertisements	38.3
Paid for television advertisements	31.1

Source: Adapted from John A. Clark, "Strategy and Symmetry in Local Political Parties," paper presented at the annual meeting of the Midwest Political Science Association, Chicago, April 1991. Reprinted with permission.

election time, they kick into high hear. Table 6.1 lists the type and frequency of electoral activity.

Local parties are less professionally organized than state parties. Although half of the local organizations maintain campaign headquarters during an election period, fewer than one-quarter operate year-round offices.[7] County chairpersons report devoting a lot of time to the party during election periods, but otherwise the post does not take much of their time. Most chairpersons lead organizations without any full-time staff, and vacancies in precinct offices are common.

The extremes in local party organization are exemplified in Los Angeles and Chicago. One analysis describes Los Angeles County in this manner: "In neither party is the Los Angeles county committee a powerful entity. Its powers are ambiguous; its meetings bog down with trivia; its funds are limited and its patronage resources more so. In each party, rival factions time after time frustrate even the appearance of solidarity in supporting a full slate of party nominees."[8] The Chicago Democratic party historically has been at the opposite end of the organizational spectrum: "The Chicago machine is both rare and impressive in the range of services offered, the cohesiveness and permanence of its structure, the professionalism and experience of its members at all levels, and, of course, its electoral successes. The difficulties the opposition party faces make its position virtually hopeless."[9] Most local parties are more akin to the Los Angeles County model than to the Chicago Democrats (who are much less cohesive than they used to be).

The Makeup of Parties   Although conservatism has experienced renewed popularity throughout the nation, the ideology of the leaders of the two parties

Figure 6.2

Ideological Distribution of Houston's Party Leaders

There are a few lonely liberals in the Republican party. Even among Democrats (in Houston, anyway), liberals make up only one-quarter of the leadership.

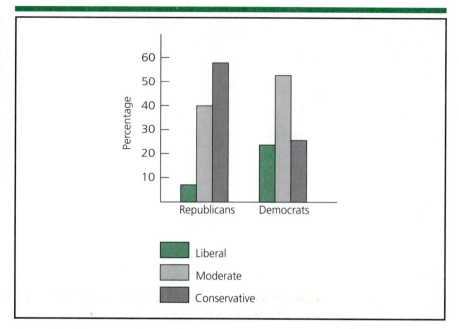

Source: Richard W. Murray and Kent L. Tedin, "Emerging Competition in the Sunbelt," in William Crotty, ed., *Political Parties in Local Areas* (Knoxville: University of Tennessee Press, 1986), p. 54. Reprinted with permission of the University of Tennessee Press.

remains distinct. A survey of Houston party leaders confirms this fact.[10] More than twice as many Republicans (56 percent) as Democrats (25 percent) labeled themselves conservatives. Liberal ideology, a grand tradition in American politics but a victim of almost hysterical denunciation in the late 1980s, clearly belongs more to Democrats (24 percent) than to Republicans (5 percent). Many of the party leaders identified themselves as "moderates," a hybrid designation. Fully 51 percent of Houston's Democratic leaders and 40 percent of the Republicans classified themselves in this way. Figure 6.2 shows the ideological distribution.

Figure 6.2 also depicts the seeds of Democratic discontent: ideological factions or subgroups within the larger organization. Whereas the Republican ideological distribution resembles a ladder of increasing conservatism, the Democratic distribution reveals that moderate party leaders buffer two equally distributed camps holding divergent ideologies. It is difficult to reconcile liberal and conservative preferences into a coherent set of policy recommendations. Whereas the Republicans find themselves in agreement on issues, Democrats are much more divided. This difficulty is reflected in the Houston leaders' responses to these policy alternatives: (a) spend less and reduce social services, or (b) continue to provide such services. Alternative *a* was favored by 83 percent of the Republican activists; alternative *b* was preferred by 16 percent of them. Among the Democrats, 43 percent selected alternative *a* and 43 percent chose alternative *b*. In short, Houston Republicans are united by an ideological bond; Houston Democrats are not. This circumstance illustrates one of the problems that a local party faces in becoming a meaningful, policy-oriented organization.

A factional challenge to local Republican parties has come from evangelical Christian activists who want to move the party to a more conservative stance. In Douglas County (Omaha), Nebraska, for example, conservative Christians had gained sufficient power by 1988 to oust the moderate head of the party.[11] The moderates responded by forming their own political action committee (PAC) to promote the Republican electoral cause. This experience is representative of what is occurring in many other locales, including North Carolina, Minnesota, Georgia, and Michigan.

Political parties continually face the problem of factions. The challenge for party leadership is to unite the factions into a winning force.

The Two-Party System

General elections in the United States are typically contests between candidates representing the two major political parties. Such has been the case for the past century and a half. The Democratic party has been in existence since the 1830s, when it emerged from the Jacksonian wing of the Jeffersonian party.[12] The Republican party, despite its label as the "Grand Old Party," is newer; it developed out of the sectional conflict over slavery of the 1850s.

There are numerous reasons for the institutionalization of two-party politics. Explanations that emphasize sectional dualism, such as East versus West or North versus South, have given way to those that focus on the structure of the electoral system. Parties compete in elections in which there can be only one winner. Most legislative races, for example, take place in single-member districts, in which only the candidate with the most votes wins; there is no reward for finishing second or third. Hence the development of radical or noncentrist parties is discouraged. Another very plausible explanation has to do with tradition. Americans are accustomed to a political system composed of two parties, and that is how we understand politics.

The assessment of former Alabama governor George Wallace that "there ain't a dime's worth of difference between Democrats and Republicans" raises questions about the need for alternative parties. Third parties (also called nonmajor or minor parties) are an unsuccessful but persistent phenomenon in American politics. There may be no substantial differences between the two major parties, but for the most part their positions reflect the public mood. When third-party options are presented to voters in national elections, voters tend to stick to the two major parties. Third parties also suffer because the two established parties have vast reserves of money and resources at their disposal; new parties can rarely amass the finances or assemble the organization necessary to make significant inroads into the system. Rarely does a Ross Perot, the independent candidate who could self-finance his 1992 presidential campaign, appear on the scene.

Figure 6.3 Party Competition in the States, 1965–1988

Interparty competition is on the increase. As recently as a decade ago, many of the competitive two-party states would have been in a one-party majority category. (Nebraska, with its nonpartisan legislative elections, is a special case.)

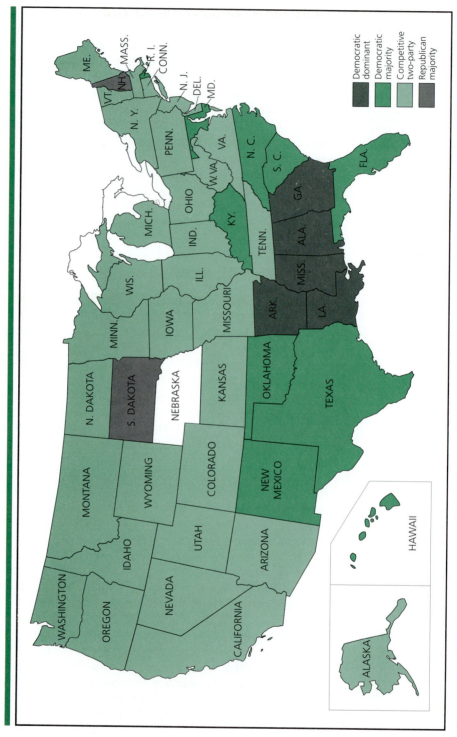

Democratic dominant

Democratic majority

Competitive two-party

Republican majority

Source: Adapted from Malcolm E. Jewell and David M. Olson, *Political Parties and Elections in American States*, 3d ed. Pacific Grove, Calif.: Brooks/Cole, 1988), pp. 26–27. Used by permission of Brooks/Cole Publishing Co.

Third parties have occasionally achieved isolated success in certain states. For example, the Socialist party elected a few state representatives in New York in the early 1900s, and the Progressive party of Robert LaFollette in Wisconsin and the Farmer Labor party in Minnesota strongly influenced the politics of those states before World War II. More recently, third parties have been formed by dissatisfied factions that have split off from a major party. This was the case with the Conservatives, who broke with the New York Republican party because it was not conservative enough for them, and with the Freedom Democratic party of Mississippi, which developed in the 1960s as an alternative to the racist official Democratic party.[13] Today, the Libertarian party and its antigovernment candidates are the most active third party.

Victory is infrequently the story of third-party electoral performance. In the eight years from 1976 to 1984, third-party candidates and independents captured less than 1 percent of the vote in state legislative races.[14] And in only five states (led by New York, with 9.2 percent) did nonmajor party candidates receive more than 2 percent of the vote. This is hardly a showing that would have set the major parties on edge. One factor that appears linked to third-party voting is the educational level of the state. States with a larger proportion of highly educated citizens are more receptive to partisan alternatives.[15]

Interparty Competition

Most states exhibit substantial two-party competition. In other words, when you look at a general-election ballot, you will find both the Democrats and the Republicans offering credible candidates. Gone are the days when one party virtually ran state government without any opposition. The extension of interparty competition to states that have lacked it is a healthy development in American politics. Citizens who are dissatisfied with the performance of the party in power have another choice.

Patterns of Competition   In measuring party competition, an important consideration is which party controls the major policymaking institutions in the state: the governor's office and the state legislature. The information in Figure 6.3 indicates party control of these institutions by state for the period 1965–1988. The assignment of states to different categories takes into consideration the closeness of the gubernatorial election and the size of the partisan majorities in the legislature.[16]

Five possible categories of competition exist: Democratic dominant, Democratic majority, competitive two-party, Republican majority, and Republican dominant. We can eliminate the last category, however, because the Republican party did not dominate the politics of any state during the twenty-four-year period. In fact, the Republican party controlled only New Hampshire and South Dakota for a majority of those years, and even these stars of Republicanism had Democratic governors for one-third of the period.

The Democrats are a different story. Georgia and Mississippi stand out among the five Democratic-dominant states, because Republicans operate at a tremendous disadvantage in state politics. When Georgia Republicans won 7 seats in the House in 1988, bringing their total to 36 (out of 180), it was an electoral coup. An editorial in the *Atlanta Journal and Constitution* was headlined "Something Is Gaining on State's Democrats."[17] Ten states are considered Democratic-majority states; Democrats usually win, but Republicans put up a spirited fight and have some victories to build on.

The majority of the states (thirty-two) have competitive two-party politics, but the institutional patterns vary. In some states, such as Oregon, one party has generally controlled the governor's office while the other has prevailed in the legislature. In others, such as California, Massachusetts, and Tennessee, Democratic control of the legislature has been offset by partisan balance in the governor's office. Exemplifying a pattern of almost perfect competition are states like Illinois, Ohio, and Pennsylvania, where institutional control has oscillated between the two parties.

Consequences of Competition   Two-party competition is spreading at a time when states are becoming the battleground for the resolution of difficult policy issues. Undoubtedly, as governors set their agendas and legislatures outline their preferences, cries of "partisan politics" will be heard. But in a positive sense, such cries symbolize the maturation of state institutions. Partisan politics will probably encourage a wider search for policy alternatives and result in innovative solutions. Consider this comment on the waning days of single-party politics in Georgia, where Republicans are making inroads into traditionally Democratic territory:

> [Georgia Democrats are] being stalked by a critter not native to these parts, an animal with hot breath, heavy footsteps and contempt for the state's ancient, ossified buddy system. . . . Sooner or later, the state's unresponsive Democrats will learn the meaning of competition. The faster complacency dies at the Capitol, the better off Georgians will be.[18]

Heated partisan competition turns a dull campaign into a lively contest. Citizen interest picks up and voter turnout increases. In the view of many, two parties are better than one.

Is the Party Over?

This impertinent question is intended to spark debate. Have political parties, as we know them, outlived their usefulness? Should they be cast aside as new forms of political organization and communication emerge?

As some have argued, a more educated populace that can readily acquire political information is likely to be less reliant on party cues.[19] Today's generation is less loyal to political parties than its grandparents were and is not so likely to vote along party lines. A *dealignment,* or weakening of individual partisan attachments, has occurred. Parties also no longer rule the roost when it comes to campaign finance. Challenges come from PACs that pour huge amounts of money into campaigns and candidates, and from political operatives who use new technology creatively to build individual election teams.

Political parties are not sitting idly by as their function in the political system is challenged. Research has shown that party organizations are making their operations more professional and have more money to spend and more staff to spend it.[20] The past several years have seen the development of party-centered advertising campaigns and a renewed commitment to get-out-the-vote drives.[21] In a few states that have publicly funded campaigns, parties as well as candidates have been designated as recipients of funds. States formerly dominated by one party now find themselves with a resilient second party on their hands. All in all, it appears that parties are still viable parts of the political system.

Political Campaigns

Like so many things these days, political campaigns aren't what they used to be. State and local campaigns are no longer unsophisticated operations run from someone's dining room table. The 1980s ushered in a new era of campaign technology and financing in which information is accessible to almost everyone through television and the mailbox. As a consequence, some argue, campaigns have taken on a different and decidedly negative tone.

A New Era of Campaigns

Campaigns of the past conjure up images of fiery oratory and county fairs. In South Carolina, for instance, candidates for statewide office used to be required by law to speak at every county seat, a practice that became widely known as the "traveling political circus." But today, campaigns orchestrated by rural court-house gangs and urban ward-bosses have given way to stylized video campaigning, which depends on the mass media and political consultants.

Mass Media The mass media, especially television, are intrinsic aspects of modern statewide campaigns. Even candidates for local offices are increasingly using mass media to transmit their messages. Campaigners can either buy their time and newspaper space for advertising or get it free by arranging events that reporters are likely to cover. These range from serious (a candidate's major policy statement) to gimmicky (a candidate climbing into the ring with a professional wrestler to demonstrate his "toughness"); either way, they are cleverly planned to capture media attention.

Using the media is an increasingly sophisticated venture. Florida state Senator Bob Graham, running in a crowded field for the Democratic gubernatorial nomination in 1978, developed what is now considered a classic approach: He held a series of "work days," spending a day each week pumping gas, clerking at a convenience store, loading trucks, digging ditches, handling baggage. The media followed him everywhere, and a disproportionate share of media attention helped him to win the nomination and ultimately the governorship. During his eight-year stint as governor, and now as a U.S. senator, Graham continues to devote one day a month to such work days.

A candidate seeking free media attention needs to create visual events, be quotable, and relentlessly attack opponents or targeted problems. But as the magazine *Campaigns and Elections* advises, he or she must integrate gimmicks with a message that appeals to the electorate. In one of its 1988 issues, this magazine contained articles aimed at candidates on "making a name for yourself," "nailing the opposition," and "effective targeting."[22]

Free media time is seldom sufficient. Candidates, particularly those running for higher-level state offices and for positions in large cities, rely on paid advertisements to reach the public. One estimate indicated that the average 1986 gubernatorial candidate produced and aired twenty to thirty different political commercials.[23] These are not inexpensive to produce or to air, although there is some variation in advertising rates around the country. A thirty-second spot on the most popular television program of 1986, "The Cosby Show," was reported to have cost $800 for all of South Dakota but $30,000 for New York City alone.[24]

Paid media advertisements these days seem to be of two distinct varieties, generic and negative. Generic advertisements include

1. *the sainthood spot,* which glorifies the candidate and her accomplishments;
2. *the testimonial,* in which other people (celebrities, average citizens) attest to the candidate's abilities;
3. *the bumper-sticker policy spot,* which emphasizes the campaign's popular and noncontroversial themes (good schools, lower taxes, more jobs); and
4. *the feel-good spot,* which identifies and capitalizes on the spirit of a place and its people (for example, "Vermont's a special place," "Nobody can do it better than Pennsylvania").[25]

Negative advertising, which has been renamed by its practitioners in a bit of linguistic chicanery as "comparative" advertising, is easily recognizable. The public has been inundated with the *flip-flop ad* and the *not-on-the-job ad,* in which an opponent's voting record and attendance rate, respectively, are presented. Comedy spots ridiculing the opponent, another type of negative ad, are difficult to produce and can backfire; but when they work, they linger in voters' minds. Another negative ad is the *hit-and-run,* in which the opponent is linked to unpopular people, causes, or events. The growing concern over negative advertising is the subject of Problem Solving 6.1.

Media advertising is important because it is frequently the only contact a potential voter has with a candidate. A candidate's personal characteristics and style—important considerations to an evaluating public—are easily transmitted via the airwaves. Advances in communications technology offer new options to enterprising candidates. One candidate for the Maryland House of Delegates distributed homemade videotapes to seven thousand targeted households in his

Problem Solving 6.1

Reforming Negative Campaign Advertising

The Problem: Over the past decade, the level of negativism in political campaign advertising has increased. Nationwide, the public is registering its disapproval of the mudslinging, take-no-prisoners campaigns that characterized the 1980s. From a systemic perspective, the strident tone projected in campaigns seems to have fueled cynicism about both government and politics.

The Solution: One approach to making campaign advertising less distorted is to treat it like product advertising. As with products, unsubstantiated claims and deceptive messages about candidates would be disallowed (although anyone who has seen the "abdominizer" ads on late-night television might question the effectiveness of such regulations). Two other approaches with the same intent are more locally based and informal. In many communities, the local newspapers have begun to report regularly on the content, presentation, and relative accuracy of television advertisements. These "truth boxes" or "spot checks," as they are often called, have had an immediate effect on campaigning, occasionally leading to the retraction or redesign of an ad. In some places, moreover, local commissions have been established to monitor the conduct of campaigns. These "Fair Campaign Practices" groups try to determine whether candidates are addressing issues of importance to the community, making accurate statements, and engaging in fair campaign tactics. Philadelphia's Fellowship Commission is a case in point. During the hotly contested mayoral race in 1991, the commission sought to rein in a spiraling cycle of charges and countercharges. Although such commissions typically have no power to impose penalties for unfair practices, their findings generate unfavorable publicity for violators of community campaign standards.

Sources: Randall Rothenberg, "Voters Complain Negative Campaigns Are Driving Them Away, *New York Times,* November 6, 1990, p. A11; Laurie Hirschfeld Zeller, "Campaign Advertising and Public Participation," *National Civic Review* 80 (Summer 1991): 275-283.

district. Curious VCR-equipped voters could tune into the candidate whenever they wanted, pause the spiel, rewind the tape, and play it again.[26]

Political Consultants Along with increased media usage, a new occupational specialty sprang up during the 1970s and 1980s: political consulting. Individuals with expertise in polling, direct mail, fund raising, advertising, and campaign management hire themselves out to campaigns, in which use of new campaign technology makes their expertise invaluable. The occupation is undoubtedly here to stay, and several colleges and universities now offer degree programs in practical campaigning.

The basic responsibility of a political consultant is to get his candidate(s) elected. In today's campaigning, this means creating the right "packaging" and ensuring that adequate funds are available. Packaging involves issues as central as identifying the campaign theme (contemporary favorites include "leadership," "integrity," and especially for gubernatorial and mayoral candidates, "business acumen") and as trivial as choosing the candidate's neckwear.

Consultants form the core of the professional campaign management team assembled by candidates for state offices. They identify and target likely voters, both those who are already in the candidate's camp and need to be reminded to vote and those who can be persuaded. They carefully craft messages to appeal to specific voters, such as the elderly, home-owners, and environmentalists. Any number of factors influence the result of an election, such as the presence of an incumbent in a race and the amount of funds a challenger has accumulated, but one significant factor is the ability to frame or define the issues during the campaign. Even in a quietly contested state legislative race, district residents are likely to receive mailings that state the candidates' issue positions, solicit funds, and perhaps comment unfavorably on the opposition. The candidate who has an effective political consultant to help set the campaign agenda and thereby put her opponent on the defensive is that much closer to victory.

Campaign Finance

To campaign for public office is to spend money—a lot of money. Collectively, the 279 candidates for governor in the 36 states conducting elections in 1990 spent $345.5 million.[27] Almost one-third of those funds were spent in two states: the hotly contested gubernatorial races in California ($53.2 million) and Texas ($50.5 million). Trailing not far behind, in terms of dollars, were the battles for the governors' seats in Florida ($25.1 million) and Illinois ($23.9 million). Gubernatorial campaign spending in 1990 represented a real (not inflated) dollar increase of 5.6 percent from the 1986 off-year elections. After examining the expenditure patterns, political scientist Thad Beyle concluded that higher campaign costs are associated with open seats, close contests, and competitive political parties.[28]

Spending in legislative races has also increased. For example, candidates for the Florida House of Representatives in 1980 were spending 50 percent more (after accounting for inflation) than their counterparts in 1972.[29] In 1983, New Jersey Assembly candidates averaged $20,000 in expenditures; two years later, the figure had climbed to $37,000.[30] Figure 6.4 shows that average campaign expenditures, with the exception of the Colorado Senate, have steadily climbed over time. California, as might be expected, was the site of the first million-dollar campaign for a legislative seat, and it is not uncommon for a competitive legislative campaign there to consume half a million dollars. At the other end of the scale are legislative races in New Hampshire, where the average candidate's expenditures in 1986 were less than $3,000. (Keep in mind, however, that the job pays $100 a year.)[31]

Just how important is money? One knowledgeable observer concluded: "In the direct primaries, where self-propelled candidates battle for recognition, money is crucial. Electronic advertising is the only way to gain visibility. Hence the outcome usually rewards the one with the largest war chest."[32] This does not bode well for an idealistic but underfunded potential candidate. Winning takes money, either the candidate's or someone else's. If the latter, it may come with a string or two attached.

Figure 6.4

Average Legislative Campaign Expenditures in Four States, 1974–1986

With rare exceptions, legislative campaign costs continue their steady climb.

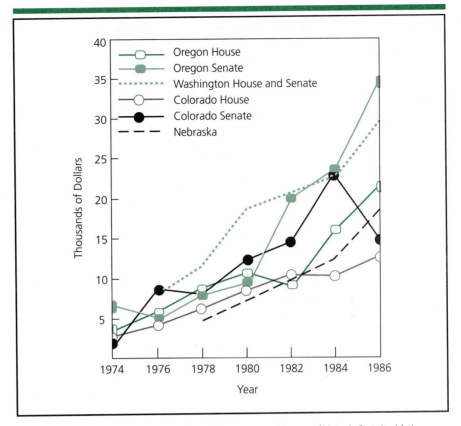

Source: Adapted from Anthony Gierzynski and David Breaux, "Money and Votes in State Legislative Elections," *Legislative Studies Quarterly* 16 (May 1991): 206. Used with permission.

State Efforts at Campaign Reform Concern over escalating costs and the influence of wealthy special interests in campaigns has led reform groups such as Common Cause to call for improved state laws to provide comprehensive and timely disclosure of campaign finances, impose limitations on contributions by individuals and groups, create a combined public-private financing mechanism for primaries and general elections, and establish an independent commission to enforce tough sanctions on violators of campaign finance laws.[33]

States have performed impressively on the first of these recommendations: In fact, all states have some sort of campaign financing reporting procedure. In response to the fourth recommendation, twenty-six states have established independent commissions to oversee the conduct of campaigns, although they have found it somewhat difficult to enforce the law and punish violators. One study of state election commissions identified only four—in California, Connecticut, Florida, and New Jersey—as displaying "consistency and vigor" in their enforcement behavior.[34]

The other recommendations have proved more troublesome. States have grappled with the issue of costly campaigns but have made only modest progress in controlling costs. A 1976 decision by the U.S. Supreme Court in *Buckley* v. *Valeo* made these efforts more difficult; the Court ruled that governments cannot limit a person's right to spend money in order to spread his views on particular issues and candidates. In essence, then, a candidate has unlimited power to spend his own money on his own behalf, and other individuals may spend to their heart's content to promote their own opinions on election-related issues. What the Court let stand, however, were state limits on an individual's contributions to candidates and parties; it also ruled that if a candidate accepts public funds, he is then bound by whatever limitations the state may impose.

Some states have established actual limits on the amount of money that organizations and individuals can contribute to a political race. In New York, for example, corporations are limited to a contribution maximum of $5,000 per calendar year, and individuals (other than official candidates) are restricted to $150,000. Florida allows corporations, labor unions, and PACs to contribute a maximum of $500 per candidate. The same limits apply to individuals, excluding the candidate's own contributions. Some states, such as Arizona, Connecticut, North Dakota, Pennsylvania, and Texas, have gone even further by prohibiting contributions from corporations and labor unions.[35] But a totally different philosophy pervades the politics of a large number of states that continue to operate their election systems without any limitations on contributions. In Colorado, Illinois, Missouri, and Utah, to name a few, organizations and individuals can contribute as much as they wish.

States have also considered the other side of the campaign financing equation: expenditures. Virtually all states require candidates and political committees to file reports documenting the expenditure of campaign funds. Nine states impose limits on a candidate's total expenditures; Hawaii uses voluntary spending limits. In Delaware, for example, statewide candidates are allowed to spend up to twenty-five cents times the number of qualified voters in the primary, and twice that figure in the general election. Michigan takes a different approach. There, publicly funded candidates (governor and lieutenant governor) are restricted to $1 million per election, with another $200,000 allowable for specific purposes. In the vast majority of states, however, candidates campaign without any spending limits.

The Need for High Financing   Does any of this really matter? Should the general public be concerned about the spiraling costs of competing for elected posts?

Recent research has confirmed several long-standing truths about the costs of campaigning.[36] For instance, close elections cost more than elections in which one candidate is sure to win, since uncertainty regarding the outcome is a spur to spending. A candidate quickly learns that it is easier to get money from potential contributors when the polls show that she has a chance of winning. Also, elections that produce change—that is, in which an incumbent is unseated or the out-party gains the office—typically cost more. Taking on an existing officeholder is a risky strategy that drives up election costs. And an open race in which there is no incumbent represents an opportunity for the party out of office to capture the seat, thus triggering similar spending by the in-party in an effort to protect the seat. It is no wonder that campaign costs continue to rise.

Major candidates, especially incumbents, do not have to look too hard to find campaign money. PACs loom larger and larger as heavy funders of state election campaigns. Data from legislative elections during the late 1980s in New Jersey, North Carolina, and Pennsylvania (see Table 6.2) make that point. Incumbents have more money to spend—in many cases, *substantially* more—and PACs provide a goodly chunk of it. In fact, Democratic incumbents in North Carolina and incumbents in both parties in Pennsylvania received more than half of their campaign funds from PACs. In New Jersey, where corporations and labor unions are allowed to make direct contributions to candidates, PACs are less important but still account for more than one-fourth of the funds available to incumbents. Political parties in the three states have adopted different funding strategies, depending on their position in the legislatures. Party contributions appear to be especially important to Republican challengers.[37]

Public Funding as a Solution Almost half the states have begun experimenting with public funding of campaigns. Individuals voluntarily contribute to a central fund, which is divided among candidates or political parties. The system is fairly easy to administer and is relatively easy for voters. In most of the public-funding states, citizens can use their state income tax form to earmark a portion (a dollar or two) of their tax liability for the fund. A check-off system of this sort does not directly increase taxpayers' tax burden. In a few states, the public fund is amassed through voluntary surcharge, or additional tax (usually $1, although California allows surcharges of $5, $10, and $25). Indiana has opted for a different approach: revenues from the sale of personalized motor vehicle license plates support the fund.

In addition to check-offs and surcharges, some of the public-funding states, including Idaho and Minnesota, offer taxpayers a tax credit (usually 50 percent of the contribution, up to a specific maximum) when they contribute to political campaigns. A more popular supplement to public funding is a state tax deduction for campaign contributions, as used in California, Hawaii, Montana, Oklahoma, and North Carolina. A final though not widely explored approach is direct state appropriation of funds. Maryland, for instance, does not use check-offs or surcharges but relies instead on a direct state appropriation to candidates for governor and lieutenant governor.[38]

Public campaign financing is supposed to rid the election process of some of its evils. Proponents argue that it will democratize the contribution process by freeing candidates from excessive reliance on special interest money. Other possible advantages include expanding the pool of potential candidates, allowing candidates to compete on a more equal basis, and reducing the cost of campaigning.[39] A study of legislative races in Wisconsin indicated that as a proportion of total contributions, public dollars increased and PAC money declined.[40] By contributing to the fund, average citizens may feel that they have a greater stake in state elections.

Table 6.2 Political Party and PAC Contributions to Incumbents and Challengers in Three States

	New Jersey		North Carolina		Pennsylvania	
	Incumbent	Challenger	Incumbent	Challenger	Incumbent	Challenger
Democrats (number of candidates)	(25)	(42)	(48)	(21)	(55)	(55)
Average PAC Contribution	$19,745	$11,457	$7,091	$4,301	$16,342	$1,789
Percentage PAC Contribution	31%	23%	52%	31%	52%	23%
Average Party Contribution	$358	$2,126	—	—	$3,366	$2,234
Percentage Party Contribution	<1%	3.6%	—	—	11%	26%
Total Revenues	$65,646	$44,953	$16,109	$13,728	$31,665	$8,718
Republicans (number of candidates)	(40)	(32)	(17)	(44)	(55)	(55)
Average PAC Contribution	$19,625	$2,672	$5,708	$741	$16,711	$1,464
Percentage PAC Contribution	26%	6%	39%	10%	52%	17%
Average Party Contribution	$14,471	$9,284	$824	$1,243	$437	$1,744
Percentage Party Contribution	18%	43%	6%	30%	1%	20%
Total Revenues	$79,166	$31,849	$17,721	$7,052	$32,475	$8,783

Note: Unopposed candidates and those in open-seat races excluded from the analysis.

Source: Adapted from Joel A. Thompson, William Cassie, and Malcolm E. Jewell, "A Sacred Cow or Just a Lot of Bull?: The Impact of Money in Competitive State Legislative Campaigns," paper presented at the annual meeting of the American Political Science Association, Washington, D.C., August 1991, Table 1. Reprinted with permission.

Yet despite the claims offered in support of public funding, it is not universally embraced. One study of legislators in eight states found that an almost equal proportion favored public funding of gubernatorial campaigns (46.2 percent) as opposed it (46.4 percent).[41] The reaction to public funding of legislative races was more one-sided: 55 percent were against it, 36 percent supported it. Opponents claim that public funding will introduce new biases into state elections while stifling competition and protecting incumbents.[42] Evidence from states with public-funding systems indicates that the mechanism itself—a check-off or a surcharge—largely determines the success of the program. When a check-off is used, the percentage of contributing taxpayers reaches the 20 to 25 percent level. With a surcharge, the participation rate falls below 5 percent. New Jersey offers a successful example of the former. Forty percent of tax filers contribute to a general fund that is allocated to gubernatorial candidates for specific campaign activities.[43] Taxpayer participation of the magnitude found in New Jersey suggests that public funding can be a useful alternative to private fund raising.

Elections

Elections are central to a representative democracy. State and local governments have traditionally relied on them for choosing top leaders. In most states, voters choose the governors, lieutenant governors, legislators, attorney generals, secretaries of state, and state treasurers; in some, they also choose the heads of the agriculture and education departments and the public utility commissioners. At the local level, the list of elected officials includes mayors and council members, county commissioners, county judges, sheriffs, tax assessors, and school board members. If state and local governments are to function effectively, elections must provide talented, capable leaders.

Primaries

In order for a party to choose a nominee and put her name on the general election ballot, a winnowing of potential candidates must occur. In the pre-Jacksonian era, party nominees were chosen by a legislative caucus—that is, a conference of the party's legislators. Caucuses gave way to the mechanism of state party conventions, which were similar to national presidential nomination conventions but without most of the spectacle; popularly elected delegates from across a state convened to select the party's nominees. Then the Progressive movement made an effort to open up the nomination process and make it more

primary system

The electoral mechanism for selecting party nominees to compete in the general election.

democratic. Political parties adopted the **primary system,** whereby voters directly choose among several candidates, to select the party's nominees for the general election.

Twelve states still allow for party conventions in particular instances, such as nominations for lieutenant governor (Michigan) and selection of nominees by third parties (Kansas).[44] Connecticut, the last state to adopt primaries, operates a unique "challenge" system, whereby party nominees for various state offices are selected at a convention; but if a contest develops at the convention and a second candidate receives as much as 20 percent of the votes, the convention's nominee and the challenger square off in a primary.[45]

closed primary

A primary in which only voters registered in the party are allowed to participate.

open primary

A primary in which voters may vote for either party's candidates.

Primaries can be divided into two types, closed and open. The only voters who can participate in a **closed primary** for a particular party are those who are registered in that party. An **open primary** does not require party membership; any voter who is qualified to vote in the general election can participate in the party's primary. However, even this basic distinction lends itself to some variation. States differ, for example, in terms of the ease with which voters can change party affiliation and participate in the closed primary of the other party. In seventeen states, a voter is an enrolled member of one party (or is an independent and may or may not be eligible to vote in either party's primary) and can change that affiliation only well in advance of the primary election.[46] Ten other closed primary states allow more flexibility, to accommodate shifts in voters' loyalties.

Open primaries account for (and perhaps contribute to) fleeting partisan loyalties among the public. The key difference among states with open primaries is whether a voter is required to identify which party's primary he is participating in. Eleven states require voters to request a specific party's ballot at the polling place. Nine other open primary states make no such demand; voters secretly select the ballot of the party in which they wish to participate.

blanket primary

A primary in which a voter is allowed to vote for candidates of both parties in a single election.

A few states fall outside the strict closed or open classification. Two western states, Alaska and Washington, use what is referred to as a **blanket primary.** Under this system, voters can vote in the primaries of both parties in a single election. In other words, voters may cross over from one party's primary ballot to the other's. A voter could select from among Democratic candidates for governor and among Republican candidates for the legislature, in effect participating in both primaries. In a sense, this is the ultimate open primary.

The other variation on the closed- versus open-primary pattern is found in Louisiana which uses a single nonpartisan primary for its statewide and congressional races. Voters can choose from among any of the candidates, regardless of party affiliation. If no one candidate receives a majority of the votes in a race, the top two vote-getters face each other in a runoff election. The nonpartisan primary is particularly disruptive to political party power. Table 6.3 groups the states according to their primary type.

The distinction between closed and open primaries obviously affects party influence in elections, but does it have any impact on the outcome? In other words, if we had completely open primaries, would different candidates win? There are no definitive answers to this question, but preliminary research on presidential primaries offers compelling evidence that primary structure does not seem to affect electoral outcomes very dramatically.[47] One possible but not very likely upset would occur if voters of one party overwhelmingly voted in the other party's primary election. This actually happened in the 1986 Democratic gubernatorial primary in Alabama.

Table 6.3
State Primary Types

States with Closed Primaries (17)	Arizona	New Mexico
	California	New York
	Connecticut	North Carolina
	Delaware	Oklahoma
	Florida	Oregon
	Kentucky	Pennsylvania
	Maryland	South Dakota
	Nebraska	West Virginia
	Nevada	
States with Flexible Closed Primaries (10)	Colorado	New Hampshire
	Iowa	New Jersey
	Kansas	Ohio
	Maine	Rhode Island
	Massachusetts	Wyoming
States with Open Primaries Requiring Party Selection (11)	Alabama	Missouri
	Arkansas	South Carolina
	Georgia	Tennessee
	Illinois	Texas
	Indiana	Virginia
	Mississippi	
States with Open Primaries (9)	Hawaii	North Dakota
	Idaho	Utah
	Michigan	Vermont
	Minnesota	Wisconsin
	Montana	
States with Blanket Primaries (2)	Alaska	Washington
States with Nonpartisan Primaries (1)	Louisiana	

Source: Malcolm E. Jewell and David M. Olson, *Political Parties and Elections in American States,* 3d ed. (Pacific Grove, Calif.: Brooks/Cole Publishing Co., 1988), p. 90. Based in part on Craig L. Carr and Gary L. Scott, *American Politics Quarterly* 12 (October 1984): 465–76, copyright 1984 by Sage Publications, Inc. Reprinted with permission of Brooks/Cole Publishing Co. and Sage Publications, Inc.

Runoff Elections

runoff election

A second election conducted if no candidate receives a majority of votes in the first election.

A **runoff election** is a second election that is held if no one candidate for an office receives a majority of votes in the primary. Runoffs became a controversial topic during the late 1980s because of the contention that different people win than would win in a system without runoffs.

Primary election runoffs have a distinct regional flavor to them. They are used by parties in nine states: Alabama, Arkansas, Florida, Georgia, Mississippi, North Carolina, Oklahoma, South Carolina, and Texas. (As we have noted, Louisiana switched from a partisan to a nonpartisan runoff election in 1975.) These have traditionally been one-party (Democratic) states, so the greatest amount of competition for an office has occurred in the Democratic party's primaries, in which as many as ten candidates might enter the race. In these states, a candidate must receive more than 50 percent of the votes in the primary to become the party's nominee. (North Carolina recently lowered the winning primary percentage to 40 percent.) When many candidates compete, it is quite probable that no one will be able to amass a majority of the votes, so the top two vote-getters face each other in a runoff election. This process ensures that the party's nominee is preferred by a majority of the primary voters. In the past, Democratic nominees in runoff states typically faced only nominal, if any, Republican opposition in the general election, so winning the Democratic primary was tantamount to being elected to office. The general election was a virtual formality.

Myths about Runoffs   Three myths have grown up around the runoff primary.[48] One is the idea that "the leader loses"—that the candidate who finishes first in primary voting is likely to lose in the runoff to the second-place finisher. Another is the "incumbent loses" myth, which suggests that an incumbent who cannot win the necessary majority in the primary is destined to lose in a runoff. Finally, some people believe in the "minority disadvantage" myth (a variation on the "leader loses" idea), which declares that a racial minority candidate who leads in the primary tends to lose to a white candidate in the runoff. Concern that these theories (especially the last one) might actually have some basis in fact has led to calls for abolishing runoff elections.

Analysis of election results does not lend much credence to the myths. Research on 215 runoffs in Georgia from 1965 to 1982 found that with the exception of some celebrated cases, primary leaders went on to win the runoff.[49] Although incumbents are more vulnerable in runoffs than are nonincumbent primary leaders, incumbents still win more often than they lose. The Georgia findings included few cases in which a minority candidate competed in a runoff, but initial results show no discernible disadvantage for these candidates. It is important to note that "minority disadvantage" was *not* mythical in North Carolina. In fact, once it was documented, the state lowered the winning threshold in first primaries to 40 percent.

Are Runoffs Divisive?   Theoretically, the rationale for the runoff primary is majority rule. But political circumstances have changed since several southern states adopted the runoff primary system in the 1920s, and the Democratic party is no longer unchallenged in the region. The growth of Republicanism produced an increasing number of meaningfully contested general elections during the 1970s and 1980s. Has the runoff primary outlived its usefulness? Worse yet, does it systematically disadvantage the political party using it? In other words, do runoffs generate such divisiveness within the party that its nominee is weakened in the general election?

A recent study of this issue supports the speculation that candidates who emerge from a bloody intraparty runoff are systematically disadvantaged in the general election.[50] Being involved in a runoff costs Democratic gubernatorial candidates in the South approximately 4.56 per 100 votes cast, on average, in the subsequent general election. (Incumbency tends to restore some of the deficit, however.) The reasons for this are complex, but they seem to reflect the factionalized majority party's inability to overcome the rancor that the two-primary structure produces.

The increasing competitiveness of the Republican party in the South has led to more crowded primaries and, hence, to greater use of runoffs. Thus, the Republicans may eventually be susceptible to the kind of divisiveness that afflicts the Democrats.

General Elections

Primaries and runoffs culminate in the general election, through which candidates become officeholders. Virtually all states hold general elections in November of even-numbered years. However, a few states—Kentucky, Mississippi, New Jersey, and Virginia among them—schedule their gubernatorial elections in odd-numbered years.

General elections typically pit candidates of the two parties against one another. The winner is the candidate who receives a majority of the votes cast. In a race in which more than two candidates compete (which occurs when an independent or a third-party candidate enters a race), the leading vote-getter is less likely to receive a majority of the votes cast. Instead, the candidate with the most votes—a **plurality**—wins.

plurality

The number of votes (though not necessarily a majority) cast for the winning candidate in an election with more than two candidates.

Political parties have traditionally been active in general elections, mobilizing voters in support of their candidates. Over time, however, their role has diminished, as general-election campaigns have become more candidate-centered and geared to the candidate's own organization.[51] One new twist in the past decade has been the emergence of legislative party caucuses as major factors in general elections. In California, for example, the Democratic and Republican leaders in both houses raised more than $7.5 million to distribute to their party nominees for the legislature in 1986.[52] That year in Illinois, the four party caucuses (two parties, two houses) spent nearly $3 million. Ohio's House Republican Campaign Committee conducts seminars on issues and on campaign management for the party's House nominees. In some states, the formal state party organization has given way to the legislative party caucus.

Nonpartisan Elections

A **nonpartisan election** removes the political party identification from the candidate in an effort to "depoliticize" the electoral campaign. Elections that have been made nonpartisan include those for many judicial offices and for many local-level positions. The special task of judges—adjudicating guilt or innocence, determining right and wrong—does not lend itself to partisan interpretation. The job of local governments—delivering public services—has also traditionally been considered nonideological. Nonpartisan local elections are likely to be found in municipalities and in school districts and special districts.

Under a nonpartisan election system, all candidates for an office compete in a first election and if there's no majority winner, a second election (runoff) is held. The occurrence of nonpartisan local elections is largely a function of region. Although 73 percent of cities use nonpartisan elections, according to a recent survey, the regional figures range from 94 percent in the West to 21 percent in the Northeast.[53] Large cities are no more likely to conduct partisan elections than smaller ones are; those that do, however, such as New York City and Chicago, tend to attract attention.

The Impact of Nonpartisan Elections   Most studies have concluded that nonpartisanship depresses turnout in municipal elections that are held independent of state and national elections. The figures are not dramatic, but in what are already low-turnout elections, the difference can run as high as 15 to 20 percent of municipal voters.[54] Nonpartisan elections seem to produce a more socioeconomically elite city council and more Republican members. One fascinating finding is that although a nonpartisan election structure seems to result in a different type of city council, the policy outcomes appear unaffected.[55] In terms of policies, nonpartisanly elected city councils are not noticeably different from partisan ones.

What It Takes to Get Elected   In the absence of political parties, candidates are forced to create their own organizations in order to run for office. They raise and spend money (much of it their own), and they seek the endorsements of newspapers and business and citizen groups. Money matters; this fact of political life cannot be understated. But endorsements are also important in local campaigns. Recent research on the impact of newspaper endorsements in six cities (Dallas, Fort Worth, San Antonio, Memphis, Peoria, and Charlotte) during a thirty-year period ending in 1980 confirmed their influence.[56] The researchers reported "considerable success for candidates receiving a newspaper endorsement."[57]

An incumbent backed by a newspaper is an almost unbeatable combination. Consider the *Tampa Tribune*'s evaluation of the three candidates competing for the mayor's post in 1987.[58] The paper claimed that one of the contenders had "served without particular distinction on the city council a few years ago." Another challenger was said to have an "absolute genius for driving people crazy." The incumbent, however, won the newspaper's resounding endorsement, because she had "demonstrated high intelligence, a talent for creative problem-solving, a strong individualistic bent, a quiet but fierce determination, and a deep and honest regard for the welfare of all [Tampa residents]." The endorsed incumbent defeated her opponents handily.

In running for a nonpartisan local office, candidates do not enjoy the good will, especially the money and grassroots support, that automatically accompanies a candidate affiliated with a major political party. In some communities, local groups function as unofficial parties in that they identify candidates whom they prefer and undertake efforts on behalf of those candidates. Citizens' groups can also be an important factor in local elections. In Austin, Texas, for example, two ideologically based citizens' groups play important roles in influencing election outcomes.[59] Liberals come together in an umbrella organization, the River City Coordinating Council, and the conservative perspective is represented by the Austin Area Research Organization. These groups provide informal support to preferred candidates. A study of Austin municipal elections from 1975 to 1985 indicates that the endorsement of these groups is "worth more than 10 percentage points of the vote."[60]

State Elections in the 1990s

Because reapportionment of state legislatures and the U.S. House of Representatives was at stake, the 1990 elections carried extra significance. As Chapter 9 details, redrawing legislative district lines is a highly partisan endeavor. Thus, winning the statehouse or gaining control of the legislature strategically advantaged a political party for the 1991–1992 reapportionment battles. And, as usual, the election outcomes were influenced by incumbency, money, partisanship, and national trends.

coattail effect

The tendency of a winning presidential candidate to carry state candidates of the same party into office.

Gubernatorial Races   Thirty-six of the fifty governor's seats were up for election in 1990. Most states schedule their statewide elections in nonpresidential election years (referred to as "off-years"), so as to prevent the presidential race from diverting attention from state races and also to minimize the possible **coattail effect**, by which a popular presidential candidate can sweep state candidates of the same party into office. The 1990 gubernatorial elections did not produce massive changes in state leadership. Voters retained some incumbents, booted others out of office, and elected two independents. In the thirty-six states with gubernatorial races on the ballot, the signs of voter disenchantment were not widespread but, rather, were tied to specific state contests.[61] Incumbent governors (ten Democrats, seven Republicans) were returned to office in seventeen states; the greatest margin of victory was recorded in South Carolina, where Republican Carroll A. Campbell, Jr., was re-elected with a comfortable 71 percent of the vote. Sitting governors, on the other hand, were ousted in six states; the most lopsided loss occurred in scandal-weary Rhode Island, where Republican Governor Edward DiPrete was beaten by Bruce Sundlun by a 74 to 26 percent margin.

Thirteen states hosted gubernatorial elections in which no incumbent competed. Republicans won six of the open seats, Democrats won five, and Independent candidates won two open seats. The victory by Independent candidates (Walter Hickel in Alaska and Lowell Weicker in Connecticut) was one of the most interesting outcomes of the 1990 gubernatorial elections. Another intriguing result occurred in Arizona, where, in a three-way race, no candidate received a majority. Because a new state law requires that the winner receive a majority, the top two candidates met in a general election "runoff" three months later. The Republican candidate, Fyfe Symington, was victorious. Women, all Democrats, were elected to the governor's office in three states: Joan Finney in Kansas, Barbara Roberts in Oregon, and Ann Richards in Texas. Excluding the races won by Independents, the vote tallies in the governors' races in 1990 and 1991 yielded a change in party control in fourteen states.

Only three states held gubernatorial elections during the off-year of 1991. In Kentucky, a new governor was elected, but the office remained in Democratic hands. In the wild Louisiana race—the subject of Profile 6.1—former Democratic governor Edwin Edwards outlasted the incumbent governor (a recently converted Republican) in the first election and solidly defeated Republican David Duke in the runoff. The Mississippi governor's race captured less national

One of the staples of the campaign season is the candidate debate. Here, primary contenders for a state senate seat square off in a public forum.

Profile 6.1

The 1991 Louisiana Gubernatorial Race

Seldom do gubernatorial elections attract national, much less international, attention. The 1991 race for governor of Louisiana was an exception. In October, Louisiana voters had to choose from a crowded field including the incumbent governor, Buddy Roemer (a Democrat who had recently switched to the Republican party); ex-governor Edwin Edwards, who had been tried twice (but not convicted) on racketeering charges; and State Representative David Duke, a former grand wizard of the Ku Klux Klan. To some, it was just Louisiana politics at its most interesting. One reporter described the state's political scene as "somewhere between stern moral drama and ribald fruitcake theater." The 1991 elections hit a new high on the "colorful" meter, even by Louisiana standards.

Candidates were competing in a nonpartisan election, itself an oddity in state politics. Prior to adopting the party-less structure in 1975, Louisiana elected its politicians much like other southern states did—with a partisan primary followed by a runoff primary if no candidate received more than 50 percent of the vote, and then a general election. In the old days, when the Democratic party was ascendant, the primaries were where the action was. When Republicans began ac-

tively contesting races with electable candidates, then-governor Edwards convinced legislators to change the system. Candidate Edwards had survived three tough races to get to the governor's office, and the specter of three intense election cycles made the open-primary/general-election structure appealing. Now, voters participate and candidates compete in a kind of free-for-all.

Louisiana voters, unhappy with Governor Roemer's tax policies, eliminated him in the October primary. The Edwards-Duke race took on an importance far beyond the simple question of who would govern Louisiana. It became a referendum on race relations. The thought of an ex-Klansman governor pushed Republicans, business leaders, and good-government types into the Edwards camp, albeit reluctantly. And fears of an ensuing economic catastrophe if Duke were elected galvanized the public. A new bumper sticker was spotted on the streets that read "Vote for the Crook, It's Important." In November, a record proportion of the Louisiana electorate (79.8 percent) turned out and former Governor Edwards was elected by a 61 to 39 percent margin.

Sources: Peter Applebome, "Rogue or Reformer, Edwards Seeks Louisiana Vindication," *New York Times,* November 11, 1991, pp. A1, C10; Peter Applebome, "In Louisiana, It Is Politics as Primal Scream," *New York Times,* November 16, 1991, pp. 1, 7; "Fast Eddie Hasn't Slowed Down Lifestyle as Louisiana's Governor," *State,* January 31, 1992, p. 6D.

attention but produced a surprising outcome nonetheless, when Republican Kirk Fordice beat incumbent Democratic Governor Ray Mabus. One interesting sidelight of the 1991 Louisiana and Mississippi governors' races was the *decline* in campaign expenditures from the level reached in the 1980s. Whether this is the beginning of a new trend, an offshoot of the recession, or simply an aberration, is too early to tell.

Legislative Races   The 1990 elections produced modest changes in the partisan makeup of state legislatures. With redistricting as the front-burner issue, state legislative elections resulted in gains for the Democratic party and losses for the Republican party. The number of Democratic-controlled legislatures increased from twenty-eight to thirty-one, whereas Republican control of both houses declined from eight to five states. In ten states, divided partisan control exists: Democrats hold a numerical edge in one house, Republicans in the other. (Legislative elections also resulted in a curious balance within three state senates: equal numbers of Democrats and Republicans.)

The Democratic Process

Elections are the key to the resurgence of state and local governments. It is through elections that we select the individuals who will serve as governors and mayors, legislators and council members, and, in many places, judges as well. If the election process is flawed, the modernized institutions of government that you will read about in the next several chapters cannot function effectively. It is the people we put into office who will make a difference in the quality of state and local government.

Elections usually involve political parties, and they almost always involve campaigning. Both elements have changed substantially in the past several years. Many of these changes have been positive, such as the increase in interparty competition; others, such as the skyrocketing costs of campaigning, have been negative. Are these processes producing the kinds of leaders needed to take state and local governments into the twenty-first century? No one has a definitive answer, but it is certainly a subject for debate. Perhaps the true test of the capacity of state and local governments will be their ability to resolve some of the difficult questions surrounding the electoral process.

Summary

Political parties, elections, and campaigns are part of the process of democratic government. This machinery is what keeps government on track and working in the public's interest. It is exciting to observe and even more exciting to participate in. Elections are the stable part of the machinery, whereas political parties are undergoing a transformation and campaigns have taken on an entirely new look. Interparty competition is on the rise at the same time that PACs are increasing their financial influence in campaigns in many states. In other states, the legislative party caucus is emerging as a real force in campaigns and elections. The tremendous fluidity of these changes makes it difficult to assess their impact on state and local government. It is important that they have a positive effect so that nonnational governments can maintain their vitality.

Key Terms

responsible party model   blanket primary
ticket-splitting   runoff election
primary system   plurality
closed primary   nonpartisan election
open primary   coattail effect

7

Governors

The Roles of the Governor: Duties and Responsibilities

Policymaker | Chief Legislator | Chief Administrator |
Ceremonial Leader | Intergovernmental Coordinator |
Economic Development Promoter | Party Leader

Today's Governors

Gubernatorial Campaigns

Formal Powers

Tenure | Appointment Power | Veto Power | Budgetary Power |
Reorganization Power | Staffing Power | The Relevance
of the Formal Powers

Informal Powers

Tools of Persuasion | Characteristics of a Successful Governor

Removal from Office

Other Executive Branch Officials

Attorney General | Lieutenant Governor | Treasurer |
Secretary of State

The Vigor of American Governors

When Democrat James J. Florio was running for governor of New Jersey in 1989, he stated publicly that an existing budget surplus meant that no new taxes would be necessary. But the national recession hit the Garden State like a hurricane, and soon that surplus was turned into a multi-million dollar deficit.

Florio, with the cooperation of Democratic majorities in both houses of the legislature, quickly pushed through a $2.8 billion tax increase to cover the budget shortfall. The tax package also hiked state aid to New Jersey's impoverished cities and to 350 poor school districts, while drastically cutting assistance to some 250 affluent districts.

The tax increase and redistribution of wealth was met with a firestorm of criticism that made the governor's name a curse word and brought his approval ratings down to some of the lowest levels in U.S. polling history. Legislators paid the price in the following year's elections; Republican majorities took control of both houses in the traditionally Democratic state and once-popular U.S. Senator Bill Bradley nearly lost his seat in Washington.

Florio had followed his liberal instincts and done what he was convinced was right. But massive voter discontent demonstrated that he had done too much, too soon, without taking time to properly "sell" his program to the people.[1] If Florio has the gumption to run for reelection in 1994, he is likely to become one more "tax loss governor." For now, he serves as a frightening example to other governors who face budget deficits and mounting social inequities.

It has been said that the American governorship was "conceived in mistrust and born in a straitjacket." Indeed, as the excesses of some colonial governors appointed by the English Crown resulted in strong dislike and distrust of executive power by the early American settlers, the first state constitutions placed political power in the legislative branch. Early governors were typically elected by the legislature rather than by the voters, were restricted to a single one-year term of office, and had little authority.[2] Two states, Pennsylvania and Georgia, even established a plural (multimember) executive. Slowly the governorships became stronger through longer terms, popular election, and the power to veto legislation; but power did not come easily. The movement for popular democracy during the Jacksonian era led to the election of other executive branch officials, and then reaction to the excesses of Jacksonian democracy resulted in numerous independent boards and commissions in the executive branch. Although governors did gain some power, they were not able to exercise independent authority over these executive boards and commissions.

In the early 1900s, along with their efforts to democratize national politics and clean up the corrupt city political machines, progressive reformers launched a campaign to reform state government. Their principal target was the weak executive branch. Efforts to improve the state executive branch have continued throughout the twentieth century. Today we are in the latter stages of a long, highly comprehensive wave of reform that began around 1965 and has affected all the states. Its essential goal has been to increase the governor's powers to make them more commensurate with the office's increased duties and responsibilities. As a result, constitutional and statutory changes have fortified the office of the chief executive, reorganized the executive branch, and streamlined the structure and processes of the bureaucracy. The capacity of governors and the executive branch to apply state resources to solve the problems of the 1990s has thus been greatly enhanced.[3]

The Roles of the Governor: Duties and Responsibilities

In performing his or her duties and responsibilities, the governor wears the hats of top policymaker, chief legislator, chief administrator, ceremonial leader, intergovernmental coordinator, economic development promoter, and political party leader. Sometimes several of these hats must be balanced atop the governor's head at once. All things considered, these roles make the governorship one of the most difficult and challenging yet potentially rewarding jobs in the world.

Policymaker

A governor is the leading formulator and initiator of public policy in his state, from his first pronouncements as a gubernatorial candidate until the final days in office. The governor's role as chief policymaker involves many other players, including actors in the legislature, bureaucracy, courts, and voting public, but few major policies that the governor does not initiate are enacted, and success or failure depends largely on how competently the governor designs and develops policy. The governor must also follow through to see that adopted policies are put into effect as originally intended.

Some issues are transitory in nature, appearing on the agenda of state government and disappearing after appropriate actions are taken.[4] These issues are often created by external events, such as federal court decisions that mandate a certain state action, a new national law requiring a state response, or an act of nature such as a tornado, flood, or forest fire. A recent example is abortion rights, which has become a key state issue since the U.S. Supreme Court's *Webster* decision in 1989 and *Planned Parenthood* v. *Casey* in 1992.

Most policy issues, however, do not emerge suddenly out of happenstance. Perennial concerns face the governor each year: education, corrections, social welfare, the environment, and economic development. Cyclical issues also appear, increase in intensity, and slowly fade away.[5] Examples of this type are consumer protection, energy conservation, ethics in government, and reapportionment.

Several factors contribute to stronger policy leadership from the chief executives in recent years, including larger and more able staffs that are knowledgeable in important policy fields; strengthened formal powers of the office, such as longer terms and the veto power; and the assistance of the National Governors' Association (NGA), which offers ideas for policy and program development. Of no small importance is the high caliber of individuals who have won the office in recent years.[6] With increasing frequency governors have even assumed the mantle of national policy leadership, most recently in public education and reform of welfare and health care.

Chief Legislator

This gubernatorial role is closely related to that of policymaker, because legislative action is required for most of the chief executive's policies to be put into effect. In fact, the governor cannot directly introduce bills; party leaders and policy supporters in the House and Senate must actually put the bills in the hopper. Dealing with legislators is a demanding role for a governor, consuming more time than any other role and representing for many the single most difficult aspect of the job.[7]

Executive-Legislative Tensions Developing a positive relationship with the legislature requires great expenditures of a governor's time, energy, and resources. Several factors hinder smooth relations between the chief executive and the legislature, including partisanship and personality clashes. Even the different natures of the two branches can cause conflict. Governors are elected by a statewide constituency and therefore tend to take a broad, comprehensive, long-range view of issues, whereas legislators represent relatively small geographical areas and groups of voters, and are more likely to take a piecemeal approach to policymaking.[8]

According to one study, the amount of strife between the two branches is influenced by three factors: the size of the majority and the minority parties, the personalities of the governor and legislative leaders, and the nearness of an election year.[9] In twenty-nine states in 1990, the governor had to deal with a one- or two-house majority from the opposing political party. When the opposition party is strong, the governor must seek bipartisan support to get favored legislation passed. Often a governor facing a large legislative majority from the opposing party has only the veto and the possibility of mobilizing public support as weapons against the legislature. Independent governors (for example, Lowell Weicker of Connecticut) don't even have a minority party to count on.

Personality clashes can make partisan conflict worse. For example, George Deukmejian, Republican governor of California, had a reputation for being an aloof and unbending conservative, and often was not able to break stalemates with the Democratic legislature. His successor, Republican Pete Wilson, showed flexibility and a willingness to listen to legislators in successfully constructing policy coalitions in the early 1990s. The approach of statewide elections can bring gubernatorial-legislative deadlock, as incumbents may be extremely cautious or overtly partisan in trying to please (or at least not to offend) the voters while discrediting their opponents. These three conflict-producing factors are intensified during debates on the budget, when the principal policy and financial decisions are made.

Even in states where the governor's own party enjoys a large majority in both houses of the legislature, factions are certain to develop along ideological, rural-urban, geographical, or other divisions.[10] Ironically, a very large legislative majority can create the greatest problems with factionalism, largely because there is no sizable opposition to unite the majority party. Apparently a legislative majority of 60 to 70 percent helps a governor; after that, the majority party tends to degenerate into intraparty rivalries beyond the governor's control.[11] As former governor Michael Dukakis of Massachusetts lamented in the face of a 4-to-1 majority of his own party in the legislature, "You've got Democrats, you've got moderate Democrats, you've got suburban Democrats, you've got urban Democrats, you've got rural Democrats, . . ."[12] Figure 6.3, you may recall, displayed the variation in party competition among the states. Now, Figure 7.1 shows the parties of the current governors.

Executive Influence on the Legislative Agenda   Despite the difficulties in dealing with the legislature, most governors do dominate the policy agenda. The governor's influence begins with the state-of-the-state address, which kicks off each new legislative session and continues with the annual budget message in most states. During the session, the governor might threaten to veto a proposed bill or appeal directly to a particular legislator's constituency.

Most of the drama, however, takes place behind the scenes. The governor might promise high-level executive branch jobs or judgeships (either for certain legislators or for their friends) to influence legislative votes. Or she might offer some sort of pork barrel reward, such as funding a highway project in a legislator's district or approving an appropriation for the local Corn Queen Festival. Private meetings or breakfasts in the governor's mansion flatter and enlist support from small groups or individual legislators. Successful governors are usually able to relate to representatives and senators on a personal level. Many are former members of the state legislature, so they know which strings to pull to win over key supporters.

In addition, all governors have one or more legislative liaisons, who are assigned to lobby for the administration's program. Members of the governor's staff testify at legislative hearings, consult with committees and individuals on proposed bills, and even write floor speeches for friends in the legislature.[13] Most governors, however, are careful not to be perceived as unduly interfering in the internal affairs of the legislature. For example, chief executives generally do not become involved in legislative elections for majority and minority leadership positions, or they act only in a quiet and very selective way.[14] Too much meddling can bring a political backlash that undermines a governor's policy program. The role of chief legislator, then, requires a balancing act that ultimately determines the success or failure of the governor's agenda.

pork barrel

Favoritism, by a governor or other elected official, in distributing government monies or other resources to a particular program or jurisdiction.

Chief Administrator

As chief executive of the state, the governor is (in name, at least) in charge of the operations of numerous agencies, departments, boards, and commissions. In

Figure 7.1   The Governors by Party, 1992

Democrats still hold a significant advantage in governorships but have lost the Old South states of Alabama and the Carolinas. Alaska's and Connecticut's governors are independents.

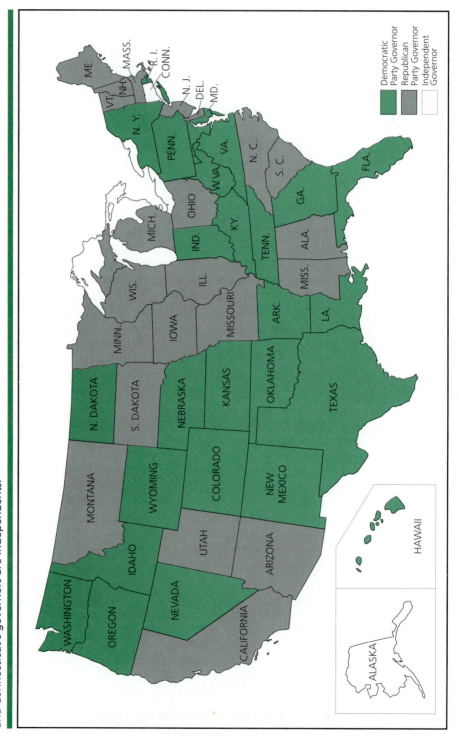

the view of many voters, the governor is directly responsible not only for pivotal matters such as the condition of the state's economy but also for such mundane things as the number and depth of potholes on state highways. Most governors are sensitive to their chief administrative responsibilities and spend a great amount of time and energy attending to them. (Problem Solving 7.1 describes how Florida's governor attacked problems in the state bureaucracy.) Constitutional and statutory reforms, including the concentration of executive power in the office of the governor and the consolidation of numerous state agencies, have considerably strengthened the governor's capacity to manage the state. (See Chapter 8 for further discussion of the bureaucracy.) The recruitment of executive support staff to help manage personnel, planning, and budgeting has also been helpful. However, most governors prefer to rely on their cabinet officials, department heads, and other staff to run state government on a day-to-day basis, while pursuing more personally rewarding activities such as policy leadership.[15]

In many respects the governor's job is comparable to that of the chief executive officer of a large corporation. The governor must manage thousands of workers, staggering sums of money, and complex organizational systems. He must establish priorities, manage crises, and balance contending interests. But there are important differences as well. For one thing, the governor is not nearly so well paid; the typical company president makes hundreds of thousands of dollars per year, whereas the average gubernatorial salary is about $80,000. More important, the governors confront several critical factors that constrain their ability to manage.

Restraints on Management   Reforms of the executive branch have allowed far more active and influential management, but significant restraints still exist. For example, the separation-of-powers principle dictates that the governor share his or her authority with the legislature and the courts, either or both of which may be politically or philosophically opposed to any given action. Changes in state agency programs, priorities, or organization typically require legislative approval, and the legality of such changes may be tested in the courts. The governor's ability to hire, fire, motivate, and punish is severely restricted by merit system rules and regulations, collective bargaining contracts, independent boards and commissions with their own personnel systems, and other elected executive branch officials, who pursue their own administrative and political agendas. Thus, the great majority of employees in the executive branch are outside the governor's formal sphere of authority and may challenge that authority almost at will. Career bureaucrats who have established their own policy direction and momentum over many years see governors come and go, but they usually march to their own tune. In sum, governors must manage through "third parties" in the three branches of government as well as in the private sector. They have very little unilateral authority.

One of the most critical functions of the governor's role as chief administrator is crisis management. Immense problems may come crashing down on the chief executive as a result of natural or manmade disasters. Some governors are

Problem Solving 7.1

Governor Lawton M. Chiles, Jr., Reinvents State Government

The Problem: Throughout the country, citizens have lost confidence in government at all levels. And there is a widespread perception that state governments, in particular, are bloated and inefficient. Florida, the fourth most populous and possibly most rapidly changing state, is a case in point.

The Solution: Reinvent state government. Lawton M. Chiles, Jr., retired from the U.S. Senate in 1986 to recover from self-diagnosed burnout. But following several years of teaching at Florida State University and the University of Florida, he ran for the governorship against incumbent Republican Robert Martinez. He won with a margin of 14 percentage points and set about transforming government in the Sunshine State.

To restore faith and confidence in state government, Chiles led a successful campaign to limit campaign contributions to $500 per donor, require public officials to report all gifts exceeding a value of $25, and give the state Ethics Commission new investigatory authority. Then he turned his attention to "rightsizing" state government.

In Chiles's view, Florida state government was too big, mismanaged, inefficient, and uninspired. As an apostle of "entrepreneurial government," the new governor proposed to cut the size of the state work force, to develop performance incentives for agencies, and to design a decentralized, customer-focused state civil service system. Moreover, he sought to reorganize the executive branch by, for example, abolishing the highway and general services departments and shifting their responsibilities to other agencies.

Most of the governor's major goals for his first year were accomplished, and his other objectives appear to be on track. Chiles's success is attributed to his bargaining and negotiation skills, his effective communications and public relations skills, and his ability to articulate a vision for Florida and determinedly stick to it. His personality and political style also have served him well. Chiles is widely respected for his honesty, values, and idealism.

The governor's abilities and skills will be tested during the remainder of his term. Florida faces severe fiscal problems and will probably have to raise taxes. Indeed, as one of the last holdouts on a personal income tax, Florida must consider a major revenue system overhaul. Chiles declares that he will seek that reform when he has fully earned the confidence of the people, but he may not have the luxury of waiting so long.

Source: Robert E. Crew, Jr., "Florida: Lawton M. Chiles, Jr., Reinventing State Government," in Thad Beyle, ed., *Governors and Hard Times* (Washington, D.C.: Congressional Quarterly, Inc., 1992), pp. 77-106.

---

unfortunate enough to have a series of crises, none of their own making, befall the state during their administration. For instance, during Milton Shapp's eight years in office, Pennsylvania suffered two terrible floods, two hurricanes, extraordinarily severe winters, major ice storms, serious forest fires, drought, and forest devastation caused by an invasion of the gypsy moth. Shapp could be forgiven for feeling like a biblical victim of God's Holy Wrath.

Governors as Managers   Because of the considerable political liabilities associated with the role of chief administrator, some of today's governors seek to avoid this responsibility. These are the **custodial (caretaker) governors,** who choose passive, perfunctory administrative roles. They generally concern themselves with ensuring that administrative agencies conduct their affairs ethically and with a reasonable degree of competence and are prepared to respond to a crisis.[16]

Managerial governors actively seek to provide policy leadership in state government and to convince the bureaucracy to follow them. Strong managerial governors during the past twenty years have included Nelson Rockefeller and Mario Cuomo of New York, Lamar Alexander of Tennessee, and Richard Lamm of Colorado. All were highly goal-directed chief administrators who managed to make a strong impact on their state bureaucracies. Carrying out the administrative role energetically and competently while paying enough attention to the competing gubernatorial roles to be re-elected appears to be the key.[17]

Former Colorado governor Richard Lamm employed a "hands on" style in managing state government. Monthly meetings were held with cabinet officers, media representatives, and gubernatorial staff. Lamm also met regularly with subgroups of agency heads and with individual cabinet members in one-on-one sessions. Occasionally, cabinet retreats were held for goal-setting.[18]

The constraints on the governor's managerial activities are not likely to lessen, nor are the potential political liabilities. The governors who courageously wade into the bureaucratic fray must invest a great deal of time and scarce political resources, yet they risk an embarrassing defeat that can drag their administrations into debilitation and disrepute. Meanwhile, social and economic changes make the management of state government increasingly complex, and the need for active managerial governors more critical than ever before. It will be instructive to observe the experiences of three former private sector executives elected governor in 1990 in Oklahoma, Nebraska, and Rhode Island.

Ceremonial Leader

Some governors thrive on ceremony and others detest it, but all spend a large portion of their time on it. Former governors remember ceremonial duties as the second most demanding of the gubernatorial roles, just behind working with the legislature.[19] Cutting the ribbon for a new highway, celebrating the arrival of a new industry, welcoming foreign businesspeople, receiving the queen of the Frog Jump Festival, announcing "Be a Good Neighbor Week," opening the state fair, and handing out high school or college diplomas are the kind of ceremonial duties that take a governor all over the state and often consume a larger portion of the workweek than any other role. Some former governors report spending more than half their time in duties relating to ceremony and public relations.[20] (See Figure 7.2 for the public schedule of Governor Lowell Weicker, Jr., on one day—April 23, 1992.)

To many management-oriented governors, the ceremonial role comprises a series of tedious events that divert them from more important responsibilities. They prefer to ask the lieutenant governor or another state official to perform

Figure 7.2

Public Schedule of Governor Lowell Weicker, April 23, 1992

Although ceremonial events dominated his formal agenda, Governor Weicker was engaged for most of the day in high pressure negotiations with union leaders concerning state spending reductions.

State of Connecticut

GOVERNOR LOWELL P. WEICKER JR.
PUBLIC SCHEDULE
April 23, 1992

Thursday, April 23

9:15 a.m.   Commissioner Jon Alander
               Commissioner Rose Alma Senatore
               Commissioner Audrey Rowe
               John Higgins-Biddle
               Executive Chambers

10:30 a.m.   * Connecticut State Fire Academy groundbreaking
               Perimeter Road
               Windsor Locks

11:30 a.m.   Litchfield High School students
               Executive Chambers

2:00 p.m.   Carol White, Susan Collins, Harry Bellardini
               U.S. Small Business Administration
               Hartford Region
               Executive Chambers

2:30 p.m.   Harry Hartley
               University of Connecticut's Men's and Women's
               Basketball Teams
               Executive Chambers

3:00 p.m.   John Wilhelm
               Hotel & Restaurant Employees International Union
               Executive Chambers

5:30-   Grassroots Tennis reception
7:30 p.m.   Governor's Residence
               Hartford

        * Governor Weicker will make brief remarks at the fire
training school groundbreaking, marking the beginning of
construction for an $11.3 million facility. A total of four
buildings with 70,000 square feet of space on 9.5 acres of land will
be built on a site at Bradley International Airport, next to the New
England Air Museum on Perimeter Road. From 4,000 to 10,000 state
firefighters are expected to be trained there every year, once the
facility is finished in 1994.

Source: Office of the governor of the state of Connecticut.

these tasks for them. But a chief executive otherwise embroiled in struggles with the legislature and the bureaucracy—as Weicker was on that day in April 1992—may welcome a chance to shake hands and visit with the people. Moreover, the ceremonial role brings favorable publicity and cultivates voter support for the next election by keeping the governor in the spotlight and in touch with constituents.

Intergovernmental Coordinator

During the 1960s and 1970s, many governors began to question whether their delegations in Congress were adequately representing state interests. The main factor that caught the governors' attention was the enormous growth in intergovernmental financial relations, as the number and size of federal grants-in-aid to states and localities mushroomed.

The governor serves as the major point of contact between his or her state and the president, Congress, and national agencies. For example, Governor Steve Cowper of Alaska coordinated cleanup efforts with the U.S. Coast Guard, the Environmental Protection Agency, and Exxon Corporation following the disastrous Exxon Valdez oil spill in April 1989. State-to-state relations in order to manage conflicts or settle disputes over water pollution and other environmental concerns are carried out through the governor's office. At the local level, governors are involved in allocating grants-in-aid, promoting cooperation and coordination in economic development activities, and a variety of other matters.

The governors' role as intergovernmental coordinator is most visible at the national level, where they are aided by the National Governors' Association and their state's Washington office. In the 1960s, the NGA was transformed from a social club into a lobbying and research organization with a staff of more than one hundred and considerable clout. It now meets two times a year in full session to adopt policy positions and to share governors' problems and policy solutions. (The governors also meet in separate regional organizations.) The NGA's Center for Policy Research analyzes important issues and distributes its analyses to the states, and the State Services Branch offers practical and technical assistance to governors. In addition, more than thirty-two states have established Washington offices to fight for their interests in Congress, the White House, and, perhaps most important, the many federal agencies that interact with states on a daily basis.[21] A governor's official inquiry can help speed up the progress of federal grant-in-aid funds or gain special consideration for a new federal facility.

The governor's role as intergovernmental coordinator is becoming more important with each passing year. It reflects the elevated position of the states in the scheme of American federalism and increasing state importance in national and international affairs. Acting together, the governors have exercised national policy leadership on critical issues such as waste management (see Chapter 18), public education (Chapter 15), welfare reform (Chapter 3), and economic development (Chapter 16).

Economic Development Promoter

As promoter of economic development, a governor works to recruit industry from out of state and promote economic growth from sources within the state. Governors attend industrial fairs, visit headquarters of firms interested in locating in the state, telephone and write promising business contacts, and welcome business leaders. The role may take the governor and the state economic development team to Japan, Korea, Germany, and other nations, but it mostly entails making the state's climate "good for business" through improving infrastructure, arranging tax and service deals, and other strategies designed to entice out-of-state firms to relocate and encourage in-state businesses to stay or to expand. Often the governor's office of economic development directs a public relations campaign organized around themes such as "Arkansas Means Business" or "Maryland—The Incentives Have Never Been Better."

When a state enjoys success in economic development, the governor usually receives (or at least claims) a major portion of the credit. Economic decline means voter disapproval.[22] For example, Michael Dukakis campaigned for the Democratic nomination for president in 1988 by emphasizing Massachusetts's surge in high-technology industry, which turned a $300 million budget deficit into a surplus of $217 million before economic growth leveled off and then nose-dived as economic recession battered New England in 1989 and 1990. Dukakis' popularity ratings fell with the Bay State economy, and he decided not to run for reelection. Tennessee's governor Lamar Alexander convinced Nissan to build small trucks and General Motors to construct its state-of-the-art Saturn plant in his state rather than in any of numerous competing states, and left office as one of the Volunteer State's most popular governors in years. Sometimes the personal touch of a governor can mean the difference between an industrial plum and economic stagnation; or, as in the case of Illinois, it can determine the nature of a summer's sports entertainment. Vigorous lobbying by Governor James R. Thompson helped keep the White Sox in Chicago.

Party Leader

By claiming the top elected post in the state, the governor becomes the highest-ranking member of his or her political party. This role is not as powerful as it was several decades ago, when the governor controlled the state's party apparatus and legislative leadership, and had strong influence over party nominations for seats in the state legislature and executive branch. The widespread adoption of primaries, which have replaced party conventions, has put nominations largely in the hands of the voters. And legislative leaders are a much more independent breed than they were, for example, in Illinois in 1969, when Governor Richard Ogilvie (1969–1973) brought up the need for income tax legislation at a breakfast meeting at the mansion. Senate President Russ Arrington angrily asked, "Who is the crazy son of a bitch who is going to sponsor this thing?" The governor calmly replied, "Russ, you are." And he did.[23]

Such an order is unheard of today. Still, some governors get involved in legislative elections through campaign aid, endorsement, or other actions. If the governor's choice wins, he or she may feel a special debt to the governor. The party remains at least marginally useful to the governor for three principal reasons.[24] Legislators from the governor's own party are more likely to support the chief executive's programs. Communication lines to the president and national cabinet members are more likely to be open when the president and the governor are members of the same party. And, finally, the party remains the most effective means by which to win nomination to the governor's office (although independents were elected in 1990 in Alaska and Connecticut).

As a growing number of states have become characterized by two competitive political parties, governors find that they must work with the opposition if their legislative programs are to pass. In state legislatures still heavily dominated by one party, the governor must try to build a majority coalition of factions in support of his or her legislative agenda.

Today's Governors

As the foregoing discussion demonstrates, being governor is a high-pressure, physically demanding, emotionally draining job. As political scientist Larry Sabato states, "Governors must possess many skills to be successful. They are expected to be adroit administrators, dexterous executives, expert judges of people, combative yet sensitive and inspiring politicians, decorous chiefs of state, shrewd party tacticians, and polished public relations managers."[25] The job is difficult from a professional perspective, but it is also hard on the governor's private life. It consumes an enormous amount of waking hours, at the expense of family activities and hobbies.

Fortunately, governorships are attracting better-qualified chief executives than ever before (Louisiana notwithstanding). These "New Breed" governors, first described by Larry Sabato in *Goodbye to Goodtime Charlie: The American Governorship Transformed,*[26] are a far cry from the figureheads of the eighteenth and nineteenth centuries and the back-slapping, cigar-smoking wheeler-dealers of the first half of the present century. Sabato's study of 357 governors holding office from 1950 to 1981 revealed "a thoroughly trained, well regarded, and capable new breed of state chief executive."[27] The trend continues in the 1990s, personified by moderate Republican governors Jim Edgar of Illinois and Pete Wilson of California. Table 7.1 provides a list of the 1992 governors.

The governor of today is younger, better educated, and better prepared for the job than his or her predecessors. The average age has declined by about five years since the 1940s. (The legal minimum age ranges from eighteen in California and Washington to thirty in most states.) Formal education has averaged around eighteen years since 1950 (the general population averages 11.1 years),[28] and approximately two-thirds of the governors since 1960 have held law degrees. More than half of today's governors paid their political dues in state

Table 7.1

1992 Occupants of Nation's State-houses

State	Governor	Party	Year of Next Election
Alabama	Guy Hunt	R	1994
Alaska	Walter J. Hickel	I	1994
Arizona	J. Fife Smythington	R	1994
Arkansas	Bill Clinton	D	1994
California	Pete Wilson	R	1994
Colorado	Roy R. Romer	D	1994
Connecticut	Lowell P. Weicker, Jr.	I	1994
Delaware	Michael N. Castle	R	1992
Florida	Lawton Chiles	D	1994
Georgia	Zell Miller	D	1994
Hawaii	John Waihee	D	1994
Idaho	Cecil D. Andrus	D	1994
Illinois	Jim Edgar	R	1994
Indiana	Evan Bayh	D	1992
Iowa	Terry E. Branstad	R	1994
Kansas	Joan M. Finney	D	1994
Kentucky	Brereton Jones	D	1995
Louisiana	Edwin Edwards	D	1995
Maine	John R. McKernan, Jr.	R	1994
Maryland	William Donald Shaefer	D	1994
Massachusetts	William Weld	R	1994
Michigan	John Engler	R	1994
Minnesota	Arne Carlson	R	1994
Mississippi	Kirk Fordice	R	1995
Missouri	John Ashcroft	R	1992

**Table 7.1
(cont.)**

State	Governor	Party	Year of Next Election
Montana	Stan Stephens	R	1992
Nebraska	E. Benjamin Nelson	D	1994
Nevada	Robert J. Miller	D	1994
New Hampshire	Judd Gregg	R	1992
New Jersey	James J. Florio	D	1993
New Mexico	Bruce King	D	1994
New York	Mario M. Cuomo	D	1994
North Carolina	James G. Martin	R	1992
North Dakota	George Sinner	D	1992
Ohio	George V. Voinovich	R	1994
Oklahoma	David Walters	D	1994
Oregon	Barbara Roberts	D	1994
Pennsylvania	Robert P. Casey	D	1994
Rhode Island	Bruce Sundlun	D	1992
South Carolina	Carroll A. Campbell, Jr.	R	1994
South Dakota	George S. Mickelson	R	1994
Tennessee	Ned Ray McWherter	D	1994
Texas	Ann W. Richards	D	1994
Utah	Norman H. Bangerter	R	1992
Vermont	Howard B. Dean	D	1992
Virginia	L. Douglas Wilder	D	1993
Washington	Booth Gardner	D	1992
West Virginia	Gaston Caperton	D	1992
Wisconsin	Tommy G. Thompson	R	1994
Wyoming	Mike Sullivan	D	1994

legislatures, gaining an understanding of important issues confronting the state, a working familiarity with influential figures in government and the private sector, and a practical knowledge of the legislative process and other inner secrets of state government. Twenty-eight percent have served previously as an elected state executive branch official, and 27 percent have a background in law enforcement (serving as solicitor, sheriff, or attorney general). Around 14 percent have held a local elective office. The attractiveness of the governor's office is evident in the fact that four current chief executives, including Carroll Campbell of South Carolina and James Florio of New Jersey, left a congressional seat to take office. Only 8 percent of the governors serving from 1970 to 1987 did not hold a previous position in government.[29]

Though still predominantly white males, today's governors are more representative of population characteristics than former chief executives were. Several Hispanics have served as governors in recent years, including Tony Anaya of New Mexico and Bob Martinez of Florida. And in 1989, the first African-American was elected governor—L. Douglas Wilder of Virginia. In earlier years, several women succeeded their husbands as governor, but since 1974 eight women have won governorships on their own: the late Ella Grasso (Connecticut, 1974, 1978), Dixy Lee Ray (Washington, 1976), Martha Layne Collins (Kentucky, 1983), Madeleine Kunin (Vermont, 1984, 1986, 1988), Kay Orr (Nebraska, 1986), and three women who took governorships in 1990: Joan M. Finney (Kansas), Barbara Roberts (Oregon), and Ann W. Richards (Texas). In addition, Rose Mofford became governor of Arizona in 1988, when Evan Mecham was forced out of office.

Gubernatorial Campaigns

The lure of the governorship must be weighed against the financial costs. It has become immensely expensive to campaign for the office. Because candidates can no longer rely on their political party to support them, they must solicit huge sums of money from donors to pay for the new technology of campaigning—political consultants, opinion polls, air travel, advertisements in the print and broadcast media, telephone banks, and direct mailings. Moreover, the growing attractiveness of the office has led to more competitive (and expensive) primary and general election races. During the 53 governors' elections from 1987 to 1990, 376 candidates actively sought the governor's office (7.1 candidates per election); 19 individuals filed for their state's top office in California alone.[30] To date, the most costly governor's race was the 1990 election in California, in which Pete Wilson defeated Dianne Feinstein; $53.2 million was spent. This official figure does not include hidden donations, such as free transportation, telephones, and other in-kind contributions from supporters.

Several expenditure patterns have been identified in gubernatorial races. Elections tend to cost more when the contest

- is close.
- involves unseating an incumbent.
- involves a partisan shift (that is, when a Democrat succeeds a Republican, or vice versa).
- is held in a highly populated state, particularly if it is also large in territory (for example, Texas, California, New York).[31]

On a cost-per-vote basis, races in states with a widely scattered population or hard-to-reach media markets, such as Alaska or Nevada, tend to be most expensive. Cost per vote in recent gubernatorial elections ranged from $114.26 in Alaska to only 69 cents in Georgia.[32]

Money means a lot in politics, but it doesn't mean everything. One contemporary veteran of political campaigns reflects that "everyone knows that half the money spent in a political campaign is wasted. The trouble is that nobody knows which half."[33] Lewis Lehrman spent $13.9 million in the 1982 race in New York, which he lost, and Tom Bradley sacrificed $8.7 million to lose in California that same year. Perhaps participants are finally beginning to discover which half is wasted. According to expenditure reports for 1982–1991, the rate of increase for the costs of governors' races is slowing. A principal reason may be that the new campaign technologies are now in place throughout the states. The tremendous leap in campaign expenditures during the 1970s and 1980s may have been a one-time phenomenon.[34]

An incumbent governor running for re-election stands an excellent chance of victory; 74 to 80 percent have retained their seats since 1970. Incumbents enjoy a number of important advantages, including the opportunity to cultivate both popularity with the voters and campaign donations from interest groups. However, re-election is no sure thing. Budget and tax woes led voters to toss several chief executives out of office in 1990, including three who, as candidates, had pledged not to raise taxes, then did so after election to their first term. Ten sitting governors eligible for re-election in 1990 chose not to run, in many cases because of voter antipathy to tax increases on their watch. Taxes will be a burning issue in the 1992 governors' races as well, and many incumbents will be running scared.

Formal Powers

formal powers

Powers of the governor derived from the state constitution.

A variety of powers are attached to the governor's office. Governor's **formal powers**—those provided for in the state's constitution—include the tenure of the office, the power of appointment, the power to veto legislation, the responsibility for preparing the budget, the authority to reorganize the executive branch, and the right to use professional staff in the governor's office. These powers give governors the *potential* to carry out the duties of office as they see fit. However, the formal powers vary considerably from state to state. Some governors' offices are considered strong and others weak. Also, the fact that

informal powers

Powers of the governor derived from nonconstitutional sources.

these powers are available does not mean that they are used fully or even partly. Equally important are the **informal powers** that governors have at their disposal. These are potentially empowering features of the job or the person that are not expressly provided for in law. Many of the informal powers are associated with personal traits on which the chief executive relies to carry out the duties and responsibilities of the office.

Both sets of powers have increased over the past several decades, and governors are more influential than ever before because of their enhanced formal powers and the personal qualities they bring to the state capital. The most successful governors are those who employ their informal powers to maximize the formal powers. The term for this concept is *synergism,* a condition in which the total effect of two distinct sets of attributes working together is greater than the sum of their effects when acting independently. An influential governor, then, is one who can skillfully combine formal and informal powers to maximum effectiveness.

Tenure

There are two aspects of the governor's tenure power: the duration (number of years) of a term of office, and the number of terms that an individual may serve as governor. Both have been slowly but steadily expanding over the past two hundred years. From the onerous restriction to a single one-year term of office placed on ten of the first thirteen governors, the duration has evolved to the standard today of two or more four-year terms (see Table 7.2). In addition, gubernatorial elections have become distinct from national elections, now that most states hold them in nonpresidential election years. As a result, there is some assurance that the voters will focus their attention on issues important to the state rather than allowing national politics to contaminate state election outcomes.

The importance of longer consecutive terms of office is readily apparent. A two-year governorship condemns the incumbent to a perpetual re-election campaign. As soon as the winner takes office, planning must begin for the next election. For a new governor, the initial year in office is typically spent getting used to the job. In addition, the first-term, first-year chief executive must live with the budget priorities adopted by his or her predecessor. A two-year governorship, therefore, does not encourage success in the role of either chief legislator or policy leader. Nor does it enable the governor to have much effect on the bureaucracy, whose old hands are likely to treat the governor as a mere bird of passage, making him virtually a lame duck when his term begins. As Governor Alfred E. Smith of New York observed after serving four two-year terms during the 1920s, "One hardly has time to locate the knob on the Statehouse door."[35]

In contrast, the governor who is restricted to a single four-year term is a bit less confined in carrying out his responsibilities. He really has only two years to put his programs and priorities in place, sandwiched on one side by the initial

Table 7.2

Tenure Provisions for Governors

Four-Year Term, No Restrictions on Re-election	Arizona California Colorado Connecticut Idaho Illinois Iowa Massachusetts Michigan	Minnesota Montana New York North Dakota Texas Utah Washington Wisconsin Wyoming
Four-Year Term, Restricted to Two Terms	Alabama Alaska Arkansas Delaware Florida Georgia Hawaii Indiana Kansas Louisiana Maine Maryland Missouri	Nebraska Nevada New Jersey North Carolina Ohio Oklahoma Oregon Pennsylvania South Carolina South Dakota Tennessee West Virginia
Four-Year Term, Consecutive Re-election Prohibited	Kentucky Mississippi	New Mexico Virginia
Two-Year Term, No Restrictions on Re-election	New Hampshire Rhode Island	Vermont

Source: *The Book of the States 1990–91* (Lexington, Ky.: Council of State Governments, 1990). Reprinted with permission. Copyright by The Council of State Governments.

"learning year" and on the other by the lame-duck period. The incumbent needs another four-year term to design new programs properly, acquire the necessary legislative support to put them into place, and get a handle on the bureaucracy by appointing competent political supporters to top posts. A duration of eight years in office also enhances the governor's intergovernmental role, particularly by giving him or her sufficient time to win leadership positions in organizations such as the National Governors' Association. The record of an eight-year chief executive stands on its own, untainted by the successes or failures of the office's previous inhabitant.

The average time actually served by governors has grown steadily since 1955 as a result of fewer restrictions on tenure. The gubernatorial graybeard is Illinois governor Jim Thompson, who stepped down after serving his fourth four-year term in 1990—a twentieth-century record. Long periods in office strengthen the governor's position as policy leader, chief legislator, chief administrator, and intergovernmental coordinator, as shown by the policy legacy left in Illinois by Thompson.[36]

There is still some resistance to unlimited tenure. More than one re-election creates fears of political machines and possible abuses of office. And, pragmatically speaking, a long period of a "safe governorship" can result in stagnation and loss of vigor in the office. Even in states that do not restrict governors to two consecutive terms, the informal custom is to refrain from seeking a third term.

Appointment Power

Surveys of past governors indicate that they consider appointment power to be the most important weapon in their arsenal when it comes to managing the state bureaucracy. The ability to appoint one's own people to top positions in the executive branch also enhances the policy management role. When individuals who share the governor's basic philosophy and feel loyal to the chief executive and her programs direct the operations of state government, the governor's policies are more likely to be successful. Strong appointment authority can even help the governor's legislative role. The actual or implicit promise of important administrative and especially judicial positions can generate a surprising amount of support from ambitious lawmakers.

Unfortunately for today's governors, Jacksonian democracy lives on in the plural executive. Most states continue to provide for popular election of numerous officials in the executive branch, including insurance commissioners, public utility commissioners, and secretaries of agriculture. Proponents of popular election claim that these officials make political decisions and therefore should be directly responsible to the electorate. Opponents contend that governors and legislators can make these decisions more properly, based on the recommendations of appointed executive branch professionals who are not beholden to special interests.

Perhaps appointment authority should depend on the office under consideration. Those offices that tend to cater to special interests, such as agriculture, insurance, and education, probably should be appointive. Less substantive offices such as secretary of state or treasurer probably should be appointive as well. However, it makes sense to *elect* an auditor and an attorney general, because they require some independence in carrying out their responsibilities. (The auditor oversees the management and spending of state monies; the attorney general is concerned with the legality of executive and legislative branch activities.)

Many governors are weakened by their inability to appoint directly the heads of major state agencies, boards, and commissions. These high-ranking officials make policy decisions in the executive branch, but if they owe their jobs in whole or in part to legislative appointment, the governor's authority as chief executive

Table 7.3

**Separately Elected
State Officials**

Office	Number of States Electing
Governor	50
Lieutenant governor	46
Attorney general	43
Treasurer	38
Secretary of state	34
Education (superintendent or board)	29
Auditor	27
Secretary of agriculture	12
Controller	10
Public utilities commissioner	8
Insurance commissioner	8
Land commissioner	5
Labor commissioner	4
Mines commissioner	1
Adjutant general (National Guard)	1

Source: Adapted from *The Book of the States, 1990–91* (Lexington, Ky.: Council of State Governments, 1990), pp. 83–84.

is diminished significantly. Though nominally in charge of these executive branch agencies, the governor is severely constrained in her ability to manage.

The fragmented nature of power in the executive branch diminishes accountability and frustrates governors. Former Oregon governor Tom McCall once lamented that "we have run our state like a pick-up orchestra, where the members meet at a dance, shake hands with each other, and start to play."[37] When the assorted performers are not appointed by the chief executive, their performance may lack harmony, to say the least.

Most reformers interested in "good government" agree on the need to consolidate power in the governor's office by reducing the number of statewide elected officials and increasing the power of appointment to policy-related posts in the executive branch. But the number of elected executive branch officials has remained virtually the same since 1965.[38] Table 7.3 shows the range and number of separately elected officials. The largest number are in North Dakota, where twelve statewide offices are filled through elections: governor, lieutenant governor, secretary of state, attorney general, agricultural commissioner, chief state school officer, treasurer, labor commissioner, tax commissioner, two insurance commissioners, and utility commissioner. At the bottom of the list are the reformer's ideal states, Maine and New Jersey, which elect only the governor. The average number of elected officials is about eight.

Why has it been so difficult to abolish multiple statewide offices? Primarily because incumbent tax commissioners, agricultural commissioners, and others have strong supporters in the electorate. Special-interest groups, such as the insurance industry, benefit from having an elected official—the insurance commissioner—representing their concerns at the highest level of state government. They can be counted on for fierce resistance to proposals to make the office appointive. Additional resistance may be credited to the legacy of Jacksonian democracy; many citizens simply like having an opportunity to vote on a large number of executive branch officials.

Appointment powers are weakened by separately elected or appointed officials, but governors do select nearly 50 percent of the top executive branch personnel. Governors have been particularly adept at winning appointment power for top posts in new state agencies for human services, the environment, natural resources, highways, and agriculture, although approval of one or both houses of the legislature must usually be obtained.[39]

Professional Jobs in State Government   The vast majority of jobs in the states are filled through objective civil service (merit system) rules and processes. Governors are generally quite content to avoid meddling with civil service positions (see Chapter 8), and a few have actually sought to transfer many **patronage** appointments—those based on personal or party loyalty—to an independent, merit-based civil service.[40] Gubernatorial sacrifice of patronage power is comprehensible in view of the time and headaches associated with naming political supporters to jobs in the bureaucracy. There is always the possibility of embarrassment or scandal if the governor accidentally appoints a person with a criminal record, a clear conflict of interest, a propensity for sexual harassment, or other inappropriate behavior. Moreover, those who are denied coveted appointments are likely to be angry. One governor is quoted as stating: "I got into a lot of hot water because I refused to appoint some of the more prominent Democrats around the state." According to another, who was about to name a new member of a state commission, "I now have twenty-three good friends who want on the Racing Commission. [Soon] I'll have twenty-two enemies and one ingrate."[41] A governor benefits from a stable, competent civil service that hires, pays, and promotes on the basis of knowledge, job-related skills, and abilities rather than party affiliation or friendship with a legislator or other politician.

The Power to Fire   The power of the governor to hire is not necessarily accompanied by the power to fire. Except in cases of extreme misbehavior or corruption, it is very difficult to remove a subordinate from office. For instance, if a governor attempts to dismiss the secretary of agriculture, he or she can anticipate an orchestrated roar of outrage from legislators, bureaucrats, and farm groups. The upshot is that the political costs of dismissing an appointee can be greater than the pain of simply living with the problem. In settings where the governor indirectly appoints top officials, it may be nearly impossible to sack an

patronage

The informal power of a governor (or other officeholder) to make appointments on the basis of party membership, and to dispense contracts and other favors to political supporters.

undesirable employee. For example, in Missouri the governor appoints eight members of the State Board of Education, who then choose a commissioner of education. The governor cannot sanction or remove the commissioner except through the State Board.[42] In the case of merit-selected civil servants, formal dismissal procedures bypass the chief executive entirely.

Several U.S. Supreme Court rulings have greatly restricted the governor's power to dismiss or remove from office the political appointees of previous governors. In the most recent case, *Rutan et al.* v. *Republican Party of Illinois* (1990), the Court found that failure to hire, retain, or promote an individual because of his or her political or party affiliation violates that person's First Amendment rights.[43] Despite these limitations, a good appointment to a top agency post is the best way for a governor to influence the bureaucracy. By carefully choosing a competent and loyal agency head, the governor can more readily bring about significant changes in the programs and operations of that agency. Where appointment powers are circumscribed, the chief executive must muster his or her informal powers to influence activities of the state bureaucracy, or rely on the reasoned judgment of professional civil servants.

Veto Power

The power to veto bills passed by the legislature is an important method for exercising the role of chief legislator. It is also a means for influencing the bureaucracy: The governor can strike out an appropriation for a particular agency's programs if that agency has antagonized the governor. Often the mere threat of a veto is enough to persuade a recalcitrant legislature to see the governor's point of view and compromise on the language of a bill. Vetoes are not easy to override. Most states require a majority of three-fifths or two-thirds of the legislature, depending on the type of veto the governor has employed.

package veto

The governor's formal power to veto a bill in its entirety.

Types of Vetoes The veto can take several forms. The **package veto,** for instance, is the governor's rejection of a bill in its entirety. All governors except North Carolina's hold package veto authority. (Almost every year the incumbent governor asks the North Carolina legislature for this power, and the request is just as regularly rejected.) The package veto is the oldest form available to governors, having been adopted first in the original constitutions of New York and Massachusetts.

line item veto

The governor's formal power to veto separate items in a bill instead of the entire piece of proposed legislation.

The **line item veto** allows the governor to strike out one or more sections of a bill, permitting the remaining provisions to become law. It is not available at the national level, much to the frustration of recent presidents. The line item veto was first adopted by Georgia and Texas in 1868 and quickly spread to other states.[44] Only Indiana, Maine, Nevada, New Hampshire, Rhode Island, Vermont, and, of course, North Carolina forbid this gubernatorial power. Eleven states permit a hybrid form of line item veto in which the governor may choose to reduce the dollar amount of a proposed item in order to hold down state expenditures or cut back support for a particular program.

pocket veto

The governor's power to withhold approval or disapproval of a bill after the legislature has adjourned for the session, thus vetoing the measure.

executive amendment

A type of veto used by the governor to reject a bill, and also to recommend changes that would cause the governor to reconsider the bill's approval.

The **pocket veto,** which is available in fifteen states, allows the governor to reject a bill by refusing to sign it after the legislature has adjourned. In three states (Hawaii, Utah, Virginia) the legislature can reconvene to vote on a pocket veto. Otherwise, the bill dies. A governor might use the pocket veto to avoid giving the legislature a chance to override a formal veto, or to abstain from going on record against a proposed piece of legislation.

A fourth type of veto is the **executive amendment,** formally provided for in fifteen states and informally used in several others. With this power a governor may veto a bill, recommend changes that would make the bill acceptable, and then send it back to the legislature for reconsideration. If the legislature concurs with the suggestions, the governor signs the bill into law.

Use of the Veto   The actual use of the veto varies by time, state, and issue. Some states, such as California and New York, often record high numbers of vetoes, while others, like Virginia, report few. On average, governors veto around 5 percent of the bills that reach their desks.[45] The variation among states reflects the tensions and conflicts that exist between the governor and the legislature. The largest number of vetoes typically occurs in states with divided party control of the executive and legislative branches. During the 1980s, Governors Bruce Babbitt of Arizona, John Carlin of Kansas, and Jim Thompson of Illinois liberally employed the veto in dealing with legislatures dominated by the opposition party.

Vetoes are cast for many different reasons, including policies and budget items opposed by the governor philosophically, as well as issues on which the governor wants to make a symbolic, and powerful, statement. Occasionally, the governor stands as the last line of defense against a flawed bill backed by the legislature because of powerful interest groups. It is not unknown for legislators to secretly ask the governor to veto a questionable bill they have just passed because it is politically popular.[46]

Although the overall rate of veto utilization has remained steady, the percentage of successful legislative overrides has increased in the past two decades from 2 to 8 percent or more, depending on the year.[47] This is an indication of the growing strength and assertiveness of state legislatures, the increase in conflict between the executive and legislative branches, and the prevalence of split-party government. Differences in party affiliation between the governor and the legislative majority probably provoke more vetoes than any other situation, especially when party ideology and platforms openly clash.

Conversely, when mutual respect and cooperation prevail between the two branches, the governor rarely needs to threaten or actually use the veto. Most governors interact with the legislature throughout the bill adoption process. Before rejecting a bill, the governor will request comments from key legislators, affected state agencies, and concerned interest groups. He may ask the attorney general for a legal opinion. And before actually vetoing proposed legislation, the governor usually provides advance notification to legislative leaders, along with a final opportunity to make amendments.[48]

The veto can be a powerful offensive weapon that may be used to obtain a legislator's support for a different bill dear to the governor's heart. The governor may, for instance, hold one bill hostage to a veto until the legislature enacts another bill that he favors. Arizona Governor Bruce Babbitt threatened to veto a popular highway bill unless a teacher salary increase was passed—"No kids, no concrete." The legislature capitulated in the end.[49] Wisconsin governor Tommy G. Thompson's creative use of the line item veto during 1987–1989 inspired a legislative revolt. Thompson applied the veto on 290 occasions, even striking out certain words and letters to radically change the meaning of text. For example, he extended the maximum time a juvenile can be held in detention from 48 hours to 10 days (by striking out certain letters in the words of the bill). The legislature responded by placing a constitutional amendment prohibiting "pick-a-letter" vetoes on the ballot in 1990; it was approved by the voters.

Budgetary Power

The governor's budget effectively sets the legislative agenda at the beginning of each session. By framing the important policy issues and attaching price tags to them, the governor can determine the scope and direction of budgetary debates in the legislature and ensure that they reflect his overall philosophy on taxing and spending. All but three governors now have the authority to appoint (and remove) the budget director and to formulate and submit the executive budget to the legislature. In Mississippi, South Carolina, and Texas, budget authority is shared with the legislature or with other elected executive branch officials. And in Mississippi as well as Texas, two budgets are prepared each year, one by the governor and one by a legislative budget board.

Because full budgetary authority is normally housed in the office of the chief executive, the governor not only drives the budgetary process in the legislature but also enjoys a source of important leverage in the bureaucracy. The executive budget can be used to influence programs, spending, and other activities of state agencies.[50] For example, uncooperative administrators may discover that their agency's slice of the budget pie is smaller than expected, while those who are attentive to the concerns of the governor may receive strong financial support. Rational, objective criteria usually determine departmental budget allocations, but a subtle threat from the governor's office does wonders to instill a cooperative agency attitude.[51]

The governor's budget requests are rarely, if ever, enacted exactly as put forward. Rather, they are usually argued and debated thoroughly in both houses of the legislature. Ultimately, "the governor may propose, but the legislature disposes." In fact, no monies may be appropriated without formal action by the legislature. (The budget process is discussed further in Chapter 8.)

Reorganization Power

Reorganization power is primarily relevant in the governor's role of chief administrator. It refers to the governor's ability to create and abolish state agencies, departments, and other offices and to reallocate administrative responsibilities among them. Reorganizations are usually aimed at the upper levels of the bureaucracy, in order to streamline the executive branch and thereby make it work more efficiently and effectively. The basic premise is that the governor, as chief manager of the bureaucracy, needs the authority to alter administrative structures and processes to meet changing political, economic, and citizen demands. For instance, serious and recurring problems in delivering social services may call for a new social services department with expanded powers. A governor with strong reorganization power can bring about such a department without approval of the legislature.

Traditionally, legislatures have been responsible for organization of state government; and in the absence of a constitutional amendment to the contrary or a statutory grant of reorganization power to the governor, they still are. A survey of thirty-nine governors during the mid-1960s asked what powers they lacked that could help them be more effective. Forty-six percent named reorganization,[52] second only to appointment power (67 percent). Apparently many of the legislatures paid attention and recognized the need to grant their chief executives more discretion in organizing the bureaucracy.

executive order

A rule, regulation, or policy issued unilaterally by the governor to affect executive branch operations or activities.

Today, twenty-four states specifically authorize their chief executive to reorganize the bureaucracy through **executive order.** This means that the governor can make needed administrative changes when she deems it necessary. All governors are permitted through constitution (eight states), statute (thirty-six), or custom (six) to issue directives to the executive branch in times of emergency, such as natural disasters or civil unrest.[53]

Administrative reorganization takes place under the assumption that properly designed government improves bureaucratic performance by cutting down on duplication, waste, and inefficiency.[54] The reorganizations that took place in Iowa in the mid-1980s and West Virginia in 1989 are cases in point. Governor Terry Branstad's restructuring program eliminated fifty departments and forty-two boards and commissions, along with almost a thousand state government positions in Iowa. Total savings were estimated at $40 million.[55] West Virginia governor Gaston Caperton, with legislative approval, consolidated 150 executive boards and agencies into 7 departments. Typically, however, reorganization achieves modest savings, if any at all.[56]

cabinet system

The organization whereby the heads of the major executive branch agencies or departments meet formally with the governor on matters of public policy and administration.

Types of Reorganization   Virtually all states have some form of cabinet structure to advise the governor and to coordinate policies and programs. There are three possible formats within a cabinet structure. The first, the **cabinet system,** is composed of state agency heads representing the most important departments, such as administration and finance, corrections, health, social services, transportation, public works, agriculture, natural resources, and labor. Cabinet size ranges from four agency heads in Wyoming to forty-two in Indiana. These members may meet regularly either as a cabinet or at the call of the governor. Such meetings can improve coordination, communications, and interpersonal relations among executive branch officials. Some governors, including James Hunt of North Carolina and Richard Lamm of Colorado, have held regular cabinet retreats away from the immediate pressures of the capital. Agency heads are key figures in the executive branch. They not only translate the governor's values and policy agenda into agency implementation but also contribute much themselves to improving state government operations. Their performance is one measure of the governor's success as chief executive.[57]

subcabinet system

The organization whereby the heads of specified state executive branch agencies or departments meet formally with the governor on matters that concern a particular problem, government function, or policy field.

A second format is the **subcabinet system,** currently in use in approximately half the states. Under this system, agency heads are assigned to functional, or working, groups to provide the governor with administrative and policy advice in specific fields such as economic development, human services, and personnel practices. Subcabinets are helpful for concentrating attention on the most pressing items on the state policy agenda and exploring methods for coordinating attacks on especially difficult problems that cut across agency lines, such as affirmative action requirements or drug-related violence.

A third organizational format is the **task force,** an ad hoc assemblage of agency heads, other high-level officials, and sometimes private-sector individuals brought together on a temporary basis to confront a special problem or issue. Several states have used this form of organization to manage block grants, to plan for the possibility of a natural disaster, or to pursue economic development opportunities.

task force

A temporary group of state executive branch officials and/or private individuals who meet with the governor to address short-term policy or administrative problems.

A growing number of states are making use of all three organizational formats to cope with increasingly complicated economic and technological policy issues. Newer experiments with executive branch reorganization are also appearing. For example, New Jersey governor Thomas Kean focused on internal (intradepartmental) restructuring of state agencies in 1982. A team of managers from the public and private sectors found that too many midlevel managers were clustered in the agencies, making the organization chart resemble "a nuclear reactor rather than a pyramid."[58] An evaluation of changes implemented during the subsequent reorganization, which included streamlining management levels, grouping similar functions together, and reallocating resources, found most public managers agreed that improved performance had resulted.

The Politics of Reorganization   Reorganization is a politically charged process. Mere talk of it sounds alarms in the halls of the legislature, in the honeycombs of state office buildings, and in the offices of interest groups. Reorganization attempts usually spawn bitter controversy and conflict inside and outside state government as assorted vested interests fight for favorite programs and organizational turf. Accordingly, reorganization proposals are frequently defeated or amended in the legislature, or even abandoned by discouraged chief executives. In a study of state reorganizations attempted between 1900 and 1975, James L. Garnett discovered that almost 70 percent resulted in rejection of the plan either in part or in entirety.[59] Even when enacted, reorganizations may generate extreme opposition from entrenched interests in the bureaucracy and, in the final analysis, be judged a failure. In the memorable words of former Kansas governor Robert F. Bennett:

> In the abstract, [reorganization] is, without a doubt, one of the finest and one of the most palatable theories ever espoused by a modern day politician. But in practice . . . it becomes the loss of a job for your brother or your sister, your uncle or your aunt. It becomes the closing of an office on which you have learned to depend. . . . So there in many instances may be more agony than anything else in this reorganization process.[60]

Table 7.4   Relative Power of the Offices of Governor

Very weak (0)*				Weak (7)				Mod-erate (38)							Strong (4)					Very strong (1)	
13	14	15	16	17	18	19	20	21	22	23	24	25	26	27	28	29	30	31	32	33	34
				RI	TX	NC	NV	OH	AL	AZ	IA	CA	CO	AK	SD	MA				MD	
							NH		ME	FL	KY	IN	CT	AR		NY					
							SC			GA	MS	IL	MI	DE		WV					
							VT			ID	MO	OR	MN	HI							
										WA	NM		NE	KS							
											ND		PA	LA							
											OH		TN	MT							
											WI		UT	NJ							
											WY		VA								

Note: Power is rated on this scale: less than 17 points, Very weak; 17 to 20 points, Weak; 21 to 27 points, Moderate; 28 to 30 points, Strong; and over 31 points, Very strong. This list is shown alphabetically by group.
* (0) Indicates number of states in this category.

Source: Thad L. Beyle, "The Powers of the Governors," *North Carolina Insight* 12 (March, 1990): 27–45. Used by permission.

Most governors who have fought the battle for reorganization would concur. Perhaps this helps explain the rarity of far-reaching executive branch restructurings in the past several years, despite its popular appeal as an antidote to fiscal ailments.[61]

Staffing Power

The governor relies on staff for policy analysis and advice, liaison with the legislature, and assistance in managing the bureaucracy. Professional staff members are a significant component of the governor's team, composing a corps of political loyalists who help the governor cope with the multiple roles of the office. From the handful of political cronies and secretaries of several decades ago, the staff of the governor's office has grown in number, quality, and diversity (with respect to gender and race).[62] The average size of professional and clerical staff rose from eleven persons in 1956 to thirty-four in 1979.[63] It is approaching fifty today. And in the larger, more highly populated states, such as New York and California, staff numbers well over one hundred. The principal staff positions of the governor's office may include the chief of staff, legislative liaison, budget director, planning director, public relations director, legal counsel, press secretary, and intergovernmental coordinator. Some governors have also established strong offices of policy management along the lines of the national Office of Management and Budget.

A question of serious concern, especially in the states whose governors have large staffs, is whether too much power and influence is being placed in the hands of nonelected officials. Clearly, professional staff members have been highly influential in developing and promoting policies for the governor in some states, particularly in cases where the governor lacks a coherent set of priorities and lets the staff have free rein. In other states the chief executive is very much in charge, relying on staff primarily for drafting bills and providing technical information.[64] Given their physical and intellectual proximity to the governor, staff members are in a highly advantageous position to influence their boss. In their role as the major funnel for policy information and advice, they can affect the governor's decisions by controlling the flow of information.

The dramatic growth in the scope and number of activities engaged in by contemporary governors demands a certain amount of staff. The institutionalized governorship appears to be a practical necessity of governance in the larger, highly populated states and a probable future development in the smaller ones as well.

The Relevance of the Formal Powers

Table 7.4 scores the states on the strength of the governor's formal powers of office. As we have noted, governors have won stronger powers during the past twenty-five years. But how helpful are the formal powers? In spite of the major transformation of the governor's office, governors remain relatively weak because of the setting of state government. They must function within a highly complex and politically charged environment with formal authority that is quite circumscribed. Because of the nature of our federal system, the national government effectively strips them of control over many policy and administrative concerns. Moreover, the business of state government is carried out in a fishbowl, open to regular scrutiny by the media, interest groups, and other interested parties. Notwithstanding the continued constraints on the exercise of their authority, however, today's governors as a group are more effective than their predecessors in carrying out their varied responsibilities. The formal powers of the office have been substantially strengthened, and highly qualified people are serving as chief executives.

In theory, governors with strong formal powers, such as those in Maryland, Massachusetts, and South Dakota, should be more effective than their counterparts in Rhode Island, Texas, and North Carolina. In practice, that tends to be true—but not always. The potential for power and influence must not be confused with action. A governor with strong formal powers enjoys the capacity to serve effectively, but she may choose not to do so or, for various reasons, be unable to utilize the formal powers properly. Alternatively, a governor with weak formal powers can nonetheless be an effective, strong chief executive if she actively and skillfully applies the levers of power embodied in the constitution.

··

Informal Powers

No doubt a governor with strong formal powers has an advantage over one without them. But at least equally important for a successful governorship is the exploitation of the informal powers of the office. These are the authoritative and influence-wielding aspects that are not directly attached to any office through statute or constitution but, rather, are associated with the human being who happens to occupy the governor's mansion.

The informal powers help transform the capacity for action into effective action. They react in synergy with the formal powers to create a successful governorship. An incumbent chief executive in the "strong governor" state of New York will be hopelessly weak unless he also uses his personal assets in performing the multiple roles of the office. Alternatively, a chief executive in a "weak governor" state such as South Carolina can be remarkably successful if he fully employs his informal powers[65] to become a "change master"—one who excels in persuading his state to adopt new ideas.[66]

The informal powers are not as easy to specify as the formal powers are. However, they generally include such tools of persuasion as popular support, public relations and media skills, negotiating and bargaining skills, prestige of the office, special sessions, pork barrel and patronage, and such personal characteristics as youth, ambition, experience, energy, and leadership.

Governor Ann Richards
of Texas responds to
questions during a
press conference.

Tools of Persuasion

Popular support refers to public identification with and support for the governor
and his or her program. It may be measured in terms of the margin of victory
in the primary and general elections or in terms of the results of public opinion
polls. A governor can parlay popular support into legislative acceptance of the
policy mandate and otherwise channel the pressures of public opinion to his or
her advantage. But popular support may erode when governors' actions alienate
the voters. In 1990, for example, Jim Florio of New Jersey and many other
newly elected governors watched their popularity ratings plummet as they began
attacking state fiscal problems with tax increases and budget cutbacks during
their first their year in office. Problem Solving 7.2 relates how one new governor
made hard choices for hard times.

Popular support can be generated and maintained through a second informal
power, *public relations and media skills*. As the leading political figure in the
state, the governor commands the "big mike": the captive attention of the
press, radio, and television. Any governor can call a press conference at a moment's notice and get a substantial turnout of the state's major media representatives, an advantage enjoyed by precious few legislators. Some chief
executives appear regularly on television or radio to explain their policy positions
and initiatives to the people. Others write a weekly newspaper column for the

Problem Solving 7.2

Hard Choices for Hard Times

The Problem: The twenty-one governors elected to office in 1989 and 1990 faced enormous—and immediate—fiscal problems. They had to balance budgets by cutting programs, raising taxes, or both. New England states were especially hard hit. In Connecticut, Governor Lowell P. Weicker, Jr., took office with a budget deficit that soon ballooned to a staggering $2.1 billion—nearly one-third of the state's fiscal 1990 budget.

The Solution: Institute a broad-based personal income tax. Weicker, a rogue Republican who lost a bid for a fourth term in the U.S. Senate in 1988, won the governorship with only 41 percent of the vote as a member of the new "A Connecticut Party." Years of profligate spending on new and existing programs during the state's boom years in the mid-1980s had created huge built-in budget costs. As the Connecticut economy faltered in 1989 and 1990, and then collapsed in 1991, the existing revenue system, based primarily on an 8 percent sales tax, could not generate sufficient monies.

Weicker proposed a tax on personal income, a 2 percent reduction in the sales tax, and various spending cuts. Citizen and legislative reaction was mostly negative. Once before, in 1971, the legislature had enacted a personal income tax, but repealed it before it could take effect because of the ensuing popular revolt. Since that time, candidates for public office in the Nutmeg State took the "no income tax pledge" if they wanted serious consideration by the electorate.

A long, fierce struggle transpired between the governor and the Democratic-controlled legislature. Weicker vetoed three consecutive budgets that he felt were constructed with sales tax hikes, false assumptions, and smoke and mirrors. After many midnight sessions, and fifty-three days into the next fiscal year without a budget, the General Assembly narrowly approved Weicker's income tax. Lieutenant Governor Eunice Groark broke a tie vote in the Senate to place the bill on Weicker's desk.

The captivating drama involved partial shutdowns of state government, raging debates, many false starts, and frantic behind-the-scenes give and take among the governor and his staff, lobbyists, and key legislators. For all practical purposes, votes were bought and sold in the halls of the capitol. Sleep and good humor were rare commodities during the last few weeks.

Even the heavens got into the act. During budget negotiations the state capitol was struck by lightning on two separate occasions, and Hurricane Bob, rising up from the tropics, blew its own hot air at all participants.

With the force of his personality and the conviction that the income tax was the right plan to resolve the crisis, Governor Weicker applied his formal and informal powers skillfully to construct a fragile voting block of Democrats and moderate Republicans. It was not a popular action. A huge crowd, variously estimated at 40,000 to 70,000 people, rallied at the capitol to demand repeal. Effigies of the governor were hung and set afire. Profane signs ("Hang the Lying Bastard") and chants ("F__k you, Weicker!") were the order of the day. But the governor and his legislative supporters held firm, despite death threats to them and their family members, and the tax took effect in late 1991. Several months later, Governor Weicker was honored with the John F. Kennedy Profile in Courage Award for his successful six-month battle.

***

Source: Various issues of the *Hartford Courant,* February 13–October 6, 1991.

same purpose. Frequent public appearances, staged events, telephone calls, and correspondence can also help the governor develop and maintain popular support. Ohio governor Richard Celeste, for instance, conducted a Donahue-style TV talk show—"School Talk with Governor Celeste." Indeed, the media can be a strong ally in carrying out the governor's programs and responsibilities. Effective governors know this instinctively and, along with Bob Graham of Florida, cultivate the press "like petunias."[67] But media relations are a two-way street. The media expect the governor to be honest, forthright, and available. If he instills respect and cooperation, observes political scientist Coleman B. Ransome, Jr., the governor's media relations can be "of incalculable value in his contest for the public eye and ear."[68]

Negotiating and bargaining skills help the governor to convince legislators, administrators, interest groups, and national and local officials to accept his point of view on whatever issue is at hand. These skills are of tremendous assistance in building voting blocks in the legislature. They also help persuade industrialists to locate in the state and effectively represent a state's interests before the national government.

Prestige of the office helps the governor open doors all over the world that would be closed to an ordinary citizen. National officials, big-city mayors, corporate executives, foreign officials, and even the president of the United States recognize that the governor sits at the pinnacle of political power in the state, and they treat her accordingly. Within the state the governor typically makes use of the prestige of the office by inviting important individuals for an official audience, or perhaps to a special meal or celebration at the mansion.

The governor's informal power to call the legislature into *special session* can be employed to focus public and media attention on a particular part of the legislative program or on a pressing issue. In this way the governor can delineate the topics that will be considered, thereby forcing the legislature's hand on divisive or controversial matters, such as insurance reform or a tax increase. In conjunction with popular support and with media and public relations skills, this informal power can work effectively to bend legislative will.

Pork barrel and *patronage* are aspects of the seamier side of state politics. Although they are utilized much less frequently than they were before the civil service reforms of the first half of this century, governors are still known to promise jobs, contracts, new roads, special policy consideration, electoral assistance, and other favors to legislators and other politicians in return for their support. All governors have some discretionary funds to help out a special friend who has constituents in need. And although patronage appointments are severely limited in most states, a personal telephone call from the governor's mansion can open the door to an employment opportunity.

Characteristics of a Successful Governor

The *personal characteristics* that make for an effective governor are discussed frequently but seldom specified, because it is nearly impossible to measure them.

Research by political scientists indicates that age is the only statistically significant predictor of gubernatorial performance: Younger governors have been more successful than older ones.[69] However, there is general agreement that leadership is a very important quality of effective governors. Leadership traits are difficult to define, but former Utah governor Scott Matheson identified the best governors as "men and women who have the right combination of values for quality public service—the courage to stick to their convictions, even when in the minority, integrity by instinct, compassion by nature, leadership by perception, and the character to admit wrong and when necessary, to accept defeat."[70]

A successful governor blends these qualities with the formal and informal powers of office in order to do a job well. For example, following the political campaign to win the election, the governor must conduct a "never-ending campaign" to win the loyalty and support of his cabinet, state employees, the legislature, and the people, if he is to be effective.[71] A case in point is Arkansas governor Bill Clinton, who successfully promoted ethics reform and education improvement campaigns. And in Florida, Governor Bob Graham fought a "Save the Everglades" campaign to protect an important vanishing natural resource.

Successful governors, particularly in "weak governor" states, know how to limit their policy agendas. Realizing that all things are not possible, they focus on several critical issues and marshal their formal and informal resources behind them. Eventually, the determined governor can wear down opponents. A successful governor exercises leadership by convincing the public that their interests are his interests, and that he is the person to pursue their vision. He prevails in the legislature by applying the pressure of public opinion and by building winning blocks of votes, and he leads the bureaucracy through personal example. Above all else, a successful governor must be persuasive.

In short, the formal powers of the office are important to any governor, but even strong formal powers do not guarantee success. They must be combined with the informal powers to be effective. For example, as chief legislator a governor may seek passage of a favorite bill by employing her budgetary and staffing powers. She may even threaten to veto an opposing legislator's pet bill. But if the governor is to win over the necessary majority of legislators' support, her negotiation and bargaining skills as well as her personal leadership qualities may be critical.

Removal from Office

All states but one provide in their constitutions for the impeachment of the governor and other elected officials (in Oregon, they are tried as regular criminal offenders). Usually impeachment proceedings are initiated in the state House of Representatives and the impeachment trial is held in the Senate. A two-thirds vote is necessary for conviction and removal of the governor in most states. Of the more than 2,100 governors who have held office, only 16 have been impeached and 8 actually convicted.

The most recent impeachment and conviction occurred in 1988 in Arizona, in the case of Republican governor Evan Mecham. The Arizona House voted to hold an impeachment trial, and Mecham was convicted by the Senate on charges of misusing state money and trying to stop an investigation of a murder threat against one of his aides. Mecham was removed from office and replaced by Secretary of State Rose Mofford. Later tried on six felony counts of perjury, he was found innocent. Unabashed, Mecham ran again for the governor's office in 1990 but finished a distant third.

Other modern governors have left office under a cloud of criminal allegations, including Illinois governor Otto Kerner, Maryland chief executives Spiro T. Agnew and Marvin Mandel, David Hall of Oklahoma, and Edwin Edwards of Louisiana (the last is back on the job). Three-term West Virginia governor Arch A. Moore, Jr., was sentenced to more than five years in prison and fined $170,000 for extortion, obstruction of justice, and tax and mail fraud shortly after leaving office in 1989. One of the most sordid governorships in recent years was Ray Blanton's in Tennessee. Blanton was convicted of conspiracy, extortion, and mail fraud and charged with numerous additional offenses, including selling liquor licenses and selling pardons to state prison inmates. But these are the gubernatorial black sheep—the oddities of contemporary state government who make interesting reading in the scandal sheets as political throwbacks to the Goodtime Charlies of yesteryear. They deflect proper attention from the vast majority of hard-working, capable, and honest chief executives who typify the American state governorship today.

Other Executive Branch Officials

The states elect more than 450 officials to their executive branches, not counting the 50 governors. This total includes 43 attorneys general, 42 lieutenant governors, 38 treasurers, 36 secretaries of state, and an assortment of other officers ranging from the Texas railroad commissioner to the commissioner of public law in New Mexico. The four most important statewide offices are described here.

Attorney General

The attorney general (A.G.) is the state's chief legal counsel. The A.G. renders formal written opinions on legal issues (such as the constitutionality of a statute, administrative rule, or regulation) when requested to do so by the governor, agency heads, legislators, local prosecutors, or other public officials. In most states, the attorney general's opinions have the force of law unless they are successfully challenged in the courtroom.

The attorney general represents the state in cases where the state government is a legal party, and conducts litigation on behalf of the state in federal and state courts. The A.G. can initiate civil and criminal proceedings in most states. Increasingly, attorneys general have actively represented their states in legal actions contesting national government statutes and administrative activities in controversial fields such as hazardous and nuclear wastes and business regulation. And activist A.G.s have taken actions to protect consumers against misleading advertisements by rental car firms, airlines, and other businesses. These "new cops on the beat"[72] constitute an aggressive group of highly competent attorneys, often working together under the auspices of the National Association of Attorneys General, to assert and protect the role of the states in American federalism.

Lieutenant Governor

This office was originally created by the states for two major reasons: to provide for orderly succession to a governor who is unable to fill out a term owing to death or other reasons, and to provide for an official to assume the responsibilities of the governor when the incumbent is temporarily incapacitated or out of the state. Seven states do not see the need for the office: Arizona, Maine, New Hampshire, New Jersey, Oregon, West Virginia, and Wyoming. Others attach little importance to it, as indicated by a very low salary ($7,200 per year in Texas) or the absence of official responsibilities. The historical reputation of the lieutenant governor was that of a do-nothing; one former occupant of the office in Nevada characterized his major responsibility as "checking the obituaries to see if I should be in Carson City."[73]

Over the past fifteen years, however, the lieutenant governorship in the majority of states has become a more visible, demanding, and responsible office. This trend is likely to continue as state governance grows increasingly complex and as additional states adopt the team election of governor and lieutenant governor. Many lieutenant governors hold important powers in the state Senate, including serving as presiding officer and making bill assignments to committees. Half (a total of twenty-five) can break a tie vote in the Senate. They are official members of the cabinet or of the governor's top advisory body in twenty states.[74] And virtually all lieutenant governors accept special assignments from the chief executive, some of which are quite visible and important. For example, Michigan's lieutenant governor acts as the state's affirmative action officer and chairs the Equal Employment and Business Opportunity Council. In general, lieutenant governors' salaries, budget allocations, and staff have grown markedly during the past two decades.

A lingering problem is that twenty states continue to elect the governor and lieutenant governor independently. This can result in conflict and controversy when the chief executive is out of state and the two officeholders are political rivals or members of opposing political parties. On several recent occasions a lieutenant governor, assuming command, has proceeded to make judicial appointments, veto legislation, convene special sessions of the legislature, and take other actions at odds with the governor's wishes. When Massachusetts governor Michael Dukakis left the country on a European trade mission in 1990, for instance, Lieutenant Governor Evelyn Murphy ordered sweeping cuts in state employment and payrolls. Dukakis's staff basically ignored Murphy, whose own campaign for governor had been struggling. Following this episode, she dropped out of the race.

In order to avoid partisan bickering and politicking in the top two executive branch offices, twenty-two states now require team election. New York was the first to adopt this innovation, in 1953; twenty-one others have followed the lead of the Empire State, most recently Iowa in 1988. In addition to avoiding embarrassing factionalism, team election has the advantages of promoting party accountability in the executive branch, making continuity of policy more likely in the event of gubernatorial death or disability, and ensuring a measure of compatibility and trust between the two state leaders.

Does the lieutenant governorship help or hinder a politician who wishes to achieve the state's top political office? Like everything else in state politics, it depends. A lieutenant governor running for the higher office does enjoy the advantage of name recognition and, potentially, a positive association with a popular governor's program. Alternatively, he or she can be linked negatively with an unpopular former governor and, for this reason, may even lose the race. Over the past thirty-five years, more than seventy lieutenant governors have won their states' top elective office. On balance, the lieutenant governorship seems to offer a boost to an aspiring chief executive.

Treasurer

The treasurer is the official custodian and manager of state funds. He or she collects revenues and makes disbursements of state monies. (The treasurer's signature is on the paycheck of all state employees and on citizens' state tax refunds.) Another important duty is the investment of state funds, including state employee pension monies.

The failure to make profitable investments can cost the treasurer his job. In 1989, West Virginia treasurer A. James Manchin was impeached by the House of Delegates for losing $279 million in state funds through bad investments.

Secretary of State

In a majority of states the duties of this office are rather perfunctory. For the most part they entail record-keeping and election responsibilities. Secretaries of state typically register corporations, securities, and trademarks, and commission people to be notary publics. In their election-related responsibilities, they determine the ballot eligibility of political parties and candidates, receive and verify initiative and referendum petitions, supply election ballots to local officials, file the expense papers and other campaign reports of candidates, and conduct voter registration programs. The typical secretary of state also maintains state archives, registers driver's licenses, files agency rules and regulations, publishes statutes and copies of the state constitution, and registers lobbyists. In some states without the office of lieutenant governor, the secretary of state is in the direct line of succession should the governor die or become incapacitated.

The Vigor of American Governors

For the past two and a half decades the states have reformed their executive branches to enhance the capability of the governor as chief executive and to make the office more efficient, effective, accountable, and responsive. Indeed, the reforms discussed in this chapter not only have extended the formal powers and capacity of the office but also have improved the contemporary governor's performance in his many demanding roles.

In addition, today's governors are better educated, more experienced in state government, and more competent than their predecessors. They are better able to employ the informal powers of their office in meeting multiple and complex responsibilities. In a word, there is greater *vigor* in the American governorships than ever before. Once out of office, many former governors continue to engage in public service. Sixteen now serve in the U.S. Senate, and, of course, several contemporary governors (including Michael Dukakis and Bill Clinton) have run for president. Two (Jimmy Carter and Ronald Reagan) have won in recent times. In 1990, moreover, seventeen retired governors founded the National Institute of Former Governors (NIFG). Its purpose is to use the individual and cumulative insight and expertise of the former chief executives to help solve the nation's most serious policy problems.

Summary

The American governorship has been transformed. Today's governors tend to be very active in their various roles, including those of policymaker, chief legislator, and chief administrator. The governor's office, historically weak in formal powers, has been significantly strengthened during the past twenty-five years. Terms of office have been extended, appointment and veto powers increased, and budgetary authority enhanced, among other things. Governors also apply various informal powers in executing their duties. These include tools of persuasion such as bargaining and negotiating skills, and personal characteristics such as leadership skills.

Key Terms

pork barrel
custodial (caretaker) governor
managerial governor
formal powers
informal powers
patronage
package veto

line item veto
pocket veto
executive amendment
executive order
cabinet system
subcabinet system
task force

8

The Bureaucracy

Everyone likes to criticize **bureaucracy.** Bureaucracy is portrayed as "the problem" with U.S. government at all levels, from the ponderous Department of Defense, to the state department of motor vehicles, to the county tax assessor's office. "Everyone knows" that bureaucracy is all-powerful and out of control, inefficient, wasteful, and drowning in red tape; that bureaucrats are insensitive and uncaring, yet stay in their jobs forever.[1] Elected officials—presidents, governors, mayors, and legislators at all levels—have stridently bashed the bureaucrats, blaming them for all imaginable sins of omission and commission (and all too often for their own personal shortcomings as well).

Why is bureaucracy "the enemy" to so many of us? Why do we simultaneously loathe and fear it? What can we do to ensure that government services are delivered in a timely, efficient, and effective manner? How, in an increasingly complex world, can we make state and local bureaucracy accountable to other political institutions and respond to the legitimate needs of society, groups, and individuals? For decades, these questions have interested political scientists and those who study and practice public administration.

A theme of this chapter is that state and local bureaucracy should not be treated as a scapegoat for all the social, economic, and political maladies that befall us. The quality and capacity of public administration have improved markedly in the country's states, municipalities, and counties during the past twenty-five years in terms of the characteristics of employees and the efficiency, effectiveness, and professionalism with which they perform their duties. In fact, studies comparing public employees with cohort groups in the private sector find no important differences between them. Government workers are just as motivated, competent, and ethical as private-sector workers. And public employees tend to be more sensitive to other human beings, and more highly educated, than their counterparts in business and industry.[2] State and local employees are providing a wider range of services, in greater quantities, to more people than ever before. They are much more accountable and responsive to political actors and to the public than they are popularly perceived to be. In truth, dedicated public employees who work for the people should be saluted, not castigated, for jobs well done under difficult conditions. When government fails to perform effectively, blame occasionally may be laid at the feet of bureaucrats. But more often than not, the fault lies with poorly designed statutes and policies, failed political leadership, and other factors beyond the control of civil servants.

State and Local Bureaucrats: Who They Are, What They Do

There are more than 15 million employees of states and localities. Their numbers have grown steadily since accurate counts were first compiled in 1929, in contrast to the number of national government employees, which has remained fairly stable at just under 3 million since 1969.[3] (This figure does not include the enormous number of private contract employees who perform work for the national government.) The distribution of government employees is also of

Figure 8.1

Distribution of Public Employment, 1929–1990

Since the end of World War II, the percentage of state and local employees, as a proportion of the total government work force, has increased.

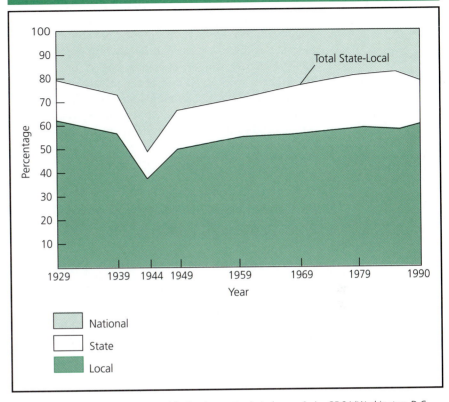

Source: U.S. Bureau of the Census, *Public Employment,* selected years, Series GE 84 (Washington, D.C.. U.S. Government Printing Office).

interest. The national percentage of civilian national government employment has declined from its World War II high of 51.5 percent in 1944 to less than l8 percent today. Correspondingly, the state and local proportions have inched upward to around 23 percent and 59 percent, respectively (see Figure 8.1). Government work tends to be highly labor-intensive, with the exception of national defense programs, which rely heavily on expensive technology. As a result of this and of inflation, personnel expenditures for states and localities have risen even faster than the number of workers. Total payroll costs for state and local governments exceeded $360 billion in 1992.

Of course, the number of employees varies greatly among jurisdictions. Generally speaking, states and localities with high populations and high levels of per capita income provide more services and thus employ larger numbers of workers than smaller, less affluent jurisdictions. Employment figures are further influenced by the number and scope of programs undertaken by governments and by the distribution of functions and service responsibilities between states and their local jurisdictions.

But such figures do not adequately account for the real people who work for states, cities, counties, towns, townships, and school districts. These include the police officer on patrol, the welfare worker finding a foster home for an abandoned child, the eleventh-grade English teacher, the highway patrol officer, and even your professor of state and local government (in public institutions). Their tasks are as diverse as their titles: sanitation engineer, zookeeper, heavy equipment operator, planner, physician, and so on. The diversity of state and local government work rivals that of the private sector. From the lowly sewer maintenance worker to the commissioner of social services, all are public servants—often known as bureaucrats. Approximately one of every six working Americans is employed by government at some level. If bureaucrats are the enemy, we have met them and they are us.

Personnel Policy in State and Local Government: From Patronage to Merit

National laws and court decisions have had a pronounced influence on state and local personnel practices, determining the parameters within which personnel policies can be set. Although national influence is important, personnel policy innovations are more likely to come from the state and local jurisdictions.

In the nation's first decades, public employees came mainly from the educated and wealthy upper class and, in theory, were hired on the basis of fitness for office. During the presidency of Andrew Jackson (1829–1837), who wanted to open up national government jobs to all segments of society, the *patronage* system was adopted to fill many positions. Hiring could depend on party affiliation and other political alliances rather than on job-related qualifications. Jackson himself continued to give jobs to competent people, but the door was open for corruption in federal hiring practices.

Moreover, patronage became entrenched in many states and cities where jobs were awarded almost entirely on grounds of partisan politics, personal friendships, family ties, or financial contributions. This made appointees accountable to the governor, mayor, or whoever appointed them, but it did nothing to ensure honesty and competence. By the beginning of the Civil War, "spoils" embraced American governments at all levels. The quality of public employees plummeted.

The Merit System

merit system

The organization of government personnel providing for hiring and promotion on the basis of knowledge, skills, and abilities rather than patronage or other influences.

The concept of the **merit system** originated with the campaign for passage of the Pendleton Act of 1883. Two key factors led to its realization. First, white Anglo-Saxon Protestants were losing political power to urban political machines dominated by "new" Americans of Irish, Italian, and Polish descent. Second, scandals rocked the administration of an alcoholic president, Ulysses S. Grant, and spawned a public backlash that peaked with the assassination of President James Garfield by a man seeking a political appointment. The Pendleton Act set up an independent, bipartisan *civil service* commission to make objective, merit-based selections for national job openings.

The *merit principle* was to determine all personnel-related decisions. Those individuals best qualified would receive a job or a promotion, for example, based on their knowledge, skill, and abilities. The merit system was originally limited to 10.5 percent of all civilian executive branch positions, but future presidents gradually extended its coverage to approximately 90 percent. The system, which is far from perfect, was thoroughly overhauled by the Civil Service Reform Act of 1978. Nonetheless, the negative effects of patronage and spoils politics in national selection practices were mostly eliminated. **Neutral competence** became the primary criterion for obtaining a national government job, as public servants were expected to perform their work competently and in a politically neutral manner.

neutral competence

The concept that public employees should perform their duties competently and without regard for political considerations.

New York was the first state to enact a merit system, in 1883, the year of the Pendleton Act, and Massachusetts followed in 1884. The first municipal merit system was established in Albany, New York, in 1884; Cook County, Illinois, became the first county with a merit system, in 1895. Ironically, both Albany and Cook County (Chicago) were later consumed by machine politics and spoils-ridden urban governance.

By 1949, twenty-three states and numerous local governments had enacted merit-based civil service systems. Congressional passage of the 1939 amendments to the Social Security Act of 1935 gave additional impetus to such systems. This legislation obligated the states to set up merit systems for employees in social service and employment security agencies and departments that were at least partly funded by national grants-in-aid under the Social Security Act. All states are thus now required to establish a merit system for a sizable segment of their work force (around 20 percent); most of them (thirty-five) have in fact developed comprehensive systems that encompass virtually all state employees (see Table 8.1). Common elements of these modern personnel systems include recruitment, selection, and promotion, in accordance with knowledge, skills, and ability; regular performance appraisals; equal employment opportunity; and position classification.

Some merit systems work better than others. In a handful of states and localities, merit systems are mere formalities, lifeless skeletons around which a shadowy world of patronage, spoils, favoritism, and incompetence flourishes.[4] Rigid personnel rules, a lack of training programs, and inadequate salaries and retirement plans continue to plague some jurisdictions. Political control over merit system employees is limited everywhere, because most cannot be fired without extreme difficulty.

State and Local Advances

On balance, however, state and local personnel systems have been greatly improved over the past twenty-five years, and the process continues.[5] Nonnational governments are experimenting with pay for performance plans and other incentive systems, participative management innovations, new performance-appraisal methods, senior executive systems, comprehensive training programs, the decentralization of personnel functions, and many other concepts. In the 1980s, virtually every state reformed its civil service in some way.

Table 8.1

Comprehensive State Merit Systems

Alabama	Kansas	New York
Alaska	Kentucky	Ohio
Arizona	Louisiana	Oklahoma
California	Maine	Oregon
Colorado	Maryland	Rhode Island
Connecticut	Massachusetts	South Dakota
Delaware	Michigan	Tennessee
Georgia	Minnesota	Utah
Hawaii	Nevada	Vermont
Idaho	New Hampshire	Washington
Illinois	New Jersey	Wisconsin
Iowa	New Mexico	

Source: 1979 Annual Statistical Report on State and Local Personnel Systems (Washington, D.C.: U.S. Office of Personnel Management, June 1980), p. 43; updated by the authors.

These reforms are designed to make the executive branch more responsive to the chief executive, to improve service capacity, to elevate efficiency and effectiveness in providing services, and to enhance flexibility for chief executives, agency heads, city managers, and other officials. Reformers remain dedicated to the principle of protecting the civil service from unnecessary and gratuitous interference by politicians with patronage considerations in mind. But they also want to increase the capacity of government executives to manage programs and people in their bureaucracies.

In addition, state and local work forces tend to be more representative of the general population than the national government work force with respect to race, gender, and other traits. And the level of professionalism, indicated by graduate degrees, government work experience, and membership in professional organizations, has risen dramatically among nonnational government employees.

Threats to the Merit Principle

As we shall see, state and local governments have taken the lead in addressing controversial questions that pose threats to the principle of merit, including affirmative action, comparable worth, and sexual harassment.

representative bureaucracy

The concept that all major groups in society should participate proportionately in government work.

Representative Bureaucracy The concept that the structure of government employment should reflect major sexual, racial, socioeconomic, religious, geographic and related components in society is called **representative bureaucracy.** The assumptions behind this idea are (1) that a work force representative of the values, points of view, and interests of the people it governs will be responsive to their special problems and concerns, and (2) that a representative bureaucracy provides strong symbolic evidence of a government "of the people, by the people, and for the people." These assumptions have been widely debated. For example, empirical research indicates that the specific agency a person works for and the profession he or she belongs to are better predictors of public policy preferences than racial, sexual, and other personal characteristics.[6] But we do know that the symbolic aspects of representative bureaucracy are important. A government that demonstrates the possibility of social and occupational mobility for all sorts of people gains legitimacy in the eyes of its citizens and expands the diversity of views taken into account in bureaucratic decisions.

One of the most controversial questions in public personnel policy is how to achieve a representative work force, particularly at the upper levels of government organizations, without sacrificing the merit principle. *Equal employment opportunity (EEO)*—the policy of prohibiting employment practices that discriminate for reasons of race, sex, religion, age, physical handicap, or other factors not related to the job—is embodied in the Fourteenth Amendment to the U.S. Constitution, the Civil Rights Acts of 1866, 1871, 1964, and 1991, the Equal Employment Opportunity Act of 1972, the Age Discrimination and Rehabilitation Acts of 1973, the Americans with Disabilities Act of 1990, and several U.S. Supreme Court decisions interpreting these acts. This policy has been the law for well over a hundred years, yet progress was very slow until the past twenty years or so.

affirmative action

Special efforts to recruit, hire, and promote members of disadvantaged groups in order to eliminate the effects of past discrimination.

Affirmative Action   In order to boost the effects of EEO, governments take special steps to hire and retain those categories of workers that have suffered discrimination in the past. These measures, known as **affirmative action,** are required under certain conditions by the U.S. Equal Employment Opportunity Commission (EEOC), the regulatory body created to enforce EEO.[7] They include goals, timetables, and other preferential selection and promotion devices to make the work forces of public and private organizations more representative of the racial, sexual, and other characteristics of the available labor pool.

Under affirmative action, the absence of overt discrimination in employment is not sufficient; organizations must implement preferential hiring schemes to redress existing imbalances. The legitimacy of affirmative action policies imposed on employers by the EEOC was seriously questioned in a series of nine U.S. Supreme Court decisions, including *Ward's Cove Packing Co.* v. *Atonio* (1989) and *Richmond* v. *Croson* (1989). *Ward's Cove* made it harder for employees to prove job discrimination.[8] And *Richmond* overturned that city's public works set-aside program for minority business contractors.[9] The 1991 Civil Rights Act reversed these Supreme Court decisions and effectively reinstated affirmative action as government policy across the United States.

Affirmative action remains highly controversial. Establishing specific numerical goals and timetables for hiring and promoting minorities does not necessarily correspond with selection or promotion of "the best person for the job." In other words, affirmative action appears to conflict with the merit principle. Furthermore, it has alienated a large proportion of white males, who feel that they have become victims of "reverse discrimination."

The Lack of Consensus   Legal clashes among the federal courts, the Congress, and the states and localities have not produced a coherent interpretation of the policy's legal standing. For example, the language of the 1972 amendment to the Civil Rights Act of 1964 prohibits state and local governments from depriving any individual of equal protection under the law. That same act forbids employers to grant preferential treatment to any individual or group on the basis of race, color, religion, sex, or national origin. Yet a hiring quota clearly denies equal protection under the law to white males by granting preferential treatment to certain other categories of people. In upholding affirmative action plans during the 1970s, the U.S. Supreme Court examined the history of the Civil Rights Act of 1964 and other laws and determined that Congress *intended* to authorize affirmative action as a means of achieving equal employment opportunity. Yet as the Court became increasingly conservative in the 1980s and 1990s, it essentially reversed direction, becoming less agreeable to affirmative action policies.

A 1984 court case shows the complexity of issues surrounding this policy. In 1980, Memphis city officials signed a federal court consent decree (an agreement among parties to a lawsuit) to increase the percentage of black firefighters to approximately the same as the proportion of blacks in the Shelby County labor pool. Facing a fiscal crisis a year later, the city announced that the fire department and other agencies would lay off a substantial number of employees, using the time-honored principle of "last hired, first fired." This meant, of course, that the new black firefighters would be the first to go.

In this case, *Memphis* v. *Stotts* (1984), a federal district court, upheld by the appeals court, prohibited the city from implementing the layoff plan if it would reduce the percentage of black firefighters.[10] The city complied, laying off white workers or reducing them in rank. On final appeal, the U.S. Supreme Court held that the district and appeals courts' actions were improper, since the original affirmative action consent decree did not mention layoffs. Moreover, the Court interpreted Title VII of the Civil Rights Act of 1964 as applying only to individuals who could prove that they themselves had been victims of illegal discrimination. There was no evidence that the Memphis blacks protected from layoff had ever suffered discrimination by the city.

The *Stotts* case had important implications for affirmative action plans containing hiring and promotion goals. The Reagan administration, consistently in opposition to affirmative action in any form, immediately called on state and local governments to terminate policies that favored a general racial or gender-based class, rather than identifiable individual victims of proven discrimination. Almost all refused to comply. State and local officials evidently feel that EEO, implemented through a policy of affirmative action, is of sufficient benefit to be retained. Ironically, most states and localities have become staunch supporters of a policy originally imposed by the national government over their strong resistance.

Substantial progress toward representative bureaucracy has been made, especially in recruiting and hiring protected-class individuals for entry-level positions. Minorities and women continue to bump against a "glass ceiling" as they try to penetrate the upper levels of state and local agencies. Nonetheless, gradual progress is being seen even in this final barrier to representative bureaucracy, as indicated both by descriptive data (for instance, the number of female city managers rose from seven in 1971 to more than one hundred in 1986) and by scholarly research on improvements in and attitudes toward minority employment.[11] In 1964, only 2 percent of the top administrative posts were held by women and 2 percent by nonwhites. By 1988, the proportions were 17 percent and 11 percent, respectively. These percentages, though low, far exceed those for female and black senior executives in the private sector.[12]

comparable worth

The principle of equal compensation for jobs of equal value to an organization.

Comparable Worth A conspicuous public personnel policy issue that has garnered a great deal of media attention is **comparable worth.** Almost everyone agrees with the principle of equal pay for equal work: Two equally productive individuals with equivalent experience and seniority, performing the *same* job, should receive equal compensation. Comparable worth takes this principle a big step further by stipulating that individuals performing *different* jobs of equal *value* should be compensated equally. For example, a vehicle maintenance worker should receive the same salary as a clerical employee if the work both people are doing is of equal worth to their employer. Supporters of comparable worth assert that it advances the merit principle by rewarding people according to the value of their contribution to the organization. Detractors claim that comparable worth threatens to undermine the merit principle by granting special pay advantage to women on the basis of their gender, instead of their performance.

Something different for government workers: Chicago police officers use all-terrain vehicles to patrol the lake front.

The Debate over Comparable Worth Comparable worth has become a prominent personnel issue because pay inequities are related to gender. Women tend to be concentrated in low-paying jobs: secretary, nurse, waitress, and so on. Nationwide, full-time working women earn an average of around 66 cents for every dollar made by men.

Advocates of comparable worth hold that women are segregated into a small number of low-paying occupations because of sex-based discrimination. From birth to adulthood, females are socialized into the "proper" occupational choice. Because their options are limited, they are paid wages that do not reflect their true value to the employer. Proponents of comparable worth argue that jobs should be comparatively evaluated for their relative worth, based on education, training, skills, effort, responsibility, and other factors associated with performance of the job. Wages should be adjusted to bring female-dominated positions in line with male-dominated jobs, and to encourage men to move into "women's jobs."

Opponents of comparable worth dispute the assertion that society segregates women into low-paying occupations. They claim that women accept these jobs freely because of personal preferences. Many women, the critics point out, leave the work force periodically to marry, have children, and provide child care. They do not accrue experience and years of service at a rate that merits the same compensation as men. Opponents also state that comparable worth is not feasible in a practical sense, as it would interfere with the forces of supply and demand that set wages in the labor market. If wages were set by some other means, tremendous disparities would occur, wreaking havoc on the nation's employers. Spokespersons for local chambers of commerce become apoplectic over the mere thought of the billions of dollars that a national comparable worth plan could cost business in the United States.

Finally, those in opposition argue that the real answer to job segregation is for women to seek out occupations that historically have been dominated by men. Little girls should be encouraged to become doctors, engineers, and police officers, not nurses and secretaries. Otherwise, the concentration of women in a narrow range of jobs will continue, whether or not they are better paid.

Comparable Worth in Court A pair of court cases brought the issue to national attention in the early 1980s. In 1981, the U.S. Supreme Court seemingly upheld sex discrimination claims based on the theory of comparable worth. In the case of *Gunther* v. *County of Washington,* the Court's 5-to-4 majority ruled that Title VII of the 1964 Civil Rights Act, which prohibits sex discrimination, applies to jobs that are similar. The suit involved a female guard in the Washington County, Oregon, jail. She based her suit on a job evaluation study that judged female jailers' work to be 95 percent as difficult as male jailers' work, but the women were paid 30 percent less.

The second case was *AFSCME* v. *State of Washington* (1983). AFSCME, a large public employee labor union, filed suit against Washington after a comparable worth study conducted by the state found substantial sex-based pay inequities, which the state did little about, primarily because of budget problems. A district court judge ruled in favor of AFSCME and instructed Washington to award several years' back pay and higher salaries to some 15,500 female employees. The judge found that Title VII did in fact call for equal pay for jobs of equal value. On appeal, however, a federal court overturned the lower court's ruling. A subsequent union appeal to the U.S. Supreme Court was dropped in December 1985, when the plaintiffs and the state of Washington reached an out-of-court settlement. Under the terms of the agreement, 34,000 workers in female-dominated state jobs received an estimated $482 million in pay adjustments over a six-year period.[13]

Washington's willingness to implement a comparable worth policy was emulated by other states. Minnesota's comparable worth plan, adopted in 1983, called for an appropriation of $21.8 million for wage adjustments for more than 8,000 employees. New Mexico joined the group later that year by allocating $3.2 million to elevate the pay ranges of twenty-three female-dominated occupations. Iowa became the fourth state in 1984, with an appropriation of $10 million.[14]

Today, at least twenty states have a written comparable worth policy in place, and seven more have conducted formal pay equity studies. Numerous local governments have implemented comparable worth policies as well. This is in stark contrast to the national government, which has moved at a snail's pace on the issue. In the private sector, large firms have begun quietly making pay adjustments in female-dominated jobs, while continuing to fight in the political arena against a national comparable worth policy.

Sexual Harassment   Sexual harassment has long been a problem in public and private employment, but it has only recently gained widespread recognition. The sexual harassment charges brought against U.S. Supreme Court nominee Clarence Thomas by Anita Hill (a former Thomas subordinate who is now a law professor at the University of Oklahoma) riveted the eyes of the nation to Senate Judiciary Committee hearings on C-SPAN. Hill's testimony on "Long Dong Silver" and other alleged verbal harassment by Thomas galvanized women's groups and dominated the TV talk shows.

Sexual harassment can consist of any of a variety of incidents: obscene or sexually oriented jokes that a listener finds personally insulting, unwanted touching or other physical contact of a sexual nature, implicit or overt sexual propositions (at issue in the Thomas hearings), or (in one of its worst forms) extortion of a subordinate by a supervisor who demands sexual favors in return for a promotion or a raise. A "hostile working environment" that discriminates on the basis of gender also constitutes sexual harassment.[15] This could involve, for example, repeated leering, sexual joking or teasing, or lewd calendars or photographs at the workplace.

Such behavior subverts the merit principle when personnel decisions are influenced by illegal or discriminatory considerations of a sexual nature, or when an employee cannot perform his or her assigned duties because of sexual harassment. There is no doubt that sexual harassment is common in the workplace. Typically, surveys of women discover that at least half of the respondents report being a victim.[16] And approximately 15 percent of men have experienced sexual harassment. Unfortunately for the recipient of unwanted sexual attention, there are seldom any witnesses. It becomes one person's word against another's. When one of the parties is the supervisor of the second party, a formal complaint is often decided in favor of the boss.

Sexual harassment is illegal according to the federal courts. Considered sex discrimination under Title VII of the 1964 Civil Rights Act and a form of punishable employee misconduct under civil service rules, it is increasingly being prosecuted in the courts.

Much of the official activity aimed at stopping sexual harassment has been concentrated in the states. Michigan was the first to adopt a sexual harassment policy, in 1979; since then, nearly every other state has adopted a statewide sexual harassment policy through legislation or executive order. Most states offer employee training programs that help workers and supervisors identify acts of sexual harassment, establish procedures for effectively addressing it, and enforce prompt, appropriate disciplinary action against offenders.[17]

The costs of sexual harassment go well beyond the personal discomfort or injury suffered by victims. The problem also results in significant financial costs to organizations whose employees lose productive work time. Such misconduct is widely considered unacceptable today in a national work force that is almost 50 percent female. Most states have responded promptly once the problem has gained recognition. Local governments are following suit—in some instances because state legislation forces them to, but more frequently because local officials also recognize the seriousness of the problem.

Unions and Collective Bargaining   Public employee unions present a potentially serious threat to the merit principle. They usually insist on seniority as the primary criterion in personnel decisions: they often seek to effect changes in merit system rules and procedures; and they regularly challenge management authority.

Until the 1960s, the growth and development of unions in the United States constituted a private-sector phenomenon, boosted by national legislation in the early 1930s. This legislation protected the rights of workers in industry to organize and engage in **collective bargaining** with their employers over wages, fringe benefits, and working conditions. Workers then organized in record numbers. By the late 1950s, however, private-sector union growth had halted. A slow but steady decline in the percentage of organized employees continues into the 1990s for a number of reasons, including the shift in the U.S. economy from manufacturing to services (banking and finance, retail sales, fast food, and so on).

collective bargaining

A formal arrangement in which representatives of labor and management negotiate wages, benefits, and working conditions.

Unions in Government   Unions in the public sector did not receive any formal recognition through national action until 1962, when President John F. Kennedy issued an executive order that recognized the rights of federal employees to join unions and to be recognized by federal agencies. Today the labor rights of national workers are covered under several executive orders and the

Civil Service Reform Act of 1978. These employees enjoy most of the rights and privileges of their counterparts in industry, with two important exceptions: Most federal workers do not have the right to negotiate over wages and benefits, and none have the right to strike.

Unionization in state and local government developed and flourished in the 1960s and 1970s, some thirty years after the heyday of private-sector unionism. During the 1960s, the number of public employee union members more than tripled. Why the sudden growth? In retrospect, several reasons are apparent.

First, the rise of unionism in government was spurred by the realization by state and local employees that they were underpaid and otherwise maltreated in comparison to their counterparts in the private sector who had progressed so well with unionization and collective bargaining. Second, the bureaucratic and impersonal nature of work in large government organizations encouraged unionization to preserve the dignity of the workers. A third reason for the rise of state and local unionism was the employees' lack of confidence in many civil service systems. Not only were pay and benefits inadequate, but grievance processes were controlled by management, employees had little or no say in setting personnel policies, and "merit" selection, promotion, and pay often were influenced by management favoritism. Fourth, public employees got caught up in the revolutionary fervor of the 1960s. They saw other groups in American society winning concessions from government authorities and they decided to join in.

Perhaps most important, the growth of unions in government was promoted by a significant change in the legal environment of labor relations. The rights of state and local employees to join unions and bargain collectively with management were guaranteed by several U.S. Supreme Court rulings, state legislation, local ordinances, and various informal arrangements that became operative during the 1960s and 1970s. Wisconsin was the first state to permit collective bargaining for state workers, in 1959. Today, forty-one states specifically allow at least one category of state or local government employees to engage in collective bargaining.

The Extent of Unionization   The extent of unionization and collective bargaining is greatest in the states of the industrial Midwest and Northeast—the same areas so fertile for the growth of private-sector unions. A handful of traditionalistic states, including Arizona, Mississippi, Utah, Virginia, and the Carolinas, continue to resist the incursion of state and local unions (see Figure 8.2). Public employees in these jurisdictions have the legal and constitutional right to join a union, but their government authorities do not have a corresponding duty to bargain with them over wages, benefits, or conditions of work.

Approximately 40 percent of all state government workers belong to unions; 50 percent of local government employees are organized. The highest proportions of union workers are found in education, highways, public welfare, police protection, fire protection, and sanitation.[18]

The surge in the fortunes of state and local unions was partially arrested by the taxpayer revolt of the late 1970s, as well as by a severe recession in the early

Figure 8.2 Collective Bargaining Rights in the States

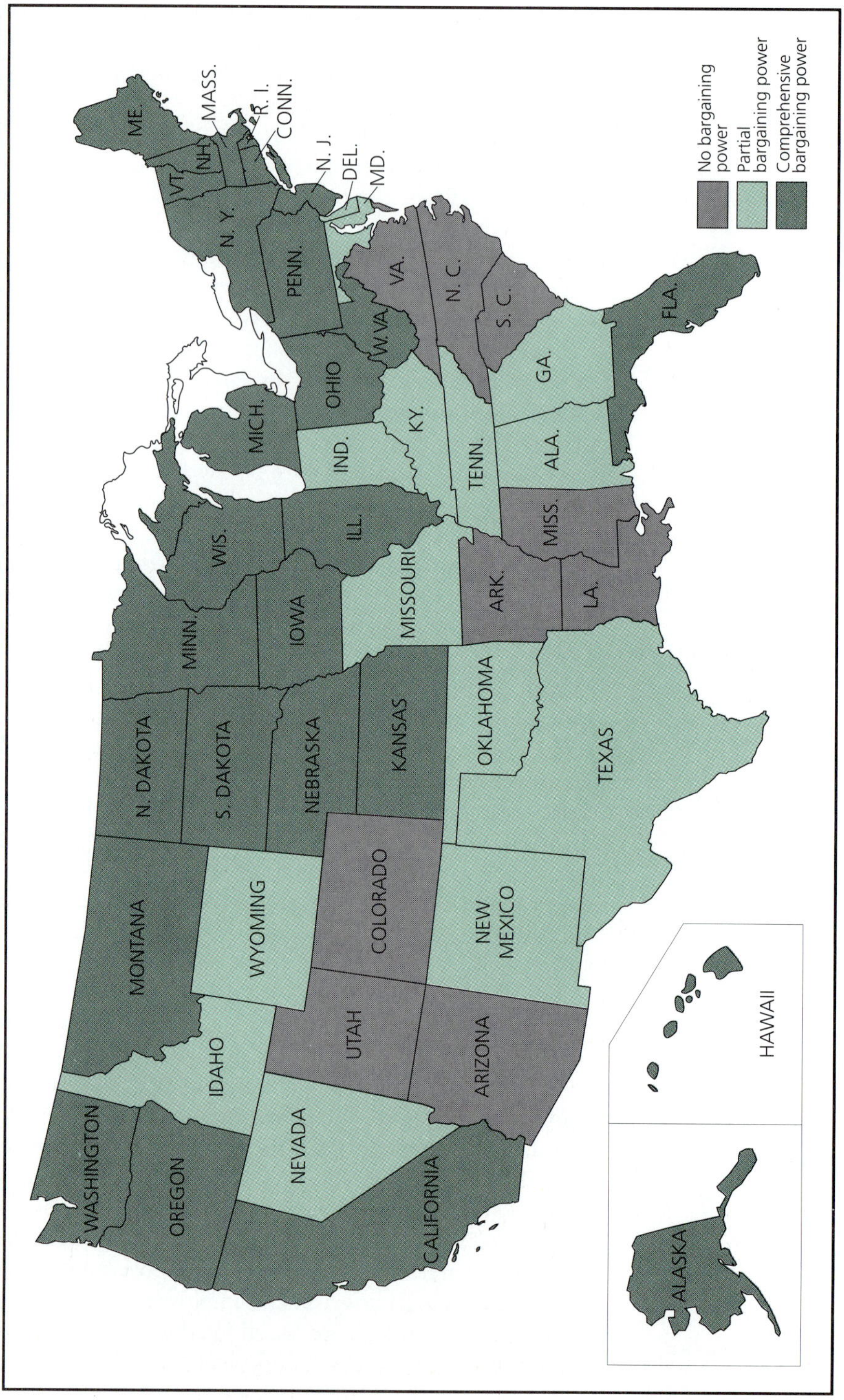

1980s that slowed the growth of government employment and also halted the rapid gains in salary levels that had accompanied the growth of unions and collective bargaining. Further resistance to unions developed from the recession of 1990–1992. Fiscal and taxpayer resistance helped stiffen the backbones of public officials, who had been criticized in some jurisdictions for giving the unions too much. Since 1976, only three additional states passed statutes that enabled major categories of state and local workers to engage in collective bargaining.

As a result of these factors, unionism in state and local government has leveled off and even declined in some jurisdictions. Substantial gains in membership and bargaining rights are not likely during the decade of the 1990s. Nonetheless, unions remain an important and highly visible component of many state and local government personnel systems.

The Impact of Collective Bargaining in State and Local Government   The outcomes of bargaining between a union and a firm in the private sector are largely determined by market forces, such as profit levels and the supply and demand for labor. In government, political factors are much more important. The technical process of negotiating over wages and other issues is very similar in business and government. But the setting makes government labor relations much more complex, mostly because the negotiating process culminates in the political allocation of *public* resources.

Jay F. Atwood has identified four factors that make government labor relations highly political.[19] First, public officials are under greater pressure than private employers to settle labor disputes. Public services are highly visible and often monopolistic in nature; for example, there are no other convenient suppliers of police and fire protection. Accordingly, elected officials who confront a controversial labor dispute in an "essential service" may fear it will derail their opportunity for re-election.

Second, public employee unions have considerable political clout. Their members can influence election outcomes, particularly at the local level. A recalcitrant mayor or city council member who opposes a hefty wage increase may suffer defeat at the polls in the next election if the municipal union members vote as a bloc. Unions may actively engage in politics through raising money, writing letters to the editor about candidates, knocking on doors to get out the vote, formally endorsing candidates, or using any of the other electoral techniques employed by interest groups. The larger unions have professional lobbyists to represent them in the state capitol or in city hall.

A third politicizing factor in government-labor relations is the symbiotic relationship that can develop between unions and elected officials. In exchange for special consideration at the bargaining table and perhaps elsewhere, the unions can offer public officials two valued commodities: labor peace and electoral support.

Finally, a hard-pressed union can use the strike or a related job action (such as a slowdown or picketing) as a political weapon. In the private sector, a strike is not likely to have widespread public repercussions unless it involves goods or services that the nation relies on for its economic well-being (such as air transportation or coal mining). In government, a strike can directly involve the health and safety of all the citizens of a jurisdiction. For instance, a general strike involving police officers, firefighters, and sanitation workers has the potential to turn a city into filthy, life-threatening anarchy.

Strikes and other job actions by public employees are illegal in most jurisdictions, although ten states permit work stoppages by "nonessential" workers under strictly regulated conditions. However, teachers, health care workers, firefighters, and others sometimes walk off the job anyway. The nightmare of a defenseless populace terrorized by acts of violence during a police strike, or the stench of garbage piling up on city streets for weeks during the hot months of July and August, has convinced many an elected official to seek a prompt settlement to a labor-management impasse.

Because of these politicizing factors, one might expect that unions in government are extravagantly successful at the bargaining table. In fact this is not the case at all. Public employee unions have raised wages and salaries an average of 4 to 8 percent, depending on the service, place, and time period under consideration (for example, teachers earn around 5 percent more if represented by a union, firefighters around 8 percent). These figures are much lower than those representing the union-associated wage impacts that have been identified in the private sector.[20] Greater success has come in winning better benefits, particularly generous pensions and health care insurance. It should be noted that union-driven wage and benefit hikes in the private sector are absorbed by profits or higher product prices. In government, the taxpayer must cough up more money, or services may be cut.

Certain personnel impacts have also been associated with collective bargaining in government. Clearly, unions have gained a stronger voice in management decision making. All personnel-related issues are potentially negotiable, from employee selection and promotion procedures to retention in the event of a reduction in force. Civil service rules, regulations, and procedures have been altered by many employers as a result of collective bargaining. In heavily unionized jurisdictions, two personnel systems coexist uncomfortably—the traditional civil service system and the collective bargaining system.[21] Certainly the rights of public employees have been strengthened by unions.

Generally speaking, governments and collective bargaining have reached an uneasy accommodation. The principle of merit in making personnel decisions is still largely in place; and it is usually supported strongly by the unions, so long as seniority is fully respected as an employment decision rule. In an increasing number of jurisdictions, unions are cooperating with management to increase productivity in government services, through participative management techniques such as Total Quality Management (see Problem Solving 8.1). Perhaps the best way to characterize the impacts of unions in government is through a "diversity thesis": The effects vary over time and place, depending on numerous variables that range from how management is structured to the personalities found on either side of the bargaining table.[22]

Problem Solving 8.1

Total Quality Management

The Problem: General public dissatisfaction with government service provision; widespread allegations of bureaucratic waste and inefficiency.

The Solution: Total Quality Management (TQM), a holistic approach to a process-oriented relationship between government managers and employees. Designed by American management guru W. Edwards Deming and widely adopted by Japanese corporations in the 1950s, TQM is now being applied in state and local government.

TQM stresses worker participation in decision making, continuous improvement in work processes, and treating organizational clients as customers, whose satisfaction is the principal goal. Quality improvement and excellence are the major values. Though still new, the TQM approach has been used with some success in a variety of settings. Officials in Madison, Wisconsin, claim that TQM helped reduce trash volume and worker injuries while raising morale among garbage collectors. In Erie, Pennsylvania, TQM improved the effectiveness of police deployment and raised arrest rates. Milwaukee County saved hundreds of thousands of dollars by instituting TQM in its vehicle main-tenance shop. And TQM saved Indiana's human services agencies an estimated $45 million through client service innovations and other changes.

Critics claim that TQM is an overblown fad—like PPBS and ZBB—that is certain to disappoint in the public sector, where its application is problematic. In government, political officials often foil the most carefully made administrative plans. An unsympathetic city manager or new governor can quickly push TQM to the back burner. And ordinary citizens may distrust certain precepts of TQM. For instance, who are the "customers" of the police department—criminals? And how do you measure—let alone enhance—"quality" in public schools and universities, when tax dollars are scarce? Public employee unions also tend to perceive TQM as a threat.

Even if TQM eventually fades away (as is likely), it will probably leave behind some lasting—and positive—legacies in government. Customer orientation, performance monitoring, and a concern for service quality are certainly laudable objectives.

Sources: Mary Walton, *Deming Management at Work* (New York: G. P. Putnam and Sons, 1990); Jonathan Walters, "The Cult of Total Quality," *Governing* 5 (May 1991): 38–42; Office of Policy and Management, "Total Quality Management" (Executive Briefing) (Hartford, Conn.: Connecticut Office of Policy and Management, August 1991).

The Politics of Bureaucracy

In an ideal world, political officials popularly elected by the people would make all decisions regarding public policy. Then it would be the duty of public administrators in the executive branch—the bureaucrats—to carry out these decisions through the agencies of state and local government. In the real world of bureaucratic politics, however, the line dividing politics and administration is transparent. Politicians have a hand in administrative matters, and administrators play politics at the state capitol and in city hall.

Joining Administration and Politics

Bureaucrats are intimately involved in making public policy, from the design of legislation to its implementation. Government workers are often the seedbed for policy ideas that grow to become law, in large part because they are more familiar with agency and departmental problems and prospects than anyone else in government. It is not unusual, for instance, for law enforcement policy to originate with police administrators, or higher education policy with university officials.

Once a bill does become law, state and local employees must interpret the language of the legislation in order to put it into effect. Because most legislation is written in very general terms, civil servants must apply a great deal of **bureaucratic discretion** in planning and delivering services and otherwise managing the affairs of government. In a very real sense, the ultimate success or failure of a public policy depends on the administrators who are responsible for its implementation. Experienced legislators and chief executives understand this, and they bring relevant administrators into the legislative process at a very early stage. The knowledge and expertise of these administrators is invaluable in developing a policy approach to a specific problem, and their cooperation is essential if a policy enacted into law is to be carried out as the lawmakers intend.

Thus, bureaucratic power derives from knowledge, expertise, and discretionary authority. It also comes from external sources of support for agency activities—that is, from the chief executive, legislators, and interest groups. Those who receive the benefits of government programs—the clientele—are also frequently organized into pressure groups. All government programs benefit some interest—agricultural policy for the farm community; social welfare policy for the poor; education policy for parents, students, teachers, and administrators—and these **clientele groups** often are capable of exerting considerable influence in support of policies that benefit them. Their support is critical for securing the resources necessary to develop and operate a successful government program. They serve as significant political assets to state agencies and municipal and county departments that are seeking new programs or additional funding from legislative and executive bodies, and they can become fearsome political infighters when their program interests are threatened.

The problem of politics and administration, then, has two sometimes incompatible dimensions. First, political intrusion into administrative affairs should be minimized, so that administrative decisions and actions can be based on neutral, professional competence, not on the politics of favoritism. Second, elected officials have the very important responsibility of ensuring that administrative decision makers are accountable and responsive to the public interest. Generally speaking, elected officials manage to avoid this responsibility. Other political and representational activities absorb so much of their time and energy that they have little left for probing the affairs of the bureaucracy. Even when elected officials want to approach the bureaucracy, they are partially constrained by merit systems, which protect public employees from dismissals, demotions, or

bureaucratic discretion

The ability of public employees to make decisions interpreting law and administrative regulations.

clientele group

A group that benefits from a specific government program, such as the poor in welfare programs.

other adverse personnel decisions. In addition, most government agencies perform their duties competently and require little direct oversight.

An example of the merger of politics and administration is the lobbying of public administrators by legislative officials. Such lobbying occurs when legislators and council members perform casework for members of their constituency. Although on occasion the legislator-lobbyist seeks favorable treatment that borders on illegality, the bulk of legislative casework is a response to a citizen's inquiry or complaint, or a request for clarification of administrative regulations.[23] Such legislative casework is useful in that it promotes both feedback on the delivery of services and helpful exchanges of information with elected officials. If inquiries determine bias in the means by which services are being delivered, corrective political actions can be taken.[24]

In sum, state and local politics are intricately joined with administration. Public policy is made and implemented through the interaction of elected officials, interest groups, and public administrators. Nonetheless, the vast majority of administrative decisions are based on the neutral competence and professionalism of public employees. An important question remains: Are administrators responsive to the public interest in their decision making?

The Public Interest

Everyone agrees that government programs should be conducted in accordance with the "public interest." The dilemma for state and local administrators lies in defining this concept. In fact, there are numerous, competing public interests with no clear set of priorities among them. Public administrators may be expected to respond to the "general" interest of the people, but who is authoritative (or presumptuous) enough to identify it? Administrators also must listen to their immediate superiors, elected and appointed officials at all levels, clientele groups, and public interest groups, and they must be aware of national and state constitutional, statutory, and administrative law.

Often various publics make demands at once. Take the case of the county animal-control officer. Her job is to keep unowned and unattended animals off the streets. Citizens call to complain about stray cats and barking dogs. Owners criticize her for making them pay to retrieve their animals. In order to have adequate space and to keep within the budget on feeding and maintenance expenses, she has to destroy unclaimed animals, which prompts regular outcries from the local animal rights groups. Yet failure to destroy the animals means a budget fight with the county administrator or county council, or a rabies epidemic that could involve state health department officials.

The point is that public administrators are required to identify and balance a variety of interests in carrying out their responsibilities. For practical purposes, there is no single, clearly identifiable public interest; nor should there be. In a sense, the bureaucracy plays an important role in integrating political demands made from a variety of interests within American government.[25] This task is accomplished largely by applying professional values and expertise to the formulation of standard operating procedures and work routines.

Bureaucratic Responsiveness

bureaucratic respon-siveness

The willingness of bu-reaucratic employees to react to demands from elected officials, interest groups, the general public, and other policy actors.

The concept of **bureaucratic responsiveness** is just as murky as that of the public interest, in part because the two are so closely linked. In essence, state and local bureaucrats are expected to be answerable, or accountable, to the public interest (however defined) for their actions. The bureaucracy must be responsible and accountable for what it does and does not do. Three basic types of administrative responsibility can be identified: objective, subjective, and professional.

Objective Responsibility   Objective responsibility means that an administrator is legally or officially responsible for some thing or action. In other words, by virtue of the constitution, a law, an administrative regulation, or some other formal requirement, x is accountable to y for z. Objective responsibility is achieved through the formal organizational structure (hierarchy) and the various political controls placed on the bureaucracy by executive, legislative, and judicial structures and processes. For example, *sunset laws* require the termination of government agencies, boards, or commissions that are unable to justify their existence on a periodic basis, and *administrative procedures laws* require government agencies to give written notice and solicit public comment before changing or eliminating administrative regulations. (See Chapter 9 for more on sunset laws.) Reorganization of the state executive branch, as described in Chapter 7, is intended to enhance objective responsibility by reducing the number of state agencies, centralizing authority in the governor's office, and other actions aimed at making high-level bureaucratic actors more directly accountable to the governor.

Similar structural reorganization efforts took place in local governments across the United States during the municipal reform movement, especially in middle-sized jurisdictions like Dayton, Ohio, and Little Rock, Arkansas (see Chapter 12). These included nonpartisan elections to eliminate the influence of political parties in urban government, at-large elections to discourage political machines and pork barrel politics, the establishment of the city manager form of government, and the development of modern personnel and budgeting systems. Although results are difficult to evaluate, a national survey of municipal department heads found that respondents from reorganized ("reformed") cities were more likely to stress efficiency, effectiveness, and equity in the delivery of services than were their colleagues in old-style cities. The respondents from reorganized localities were also judged to be more responsive to the needs of individual citizens and minorities.[26]

Subjective Responsibility   The second category of administrative responsibility, *subjective responsibility*, concerns a personal feeling of moral obligation: A public employee should *feel* responsible for behaving legally and properly. This feeling is associated with a sense of loyalty or conscience. Almost all states and many of the larger local governments have enacted laws that set forth standards on what conduct is and is not considered ethical. Unfortunately, such ethics laws have been of limited use. They tend to issue grand exhortations and to impose sweeping moral judgments that cannot be enforced.

Professional Responsibility   A more pragmatic means of seeking bureaucratic responsiveness is through professional responsibility.[27] This concept is based, first, on the professional public servant's dedication to and confidence in the expert knowledge and skills that he has developed and, second, on the use of his knowledge and skills in conformity with standards and norms established by the profession in pursuit of the public interest.

Professionals in State and Local Government

The growth of professionalism in government is a controversial phenomenon that has generated much discussion among scholars.[28] Virtually every profession in the United States is represented in state and local government. Some, such as law, medicine, and teaching, have been recognized for many years. Newer professions include certified public accounting, social work, librarianship, and city planning. And there is the emerging profession of public administration itself, which embraces administrative generalists such as city managers and department heads.

The Rise of Professionalism   The proportion of professionals in state and local government employment has risen steadily, and an increasing number of government workers hold graduate degrees or professional licenses. The professions and government are highly interdependent. Indeed, only government can provide employment for some professionals, such as military specialists and city managers. And it is not uncommon for a particular profession's values and goals to dominate a public organization; examples include doctors in a state department of public health and engineers in a state highway department. In local government, too, the city management profession has exerted substantial influence over policies, programs, and techniques.

Critics bemoan professionalism in government. It is said that each profession has its own view of the world, grounded in its education process and specialized knowledge. Some fear that a professionalized bureaucracy pursues its own limited notion of what is in the public interest (and in the interest of the profession), rather than balancing the interests of the citizenry, clientele groups, elected officials, and others. Other critics have associated the dangers of professionalism with those of bureaucracy generally, by saying that professionalized agencies are not accountable to the public interest and that the original goals of public agencies and programs are displaced by professional goals.[29]

Professionalism and Bureaucratic Responsiveness   Actually, a strong case can be made that professionalism encourages bureaucratic responsiveness.[30] Professional responsibility, as embodied in the public-serving norms and standards of the professions, can lead the administrator to respond neutrally, objectively, and competently to competing interests in government. Professional norms, standards, and codes of ethics provide the public administration professional with a means for deciphering and responding to a multifaceted public interest by promoting accountability for work behavior and encouraging a sense of personal duty.[31]

An excellent example of the value of professionalism can be found in case studies of urban service delivery, in Houston, Chicago, San Antonio, Oakland, Detroit, and other cities. These studies reveal that bureaucratic rules, usually developed in accordance with professional standards, serve as the basis for allocating services in police and fire protection, recreation, street repair, and other areas. This finding is important, because it indicates that urban services are generally provided without discrimination on the basis of wealth or race.[32] When, for example, the municipal department of roads and streets must decide which transportation routes to repave, the decisions are seldom made on the basis of political favoritism. Applied instead is a formula that takes into account such factors as date of the last repaving, intensity of public usage, and the condition of the road.

Professional organizational goals and the public interest do not necessarily conflict. Indeed, they have evolved and interacted over time. Public administrators tend to be committed to their profession, but even more strongly committed to their immediate employer and to the broader institutions and processes of American government.[33] Other factors also should alleviate apprehension. First, there is healthy debate in most professions regarding the interpretation of ethics, values, and goals. Second, representative bureaucracy helps restrain professional dominance by ensuring that professionals in public organizations have diverse backgrounds. This enhances the legitimacy of agency decision making and expands the diversity of views taken into account. Finally, there are the numerous formal and informal constraints on professional and bureaucratic discretion noted earlier, including interest groups and the checks and balances of the three branches of government.[34]

Improving Government Performance   State and local government employment has burgeoned since the 1960s, at a rate much faster than that of population growth. The number of Texas state workers jumped from 112,000 in 1970 to 223,000 in 1990; in New Jersey, the twenty-year increase was from 58,000 to 112,000. The total state and local government payroll is $360 billion per year, for about 15.5 million workers.[35] Explanations for this huge expansion in the size and costs of government are numerous, including federal mandates, public employee unionization, political partisanship, and institutional inertia.[36]

Are the quantity and quality of services better than ever? Not according to most citizens, as we pointed out in the beginning of this chapter. Instead, taxpayer ire and criticism of government at all levels have reached new heights. So have calls for making government more efficient and effective. Many new strategies are being tried in an effort to improve the performance and productivity of state and local governments. Two of the most popular of these are discussed here.

Privatization, such as contracting out services to a private firm, was a widely heralded reform during the 1980s; and it continues to garner much support today, especially among conservatives, Republicans, and others who want to see a "business-like" approach to government. Virtually any government service is a candidate for contracting out, from jails to janitorial work, and from teaching to trash collection. (In theory, most government facilities could even be sold to private interests and operated like businesses. Airports and bridges are obvious examples.)

But privatization isn't as easy as it sounds. Insufficient oversight on the part of some jurisdictions has resulted in cost overruns, poor service delivery, and fraud and corruption by the contractor. Indeed, successful contracting requires not only careful government planning, design, and analysis of what the jurisdiction wants to have done but also continuous assessment of a contractor's performance. Contract monitoring thus needs to include inspections, performance reports, and investigations of citizen complaints.[37]

To keep contractors honest, some governments use multiple, competing firms or nonprofit organizations to deliver the same service to different state agencies or geographic areas. Phoenix, for instance, devised a garbage collection plan in 1978 that permitted the city public works department to compete against private collectors for long-term contracts in five service districts. Until 1984, the city workers were consistently the highest bidders. But after garbage truck drivers redesigned routes and work schedules and adopted one-person collection vehicles, the public works department eventually won back all five district contracts. (See Problem Solving 8.2 for another employee-centered approach.) In this case, government was able to do more with less, and to achieve greater operating efficiencies than private firms could.[38]

Improvements in technology also offer promise for productivity and performance gains. Some improvements are rather mundane and common-sensical. In Wisconsin, for example, renewal of auto licenses and registrations—always a headache for vehicle owners—can be done by telephone and paid for with a credit card. Other improvements are more futuristic. In Santa Monica, California, residents can use personal computers at home or at public terminals located throughout the city to access a variety of city data bases, including library card catalogues and recycling information. A similar videotext system has been set up in Peoria, Illinois. Such systems are fast, efficient, and available twenty-four hours a day, seven days a week.[39] Another innovation, videoconferencing, saves travel costs in large states, as do video workshops and training modules.

....

Budgeting in State and Local Government

The budget is the very lifeblood of state and local organizations. Without a budgetary appropriation, they would cease to exist. The monies are allocated (usually on an annual basis) by legislative bodies, but the politics of the budgetary process involves all the familiar political and bureaucratic players: chief executives, interest and clientele groups, other government employees, the general public, and, of course, the recipients of legislative appropriations—the state highway department, the municipal police department, the county sanitation

Problem Solving 8.2

Enterprise Management

The Problem: The head of Minnesota's Department of Administration wanted to improve its efficiency and productivity.

The Solution: Small business enterprises were created within state government, thereby combining the best aspects of both the public and the private sectors.

Minnesota's Department of Administration (DOA) was known as a highly bureaucratized, nonproductive staff agency that sometimes seemed more of an obstacle than a facilitator for other state agencies it was intended to serve. (The joking definition for DOA was "Dead on Arrival.") But Commissioner Sandra J. Hale turned DOA around through Enterprise Management. Various DOA functions were redesigned as small businesses, using marketplace dy-

namics to determine their costs and service quality and to make improvements. Thus, the motor pool, purchasing, computer operations, micrographics, printing, equipment leasing, and other activities were treated as business enterprises. The unit costs and revenues were separately identified for each activity and its major product or service. Flexibility and problem solving were emphasized instead of bureaucratic rules and red tape.

Enterprise Management did indeed succeed in cutting DOA costs and improving service quality. DOA purchases for state agencies, for example, were speeded up from an average time of forty days to only sixteen. Moreover, prices for DOA services grew at an average annual rate of only 0.8 percent over five years, while inflation averaged nearly 5 percent per year.

Source: Sandra J. Hale, *Lessons for Florida; The Minnesota Approach to Revitalizing Government* (Tallahassee, Fla.: Florida State University Center for Public Management, 1991).

office, and so on. In a phrase, budget making is a highly charged political poker game with enormous stakes. To understand bureaucracy one must have a grasp on budgetary politics.

An often-quoted definition of politics is Harold Lasswell's famous line, "Politics is who gets what, when, where, and how."[40] The budget document provides hard dollars-and-cents data for this statement. It is a political manifesto—the most important one you will find in state and local government. It is a policy statement of what government intends to do (and not do) for the next year, detailing the amount of the taxpayers' resources that it will dedicate to each program and activity. The outcomes of the budgetary process represent the results of a zero-sum game—for every winner there is a loser—because public resources are limited. An extra million dollars for corrections can mean that much less for higher education; an expensive new fleet of sanitation trucks requires higher taxes or fees from the homeowner.

The Budget Cycle

The process of governmental budgeting is best understood as a cycle with overlapping stages, five of which can be identified: preparation, formulation, adoption, execution, and audit (see Figure 8.3). Several stages are taking place at any single time. For example, while the 1993 budget is being executed and revenues and expenditures are being monitored to guard against an operating deficit, the governor and the legislature are developing the 1994 budget. Meanwhile, the 1992 budget is being audited to ensure that monies were properly spent and otherwise accounted for.

Budgets are normally based on a *fiscal* (financial) *year* rather than on the calendar year. Fiscal years for all but four states run from July 1 through June 30 (the exceptions are Alabama, Michigan, New York, and Texas). Eleven states, including Oregon, Montana, and Kentucky, have biennial (two-year) budget cycles. Most local governments' fiscal years also extend from July 1 to June 30, but a substantial minority budget on the calendar year. (The national government's budget cycle begins on October 1 and ends on September 30.)

Figure 8.3

The Budget Process

The budget process has built-in "checks and balances," since all spending is approved or audited by more than one agency or branch.

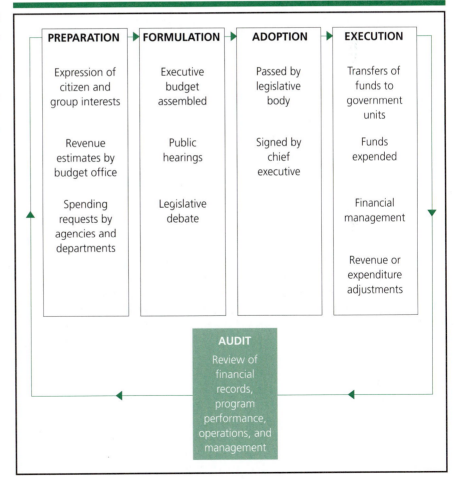

PREPARATION	FORMULATION	ADOPTION	EXECUTION
Expression of citizen and group interests	Executive budget assembled	Passed by legislative body	Transfers of funds to government units
Revenue estimates by budget office	Public hearings	Signed by chief executive	Funds expended
Spending requests by agencies and departments	Legislative debate		Financial management
			Revenue or expenditure adjustments

AUDIT

Review of financial records, program performance, operations, and management

The initial phase of the budget cycle involves demands for slices of the budget pie and estimates of available revenues for the next fiscal year. State and local agency heads join the chorus of interest groups and program beneficiaries seeking additional funding. Large state agencies are typically represented by their own lobbyists, or "public information specialists." State and local administrators develop estimates of revenues based on past tax receipts and expected economic conditions, and communicate them to their respective state agencies or municipal departments, which then develop their individual spending requests for the fiscal year. Revenue projections are revised as new data become available.

Formulation, or development, of the budget document is the responsibility of the chief executive in most states and localities. Exceptions include states in which the balance of power rests with the legislature (such as Arkansas, Mississippi, and South Carolina) and local governments in which budgeting is dominated by a council or commission. The executive budget of the governor or mayor is prepared by budget office staff (for example, an office of management and budget) and submitted to the chief executive for the final touches. The executive budget is then presented to the appropriate legislative body for debate and review. (In many New England local governments, budgets are approved by citizens attending a town meeting or through a public referendum.) The lengthy review process that follows allows agencies, departments, interest groups, and citizens to express their points of view. Finally, the budget is enacted by the legislative body.

The state legislature or city council must ensure that the final document balances revenues with expenditures. Balanced-budget requirements are contained in the constitutions or statutes of most states and operate through precedent in the others. These requirements usually apply to local governments as well. Balanced-budget requirements force state and local governments to balance expenditures with revenues, but they may be circumvented to some extent.[41] One popular device is the "off-budget budget," in which costs and revenues for public enterprises such as government corporations and development banks are exempt from central review and are not included in budget documents and figures. Another tactic is to borrow money from employee pension funds to cover the current year's deficit. Before the budget bill becomes law, the chief executive must sign it. Last-minute executive-legislative interactions may be needed to stave off executive vetoes or to override them. Once the chief executive's signature is on the document, the budget goes into effect as law, and the execution phase begins.

State budget making during the 1991 recession year illustrates the trauma of trying to make ends meet when revenues are declining and expenditure demands are rising. Nine of the forty-six states involved in budget making went beyond legal deadlines before they could ratify the final document. Each had to raise taxes, cut services, or use some combination of both to balance the budget—unpopular choices all. During the budget impasses, governors imposed a variety of money-saving measures, including hiring and travel freezes, layoffs, furloughs, and across-the-board spending reductions. The governors of Maine and Connecticut, in particular, shut down all nonessential state services, provoking angry demonstrations by state employees. Similar problems were encountered by five states that missed budget deadlines in 1992. One of them, California, had to issue IOUs to state employees in order to meet its payroll as budget negotiations between the governor and the legislature reached an impasse.

During budget execution, monies from the state or local "general fund" are periodically transferred to agencies and departments to meet payrolls, purchase goods and materials, fulfill service contracts, write checks for welfare recipients and pensioners, and try to achieve program goals. Accounting procedures and reporting systems continually track revenues and outlays within the agencies. If revenues have been overestimated, the chief executive must make adjustments to keep the budget in the black. He or she may draw on a "rainy day fund" to meet a shortfall or, if the deficit is a large one, order service reductions or layoffs. In a crisis the governor may call the legislature into special session, or the mayor may request a tax increase from the city council.

The final portion of the budget cycle involves several types of audits, or financial reviews—each with a different objective. Fiscal audits seek to verify that expenditure records are accurate and that financial transactions have been made in accordance with the law. Performance audits examine agency or department activities in relation to goals and objectives. Operational and management audits review how specific programs are carried out and assess administrators' performance. The auditors may be employed by either the executive or the legislative branch. Some jurisdictions retain professional auditors from the private sector in order to ensure objectivity.

The Actors in Budgeting

There are three main actors in the budget process: agencies, the chief executive, and the legislative body. The role of the agency or department is to defend the base—the amount of the last fiscal year's appropriation—and to advocate spending for new or expanded programs. Agency and department heads are professionals who believe in the value of their organization and its programs, but they often find themselves playing Byzantine games to get the appropriations they want, as set forth in Table 8.2.

Aaron Wildavsky describes the basic quandary of agency and departmental representatives as follows:

> Life would be simple if they could just estimate the costs of their ever-expanding needs and submit the total as their request. But if they ask for amounts much larger than the appropriating bodies believe is reasonable, their credibility will suffer a drastic decline. . . . So the first decision rule for agencies is: do not come in too high. Yet the agencies must also not come in too low, for the assumption is that if the agency advocates do not ask for funds they do not need them.[42]

What agency heads usually do is carefully evaluate the fiscal-political environment. They take into consideration what happened last year, the composition of

Table 8.2

The Games Spenders
Play

The following are suggestions directed to state and local officials for maximizing their share of the budget during negotiations and hearings with the legislative body.

Massage your constituency.	Locate, cultivate, and utilize your clientele groups to further the organization's objectives. Encourage them to offer committee testimony and contact legislative members on your behalf.
Always ask for more.	If your agency or department doesn't claim its share of new revenues, someone else will. The more you seek, the more you will receive.
Spend all appropriated funds before the fiscal year expires.	An end-of-year surplus indicates that the elected officials were too generous with you this year; they will cut your appropriation next time.
Conceal new programs behind existing ones.	Incrementalism means that existing program commitments are likely to receive cursory review, even if an expansion in the margin is substantial. An announced new program will undergo comprehensive examination. Related to this game is **camel's nose under the tent,** in which low program start-up costs are followed by ballooning expenses down the road. (The U.S. defense industry has mastered this one.)
Here's a knife, cut out my heart while you're at it.	When told that you must cut your budget, place the most popular programs at the front of the line to the chopping block. Rely on your constituency to organize vocal opposition.
A rose by any other name.	Conceal unpopular or controversial programs within other program activities. And give them appealing names (for instance, call a sex education class "Teaching the Values of Family").
Let's study it first (or maybe you won't be re-elected).	When told to cut or eliminate a program, argue that the consequences would be devastating and should be carefully studied before action is taken.
Smoke and mirrors.	Support your requests for budget increases with voluminous data and testimony. The data need not be especially persuasive or even factual, just overwhelming.

the legislature, the economic climate, policy statements by the chief executive, the strengths of clientele groups, and other factors. Then they put forward a figure somewhat larger than they expect to get.[43]

The chief executive has a very different role in the budget process. In addition to tailoring the budget to his program priorities as closely as possible, he acts as an economizer. Individual departmental requests must be reconciled, which means that they must be cut, since the sum total of requests usually greatly exceeds estimated revenues. Of course, an experienced governor or mayor recognizes the games played by administrators; he knows that budget requests are likely to be inflated in anticipation of cuts. In fact, various studies on state and local budgeting indicate that the single most influential participant is the chief executive.[44] Not surprisingly, astute administrators devote time and other resources to cultivating the chief executive's support for their agency's or department's activities.

The role of the legislative body in the initial stage of the budget cycle is essentially to respond to the initiatives of the chief executive. The governor, mayor, or city manager proposes, and the legislature or council reacts. Later in the budget cycle, the legislative body performs an important function through its review of agency and department spending and its response to constituents' complaints.

Pervasive Incrementalism

In a perfect world, budgeting would be a purely rational enterprise. Objectives would be identified, stated clearly, and prioritized; alternative means for accomplishing them would be considered; revenue and expenditure decisions would be coordinated within the context of a balanced budget.

That is how budgeting *should* be done. But state and local officials have to allocate huge sums of money each year (about $1 trillion in 1992) in a budgetary environment where objectives are unclear or controversial and often conflict with one another. It is nearly impossible to prioritize the hundreds or thousands of policy items on the agenda. Financial resources, time, and the capacity of the human brain are severely constrained.

In order to cope with complexity and minimize political conflict over scarce resources, decision makers muddle through.[45] They simplify budget decision making by adopting decision rules. For example, instead of searching for the optimal means for addressing a public problem, they search only until they find a feasible solution. As a result, they sacrifice comprehensive analysis and rationality for **incrementalism** in which small adjustments (usually an increase) are made to the funding base of existing programs. Thus the policy commitments and spending levels of ongoing programs are accepted as a given—they become the base for next year's funding. Decisions are made on a very small proportion of the total budget: the increments from one fiscal year to the next. If the budget has to be cut, it is done decrementally; small percentage adjustments are subtracted from the base. In this way, political conflict over values and objectives is held to a minimum.

incrementalism

A decision-making approach in the budgetary process in which last year's expenditures are used as a base for this year's budget figures.

The hallmarks of incremental budgeting are consistency and continuity: The future becomes an extension of the present, which is itself a continuation of the past. Long-range commitments are made, then honored indefinitely. This is not to say that state and local budget making is a simple affair. On the contrary: It is as tangled and intricate as the webs of a thousand spiders.

Types of Budgets

A budget document can be laid out in various ways, depending on the purposes one has in mind: control, management, or planning. Historically, *control,* or fiscal accountability, has been the primary purpose of budgeting, incrementalism the dominant process, and the line item budget the standard document.

line item budget

A budget that lists detailed expenditure items such as computers and automobiles, with no attention to goals or objectives of spending.

Control Through Line Item Budgets   The **line item budget** facilitates control by specifying the amount of funds each agency or department receives and monitoring how those funds are spent. Each dollar can be accounted for with the line item budget, which lists every object of expenditure, from earth-moving vehicles to toilet paper, on a single line in the budget document. A police department's line items would typically include firearms, ammunition, gasoline for squad cars, uniforms, telephone costs, and so forth.

Line item budgets are useful for finding out where the money goes and tracking the annual incremental changes, but they do not tell us how effectively the money is spent. They do not inform us on important matters such as the impact of police spending on crime rates or clearance (arrest) rates, nor do they provide a clue as to the performance of a new program intended to reduce violent crimes or parking violations. Line item budgets facilitate incrementalism by emphasizing changes in the same expenditure categories year after year.

Budgeting for Management and Planning   Budget formats that stress *management* and *planning* are intended to help budget makers move beyond the narrow constraints of line items and incrementalism toward more rational and flexible decision-making techniques that focus on program results. Chief executives and agency officials seek to ensure that priorities set forth in the budget are properly carried out by organizational units—the management aspect of budgeting. The planning part involves orienting the budget process toward the future by anticipating needs and contingencies. A budget format that emphasizes planning is one that specifies objectives and lays out a financial plan for attaining them.

Several techniques permit budgeting for management and planning. The most important are performance budgets; planning, programming, and budgeting systems (PPBS), which require identification of program objectives and output measures; and zero-based budgeting (ZBB), which reviews the expenditure base each year. All of these systems are designed to address a single fiscal year's operating revenues and expenditures. Most state and local governments

capital budget

A budget that plans large expenditures for long-term investments, such as buildings and highways.

performance budgeting

Budgeting that is organized to account for the outcomes of government programs.

also use **capital budgets,** which allocate funds over a period of years to pay for expensive, one-time projects. These budget systems are much more demanding than the simple line item budget, but if properly implemented, they can significantly improve agency management and planning.

In **performance budgeting,** the major emphasis is on activities, or programs. The idea is to focus attention on how efficiently and effectively work is being done rather than on what things are acquired. Whereas line item budgets are input oriented, performance budgets are output oriented. For example, the performance of a state highway department can be evaluated by examining the unit costs of resurfaced highways or rebuilt bridges. By focusing on program objectives and work performance, performance budgets can assist managers, elected officials, and citizens in assessing the efficiency of government operations. This form of budget has been criticized, however, because suitable measures of program performance are difficult to find. For example, a new garbage truck might double the amount of trash collected in a given time period, but it might also leave a trail of garbage in its wake. Is this improved performance? State and local governments usually try to employ several indicators to gauge the efficiency and effectiveness of their programs, and they have made a great deal of progress in performance measurement. Still, it remains very difficult to judge the quality of service delivery in those government activities, such as social services and criminal justice, that deal with changes in human behavior and attitudes.

Planning, Programming, and Budgeting System   Introduced by Secretary of Defense Robert McNamara in the early l960s, a planning, programming, and budgeting system attempts to move public budgeting one step closer to the rational allocation of dollars among competing agencies, departments, and programs. The process of PPBS involves identifying (planning) goals and objectives, designing (programming) systems to put them into effect, and budgeting to finance each program adequately. President Lyndon B. Johnson ordered all national agencies to adopt PPBS in 1965. Many states and several large cities experimented with the technique as well, but found the process to be very time-consuming, complex, and expensive.[46] In the several states and localities that continue to use it, PPBS has been substantially modified.

Zero-Based Budgeting   Zero-based budgeting, or ZBB, was first applied to a government setting in Georgia in the early 1970s by then-governor Jimmy Carter. When Carter won the presidency in 1976, he ordered its usage throughout the national government. By 1985, more than twenty states had adopted the technique in whole or in part.

ZBB directly attacks incrementalism by formally and regularly re-examining the primary objectives and baseline funding of programs. Thus, programs compete each fiscal year, on an equal footing, for scarce government dollars. The base expenditures for existing programs are evaluated and may be cut or even eliminated.

Unfortunately, ZBB is a very time-consuming activity for managers. Reassessing all programs in a single jurisdiction is impossible in most settings, and most expenditures are uncontrollable in the short term anyway, because they have been allocated for ongoing programs. In general, the widely trumpeted promise of ZBB has gone unrealized. The technique has been useful, however, when applied on a limited basis in state and local government. Research indicates that legislators and administrators can reduce demands on their time and energy by examining as little as 20 percent of existing programs each year.[47]

No new budgeting technique that promises to wipe out incrementalism is on the horizon, but the innovations discussed above have nudged the budget process in the direction of rationalism and comprehensiveness. States and localities have moved beyond the limited control function of budgeting in a quest for improvements in management and planning. Incrementalism remains the norm, but program performance is now taken into consideration along with dollar outlays for personnel and material goods. Efficiency and effectiveness measures are increasingly used to evaluate how well governments use the taxpayers' dollars, and budgeting has been linked to planning beyond the immediate constraints of the next fiscal year. Of equal importance, perhaps, state and local governments are developing tailor-made budget systems by incorporating the elements of performance budgeting, PPBS, and ZBB that best suit their needs.[48]

Capital Budgets   The budget formats described above are utilized for operating allocations that are depleted within a year. Capital outlays are made over a longer period of time and are composed of "big ticket" purchases such as hospitals, university buildings, libraries, new highways, and major computer systems. They represent one-time, nonrecurring expenditures that call for special funding procedures, or a capital budget. Because such items cannot be paid for within a single fiscal year, governments borrow the required funds, just as most individuals borrow when buying a house or an expensive automobile. The debt is paid back in accordance with a predetermined schedule.

Capital projects are funded by selling general obligation or revenue bonds. *Bonds* are certificates of debt sold by a government to a purchaser, who eventually recovers the initial price of the bond plus interest. *General obligation bonds* are paid off with a jurisdiction's regular revenues (from taxes and other sources). The "full faith and credit" of the government is pledged as security. *Revenue bonds* are usually paid off with user fees collected from use of the new facility (for example, a parking garage, auditorium, or toll road). Payments for both types of bonds are scheduled over a period of time, which usually ranges from five to twenty years. The costs of operating a new facility, such as a school or recreation area, are met through the regular operating budget and/or user fees.

Capital budgeting lends itself to a more rational approach than do operating budgets. Payments must be scheduled years in advance, and most state and local governments have constitutional or statutory limitations on how much they can borrow. Thus, capital purchases must be anticipated and prioritized well into the future by agency heads, program administrators, and elected officials. Fiscal austerity, however, can throw the operating and capital budgets out of sync. For example, Connecticut finished construction of three new prisons in 1991 but could not afford to put inmates in them for at least two years.

....

The Quality and Capacity of Bureaucracies

In spite of the amount of criticism hurled at government bureaucracies by the popular media, elected officials, and others, the quality of public administration in state and local government has improved markedly. Of course, there is considerable variance among jurisdictions; the quality of administration is higher in those that are affluent, highly educated, industrialized, and urban.[49] But for the most part, patronage systems have been replaced by merit-based personnel systems, and bureaucracies are more representative of race, gender, and other characteristics of the American people. In addition, pay disparities based on gender are gradually being rectified through comparable worth, and some forty states now have comprehensive labor-relations policies in place.

Administrative quality is a critical factor in support of the resurgence of the states and the revitalization of localities. State and local governments have the capacity to do more things on a grander scale than ever before, and this trend is continuing in the 1990s. The basics of providing service, from disposing of dead animals to delivering healthy human babies, depend on government employees for high standards of performance and professionalism. To an increasing degree, those who work in state and local bureaucracies represent the values of professionalism and neutral competence.

....

Summary

Much of the popular criticism of state and local bureaucracy is misplaced. Innovation and capacity-building are two important characteristics of bureaucracy in state and local government. Advances include merit systems, representative bureaucracy, fair pay policies, labor-management relations policies, and increased professionalism and responsiveness in public administration. Budgeting in the nonnational governments is more oriented toward management and planning, although exercising financial controls is still important.

Key Terms

bureaucracy
merit system
neutral competence
representative bureaucracy
affirmative action
comparable worth
collective bargaining

bureaucratic discretion
clientele group
bureaucratic responsiveness
incrementalism
line item budget
capital budget
performance budgeting

State Legislatures

A murmur rushed through the packed galleries of the Oklahoma House of Representatives as the votes were tallied. Seventy-two yeas, twenty-five nays, and with that, the Oklahoma legislators had unceremoniously ousted their leader, the Speaker of the House. This event, known as "the revolt of the T-Bar Twelve" after the group of insurgent Democrats who plotted the coup in a seldom-used back room at the T-Bar Restaurant in Oklahoma City, carried great significance. Oklahoma had changed during the 1980s and the legislature was changing along with it.[1]

The Essence of Legislatures

"They're ba-a-ck." The announcement by the little girl in the movie *Poltergeist II* about her other-world friends could easily be applied to state legislators converging on the state capitol year after year. Every January (or February or April in a few states; every other January in a few others), state legislatures reconvene in session to do the public's business. More than seven thousand legislators hammer out solutions to intricate and often intransigent public problems.

Legislative Functions

Legislatures engage in three principal functions: *policymaking, representation, and oversight*. The first, policymaking, includes enacting laws and allocating funds. During the early 1990s, legislators debated such issues as school choice, Medicaid cost containment, and prison overcrowding. These deliberations resulted in the revision of old laws, the passage of new laws, and changes in spending. This is what policymaking is all about. Legislatures do not have sole control of the state policymaking function—governors, courts, and agencies also determine policy, through executive orders, judicial decisions, and administrative regulations, respectively—but they are the dominant policymaking institution in state government.

In their second function, legislators are expected to represent their constituents—the people who live in their district—in two ways. At least in theory, they are expected to speak for their constituents in the state capital—to do "the will of the public" in designing policy solutions. This is not an easy task. On "quiet" issues, a legislator seldom has much of a clue as to what the public's will is. On "noisy" issues, constituents' will is rarely unanimous. Individuals and organized groups with different perspectives may write to or visit their legislator to urge her to vote a certain way on a pending bill. In the other method of representation, legislators act as their constituents' facilitators in state government. For example, they may help a citizen deal with an unresponsive state agency. This kind of constituency service, or casework, as it is often called, can pay dividends at re-election time, since voters tend to look favorably on a legislator who has helped them out.

The oversight function is one that legislatures have taken on recently. Concerned that the laws they passed and the funds they allocated frequently did not produce the intended effect, lawmakers began to pay more attention to the performance of the state bureaucracy. Legislatures have adopted a number of methods for checking up on agency implementation and spending. The oversight role takes legislatures into the administrative realm and, not surprisingly, is little welcomed by agencies, although legislatures see it as a logical extension of their policymaking role.

A History of Legislative Malfunction

The dawning of the twentieth century found state legislatures in poor shape, and they continued to languish well into the 1960s. One widely cited criticism was that state legislatures were using horse-and-buggy methods to solve jet-age problems.[2]

Malfunctioning legislatures were the result of three conditions: not enough pay, not enough time, and not enough help.[3] Until the mid-1960s, pay was so low that legislative service attracted only the independently wealthy, the idle, and young careerists on the rise. (For example, lawyers who were just beginning their practice often campaigned for the legislature as a way of getting their name known, in hopes that it might bring some business their way.) Annual legislative salaries ranged from $100 in New Hampshire to $10,000 in New York. Serving in the legislature was a part-time vocation, and most members had to supplement their salaries with other jobs. Others collected unemployment compensation; and some sought income from legal fees, retainers from corporations, public utilities, or interest groups, or outright payoffs from lobbyists for votes or other assistance in the legislative process.

The length and frequency of legislative sessions were additional problems. Some were restricted to as few as 36 days in session (in Alabama, for example), and most met on a biennial basis. For instance, the Texas constitution required the legislature to meet once every 2 years for 140 days. (Critics have suggested that the constitution really meant for the legislature to meet once every 140 years for 2 days.) As the policy problems confronting state government became more numerous and complex, legislators found themselves overburdened with work and without the time to give much more than cursory examination to most of the proposed legislation that passed across their desks.

As for help, legislatures in the early 1960s were woefully understaffed and poorly equipped to process information, to study problems, or to respond to the needs of citizens. Many states did not make transcripts of committee hearings or floor debates, and thus had no formal legislative history. Some states turned to organizations like the state bar association for assistance in drafting bills. Without enough staff, legislatures lacked an independent research capability. It was virtually impossible for them to accumulate information and systematically analyze possible solutions to contemporary problems. Instead, they tended to rely on the governor and the executive branch as well as on lobbyists for special interests, who set the policy agenda and controlled the flow of information.

State legislatures could not function as effective policymaking institutions under these conditions. Despite the pervasive sense that matters had to improve, it took two factors to shake legislatures out of their lethargy: first, the federal court decisions in *Baker* v. *Carr* (1962) and *Reynolds* v. *Sims* (1964), which mandated reapportionment of both the lower and upper houses of state legislatures (compliance with these rulings eventually changed the composition of legislatures); and, second, the activities of private reform groups of the 1960s such as the Committee on Economic Development and the Citizens Conference on State Legislatures, which promoted the modernization of state legislatures to make them more capable institutions. The success of the reformers has produced legislative assemblies that are far more professional than they were in the past.

Legislative Dynamics

State legislative bodies are typically referred to as "the legislature," but their formal titles vary. In Colorado, it is the General Assembly that meets every year; in Massachusetts, it is the General Court; and in Oregon, it is the Legislative Assembly. The legislatures of forty-three states meet annually; in seven (Arkansas, Kentucky, Montana, Nevada, North Dakota, Oregon, and Texas), they meet every two years. The length of the legislative session varies widely. For example, the Massachusetts General Court convened on January 4, 1989, and did not adjourn until January 2 of the following year—a total of 364 calendar days in session. In Utah, by contrast, the legislature gathered in Salt Lake City on January 9, 1989, and was out of town by February 22, 1989, for a total of 45 calendar days in session.[4]

The Senate and the House

State legislatures have two houses or chambers, similar to those of the U.S. Congress. Forty-nine states are bicameral (the exception is Nebraska, which in 1934 established a unicameral legislature). Bicameralism owes its existence to the postcolonial era, in which an "upper house," or Senate, represented the interests of the propertied class, and a "lower house" represented everyone else. Even after this distinction was eliminated, states stuck with the bicameral structure, ostensibly because of its contribution to the concept of checks and balances. It is much tougher to pass "bad" bills when they have to survive the scrutiny of two legislative houses. Having a bicameral structure, then, reinforces the status quo. Unicameralism might improve the efficiency of the legislature, but efficiency has never been a primary goal of the consensus-building deliberative process.

In the forty-nine bicameral states, the upper house is called the Senate; the lower house is usually the House of Representatives. The average size of a state Senate is forty members; Houses typically average about one hundred members. As with most aspects of state legislatures, chamber size varies substantially—from the Alaska Senate with twenty members to the New Hampshire House with four hundred representatives. For senators, the term of office is usually four years; approximately one-quarter of the states use a two-year Senate term. In many states, the election of senators is staggered. House members serve two-year terms, except in Alabama, Louisiana, Maryland, and Mississippi, where four-year terms prevail.

There are 7,461 state legislators in this country: 1,995 senators and 5,466 representatives. Democrats outnumber Republicans 60 percent to 40 percent; men outnumber women 82 to 18 percent; and whites outnumber nonwhites 95 to 5 percent. Yet even this small proportion of women and nonwhites represents a substantial increase, relative to their virtual absence from most pre-1970s legislatures. (Profile 9.1 examines the issue of women in the legislature.) In terms of occupations, lawyers and business owners predominate, followed by employees of someone else and farmers.[5] Figure 9.1 shows the breakdown in professions.

Legislative Districts

Legislators are elected from districts. Each state is divided, or apportioned, into legislative districts, and the delineation of these districts is an intensely political process. Legislative decisions about districting effectively structure the balance of power in a state. In the 1960s, for example, the less populated panhandle area of Florida was overrepresented in the legislature at the expense of the heavily populated southern areas of the state. The balance of power lay with the northern rural regions. Therefore, despite Florida's rapid urbanization during that period, public policy continued to reflect the interests of a rurally based minority.

malapportionment

Skewed legislative districts that violate the "one person, one vote" ideal.

Malapportionment   Political decisions on districting have often resulted in this sort of **malapportionment,** or unequal representation. For example, before reform, some states had simplified the senatorial districting system by allocating an equal number of senators to each county. (This system calls to mind the U.S. Senate, which has two senators per state.) Because counties vary in population size, some senators were representing ten or twenty times as many constituents as their colleagues were. New Jersey offered one of the most extreme cases. In 1962, one county contained 49,000 residents and another had 924,000; yet each county was allocated one senator, and each senator had one vote in the Senate.[6] This kind of imbalance meant that a small group of people had the same institutional power as a group that was nineteen times larger. Such dispropor-

Profile 9.1

Women's Work: Serving in the State Legislature

A T-shirt popular at women's political rallies in the 1980s reads "A woman's place is in the House . . . and in the Senate." In some states, the slogan has become reality. By 1992, 18 percent of the country's state legislators were women. Though far from achieving gender parity in the legislature, women are a more visible and forceful presence than ever before. Every state has female legislators. The representation of women is greatest in Arizona (34 percent), Washington (33 percent), Maine (32 percent), Vermont (31 percent), and Colorado (31 percent). Women occupy 14 percent of the legislative leadership posts and 11 percent of the committee chair positions.

The growing number of women in the legislature begs the "what difference does it make?" question. Surveys show that women state legislators think of their female constituents as a special responsibility. And although their legislative interests run the gamut, they often identify issues such as equal pay, comparable worth, child abuse, day care, child support, and infant mortality as legislative priorities. State

legislatures with greater numbers of women among their ranks tend to consider and pass more of this priority legislation than do legislatures with lower female representation.

In addition, once women legislators reach positions of leadership within a chamber, they operate differently from their male counterparts. For instance, one study of legislative leaders in twenty-two states found that womens' leadership styles tended toward coordination or consensus-building rather than the more traditional command style. In the words of Vera Katz, the Speaker of Oregon's House of Representatives, it is "the feminization of leadership."

Women are no longer oddities in the legislature. Indeed, as the public becomes more disenchanted with "politics as usual," they stand a good chance of increasing their numbers.

Sources: "Women in Elective Office 1992," Center for the American Woman and Politics (New Brunswick, N.J.: Rutgers University, 1992); Sue Thomas, "The Impact of Women on State Legislative Policies," *Journal of Politics* 53 (November 1991): 958–976; Malcolm E. Jewell and Marcia Lynn Whicker, "Women as State Legislative Leaders," paper presented at the annual meeting of the Southern Political Science Association, Tampa, November 1991; Foster Church, "Just Like a Woman," *Governing* 3 (September 1990): 26.

tionate power is inherently at odds with representative democracy, in which each person's vote carries the same weight.

Until the 1960s, the federal courts ignored the legislative malapportionment issue. It was not until 1962, in a Tennessee case in which the malapportionment was especially egregious (House district populations ranged from 2,340 to 42,298), that the courts stepped in. In that case, *Baker* v. *Carr*, the U.S. Supreme Court ruled that the Fourteenth Amendment guarantee of equal protection applies to state legislative apportionment.[7] With that ruling as a wedge, the Court ruled that state legislatures should be apportioned on the basis of population. In *Reynolds* v. *Sims* (1964), Chief Justice Earl Warren summed up the apportionment ideal by saying, "Legislators represent people, not trees or acres."[8] Accordingly, districts should reflect population equality: one person, one vote. This decision, which overturned the apportionment practices of six states, caused a **reapportionment** fever to sweep the country, and district lines were redrawn in every state.

reapportionment

The redrawing of legislative district lines to conform as closely as possible to the "one person, one vote" ideal.

The State House as a Second Job, 1986

A 1986 survey determined that 11 percent of legislators do not have an outside occupation, and that the proportion of full-time legislators is on the rise.

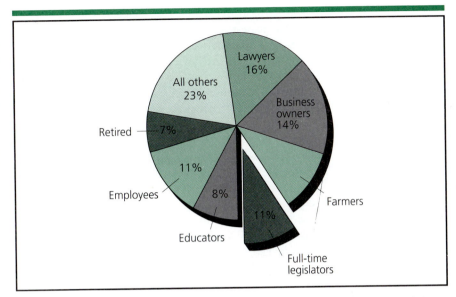

Source: Elizabeth Kolbert, "As Workload Grows, Number of Part-time Legislators Falls," *New York Times*, June 4, 1989, p. 13. Copyright © 1989/91 by The New York Times Company. Reprinted by permission.

Reapportionment provided an immediate benefit to previously underrepresented urban areas, and increased urban representation led to a growing responsiveness in state legislatures to the problems and interests of cities and suburbs. Where reapportionment had a partisan effect, it generally benefited Republicans in the South and Democrats in the North. Other impacts of reapportionment have included the election of younger, better-educated legislators and, especially in southern states, better representation of blacks.[9] In addition, state legislatures, in the opinion of those who served during the reapportionment period of 1967–1977, took a discernibly liberal turn.[10] All in all, reapportionment is widely credited with improving the representativeness of American state legislatures.

Reapportionment after the 1990 Census State legislatures are reapportioned after the United States census, which is taken every ten years. This arrangement allows population fluctuations—growth in some areas, decline in others—to be reflected in redrawn district lines. Thirty-nine legislatures do the job themselves; nine states attempt to depoliticize the process by using impartial commissions to develop their reapportionment plans.[11] In two states, Alaska and Maryland, the governor plays a dominant role in redistricting.

In apportioning a legislature, the tradition has always been to draw district lines so as to maximize the strength of the party in power. The art of drawing district lines creatively was popularized in Massachusetts in 1812, when a political cartoonist for the *Boston Gazette* dubbed one of Governor Elbridge Gerry's district creations a **gerrymander** because the district, carefully configured to

gerrymander

The process of creatively designing a legislative district to enhance the electoral fortunes of the party in power.

reflect partisan objectives, was shaped like a salamander. Gerrymandering has not disappeared. In fact, when Indiana's districting plan was challenged in the courts in 1986, the Republican Speaker of the House acknowledged that the intent was "to save as many Republicans as possible."[12]

Reapportionment has become a sophisticated operation in which statisticians and geographers use computer mapping to assist the legislature in designing an optimal districting scheme. Allowable deviation from the population-equality standard varies, but 5 percent appears to be the maximum. Although "one person, one vote" is the official standard, some unofficial guidelines are also taken into consideration. Ideally, districts should be geographically compact and unbroken. Those who draw the lines pay close attention to traditional political boundaries such as counties and to the fortunes of political parties and incumbents. As long as districts adhere fairly closely to the population-equality standard, federal courts tolerate the achievement of unofficial objectives. But it does make for some oddly shaped districts resembling lobsters, spiders, and earmuffs.[13] Figure 9.2 shows the design of several districts drawn by the Florida House of Representatives in 1992.

Increasingly, legislatures have to pay attention to the effects of their reapportionment schemes on minority voting strength. In fact, amendments to the Voting Rights Act and subsequent court rulings instruct affected states to create districts in which racial minorities will have majority status. Mississippi found out just how serious the U.S. Department of Justice was about enhancing minority representation when the state's redistricting plan was rejected in 1991.

Figure 9.2

Florida Reapportionment

In reapportioning Florida in 1992, legislators worked toward an ideal "one person, one vote" ratio of 107,816 people per district. Creating districts with equal populations meant that some counties were split up and others were combined, as this map of northeastern Florida shows. The population deviation from any one of these districts to another is less than 2 percent.

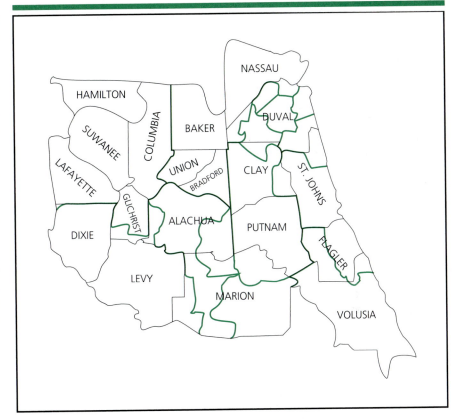

Source: Committee on Reapportionment, Florida House of Representatives.

In the Magnolia State, where African-Americans make up 35.6 percent of the population (and 16 percent of the House and 4 percent of the Senate), the Justice Department concluded that the legislature's plan did not create enough majority-black districts.[14] Mississippi lawmakers went back to the drawing board to create a more acceptable plan.

The answer to the "how many districts?" question is frequently determined by the formula that is used to define a majority-black district. In Georgia, for example, two redistricting plans emerged during the 1991 special session on reapportionment. The state's official plan used a 70-percent-black threshold, thus creating 37 majority-black House seats and 11 majority-black Senate seats. A rival plan set the threshold at 60 percent and was therefore able to carve out 51 majority-black House seats and 15 in the Senate. Establishing a higher threshold makes it more likely that a black candidate will be elected from the district, but it has another impact, too: A study of South Carolina Senate reapportionment demonstrated that "packing" blacks into districts diluted the Democratic vote of nearby districts, thereby allowing Republicans to win.[15] Both blacks and Republicans have benefited from such reapportionment.

During the redistricting that followed the 1990 Census, racial minorities and the Republican party formed a curious alliance in some southern states. In Texas, a state covered under the Voting Rights Act, the federal judiciary played an unusually intrusive role. Minority groups and Republicans challenged the reapportionment plan passed by the Democratically controlled legislature in 1991. Eventually, a three-judge federal panel substituted its own redistricting map in place of the plan designed by the Texas legislature.[16] The judicial plan had a decidedly Republican tilt to it. Consequently, for the first time since Reconstruction, Republican control of the state Senate seemed within the realm of possibility.

Legislative Pay

Legislative compensation has increased handsomely in the past two decades, again with some notable exceptions. Before the modernization of legislatures, salary and per diem (money for daily expenses) levels were set in the state constitution and, hence were impossible to adjust without a constitutional amendment. By the early 1990s, only six states continued to have constitutional restrictions on legislative compensation.[17] Lifting these limits put legislatures, as the policymaking branch of state government, in the curious position of setting their own compensation levels. Recognizing that this power is a double-edged sword (the legislators can vote themselves pay raises and the public can turn around and vote them out of office), almost half of the states have established compensation commissions or advisory groups to make recommendations on legislative remuneration.

As of 1992, annual salaries of legislators (excluding per diem) ranged from a low of $100 in New Hampshire to a high of $57,500 in New York.[18] Eight states paid their legislators more than $30,000 annually. Compare these figures with the more modest pay levels of legislators in Arizona ($15,000), Georgia ($10,500), and West Virginia ($6,500). States paying a more generous compensation typically demand more of a legislator's time than do low-paying states, however. The data in Table 9.1 reflect the link between legislative salaries and legislative session length.

Legislative Leadership

Legislatures need leaders, both formal and informal. Each chamber usually has four formal leadership positions. In the Senate, a president and a president pro tempore (who presides in the absence of the president) are in charge of the chamber; in the House, the comparable leaders are the Speaker and the Speaker pro tempore. These legislative officials are chosen by the members. Both houses have two political party leadership positions: a majority leader and a minority leader.

The leaders are responsible for making the legislature run smoothly and see-ing that it accomplishes its tasks. In a typical chamber, the presiding officer

Table 9.1

Legislative Salaries
and Length of Ses-
sions in Ten States

State	Annual Salary	Duration of 1989 Session
California	$52,500	December 5, 1988–September 15, 1989
Illinois	37,230	January 10, 1989–November 3, 1989
New Jersey	35,000	January 10, 1989–January 8, 1990
Ohio	42,427	January 3, 1989–December 31, 1989
Pennsylvania	47,000	January 3, 1989–January 2, 1990
Indiana	11,600	November 22, 1988–April 23, 1989
Maine	7,125	December 7, 1988–July 1, 1989
Mississippi	10,000	January 3, 1989–April 10, 1989
Oregon	11,868	January 9, 1989–July 4, 1989
Texas	7,200	January 10, 1989–May 29, 1989

Source: "Legislative Salaries and Length of Sessions in Ten States," from *The Book of States, 1990–91*.
© 1991 The Council of State Governments. Reprinted with permission.

appoints committee members, names committee chairs, controls the activity on the floor, allocates office space and committee budgets, and, in some states, selects the majority leader and the holders of other majority-party posts.[19] The actual influence of the leadership varies from one chamber to another. One factor that affects leaders' power is whether the positions are rotated or retained. Leaders who have the option of retaining their position can build power bases; in the case of rotation, however, one set of leaders is replaced with another on a regular basis, so the leaders are lame ducks when they assume the posts.

Leadership in legislatures is linked to political parties. In states with competitive political parties, legislative behavior and decisions have a partisan cast. There are Democratic and Republican sides of the chamber and Democratic and Republican positions on bills. The parties meet in caucuses to design their legislative strategies and generate camaraderie. In states dominated by one political party, partisanship is less important. In one-party settings, the dominant party typically develops splits or factions at the expense of party unity. However, when the vastly outnumbered minority party begins to gain strength, the majority party usually becomes more cohesive. In the Texas House, traditionally a bastion of Democratic party strength, Republicans now hold about one-third of the seats. By way of response, the Democrats have coalesced and organized a truly partisan Democratic caucus.[20] As a result, legislative voting patterns among Democrats show less fractionalization.

One reward for party loyalty comes when pork barrel projects are dispersed. The way this process works in the Democratic-controlled North Carolina legislature is instructive.[21] Requests for local appropriations (to construct a civic center in district *x*, a sewer system in district *y*) are consolidated into an omnibus "pork" bill (affectionately known as the "Christmas tree" bill). The leaders determine what is in and what is out. Which projects are included depends largely on partisanship (Democrats get more than Republicans) and loyalty (party members who occasionally vote with Republicans get less than "true" Democrats).

Legislative Committees

The workhorse of the legislature is the committee. Under normal circumstances, a committee's primary function is to consider bills—that is, to hear testimony, perhaps amend the bills, and ultimately approve or reject them. A committee's action on a bill precedes debate in the House or Senate.

All legislative chambers are divided into committees, and most committees have created subcommittees. Committees can be of several types. A *standing committee* regularly considers legislation during the session. A *joint committee* is made up of members of both houses. Some joint committees are standing; others are temporary and are convened for a specific purpose, such as investigating a troubled agency or a particularly challenging public policy problem. Most states use *interim committees* during the period when the legislature is not in session to get a head start on an upcoming session. The number of committees varies, but most Senates and Houses have standing committees on the topics listed in Table 9.2.

A substantive standing committee tends to be made up of legislators who are interested in that committee's subject matter.[22] Thus you find farmers on the Agriculture Committee, teachers on the Education Committee, bankers on the Commerce Committee, lawyers on the Judiciary Committee, and so on. These legislators bring knowledge and enthusiasm to the committee; they also bring a certain bias since they tend to function as advocates for their career interests.

The central concern of a standing committee is its floor success—getting the full chamber to accede to its recommendations on a bill. There are a number of plausible explanations for a committee's floor success.[23] For one thing, a committee with an ideological composition similar to that of the chamber is likely to be more successful than one whose members are at odds with the chamber. Also, committees full of legislatively experienced members generally have more floor success than committees composed of legislative novices. And committees that have a reputation for being tough have more floor success with their bills than committees that are easy and pass everything that comes before them.

How a Bill Becomes Law

A legislative bill starts as an idea and travels a long, complex path before it emerges as law. It is no wonder that of the 2,094 bills introduced in the Michigan legislature in 1991, only 201 had become law by the end of the session.[24] A legislative session has a rhythm to it. Minor bills and symbolic issues tend to be resolved early. Major, potentially divisive issues take a much longer

Table 9.2	Both houses of state legislatures typically have standing committees dealing with these substantive issues:
Standing Commit-tees of the Legislature	Agriculture Banking/Financial Institutions Business and Commerce Communications Education Elections Energy Environment and Natural Resources Ethics Government Operations Health Insurance Judiciary and Criminal Justice Local Affairs Public Employees Rules Social/Human Services Transportation In addition, both houses have standing committees that address the raising and allocating of state funds. These committees may have different names in different chambers: Appropriations Finance and Taxation Ways and Means

time to wend their way through the legislative labyrinth. The budget or appropriations bill is typically one of the last matters that the legislature debates during the session.

We seldom think of meat processing and bill processing as similar, but legislative veterans frequently comment that there are two items that people should not see being made: sausage and laws. This comparison is probably unfair to the meat-processing industry. Figure 9.3 diagrams the law-making process.

The Birth of a Bill: Idea and Introduction

Bills do not emerge out of thin air; they come from the recommendations of interest groups and their lobbyists, state agencies, constituents, and citizen groups. Governors are initiating legislation at an ever-increasing rate.

Suppose that an organization you have joined, Students Opposed to Toxins (SOT), has come up with a plausible solution to the toxic waste problem

Figure 9.3

How a Bill Becomes Law

At each of the stages in the process, supporters and opponents of a bill clash. Most bills stall at some point and fail to make it to the end.

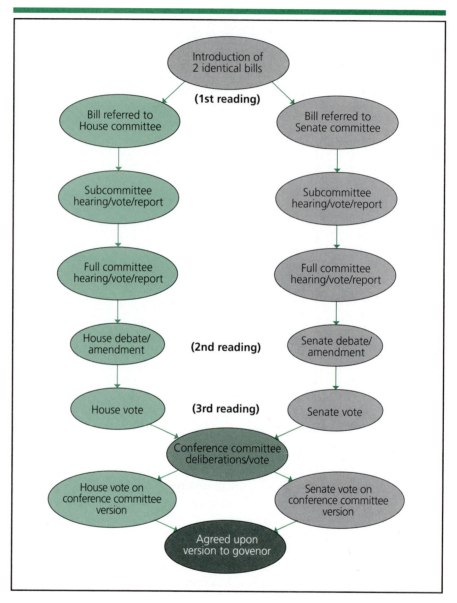

plaguing your state. The first step is to find a legislator who would be willing to introduce your solution in the form of legislation. In other words, you have to find someone to sponsor the bill. Introduction ("putting the bill in the hopper") gives the proposal legislative life.

The new bill will be assigned a number (for example, House Bill 1520) and given *first reading*. In this stage, it is announced to the House (this usually involves reading its title) and referred by the Speaker to a committee. Committee referral matters. The Speaker can assign H.B. 1520 to the Committee on Environment, which is likely to be receptive to its contents, or to the Committee on Commerce, which may be less than enthusiastic about it. If the bill goes to Environment, it will be scheduled for a hearing. If it goes to Commerce, it stands a good chance of being assigned to a subcommittee that will never meet. If no action is taken in committee, the bill has been *pigeonholed* or *bottled up* and, in all likelihood, will die there. (This potential for committees to become bill graveyards has caused many legislatures to adopt procedures to force a committee to hear a bill.) If H.B. 1520 will cost the state money, it is referred to the Committee on Appropriations in addition to a substantive committee.

Committee Action

For the sake of argument, let's assume that good fortune visits SOT, and that the Speaker is an environmentalist (or fears the wrath of the Environment Committee chairperson if the bill is assigned to Commerce) and refers H.B. 1520 to the Committee on Environment. The bill will be assigned by the committee chairperson to a subcommittee for study and recommendation. The committee staff, knowledgeable about environmental issues, will evaluate it. At the subcommittee hearing, you and SOT will have a chance to present arguments in favor of it, and the bill's sponsor will also attend, probably rushing into the hearing room from another committee meeting. Opponents will also be heard. As a consequence of the discussion, members of the subcommittee may offer amendments to the bill. This is another critical point, as some amendments may not be supportive of the bill's content. For example, if a subcommittee member raises his hand and suggests that the subcommittee strike everything after the enacting clause (the introduction), he has proposed an *unfriendly amendment*, effectively killing the bill by deleting all of its substance. For the sake of this example, let's assume that only friendly, clarifying amendments are attached to H.B. 1520 and that the subcommittee recommends it favorably to the full committee.

The Committee on Environment will schedule the bill, with the subcommittee's amendments, for a full committee hearing. You can be sure that the bill's opponents, unhappy at failing to get the bill pigeonholed or reported unfavorably by the subcommittee, will have contacted the members of the full committee to make their case. Anticipating this, SOT should engage in its own lobbying of committee members in support of the bill. (You cannot expect the merits of the bill to carry the day. You have to convince committee members that voting for H.B. 1520 is in their interest.) Both the bill's sponsor and the groups that testified before the subcommittee typically reappear at the full committee hearing.

Given the number of bills introduced and the proportion that ultimately become law, SOT should be pleased that its idea has gotten this far. Since so many legislatures operate with absolute limits on session length, they often run out of time before they can consider all of the bills that have been introduced.[25]

Time is an interesting concept in a legislature, and skillful legislators use time to their advantage. Common explanations for legislative action (or inaction) are "because of a lack of time" or "owing to time pressures."

Let's assume that H.B. 1520 is supported by the committee, although it is subjected to a variety of amendments. Someone on the committee might move that the committee offer a substitute for H.B. 1520. It will probably be wise for the sponsor to accept the motion, because reporting a committee substitute adds the weight of the committee to what was originally an individually sponsored bill. The next critical juncture is getting the bill through the scheduling committee, often called the Committee on Rules and Calendar. While the Committee on Environment was considering H.B. 1520, twenty other committees were also considering bills. The Rules and Calendar Committee is a point at which bills can pile up. Some may languish on the back burner while the committee schedules the bills it prefers or considers most pressing for floor debate. Thus SOT has to make certain that H.B. 1520's sponsors (the Environment Committee and the original sponsor) actively urge the Rules and Calendar Committee to schedule the bill for prompt floor action.

Floor Action

Some time usually passes between standing committee passage and floor action, so SOT and other supporters of the bill should use the time to contact legislators and acquaint them with the positive features of H.B. 1520. Again, you can be certain that the bill's opponents have not conceded defeat. Opposing interests will be lobbying hard against H.B. 1520.

When the bill is scheduled for floor action, it is given *second reading,* which means that it is put formally before the House for consideration. Arguments for and against ensue, and amendments are offered and accepted or rejected. If H.B 1520 survives this part of the process, its supporters can breathe a sigh of relief. True, it still faces *third reading,* which is a vote on final passage; but in most states second reading spells a bill's fate. Third reading becomes a formality, and you may find that some of H.B. 1520's opponents vote for the bill at this point, in grudging recognition that they have lost the battle. (This maneuver often confuses voters when they try to evaluate a legislator's voting record. A legislator may be actively opposed to a particular bill right up until third reading, at which time he votes in favor of it.) Virtually all states require a *roll call vote* on third reading, which means that an individual legislator's vote is recorded. Watching the electronic toteboard flash a green (yes) or a red (no) light next to a legislator's name is the key moment both for the bill and for SOT members.

The Other Chamber

H.B. 1520 now goes to the Senate, where it will experience a similar routine of referral, committee hearings, and floor action. Because this process can be lengthy, SOT would have been well served to have had a senator introduce a companion bill to H.B. 1520 at the beginning of the session, so the bills could move through the two houses simultaneously. Whichever bill passes first can be substituted for the companion in the other chamber, if the other chamber agrees. This saves time, an important commodity in legislatures with short sessions.

If the Senate further amends H.B. 1520, the two versions of the bill will have to be reconciled. If the House refuses to accept the Senate's amendments, the presiding officers of the two chambers appoint a *conference committee* to devise some kind of compromise. This can be a challenging process, depending on the extent of disagreement and the intensity of the conferees' views. Their compromise is called a conference committee report and is voted on by both houses. If both chambers approve the conference committee report, the bill is *enrolled*—certified and signed by the presiding officers—and sent to the governor for her signature.

The Governor

The law-making process is not over until the governor acts (or fails to act). Bills passed by the legislature can be signed by the governor, vetoed by the governor, or not acted on by the governor. If the governor signs H.B. 1520, it becomes law. If the governor vetoes it, it still has a chance to become law, if the legislature can *override* the veto. An override typically requires an extraordinary majority (a two-thirds vote) in both houses. If the legislature feels strongly about H.B. 1520, it might be able to muster the necessary votes. But if the governor's veto comes after the legislature has adjourned, a special session must be called to consider the veto. (This is why some legislatures do not officially adjourn until the governor has acted on all bills.) If the session has ended and the governor has not acted on H.B. 1520, in most states the bill becomes law without the governor's signature (the unsigned bill is a symbolic gesture of the governor's lack of support). In other states, the governor's inaction is a *pocket veto* of the bill (see Chapter 7), and the bill is dead.

After reading about the law-making process, you might be amazed that any good idea survives to become law. In one sense, that is a valid assessment, because without pushes and nudges along the way—without active and skillful lobbying, without the support of key legislators, and without fortuitous timing—few bills would become law. A consensus has to be built around the issue, and the bill has to be widely perceived as the appropriate solution, before proposed legislation becomes statutory.

....

Legislative Behavior

Legislatures have their own dynamics, their own way of doing things. Senate and House rule books spell out what can and cannot be done, in the same way that an organization's by-laws do. Legislatures, for the most part, function as self-regulating institutions; it is especially important, therefore, that participants know what is expected of them. To make certain that the chamber's rules are understood, most legislatures conduct orientation sessions for new members.

Legislative Norms

An understanding of the legislature involves not only knowledge of formal structures and written rules but also an awareness of informal norms and unwritten policies. For example, nowhere in a state's legislative rules does it say that a freshman legislator is prohibited from playing a leadership role, but the unwritten rules of most legislatures place a premium on seniority. A primary rule of legislative bodies is that "you gotta go along to get along," a phrase that emphasizes teamwork and "paying your dues." Legislators who are on opposite sides of a bill to regulate horse racing might find themselves on the same side of a bill outlawing the sale of handguns known as Saturday night specials. Yesterday's opponent is today's partner. For this reason, no one can afford to make bitter enemies in the legislature and expect to flourish. Legislators also learn early that concealing the real purpose of a bill in order to secure its passage will get them in trouble.[26] During the 1988 session, for instance, a freshman legislator in Tennessee wrote in his diary that he planned to watch one of his colleagues more closely, because "he slipped in an amendment increasing legislative pensions without disclosing what he was doing."[27]

Those who aspire to rise from rank-and-file legislator to committee chairperson and perhaps to party leader or presiding officer find consensus-building skills quite useful. These skills come in handy because many norms are intended to reduce the potential for conflict in what is inherently a setting full of conflict. For instance, a freshman legislator is expected to defer to a senior colleague. Although an energetic new legislator might chafe under such a restriction, one day he will have gained seniority and will take comfort in the rule. Moreover, legislators are expected to honor commitments made to each other, which encourages reciprocity: "If you support me on my favorite bill, I will be with you on yours." A legislator cannot be too unyielding. Compromises, sometimes principled but more often political, are the backbone of the legislative process. Very few bills are passed by both houses and sent to the governor in exactly the same form as when they were introduced.

It is worth noting that the internal organization of legislatures varies, as a study of three legislatures—New York, Connecticut, and California—emphasizes.[28] New York has a stable organizational system in which seniority is the major criterion for advancement. Empire State legislators tend to be careerists who expect a long tenure in office. In Connecticut, where an unstable system prevails and few career incentives exist, members stay in the legislature a short time and then return to private life. California has an unstable system that is not seniority oriented, and talented legislators can advance quickly; therefore, California legislators tend to be politically ambitious, and the system allows them to act as entrepreneurs. The informal rules in these three legislatures are quite different, and the institutions tend to attract different types of legislators. Accordingly, the New York legislature is considered career oriented, Connecticut's legislature a dead end, and California's a springboard.[29]

Informal rules are designed to make the legislative process flow more smoothly. Legislators who cannot abide by the rules, those who refuse to "go along," find it difficult to get along. They are subjected to not-so subtle behavior modification efforts, such as powerful social sanctions (ostracism and ridicule) and legislative punishment (bottling up their bill in committee or assigning them an unpopular committee), to promote adherence to norms.

Legislative Cue-Taking

Much has been written about how legislators make public policy decisions, and a number of explanations are plausible. Legislators may adopt the policy positions espoused by their political party. They may follow the dictates of their conscience—that is, do what they think is right. They may yield to the pressures of organized interest groups. They may be persuaded by the arguments of other legislators, such as a committee chairperson who is knowledgeable about the policy area or a trusted colleague who is considered to be savvy; or they may succumb to the entreaties of the governor, who has made a particular piece of legislation the focus of her administration. Of course, legislators may also attempt to respond to the wishes of their constituents. On a significant issue—one that has received substantial media attention—they are likely to be subjected to tremendous cross pressures.

One remarkably candid assessment of how legislators make public policy decisions was offered by a freshman in the Tennessee House of Representatives. He identified two often unspoken but always present considerations: "Will it cost me votes back home?" and "Can an opponent use it against me [in the] next election?"[30] These pragmatic concerns intrude on the more idealistic notions of decision making. They also suggest a fairly cautious approach to bold policy initiatives.

Assuming that legislators are concerned about how a vote will be received back home, it seems logical that they would be particularly solicitous of public opinion. Some research on the subject, however, has shown that state legislators frequently hold opinions at odds with those of their constituents.[31] Moreover, they misperceive what the public is thinking, so it is difficult for them to act as

delegate

A legislator who functions as a conduit for constituency opinion.

mere **delegates** and simply fulfill the public's will. To improve the communications link, some legislators use questionnaires to poll constituents about their views, and some hold town meetings at various spots in the district to assess the public's mood.

It is quite probable that first-term legislators feel more vulnerable to the whims of the public than legislative veterans do. Hence the new legislator devotes more time to determining what the people want, while the experienced

trustee

A legislator who votes according to his or her conscience and best judgment.

legislator "knows" what they want (or perhaps knows what they need) and thus functions as a **trustee**—someone who follows his or her own best judgment. Since the vast majority of legislators are returned to office election after election, it appears that there is some validity to this argument. Recent research on Oklahoma and Kansas legislators, for example, found that the members' personal values were consistently important in their decision choices.[32]

In the final analysis, the issue under consideration appears to be the determining factor in how legislators make decisions. "When legislators are deeply involved with an issue, they appear to be more concerned with policy consequences" than with constituency preferences.[33] In this situation, legislators are not simply bent on re-election. But if legislators are not particularly concerned about an issue that is important to their constituents, they will follow their constituents' preference. In that sense, they act as **politicos**, adjusting as the issues and cues change.

politico

A legislator who functions as a delegate or a trustee, as circumstances dictate.

Legislative Reform and Capacity

It was not easy to get state legislatures where they are today. During the 1970s, fundamental reforms occurred throughout the country as legislatures sought to increase their capacity and to become more professional. The modernization process never really ends, however.

The Ideal Legislature

In the late 1960s, the Citizens' Conference on State Legislatures (CCSL) studied legislative performance and identified five characteristics critical to legislative improvement.[34] Ideally, a legislature should be functional, accountable, informed, independent, and representative; the acronym is FAIIR.

The *functional* legislature has virtually unrestricted time to conduct its business. It is assisted by adequate staff and facilities, and has effective rules and procedures that facilitate the flow of legislation. The *accountable* legislature's operations are open and comprehensible to the public. The *informed* legislature manages its workload through an effective committee structure, legislative activities in between sessions, and a professional staff; and it conducts regular budgetary review of executive branch activities. The *independent* legislature runs its own affairs independent from the executive branch. It exercises oversight of agencies, regulates lobbyists, manages conflicts of interest, and provides adequate compensation for its members. Finally, the *representative* legislature has a diverse membership that effectively represents the social, economic, ethnic, and other characteristics of the constituencies.

CCSL evaluated the fifty state legislatures and scored them according to the FAIIR criteria. The rankings, which appear in Table 9.3, offered a relatively scientific means of comparing one state legislature with another. Overall, the "best" state legislatures were found in California, New York, Illinois, Florida, and Wisconsin. The "worst," in the assessment of CCSL, were Alabama, Wyoming, Delaware, North Carolina, and Arkansas.

The CCSL report triggered extensive self-evaluation by legislatures around the country. The results are readily apparent. In terms of the CCSL criteria, states have made tremendous strides in legislative institution building. Re-examination of the criteria reveals these facts:

1. *Staffing.* Individual legislators now have vastly more staff resources at their disposal than they did twenty years ago. Many states provide year-round staff for legislators (especially senators) at the state capital, and some states make personnel available in a legislator's district office. (A few states limit staff to the session only.) Professionals serve on at least some legislative committees in all states, and the legislative leaders' staff has increased. These factors have helped make legislatures more independent and informed.

2. *Compensation.* Serving in the legislature is more lucrative today than it was twenty years ago. In about one-quarter of the states, legislators can afford to be full-time, or professional, legislators. Legislative leaders typically enjoy a higher level of remuneration than members. For example, when the Tennessee legislature increased annual legislative salaries by 32 percent (from $12,500 to $16,500), it tripled the salaries of House and Senate speakers (from $18,500 to $47,500).[35]

3. *Time.* Annual sessions are the rule, not the exception. However, thirty-eight state legislatures continue to operate with constitutional or statutory limits on session length. In order to remain ready to respond to a crisis, some legislatures that have the authority to do so will recess temporarily rather than adjourn. In this way the presiding officers can call legislators back into session without the formality of a special session.[36]

4. *Committee structure.* In response to CCSL recommendations, most states have tinkered with legislative committee structure. Over time, however, they have not pared their committees back as drastically as CCSL advocated. Legislators are stretched thin when they are assigned to four committees. However, legislatures do use their committees more effectively now, especially by scheduling committee meetings during the period when the legislature is not officially in session.

5. *Facilities.* Legislative surroundings have improved, in some states quite dramatically. New legislative buildings have been built, and some states, such as Florida, have erected new capitols. Legislators have private offices, ample meeting space, and computerized bill-tracking and vote-tallying systems.

6. *Leadership.* Legislatures have experienced substantial democratization in the years since the CCSL study. Legislative leaders' control over "information, favors, and finances" has diminished,[37] and there is an increasing tendency to rotate leadership assignments.

7. *Rules and procedures.* Legislatures have begun to realize that their rules and procedures are not cast in stone. Periodic review of rules and procedures is not uncommon. For example, legislatures have imposed limitations on the number of bills that can be introduced, instituted more equitable committee hearing procedures, and established deadlines for committee action.

Table 9.3

FAIIR Rankings of State Legislatures

Overall	State	Functional	Account-able	Informed	Independ-ent	Represen-tative
1	Calif.	1	3	2	3	2
2	N.Y.	4	13	1	8	1
3	Ill.	17	4	6	2	13
4	Fla.	5	8	4	1	30
5	Wis.	7	21	3	4	10
6	Iowa	6	6	5	11	25
7	Hawaii	2	11	20	7	16
8	Mich.	15	22	9	12	3
9	Nebr.	35	1	16	30	18
10	Minn.	27	7	13	23	12
11	N. Mex.	3	16	28	39	4
12	Alaska	8	29	12	6	40
13	Nev.	13	10	19	14	32
14	Okla.	9	27	24	22	8
15	Utah	38	5	8	29	24
16	Ohio	18	24	7	40	9
17	S. Dak.	23	12	15	16	37
18	Idaho	20	9	29	27	21
19	Wash.	12	17	25	19	39
20	Md.	16	31	10	15	45
21	Pa.	37	23	23	5	36
22	N. Dak.	22	18	17	37	31
23	Kans.	31	15	14	32	34
24	Conn.	39	26	26	25	6
25	W. Va.	10	32	37	24	15

8. *Size.* CCSL reformers argued that a legislature composed of between 100 and 150 senators and representatives would be about right. Almost 40 percent of today's legislatures exceed that size; and, not unexpectedly, large legislatures balk at reducing the number of legislators. One noteworthy reduction came when Illinois voters cut their House by one-third, to 118 representatives. But size is a tricky issue. A large legislature reduces the citizen-to-legislator ratio and thus increases the potential for representation, but it also probably functions less efficiently than a small one. Which value should be maximized?

9. *Ethics.* Legislatures have made substantial efforts to promote ethical behavior in the institution. They have adopted financial disclosure and conflict-of-interest laws for members, and a few have begun to impose restrictions on a former legislator's ability to hire himself out as a legislative lobbyist. Problem Solving 9.1 elaborates on some of the most recent ethics reforms.

Table 9.3 (cont.)

Overall	State	Functional	Account-able	Informed	Independ-ent	Represen-tative
26	Tenn.	30	44	11	9	26
27	Ore.	28	14	35	35	19
28	Colo.	21	25	21	28	27
29	Mass.	32	35	22	21	23
30	Maine	29	34	32	18	22
31	Ky.	49	2	48	44	7
32	N.J.	14	42	18	31	35
33	La.	47	39	33	13	14
34	Va.	25	19	27	26	48
35	Mo.	36	30	40	49	5
36	R.I.	33	46	30	41	11
37	Vt.	19	20	34	42	47
38	Tex.	45	36	43	45	17
39	N.H.	34	33	42	36	43
40	Ind.	44	38	41	43	20
41	Mont.	26	28	31	46	49
42	Miss.	46	43	45	20	28
43	Ariz.	11	47	38	17	50
44	S.C.	50	45	39	10	46
45	Ga.	40	49	36	33	38
46	Ark.	41	40	46	34	33
47	N.C.	24	37	44	47	44
48	Del.	43	48	47	38	29
49	Wyo.	42	41	50	48	42
50	Ala.	48	50	49	50	41

Source: Citizens' Conference on State Legislatures. *The Sometime Governments: A Critical Study of the 50 American Legislatures,* 2d ed. (Kansas City, Mo.: CCSL, 1973).

The Effect of Reform

The jury is still out on whether increased professionalism in state legislatures represents a total victory. Initial research suggested that legislative profession-alism had an independent, positive effect on social welfare policy.[38] In other words, policymaking in professional legislatures seemed to be more responsive to the needs of lower-income citizens. However, subsequent research arrived at a different conclusion: Professionalized legislatures did not seem to affect the direction of state public policy.[39] More recent studies have sought to clarify the relationship between the characteristics of a legislature and its public policy outputs. They have led to the recognition that legislative characteristics *and* a variety of other factors, such as a state's socioeconomic conditions and executive branch strength, affect policy decisions.[40]

Problem Solving 9.1

Votes for Sale

The Problem: It was like a made-for-TV movie, only better. Selected members of the Arizona legislature had starring roles in an elaborate sting operation conducted by the Phoenix Police Department and the Maricopa County prosecutor during the 1991 session. As they pocketed wads of cash, a hidden video camera and microphone recorded one lawmaker flatly stating, "I don't give a ____ about issues. I do deals." A state senator was equally direct on film: "We all have our prices." In all, seven legislators took money from an actor posing as "Tony V." in return for their support of a bill to legalize casino gambling. In other words, these lawbreaking solons sold their votes.

Arizona was not the only state in which legislators supplemented their salaries with tainted cash. In South Carolina, the FBI, using a lobbyist-turned-informer as its operative, snared seventeen legislators in a sting dubbed "Operation Lost Trust." Once again, concealed video cameras and microphones recorded legislators taking money to vote in favor of a gambling bill—in this instance, one concerned with pari-mutuel betting. Eventually, sixteen legislators were convicted of selling their votes; one was exonerated in a jury trial.

The Solution: The well-publicized legislative scandals in Arizona and South Carolina, as well as incidences of corruption in other states, have triggered an array of ethics reforms. State laws regulating campaign financing have been strengthened, conflict-of-interest statutes have been broadened, codes of ethics have been adopted, and ethics commissions have been created. In some states, the new rules have put a definite crimp in the legislator-lobbyist relationship. In Wisconsin, for example, legislators are required to pay their own way at receptions hosted by lobbyists. California requires lobbyists, legislators, and their aides to attend an annual seminar on ethics. And in South Carolina, public officials are now prohibited from accepting *anything* of value from a lobbyist.

The ethics reforms of the early 1990s may have solved the immediate problems, but larger questions remain about ethical behavior in a system that is fundamentally about power and influence.

Sources: Susan Biemesderfer, "Making Laws, Breaking Laws," *State Legislatures* 17 (April 1991): 12–18; Linda Wagar and Elaine S. Knapp, "The Truth about Ethics," *State Government News* 34 (June 1991): 5–9, 32; Don Harris, "It Will Never Be Behind Us," *State Legislatures* 17 (July 1991): 38–40.

In the late 1980s, legislative capacity gained attention. Recent analysis has confirmed the significance of the variables that CCSL used. Legislatures that are closer to the FAIIR standards appear to have greater capacity than the remaining "less FAIIR" institutions do.[41]

Political scientist Alan Rosenthal, who has closely observed legislative reform, has warned that "the legislature's recent success in enhancing its capacity and improving its performance may place it in greater jeopardy than before."[42] That certainly was not an intended effect of the reform efforts. Rosenthal's argument is that a constellation of demands pulls legislators away from the legislative core. That is, the new breed of legislators get caught up in the demands of re-election, constituent service, interest groups, and political careerism and thus neglect institutional matters such as structure, procedure, staff, image, and community. The legislature as an institution suffers, because it is not receiving the necessary care and attention from its members.

Consider the idea of a citizen-legislator, one for whom service in legislature is a part-time endeavor. Since the onset of reform, the proportion of legislators who are lawyers, business owners, or insurance or real estate executives has dropped from almost one-half to slightly over one-third.[43] This has been accompanied by a rise in the number of full-time legislators. In states such as Michigan, Pennsylvania, and Wisconsin, roughly two-thirds of the lawmakers identify themselves as "legislators," with no other occupation. The critical issue is whether the decline of the citizen-legislator is a desirable aspect of modernization. Should a state legislature represent a broad spectrum of vocations or should it be composed of career politicians? One perspective is this: "If I'm sick, I want professional help. I feel the same way about public affairs. I want legislators who are knowledgeable and professional."[44] Another view is represented by a Michigan legislator who believes that his careerist colleagues have lost touch with their constituents. "When you spend all your time in Lansing, you're more influenced by the lobbyists than by your constituents."[45]

In effect, state legislatures are becoming more like the U.S. Congress. Legislators are staying in the legislature in record numbers. Modernization has made the institution more attractive to its members, and thus turnover rates are declining. Do we really want fifty mini-Congresses scattered across the land? Today's legislatures are more "FAIIR" than in the past, but reform has also brought greater professionalization of the legislative career, increased polarization of the legislative process, and more fragmentation of the legislative institution.[46]

Term Limits

The "revolt of the T-Bar Twelve," the vignette that opened this chapter, was but the tip of a much larger chunk of ice. In September 1990, Oklahoma voters overwhelmingly approved a ballot measure limiting the tenure of state legislators and statewide officers. Limiting terms was not just a Sooner thing. Within two months, voters in California and Colorado had followed suit. And, although Washington state voters defeated a similar measure, a wave of term limitation mania was threatening to sweep the country. By the summer of 1991, 145 bills to limit legislators' terms had been introduced in forty-two states.[47] As many as twenty states were anticipating term limitation questions on their November 1992 ballots.

In Oklahoma, California, and Colorado, voters have limited their legislators to a specific number of years in office. In Oklahoma, a legislator is limited to twelve years in total legislative service, whether in the House, in the Senate, or in combination. The California and Colorado measures imposed specific limits for each chamber. In California, members of the State Assembly are limited to three two-year terms and members of the Senate to two four-year terms. Theoretically, a state assemblywoman could complete six years in the Assembly and then run for the Senate, where she could serve for eight years. Colorado voters imposed an eight-year limitation on service in each chamber. Although angry

California lawmakers claimed that term limits were unconstitutional, the measure has survived legal challenges in the courts.

The success of term limits in these three states has made the movement a coast-to-coast phenomenon.[48] In Oregon, a group called LIMITS (Let Incumbents Mosey into the Sunset) grew out of a tax limitation organization. In Wisconsin, a coalition known as "Badgers Back in Charge" has taken up the term limitation cause. And political activists of many stripes—populists, conservatives, and libertarians—have found a home in the term limitation movements in Florida, Michigan, and Texas.

Term limits are likely to have three consequences. First, and most obvious, the domination of a chamber by powerful entrenched veteran legislators will end. Second, in any one session, the proportion of first-termers is likely to be substantial. These two consequences mean that the distribution of power within a legislature will fluctuate. Third, groups that have been underrepresented in the legislature, women and minorities, will have greater electoral opportunities because of the guarantee of open seats. These three consequences beg the question: Will term limits result in better legislation? It remains to be seen.[49]

Why, after two decades of legislative reform, are voters saying "no mas" to their legislators? The primary explanation has to do with the low level of public confidence in legislative institutions generally. The scandals that rocked the legislatures in Arizona and South Carolina, the subject of Problem Solving 9.1, portrayed a powerfully negative impression of contemporary lawmakers. In addition, the intractable problems that confront states, especially those with declining economies, are difficult for even the most effective legislatures to resolve.

Relationship with the Executive Branch

In Chapter 7, you read about strong governors leading American states boldly into the twenty-first century. In this chapter, you have read about strong legislatures charting a course for that same century. Do these institutions ever collide in their policymaking? Is there conflict between the legislature and the governor in a state? Of course there is. Probably the most pitched governor-versus-legislature battle of 1992 occurred in New Jersey. There, uncompromising politicians wrestling with nagging fiscal problems engaged in threats and maneuvers to achieve their objectives. Eventually, Governor James Florio vetoed the entire state budget; the legislature did him one better and overrode the veto eight hours before the fiscal year began. In the words of one observer, "Conflict is the chief manifestation of a new calculus of political and institutional power in state government today."[50]

Interinstitutional tension is inevitable, but it is not necessarily destructive. It is inevitable because both governors and legislators think that they know what is best for the state. It is not necessarily destructive because during the posturing, bargaining, and negotiating that produces a consensus, governors and legislators may actually arrive at the "best" solution.

Connecticut lawmakers celebrate the passage of the state budget, a process made all the more difficult because of conflict with the governor.

Dealing with the Governor

The increased institutional strength of the legislature and its accompanying assertiveness have made for strained relations with a governor accustomed to being the political star. When a legislature is dominated by one party and the governor is of the other party, a condition referred to as **split party control** of state government, the ingredients for conflict are assembled. This is a fairly new phenomenon in the Democratic-dominated southern states, which elected their first Republican governors since Reconstruction during the 1970s (in the Carolinas and Texas), 1980s (in Alabama and Louisiana), and 1990s (in Mississippi). In some states in the Rocky Mountain area, the reverse was the case. During the 1980s, popular Democratic governors and Republican-dominated legislatures governed Arizona, Colorado, Utah, and Wyoming. The result of split party control can be finger-pointing and blame-shifting.

But having a governor and a legislature controlled by the same party does not necessarily make for easy relations. In fact, it may actually increase the strain between the two branches. Especially in states where the two parties are competitive, legislators are expected to support the policy initiatives of their party's governor. Yet the governor's proposals may not mesh with individual legislators' attitudes and ambitions.

split party control

A situation in which the governorship is controlled by one party and the legislature by the other party.

Executives have a media advantage over deliberative bodies like a legislature. We saw media use developed to a veritable art form at the national level during the Reagan years, when the media conveyed images of the president as leader and the Congress as a collection of self-interested politicians. A similar situation exists at the state level. The governor is the visible symbol of state government and, as a single individual, fits into a media world of thirty-second sound bites. The Colorado Senate president explains it from a distinctly legislative perspective: "We never win in Colorado in the public's eye. We, the legislature, are always the bad guys, and the governor is the white hat, and he has been very successful in making that appeal to the public through the news media."[51] In contrast, media images of the legislature often portray deal-making, pork barrel politics, and general silliness.

Another weapon of the governor is the veto. In 1987, the Wisconsin legislature found out just how powerful this can be, when the Republican governor used 290 partial vetoes (the deletion of specific items) to virtually rewrite the budget produced by the Democratic legislature.[52] The governor's explanation was that the legislature was testing him by passing a budget bill that was "porked up."[53] In the 1988 session, the legislature changed its strategy; according to the Speaker of the House, "We put more controversial items in bills where he couldn't use his partial veto, where he had to veto the whole bill or sign it."[54]

Sometimes governors who have previously served as legislators seem to have an easier time dealing with the law-making institution. For example, former Governor Madeleine Kunin of Vermont assumed the office after three terms in the legislature and one term as lieutenant governor, "knowing the needs of legislators, the workings of the legislative process, the sensitivities of that process."[55] Usually about two-thirds of the governors have had legislative experience, although the proportion has recently declined. In 1992, for example, twenty-eight of the fifty governors had put in time in the legislative ranks.

The legislature is not without its weapons. In recent years a popular battleground has been the state budget. As the New Jersey example showed, if the legislature can muster the votes, it can override a gubernatorial veto. Legislatures have enacted other measures designed to enhance their control and to reduce the governor's flexibility in budgetary matters.[56] For example, some states now require the governor to get legislative approval of budget cutbacks in the event of a revenue shortfall. Others have limited the governor's power to initiate transfers of funds among executive branch agencies. These actions reflect the continuing evolution of legislative-executive relations.

Overseeing the Bureaucracy

Legislative involvement with the executive branch does not end with the governor. State legislatures are increasingly venturing into the world of state agencies and bureaucrats, with the attitude that "we've authorized the program, we've allocated funds for it, so let's see what's happening." Legislative oversight involves four activities: policy and program evaluation, legislative review of administrative rules and regulations, sunset legislation, and review and control of federal funds received by the state.[57]

Policy and Program Evaluation   Legislatures select auditors to keep an eye on state agencies and departments (in a few states, auditors are independently elected officials). Auditors are more than superaccountants; their job is to evaluate the performance of state programs as to their efficiency and effectiveness (sometimes known as the postaudit function). In particular, they conduct periodic performance audits to measure goal achievement and other indicators of progress in satisfying legislative intent, a process that has been credited with both saving money and improving program performance.[58] The key to a useful auditing function is strong legislative support (even in the face of audits that turn up controversial findings) and, at the same time, a guarantee of a certain degree of independence from legislative interference.[59]

Legislative Review of Administrative Rules   All state legislatures are involved in reviewing administrative rules and regulations, but they vary in the way they do it. They may assign the review function to a special committee (such as a Rule Review Committee) or to a specific legislative agency, or they may incorporate the review function in the budgetary process.

Legislative review is a mechanism through which administrative abuses of discretion can be corrected. Legislative bills frequently contain language to the effect that "the Department of Youth Services shall develop the necessary rules and regulations to implement the provisions of this act." This gives the agency wide latitude in establishing procedures and policies. The legislature wants to be certain that, in the process, the agency does not overstep its bounds or violate legislative intent. If it is found to have done so, then the legislature can overturn the offensive rules and regulations through modification, suspension, or veto, depending on the state.

legislative veto

An action whereby the legislature overturns a state agency's rules or regulations.

This is a true gray area of legislative-executive relations, and court rulings at both the national and state levels have found the most powerful of these actions, the **legislative veto,** to be an unconstitutional violation of the separation of powers. If legislative vetoes and similar actions are determined to be unconstitutional, more states will return to the traditional means of reviewing agency behavior—through the budgetary process. Increasingly, legislatures are requiring state agencies to furnish extensive data to justify their budget requests, and they can use their financial power to indicate their displeasure with agency rules and regulations.

sunset laws

Statutes that set automatic expiration dates for specified agencies and other organizations.

Sunset Legislation   Half the states have established **sunset laws** that set automatic expiration dates for specified agencies and other organizational structures in the executive branch. An agency can be saved from termination only by an overt renewal action by the legislature. Review occurs anywhere from every two years to every twelve years, depending on individual state statute, and is conducted by the standing committee that authorized the agency or by a committee established for sunset review purposes (such as a Government Operations Committee).

During the 1970s, sunset legislation was widely hailed as an effective tool for asserting legislative dominion over the executive branch, but fifteen years' experience with the technique has produced mixed results, and some states have repealed their sunset laws. Agency reviews tend to be time consuming and costly. Nevertheless, they do acquaint the legislature with the intricacies of agency operations. Termination is more a threat than an objective reality.

State Legislative Review   Since the early 1980s, legislatures have played a more active role in directing the flow of federal funds once they have reached the state. Before this time, the sheer magnitude of federal funds and their potential to upset legislatively established priorities caused great consternation among legislators. The executive branch virtually controlled the disposition of these grant funds by designating the recipient agency and program. In some cases, federal money was used to fund programs that the state legislature did not support. Federal dollars were simply absorbed into the budget without debate and discussion, and legislators were cut out of the loop. By making federal fund disbursement part of the formal appropriations process, however, legislators have redesigned the loop.

If legislatures are to do a decent job in forecasting state priorities, some control of federal funds is necessary. In the face of reduced federal aid to states, it is critical for legislators to understand the role that federal dollars have played in program operation. When funding for a specific program dries up, it is the legislature's responsibility to decide whether to replace it with state money.

How effectively are legislatures overseeing state bureaucracies? As with so many questions, the answer depends on who is asked. From the perspective of legislators, their controls increase administrative accountability. A survey of legislators in eight states found legislative oversight committees, the postaudit function, and sunset laws to be among the most effective bureaucratic controls available.[60] Another effective device, and one that legislatures use in special circumstances, is legislative investigation of an agency, an administrator, or a program. But from the perspective of the governor, many forms of legislative oversight are simply meddling and, as such, they undermine the separation of powers.[61]

Legislatures and Capacity

State legislatures are fascinating institutions. Although they share numerous traits, each maintains some uniqueness. Despite their newfound seriousness of purpose, legislatures still address items that most observers would deem trivial. The Colorado legislature, for example, spent some of its precious 1991 session time debating a bill that would make those who unfairly disparage food products the targets of civil suits. That same legislature, however, gave considerable time and energy to much more compelling problems, such as health care and workers' compensation. Table 9.4 lists some of the major issues with which legislatures will grapple in the 1990s.

Table 9.4

Ten Hot Legislative
Issues for the 1990s

The Issue	What's Going On
Term Limits	Public unhappiness with the performance of state legislatures fuels this movement to force lawmakers out of office after a fixed number of years/terms.
Medicaid Cost Containment	Medicaid is an increasingly large chunk of a state's budget. Options include Oregon's rationing plan and the more popular "managed care" approach.
Workers' Compensation	High medical costs, frequent litigation, and allegations of unsafe conditions and benefits abuse make this a complex subject. Alternatives to raising rates are being sought.
Privatization	An effort is under way to make government services more efficient by contracting them out to the private sector. Expect more private toll roads.
School Choice	States are attempting to force schools to improve by allowing students to choose which school they will attend. The big question is whether private schools should be part of the choice options.
School Finance Equity	Finance equity is a response to the problem of disparities between rich and poor school districts.
Childhood Lead Poisoning	This is reportedly the leading environmental health hazard to children. Children in older homes are especially at risk. Proposals advocate more screening of children and cleanup of hazards.
Prenatal Care	Such care is a response to the persistent problem of high infant mortality. Measures seek broadened eligibility and expanded programs.
Sexual Harassment	The Clarence Thomas–Anita Hill hearings transfixed the nation. Prohibitions against sexual harassment and provisions for damages are on the agenda.
Alternative Prison Sentencing	Prison overcrowding persists; under consideration are options other than jail time, such as boot camps and work release programs.

Source: "Ten Legislative Issues to Watch in 1992," *Governing* 5 (January 1992): 38–39. Reprinted with permission.

The demands placed on state legislatures are unrelenting. Challenges abound. The ability of the legislatures to function effectively in these times depends on institutional capacity. The extensive modernization that virtually all legislatures underwent in the 1970s is evidence of institutional renewal. Structural reforms and a new breed of legislator have altered state legislatures and are sending them in the direction of increased capacity. How ironic, then, that with all their institutional success, reformed legislatures continue to struggle with their public images.[62]

Summary

Overcoming a history of legislative malfunction, state legislatures have embarked on an aggressive effort at reform and modernization. These changes have affected their three major functions: policymaking, representation, and oversight. Today's legislatures have become more functional, accountable, informed, independent, and representative, or FAIIR.

Legislatures are deliberative bodies with their own informal rules and behavioral norms. Today's legislator is more likely than ever before to consider herself or himself a full-time legislator, a situation that has led to some debate over whether the institutions are becoming "congressionalized." Meanwhile, legislatures' relationship with governors and the executive branch continues to move in the direction of greater interaction.

Key Terms

malapportionment
reapportionment
gerrymander
delegate
trustee

politico
split party control
legislative veto
sunset laws

10

The Judiciary

I n the case of *Barnes* v. *Glen Theatre Inc.* (1991), a prudish U.S. Supreme Court ruled that nude dancing, being dangerous to "order and morality," is not protected as free expression under the First Amendment of the Constitution. This case, which arose in Indiana, was tried in the federal courts under national constitutional law.

Yet in Boston, a city once known for banning all manner of objects and activities deemed to be immoral, totally naked women grind, bump, and pirouette at tacky cabarets, fully confident that their activities are legal. In Massachusetts, the voluntary display of a naked body has been protected under the *state* constitution as a form of expression since the state supreme court ruled it so in 1984.[1] As the U.S. Supreme Court has become increasingly conservative from the Chief Justiceship of Earl Warren (1953–1969) to today's Rehnquist Court, state courts have become more and more popular with individuals and groups advocating liberal causes such as civil rights, free speech, and freedom of expression. All sorts of conflicts and problems find their way to state and local courts, from the profound (abortion rights) to the profane (nude dancing).

Sometimes, state supreme courts act as policymakers. As the third branch of government, the judiciary is, after all, the final authority on the meaning of laws and constitutions and the ultimate arbiter of disputes between the executive and legislative branches. It also makes public policy through rulings on questions of political, social, and economic significance and may serve as the last chance for minority interests to defend themselves from the decisions of the majority. As noted in Chapter 4, state courts have become more active policymakers in recent years and have increasingly based important decisions on state constitutions rather than on the national Constitution. And like the other branches of state government, their structures and processes have been greatly reformed and modernized in recent years. In our lifetimes, nearly all of us will experience the judicial branch as direct participants. At times, the courts are more accessible to us than are the other branches of government.

The work of the fifty state court systems is divided into three major areas: civil, criminal, and administrative. In **civil cases,** one individual or corporation sues another over an alleged wrong. Typical civil actions are property disputes and suits for damages arising from automobile or other accidents. **Criminal cases** involve the breaking of a law by an individual or a corporation. The state is usually the plaintiff; the accused is the defendant. Murder, assault, embezzlement, and speeding are common examples. **Administrative cases** concern court actions such as probating wills, revoking drivers' licenses, or determining custody of a child of divorced parents. Some administrative cases involve administrative law judges and quasi-judicial (less formal) proceedings.

civil case

A case that concerns a grievance involving individuals or organizations, not the breaking of a law.

criminal case

A case that involves the breaking of a law.

administrative case

A legal dispute not involving a civil suit or a criminal matter.

The Development and Structure of State Court Systems

State courts have evolved in response to changes in their environment. In colonial days, they developed separately, influenced by local customs and beliefs.

Owing to a shortage of trained lawyers and an abiding distrust of English law, the first judges were laymen who served on a part-time basis. It did not take long for the courts to become overwhelmed with cases: Case overloads were reported as long ago as 1685.[2] More than three hundred years later, case backlogs still plague our state judiciaries.

As the population and the economy grew, so did the amount of litigation. Courts expanded in number and in degree of specialization. Their names reflected the problems they were designed to address: small claims court, juvenile court, traffic court. However, their development was not carefully planned. Rather, new courts were added to existing structures. The results were predictably complex and confusing, with overlapping, independent jurisdictions and responsibilities. For instance, Chicago offered an astounding array of jurisdictions, estimated at one time to number 556.[3] State court systems were beset not only by numerous overlapping and independent jurisdictions but by a host of other serious problems, including administrative inefficiency, congestion, and excessive delays. In short, the American system of justice left much to be desired.

The organization of the state courts is important because it affects the quality and quantity of judicial decisions and the access of individuals and groups to the legal system. It also influences how legal decisions are made. An efficiently organized system, properly staffed and administered, can do a better job of deciding a larger number of cases than a poorly organized system can. Court structure is of great interest to those who make their living in the halls of justice—namely, lawyers and judges. It can also be an issue of concern to others who find themselves in court.

The Three Tiers

original jurisdiction

The power of a court to hear a case first.

appellate jurisdiction

The power of a court to review cases previously decided by a lower court.

States today have a three-tiered court structure: limited jurisdiction courts, trial courts, and appellate courts. Each tier, or level, has a different *jurisdiction,* or range of authority. Courts in the lowest tier—*limited jurisdiction courts*—have **original jurisdiction** over specialized cases, such as those involving juveniles, traffic offenses, and small claims (see Problem Solving 10.1). This means that these courts have the power to hear certain types of cases first, in contrast to **appellate jurisdiction,** which means the courts review cases on appeal after they have been tried elsewhere. Most states have three to five courts of limited jurisdiction, with names that reflect the type of specialized case: traffic court, police court, probate court, municipal court, and so on. Criminal cases are usually restricted by law to violations of municipal or county ordinances and are punishable by a small fine, a short jail term, or both. It would not be surprising if additional courts of limited jurisdiction were created in the future to deal with special types of cases or circumstances. For example, some jurisdictions have established "drug courts" to process the increasingly large number of drug-related cases more efficiently and consistently.

The middle tier of the state judiciary is composed of *major trial courts,* which exercise general authority over civil and criminal cases. Most cases are filed

Problem Solving 10.1

Taking Your Case to Small Claims Court

The Problem: You feel that you have been ripped off by your landlord, or by the slick-talking salesperson who convinced you to purchase that off-brand CD player.

The Solution: Almost all states offer a relatively simple and inexpensive way to settle minor civil disputes without either party having to incur the financial and temporal burdens of lawyers and legal procedures. Small claims courts are usually divisions of county, city, or district trial courts. The plaintiff (the person bringing the suit) asks for monetary recompense from the defendant (the individual or firm being sued) for some harm or damage. Claims are limited to varying amounts, depending on the state. The average maximum is around $900. Some states allow claims as high as $3,000. The cost of taking a case to small claims court is usually $25 or less.

The proceedings are informal. Each party presents the relevant facts and arguments to support his or her case to a judge. The party with the preponderance of evidence on his or her side wins. Most disputes involve tenant-landlord conflicts, property damage, or the purchase of merchandise (for example, shoddy merchandise or the failure of a customer to pay a bill).

According to a 1978 study by the National Center for State Courts, the plaintiff usually wins. About half the time, defendants do not show up to plead their case and thereby lose by default. In contested cases, plaintiffs win around 80 percent of the time. Of course, collecting the award is quite a different matter, sometimes requiring the services of the local sheriff.

The Consumer's Union, the publisher of *Consumer Reports* magazine, offers an instruction booklet on small claims court. It recommends the following steps in handling your case:

1. *Properly identify your opponent.* The legal name of a business may not be the same as the advertised name. Look at the business license, which must be posted. Individuals can often be identified through automobile registration files.
2. *Send a warning letter* stating your claim, the facts of the case, and that you will file a suit in small claims court if you do not receive a satisfactory reply within a specified period of time.
3. *Find the court.* Try the telephone book under small claims, municipal, or county courts. Another option is to call the state or local office of consumer affairs.
4. *File a claim and pay the filing fee.* Follow the exact procedures specified.
5. *Notify the defendant.* The court will usually do this for you, but if its initial effort does not meet with success, it becomes your responsibility. The local sheriff may deliver the notification for a fee.
6. *Assemble the evidence.* This includes all relevant documents, photographs, witnesses, and objects.
7. *Consider an out-of-court settlement* if offered by the defendant.
8. *Present your case to the judge.* A dress rehearsal in front of a friend or family member is advised.

Source: ''Role of the Small-claims Court,'' *Consumer Reports,* November 1979, pp. 666–670. Copyright 1979 by Consumers Union of United States, Inc., Mount Vernon, NY 10553. Reprinted by permission from *Consumer Reports.*

initially under a major trial court's original jurisdiction. However, trial courts also hear cases on appeal from courts of limited jurisdiction. Major trial courts are often organized along county or district lines. Their names—circuit courts, superior courts, district courts, courts of common pleas—vary widely.

The upper tier consists of **supreme courts** (sometimes called courts of last resort) and, in most states, **intermediate appellate courts.** Oklahoma and Texas have two supreme courts, one for criminal cases and the other for civil disputes. Thirty-five states have intermediate appellate courts (Alabama, Oklahoma, Oregon, Texas, Pennsylvania, and Tennessee have two, typically one each for criminal and civil cases). Most are known as superior courts or courts of appeals. Their work generally involves cases on appeal from lower courts. Thus, these courts exercise appellate jurisdiction. State supreme courts also have original jurisdiction in certain types of cases, such as those dealing with constitutional issues.

Appellate court decisions are rendered by a panel of judges, in contrast to a single judge or a jury, which decides lower court cases. Majority rule determines case outcomes. Usually, the judges write majority and minority opinions. The typical supreme court consists of a chief justice and six associate justices, although several states have a total of nine justices and some have only five. The number of intermediate appellate court justices varies widely from state to state; Texas has eighty, Arizona and four other states only three.

Intermediate appellate courts constitute the most notable change in the structure of the state court system during the past twenty-five years. They are intended to increase the capability of supreme courts by reducing their caseload burden, speeding up the appellate process, and improving the quality of judicial decision making. The bulk of the evidence points to moderate success in achieving each of these objectives.[4] Case backlogs and delays have been reduced, and supreme court justices are better able to spend an appropriate amount of time on significant cases.

If a state supreme court so chooses, it can have the final word on any state or local case except one involving a national constitutional question, such as First Amendment rights. Some cases can be filed in either federal or state court. For example, a person who assaults and abducts a victim and then transports him across a state line can be charged in state court with assault and in federal court with kidnapping. Some acts violate nearly identical federal and state laws; possession or sale of certain illegal drugs is a common example. Other cases fall entirely under federal court jurisdiction, such as those involving the theft of mail, treason, or violation of currency laws. Thus, there is a *dual system* of courts in the United States. Generally, state courts adjudicate, or decide, matters of state law, whereas federal courts deal with national law. The systems are separate and distinct, although state courts cannot decide against federal law but can base certain rulings on the federal constitution. For example, it is very unusual for a case decided by a state supreme court to be heard by the U.S. Supreme Court or any other federal court. Such a dual hearing occurs only when the case involves a federal question—that is, an alleged violation of federal constitutional or statutory law.

supreme court

The highest state court, beyond which there is no appeal except in cases involving federal law.

intermediate appellate court

A state appellate court that relieves the case burden on the supreme court by hearing certain types of appeals.

appellate court

A court that considers appeals of a lower court's decision.

Structural Reforms

The court reform movement that swept across the states in the 1960s and 1970s sought, among other things, to reorganize the state courts into more rational, efficient, and simplified structures. One important legacy of that movement is the *unified court system*.[5]

Although the three tiers of state courts appear to represent a hierarchy, in fact they do not. Courts in most states operate with a great deal of autonomy. They have their own budgets, hire their own staff, and use their own procedures. Moreover, the decisions of major and specialized trial courts usually stand unchallenged. Only around 5 percent of lower court cases are appealed, mostly because great expense and years of waiting are certain to be involved.

Unified court systems consolidate the various trial courts with overlapping jurisdictions into a single administrative unit and clearly specify each court's purpose and jurisdiction. The aim of this arrangement is to make the work of the courts more efficient, saving time and money and avoiding confusion. Instead of having each judge running his or her own fiefdom, rule making, record keeping, budgeting, and personnel management are standardized and centralized, usually under the authority of the state supreme court.

Such centralization relieves judges from the mundane tasks of day-to-day court management so that they can concentrate on adjudication. Additional efficiencies are gained from *offices of court administration,* which exist in all states. Some of these offices do little more than collect and disseminate statistics, but administration in an increasing number of states involves active managing, monitoring, and planning of the courts' resources and operations.

In spite of consolidation and centralization, court structures and processes continue to vary widely among the states, as shown in Figure 10.1. Generally, the most modern systems are found in the western states, including Alaska and Hawaii. Further improvements could usefully be made in most states, but the staggering number of changes made in state court structures and procedures in recent years has produced a system that "would hardly have been recognizable twenty-five years ago."[6]

How Judges Are Selected

In large part, the quality of a state court system depends on the selection of competent, well-trained judges. According to the American Bar Association (ABA), the leading professional organization for lawyers, judges should be chosen on the basis of solid professional and personal qualifications, regardless of their political views and party identification. Judges should have "superior self-discipline, moral courage, and sound judgment."[7] They should be good listeners. They should be broadly educated and professionally qualified as lawyers. An appellate or general trial court judge should also have relevant experience in a lower court or as a courtroom attorney. Even the three states that do not require judges to be members of the state bar (namely, Massachusetts, New

Figure 10.1

Simplicity and Complexity in State Court Systems

State court systems can vary from the simple to the very complex, as illustrated by these two models.

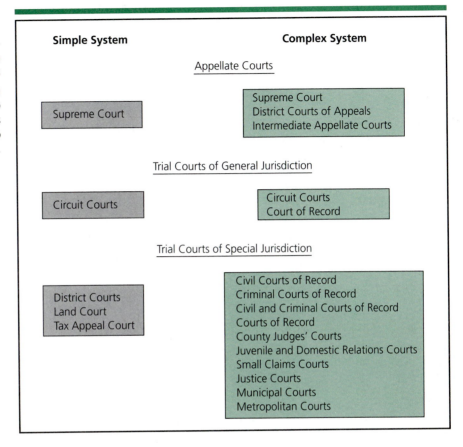

Simple System	Complex System

Appellate Courts

| Supreme Court | Supreme Court
District Courts of Appeals
Intermediate Appellate Courts |

Trial Courts of General Jurisdiction

| Circuit Courts | Circuit Courts
Court of Record |

Trial Courts of Special Jurisdiction

| District Courts
Land Court
Tax Appeal Court | Civil Courts of Record
Criminal Courts of Record
Civil and Criminal Courts of Record
Courts of Record
County Judges' Courts
Juvenile and Domestic Relations Courts
Small Claims Courts
Justice Courts
Municipal Courts
Metropolitan Courts |

Hampshire, and Rhode Island, which also have no U.S. citizenship, residence, or minimum age requirements) rarely permit anyone who is not a lawyer to receive an appointment to the bench.[8]

For a great many years, however, controversy has swirled over the selection of state judges. Should they be elected by popular vote? Should they be appointed by the governor? By the legislature? Many critics insist that judicial selection be free from politics and interest group politics. Others claim that judges should be held accountable to the people or to elected officials for their decisions.

The conflict between judicial independence and accountability is manifest in the five types of selection systems used in the states: legislative election, partisan popular election, nonpartisan popular election, merit plans, and gubernatorial appointment. Thirty-nine states use a single selection system for all appellate and major trial court judges. The other states take separate approaches to selecting judges, depending on the tier. Table 10.1 shows these selection techniques for appellate and major trial courts. Some states have rather elaborate systems. Oklahoma, for example, utilizes a merit plan for the supreme court and court of criminal appeals, partisan elections for its other appellate courts and district courts, and city council appointment of municipal judges.

Table 10.1

Appellate and Major
Trial Court Selection
Plans

State	Appellate Courts					Major Trial Courts				
	Leg. elec.	Gub. appt.	Part elec.	Non-part. elec.	Merit plan	Leg. elec.	Gub. appt.	Part elec.	Non-part. elec.	Merit plan
Ala.			X					X		
Alaska				X						X
Ariz.				X					X	X
Ark.			X					X		
Calif.				X					X	
Colo.				X						X
Conn.	X					X				
Del.		X					X			
Fla.				X					X	
Ga.			X				X	X		
Hawaii				X						X
Idaho				X						X
Ill.			X					X		
Ind.				X				X		
Iowa				X						X
Kans.				X					X	
Ky.				X					X	
La.				X					X	
Maine		X						X		
Md.				X						X
Mass.				X						X
Mich.			X						X	
Minn.			X						X	
Miss.			X					X		
Mo.				X				X		X

Legislative Election

This method is found in only four states, all of them original colonies. In Rhode Island, South Carolina, and Virginia, the legislature elects judges from among announced candidates by majority vote. And Connecticut's judicial candidates are nominated by the governor, then appointed by legislative vote. Not surprisingly, the vast majority of judges selected under this plan are former legislators (in South Carolina, the proportion is close to 100 percent).[9] In these four states, a judgeship is viewed as a highly valued reward for public service and a prestigious cap to a legislative career.

Few people other than legislators approve of legislative election. Indeed, the method seems open to criticism. The public has no role in either choosing

Table 10.1 (cont.)

State	Appellate Courts					Major Trial Courts				
	Leg. elec.	Gub. appt.	Part elec.	Non-part. elec.	Merit plan	Leg. elec.	Gub. appt.	Part. elec.	Non-part. elec.	Merit plan
Mont.				X					X	
Nebr.					X					X
Nev.				X					X	
N.H.		X					X			
N.J.		X					X			
N. Mex.					X					X
N.Y.		X	X				X			
N.C.			X				X			
N. Dak.				X					X	
Ohio				X					X	
Okla.				X	X				X	
Ore.				X					X	
Pa.			X					X		
R.I.	X						X			
S.C.	X					X				
S.D.					X				X	
Tenn.			X		X			X		
Tex.			X					X		
Utah					X					X
Vt.					X					X
Va.	X					X				
Wash.				X					X	
W. Va.			X					X		
Wis.				X					X	
Wyo.					X					X

Source: Adapted from "Selection and Retention of Judges," *The Book of the States, 1992/93,* Table 4.4, pp. 233–35. © 1992 The Council of State Governments. Used by permission.

judges or re-electing them, so accountability is minimal. The judges may be independent, but since the major criterion for selection is service as a legislator, they often lack other qualifications. Legislative service has little connection to the demands of a judgeship.

Partisan Popular Election

Judges for courts in one or more tiers run for popular election on a party ballot in fifteen states. More than half of the partisan election states are located in the

South; Mississippi was the first to adopt this system, in 1832. All except one (New Mexico) are in the eastern half of the United States. This plan enjoyed popularity during the Jacksonian era as a means of ensuring a judiciary answerable to the voters.

In theory, partisan election maximizes the value of judicial accountability. Judges, identified by party label, must run for office, on the same ticket as candidates for other state offices. Like other candidates, they must raise and spend money for their election campaigns and publicly deal with political issues. The American Bar Association Code of Judicial Conduct forbids judicial campaigning on legal issues, but this prohibition is sometimes overlooked in close contests and where crime-related concerns claim voters' attention. And as in other electoral contests, negative campaigning is on the rise. A more serious problem occurs when judges elected on a partisan ballot are accused of pandering to special interests during election campaigns and of favoring them in court decisions. In Texas, for instance, supreme court justices deciding a $10.5 billion judgment against Texaco in favor of Pennzoil were criticized for accepting huge campaign contributions from both parties. Nonpartisan elected judges are open to similar charges.

Nonpartisan Popular Election

In eleven states, appellate judges are elected from a ballot on which party identification is not listed; thirteen states use this method for trial court judges. This selection technique won favor during the first half of the twentieth century, when reformers sought to remove partisanship from the election of judges and certain other officials in state and local government. Political parties are prohibited from openly taking sides in nonpartisan judicial elections. In fact, however, they sometimes play a covert role in such contests. Approximately 95 percent of all judges have a political party preference;[10] most list it in the official biographies that are available to interested voters during campaigns.

Nonpartisan elections tend to reduce voter participation, since party identification is an important voting cue for many citizens. However, voter turnout is very low in most judicial elections anyway, whether partisan or nonpartisan. This is a major criticism of both methods of electing judges: The winners are not truly accountable to the people, which is the principal advantage commonly associated with elections. Low rates of voter interest and participation combine with low-key, unexciting, and issueless campaigns to keep many incumbent judges on the bench as long as they run for re-election. In addition, popular elections are criticized for the growing amount of money necessary to win a state judgeship. In some cases, in both partisan and nonpartisan elections, the implication is that judges have sacrificed their independence and professionalism for crass electoral politics.

Texas's partisan election system illustrates the problems with both partisan and nonpartisan elections. During the aforementioned lengthy court battle between Pennzoil and Texaco during the 1980s, Pennzoil and its attorneys legally contributed over $315,000 to the campaigns of Texas supreme court justices. Texaco, which lost the lawsuit, doled out $190,000. During the next election, in 1988, nine judgeships were at stake. It is estimated that $10 million was spent on that election. In the eyes of some observers, Texas "justice" is for sale.[11]

Following the trend set in executive and legislative contests, judicial campaign spending has also skyrocketed in other states that elect judges. The 1987 Ohio race for supreme court chief justice cost $2.7 million, $1.7 of which was spent by the loser. (In 1980, the two chief justice candidates spent only $99,192.) The largest campaign contributors are usually trial lawyers and other groups with a stake in judges' decisions, such as labor unions, business interests, and various professions.[12]

It looks as though judges running for election are forfeiting their independence in certain legal disputes while offering accountability only to the highest bidders instead of to the general public. If, indeed, this is the case, neither independence nor accountability is achieved. According to the president of the Ohio State Bar Association, "The people with money to spend who are affected by court decisions have reached the conclusion that it's a lot cheaper to buy a judge than a governor or an entire legislature, and he can probably do a lot more for you."[13]

If, as some people argue, it is unethical for a judge to rule on a case in which he or she has accepted money from one or more of the interested parties, then it would be difficult to bring together enough judges to hear cases in Texas and Ohio. As a direct consequence of the burgeoning costs and questionable ethics of judicial elections, other states are joining Texas in actively considering alternative selection plans, or at least in imposing spending and contribution ceilings for judicial contests. Increasingly, the general sentiment is that judges should be both qualified and dignified, and that elections do not further either objective. Three states—Montana, North Carolina, and Wisconsin—have public financing for judges' campaigns to help contain spiraling costs. After a mud-slinging state supreme court election in 1990, North Carolina also created a statewide committee to oversee judges' elections and published a twelve-page voters' guide to educate the electorate on judicial elections.[14]

Judicial elections are under attack from the federal courts and the U.S. Justice Department as well. The Voting Rights Act of 1965 has been applied to the election of judges in states with a history of voting rights violations. At-large systems for electing judges have been declared illegal in Mississippi (1987) and Georgia (1990) because they discriminate against blacks by diluting group voting power. The implication, as in the case of legislative elections, is that judges will have to be elected from single-member districts, and that some of these districts will have to be redrawn to maximize the opportunity for electing a minority.

Merit Plans

Dissatisfaction with the other methods for selecting judges has led to the popularity of so-called *merit plans.* Incorporating elements of gubernatorial appointment and elective systems, merit plans attempt to provide a mechanism for appointing qualified candidates to the bench while permitting the public to evaluate a judge's performance through the ballot box.

First recommended by the ABA in 1937 and strongly supported today by virtually the entire legal community, merit plans have been adopted by all but two of the states that have changed their selection systems since 1940. Missouri became the initial adopter in 1940; Kansas followed eighteen years later. Since then another twenty states have adopted merit plans, and others are considering merit selection.

The Missouri Plan   Commonly referred to as the Missouri Plan, the basic merit plan involves three steps:

1. A judicial nominating commission meets and recommends three or more names of prospective judges to the governor. Members of this bipartisan commission usually include a sitting judge (often the chief justice), representatives chosen by the state bar association, and laypersons appointed by the governor. In a few states, nominations are made by a group of judges. The nominating commission solicits names of candidates, investigates them, chooses those it believes to be the three or more best-qualified individuals, and then forwards their names and files to the governor.
2. The governor appoints the preferred candidate to the vacant judgeship.
3. A retention election is held, usually after one or two years, in which the newly appointed judge's name is placed before the voters on a nonpartisan ticket. The voters decide whether or not the judge should be retained in office. If he or she is rejected by a majority vote, the judicial nominating commission begins its work anew. Subsequent retention elections may be held every eight or twelve years, depending on the merit plan's provision.

Various hybrids of the basic plan are used in several states. For example, the California Plan for choosing appellate judges begins when the governor identifies a candidate for a vacancy on the bench and sends that person's name to the Commission on Judicial Appointments. The commission, composed of two judges and the attorney general, hears testimony regarding the nominee and votes to confirm or reject. The new judge is then accepted or rejected in a retention election in the next regularly scheduled gubernatorial contest.[15] Thus, although the governor appoints, the new judge is subject to confirmation by both the Commission on Judicial Appointments and the voters. In New Mexico's multistage merit plan, adopted in 1988, a judge is nominated by a commission and appointed by the governor. During the next general election the judge must run in a partisan election. If she wins, she must run unopposed in a nonpartisan retention election on the next general-election ballot.

The object of merit plans is to permit the governor some appointive discretion while removing politics from the selection of judges. If they work as intended, popular and legislative elections as well as direct gubernatorial appointments (all of which are highly politicized procedures) are replaced by a careful appraisal of candidates' professional qualifications by an objective commission. The process is intended to ensure the basic independence of judges and their accountability to the people.

The Politics of Merit Selection

The merit plan looks great on paper, but in practice it has not fulfilled its promise. First of all, it certainly has not dislodged politics from its preeminent position in judicial selection. A judgeship is too important a political office in any state ever to be immune from politics. It is a prized job and an important point of judicial access for numerous individuals, firms, and interest groups, especially the powerful state bar association.

Studies of judicial nominating commissions show that politics is rampant in the review and nomination of candidates.[16] For better or worse, the legal profession often dominates the process. Counting the judge who presides over the nominating commission, lawyers make up a commission majority in at least nine of the states with merit plans. Bar association lobbying is often the prime reason that merit plans are adopted in the first place. However, the legal profession is not monolithic in its politics, and it often divides into two camps: plaintiff's attorneys and defendant's attorneys.

Furthermore, the governor's influence can be exceptionally strong. The laypersons he or she appoints to the nominating commission may hold the judge in awe, but they are there to represent the governor's point of view and sometimes to promote specific candidates or the agenda of the governor's political party.[17] In six states, the majority of commission members are laypeople. The judge may also respect the governor's preferences, particularly if he owes his appointment to that chief executive.

A second criticism of merit plans in action is that the procedure intended to ensure judicial accountability to the people—the retention election—rarely generates any voter interest and almost never results in an incumbent judge being turned out of office.[18] Turnout in retention elections is normally very low, sometimes even lower than the abysmal participation levels in local bond referenda. Fewer than 3 percent of incumbent judges have been voted out in retention elections—only a handful of judges in more than fifty years. In effect, merit selection has been a lifetime appointment in most states, and some have argued that this was its intended purpose.[19]

Recently, however, voter backlashes have occurred against judges whose decisions are distinctly out of step with public opinion. In November 1986, California Chief Justice Rose Bird and two associate justices were swept from the state supreme court by large margins in retention elections, as voters reacted negatively to a series of supreme court rulings that significantly expanded the rights of the accused and of convicted felons. Bird had voted to overturn all sixty-one capital punishment cases brought to the court during a period when polls showed 80 percent support for the death penalty in California.[20] Sometimes a single issue can loom large in retention elections. Judge Leander J. Shaw, Jr., nearly lost his Florida supreme court seat in 1990 due to a ruling striking down a state law requiring a pregnant teenager to obtain a parent's consent to have an abortion. Judges are more likely to be defeated as retention elections become increasingly politicized in the 1990s.

The final charge leveled against merit plans is that, despite reformers' claims to the contrary, they do not result in the appointment of better-qualified judges or of more women and minorities. When background, education, experience, and decision making are taken into account, judges selected by the merit plan are very comparable to those selected with other plans.[21] Virtually all are white males. Most leave private practice for the bench in their forties and stay there until retirement, often moving up the three tiers of courts. Approximately 20 percent come from a family in which the father or grandfather held political office (often a judgeship).[22] Almost all state judges are qualified attorneys. A substantial majority were born, raised, and educated in the state in which they serve. A majority are members of the Democratic party, but the percentage of Republican judges has been rising since the early 1980s.

Gubernatorial Appointment

This is the method of choice in six states for appellate or major trial courts, or both. Usually the Senate is required to confirm gubernatorial appointees. All six states using this method are former colonies, reflecting the early popularity of the plan. As a method, gubernatorial appointment rates fairly high on independence, since the judge is appointed without an election; but it is weak on accountability, because the judge is beholden to only one person for his or her job.

Although only six states formally recognize it, gubernatorial appointment is in fact the most common method for selecting a majority of appellate and major trial court judges in the United States. Judges in states with popular elections or merit plans often resign or retire from office just before the end of their term.[23] Under most state legal systems, the governor has the power to make interim appointments to vacant seats until the next scheduled election or the commencement of merit plan selection processes. The governor's temporary appointee then enjoys the tremendous advantage of running as an incumbent for the next full term. Gubernatorial appointment is also used to replace a judge who dies before the expiration of the term.

A study of state trial courts in California by Philip L. Dubois found that 84.3 percent of the judges selected for the superior court from 1959 to 1978 were initially appointed by the governor to fill vacancies, in spite of the formal requirement for nonpartisan election. The importance of such initial selection is evident in the astounding success of these California judges when running for election to a full term: 99.4 percent won.[24]

What criteria does a governor apply in making appointments to the bench? Political considerations usually come first. The governor can use the appointment to reward a faithful legislator, to shore up support in certain regions of the state, to satisfy the demands of party leaders and the state legal establishment, or to appeal to women's groups or to racial or ethnic groups.[25] Of course, a poor choice can sometimes backfire politically, so governors must pay close attention to the judge's background, education, experience, and legal philosophy.[26]

Dubois's California study sheds some light on how governors choose judges. Although California formally uses a merit plan, its governor has so much input in the judge selection process that it is useful to look at the way certain governors made their choices. Dubois examined the governorships of three very distinctive individuals: Edmund G. "Pat" Brown (1958–1966), Ronald Reagan (1966–1974), and Edmund G. "Jerry" Brown, Jr. (1974–1982). He found that all three governors used a similar process to identify, evaluate, and select judges. Each one's staff received nominations from legislators, lawyers, interest groups, and other interested individuals (including the candidates themselves), and then checked out each nominee's background. Consultations were held with judges, lawyers, and legislators from the local district where the vacancy existed. Names of the most promising candidates were sent to the California State Bar for confidential assessment and rating.[27] Each governor selected more than 80 percent of his appointees from candidates within his own political party who shared his general political ideology.[28] Differences in educational background and legal experience were minimal. All three governors picked a majority of appointees from private law practice, although Governor Jerry Brown did select a greater percentage of women and minorities than did his father or Governor Reagan.

Which Selection Plan Is Best?

The ongoing debate over which is best among the five formal selection systems is unlikely to be decided convincingly. Legislative election and gubernatorial appointment are probably the least desirable, because judges selected under these systems tend to come from a rather specific political occupation (the legislature), and the general public has little opportunity to hold these judges accountable. Yet none of the three remaining systems produces "better" judges or decisions. Elections emphasize accountability, while merit plans favor judicial independence. And minorities have not done well under any selection plan. Blacks fill less than 4 percent of state court seats. Gubernatorial appointment and legislative election apparently increase the selection opportunities for African-American judges, but significant gains probably await the development of a larger pool of black attorneys.[29] Politics, of course, is what raises all judges into office, regardless of the selection method. Ultimately, the voters and their elected representatives must determine the selection system that is most acceptable. Experimentation with new selection systems will continue, for no "perfect" arrangement is likely to be discovered.

Removal of Judges

Like anyone else, judges can break the law, go mad, suffer senility, or become physically incapable of carrying out their responsibilities. If a judge displays serious deficiencies, he or she must be removed from the bench. Forty-five states provide for the rather clumsy process of impeachment, wherein charges are filed in the state House of Representatives and a trial is conducted in the Senate. Other traditional means for removing justices include the legislative address (nineteen states) and popular recall (five states).[30] In the legislative address, both houses of the legislature by two-thirds vote must ask the governor to dismiss a judge. Popular recall requires a specified number of registered voters to petition for a special election to recall the judge before the term has expired. These traditional mechanisms are slow, cumbersome, uncertain, and hence seldom used.

In recent years, states have begun utilizing more practical methods for removing judges. Problems related to senility and old age are dealt with in at least thirty-seven states by a mandatory retirement age (generally seventy years) or by the forfeiture of pensions for judges serving beyond the retirement age. This has the added benefit of opening up the courtrooms to new, and younger, judges, even where advancing age does not impair performance.[31] Most states have established special entities to address behavioral problems. *Courts of the judiciary,* whose members are all judges, and *judicial discipline and removal commissions,* composed of judges, lawyers, and laypersons, are authorized to investigate complaints about judges' qualifications, conduct, or fitness. These entities may reject allegations if they are unfounded, privately warn a judge if the charges are not serious, or hold formal hearings. Hearings may result in dismissal of the charges, recommendation for early retirement, or, in some states, outright suspension or removal.[32]

The discipline, suspension, or removal of state court judges is uncommon, but it becomes necessary in all states at one time or another. Judges have been found guilty of drunkenness and drug abuse, sexual misconduct with witnesses and defendants, soliciting and accepting bribes, and just about every other kind of misconduct. Sometimes judicial ethics seem to be seriously in short supply. In 1988, fifteen Philadelphia municipal judges resigned or were removed from office in connection with taking bribes and other scandals. And eleven Cook County, Illinois, judges were convicted in the late 1980s as a result of Operation Greylord, which investigated various charges of judicial corruption, including the buying and selling of verdicts.

Judicial Decision Making

What factors influence the rulings of state court judges? Why are some judges widely recognized as "liberal" and others as "tough on crime"? Why does a prosecutor prefer to file a case before one judge rather than another? Isn't justice supposed to be blind, like its symbol of the woman holding the scales?

Judges, alas, are mortal beings just like the rest of us. The legal formalities and mumbo jumbo of the courtroom tend to mask the fact that judges' decisions are no less discretionary and subjective than the decisions of a governor, legislator, or agency head. Before we examine the factors that affect judicial decision making, however, we must distinguish between the legal settings of appellate courts and trial courts.

In and Out of the Trial Court

It has been estimated that 90 percent of all civil and criminal cases are actually resolved outside of the courtroom. In many civil cases, the defendant never appears in court to defend himself, and so he implicitly admits his guilt and loses the case by default. Other civil cases are settled in a pretrial conference between the defendant and the plaintiff (where, for instance, payments on an overdue debt might be rescheduled).

plea bargaining

Negotiation between a prosecutor and a criminal defendant's counsel that results in the defendant's pleading guilty to a lesser charge or pleading guilty in exchange for a reduced sentence.

The process of settling criminal cases out of court at the discretion of the prosecutor and the judge is called **plea bargaining.** Although some defendants plead guilty as originally charged, acknowledging guilt for a lesser charge is more typical in criminal proceedings. With the possible exception of the victim and the general citizenry, everyone potentially benefits from plea bargaining, a fact that accounts for its extensive use. The accused gets off with lighter punishment than she would face if the case went to trial and she lost. The defense attorney frees up time to take on additional legal work. The prosecuting attorney increases his conviction rate, which looks good if he has political ambitions. The judge helps cut back the number of cases awaiting trial. Even police officers benefit by not having to spend time testifying (and waiting to testify) and by raising the department's clearance rate (the number of cases solved and disposed of).

Out-of-court settlements through plea bargaining are negotiated in a very informal atmosphere in the judge's chamber, or between attorneys in the halls of the court building, or over drinks in a neighboring tavern. This is a disturbingly casual way to dispense justice. The process is secretive and far removed from any notion of due process. The prosecuting (district) attorney enjoys enormous discretion in making deals. Often her propensity to settle depends on the length of her court docket or her relationship with the accused's attorney, not on the merits of the case. All too often an innocent person pleads guilty to a lesser offense for fear of being wrongly convicted of a more serious offense, or because he cannot post bail and doesn't want to spend any unnecessary time behind bars. Equally disturbing—particularly to a victim—is the fact that plea bargaining can soon put a guilty person back on the streets, perhaps to search for another victim.

Nonetheless, plea bargaining is widely practiced. It is almost inevitable when the prosecutor's case hinges on weak evidence, police errors, a questionable witness, or the possibility of catching a bigger fish. Negotiation of a guilty plea for a lesser offense can occur at any stage of the criminal justice process. Sometimes it is abetted by a judge, who promises a light sentence in exchange for a guilty plea.

bench trial

Trial by a single judge, without a jury.

trial by jury

A trial in which a jury decides the facts and makes a finding of guilty or not guilty.

If the accused is unable to reach a compromise with the prosecuting attorney, he faces either a **bench trial** by a single judge or a **trial by jury.** Both involve a courtroom hearing with all the legal formalities. In some jurisdictions and for certain types of cases, the defendant has a choice. In other situations, state legal procedures specify which trial format will be utilized. For murder cases, a jury is always mandatory. Problem Solving 10.2 discusses some suggestions for improving the jury system.

In a bench trial, the judge alone hears all arguments and makes rulings on questions of law. Jury trials depend on a panel of citizens who share decision-making power. Although at least one study has found that juries and judges come to identical decisions in more than 75 percent of criminal cases,[33] the uncertainty introduced by twelve laypersons is usually great enough to convince a defendant to choose a bench trial. Fewer than 1 percent of all cases are resolved by jury trial.

Attorneys seek to limit the unpredictable nature of juries by extensively questioning individuals in the jury pool. Each side in the dispute has the right to strike the names of a certain number of potential jurors without giving a specific reason. Others are eliminated for cause, such as personal knowledge of the case or its principals. In high-stakes cases, the jury selection process involves public opinion surveys, individual background investigations of potential jurors, and other costly techniques.

Inside the Appellate Court

Appellate courts are substantially different from trial courts. No plaintiffs, defendants, or witnesses are present. The appeal consists of a review of court records and arguments directed by the attorneys, who frequently are not the same lawyers who originally represented the parties. There is no bargaining and no opportunity for predecision settlement. Appellate court rulings are issued by a panel of at least three judges. Unlike decisions in most trial courts, appellate court decisions are written and published. The majority vote prevails. Judges voting in the minority have the right to make a formal, written dissent that justifies their opinion.

There is marked variation in the dissent rates characterizing state appellate courts. Some courts maintain a public aura of consensus on even the most controversial matters by almost always publishing unanimous opinions. Other courts are racked by public battles over legal questions. Personal, professional, partisan, political, and other disagreements can spill over into open hostility over casework.[34] Supreme courts in states such as California, New York, and Michigan have a history of contentiousness, while others, like those in Rhode Island and Maryland, are paragons of harmony. Dissent rates appear to be related to state social and political factors, such as urbanization and partisan competition. More dissent occurs in courts with a large number of justices[35] and in states with intermediate appellate courts. According to one analysis of quarreling on the Missouri Supreme Court, the more time the justices have at their disposal, the

Problem Solving 10.2

Improving the Jury System

The Problem: Citizens serving jury duty in most courtrooms must sit quietly and listen to the proceedings, absorbing the evidence and testimony. Then, sometimes frustrated and confused, they meet together in the jury room and attempt to decide the accused or respondent's guilt or innocence.

During long or complex trials, jurors may forget important details, lose track of what is going on, or have questions that they wish they could ask.

The Solution: Permit juror note-taking and questions. Some trial judges are using their discretionary authority to permit jurors to jot down notes during the trial and, at the conclusion of testimony by each witness, to write down questions. The judge and attorneys meet in private and decide which written questions to ask of the witness when they return to the courtroom. (Direct verbal questions by jurors are not allowed because they might cause a mistrial.)

University researchers at Northwestern University and the University of Minnesota have obtained a $111,000 grant from the State Justice Institute to conduct an experiment with these innovations. In 350 trials across the county, participating judges are asked either to permit note-taking, allow questions, permit both, or prohibit both. Then questionnaires are completed by the judges to record their assessments of whatever procedures are employed.

Early indications are that taking notes and asking questions render jurors more attentive and better informed to make decisions more confidently and efficiently. Time is saved by clarifying questions that help preclude the need to read back witnesses' testimony to the jurors. Critics, however, fear that taking notes causes important testimony to be missed by busily writing jurors and creates problems when jurors make mistakes in their notes.

––––––––

Source: Adapted from Bruce Maxwell, "Judges Experiment, Reshaping the Role the Jury Plays," *Governing* 3 (January 1990): 62–63. Used by permission.

more likely they are to find reasons to disagree. In Missouri argot, "if a mule is pulling, he can't kick."[36]

On the average, state appellate court dissent rates are much lower than those in federal courts. This finding reflects the tradition of unanimity in some states, the similar backgrounds of state justices, and the way in which cases are managed. For example, unanimous decisions are partly a result of the common practice of coping with heavy caseloads by making one judge responsible for writing the opinion on each case. In such instances, the other judges tend to concur without careful review.

Influence of the Legal System

In addition to the facts of the case itself, judicial decision making is influenced by factors associated with the legal system, including institutional arrangements, accepted legal procedures, caseload pressures, and the ease with which interested parties gain access to the legal process.

An attorney sums up
his case before a
Texas jury.

1. *Institutional arrangements.* Where court organization includes an intermediate appellate court, supreme court judges have more time to consider important cases. The level, or tier, of court is another structural characteristic that influences decision making. Trial court judges enforce legal norms and routinely *apply* the law as it has been written and interpreted over the years. The trial court permits direct interpersonal contacts among the judge, the jury, and the parties (usually individuals and small businesses). Divorce cases, personal injury cases, and minor criminal cases predominate in trial courts.

Appellate courts are more apt to *interpret* the law and create public policy. Cases typically involve governments and large corporations. State constitutional issues, state-local conflicts, and challenges to government regulation of business are the kinds of issues likely to be found in appellate courts. From time to time a particular case in a high court has an enormous impact on public policy, as judges depart from established precedent or offer new interpretations of the law. Rulings on capital punishment, abortion, affirmative action, and the financing of public education offer good examples, as does court settlement of executive-legislative disputes.

Other important institutional arrangements concern selection procedures for judges. Judicial decisions may be influenced by partisan electoral competition. When an elected judge votes on an issue highly salient to voters, public opinion can affect the judge's ruling.[37]

precedent

The legal principle that previous court decisions influence future decisions.

Precedent means that the principles and procedures of law applied in one situation are applied in any similar situation. Lower courts are supposed to follow the precedents established by higher courts. Although an individual decision may seem unimportant in itself, when taken in the context of other, similar cases, it helps judicial policy evolve. Through this practice the doctrine of equal treatment before the law is pursued. When lower court judges refuse to follow precedent or are ignorant of it, their decisions are likely to be overturned on appeal.

Where do judges look to find existing precedent? Within a state, supreme court decisions set the norms. Supreme courts themselves, however, must scan the legal landscape beyond state boundaries. In the past, decisions of the U.S. Supreme Court heavily influenced them. Increasingly, however, state supreme courts are looking to one another for precedent. According to political scientist Gregory A. Caldeira, state appellate judges have taken a cue from legislators in borrowing from the experiences of other states.[38] They especially tend to rely on the more professional, prestigious supreme courts, such as those of California, Massachusetts, and New York, whose decisions are generally applicable in other states and times. State courts also tend to "network" with courts in the same region of the country, where cultural and other environmental factors are similar.[39] The closer two supreme courts are geographically, the more likely they are to communicate. This sort of judicial cross-fertilization puts legal distance between the state and federal supreme courts.

2. *Legal procedures.* Legal procedures other than precedent affect judicial decision making. These include the formal and informal rules of interaction among appellate judges on a panel and between trial court judges and the lawyers and litigants who appear before them. Examples are the procedure for assigning written majority and minority opinions, and the order in which judges vote.[40] Another important procedural factor is the degree of administrative oversight exercised over a lower court by a higher one.

3. *Caseload pressures.* Caseload affects the decisions of judges. The number of cases varies in accordance with crime rates, socioeconomic characteristics of the jurisdictions, state laws, the number of judges, and many other variables. It stands to reason that the quality of judicial decision making is inversely related to caseload. Judges burdened by too much litigation are hard-pressed to devote an appropriate amount of time and attention to each case before them.

4. *Access to the system.* The final characteristic that affects judicial decisions is the access of individuals, organizations, and groups to the court system. Wealthy people and businesses are better able to pay for resources (attorneys, legal research, etc.) and therefore enter the legal system with an advantage over poorer litigants. Special interest groups also enjoy certain advantages in affecting judicial decisions. They often have specialized knowledge in areas of litigation, such as environmental or business regulation. Lobbying by interest groups is much less prominent in the judicial branch than in the legislative and executive branches, but groups can affect outcomes by providing financial aid to litigants in important cases and by filing *amicus curiae* (friend of the court) briefs supporting one side or the other in a dispute.

Most of the legal-system factors influencing judicial decision making are subject to manipulation by elected officials, who can add judges, pass laws, alter procedures, and ease caseloads through various reforms. However, the second set of factors related to decision making in the courts, judges' values and attitudes, are rather immutable.

Personal Values and Attitudes of Judges

Simply put, judges do not think and act alike. Each is a product of his or her individual background and experiences, which in turn influence decisions made in the courtroom. Studies of state supreme court justices have found that decisions are related to the judges' party identification, political ideology, prior careers, religion, ethnicity, age, and sex. In other words, personal characteristics predispose a judge to decide cases in certain ways.

For example, political scientist Stuart Nagel found that Democratic judges tend to favor the claimant in civil rights cases, the government in tax disputes, the employee in worker's compensation cases, the government in business regulation cases, the defendant in criminal contests, the union in disagreements with management, and the tenant in landlord-tenant cases. Republicans tend to support the opposite side on all these issues.[41] Female judges are more supportive of women in feminist issues and in general are more liberal than their male colleagues.[42] (Future research will no doubt focus on the Minnesota Supreme Court, which in January 1991 became majority female.) Obviously, these distinctions do not hold in all situations, but the point is that "justice" is a complex concept subject to individual interpretation. No wonder attorneys try to shop around for the most sympathetic judge before filing a legal action.

"New Wave" Courts: Activism in the States

During the 1950s and 1960s, the U.S. Supreme Court was far and away the leading judicial actor in the land. Under the chief justiceship of Earl Warren (1953–1969) and his liberal majority, the Court handed down a long series of rulings that overturned legally imposed racial segregation, mandated legislative reapportionment, extended voting rights, and expanded the rights of accused criminals. Significant reversals of state court decisions were commonplace.

Beginning with Chief Justice Warren Burger (1969–1986) and a growing faction of conservative judges, however, the Supreme Court changed direction in the 1970s and 1980s.[43] By 1988, a conservative majority was firmly in control. This fact was reflected in the Court's new hesitance to intrude in many areas and in some backtracking on Warren Court "minimum standards." The Supreme Court's caution created a vacuum of sorts, which some activist state high courts rushed to fill.

Judicial Activism

judicial activism

Judges' making of public policy through decisions that overturn existing law or effectively make new laws.

Judicial activism is a term that has value-laden and ideological dimensions.[44] Usually associated with political liberalism, it is therefore decried by conservatives. However, conservative judges have also been accused of activism. For example, liberals accuse the U.S. Supreme Court under Chief Justices Warren Burger and William Rehnquist of reversing rulings made by the Warren Court in such areas as civil liberties and criminal procedure. Activist judges can be either liberals or conservatives, but all tend to show strong ideological tendencies.[45]

An objective definition of judicial activism, then, points to court-generated change in public policy that is perceived as illegitimate by opponents who favor the status quo.[46] Judicial activism is in the eye of the beholder; it holds a pejorative association for some people and a positive one for others, depending on the issue at hand.

Regardless of one's feelings on the matter, state supreme courts have clearly become *more* activist by expanding into new policy areas. They are more likely to be involved in the policymaking process by making decisions that affect policy in the executive branch, and they even appear to pre-empt the lawmaking responsibility of the legislature. Ironically, some of the most spectacular examples of state court activism are based on prior rulings by the U.S. Supreme Court. Indeed, since 1970 state supreme courts are estimated to have issued more than three hundred opinions that have taken certain minimum standards established by the federal Supreme Court and expanded them within the jurisdiction of the states. Examples include the following:

- California, Connecticut, and Massachusetts courts have expanded women's right to abortion on demand and the right to financial aid from the state for abortions.
- Courts in New York, Pennsylvania, and other states have struck down sodomy laws as violations of their state constitutions' right to privacy. The U.S. Supreme Court has upheld state sodomy prohibitions. Courts in New York, Wisconsin, Mississippi, and elsewhere have rejected a Burger Court ruling that permits prosecutors to introduce evidence obtained through a defective search warrant.
- The California Supreme Court has upheld the right of people to collect petition signatures in a private shopping center, after the U.S. Supreme Court ruled that owners of shopping malls could prohibit such activities.
- The supreme court of Oregon has rejected a U.S. Supreme Court decision that provided guidelines for declaring certain printed and visual materials to be obscene. The Oregon court noted that its state constitution had been authored "by rugged and robust individuals dedicated to founding a free society unfettered by the governmental imposition of some peoples' views of morality on the free expression of others." "In this state," declared the Oregon Supreme Court, "any person can write, print, read, say, show or sell anything to a consenting adult even though that expression may be generally or universally considered 'obscene.' "[47]

How can the state courts override the decisions of the highest court in the land? The answer is that they are grounding their rulings in their own constitutions instead of in the national constitution.[48] The Bill of Rights protections of many states are more precise and broader in scope than the rights set forth in the first ten amendments to the U.S. Constitution. In several decisions, the Burger Court specifically upheld the right of the states to expand on the minimum rights and liberties guaranteed under the national document. Chief Justice William Rehnquist, who replaced Warren Burger in 1986, is sympathetic to this position.[49] Of course, when there is an irreconcilable conflict between state and federal law, the latter prevails.

Current Trends in State Courts

The new wave of state court activism is not carrying all the ships of state with it; a majority of state supreme courts remain caught in the doldrums, consistently endorsing—rather than repudiating—Supreme Court decisions. Some of them are so quiet, as one wag suggested, "that you can hear their arteries harden." But even traditionally inactive courts, in states such as Wisconsin and Mississippi, have been stirred into independent actions recently, and the trend is continuing.[50] The U.S. Supreme Court will have a conservative majority for many years to come, which will permit the state courts to explore the legal landscape further. State court activism seems to be contagious, as courts utilize their own information and case networks instead of those of the Supreme Court.

Of course, with rare exceptions, judges cannot seize issues as governors and legislators can; they must wait for litigants to bring them to the courthouse. And although judges can issue rulings, they must depend on the executive and legislative branches to comply with and enforce those rulings. Nonetheless, many state supreme courts are becoming more active in the policymaking process. A case in point is the supreme court of New Jersey, which has clearly departed from several U.S. Supreme Court rulings on issues including free speech, search and seizure, mandatory drug testing, and public financing of abortion rights for poor women. The reluctance of the federal courts to address important and controversial issues comprehensively has resulted in more cases for state supreme courts to decide.

State court activism does have some negative points. Some courts may overstep their authority and try to go too far in policymaking, intruding into the domain of executive and legislative actors. Judges have little expertise in the substance of public policy or in the policymaking process. They have no specialized staff to perform in-depth policy research on particular policy issues, and they cannot realistically depend on lawyers to do policy research for them. Attorneys are trained and practiced in legal reasoning, not social science or political science.[51] Another problem is that in state constitutional rights, geography is destiny. A state-by-state approach may not be appropriate for such policies as civil rights, which should probably be equal for all citizens.

....

New Directions in State Court Reform

We have already discussed several important judicial reforms: intermediate appellate courts, court unification and consolidation, administrative improvements, merit selection plans for judges, and more practical means for disciplining and removing judges. Administrative and organizational issues remain important, as shown by the growing number of states that are centralizing court budgeting and finance.

Financial Improvements

More than half of the states have assumed full financial responsibility for the operation of state and local courts. In 1969, the states paid only about 25 percent of all costs; counties and municipalities took care of the remainder. The alternative to full state funding—state and local sharing of costs—tends to be associated with spending disparities between courts and between judicial districts, and with an absence of evaluation and control of court operations.

First recommended by the American Bar Association in 1972, centralized budgeting has been adopted by approximately twenty states. Also referred to as *unified court budgeting,* this reform entails a consolidated budget for all state and local courts, prepared by the chief administrative officer of the state court system, that details all personnel, supplies, equipment, and other expenditures.[52] It is intended to enhance financial management and help maintain judicial independence from the executive and legislative branches, which lose their authority to alter the judiciary's budget. A unified court system, centralized financing, and unified budgeting are all similar in that the objective is to bring a state's entire court system under a single authoritative administrative structure.

Dealing with Growing Caseloads

Recently, court reformers have been attending to the need to deal more effectively with case backlogs. State courts confronted more than 98 million new cases in 1988. Some judges participated in more than 300 opinions that year. Delays of two years or more have not been uncommon for appellate court hearings, and the unprecedented pressure is growing.

Excessive caseloads are caused by numerous factors, including the greater propensity of losing parties to appeal lower court decisions, the tremendous growth in litigation, huge increases in drug-related and drunk driving cases, and poor caseload management procedures. The facts that the number of lawyers in the United States has tripled over the past three decades and that two-thirds of the world's lawyers live in this country also contribute significantly. The paramount concern is that long delays thwart the progress of justice. The quality of evidence deteriorates as witnesses disappear or forget what they saw, and victims suffer from delays that prevent them from collecting damages for injuries incurred in a crime or an accident. Even accused (and perhaps innocent) perpetrators can be harmed by being held in prison for long periods while awaiting trial.

Reducing excessive caseloads is not a simple matter. Common sense dictates establishing intermediate appellate courts and adding new judgeships; but much like a new highway draws traffic, intermediate appellate courts tend to attract more appeals by their very existence.[53] Additional judges speed up the trial process in lower courts but can add to appellate backlogs. Expanding the number of judges in an appellate court is also problematic; hearings may actually take longer because of more input or factional divisions among judges.[54]

The stubborn persistence of case backlogs has led to some interesting and promising new approaches.

1. *Alternative dispute resolution.* Pennsylvania and at least twenty-three other states use mediation, arbitration, or other techniques to help settle litigation prior to a formal courtroom proceeding. Third-party mediation by retired judges or attorneys and voluntary binding arbitration are promising approaches. In South Carolina most civil cases under appeal are eligible for binding settlement by a three-member panel of retired judges or lawyers. A two-year appellate court backlog in civil cases was reduced to four to five months after this system was first implemented.[55] In some states, including California and Washington, litigants in search of timely settlement have hired private judges to decide their disputes.[56]

2. *New legislation or court rules.* These provide for monetary fines to be levied by judges against lawyers and litigants guilty of delaying tactics[57] or, in twenty-three states, for violating standards that require cases to be heard within a specified time period.

3. *Case management systems.* This is probably the most promising innovation. Although individual systems vary widely, a typical approach is *multitracking,* which distinguishes between simple and complex, and frivolous and potentially significant cases, and treats them differently. Complex and significant cases are waved on down the traditional appellate track. Simple and frivolous cases take a shorter track, usually under the direction of staff attorneys. Experiments with multitracking have been successful in reducing case delays in Arizona, Maine, New Hampshire, and several other states. Another case management practice to speed up the wheels of justice is case channeling, in which environmental law disputes, drug cases, or others with special characteristics are placed on dockets with judges experienced in the relevant field.

4. *New technology.* Technological innovations are improving the quality and quantity of court operations as well. Electronic databases (for example, LEXIS and WESTLAW) are being used to store case information and legal research and to transmit information from law offices to courts. Automation helps track child support payments, court administrative systems, and traffic tickets. Videotaping of witnesses' testimony is becoming commonplace. Ar-

raignment procedures, during which suspects are formally charged, are also videotaped to save time or to prevent potential problems from a disruptive defendant. Kentucky has instituted "video courtrooms" in which trials are filmed by TV cameras. This arrangement creates a more accurate trial record and costs much less than a written transcript by a court stenographer.[58] And the audiovisual technology in Brevard County, Florida, permits hearings, motions, pleas, sentencing, and other proceedings to be conducted long distance, between the jail and the courthouse, thereby both saving money and enhancing security.[59]

5. *Higher salaries for judges.* Judicial salaries declined markedly during the 1960s and 1970s compared to inflation and to the earnings of attorneys. One study found that whereas the salaries of lawyers increased by 9 percent in noninflationary terms from 1974 to 1984, the salaries of state supreme court justices dropped 15 percent.[60] Workloads burgeoned while compensation declined.

Compensating the Judges

At first glance, judicial salaries seem high enough. In 1990, state supreme court judges earned an average of approximately $81,337. (The variation was great. New York justices make more than twice as much as their counterparts in Montana.) Trial court judges were paid 10 to 20 percent less. However, these amounts are substantially below what an experienced, respected attorney can expect to make. A successful lawyer who gives up private practice for the bench must be willing to take a considerable cut in income. Unlike legislators, state judges are permitted very little outside income. Therefore, it is reasonable to ask whether the best legal minds will be attracted to judgeships, when judicial compensation is relatively low.[61] This is a dilemma at all levels and in all branches of public service, from the municipal finance officer to the highway patrol officer, since most state and local government compensation lags behind pay for comparable jobs in the private sector. If we expect our judges, law enforcement officers, and other public employees to be honest and productive, they must be compensated adequately. Recent salary increases for state judges seem to recognize this principle.

....

State Courts Enter the Modern Age

As is the case with the other two branches of government, state judicial systems have been touched significantly by reform. Court systems have been modernized and simplified, intermediate appellate courts have been added, processes have been streamlined, judicial selection has been moved toward the merit ideal, and case delays have been reduced. Moreover, disciplinary and removal commissions make it easier to deal with problem judges. As a result, courts are striving for greater independence from political pressures and favoritism and more accountability for their actions. Justice at times may still appear to be an ephemeral ideal, and damned expensive, but it is more likely to be approximated in state judicial decisions today than ever before.

The changes in state court systems during the past quarter-century have not gone far enough in some instances, but it is still remarkable that so much has happened in such a short period of time to such a conservative, slow-moving institution of government. The courts, like the rest of society, are no longer immune to the technological age and its prime tool, the computer. New innovations and approaches will follow the recommendations of commissions in Virginia, Arizona, and other states studying the needs of state judicial systems in the twenty-first century.[62]

Court modernization and reform have been accompanied by increased judicial activism. The "new wave" state courts have far surpassed the federal courts in public policy activism. They sometimes blatantly disagree with federal precedents and insist on decisions grounded in state constitutional law rather than in the national constitution. In sum, the resurgence of the states has not left the state courts behind.

....

Summary

The state courts are political institutions with public policy implications. They sort out hundreds of thousands of conflicts each year on an astonishing variety of topics. Yet like the executive and legislative branches, the judiciary has come in for its share of criticism. Byzantine court organization, judicial selection systems, and excessive delays are just three examples of problems confronting state courts during the past two decades.

The trends in court organization are toward greater centralization, control, and efficiency. Merit plans are replacing other judicial selection methods. Various court reforms have cut down case backlogs. "New wave" activist courts have developed in the states, and reform continues to improve the operation of state judiciaries.

Key Terms

civil case
criminal case
administrative case
original jurisdiction
appellate jurisdiction
supreme court
intermediate appellate court

appellate court
plea bargaining
bench trial
trail by jury
precedent
judicial activism

11

The Structure of Local Government

Orientations to American Communities

Five Types of Local Governments

Counties | Municipalities | Towns and Townships |
Special Districts | School Districts

Interlocal Cooperation

The Issue of Governance

W here would you find the most typical community in the United States, the proverbial "Anytown, USA"? Probably not on either of the coasts. A place located more toward the center of the country would be preferable. And it should not be too big or too small—no New York City or Cicely, Alaska. What we're looking for is a medium-sized community inhabited by hard-working, fun-loving, average Americans. Actually, locating this representative city is not all that difficult. Using the 1990 Census data, market researchers have determined that Tulsa, Oklahoma, is the most typical American city.[1] By analyzing demographic characteristics such as age distribution, racial mix, and housing prices, they have concluded that Tulsa is the place that most closely mirrors the national average. The city of 367,000 is the microcosmic American community. Finding the average local government, however, is not as easy as identifying a typical community.

American local governments were not planned according to some grand design. Rather, they grew in response to a combination of citizen demand, interest group pressure, and state government acquiescence. As a consequence, no scientific system of local governments exists. What does exist is a collection of autonomous, frequently overlapping jurisdictional units. Consider the Pittsburgh metropolitan area. Packed into its 3,000 square miles are 4 counties, 195 cities (55 of which have fewer than 1,000 residents), 117 townships, 331 special districts, and 92 school districts.[2] That is a lot of local government.

What do citizens want from local governments? The answer is, to be governed well. But as this chapter demonstrates, "governed well" is hard to define.

....

Orientations to American Communities

In the early days of the United States, communities were idealized as *civic republics*.[3] In a civic republic, community government is based on the principle of mutual consent. Citizens share fundamental beliefs and participate in public affairs. Their motivation for civic involvement is less materialistic self-interest than altruistic concern for community welfare. Although this conception continued to have theoretical appeal, its reality was threatened by the growing and diverse nineteenth-century populace, which preferred to maximize individual liberty and accumulation of wealth. An economically inspired conception of the community, that of the *corporate enterprise,* gradually emerged. Economic growth and the ensuing competition for wealth sparked extensive conflict.[4] Local governments created rules and mediated between the clashing interests.

These two theoretical orientations, the community as a civic republic and the community as a corporate enterprise, remain viable. A new orientation is emerging, however—one that portrays the community as a *consumer market,*[5] in which citizens are consumers of public services and governments are providers. This idea places increased emphasis on quality of life and cost-effectiveness. Whether this orientation will demonstrate the staying power of the other two is uncertain, but the consumer-market model is attracting substantial scholarly attention.

A quarter-century ago, a study conducted in Michigan pointed out four types of communities, as identified by officials and candidates for local public offices.[6] The four types were as follows:

1. *the boosteristic city:* the city as a promoter of economic growth.
2. *the amenities city:* the city as a provider and preserver of life's comforts.
3. *the caretaker city:* the city as a maintainer of traditional services.
4. *the brokerage city:* the city as an arbiter of conflicting interests.

Even today these types can be loosely associated with certain kinds of places. For example, many medium-sized communities stretching from the South Atlantic seaboard through the Southwest to the Pacific Coast display characteristics of boosterism—an avid devotion to growth and expansion. Upper-middle-income suburbs of large central cities prefer to focus on conserving community amenities such as residential landscaping. Small towns in all regions that are content to remain small are caretaker communities. It's in large cities experiencing population loss and economic stresses that a brokerage style of government is likely to emerge. Of course, all communities have governments; in fact, they have a variety of governments. In the next section, we examine the five types of local governments.

Five Types of Local Governments

general-purpose local government

A local government that provides a wide range of functions.

single-purpose local government

A local government, such as a school district, that performs a specific function.

Local government is the level of government that fights crime, extinguishes fires, paves streets, collects trash, maintains parks, provides water, and educates children. Some local governments are engaged in all of these activities; others provide only some of these services. A useful way of thinking about them is to distinguish between general-purpose and single-purpose local governments. **General-purpose local governments** are those that perform a wide range of governmental functions. These include counties, municipalities, and towns and townships. **Single-purpose local governments,** as the label implies, have a specific purpose and perform one function. School districts and special districts are single-purpose governments. In the U.S., the number of local governments exceeds 83,000. Table 11.1 classifies those governments.

Regardless of the purpose of a local government, we must remember that it has a lifeline to state government. In short, state government gives local government its legal existence. This relationship is not quite the equivalent of a hospital patient hooked up to a life-support system, but it is a basic condition of nonnational government organization. Local citizens may instill a local government with its flavor and its character, but state government makes local government official.

Being so close to the people offers special challenges to local governments. Citizens are well aware when trash has not been collected or when libraries do not carry current best sellers. They can contact local officials and attend public hearings. Local government can be very interactive.

Table 11.1

Number and Types of Local Government

Type of Local Government	Number
County	3,042
Municipality	19,200
Town/Township	16,691
School District	14,721
Special District	29,532
Total	83,186

Source: U.S. Bureau of the Census, *1987 Census of Governments* (Washington, D.C.: U.S. Government Printing Office, 1987).

Counties

Counties are general-purpose units of local government. With a few exceptions, most Americans are in a county right now. The exceptions occur in Connecticut and Rhode Island, where there are no functional county governments; Washington, D.C., which is a special case in itself; municipalities in Virginia that are independent jurisdictions and are not part of the counties that surround them; and cities like Baltimore and St. Louis, which, as the result of past political decisions, are not part of a county. Even in places where you do not ever hear about county government—New York City, Philadelphia, Boston, and San Francisco—you are actually in one; long-time consolidated city-county government structures exist in these major cities. State governments have carved up their territory into 3,042 discrete subunits called counties (except in Louisiana, where counties are called parishes, and Alaska, where they are called boroughs).

Not All Counties Are Alike   Seldom does anyone confuse Los Angeles County, California, with Gilmer County, West Virginia. Obviously, counties can be differentiated according to their urban/rural nature.[7] There are three types of *metropolitan* counties, some of which contain large cities (the core counties) and others which abut the core county (the fringe counties). The core county is likely to serve as the work destination of the residents of the fringe counties. Fewer than 10 percent of the counties in the United States are core or fringe, but these are the highly urbanized counties that we hear about most—places like Dade County (Miami), Cook County (Chicago), and Fulton and DeKalb counties (Atlanta). The third kind of metropolitan county is the single-county metropolitan area. It differs from the core and fringe counties in that its largest cities do not attract commuters from nearby areas. (Approximately 15 percent of American counties fall into this category.)

Even though most Americans live in metropolitan areas, most counties are *nonmetropolitan,* and there are three types of these, too. Those that contain one or more growing small cities (the urbanized counties) act as service centers for surrounding rural areas. These are the nonmetropolitan equivalents of the metropolitan core counties. Counties categorized as "less urbanized" are those with populations in the 2,500-to-20,000 range, containing only one small city. The most rural of all the counties are the "thinly populated centers," and they have no incorporated places with more than 2,500 residents. Loving County, Texas, with its 107 residents, gives meaning to the phrase "thinly populated."

Why We Have County Governments   Counties were created by states to function as their administrative appendages. In other words, counties were expected to manage activities of statewide concern at the local level. Their basic set of functions traditionally included property tax assessment and collection, law enforcement, elections, land transaction record keeping, and road maintenance.[8] The county courthouse was the center of government.

The twin pressures of modernization and population growth placed additional demands on county governments. As a result, their service offerings have expanded. Counties these days handle health care and hospitals, pollution control, mass transit, industrial development, social services, and consumer protection.[9] They are increasingly regarded less as simple functionaries of state government and more as important policymaking units of local government. Organizational change and reform have occurred at the county level: State governments have awarded greater decision-making authority and flexibility to counties through *home rule* (see Chapter 2). By 1991, thirty-six states had adopted home rule provisions for at least some of their counties.[10]

Even with their gradual empowerment, counties, like other local governments, continue to chafe at the traditionally tight reins of state government control. In a recent survey, county officials blamed "state requirements without state funding" for many of the problems plaguing their government.[11] Also ranking high on their list of complaints were "state limits on authority." The issue of empowerment is unlikely to fade away during the 1990s.

How County Governments Are Organized   The typical structure of county government is based on an elected governing body, usually called a board of commissioners or supervisors, which is the central policymaking apparatus in the county. The board enacts county ordinances, approves the county budget, and appoints other officials (such as the directors of the county public works department and the county parks department). One of the board members acts as presiding officer. This form of government is the most popular; about three-quarters of the United States' counties use it. A typical county commission has three or five members and meets in regular session twice a month.

The board is not omnipotent, however, inasmuch as a number of other county officials are elected as well. In most places, these include the sheriff, the county prosecutor (or district attorney), the county clerk (or clerk of the court), the county treasurer (or auditor), the county tax assessor, and the coroner.

Figure 11.1

Traditional Organization of County Government

The most common form of county government lacks a central executive.

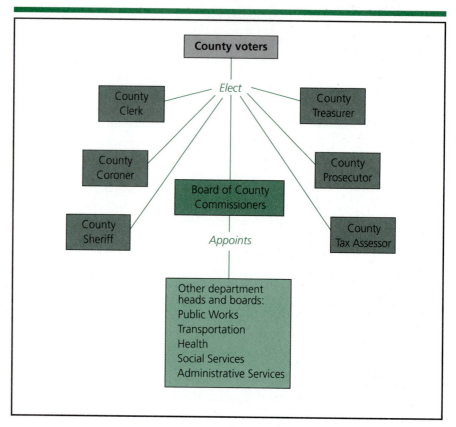

These officials can become powerful political figures in their own right by controlling their own bureaucratic units. Figure 11.1 sketches the typical organizational pattern.

There are two primary criticisms of this type of organization. First, there is no elected central executive official, like the mayor of a city or the governor of a state. County government is run by a board. Second, there is no single professional administrator to manage county government, the way a city manager does in a municipality. Elected officials are responsible for administering major county functions.

These criticisms have led to two alternative county structures. In one, called the *county council–elected executive plan,* the voters elect an executive officer in addition to the governing board. The result is a clearer separation between legislative and executive powers—in effect, a two-branch system of government. The board still has the power to set policy, adopt the budget, and audit the financial performance of the county. The executive's role is to prepare the budget, administer county operations (in other words, implement the policies of the board), and appoint department heads. Slightly under 400 counties have adopted this arrangement. In the other alternative structure, the *council-*

Table 11.2

The Most Pressing
Problems for County
Government

Problem	Percentage of Counties in Which the Problem is "Very Important"
Promotion of business and industrial development	70.8
Financial management	63.2
Roads	61.2
Toxic waste management	51.0
Public transportation	45.7
Jail expansion	40.4
Law enforcement planning	36.5
Land-use planning and zoning	35.0

Source: Barbara P. Greene, "Counties and the Fiscal Challenges of the 1980s," *Intergovernmental Perspective* 13 (Winter 1987): 16.

administrator plan, the county board hires a professional administrator to run the government. The advantage of this form of government is that it brings to the county a highly skilled manager with a professional commitment to efficient, effective government. Approximately eight hundred counties have variations of the council-administrator structure.

Determining the most effective structural arrangements for county government is an ongoing issue. Defections from the long-standing commission form of county government and experimentation with alternatives continue.

Hot Topics in County Government   Myriad problems confront county governments. Table 11.2 lists the most pressing of these, according to county officials. In almost every county, the promotion of business and industrial development is the most critical concern. County governments are increasingly devoting time and resources to promoting their area as a place to do business. Other concerns include financial management (primarily a matter of achieving a balance between revenues and expenditures), roads (a long-time county concern), and toxic waste management (a new problem). Public transportation, jail expansion, law enforcement planning, and land-use planning and zoning are very important issues in at least one-third of American counties.

County Performance   The last word on counties has not been written. Since the 1970s they have been said to be improving, modernizing, or exhibiting some other positive behavior. Granted, counties are now more prominent than they were in the old days, when they were considered the shadowy backwaters of local governments. As urban populations spill beyond the suburbs into the unincorporated territory of counties, the pressure on local governments grows.[12]

Fearful that these pressures have already overwhelmed county governments, the Speaker of the California Assembly introduced legislation in 1991 to create a tier of regional governments in his state.[13] Under the proposal, California would be divided into seven regions that would be governed by thirteen-member elected boards. These regional "super" governments would assume many of the development and infrastructure functions currently assigned to county governments. Although the bill did not pass, the issue has not disappeared. County governments must continue to modernize and focus on the "big picture" or run the risk of being bypassed.

Municipalities

Municipalities are cities; the words are interchangeable, and they refer to a specific, populated chunk of territory, typically operating under a charter from state government. Cities differ from counties in terms of how they were created and what they do. Historically, they have been the primary units of local government in most societies—the grand enclaves of human civilization. Augustine wrote of a city of God and Cotton Mather of a heavenly city, but more recent formulations speak of ungovernable[14] and unheavenly[15] cities. Whatever the appropriate image, they are fascinating places.

Creating Cities   A city is a legal recognition of settlement patterns in an area. In the most common procedure, residents petition the state for a charter of incorporation. The area slated for incorporation must meet certain criteria, such as population or density minimums. In most cases, a referendum is required. The referendum enables citizens to vote on whether they wish to become an incorporated municipality. Frequently, citizens are also asked to vote on the name of the municipality and its form of government. If the incorporation measure is successful, then a charter is granted by the state, and the newly created city has the legal authority to elect officials and to provide services to its residents. Not all cities have charters, however. Most California cities, for example, operate under general state law.

New cities are created every year. For instance, in 1991, twenty-four places incorporated (and five cities disincorporated, or ceased to exist).[16] Although most new cities tend to be small, some had sizable populations from the start. California's new cities, Santa Clarita and Mission Viejo, had populations of more than 65,000 and 50,000, respectively, when they incorporated in the late 1980s.

Like counties, cities are general-purpose units of local government. But unlike counties, they typically have greater decision-making authority and discretion. Most states have enacted home rule provisions for cities, although in some states, only those cities that have attained a certain population size can exercise this option. In addition, cities generally offer a wider array of services to their citizenry than most counties do. Public safety, public works, parks, and recreation are standard features, supplemented in some cities by publicly maintained cemeteries, city-owned and operated housing, city-run docks, and city-constructed convention centers. It is city government that picks up garbage and trash, sweeps streets, inspects restaurants, maintains traffic signals, and plants trees.

City Governmental Structure   City governments operate with one of three structures: a mayor-council form, a city commission form, or a council-manager form. In each structure, an elected governing body, typically called a city council, has policymaking authority. What differentiates the three structures is the manner in which the executive branch is organized.

1. *Mayor-council form.* In the mayor-council form of government, executive functions such as the appointment of department heads are performed by elected officials. This form of government can be subdivided into two types, depending on the formal powers held by the mayor. In a strong-mayor–council structure, the mayor is the source of executive leadership. Strong mayors run city hall like governors run the statehouse. They are responsible for daily administrative activities, the hiring and firing of top-level city officials, and budget preparation. They have a potential veto over council actions. In a weak-mayor–council structure, the mayor's role is that of executive figurehead. The council (of which the mayor may be a member) is the source of executive power. The council appoints city officials and develops the budget, and the mayor has no veto power. He performs ceremonial tasks such as speaking for the city, chairing council meetings, and attending ribbon-cutting festivities. A structurally weak mayor can emerge as a powerful political figure in the city, but only if she possesses informal sources of power. Figure 11.2 highlights the structural differences between the strong- and weak-mayor–council forms of city government.

Mayor-council systems are popular in large cities (where populations are greater than 250,000) and in small cities (with populations under 10,000). More than half of the cities in the United States use a mayor-council structure. Some large cities, in which the administrative burdens of the mayor's job are especially heavy, have established the position of general manager or chief administrative officer.

2. *City commission form.* Under the city commission form of government, illustrated in Figure 11.3, legislative and executive functions are merged. Commissioners not only make policy as members of the city's governing body, but they also head the major departments of city government. They are both policymakers and policy executors. One of the commissioners is designated as mayor simply to preside over commission meetings.

The commission form of government was created as a reaction to the mayor-council structure. Its origins can be traced back to the inability of a mayor-council government in Galveston, Texas, in 1900, to respond to the chaos caused by a hurricane that demolished the city and killed six thousand people. Bowing to gubernatorial pressure, the Texas legislature authorized the creation

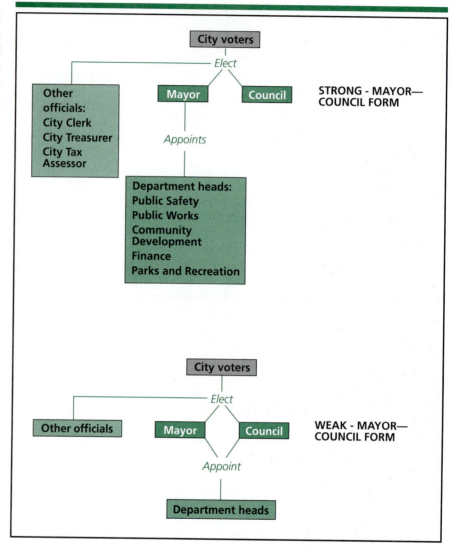

Figure 11.2

Mayor-Council Form of Government

The primary difference between these two structures concerns the power and authority possessed by the mayor. Strong mayors are more ideally situated to exert influence and control.

of a totally new form of city government—a commission form—and by 1904, the new city government had entirely rebuilt Galveston.[17] The success of the commission led to its adoption first by other Texas cities (Houston, Dallas, Fort Worth) and, within a decade, by 160 other municipalities (such as Des Moines, Pittsburgh, Buffalo, Nashville, and Charlotte). Its appeal was its ostensible reduction of politics in city government.

But almost as fast as the commission form of government appeared on the scene, disillusionment set in. One problem stemmed from the predictable tendency of commissioners to act as advocates for their own departments. Each commissioner wanted a larger share of the city's budget allocated to his or her

Figure 11.3

City Commission Form of Government

Executive leadership is fragmented under a commission form of government. Individually, each commissioner heads a department; together they run city hall.

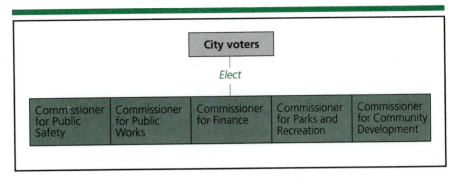

department. Another problem had to do with politicians acting as administrators: elected officials do not always turn out to be good managers. As quickly as it had appeared, the commission form declined. One study showed that of the almost two hundred cities reporting a commission structure in 1970, more than 42 percent had replaced it with another form by 1980.[18] By the 1990s, only a few cities were operating with a commission structure. Notable among them were Mobile, Topeka, Portland (Oregon), and Chattanooga.

3. *Council-manager form.* The third city government structure, the council-manager form, emphasizes the separation of politics (the policymaking activities of the governing body) from administration (the execution of the policies enacted by the governing body). Theoretically, the city council makes policy, and administrators execute policy. Under this structure, the council hires a professional administrator to manage city government. Figure 11.4 sketches this structure.

The administrator (usually called a city manager) appoints and removes department heads, oversees service delivery, develops personnel policies, and prepares budget proposals for the council. These responsibilities alone make the manager an important figure in city government. But add to them the power to make policy recommendations to the city council, and the position becomes very powerful. When offering policy recommendations to the council, the manager is walking a thin line between politics and administration. Managers who, with the acquiescence of their council, carve out an activist role for themselves may be able to dominate policymaking in city government.[19] In council-manager cities, the two contending parties typically have a working understanding about just how far the manager can venture into the policymaking realm of city government.[20]

The council-manager form of city government predominates in cities of 10,000 to 25,000 people, especially in homogeneous suburban communities and in the newer cities of the Sunbelt region.

Which Form of City Government Is Best? Experts disagree about many things, and one of them is which city government structure is best. Most would probably agree that structures lacking a strong executive officer are generally less

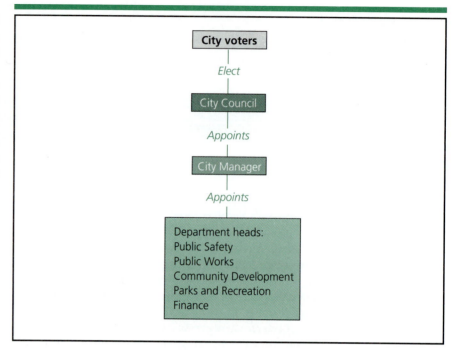

preferable than others. By that token, the weak-mayor–council and the commission forms are less favorable. The strong-mayor–council form of government
is extolled for fixing accountability firmly in the mayor's office, and the council-
manager system is credited with professionalizing city government by bringing
in skilled administrators to run things. It is up to the people to decide which
form of government they want, and they have been doing just that.

In 1984, voters in Rochester, New York, replaced their long-standing council-
manager form with a strong-mayor–council structure. And in 1990, Tulsa installed a mayor-council form in place of what many voters felt was an antiquated
commission system. Not all proposed switches meet with success, of course. In
Toledo in 1986, for example, voters defeated a proposal to abandon the council-
manager plan in favor of a strong mayor. Voters in Kansas City in 1989 rejected
a plan to change from a weak-mayor to a strong-mayor structure. The best
advice may be for a city to use whichever form of government works while
remaining receptive to structural improvements.

Pressing Issues in City Government   The pressing issues in city governments
these days include planning and land use, annexation, finances, and representation. Although the issues are discussed separately below, they are frequently
intertwined. For instance, decisions about land use can affect the city's finances.
The annexation of new territory may alter representation.

1. *Planning and Land Use.* Land is important to city governments, for it is
crucial to their economic and political well-being.[21] City governments control

land uses within their boundaries. They frequently use a comprehensive plan (often called a general or master plan) to guide them. The plan typically divides the city into sections for commercial, industrial, and residential uses. In addition, a city might set aside areas for recreation and open space. For example, the general plan for Santa Barbara, California, designates portions of the city for parks, bikeways, and a bird refuge.

New York City enacted the first modern zoning ordinance in 1916 and, since then, cities have used *zoning* to effectuate land use planning and control.[22] Through zoning, the designations established in a city's plan are made specific. For example, land set aside for residential use may be zoned for single-family dwellings, multifamily units, or mobile homes. Commercial areas may be zoned for offices, shopping centers, or hotels. Industrial sections of the city are often separated into "light" and "heavy" zones. Additionally, cities can overlay special zones onto existing ones. For example, cities bent upon restoration of older sections of the commercially zoned downtown area may establish historic preservation zones. Once designated, property owners are prohibited from tearing down old structures and, instead, are encouraged to renovate them. A city anxious to transform the appearance of a particular area may create special zones in order to regulate architectural style or height of buildings such that the right "look" can be achieved. Undesirable uses, such as pornographic bookstores and XXX theaters, are often clustered together in special adult entertainment zones.

Once set, zoning can be altered through applications for variances and rezoning, usually heard by a city's planning commission. A variance is a nonconforming use, such as professional offices in an area zoned for duplex housing. Rezoning involves a change in zoning designation, either to allow more intense use of the land (an upzoning) or to restrict use (downzoning). Sometimes, applications for variances and rezoning can be controversial. A study of fourteen years' worth of applications to upzone parcels in Wilmington, Delaware, demonstrated that community opposition played an important role in the outcome.[23] When community opposition existed, such as a protest by neighborhood organizations against an upzoning application, 70 percent of the applications failed. When no community opposition emerged, 80 percent of the upzoning requests were approved.

Zoning is, ultimately, a political exercise with economic consequences. It is a high-stakes activity for city governments. Cities use zoning to promote "good" growth such as upscale residential areas and to limit "bad" growth such as low-income housing.[24] Some cities have engaged in a practice that became known as *exclusionary zoning*. For example, a city might restrict its residential zones to 3,500 square-foot single-family dwellings on five-acre lots. The resulting high cost of housing would effectively limit the potential residents to the wealthy. Court decisions have not only found exclusionary zoning illegal; they have instructed local governments to engage in inclusionary zoning. The New Jersey Supreme Court led the way in its *Mount Laurel* decisions, in which municipalities in the state were ordered to provide housing opportunities for low- and moderate-income people.

2. *Annexation.* Annexation has historically been a popular means of adding territory and population. In the past thirty years, many cities have found them-

selves squeezed by the rapid growth and incorporation of territory just outside city limits, and therefore beyond their control. What is worse (from a central city's perspective), some of these suburban cities have begun to threaten the central city's traditional dominance of the metropolitan area. People and jobs are fleeing the central city. To counteract this trend and to assure themselves of adequate space for future expansion, some cities have engaged in annexation efforts.

Not all cities can annex, however. They run up against two realities: the existence of incorporated suburbs (which makes that territory nonannexable) and the strictures of state laws. State governments determine the legal procedures for the annexation process, and they can make it easy or hard. Texas is a state that makes it easy for cities to annex, and not surprisingly, big Texas cities (in terms of population) have vast territories: Houston covers 539 square miles, Dallas 342 square miles, and San Antonio 333 square miles.

extraterritorial jurisdiction

The ability of a city government to control certain practices in an adjacent unincorporated area.

In Texas, cities use their power of **extraterritorial jurisdiction** (ETJ) to supplement annexation. Under ETJ, they can control subdivision practices in unincorporated bordering territory. (The amount of territory varies from a half-mile for small cities to five miles for cities with over 250,000 people.) Addi-

Rural villages, shown in the first and fourth panels, have two development options. Under most conventional land use plans, villages take on suburban characteristics, as reflected in the second panel. An alternate approach to land use, one that reinforces the traditional character of small towns and protects the landscape, is modeled in the third panel.

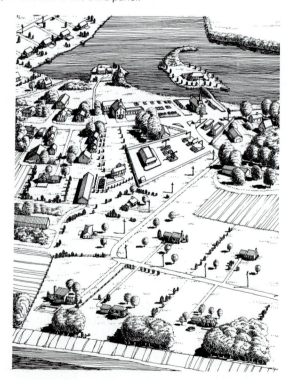

tionally, a Texas city can annex up to 10 percent of its territory annually without a referendum. The city simply has to provide adequate notice to the about-to-be-annexed residents. Houston has elevated this practice to an art form: It has annexed along major transportation arteries extending out of the city, thereby astronomically increasing its extraterritorial jurisdiction and reserving for itself vast territories for future annexation.[25]

Some states make it difficult for cities to annex. Cities may have to wait for land owners in an adjacent area to petition to be annexed. Even when a majority of the land owners request annexation, if the proportion is less than 75 percent, referendum elections must be held. State law may require that the annexation be approved by referendum by both the existing city and the area to be annexed. This is known as a "dual majority," and it effectively makes annexation difficult.

Some of the United States' most prominent cities have rather confined city limits. For example, of the fifty most populated cities in the country, twenty-two control less than one hundred square miles of territory. The most extreme cases are Newark (covering 24.1 square miles), Miami (34.3), Buffalo (41.8), San Francisco (46.4), and Boston (47.2).[26] In the older, established metropolitan areas there is little room for a central city to expand, because it is hemmed in by incorporated suburbs. Suburban areas incorporate—that is, become legal municipal—entities, for many reasons. Among those reasons is annexation. Recent research has shown that the threat of annexation frequently stimulates the creation of new cities.[27]

Table 11.3

The Proportion of Cities Expecting Revenue-Expenditure Imbalances Worse than −5 Percent

	Percentages of Cities 1990	1991
All Cities	11	26
Broken Down by Region		
Northeast	7	15
Midwest	9	28
South	12	21
West	15	40
Broken Down by Population Size		
300,000 and over	3	9
100,000–299,999	6	15
50,000–99,999	12	29
10,000–49,999	13	30

Source: Adapted from Michael A. Pagano, *City Fiscal Conditions 1991* (Washington, D.C.: National League of Cities, 1991), p. 11. Used by permission.

3. *Finances.* City governments, just like other local governments, have to balance their fiscal resources against their fiscal needs. Unlike the national government, however, these governments have to operate within the constraints of a balanced budget. The option of ending the fiscal year in debt or printing new money does not exist for them. As a result, they have become fairly creative at finding new sources of revenue in hard times.

A 1991 National League of Cities (NLC) survey of 525 city finance directors indicated just how serious the revenue issue is in city governments.[28] Sixty-one percent of the cities reported that their general fund expenditures would exceed their general fund revenues. (The general fund is the entity through which most major operations of the city are conducted.) Minor shortfalls can be covered (for example, cities may be able to transfer dollars out of another fund into the general fund), but more substantial gaps are cause for alarm.

Table 11.3 reports the percentage of cities in which the imbalance between general fund revenues and expected expenditures was worse than minus 5 percent. It is evident from the table that the proportion of cities experiencing imbalances more than doubled between 1990 and 1991. The regional breakdowns indicate that the problem was somewhat less acute for cities in the Northeast; but for the most part, the percentages were fairly constant across regions. The population breakdowns present quite a different picture. Small- to

Table 11.4

City Responses to Fiscal Stress

Corrective Action	Percentage of Cities Using the Action
Increased level of fees/charges	73.1
Reduced growth rate in operating spending	58.5
Increased property tax rates	43.4
Reduced actual level of capital spending	43.2
Implemented new fees/charges	40.0
Contracted out services	36.6
Froze municipal hiring	36.2
Reduced number of city employees	29.3
Imposed or raised development or impact fees	22.9
Increased rates of other taxes	13.3
Implemented a new tax or taxes	11.4
Reduced city service levels	9.5
Increased sales tax rates	4.4
Shifted service responsibilities to another government	3.4
Increased income tax rates	1.1

Source: Michael A. Pagano, *City Fiscal Conditions 1991* (Washington, D.C.: National League of Cities, 1991), p. 25. Reprinted by permission.

medium-sized cities, those in the 10,000–to–99,999 categories, have been hardest hit by the revenue-expenditure imbalance, and this is a growing problem. In a more advantageous situation are large cities—those with populations of 300,000 or more. Only 9 percent of the latter showed a serious imbalance in 1991, although the percentage was rising.

Given these figures, what can cities do to adapt? The NLC survey asked just that question. The responses from city officials appear in Table 11.4. The most relied-upon corrective action was to increase fees and charges. More than 70 percent of the cities did so during the previous fiscal year. For instance, a city might increase the cost of a building permit or charge more for health inspections at restaurants. And the cost of parking in a metered space or in a city-owned parking garage can be hiked. (Commuting students at urban colleges with inadequate parking have probably marveled at how adept city officials are at the "make students pay" strategy.) Indeed, cities can boost revenues in a variety of seemingly small ways. More than one-third of the cities indicated that they were imposing new fees and charges. A city service that used to be free, such as a city park, may now have an admission fee.

An alternative to raising more money is to cut costs. Cities in the NLC survey indicate that this too is a popular option. Almost 60 percent of the cities reduced the growth rate of their operational spending (expenditures for city services), and more than 40 percent cut their capital spending (items such as construction projects). However, as fiscal stress forces cities to reconsider their spending priorities, many people are concerned that, in doing so, cities will assign social services (such as programs for the poor) a low priority.

The list in Table 11.4 suggests that cities are responding inventively to the revenue-expenditure imbalance. City officials bite the political bullet and increase fees and taxes; they try to achieve savings in service delivery in a number of ways. Yet in some cities, such as Scranton, Pennsylvania, minor adjustments have not worked. After three years' worth of budget deficits, the state ruled that Scranton was a "distressed municipality" and appointed an outside administrator with the authority to make tough choices for the city.[29] Although most cities are not in such dire straits, concern over balancing revenues and expenditures persists.

4. *Representation.* Representation in city government is another fundamental concern. How can citizens' preferences be effectively represented in city hall? In the colonial days of town meetings and civic republics, it was simple: A citizen showed up at the meeting hall, voiced his opinion, and the majority ruled. When this proved to be unwieldy, a system of representative democracy seemed just the ticket.

In city governments, city council members are elected in one of two ways: either at large or by districts (also called wards). In **at-large elections,** a city voter can vote in each council race. In **district elections,** a city voter can vote only in the council race in her district. From the perspective of candidates, the at-large system means that a citywide campaign must be mounted. With districts, the candidate's campaign is limited to a specific area of the city. As discussed in Chapter 12, the structural reform movement advocated at-large elections as a means of weakening the geographic base of political machines.[30] Candidates running in citywide races must appeal to a broad cross-section of the population to be successful.

There are significant consequences for the use of at-large electoral systems. An in-depth study of almost one thousand city council members across the country revealed that at-large members tend to be wealthier and more highly educated than council members elected from districts.[31] At-large council members also differ from district members in terms of their relationships with constituents. Council members elected at large devote less time to answering individual complaints and direct their attention to a citywide and business constituency.

Almost half of U.S. cities with populations of 2,500 or more use an at-large method for electing their council members. The popularity of the method decreases as city population size increases, however. For example, only 15 percent of cities with populations above the half-million mark use at-large elections. This approach to city council representation is increasingly under attack for diminishing the likelihood that a member of a minority group can be elected. Research on 313 cities indicated that when cities shifted from an at-large system

at-large elections

Citywide (or countywide) contests to determine the members of a city council (or county commission).

district (ward) elections

Elections in which the voters in one district or ward of a jurisdiction (city, county, school district) vote for a candidate to represent that district.

to a district or mixed format (a combination of at-large and district seats), more blacks were elected to the council.[32] Other research has amplified those findings, especially in cities where the black population is more than 20 percent.[33] When New York City redrew city council district lines in 1991, the racial and ethnic composition of the resulting council was quite different, as Problem Solving 11.1 relates.

Some studies have shown that changing the electoral system from at large to districts produces an overall increase in citizen participation, in terms of greater attendance at council meetings, higher voter turnout, and a larger number of candidates.[34] It is not altogether clear that changing to districts will translate into policy benefits for the previously underrepresented sectors of the city, however.[35] Research has shown that in terms of policy attitudes, there is really no significant difference between council members elected at large and those elected from districts.[36]

Towns and Townships

The word *town* evokes an image of a small community where everyone knows everyone else, where government is informal, and where local leaders gather at the coffee shop to make important decisions. This is both accurate and inaccurate. Towns generally are smaller, in terms of population, than cities or counties. And the extent of their governmental powers depends on state government. But even where they are relatively weak, town government is increasingly becoming more formalized.

How Do We Know a Town When We See One?   Towns and townships are general-purpose units of local government, distinct from county and city governments. Only twenty states, primarily in the Northeast and Midwest, have official towns or townships. In some states these small jurisdictions have relatively broad powers; in others they have a more circumscribed role.

New England towns, for example, offer the kinds of services commonly associated with cities and counties in other states. Many New England towns continue their tradition of direct democracy through a town meeting form of government. At a yearly town meeting, residents make decisions on policy matters confronting the community. They elect town officials, pass local ordinances, levy taxes, and adopt a budget. In other words, the people who attend the town meeting function as a legislative body.

New England towns, along with those in New Jersey, Pennsylvania, and to some degree Michigan, New York, and Wisconsin, enjoy fairly broad powers. In large measure, they act like other general-purpose units of government. In the remainder of the township states (Illinois, Indiana, Kansas, Minnesota, Missouri, Nebraska, North Dakota, Ohio, and South Dakota), the nature of township government is more rural. Rural townships tend to stretch across thirty-six square miles of land (conforming to the surveys done by the national government before the areas were settled), and their service offerings are often limited

Problem Solving 11.1

The "New" New York City

The Problem: New York City grappled with an array of problems in the early 1990s—the loss of business firms to other jurisdictions, rapidly diminishing federal aid, and an upsurge in interracial conflict. It was not that these problems were unique to New York; on the contrary, many cities faced similar conditions. But New York City, by virtue of its 7.2 million residents, operates on a massive scale. And as social and economic problems festered, the city faced a growing political challenge—increasing minority representation on the city council.

A new city charter, ratified in 1989, had increased the powers of the city council and expanded its membership from 35 to 51 members. A Districting Commission was established to create what would be, in fact, a new political map for the city. The new map was intended to reflect the multiracial nature of New York City. The old 35-member council, with 26 whites, 6 blacks, and 3 Hispanic members, failed to do so in a city with a minority population of approximately 57 percent. By enlarging the council membership and drawing district boundaries creatively, the new council would likely capture the city's diversity.

The Solution: After months of wrangling, the Districting Commission proposed a plan that, according to commission members, would increase the number of seats held by minorities. To increase the likelihood that minority candidates would have a chance to win, the plan created a number of districts in which the minority population was 60 percent or higher.

(Because minority neighborhoods tend to have lower voter registration and turnout rates, 60 percent is considered the minimum needed to give minority candidates a fair shot at winning the election.) Of course, the new districts meant that some incumbents would lose their jobs.

The Districting Commission's plan was immediately discredited by diverse groups aspiring for greater representation, such as African Americans, Hispanics, homosexuals, Republicans, and Asian-Americans, and by a group of incumbents fighting to protect their seats. In response, the commission reconvened and offered a new plan, one that would create thirteen black and eight Hispanic districts. But its job was not over. The U.S. Justice Department, which under the Voting Rights Act has final approval over changes in New York City's election procedures, rejected the plan just months before the September 1991 primary elections were to be held. The commission returned to the drawing boards and produced a modified plan that increased the number of Hispanic districts to ten. Once the Justice Department approved the plan, council elections were held as scheduled. The new districts performed as expected in most instances. Minority representation increased to about 40 percent, more closely mirroring the city. The diverse interests that influence New York City politics in the 1990s have another goal in mind as well: winning the mayor's seat in 1993.

Sources: Felicia R. Lee, "New York City Plan Seeks More Minorities on Council," *New York Times,* May 2, 1991, p. B12; Robert Pear, "U.S. Bars New York District Plan, Finding Hispanic Voters Are Hurt," *New York Times,* July 20, 1991, pp. 1, 10; Jerry Gray, "New Prize in New York City's Tug-of-War on Council Redistricting," *New York Times,* August 5, 1991, p. A14.

to roads and law enforcement. The closer these rural townships are to large urban areas, the more likely they are to offer an expanded set of services to residents.

Townships and the Future   The demise of the township type of government has long been expected. As rural areas become more populated, they will eventually meet the population minimums necessary to become municipalities. Even in New England, questions of town viability have arisen. For example, many Connecticut towns with populations exceeding 15,000 have found it increasingly difficult to operate effectively through town meetings.[37] Consequently, some are adding professional managers, whereas others are considering a shift to a strong-mayor form of government. Other towns face a different problem. Many are experiencing substantial population exodus and, in the process, losing their reason for existence. These towns may die a natural death, with other types of government (perhaps counties or special districts) providing services to the remaining residents. The question is whether towns and townships make sense in contemporary America. Despite dire predictions, towns and townships have proved to be remarkably resilient. According to the Census Bureau, there were 16,700 of them in 1987, down only 100 from the 1977 figure.

Townships have not sat idly by as commentators speculated on their dim future. Many small towns have embarked upon ambitious economic development strategies: industrial recruitment, tourism promotion, and amenity enhancement.[38] They formed an interest group, the National Association of Towns and Townships, to lobby on their behalf in Washington, D.C. Moreover, as general-purpose units of local government, townships qualified for General Revenue Sharing (GRS) funds from the national government when those funds were still available, and were thus helped through times of financial stress. The U.S. Advisory Commission on Intergovernmental Relations (ACIR) went so far as to opine that townships were being "propped up by GRS largesse."[39]

Now that GRS has run its course, however, the long-anticipated demise of some townships may come to pass. In fact, one observer has called for a triage strategy for allocating funds to small towns.[40] This approach would concentrate funds on towns with the prospect of survival, not on those that are dying or flourishing. Taking a different tack, a political scientist and a state senator in Vermont teamed up to advocate redesigning their state government around a system of reinvigorated towns and regional governments they called *shires*.[41] In fact, they see towns and their grassroots governments as the last hope for democracy in the twenty-first century.

Special Districts

Special districts are supposed to do what other local governments cannot or will not do. They are created to meet service needs in a particular area. If, for example, residents of an unincorporated area want fire protection but the closest city refuses to extend its coverage and the county is unable to provide adequate service, the residents may establish a special fire district. The process usually requires that the residents petition the state to hold a referendum on the question. If the vote is favorable, a fire service district will be established, employees will be hired, and fire protection will be provided. Residents will pay a special tax or fee for the operation of the district. There are approximately 29,000 special districts around the country, and that number is increasing.

Not all special districts are organized alike. Ninety percent of them provide a single function, such as irrigation or mosquito control. Governing bodies can be independently elected or, in the case of weaker special districts, appointed by another government, such as the county. The budget and staff size of special districts ranges from minuscule to mammoth. Some of the more prominent include the Port Authority of New York and New Jersey, the Chicago Transit Authority, the Washington Public Power Supply System, and the Los Angeles County Sanitation District.

Yes, But Do We Really Need Them?   Special districts overlay existing general-purpose local governments, and some question their necessity. The ACIR puts the question bluntly: "If general-purpose local governments are set up to perform a broad spectrum of functions and if they collectively cover practically every square foot of territory in a state, why [are] special districts needed at all?"[42] The answer has traditionally focused on the deficiencies of general-purpose local governments.[43] Three general categories of "deficiencies" are worth examining.

First are the technical conditions of a general-purpose local government. In some states, cities cannot extend their service districts beyond their boundaries. Moreover, the problem to be addressed may not fit neatly within a single jurisdiction. A river that runs through several counties may periodically overflow its banks in heavy spring rains. The problem affects small portions of many jurisdictions. A flood control district covering only the affected areas may be a logical solution. Furthermore, there are problems of scale. A general-purpose local government simply may not be able to provide electric service to its residents as efficiently as a special utility district that covers a multitude of counties. Finally, there may be prohibitions against jurisdictional coventuring. For example, some states do not allow their counties to offer services jointly with other counties. Management of a two-county library requires that a special two-county library district be established.

A second set of deficiencies has to do with financial constraints. Local general-purpose governments commonly operate under debt and tax limitations. Demands for additional services that exceed a jurisdiction's revenue-raising ceiling or lead to the assumption of excessive debt cannot be accommodated. By using special districts, existing jurisdictions can circumvent the debt and tax ceilings. Special districts are better suited than general-purpose governments for service charge or user fee financing, whereby the cost of the service can be directly apportioned to the consumer, as with water or sewer charges.

Technical and financial deficiencies of general-purpose local governments help to explain the creation of special districts, but political explanations shed even more light. Restrictive annexation laws and county governments with limited authority are political facts of life that encourage the use of special districts. For residents of an urban fringe area, a public service district (which may provide more than one service) may be the only option. Some special districts owe their existence to a federal mandate. For example, national government policy has spurred the creation of soil conservation and flood control districts throughout the country.

Profile 11.1

The Nation's Top Tourist Attraction Is a Special District?

In 1967, the Florida legislature created an extra-special special district, the Reedy Creek Improvement District (RCID). You may know it by another name: Disney World. Yes, the home of Mickey Mouse, Space Mountain, and EPCOT is a special district.

The reason for the establishment of the district was quite simple: Disney World's creators wanted to be protected from the whims of local and state politicians. A special district, with Disney as the sole landowner, would do just that. And if the state would not comply with their request for a special district, Disney threatened to choose a non-Florida location. With only one dissenting vote, the Florida legislature approved RCID and, in 1971, Disney World opened for business.

Covering 27,400 acres that were once orange groves and pine trees, Disney World's impact has been substantial. With 33,000 workers, it is central Florida's largest employer. In 1990, the Florida Department of Commerce estimated that 28.5 million people visited the facility, making Disney World the most popular tourist attraction in the country. Once Disney World was in place, additional development quickly followed. The new hotels, restaurants, shops, and other theme parks have had a tremendous impact on government. Sales tax revenue in the two counties where spin-off development has occurred rose from $3.3 billion in 1970 to $45.2 billion in 1990. Not all of the spin-offs have been positive, however. Although RCID has been effectively planned and managed, adjacent jurisdictions have had to contend with traffic congestion, overburdened infrastructure, and pollution problems.

As the label implies, special districts are indeed special. Perhaps the Reedy Creek Improvement District ought to be considered a *unique* district.

Sources: "Disney World, 20, Throws Itself a Party," *The State*, September 29, 1991, p. 3A; "'67 Florida Law Lets Disney World Govern Itself," *The State*, September 29, 1991, p. 3A.

Once created, a special district may become a political power in its own right. In places where general-purpose governmental units are fully equipped legally, financially, and technically to provide a service, they may encounter resistance from special-district interests fighting to preserve the district.

Uneasiness about Special Districts   The arguments in favor of special districts revolve around their potential for efficient service provision and the likelihood that they will be responsive to constituents whose demands are not otherwise being met.[44] But for the most part, scholarly observers look at special districts with a jaundiced eye. The most frequently heard complaint is that special districts lack accountability. The public is often unaware of their existence, so they function free of much scrutiny. It has been said that special districts "operate in dim lights at the outermost fringes of public consciousness."[45] Profile 11.1 tells the story of a well-known tourist attraction that is actually a little-known special district.

The proliferation of special districts complicates the development of comprehensive solutions to public problems. The metropolitan areas of two large Texas cities, Houston and Dallas, contain 779 active special districts.[46] The presence of such an array of districts makes it difficult for general-purpose governments to set priorities.[47] It is not uncommon for cities and counties to be locked in governmental combat with the special districts in their area. There is a natural tendency for these governmental units to be turf-protecting, service-providing rivals.

Cognizant of these concerns, state governments are looking more closely at special districts and the role they play in service delivery. Colorado, Arizona, and Florida have taken actions that give their general-purpose local governments more input into the state's decision to create special districts.[48]

School Districts

School districts are a type of single-purpose local government. They are a special kind of special district and, as such, are considered one of the five types of local government. The trend in school districts follows the theory that fewer is better. Before the Second World War, more than 100,000 school districts covered the countryside. Many of these were rural, one-school operations. In many small towns, community identity was linked to the local schoolhouse. Despite serving as a source of pride, small districts were so expensive to maintain that consolidations occurred throughout the nation, and by 1987 the number of districts was less than 15,000.

School Politics   The school board is the formal source of power and authority in the district. The board is typically composed of five to seven members, usually elected in nonpartisan, at-large elections. Their job is to make policy for the school district. One of the most important policy decisions involves the district budget—how the money will be spent.

School districts are governed by boards and managed by trained, full-time educational administrators. Like city governments, school districts invested heavily in the reform model of governance, and the average district has become more professional in operation in the past thirty years. An appointed chief administrator (a superintendent) heads the school district staff, the size of which is dependent on the size of the district.

During the 1970s, the criticism of school districts was that professional experts had seized control of the educational system, thus reducing the governing function of school boards to mere rubber-stamping of administrators' recommendations.[49] This appears to be less true as time passes. The 1980s were a time of rediscovery of public education, leading to a repoliticization of school districts. The issue of who is in charge, however, has another claimant: the parents of schoolchildren.

Parental influence in school district policy is most clearly emerging in the matter of school choice. School districts around the country are beginning to adopt measures that allow parents to decide whether their child will attend the school in the neighborhood or one elsewhere in the district. In effect, schools are competing for students. They are anxious to attract students, because district and state funds are allocated on a per-pupil basis. To attract students, some schools specialize in a particular academic area, such as arts or sciences; others emphasize certain teaching styles. As one administrator put it, "Public schools of choice is an on-rushing train."[50] The tradition of neighborhood schools, disrupted by busing and redrawing of school boundary lines in efforts to achieve racial balance, is being further eroded.

Advocates of parental choice claim that the approach offers poor families some of the options that wealthy families have always had with private schools. They argue that competition among schools will generate creativity and responsiveness among teachers and principals. Opponents of parental choice voice concerns about equity. They fear that students left in the less preferred schools (perhaps because their parents cannot afford to take them to a distant school and the school district does not provide transportation) will receive lower-quality education.

School District Concerns   There are always controversies in education. The burning issues in school districts range from corporal punishment to the dropout rate, but one recurring central issue is finances. Although the relationship is a bit more complex than "you get what you pay for," there is widespread agreement that children in well-funded school districts are better off than those in poorly funded ones.

A history of serious disparities in school funding, caused by great differences in the available property taxes that provide most of the revenue, has led to the increasing financial involvement of state government in local school districts. State governments use an **equalization formula** to distribute funds to school districts in an effort to reduce financial disparities. Under this formula, poorer school districts receive a proportionately larger share of state funds than wealthier districts do. Although these programs have increased the amount of funding for education, they have not eliminated the interdistrict variation. Wealthier districts simply use the state guarantee as a foundation on which to heap their own resources. Poorer school districts continue to operate with less revenue. By 1990, this situation had prompted state courts in Montana, Texas, New Jersey, and Kentucky to declare their public-school finance systems unconstitutional. In those states, the legislatures struggled to design new, more equitable financial arrangements. Texas, for example, responded with a controversial property-tax sharing system. By 1991, suits challenging the constitutionality of school financing were pending in nineteen states.[51] Some efforts at equalization are locally based. For instance, in 1992 the school district of La Crosse, Wisconsin, used family income as a criterion for assigning students to elementary schools.[52] By doing so, the district intended to create socioeconomically mixed schools. Chapter 15 looks in depth at school administration, innovations in education, and school finances.

equalization formula

A means of distributing funds (primarily to school districts) to reduce financial disparities among districts.

....

Interlocal Cooperation

Local governments of all stripes are re-examining the "go it alone" approach to problem solving. Central cities and suburban town governments are banding together, and cities and counties are joining in efforts to forge areawide solutions to contemporary problems. Governments of all types are expanding their involvement with the private sector. This is not to say that concerns over turf or interjurisdictional jealousies are things of the past, but there is a new appreciation of common problems.

A large portion of interlocal cooperation is fairly modest in application. Adjoining cities may operate a sanitary landfill together; a city and a county may agree to use the same jail facility; three school districts may share student transportation vehicles. Despite their seemingly inconsequential nature, even these small steps represent service delivery alternatives that were seldom examined in the past.

The explanation for such cooperative behavior is in large part financial. Simply put, the cost of independently providing a service may exceed the preference for it. Another part of the explanation is uneasiness about existing arrangements and, perhaps, the dawning awareness that cooperative approaches may be more effective than individual jurisdictional solutions. Whatever the explanation, the phenomenon appears to be growing.

In the past, areawide solutions were attempted through the organizational mechanism of a regional planning council. These councils, as noted in Chapter 13, owed their genesis to national-level decisions about how local governments should act. As is often the case with externally imposed solutions, the regional planning council concept met with indifference at best, opposition at worst, in local governments around the country. As a result, these "glamour organizations of the 1960s [have] become major disappointments all over the country."[53] Local governments are much more likely to succeed in jurisdictional cooperation when they themselves initiate it. The kind of interlocal cooperation that is catching on now has been given the label "intercommunity partnerships."[54] The key to these partnerships is that they involve private-sector organizations, the academic community, and citizen leagues. An example is the Intergovernmental Cooperation Program (ICP) in the Pittsburgh area. The central purpose of the ICP is "to identify emerging issues that offer timely opportunities for intergovernmental cooperation, to assemble resources for designing cooperative projects, and to monitor the implementation of cooperative projects."[55] The ICP has created a weighty agenda for itself.

Less formal than the ICP are coalitions that pursue common objectives. In the Seattle metropolitan area, in an effort to secure passage of referenda on low-income housing and a downtown art museum, supporters of each project established an informal alliance for joint fund raising, political organizing, and marketing.[56] The motto for this unlikely coalition is "Art, like low-income housing, serves the public interest."[57] Another coalition composed of naturalists, business interests, and civic activists emerged in support for a bond issue to upgrade the local zoo. These efforts in Seattle have generated a strategic consensus on behalf of interlocal cooperation that is likely to spread. Local governments are inveterate borrowers of good ideas from other local governments.

The Issue of Governance

Intercommunity partnerships return us to the governance issue raised early in this chapter and alluded to throughout it. How do we know when a community is well governed? We have seen communities restructure their governments with the intent of improving governance. Voters defeat incumbents and elect new council members in a similar effort. Conflict over local government spending priorities ensues. There is no set of universally accepted criteria for evaluating the quality of governance. The National Municipal League, a group that got its start during the reform movement, annually bestows its "All-American City" designation on a few select communities that display "civic energy."[58] Perhaps the key to governance is energy.

One attempt to isolate characteristics that are plausibly related to governance settled on seven elements.[59] According to this study, well-governed communities exhibit

1. tranquility among public officials—an absence of squabbles and bloodletting;
2. continuity in office of top-level managerial officials—a stable corps of administrative personnel;
3. use of analytical budgeting and planning processes—reliance on comprehensive, multiyear methods;
4. participative management—less commitment to hierarchical models and more employee-oriented management;
5. innovativeness—receptivity to new ideas;
6. active public-private partnerships—a minimization of the traditional barrier between government and the private sector; and
7. citizen input into government decisions—the use of formal mechanisms to increase public involvement in government.

The governance question goes back to Plato and Aristotle, and we are unlikely to resolve it here. But these seven elements do offer some guidance for continued rumination about government structure and function.

Summary

Communities can be considered civic republics, corporate enterprises, or consumer markets. The prevailing orientation affects the structure of government, and the structure in turn affects the way government functions.

The American landscape is awash in local governments, all delivering services to the public. General-purpose governments (counties, cities, towns, and townships) cover the country. Superimposed on them are thousands of single-purpose governments (special districts, school districts). These governments continue to tinker with their structures in an effort to find the right balance between the twin goals of efficiency and responsiveness. Additionally, local governments are experimenting with new jurisdictional partnerships.

Key Terms

general-purpose local government   at-large elections
single-purpose local government   district (ward) elections
extraterritorial jurisdiction   equalization formula

12

Local Leadership

The Meaning of Leadership

Community Power

The Elite Theory | The Pluralist Theory |
A Return to New Haven: Is It All in the Approach? |
The Dynamics of Power

Local Executives

Mayors | City Managers

Local Legislatures

City Council Members: Old and New | Councils
in Action: Increasing Conflict | Reshaping a
Council: The Case of Houston | Women as
Local Government Leaders

Political Leadership Versus Professional Leadership

Council-Manager Interactions | Perceptions of
Governmental Systems

Policy Innovation at the Local Level

Leadership *Is* Capacity

B ack in the mid-1980s, voters in San Jose, California, amended their city charter to strengthen the office of mayor. Under the revised charter, the mayor became responsible for nominating a city manager and for drafting budget proposals. Little did the public know that these minor structural alterations would fundamentally rearrange the relationships that their mayor had with the city council, professional staff, and the citizenry. By skillfully using his new powers, Mayor Tom McEnery, who served until 1992, was able to become the premier power broker in San Jose.[1] And the strong-mayor structure suits the new mayor, Susan Hammer, just fine.

Leadership is critical to local governments. It can make the difference between an effectively functioning government and one that lurches from one crisis to another. The terms that conjure up images of leadership in local government circles these days include initiative and inventiveness, risk-taking, high energy level, persistence, entrepreneurship and innovation, vision. These words share a common element: they denote activity and engagement. Leaders are people who "make a difference."[2]

....

The Meaning of Leadership

Every community needs leaders. Good leadership is good leadership, whether in the public or the private sector. *In Search of Excellence,* a study of sixty-two private-sector organizations, identified several interrelated factors that made for excellent companies—and, by inference, excellent governments as well.[3] These included

1. an organizational tendency toward action;
2. closeness to the customer;
3. autonomy and entrepreneurship;
4. productivity through employees;
5. a hands-on, value-driven approach; and
6. a simple organization with a lean staff.

The authors did not spell it out, but each of these characteristics is essentially about leadership. In a sequel to *In Search of Excellence,* in fact, the authors acknowledge that leadership is the "one element that connects all the others."[4] Another study that focused on leaders and their behavior found that effective leadership in organizations involves four strategies:

1. *Attention through vision:* creating a focus for what needs to get done.
2. *Meaning through vision:* communicating the vision, gaining its acceptance, and imparting its meaning to the organization's employees.
3. *Trust through positioning:* developing a set of actions necessary to implement the leader's vision.
4. *Deployment of self through positive self-regard:* recognizing personal strengths and compensating for weaknesses, nurturing one's own skills, and matching individual skills with organizational needs.[5]

The findings from these studies offer some important lessons for local government officials. As the models recommend, good leaders tend to be people who aim for results. They think in terms of desired outcomes.[6] Leaders are also people-oriented: They interact positively with others and are able to mobilize them in support of organizational objectives.

The final word on leadership belongs to scholars at the Center for Excellence in Local Government. In trying to identify the essential kernel that is leadership, they relayed a comment about former Baltimore mayor (now Maryland governor) William Donald Schaefer: "Schaefer just doesn't run Baltimore, he *is* Baltimore. The same goes for other excellent leaders. They *are* what they lead."[7]

....

Community Power

Real questions about who is running the show in local government do arise. At the risk of being accused of naiveté, we might suggest that "the people" run government, local and otherwise. Unfortunately, there is much evidence to persuade us otherwise. But we should not become too cynical, either. Citizen preferences do have an impact on public policy decisions. Can we assume, therefore, that those who occupy important positions in government, such as the mayor and the city council, are in fact in charge? Are they the leaders of the community? This is a question that has interested scholars for more than sixty years.

In sorting through the issue of "who's running the show," we find that two theories predominate. One, the **elite theory,** argues that a small group of leaders called an elite possesses power and rules society. The **pluralist theory,** conversely, posits that power is dispersed among competing groups, whose clash produces societal rule.

elite theory

A theory of government which asserts that a small group possesses power and rules society.

pluralist theory

A theory of government which asserts that multiple, open, competing groups possess power and rule society.

The Elite Theory

One of the earliest expositions of the elite theory argued that in any society, from underdeveloped to advanced, there are two classes of people: a small set who rule and a large clump who are ruled.[8] The rulers allocate values for society and determine the rules of the game; the ruled tend to be passive and ill-informed, and are unable to exercise any direct influence over the rulers. This division is reflected elsewhere in society. In organizations, for example, power is inevitably concentrated in the hands of a few people.[9] Given the pervasiveness of elite systems, should we expect decision making in communities to be any different?

A famous study of community power in Middletown (actually Muncie, Indiana) in the 1920s and 1930s discovered an identifiable set of rulers.[10] The researchers, sociologists named Robert and Helen Lynd, determined that "Family X" (the Ball family) was at the core of this ruling elite. Through their economic power, Family X and a small group of business leaders called the shots in Middletown. Government officials simply did the bidding of Family X and its cohorts.

Another widely read study of community power confirmed the basic tenets of elitism. Floyd Hunter's study of Regional City (Atlanta) in the 1950s and 1970s isolated the top leadership—a forty-person economic elite—that dominated the local political system.[11] Hunter argued that an individual's power in this city was determined by his role in the marketplace. Local elected officials simply carried out the policy decisions of the elite. To illustrate this point, Hunter compared the relatively limited power enjoyed by the mayor of Atlanta to the extensive power possessed by the president of Coca-Cola.[12]

Assuming for a moment that the elitist interpretations of community power are accurate, where do they take us? Do not be confused about the intent of an economic elite: They are not running the community out of a sense of benevolence. The following statement captures the larger meaning of elitism: "Virtually all U.S. cities are dominated by a small, parochial elite whose members have business or professional interests that are linked to local development and growth. These elites use public authority and private power as a means to stimulate economic development and thus enhance their own local business interests."[13] To many, this is a fairly disturbing conclusion.

The Pluralist Theory

The findings of these sociologists did not square with the prevailing orthodoxy of American political science: pluralism. Not everyone saw community power through the elitist lens, and many questioned whether the findings from Middletown and Regional City applied to other communities.

Pluralist theory views the decision-making process as one of bargaining, accommodation, and compromise. According to this view, no monolithic entity calls the shots; instead, authority is fragmented. There are many leadership groups, any one of which, given the importance of the issue at hand, can become involved in decision making. Granted, the size, cohesion, and wealth of these groups vary. But no group has a monopoly on resources. Pluralism sets forth a much more accessible system of community decision making than the grimly deterministic tenets of elitism do.

A study conducted by Robert Dahl in New Haven, Connecticut, challenged the sociologists' findings, particularly those of Hunter.[14] According to Dahl, decisions in New Haven in the 1950s were the product of the interactions of a system of groups with more than one center of power. Except for the mayor, no one leader was influential across a series of issue areas, and influential actors were not drawn from a single segment of the community.

Further explication of the pluralist model revealed that, although community decision making is limited to relatively few actors, the legitimacy of such a system hinges on the easily revoked consent of a much larger segment of the local population.[15] In other words, the "masses" may acquiesce to the leaders, but they can also rise up when they are displeased. Success in a pluralistic environment is determined by a group's ability to form coalitions with other groups. Pluralism, then, offers a more hopeful interpretation of community power.

A Return to New Haven: Is It All in the Approach?

reputational approach

A method for studying community power in which researchers ask informants to name and rank influential individuals.

New Haven, the setting for Dahl's affirmation of pluralist theory, has been examined and re-examined by skeptical researchers. Some of the debate between elitists and pluralists is a function of methodology—that is, the approach that is used in studying community power. Sociologists have tended to rely on what is called a **reputational approach.** They go into a community and ask informants to name and rank the local leaders. Those whose names repeatedly appear are considered to be the movers and shakers. This approach is criticized on the grounds that it measures not leadership per se but the reputation for leadership. Political scientists approach the power question differently, through a **decisional method.** They focus on specific community issues and, using a variety of sources, try to determine who is influential in the decision-making process. It is easy to see that the two different approaches can produce divergent findings.

decisional method

A method for studying community power in which researchers identify key issues and the individuals who are active in the decision-making process.

Users of the decisional method claim that it allows them to identify overt power rather than just power potential.[16] Additionally, it offers a realistic picture of power relationships as dynamic rather than fixed. Defenders of the reputational method argue that when researchers select key issues to examine, they are being arbitrary. Also, it may be that a study of decision making ignores the most powerful actors in a community—those who are able to keep issues *off* the agenda, who are influential enough to keep certain issues submerged.[17]

New Haven was found by Dahl to be a pluralist's delight. Convinced that the finding was affected by Dahl's methods, another researcher, G. William Domhoff, examined New Haven and emerged with a contrary view of the power structure.[18] He claimed that Dahl missed the big picture by focusing on issues that were of minor concern to the New Haven elite, so that Dahl's finding of an accessible decision-making process in which many groups were involved was not an adequate test of the presence of an elite. Domhoff investigated the urban redevelopment issue and discovered that the long-time mayor, whom Dahl had seen as leading an executive-centered coalition, was in fact being actively manipulated by a cadre of local business leaders. New Haven, Domhoff contended, was not quite the pluralistic paradise it was made out to be.

The Dynamics of Power

The work of Hunter and Dahl remains significant, but neither elitism nor pluralism adequately explains who's running the show. In fact, some observers claim that "no single descriptive statement applies to community leadership in general in the United States today."[19] Not all communities are organized alike;

and even within a single community, power arrangements shift as time passes and conditions change. One group of political scientists, Robert Agger, Daniel Goldrich, and Bert Swanson, argued that an understanding of community power requires an assessment of two variables: how power is distributed to the citizens, and the extent to which there is ideological unity among the political leaders.[20]

The effort of a Chicago growth coalition to promote the 1992 World's Fair offers an instructive example of how the power structure sometimes loses.[21] The 1992 Fair Corporation, a well-connected nonprofit group of economically powerful and socially prominent people, wanted to bring the 1992 World's Fair to Chicago. World's fairs have value to a community, secondarily from the show and spectacle, but primarily because of the long-term development consequences. To land the fair, the group had to convince the city's political leadership of the event's importance. They were in the process of doing so when the political dynamics suddenly changed. A supportive mayor, Jane Byrne, was defeated in 1983, and the new mayor, Harold Washington, was indifferent to the project. That was just the wedge that opponents of the fair needed. In the words of one commentator, "Chicago's new reform-minded black mayor and more open city council gave legitimacy to Fair critics."[22] Grassroots and political opposition intensified. Eventually, enough questions were raised that the state legislature refused to allocate the funds necessary to continue planning for the fair, and the 1992 Fair Corporation was forced to admit defeat. In this instance, power had shifted to a temporary coalition of forces.

If the elite can be beaten in Chicago, is pluralism likely to triumph in communities across the land? Probably not. The penetration of the government's domain by private economic interests in American communities is deep.[23] Clarence Stone uses the concepts of "systemic power" and "strategic advantage" to explain why community decisions so frequently favor upper-strata interests.[24] The starting point of his argument is that public officials operate in a highly stratified socioeconomic system in which there is a small upper class, a large, varied middle class, and a relatively small lower class. According to Stone, "Public officeholders are predisposed to interact with and to favor those who can reciprocate benefits."[25] Two considerations define the environment in which public officials operate: electoral accountability (keeping the majority of the public satisfied) and systemic power (the unequal distribution of economic, organizational, and social resources). Decision makers are likely to side with majority preferences on highly visible issues; but on less visible ones, the upper strata will win most of the time. The latter, in other words, enjoy a strategic advantage.

The final word on community power structures has not been written. That some interests, especially those of the economically powerful, seem to prevail more often than others is certain. Yet different communities have developed different arrangements for governance.[26] In some places, weak political leadership and a dispersed business elite have resulted in a condition called *hyperpluralism*. In hyperpluralistic communities, where many interests clash, competing groups are unable to form coalitions. Public policy, as a consequence, may become incoherent and increasingly ineffective. By the early 1990s, Chicago,

Detroit, Los Angeles, Miami, New Orleans, Philadelphia, and San Francisco were exhibiting signs of hyperpluralism.[27] Unfortunately, in Los Angeles in 1992, hyperpluralistic conditions took a tragic turn in the rioting that followed the not guilty verdict in the Rodney King–police brutality case. The question of who's in charge remains an interesting one.

Local Executives

The mantle of leadership in local government falls most often on chief executives: mayors and managers. Although it is possible for chief executives to eschew a leadership role, it is unlikely.

Mayors

Mayors tend to be the most prominent figures in city government, primarily because their position automatically makes them the center of attention. Occasionally a city council member emerges as a leader on a specific issue or stirs up some interest with verbal attacks on the mayor (which many observers interpret as jockeying for position to run against the mayor at the next election). This occurred in Chicago in the mid-1980s, when city alderman Edward Vrdolyak locked horns with incumbent mayor Harold Washington in his bid to win the office. But for the most part, attention is drawn to the mayor.

Differences Between Strong and Weak Mayors   Because of the structure of local government, some mayors have a greater opportunity for leadership than others. They are referred to as **strong mayors,** while those who lack the leadership-inducing structure are referred to as **weak mayors.** It is important to note that these labels refer to the position, not to the person who occupies it. A structure simply creates opportunities for leadership, not the certainty of it. True leaders are those who can take what is structurally a weak-mayor position and transform it into a strong mayorship.

As explained in Chapter 11, a strong-mayor structure establishes the mayor as the sole chief executive who exercises substantive policy responsibilities. In this kind of structure there is no city manager, who could expand on an administrative role and become a policy rival to the mayor. A strong mayor is directly elected by the voters, not selected by the council; serves a four-year, not two-year, term of office; and has no limitations on re-election. She also has a central role in budget formulation, extensive appointment and removal powers, and veto power over council-enacted ordinances.[28] The more of these powers a mayor has, the stronger her position is and the easier it is for the mayor to become a leader.

A weak-mayor structure does not provide these elements. It is designed such that the mayor shares policy responsibilities with the council and perhaps a

strong mayor

An elected chief executive who possesses extensive powers in the city government structure.

weak mayor

An elected chief executive who shares power with other officials in the city government structure.

manager and serves a limited amount of time in office. (In an especially weak-mayor system, the job is passed around among the council members, each of whom takes a turn at being mayor.) A weak-mayor structure often implies strong council involvement in budgetary and personnel matters.

The mayoral structures of most American cities reveal a suspicion about powerful elected executives and a preference for weak mayors. In some smaller cities, the mayor is structurally strong and has the powers that the average governor has at the state level. In most cities, however, if the mayor is to become a leader, he has to exceed the job description.

An example of a mayor who was able to do just that is Pete Wilson (now California's governor), who was mayor of San Diego from 1971 to 1982. In terms of structure, the San Diego mayor is weak, since he has to share power with a manager. Mayor Wilson quickly learned that "his ability to lead the city depended on his power of persuasion, not the formal power of the charter."[29] Wilson was able to capitalize on a time of flux in community core values (the citizens were rethinking issues such as growth rates and development patterns) and use his talents to restructure the role of the mayor informally. During this period, San Diegans voted down charter amendments that would have formally established a strong-mayor structure. Instead, Wilson made internal organizational changes, such as creating a city council subcommittee system and expanding the staff of the mayor's office, that effectively diminished the manager's power. Within three years of taking office, Wilson was the acknowledged leader of San Diego—a city that ten years before had no city officeholders among its thirty-person power structure.

Requirements for Leadership   What transforms a mayor into a leader? Three factors stand out. One is the individual's ability to use the resources of the office effectively. This is a special challenge for structurally weak mayors. Another factor is the personal and political skills of the individual. The ability to use the media skillfully, to exploit connections with state and national officials, and to maintain popularity with the electorate is what a leader needs. And not enough can be said about timing, the third leadership factor and the one most beyond the control of the mayor. The circumstances, or conditions, at a given time must be conducive to the leadership transformation. So, in the final analysis, Pete Wilson's personal and political skills notwithstanding, he "was the right person at the right time in San Diego."[30]

Problems can arise when a strong person occupies a structurally weak mayoral post. If politically powerful citizens in the city want a star, they design a government structure to accommodate stardom. But if they have installed a structure intended to minimize individual leadership, a would-be leader may find his efforts at establishing a statewide reputation disrupted by squabbles back home.

Mayoral Types   Of course, not everybody wants to be a leader. Some mayors are comfortable just being mayor; they may find the position appealing because of the social benefits that accompany the office. And a mayoral style that is acceptable in one community might not fit in other places. One typology identified four styles of mayoral behavior:

- *the crusader mayor,* who wants to solve urban problems and produce signficant policy innovations but is hindered by weak political and financial resources;
- *the entrepreneurial mayor,* who, like the crusader, is predisposed toward activism in urban policymaking but, unlike the crusader, is blessed with strong political and financial resources;
- *the boss mayor,* who, unlike the crusaders or entrepreneurs, is not particularly interested in solving urban problems but has strong political and financial resources at his disposal; and
- *the broker mayor,* who lacks both resources and will and therefore devotes much of his time to balancing and adjusting demands and conflicts.[31]

Given these variations in resources and predispositions, we can expect different responses to common problems. The crusading mayor will devote his energies to symbolic politics and crisis management. Given a deficient resource base, he has to build a supportive constituency in order to pursue his objectives. This type of mayor often does not seek re-election, because he is frustrated that the policy return does not justify the energy expended. The entrepreneurial mayor, by contrast, has the luxury of resources to go with her activist style. This kind of mayor is most likely to be considered a leader. The entrepreneur can control the policy agenda and build the necessary political alliances to centralize power in her office.[32] Mayors with ample resources but without the inclination to engage in innovative policymaking tend to focus on enhancing their own political base. Policymaking is pragmatic, not ideological, for these boss mayors. And finally, broker mayors, who lack resources and policymaking verve, really function as mediators and referees in the city government system. They are not the stuff of which local government leadership is made.

Black Mayors   Black mayors were interesting in the past simply because there were so few of them, but today their uniqueness has worn off. By the early 1990s, there were black mayors in more than three hundred cities across the country. (About fifty are women.) African-American mayors are interesting now because of the different nature of the challenge they confront and the subtle shift in their orientation to it. Called by some scholars a "new generation," these mayors consider themselves problem solvers, not crusaders; political pragmatists, not ideologues.[33]

A roll call of the black mayors who were "firsts"—that is, the first blacks to be elected to the mayor's office in major cities—includes some powerful names from the past: Carl Stokes in Cleveland; Richard Hatcher in Gary, Indiana; Kenneth Gibson in Newark; Ernest Morial in New Orleans; Harold Washington in Chicago. Some powerful names of the present are also on the list: Coleman Young of Detroit, Tom Bradley of Los Angeles, and Maynard Jackson of Atlanta. For many of these pioneering mayors, a prominent item on the agenda has been civil rights.

Table 12.1

**Big-City Black
Mayors***

City	Blacks as Percentage of City Population	Mayor
New York City	28.7%	David Dinkins
Los Angeles	13.9	Tom Bradley
Detroit	75.7	Coleman Young
Baltimore	59.2	Kurt Schmoke
Memphis	54.8	Willie Herenton
Washington, D.C.	65.8	Sharon Pratt Kelly
Cleveland	46.5	Michael White
Seattle	10.1	Norman Rice
New Orleans	61.9	Sidney Barthelemy
Denver	12.8	Wellington Webb
Kansas City	29.5	Emmanuel Cleaver
Atlanta	67.0	Maynard Jackson
Oakland	43.8	Elihu Harris
Newark	58.4	Sharpe James
Birmingham	63.2	Richard Arrington

* As of 1992. Listed in descending order according to city size.

Source: Data for percentages of blacks from U.S. Department of Commerce, *Census of the Population* (Washington, D.C.: U.S. Government Printing Office, 1991).

For second-generation African-American mayors, the focus tends to be city-wide development issues rather than civil rights and empowerment of minorities.[34] According to Richard Arrington, the mayor of Birmingham, "What black voters want now is a chunk of the city's commercial and economic development boom."[35] In addition, second-generation black mayors have found that winning the election means building coalitions among white voters. Table 12.1 lists big-city black mayors and the corresponding black population percentages.

Increased success by blacks in mayoral elections has led some observers to talk of *deracialization*, or the deemphasis of race as a campaign issue in an effort to attract white voter support.[36] Instead of making racial appeals, candidates offer a race-neutral platform that stresses their personal qualifications and political experience.[37] In cities where the white electorate outnumbers the black electorate, such as Seattle and Kansas City, neither Norman Rice nor Emmanuel Cleaver could have been elected without the support of white voters. And even in cities where white voters constitute a minority, they often control the elec-

Sharon Pratt Kelly's election-night smile lost some of its luster during a tough first year as mayor of Washington, D.C.

toral balance. For example, in Cleveland in 1989, two black candidates were pitted against each other in the mayoral runoff election. State senator Michael White defeated city council president George Forbes, in large measure, by receiving 80 percent of the white vote. White's campaign succeeded, according to a local county commissioner, because "he doesn't poke the white middle class in the eye and call them racists. He compels them with the sense of his arguments."[38] Deracialization of local campaigns, and the manner in which a mayor elected by a multiracial coalition governs once in office, remains a highly debated issue.

The defeat in 1987 of Harvey Gantt, the first black mayor of Charlotte, North Carolina, demonstrates the fragility of biracial coalitions in city politics. Charlotte's population is 30 percent black. Gantt, with overwhelming support in the black community, had won in 1983 with 36 percent of the white vote and in 1985 with 46 percent. Although race was not the key issue in the campaign (traffic congestion was), a white challenger unseated him when Gantt's proportion of the white vote dropped to 34 percent and turnout among black voters declined. Results from the 1989 mayoral race in Chicago raised disturbing questions about racial polarization in the voting there: More than 90 percent of the black voters voted for black candidates; more than 90 percent of the white electorate voted for white candidates.[39] And, finally, in many cities the term *biracial* understates the degree of diversity in the community. In the 1991

Houston mayoral election, for example, the African-American candidate was defeated by a coalition of moderate to conservative whites and Hispanics.

City Managers

City managers (as well as county administrators and appointed school superintendents) exemplify the movement toward reformed local government. Local government reform was a Progressive Era movement that sought to depose the corrupt and inefficient partisan political machines that controlled many American cities. To the reformers, local government had become too political; and what was needed, they believed, was a government designed along the lines of a business corporation. In the words of one reformer, party government had led to the "injection of political virus" into municipal government, which had "poisoned the system."[40] To achieve their goals, reformers advocated fundamental structural changes in local government such as the abolition of partisan local elections, the use of at-large electoral systems, and the installation of a professionally trained city manager. Altering the structure of local government has had profound consequences for local government leadership, as the latest round of reforms discussed in Problem Solving 12.1 indicates. City managers, the professional, neutral experts whose job it is to run the day-to-day affairs of the city, have become a force in their own right.

In the original conception, managers were to implement but not formulate policy. Administration and politics were to be kept separate. The managers' responsibility would be to administer the policies enacted by the elected officials—the city councils—by whom they were hired (and fired). But it is impossible to keep administration and politics completely separate. City managers are influenced not only by their training and by the councils that employ them but also by their own political ideologies.[41] When it comes to making choices, they balance professional norms, the politics of the issue, and their own predispositions. Hence city managers typically end up being far more influential on the local government scene than their neutral persona might suggest. A case in point is the city manager of Austin, Texas: Camille Barnett. She has consciously adopted a high-visibility role that, some argue, overshadows the mayor and the council of this city of 466,000 people.[42]

Managers as Policy Leaders   As time has passed and more governments have adopted the council-manager form, the issue of whether the city manager should be a policy leader or a functionary of the city council has become paramount.[43] Should a city's policy initiation and formulation process involve a well-trained, highly competent administrator?

The International City Management Association, the city managers' professional association (and lobbyist), says yes: The role of the manager is to help the governing body function more effectively.[44] The manager-in-training is taught that "the manager now is also expected to be a full partner in the political side of the policymaking process."[45] Ways in which the manager can assume a larger

Problem Solving 12.1

Reinventing Local Government, or Reforming the Reforms

The Problem: The structures established during the Progressive Era—intended to make local government efficient and equitable—emphasized rules, standardization, and control. Now, according to some, these structures have outlived their usefulness. Bureaucracies have become cumbersome, the policy process a tangled maze. No wonder, then, that confidence in government is at an all-time low. One of the reasons for this situation is that today's local governments were designed for yesterday's conditions. Critics describe local government structures as "luxury ocean liners in an age of supersonic jets." Do we really need a governmental apparatus geared to solving the problems created by the partisan political machines of the early twentieth century? Increasingly, the answer is "no." What is needed is a fresh vision complemented by new structures and new behaviors, so that local governments can lead the way into the twenty-first century.

The Solution: The question that has separated conservatives and liberals—"How much government?"—misses the point. The fundamental question is, instead, "What kind of government?" The answer, if the new reformers are right, is an *entrepreneurial government*—one that is innovative and market-oriented. One that focuses on goals and empowers citizens.

Entrepreneurial governments promote competition between service providers. In Phoenix, Arizona, for example, the public works department competes with private companies for contracts to collect garbage and repair streets. Contained costs and high-quality services result. Entrepreneurial governments also redefine clients as customers, as did the ravaged East Harlem school district in New York City. Now students and their parents choose the school that fits their needs and interests rather than being assigned to the school closest to their home. Another characteristic of these forward-thinking governments is decentralized authority. Some California communities, for instance, use an expenditure-control budgeting system that allows managers to allocate resources in response to changing needs. Funding decisions are made by the officials nearest the situation, rather than by those farther up the chain of command. Entrepreneurial governments act as catalysts, bringing private-sector enterprises and nonprofit organizations into the fold. For instance, when St. Paul, Minnesota, decided to redevelop areas of the city, it created several private, nonprofit corporations to undertake the effort.

Instituting new structures and approaches requires a rethinking about government and its role in our lives. After all, if Eastern Europe can break the stranglehold of entrenched governmental bureaucracy, can it be that difficult to free American local governments?

_____

Source: Adapted from David Osborne and Ted A. Gaebler, "Bringing Government Back to Life," *Governing* 5 (February 1992): 46–50.

role in policymaking include proposing community goals and service levels; structuring the budget preparation, review, and adoption process so that it is linked to goals and service levels; and orienting new council members to organizational processes and norms.

One indisputable role is as an information source for the busy, part-time city council. For instance, suppose that some enterprising college students are requesting a change in a city ordinance that prohibits street vendors. The council asks the manager to study the pros and cons of street vending. At a subsequent meeting, he reports on other cities' experiences: Has it created a litter problem? Does it draw clientele away from established businesses? How much revenue can be expected from vendor licensing fees? The manager then offers alternative courses of action (allow street vending only at lunchtime, restrict pushcarts to Main Street) and evaluates their probable consequences. In some councils, the manager is asked to make a formal recommendation; in others, his recommendation is more along the lines of "Well, what do you think?" At some point, a vote will be called and the council will make a formal decision.

Managerial Types   Let us reconsider San Diego in the 1970s. From the perspective of mayoral leadership it was a success story, but from the view of city management it was a disaster. During Mayor Pete Wilson's eleven-year tenure, San Diego went through five city managers.[46] Few of the new breed of managers trained to be policymakers wanted to return to the weakened managerial position that Wilson had instituted.

Like mayors, city managers are not cut from one mold. The trick is to match the managerial "type" with the right community. Four general local managerial types have been identified:

- *the community leader,* who sees himself or herself as an agent for community change, as an innovator, full of energy and idealism;
- *the chief executive,* the experienced community leader whose innovativeness and idealism have been tempered by pragmatism;
- *the administrative innovator,* an inward-focused manager who is interested in change within the organization by promoting technical and procedural improvements; and
- *the administrative caretaker,* who values order and routine and concentrates on the housekeeping functions of local government.[47]

For any of these administrators to be successful, he or she must fit with the community. We can match the managerial types with the four community types introduced in Chapter 11. The brokerage community, for example, would benefit from the enthusiasm and commitment of a community leader who could put his skills to work resolving conflicts. The boosteristic community would be a good place for the savvy chief executive who has "been around"; in such a setting, the manager's job would entail promoting the community and managing growth, two functions that often do not complement one another. The amenities community would be an ideal spot for an administrative innovator, an environment in which her skills would be valued; preserving the quality of life and providing services efficiently would probably be the major responsibilities of the post. Finally, the caretaker community and the administrative caretaker are made for each other as well: This community type prefers minimal government, and the manager would want little challenge.

When managerial type and community type correspond, local government should function well. A perfect fit is difficult to achieve, however. City councils get replaced, local tax bases suffer disruptions, and managers shift their orientation to the job. Communities search for the perfect manager; managers seek out the perfect community.

....

Local Legislatures

Local legislatures include city councils, county commissions, town boards of aldermen or selectmen, special district boards, and school boards. They are representative, deliberative bodies. In this section we focus on city councils, because that is where most of the research has taken place, but many of the points made are applicable to the other local legislative bodies as well.

City Council Members: Old and New

A former member of the city council of Concord, California, defines "the good old days" on local governing boards with this comment: "When I first came on the city council, it was like a good-old-boys' club."[48] The standard description was that the city council was a part-time, low-paying haven for public-spirited white men who did not consider themselves politicians. Most councils used at-large electoral mechanisms, so individual council members had no specific territorially based constituency. Council members considered themselves volunteers.[49] Research on city councils in the San Francisco Bay–area cities in the 1960s found that these volunteer members were fairly unresponsive to public pressures and tended to vote their own preferences.

These days, circumstances have changed. As pointed out in Chapter 11, city councils are less white, less male, and less passive than they were in the past. Some of this change is due to modifications in the electoral mechanism. Many cities, such as San Antonio, have abandoned citywide elections and switched to district (or ward) elections. In San Antonio, a council-manager city, only the mayor is currently elected at large. Other cities have chosen to retain some at-large seats while dividing the city into electoral districts. Houston, a strong-mayor city, is an example: Of the fourteen members of the Houston city council, five are elected at large and nine are elected from districts. (Table 12.2 shows the wide variation in both council size and number of members elected at large and from districts.) In both San Antonio and Houston, and in cities across the nation, changes in election mechanism signaled a change in council composition. There are more African-Americans, Hispanics, and women on city councils than ever before, and they are taking their governance roles quite seriously.

Councils in Action: Increasing Conflict

In earlier times, when members of the council came from the same socioeconomic stratum (in some communities, *all* members of the at-large council came

Table 12.2

City Councils of the Twenty Largest U.S. Cities

Table 12.2

City Councils of the Twenty Largest U.S. Cities

City	1990 Population	Council Size	Number at Large	Number of Districts
New York	7,323,000	51	0	51
Los Angeles	3,485,000	15	0	15
Chicago	2,784,000	50	0	50
Houston	1,631,000	14	5	9
Philadelphia	1,586,000	16	0	16
San Diego	1,111,000	7	0	7
Detroit	1,028,000	9	9	0
Dallas	1,007,000	6	6	0
Phoenix	983,000	9	1	8
San Antonio	936,000	11	1	10
San Jose	782,000	10	0	10
Baltimore	736,000	19	1	18
Indianapolis	731,000	7	2	5
San Francisco	724,000	11	11	0
Jacksonville	635,000	19	5	14
Columbus	633,000	7	7	0
Milwaukee	628,000	16	0	16
Memphis	610,000	13	6	7
Washington, D.C.	607,000	13	5	8
Boston	574,000	13	4	9

Sources: Adapted from International City Management Association, *The Municipal Year Book 1987* (Washington, D.C.: ICMA 1987); National League of Cities, *Directory of City Policy Officials* (Washington, D.C.: NLC, 1991); U.S. Department of Commerce, *Census of the Population* (Washington, D.C.: U.S. Government Printing Office, 1991).

from the same neighborhood) and when they shared a common political philosophy, governing was a lot easier. The council could meet before the meeting (usually at breakfast) and discuss the items on the agenda. That way they could arrive at an informal resolution of any particularly troubling items and thereby transform the actual council meeting into a rubber-stamp exercise. No wonder that the majority of council votes were unanimous; members were merely ratifying what they had already settled on.

Council members elected by districts report more factionalism and less unanimity than do their counterparts elected at large. Data from surveys of council

	None	Some	Sharp	
Factions on the Council (Percentage of Councils)	19%	36%	45%	
Unanimous Votes (Percentage of Time)	75% 42*	50–74% 31	25–49% 14	<25% 12

Intergroup Rivalry	(Percentage by Degree of Importance)		
	Very	**Somewhat**	**Not Very**
Development Interests vs. Others	44%	41%	15%
Business vs. Neighborhoods	32	42	27
Tax Cutters vs. Opponents	27	45	28
One Area vs. Another	20	39	42
Liberals vs. Conservatives	19	40	40
Business vs. Labor	12	33	56
Whites/Anglos vs. Others	12	27	62
Democrats vs. Republicans	12	26	63
Political Machine vs. Reformers	12	25	64

* Forty-two percent of the cities have unanimous votes 75 percent or more of the time, 31 percent have them 50–74 percent of the time, and so forth.

Source: Based on Susan Welch and Timothy Bledsoe, *Urban Reform and Its Consequences* (Chicago: University of Chicago Press, 1988), p. 96. Reprinted by permission of The University of Chicago Press.

members in 218 cities in 42 states shed more light on this question.[50] Conflict on councils revolves around three types of rivalries: development interests versus others, business versus neighborhoods, and tax-cutters versus opponents. The level and focus of such conflict are detailed in Table 12.3. The growing tendency of cities to move away from complete reliance on at-large electoral mechanisms suggests that council conflict will be on the rise in the future. Fifty-five percent of the city council members responding to a recent national survey reported that council member conflict was a serious source of frustration to them.[51] Ten years earlier, only 33 percent voiced a similar concern.

Reshaping a Council: The Case of Houston

Houston, the nation's fourth largest city, has weathered several changes in the functioning of its government. It adopted the plural-executive commission structure during the reform movement but abandoned it for a fling with the council-manager structure from 1942 to 1946. During the late 1940s, Houston adopted a strong-mayor structure. In 1979, the eight-member, elected at-large council system was junked in favor of the fourteen-member system described above. This change represented a definite revision in terms of council composition. In 1981, a new mayor, Kathryn J. Whitmire, was elected with the explicit intent of executive branch reform.[52] Thus, a newly aggressive council encountered a mayor with a mission. The consequences were predictable: The mayor thought the council was intent on encroaching on her authority, and the council was convinced that the mayor was engaging in empire-building.

In the ensuing years, the mayor and the council hammered out a working relationship that entailed greater council involvement in the affairs of city government. The old "council as [a] rubber stamp of the mayor and the city's business interests" is gone.[53] This is not to say that an expanded role for the council has been created without bitter antagonism between the executive and the legislative branches—far from it. But the council's larger role reflects both a recognition of its representational function and an appreciation of the need for institutional partnerships.

Recently, members of Houston's large Hispanic community filed a lawsuit against the city to get rid of the at-large seats. Their claim that the structure discriminated against them lost some of its legitimacy when a Hispanic female, Gracie Saenz, won a citywide council seat in 1991.[54] The 1991 city elections may have set in motion a new round of mayor-council squabbling. Houston voters not only rejected Mayor Whitmire's bid for a sixth term and elected a wealthy businessman; they also approved a proposition limiting elected city officials to three two-year terms.

Women as Local Government Leaders

Do women officeholders act differently and pursue different interests from men in public office? As the number of female officeholders in local government increases, this question becomes especially compelling. Nationally, women constitute 9 percent of county governing boards, 14 percent of mayors and city councils, and 37 percent of school boards.[55] Alaska and Hawaii consistently report female officeholding far above these national averages; Georgia and North Dakota are examples of states in which the proportion of women in local public office is substantially lower. Recent data on mayors indicate that a greater percentage of black than white elected officials are women: In 1985 12 percent of black mayors were women whereas the figure for white mayors was 8.2 percent.[56] In the South, a study of city councils in medium-to-large-sized cities found that the percentage of councils without female members ranged from lows of 13 percent and 18 percent in Virginia and North Carolina, respectively, to highs of 70 percent in Arkansas and 73 percent in Alabama.[57] And a recent national survey of city council members showed that, compared to males, female council members are much more likely to view the representation of women, environmentalists, abortion rights activists, racial minorities and good government organizations as very important.[58]

A review of the research suggests that women officeholders frequently differ not only from their male counterparts but also from one another.[59] Four basic types of female political actors have been hypothesized: the traditional politician, the traditional liberal feminist, the caring humanist, and the change-oriented feminist. Women who are traditional politicians articulate no particular gender differences and do not expect much divergence between men's and women's interests. Traditional liberal feminists, on the other hand, are concerned with what have been termed "women's issues," such as abortion, rape, domestic violence, pornography, child care, and education. In addressing these issues, they work within the norms and practices of the established political system. Female officeholders of the caring humanist–type, though concerned with women's issues, place a higher priority on matters of social justice and ecological balance. They also tend to be somewhat estranged from the established order. And change-oriented feminists see sexism as a fundamental characteristic of our society and, therefore, have no interest in being assimilated into established male structures. Instead, they want to create a new order based on female sex-role expectations.

Although all four types are represented among women holding local public office, most female officeholders have tended to cluster in the first two types. And, while the discussion in Profile 12.1 does not directly relate to women's issues, how would you classify the mayors described there?

Black female local elected mayors and council members are worthy of special mention. Frequently they are double-counted; that is, they are counted among both female officials and black officials. Yet regardless of the interests that link them to both groups, race and gender differentiate them. They belong; but then again, they do not. The National League of Cities's convention, where as many as five thousand local elected officials from throughout the country gather each year, offers a telling example. Although black female mayors and council members are welcomed by and participate in NLC's Women in Municipal Government and NLC's National Black Caucus of Local Elected Officials organizations, they have established their own informal group. To them, it is a matter of common interests and, no less important, feeling like they belong.

Political Leadership Versus Professional Leadership

The issue of politics versus administration is not confined to the local level of government. Congress battles with federal agencies, and state legislatures fight with state agencies. There is a natural struggle between officials who make policy and those who implement it, and between those who allocate funds and those who spend them. What distinguishes the local level is the relentlessness of the conflict. The elected representatives of the public—the members of the city council—are pitted against the best professional management that money can buy—the city administrator and her staff. In strong-mayor cities, the dynamic is slightly different, inasmuch as an elected official heads the bureaucracy. In that

Profile 12.1

Three Female Mayors: Different Cities, Different Styles

Examples of female mayors abound—Susan Weiner in Savannah, Kay Granger in Ft. Worth, DeeDee Corradini in Salt Lake City, Jan Laverty Jones in Las Vegas. But only three have been selected for discussion in this profile. Just as Pittsburgh, Washington, D.C., and Tampa face similar and different problems, each of the mayors is both typical and unique.

Sophie Masloff, the steel city's first female mayor, had served twelve years on the city council and one year as interim mayor before winning an upset victory over five males in the Democratic primary in 1989. (She ran unopposed in the general election.) Considered to be nurturing and compassionate, Mayor Masloff frequently refers to herself as "an old Jewish grandmother." Yet the down-to-earth manner that has made her so popular with Pittsburgh's voters has made her decidedly unpopular with some insiders at city hall. Her critics label her ineffective and lacking in vision. It is unlikely that she will lack opponents when she runs for re-election in 1993.

Sharon Pratt Kelly, a political newcomer, took the oath of office as mayor of the nation's capital in 1991 amid almost euphoric celebration. The citizens, emotionally drained from the turmoil surrounding former Mayor Marion Barry and deeply troubled by the array of social problems plaguing the city, placed high hopes in the new mayor. Yet her first year in office proved that many of D.C.'s problems elude easy resolution. Short of money, and with no let-up in the pervasive drug-driven violence, Mayor Kelly has had to turn to the city's most powerful resident, the federal government, for financial help. A $100 million infusion of federal funds eased the immediate crunch, and the mayor's plans to increase police presence on the streets calmed a fearful public; but longer-term solutions are needed.

Like Mayors Masloff and Kelly, Sandra Freedman was the first female mayor in her city, Tampa. But, unlike the others, Freedman is serving her second full term as mayor. In 1991, she retained the mayoralty with a comfortable margin of 70 percent of the vote in a three-candidate race. Fewer than one-third of Tampa's voters turned out on election day, further suggesting satisfaction with Mayor Freedman's performance in office. Although it is difficult to identify precisely what makes for a popular incumbent, Tampa's decreasing crime rate and stable growth certainly helped. Addressing her supporters at a victory celebration, Mayor Freedman commented, "It's an indication to me that we are on the right track."

Sources: Michael deCourcy Hinds, "Grandma Mayor Takes Up Hardball," *New York Times,* January 22, 1992, p. A9; B. Drummond Ayres Jr., "New Mayor of Nation's Capital Finds Sober Reality Dulls Bright Promise," *New York Times,* December 11, 1991, p. A12; Preston Trigg and Wayne Garcia, "Freedman Rolls to Re-election, Crushes Rivals," *Tampa Tribune,* March 6, 1991, pp. 1, 7.

setting, the chief executive balances a political role with an administrative one. In both instances, the functioning of local government depends on the creation of a workable relationship.

Council-Manager Interactions

The interactions between the council and the manager cover more than the traditional division of politics and administration. Interviews with elected and

Figure 12.1

Four Dimensions of the Governmental Process

Local government officials, both elected and appointed, want to protect their turf— their designated dimension.

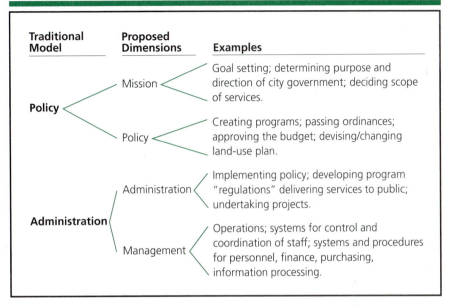

Traditional Model	Proposed Dimensions	Examples
Policy	Mission	Goal setting; determining purpose and direction of city government; deciding scope of services.
	Policy	Creating programs; passing ordinances; approving the budget; devising/changing land-use plan.
Administration	Administration	Implementing policy; developing program "regulations" delivering services to public; undertaking projects.
	Management	Operations; systems for control and coordination of staff; systems and procedures for personnel, finance, purchasing, information processing.

Source: James H. Svara, "The Complementary Roles of Officials in Council-Manager Government," in *International City Management Association, The Municipal Year Book 1988* (Washington, D.C.: ICMA, 1988), p. 24. Reprinted by Permission.

administrative officials in five North Carolina cities convinced one researcher that this dichotomy did not describe reality.[60] Every city revealed instances when administrators had engaged in policymaking (for example, when they initiated proposals and drafted the budget) and when council members had intruded on the administrative sphere (say, with legislative oversight of program implementation). A more realistic model of council-manager interaction posits four functions of the government process: mission, policy, administration, and management. Figure 12.1 depicts these dimensions.

The *mission* function involves setting goals and establishing the purpose and direction of city government. The *policy* function covers middle-range actions such as passing ordinances, making spending decisions, and creating programs. The *administration* function includes policy implementation, service delivery, and promulgation of regulations. And the *management* function involves the day-to-day operations of city government—organizational procedures and actions.

The mission function is primarily the province of elected officials, just as the management function belongs to administrative personnel (although the council is an "interested observer" in hiring and firing decisions and contract awards). Predictably, the policy and administration functions are more difficult to sort out. Elected officials and managers share these functions to a considerable extent. Managers make policy recommendations; elected officials field citizen complaints and participate in some implementation decisions.[61] The key to effective government is a mutual understanding of the mixed responsibilities involved in both policy and administration.

Perceptions of Governmental Systems

This chapter and the preceding one emphasize government structure. The basic point is that structure reflects orientations to and expectations of government. A strong-mayor system reflects a polity in which accountability is valued and politics is not a dirty word. A council-manager form is characteristic of a polity that emphasizes professional management and efficiency. This distinction certainly does not mean that a strong-mayor system is inevitably less efficient or that a council-manager form is not accountable to the public. It simply suggests that the orientations and expectations are different.

This difference is borne out in the internal workings of local governments. Table 12.4 shows the degree to which council members and department heads agree with four statements about the way their governments work.[62] Responses from officials in council-manager cities tend to be at odds with responses from those in strong-mayor systems.

With respect to the basic question of whether the council and the chief executive officer (a manager in the council-manager cities, a mayor in the strong-mayor cities) have a good working relationship, there is striking variation among the answers of officials in the two structures. Virtually all of the council members and three-quarters of the department heads in council-manager systems report good working relationships; in strong-mayor systems, only about half of the council members and the department heads report this. Council members in council-manager systems are much more satisfied with the process of arriving at policy alternatives than are council members in strong-mayor structures. And in compelling affirmation of the different nature of service delivery and constituency relations in the two forms, nearly twice as many council members in strong-mayor structures report that council intervention is necessary to get the bureaucracy to respond to citizen complaints.

These findings suggest that structural differences can have consequences. It is important to remember, however, that inidividuals who work within structures are the essential factor. As we saw in the case of San Diego, leaders can make structures work for them (sometimes by performing minor surgery on the structure to ensure that it does). Consider the comment made by the mayor of Rochester, New York, a city that switched from a council-manager system to a strong-mayor form: "The bottom line is good people committed to good governance."[63]

Policy Innovation at the Local Level

Earlier in this book, the point was made that state and local governments function as sources of innovation. Reflect on the words of former President

Table 12.4

Perceptions
of Council–
Chief Executive
Relations

Description	Form of government*			
	Council-Manager†		Strong-Mayor–Council‡	
	Council Members Agree (%)	Department Heads Agree (%)	Council Members Agree (%)	Department Heads Agree (%)
The council and manager (or mayor) have a good working relationship	100.0	75.7	56.5	52.1
The manager [or] mayor provides council with sufficient alternatives for policy decisions	76.9	90.9	29.1	56.2
The council effectively draws on the expertise of professional staff	76.9	76.1	54.2	47.9
Intervention by a council member is necessary to get adequate response to citizen complaints	34.6	7.5	66.7	14.6

* The forms of government in this table included six council-manager and five strong-mayor–council cities.
† In the council-manager cities, twenty-six council members and sixty-seven department heads responded.
‡ In the strong-mayor–council cities, twenty-four council members and forty-eight department heads responded.

Source: James H. Svara, "The Complementary Roles of Officials in Council-Manager Government," in *International City Management Association, The Municipal Year Book 1988* (Washington, D.C.: ICMA, 1988), p. 25. Reprinted by permission.

Reagan in his January 1988 state-of-the-union message; he mentioned "a thousand sparks of genius" and suggested that some of these sparks would catch fire and "become guiding lights."[64]

To be innovative means simply to try something new. But to do something new implies taking risks. Innovators often behave in an entrepreneurial manner. True leaders—individuals who are unequivocally perceived as leaders by relevant observers—tend to be innovative *and* entrepreneurial.[65] They do things that others cannot or will not do.

Innovative communities are those that do things first, that are receptive to creative solutions to problems. One example of a recent local government innovation is the restriction or banning of billboards. With the aim of reducing visual pollution, cities across the nation, especially those in the growing Sunbelt areas, have enacted antibillboard ordinances. In 1987, voters in Jacksonville, Florida, approved a measure designed to remove all billboards from city streets by 1992.[66] Other cities are following suit, though not to the point of total removal. Denver, for example, has frozen the allowable number of billboards at the 1988 level and has mandated the removal of all billboards along historic boulevards. Houston and Phoenix have taken similar actions.

Another example of innovation is found in environmental issues. In 1988, Suffolk County in New York became the first jurisdiction in the country to outlaw the use of nonbiodegradable containers. The ban includes "clamshell" packaging for fast foods, plastic-foam meat trays, and certain plastic grocery sacks.[67] This behavior is not aberrant for Suffolk County; in 1981, it was the first to prohibit the nonreturnable bottle. The Long Island county's innovativeness is partly the result of a waste problem. As in other jurisdictions, the local waste dumps are at capacity and scheduled for closure, and plastic packaging of the kind that has been banned cannot be safely incinerated. Innovation is the product of need: The county had to do something to reduce the volume of waste.

After listening to the business community complain that high school graduates frequently lacked basic skills, Prince George's County in Maryland created a "guaranteed employability certificate."[68] It is awarded to students who can read, compute, and reason, and who have personal qualities, such as good attendance, that suggest success in the workplace. The certificate is like a warranty; if a certificated graduate proves deficient in entry-level skills, the school district is obligated to provide additional training.

As noted previously, solutions often spread from one community to another. Minneapolis, Salt Lake City, and New York City, for example, have enacted local ordinances that ban cigarette vending machines from many public places.[69] The primary intent of these actions was to prevent the sale of cigarettes to children. With these cities leading the way, other communities beset by similar concerns followed suit.

An action by the Los Angeles County Transportation Commission produced shock waves that reverberated globally.[70] The Los Angeles area has a $150 billion, 300-mile rail mass transit system under construction. In early 1992, the commission canceled a contract to buy $122 million worth of rail transit cars from a Japanese company. The commission was reacting to bitter public protest, driven partly by a faltering southern California economy, but also by a national backlash against Japan's economic prowess and the complementary "Buy American" movement. Now, the commission has proposed constructing its own factory to lease to American manufacturers who would build the cars. Although others might disagree, many Los Angeles officials see themselves as designing innovative industrial policy for the nation. Whether other cities will follow suit remains to be seen.

Some innovations have symbolic value. Madison, Wisconsin, the home of the University of Wisconsin, elected and re-elected a Socialist as its mayor in the 1970s. And in the 1980s, Madison led the rest of the country with its adoption of three innovations dealing with foreign affairs. The city declared itself a nuclear-free zone, which means that no nuclear weapons can be developed, stored, or transported through the community, and it became a sanctuary for Central American refugees. In addition, the Madison city council adopted a

resolution calling for a comprehensive nuclear testing ban. These actions placed the city at the forefront of a group of politically liberal communities scattered across the country.

Occasionally, however, a local government's innovation does not survive judicial scrutiny. For example, San Francisco's innovative ordinance that regulated the use of video display terminals in the workplace was struck down by the courts in 1992. The ordinance, which required adjustable chairs, proper lighting, detached keyboards, and rest breaks, was designed to prevent some of the physical problems that result from prolonged use of computer terminals. The court concluded that California law allowed the state, not individual cities, to regulate workplace safety. Yet at the state level, business opposition to such rules makes it difficult to get them enacted.[71]

Leadership *Is* Capacity

In the final analysis, leadership remains somewhat ephemeral. But regardless of the difficulty in pinning it down, it is a central, critical concern in local government. For example, Oshkosh, Wisconsin, is hailed as a Midwestern success story because of the rejuvenation of its declining economy. Replicating this success in other cities is a difficult task, though, since "so much is dependent upon the charisma, vision, skill, and commitment of particular business leaders, city politicians, and managers."[72] In other words, success depends on leadership.

Leaders see problems as opportunities. The challenge comes in devising effective solutions. For example, in a 1989 poll, New York City residents reported profound pessimism about the city's future and identified drugs and crime as intractable problems crying out for solution.[73] When asked about their long-range view of the city, only 22 percent believed that New York would be a better place to live; more than twice that figure thought that it would be a worse place. Local leaders in New York City and in many other communities have their work cut out for them.

Summary

Leaders display a penchant for action, and leading communities behave similarly. In every community, there are a few leaders and many followers; the same is true for each region and its constituent communities. Whether the focus is on individual leaders or leading communities, some of the important characteristics are initiative, energy, persistence, and vision.

Researchers who study power in communities have found variations of elitism and pluralism. And as political scientists, we have concentrated in this chapter on leadership positions in local government—mayors, managers, councils, and commissions. But this focus does not deny the existence of unofficial power and the central role played by the private sector.

Key Terms

elite theory

pluralist theory

reputational approach

decisional method

strong mayor

weak mayor

13

State-Local Relations

Harris County (Texas) officials were quite proud of their new state-of-the-art jail. Finally, they thought, they had adequate space to house area prisoners. Within months after the facility opened, the jail was full, but not with local lawbreakers. The state of Texas, getting tough on crime, had more inmates than space in state penitentiaries. So the state engaged in "inmate dumping": It forced county jails to hold state prisoners. In 1991, ten thousand state inmates were housed in Texas county jails. For the counties, this practice cost millions of dollars and posed security risks. Their repeated complaints fell on deaf ears, however, and it was only after several counties sued the state over its inmate transfer policy that Texas acted. In its 1991 session, the Texas legislature passed a $1.6 billion reform package that will create almost thirty thousand new prison beds and explore alternatives to incarceration.[1] And the counties rejoiced.

States and their communities have a strained relationship. On the one hand, it is state government that gives local governments life. Local governments exist only with state approval. On the other hand, state governments historically have not treated their local governments very well. It appears, however, that states are beginning to realize that mistreating their governmental offspring is counterproductive, and many have launched a sometimes uncoordinated process of assistance and empowerment of local government.

Capturing this evolution is the statement of the National Conference of State Legislatures (NCSL) Task Force on State-Local Relations: "Legislators should place a higher priority on state-local issues than has been done in the past. The time has come to change their attitude toward local governments—to stop considering them as just another special interest group and to start treating them as partners in our federal system."[2] Stronger, more competent local governments are an asset to state government.

Chapter 14 will address the financial relationship between state and local governments. This chapter examines broader issues and related trends. Let us first consider the most fundamental issue: the distribution of authority between the state and its constituent units.

··

The Distribution of Authority

In the words of the U.S. Advisory Commission on Intergovernmental Relations, (ACIR), "State legislatures are the trustees of the basic rules of local governance in America. The laws and constitutions of each state are the basic legal instruments of local governance."[3] For example, in 1988, when the eight communities known as the Illinois Quad Cities were considering merging to become a "supercity," they could not proceed without enabling legislation from the Illinois General Assembly.[4] Both the ACIR statement and the Quad Cities example denote the essence of the distribution of authority between a state and its localities. Simply put, it is up to the state to determine the amount and type of authority a local government may possess. As specified by Dillon's Rule (see Chapter 2), local governments are creatures of the state; therefore, they depend on the state to imbue them with enough powers to operate effectively.

The Amount and Type of Authority

There is wide variation in how much and what kind of authority states give their local governments. Some states grant their localities wide-ranging powers to restructure themselves, to impose new taxes, and to take on additional functions. Others, much more conservative with their power, force local governments to turn to the legislature for approval to act. Empowerment also depends on the type of local government. General-purpose governments such as counties, cities, and towns typically have wider latitude than special-purpose entities like school districts. Even among general-purpose governments there are different degrees of authority; counties tend to be more circumscribed in their ability to modify their form of government and expand their service offerings than cities are.[5]

No local government today, however, suffers the powerlessness that South Carolina historically imposed on its counties. Until the late 1960s, the South Carolina legislature passed each county's budget (called a *supply bill*) and set local tax rates.[6] The legislative delegation was in fact the real government of the county. It was only two decades ago that the legislative changes brought by reapportionment and the pressures of urbanization forced the state to strengthen county governments.

The ACIR examined the distribution of authority between states and their cities and counties as the 1980s began.[7] It measured the amount of discretion a local jurisdiction possessed regarding its structure, personnel, finances, and functions and ranked the states according to the degree of local-government discretionary authority present. Leading the list were Oregon, Maine, North Carolina, Connecticut, and Alaska. Localities in those states enjoy substantially more discretion to manage their own affairs than do their counterparts in low-ranking states such as Idaho, West Virginia, New Mexico, South Dakota, and Nevada.

As emphasized in Chapter 3, the 1980s saw a shift in power from the national government to state capitals. A smaller version of this phenomenon has occurred between states and their local governments. The more recently a state has adopted its constitution, the more likely the document is to contain provisions that strengthen local governments.[8] Some state constitutions set forth a provision for home rule (see Chapters 2 and 11), the true meaning of which becomes evident when state and local governments try to sort out which issues are local and which are of state concern. For the most part, however, real home rule has been somewhat elusive. Only about one-half of the states extend truly proprietary policymaking powers to their city governments; even fewer accord similar powers to counties.[9]

Table 13.1

Local Government Influence in State Highway Matters

Issue: If local officials wish to modify a state road or highway plan or project that affects their area, how likely are they to be able to convince state highway officials to make the changes they desire?

Likelihood of Convincing State	Type of Local Official			
	Township	Municipal	County	Regional Council
Very likely	0.0	15.2	8.3	20.0
Somewhat likely	44.4	72.7	52.8	63.3
Hardly likely	55.6	12.1	27.8	13.3
Not at all likely	0.0	0.0	0.0	0.0
Don't know	0.0	0.0	11.1	3.3

Source: U.S. Advisory Commission on Intergovernmental Relations, *Local Perspectives on State-Local Highway Consultation and Cooperation* (Washington, D.C.: ACIR, July 1987), p. 13.

How Distribution of Authority Works

The concept of distribution of authority becomes clearer when we apply it to an actual situation, such as highway planning, funding, and construction. State and local governments share the responsibility for this function and over time have fashioned a workable relationship.[10] For example, state officials consult local officials regarding the planning and construction of state roads and highways in their jurisdictions. Consultation does not mean that local approval is required; only occasionally is local approval sought. But consultation does guarantee room for local maneuvering, according to a 1987 nationwide survey of executive directors of state associations of counties, cities, towns, and regional councils (see Table 13.1).

Local officials are frequently able to convince state highway officials to modify highway plans to accommodate local preferences. Among city officials and regional councils, the reported ability to influence state highway officials is strong. The group with the least influence—township officials—represents the smallest jurisdictions, both in area and population. All in all, although local officials tend to be satisfied with the amount of highway consultation in their area, they would prefer more influence. This comparatively harmonious relationship does not necessarily extend to other interactions between state and local officials. Land management, for example, can generate considerably more friction, as explained in Problem Solving 13.1.

A Tug of War

Local governments want their states to provide them with adequate funding and ample discretion. Local officials are supremely confident of their abilities to

Problem Solving 13.1

Cooling Off Red-Hot Growth Without Putting Out the Fire Altogether

The Problem: Florida and many of its communities face an unusual side of the growth and development problem: too much. From 1950 to 1990, Florida's population skyrocketed by 367 percent. By 1990, thirteen million people called the now-fourth largest state home. Many of the new residents settled in environmentally sensitive areas along the Atlantic and Gulf coasts. Fearing that an overcrowded Florida will be unattractive to visitors and thus kill its tourist-based economy, the state is attempting to solve the fast-growth problems.

The Solution: After many false starts and much confusion, the Florida Growth Management Act, passed in 1985, began to have an impact in 1990. The law requires that communities have the requisite roads, sewers, parks, and other pieces of infrastructure in place "concurrent" with—that is, at the same time as— the new development projects that will use them.[1] If the infrastructure is not there, the development project—a new subdivision, a shopping mall, whatever—cannot be built. The amount of infrastructure, or what is referred to in the law as "level of service," is determined by local governments and subject to the approval of the state. Managing the level of service will allow local governments to pace their growth and development. Local governments pay for their infrastructure improvements with impact fees, a one-cent local option sales tax, and a four-cent gasoline tax.

The law also requires that local growth management plans be consistent with regional plans, and that regional plans be consistent with the state plan. In other words, the plans of the various units of local government are "nested."

Florida's implementation of its Growth Management Act is being watched carefully by other states feeling growth pressures. Its impact is potentially tremendous. In populous Broward County, where Fort Lauderdale is located, the inability to meet the concurrency requirement forced a building moratorium.[2] In other counties where growth has outstripped government services, the rate of growth has slowed drastically. Meanwhile, the law is under attack from both sides: No-growth advocates claim that it does not go far enough, whereas pro-growth adherents complain that it goes too far.

1. Robyne S. Turner, "Intergovernmental Growth Management: A Partnership Framework for State-Local Relations," *Publius* 20 (Summer 1990): 79–95.
2. William Fulton, "Addicted to Growth," *Governing* 4 (October 1990): 68–74.

govern, given sufficient state support. But county officials express concern that neither their policymaking power nor their financial authority has kept pace with the increased administrative responsibilities placed on them by state government.[11] The recognition and correction of such conditions are the states' responsibility.

Evidence from New York indicates that state and local officials evaluate the condition of their relations differently.[12] Using a scale on which 100 represented ideal state-local relations, state officials were generally more positive, scoring 56.2 in contrast to the local officials' range of 43.2 to 50.0 (depending on the type of local government). These scores reflect an improvement (a gain of 11.2 points) from state officials' assessment of the relationship five years earlier. Local officials, however, did not think any progress had been made. The state received relatively high marks for its provision of technical assistance, but it fared less well on both financial assistance provided to local governments and discretion in the use of the funds.

To a certain extent, the evaluation of state-local relations depends on who is doing the assessment. State officials are apprehensive of awarding local governments carte blanche authority. Local officials, though they angle for more authority, really want more money. The tug of war will continue.

State Mandates

Although local governments generally want more autonomy, state governments share their policymaking sphere with reluctance. They have demonstrated a tendency to be fairly comfortable with a command approach. In other words, rather than let subgovernments devise their own solutions to problems, states frequently prefer to tell them how to solve them. They do this through a mechanism called a *mandate,* a subject that will be discussed in Chapter 14 in the context of state-local finances. The New York survey of state and local officials identified unfunded mandates as the most persistent source of friction between the levels of government.[13]

From the perspective of state government, mandates are necessary to ensure that vital activities are performed and desirable goals are achieved. State mandates promote uniformity of policy from one jurisdiction to another (for instance, the length of the public school year or the operating hours of precinct polling places). In addition, they promote coordination, especially among adjacent jurisdictions that provide services jointly (such as a regional hospital or a metropolitan transportation system).

Local governments see the issue quite differently. They have three basic complaints:

1. State mandates (especially those that mandate a new service or impose a service quality standard) can be quite expensive for local governments.
2. State mandates displace local priorities in favor of state priorities.
3. State mandates limit the management flexibility of local governments.[14]

mandate-reimbursement requirements

Measures that take the sting out of state mandates.

Taken together, these problems make for unhappy local officials. Recognizing the problem, sixteen states have adopted **mandate-reimbursement requirements**. These measures require states either to reimburse local governments for the costs of state mandates or to give local governments adequate revenue-raising capacity to deal with them. Mandate-reimbursement requirements tend to make state officials unhappy. They argue that mandates are frequently necessary to prod reluctant local governments into assuming their rightful responsibilities. And, as for paying for them, state governments protest that they cannot afford it. Given the opportunity to speak out on the mandate question, voters have sided with local governments. The mandate-reimbursement question was on the Florida and Wisconsin ballots in 1990. In both states, the measures passed with substantial margins.[15] In Louisiana in 1991, voters approved a constitutional amendment that allows localities to ignore state mandates unless the state provides funding or authorizes local fund-raising mechanisms.[16] If each legislative session unleashes a flood of new mandates on fiscally stressed local governments, the pressure for mandate-reimbursement requirements is likely to spread.

It is no wonder that the NCSL's Task Force on State-Local Relations has urged states to consider relaxation or elimination of mandates and assumption of the cost of complying with them.[17] Mandates dealing with local personnel policies, environmental standards, service levels, and tax-base exemptions are due reconsideration. Massachusetts has gone a long way toward this end; its Division of Local Mandates in the Department of the State Auditor reviews mandates every five years and recommends their continuation, modification, or termination. Other states are likely to adopt similar provisions.

State-Local Organizations

Although the structure of the federal system has created a set of legal, administrative, and financial ties between state and local governments, it has not necessarily embraced state understanding of or sympathy toward local governments. To rectify this condition, state governments have established numerous organizations such as local government study commissions and advisory panels of local officials. Three popular approaches are examined here.

Task Forces

Task forces tend to be focused organizations set up by the governor or the state legislature in response to a perceived local-level problem. If a state wants to investigate the ramifications of changing its annexation statutes, the legislature might create a Task Force on Annexation and Boundary Changes or something similar. The task force would probably be composed of state and local officials, community leaders, and experts on the subject of annexation.

The task force would proceed in this manner: First it would collect information on how other states handle the annexation question. Next it would conduct a series of public hearings to get input from individuals and groups interested in the issue; and finally it would compile a report that included recommendations suitable for legislative action. Its work completed, the task force would then disband, although individual members might turn up as advocates when the task force recommendations received legislative attention.

Task forces are quick organizational responses to local problems that have become too prominent for state government to ignore. A task force is a low-cost, concentrated reaction that gives the appearance of action and, in some instances, actually influences legislative deliberations.

Advisory Commissions on Intergovernmental Relations

In an ongoing, comprehensive effort at state-local cooperation, many states have created state-level advisory commissions on intergovernmental relations, modeled after the commission created by the U.S. Congress in 1959. State-level ACIRs are designed to promote more harmonious, workable relations between the state and its governmental subdivisions. They are intended to offer a neutral forum for discussion of long-range state-local issues—a venue where local officials can be listened to and engaged in focused dialogue; conduct research on local developments and new state policies; promote experimentation in intergovernmental processes, both state-local and interlocal; and develop suggested solutions to state-local problems.[18] And to prevent their recommendations from gathering dust on some forgotten shelf, many state-level ACIRs have added marketing and public relations to their list of activities.[19]

By 1991, twenty-six states had instituted their own ACIRs. Colorado, where state-local issues have been termed "complex," created its ACIR in 1988.[20] The membership of the Colorado ACIR is evenly split between state and local interests. On the twenty-four-member panel sit three representatives of the Colorado Municipal League, three from Colorado Counties, Inc., three from the Special Districts Association, and three from the Association of School Boards. From the state side are four senators, four representatives, and four members of the executive branch. Unlike most state ACIRs, the Colorado organization operates without the backing of a legislative enactment or an executive order. Consequently, it does not have its own source of funding. Instead, it relies on in-kind resources provided by the membership. Although this organizational insecurity limits the ACIR's ability to solve state-local problems, it has provided a forum for discussion and research.

Generally, state-level ACIRs return real benefits to local government. Whether in their narrowest form, as arenas for discussion of local issues, or in their broadest, as policy developers and initiators, ACIRs are useful to state and local governments. But their greatest impact of all will occur if they are given the authority and resources to do something more than simply discuss issues. The remainder of the 1990s will probably see other states exploring this organizational possibility.

Departments of Community Affairs

Another way in which states can generate closer formal ties with their local governments is through specialized administrative agencies. All fifty states have created departments of community affairs (DCA) that are involved in local activities. They have different labels (Kentucky calls its DCA the Department for Local Government; Ohio's is the Department of Economic and Community Development), but their function is similar: to offer a range of programs and services to local governments.[21] DCAs are involved in housing, urban revitalization, antipoverty programs, and economic development; they also offer local governments such services as planning, management, and financial assistance.

DCAs vary on several dimensions: their niche in state government, the sizes of their budget and staff, and whether they include an advisory board of local officials. Each of these dimensions contributes to the clout wielded by any DCA. For example, a DCA that has cabinet-level status (as thirty-five of them do) is likely to be more influential than one located within another state agency (nine states) or within the governor's office (six states). DCAs with bigger budgets and staffs should have more influence. As of 1980, the budgets of these organizations ranged from under $200,000 to $70 million, and their staff sizes ranged from fewer than fifty to more than five hundred. The existence of an advisory board is problematic, however. Half of the DCAs have advisory boards, but few of these are active or effective in an array of local policy areas.[22]

Compared to their state-level ACIR counterparts, DCAs function much more as service deliverers and much less as policy initiators. Therefore, these two types of organizations tend to complement rather than compete with one another. Both, however, function as advocates for local government at the state level.

Metropolitics: A New Challenge for State Government

State governments find their dealings with local governments confounded by the side effects of urbanization. Regardless of which state we examine, its urban areas show the effects of three waves of suburbanization. An early wave occurred during the 1920s, when automobiles facilitated the development of outlying residential areas. Although the dispersion slowed during the Depression and World War II, its resurgence in the 1950s triggered a second wave, during which retail stores followed the population exodus. The "malling of America" has led to the third wave of suburbanization: the development of office space beyond the central city.[23] This is happening with a vengeance in New York City and Atlanta, in Cheyenne and Nogales. It is this third wave that has caught the attention of state governments.

As a result of the transformation of American metropolitan areas in the 1980s, central cities have lost their prominence as the social, economic, and political focal points of their areas. People have moved to surrounding suburbs and beyond; businesses and firms have sprung up in the hinterlands; communities have formed their own service and taxing districts. The outward flow of people and activities has fundamentally altered metropolitan areas, which are now composed of "a series of relatively self-contained and self-sufficient decentralized regional units."[24] Not simply residential, these new "boom towns" include business, retail, and entertainment activities. The de-emphasis of the central city suggests the need for changes in outmoded state government policy toward metropolitan jurisdictions.

A serious concern is that rapid, unplanned growth is producing "accidental cities" and fostering "shadow governments." A logical question is, What is state government doing while all of this is occurring? In the early 1990s, the answer was not much.

Accidental Cities

accidental cities

The unplanned transformation of suburban communities and small towns into homogenized, congested places.

The term that the Conservation Foundation has coined for the conversion of suburban communities and small towns into homogenized, traffic-clogged places is **accidental cities**.[25] The forces of rapid, unplanned growth are said to threaten the distinctive character of small towns and the community life of extant suburbs. Residents watch the conversion occurring around them, as a stand of pine trees is leveled for a car wash, a locally owned drug store becomes the site of a new office tower, and homes located along two-lane roads are converted to professional offices, then razed when the road is widened to six lanes and the property is rezoned as commercial.

To the Conservation Foundation, the spread of accidental cities raises questions about livability and quality of life. Others, however, see the sprawl as a natural progression in the urbanization process. A *Washington Post* reporter Joel Garreau, spent several years exploring these places, which he calls *edge cities*.[26]

As recently as the 1950s, Tysons Corner was a quiet crossroads with a general store. Explosive growth has transformed this northern Virginia community into the largest edge city in the state.

With their office towers, shopping malls, and jogging paths, edge cities are the new frontier for an urbanized United States. The areas surrounding Phoenix and Honolulu offer interesting cases of governmental responses to growth.

The Phoenix Area   Phoenix, the fastest-growing large city in the country, has three edge cities; four growth "hot spots" are emerging as edge cities, and another five are likely by the year 2000.[27] The map in Figure 13.1 shows their location. Phoenix was the first city in the United States to acknowledge these emerging urban centers officially in its planning process, thus suggesting that the growth areas will be targeted for public infrastructure investments—parks, libraries, government offices, hospitals—in anticipation of development rather than in reaction to it. Among city officials, the hope is that the state of Arizona will provide enough resources to help Phoenix prepare for the growth. As an initial step in the late 1980s, the legislature commissioned a study of growth management strategies for the area.[28]

The Honolulu Area   Honolulu has taken an innovative approach in addressing the excesses of rapid urbanization on the eastern side of the island of Oahu. The state of Hawaii and Honolulu County have joined forces to create a new municipality twenty miles from Waikiki Beach.[29] Plans for the new city include waterfront resort hotels largely financed by Japanese investors, a defined downtown center, an industrial park, large residential neighborhoods, shopping centers, and office buildings. Government officials hope to recreate the look of old Honolulu in the new city of Kapolei and to avoid the high-rise concrete jungle that characterizes downtown Honolulu today. Of course, it is much easier to improve on the past when you have the luxury of starting from the ground up (quite literally in this case) than when you are confronted with years of accumulated land uses.

Shadow Governments

shadow governments

Entities, especially unofficial ones, that function like governments.

Accidental cities are appearing and new forms of governance are emerging. **Shadow governments** may or may not be official government units, but in many important ways they behave like governments: They levy taxes, regulate behavior, and provide services. Three types of shadow governments exist: private enterprise shadow governments, such as homeowners' associations; public-private partnership shadow governments, a common example of which is development corporations (see Chapter 16); and subsidiaries of conventional governments with unusual powers, such as areawide planning commissions (see the discussion of regional coordination later in this chapter).[30] These bodies exist within the confines of state law, but states have thus far displayed a curious hands-off posture toward them.

Estimates place the number of private enterprise shadow governments at about 120,000, approximately 60 percent of which are located in suburban areas.[31] Condominium communities are a good illustration. The property

Figure 13.1

Living on the Edge in Phoenix

In the fast-growing Phoenix area, new work-play-sleep communities are springing up beyond downtown.

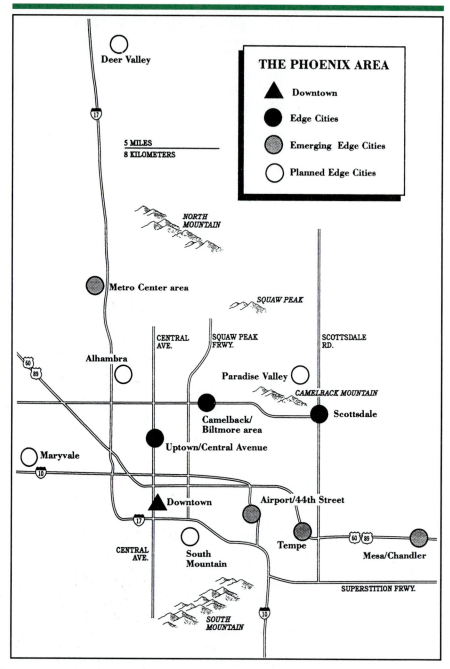

Source: From *Edge City* by Joel Garreau, © Joel Garreau. Used by permission of Doubleday, a division of Bantam Doubleday Dell Publishing Group, Inc.

The developers of the planned city Kapolei hope to capture the flavor of "old Hawaii." This mixed-use district is designed for both commercial and residential activities.

owners' association makes rules for residents (from the speed limit on community streets to the color of the condo), provides services (security, maintenance, landscaping), and assesses fees (based on the size of the unit). Residents typically vote for the board of directors of the association (in some instances, developers of the project retain seats on the board), and votes tend to be weighted according to the value of the housing unit. Residents with a greater financial investment have a greater say in the governing of the community. This is a far cry from the one-person, one-vote principle.

Shadow governments, regardless of type, raise questions about matters of power and equity. (There are few questions about their efficiency, because by most accounts they tend to operate fairly efficiently.) The power issue centers on information, influence, and accountability. Shadow governments control information, restrict influence to those who belong or can pay, and have no public accountability. They are not subject to the same legal standards as are "real" governments.[32] The equity issue addresses the class discrimination inherent in these governments. A poor family out for a Sunday drive may be able to traverse city streets, but if they turn their ramshackle automobile off onto a private street patroled by private police, they are likely to be followed and perhaps even stopped, questioned, and escorted out of the neighborhood.

Whatever our uneasiness over power and equity, the number of shadow governments is increasing, not decreasing. In metropolitan areas, where in the words of one observer "local government boundaries are totally out of whack with the realities of economic geography or development patterns,"[33] shadow governments are especially popular. Their vaunted efficiency makes them a force to be reckoned with.

The social and economic changes in the United States' metropolitan areas have had a tremendous impact on urban governance. Accidental cities and shadow governments make up extended webs of interdependent jurisdictions. How can these places best be governed? Thus far, state governments do not have much idea. Idealistic metropolitan reformers have called for regional government; more pragmatic observers have advocated regional coordination.

Regional Government

One alternative to specialized minigovernments is the creation of **regional government,** a structural recognition of the interdependence of proximate communities. Under a regional government, local jurisdictions give up some of their power and authority to a larger government in exchange for areawide solutions to local problems. State legislatures are important players in this process because, aside from the state constitution, they create the rules of the game. Their actions either facilitate or hinder local government reorganization into regional units.

regional government

An areawide structure for local governance, designed to replace multiple jurisdictions.

In the United States, the closest thing to regional government is **city-county consolidation**, whereby area jurisdictions are absorbed into a single countywide government. Structure and function are unified. In a pure form of consolidation, there is one police department, one fire department, one water and sewer system. The functions of local government—public safety, public works, health and human services, community and economic development, and recreation and arts programs—are provided by a single jurisdiction. There are twenty-three city-county consolidated governments; Indianapolis/Marion County, Indiana; Jacksonville/Duval County, Florida; and Nashville/Davidson County, Tennessee, are among the most prominent examples. Table 13.2 lists the twenty largest consolidated governments.

city-county consolidation

The merger of city and county governments into a single jurisdiction.

Regional government seems so rational, yet it has proven to be quite elusive, inasmuch as many attempts at city-county consolidation were defeated at the polls in the 1960s and 1970s. The logic is straightforward: If small local governments in a metropolitan area merge to form a larger local government, two positive outcomes will occur. First, stubborn public policy problems can be tackled from an areawide perspective. For example, the pollution generated by city A that affects city B can be handled as a regional problem rather than as a conflict between the two cities. Second, combining forces produces *economies of scale* in service delivery. Instead of each jurisdiction constructing and operating jails, for example, one large regional facility can be maintained. Jail service can be provided at a lower cost to each participating jurisdiction. These outcomes are persuasive; and local governments, even in places where voters have previously rejected consolidation, such as Tallahassee and Sacramento, continue to explore the possibility.

Table 13.2

Consolidated City-County Governments

Jurisdiction	Year Organized
Anaconda–Deer Lodge County, Montana	1976
Anchorage–Anchorage Borough, Alaska	1975
Athens–Clarke County, Georgia	1990
Baton Rouge–East Baton Rouge Parish, Louisiana	1947
Boston–Suffolk County, Massachusetts	1821
Butte–Silver Bow County, Montana	1976
Carson City–Ormsby County, Nevada	1969
Columbus–Muscogee County, Georgia	1970
Denver–Denver County, Colorado	1904
Honolulu–Honolulu County, Hawaii	1907
Houma–Terrebonne Parish, Louisiana	1984
Indianapolis–Marion County, Indiana	1969
Jacksonville–Duval County, Florida	1967
Juneau–Greater Juneau Borough, Alaska	1969
Lexington–Fayette County, Kentucky	1972
Nashville–Davidson County, Tennessee	1962
New Orleans–New Orleans Parish, Louisiana	1805
New York–New York County, New York	1847
Philadelphia–Philadelphia County, Pennsylvania	1854
San Francisco–San Francisco County, California	1856

Source: Victor S. DeSantis, "Profiles of Individual Cities and Counties," in International City Management Association, *The Municipal Year Book 1988* (Washington, D.C.: ICMA, 1988), pp. 199–200. Reprinted by permission. Updated by the authors.

Regional government does not always perform as expected. Recent research compared the taxing and spending policies of a consolidated jurisdiction with a comparable but unconsolidated area in the same state.[34] In Florida, both taxes and expenditures increased in consolidated Jacksonville/Duval County compared to those of unconsolidated Tampa/Hillsborough County. Another criticism of regional government is that it can be inaccessible and destructive of the hard-won political gains of minorities. Compared to a city or town government, regional government is farther away, both literally and figuratively. The effect on minority political strength, while not as obvious, is no less troublesome. Because the proportionate number of minorities may be lessened when jurisdictions are combined, their voting strength can be diluted. Minorities will likely find it more difficult to elect one of their own to the regional governing board. This concern led the U.S. Department of Justice to reject, under the Voting Rights Act, the consolidation of the city of Augusta and Richmond County, Georgia, in 1991.

Given the reluctance of voters to endorse consolidated city-county government, some reformers have turned their attention to an old-fashioned way of merging governments—by state legislative action. In the nineteenth century, legislatures simply combined local governments when they thought it necessary. The sole successful modern example of consolidation by a state legislature is Indianapolis/Marion County, Indiana. (Nevada's state legislature consolidated Las Vegas and Clark County in 1975, but the action was subsequently overturned by the state supreme court as unconstitutional.)[35] Since the action of the Indiana legislature, both Alabama and Georgia seriously considered consolidation of Birmingham and Jefferson County and Atlanta and Fulton County, respectively. In each case, the legislative action fell short of the necessary votes.

Regional Coordination

substate districts

Formal organizations of general-purpose governments in an area, intended to improve regional coordination.

Regional coordination is an alternative to regional government. **Substate districts,** usually called councils of government or regional planning commissions, are examples. Substate districting does not involve a formal merger or combination of governments; instead, districts are loose collections of local governments designed to increase communication and coordination in an area. State governments were not active in the creation of substate districts; national government programs spurred their development. The Housing Act of 1954, for example, provided funds for metropolitan planning; but the real impetus came through the Model Cities Act of 1966, which required metropolitan planning agencies to review grant applications. The review process, known as A-95, stimulated the creation of regional planning organizations in both metropolitan and nonmetropolitan areas. By 1980, 650 such entities were supported by federal grants and payments from member governments.

Although areawide planning remains the most common activity of councils of government, they do other things as well. Member governments can turn to them for technical assistance (such as help in writing federal grant applications), professional services (planning, budgeting, engineering, legal advice), and information (economic data for the region).[36]

The impact of these councils has been less significant than their creators hoped, but they have had two positive effects. First, councils have elevated the concept of areawide policy planning from a pipe dream to a reality. They have been heavily involved in criminal justice, water quality, housing, and transportation planning. Second, councils have substantially improved the operational capacity of rural local governments, by providing expertise to small local jurisdictions that cannot afford to hire specialized staff.

During the 1980s, councils suffered several blows that threatened their survival. In 1983, the Reagan administration rescinded the A-95 order, thus ending the councils' mandatory grant-review function. In addition, less money was available from the national government for areawide planning. The councils' standing was further threatened by defections by member governments. In some instances, local officials resented their power; in other cases, the governments could no longer afford to pay the necessary dues.

State governments will play an important role in determining the fate of regional councils in the future. The Reagan administration's substitute for A-95 was Executive Order 12372, which emphasizes a state-determined review process for federal financial assistance. Although states vary in their commitment to regional coordination, the majority have continued to utilize a regional council structure in their grant process.[37] North Carolina, for example, has chosen to use regional councils to link the state and its communities. In addition, the state hires regional organizations to conduct studies and produce research reports. Not all states have exhibited this level of support, however; and, to survive, regional councils have redirected their organizational mission toward providing services to member governments.[38]

Some localities have taken a more informal route to regional coordination through service-sharing. In service-sharing, jurisdictions agree to consolidate specific services, cooperate in their provision, or exchange them.[39] Recreational facilities may be jointly provided by several jurisdictions; one government may "rent" jail space from another; county residents may use the city library in return for city residents' use of the county's solid waste landfill. Service-sharing arrangements are popular because they hold the promise of greater efficiency in service delivery *and* they do not threaten the power and autonomy of existing jurisdictions.

....

States and Urban Policy

If you had attended an urban policy conference in the early 1990s, you would have heard the phrase *state government* used repeatedly. When people mentioned the national government, they did so more wistfully than hopefully. Even government interest groups that have built solid reputations on their ability to represent urban interests before the national government, such as the National League of Cities and the U.S. Conference of Mayors, are increasingly concentrating on state capitols.

One action that symbolized the cities' steep fall from national grace was congressional action in 1988 that eliminated the locally popular Urban Development Action Grant (UDAG) program. Members of Congress who wanted to kill the program argued that UDAG had accomplished much of the original intent (funneling money to the nation's distressed cities) and that significant diversion was occurring (amendments allowed economically healthy cities to receive one-third of the funds).[40] Regardless of the assets of the

program and communities' need for it, congressional decision makers concluded that UDAG was not a priority and shifted its funds into space exploration. Such national actions make state government the alternative savior of
urban areas.

Two significant contemporary issues, housing and infrastructure, are of particular interest in an urban environment, simply because of the large number of
people who are affected. Let us consider each of these in terms of state-local
interaction.

Housing Policy

For middle- and upper-income city residents, the housing market can be
counted on to produce "affordable" units; but what is affordable to these
residents is out of reach for low-income households. The mechanics of market
economics effectively shut them out of the system. Low-cost housing does not
generate the return that higher-cost housing does. As a result, governments
have intervened to create incentives for developers to produce low-income housing units and, where incentives do not work, to become providers of housing
themselves. One of the aims of the federal Housing Act of 1949 was "a decent
home in a suitable living environment" for all Americans.

Over time, the national government has backed away from this aim and
altered its approach to housing. In 1968 it was willing to become the nation's
houser of last resort, but by 1982 the push was to deregulate and let market
forces prevail.[41] Modifications of the national tax laws have had a negative effect
on rental housing stock. Deliberate actions and inaction have resulted in a
decline in home ownership, an increase in the proportion of household income
that is spent on housing, a decrease in the number of affordable rental units, an
increase in the number of physically inadequate and abandoned structures, and
an increase in the number of homeless people.

In response, state governments have set up housing finance agencies, nonprofit corporations have entered the low-income housing market, and local
governments have adopted regulations to preserve their affordable housing
stock. New Jersey, for example, mandated that all of its 567 communities provide their "fair share" of affordable housing for low- and moderate-income
people. In some places, housing vouchers—a form of consumer subsidy that
would open up currently nonaffordable housing to low-income residents—are
being discussed. Another approach is for local governments to require developers to include a fixed proportion of affordable units in their market-rate
projects as a condition for approval of a building permit. This approach works,
however, only where developers are clamoring for access.

Connecticut has been particularly innovative in addressing its affordable housing problem. As part of its new statewide plan, the state conducted a "housing
needs assessment."[42] The bottom line is that "poor people don't make enough
money to buy decent shelter at a price that the market can economically provide."[43] In a pilot program, Connecticut will enter into mediated negotiations

with local jurisdictions in a specified area to develop a fair-housing compact for the area. To encourage local jurisdictions to pursue the goals of the compact, Connecticut has established a housing infrastructure fund to provide state financial assistance. The state's effort to address the scarcity of affordable housing is likely to be emulated by other states.

Infrastructure Policy

Infrastructure—public works projects and services—is the physical network of a community, that is, its roads and bridges, airports, water and sewer systems, and public buildings. It is important because it is crucial for development; the simplest equation is, no infrastructure = no development. Infrastructure has become an issue in many communities because of its crumbling condition and the high cost of repair or replacement.[44]

States take different approaches in financing local public works, and tradition is a powerful explanation of this behavior.[45] Generally, they are providing more financial support for local public works today than they did in the early 1980s, through grants, dedicated revenues (the money collected from a particular tax), loans, and bonds. States that have been particularly inventive in public works assistance include Pennsylvania, Massachusetts, Virginia, Wisconsin, and Wyoming.[46] Pennsylvania, for instance, allows cities to become financial partners in constructing roads to shopping malls and industrial sites. And Massachusetts, through its Aquifer Land Acquisition Program, purchases property or development rights to protect public drinking-water supplies.

Texas has embarked on one of the greatest infrastructure adventures in modern times with its bullet-train project. If all goes as expected, the cities of Houston, Dallas, and San Antonio will be linked by a high-speed rail system by the year 2000. Passengers would hurtle past startled cowpokes at speeds up to two hundred miles per hour. The project hinges on the successful sale of $5 billion worth of tax-exempt bonds, which is on a scale never before attempted in public finance markets.[47] Although the state of Texas will not be putting any of its funds into the project, promoters hope to secure enough federal and local funds to fill any financial gaps that might occur.

The stock of aging, sometimes unsafe, infrastructure—coupled with declining federal aid for public works—has found states casting about for solutions. In transportation infrastructure, one approach that is receiving greater scrutiny is privatization. Virginia has approved legislation to allow the construction of a private toll highway; California has four private toll road projects pending.[48] Another dozen states are considering the idea. Private highway projects are criticized on two accounts. Some argue that private roadways will produce a "have/have-not" distinction, with the affluent traversing pay roads and the poor being dispatched to congested freeways. Others claim that privatization offers a band-aid solution to the enormous transportation problems facing the nation. Despite these concerns, privatization remains an attractive option to governors and legislatures intent upon holding down highway taxes.

States and Their Rural Communities

When the local Dairy Queen closes its doors, a small town in rural America knows that it is in trouble. The Dairy Queen, like the coffee shop on Main Street, serves as a gathering place for community residents. Its demise symbolizes the tough times that a lot of rural communities face. In fact, some analysts argue that the major distinctions in regional economics are no longer between Sunbelt and Frostbelt or East Coast and West Coast but between metropolitan America and the countryside.[49]

Not all rural areas are suffering. Four community growth types can be identified from economic and demographic trends.[50] A dynamic growth community is one in which both population and economic growth are occurring. Its opposite is the declining community, which is losing both its population and its economic base. Typically, declining communities have had economies based on farming, mining, or manufacturing. "Strain" communities experience population growth without proportionate gains in personal income; and, finally, preservation communities have stable or declining populations but enjoy growth in personal income. Even prosperous communities have difficulties, as leaders ponder whether growth will disturb their rural flavor and identity.

The distressing news for declining communities is that, compared to the other types, their local leaders are the least supportive of administrative modernization and change.[51] Local governments in these communities are less capable of responding creatively to the problems they face. Consequently, the gap between places where dynamic growth is occurring and the declining communities is likely to increase. The fear is that this will become a self-perpetuating phenomenon, until some communities simply disappear. Research on rural communities in the Midwest lends some credibility to this contention: The communities that have withstood economic downturns are those that have had the administrative capacity to identify and pursue opportunities.[52] Macon County, Missouri, is an example. With "hard work, luck, and heads-up opportunism," Macon County transformed itself from a declining community into a dynamic growth community.

What can state governments do to encourage the right kind of growth in rural areas? Short of pumping enormous amounts of money into the local economy, they can encourage the expansion of local intergovernmental cooperation, whereby small rural governments join together to increase their administrative capacity to deliver services and achieve economies of scale. Two state actions facilitate such cooperation. One is reform of state tax codes, so that jurisdictions can share locally generated tax revenues. Rather than competing with one another for a new manufacturing plant or a shopping mall, local governments can cooperate to bring the new facility to the area; regardless of where this facility is located, all jurisdictions can receive a portion of the tax revenue. A second useful state action is the promotion of statewide land-use planning. As one observer has noted, "Currently too many rural local governments engage in wasteful inter-community competition, mutually antagonistic zoning, and contradictory development plans."[53]

In 1990, a new federal initiative offered states a means of redesigning their rural development efforts. Concerned that existing rural programs were fragmented and only partially successful, the national government selected eight states for a pilot study.[54] In those states, newly established Rural Development Councils brought together—for the first time—federal, state, and local officials involved in rural development. And rather than mandating the structure of the councils and their agendas, the federal government assumed a hands-off posture and simply provided the necessary start-up funds. During the following year, each of the councils designed its own initiative aimed at specific conditions and problems confronting the state. Mississippi, for example, is working on a tourism and recreation project, South Dakota is developing an on-line resource data base, and Washington is taking up the issues of affordable housing and job retraining. The promise of these state-based interorganizational networks is substantial, but it will be several years before their success can be gauged. Thinking optimistically, the federal government plans to extend the initiative to an additional sixteen states.

The Interaction of State and Local Governments

State governments benefit from positive relationships with their local governments. Local governments benefit from positive relationships with their state government. Nonetheless, the two levels of government frequently clash. And those clashes can have drastic consequences, as Problem Solving 13.2 details.

Constitutionally, state governments are supreme in their dealings with local governments; even New York City, seven million strong and larger than many states, has to do what the government in Albany says. Yet there is evidence that the state-local relationship is shifting. Leaders in state government are increasingly aware that creating clinging vines—local governments with limited legal and fiscal authority—does not suit their purposes. During the 1990s, states will be strengthening those vines so that they can grow and prosper. Strong local governments make for resurgent state governments.

An interesting test of this prediction is likely to occur in western Washington. The Puget Sound region, a four-county, seventy-one-city area experiencing tremendous growth, faces infrastructure problems that crisscross the boundaries of individual jurisdictions.[55] Streets, bridges, and water and sewer systems need repair, replacement, and expansion. State government is ideally suited to devise a regionwide solution to these growth problems, but local jurisdictions are reluctant to give up their existing authority. Perhaps the best solution is something that has been called home-grown regionalism, in which regional goals are set at the local level and then implemented with state incentives.[56]

Of course, there are still examples of states withholding power from local governments. In its 1989 session, the Virginia legislature passed a bill that gives

Problem Solving 13.2

California: Like It or Leave It . . . Twenty-Seven Counties Consider Leaving

The Problem: Many residents of twenty-seven northern California counties are unhappy with state politicians whom they consider to be unresponsive to their needs. Some of these thinly populated rural counties, struggling under the weight of unfunded state mandates, face bankruptcy.

The Solution: Secede from California. Most secessionists favor becoming a new state, although some want to be annexed by neighboring Nevada.[1]

California has a long history of secessionist threats. More than two dozen secession plans, some half-baked, some carefully studied, have been floated since the state was admitted to the Union in 1850. Because secession requires the approval of both the California legislature and the U.S. Congress, the proposed splits have never occurred.

Unlike most earlier plans, the proposal introduced in the state legislature in 1992 does not divide the state midway between San Francisco and Los Angeles. Instead, the carefully drawn dividing line begins north of San Francisco above Marin County and moves eastward, with an abrupt turn to the north to avoid Sacramento, eventually winding south and east to include the counties bordering Lake Tahoe.

The geographical isolation of the northern third of California and the political estrangement felt by its two million residents have fueled secessionism. The affected counties, full of dramatic scenery and natural resources, lack the ethnic and cultural diversity that characterizes the rest of the state.[2]

With the majority of Californians decidedly cool to the split, the secession proposal faced almost insurmountable odds in California's General Assembly. Meanwhile, proponents of the measure engaged in wishful thinking about a name for their new state ("Jefferson" had a presidential ring to it; "Superior California" captured their feelings) and the location of the new state's capital.

1. "California Counties Rebelling, Plan Secession," *The State,* October 24, 1991, p. 10A.
2. Katherine Bishop, "California Dreaming, 1991 Version: North Secedes and Forms 51st State," *New York Times,* November 30, 1991, p. 6.

the state sole authority to regulate smoking.[57] In short, local governments in Virginia are prohibited from enacting their own clean indoor-air bills. The state's explanation for its action was uniformity: A state law would prevent a patchwork of different and perhaps conflicting local ordinances. An example like this speaks volumes about the power of the tobacco industry in Virginia politics; it also underscores the limitations of local government authority.

Summary

State-local relations are always in flux. The trend over the past two decades has been toward increased state assistance and empowerment of local jurisdictions.

Localities have wrested more authority from state government in matters of taxation and service consolidation. The imposition of mandates remains a source of conflict. Until the mandate issue is resolved, localities will be hard-pressed to achieve meaningful grassroots governance.[58]

States have established a number of organizations in an effort to better understand and assist local governments. The consequences of growth (and, in some jurisdictions, stagnation) are likely to culminate in increasing state-local conflict. Local governments do not want to be neglected by the state, but neither do they want the state to become too involved in their affairs. There is a fine line between state assistance and state interference. Where the line is drawn depends on which level of government is holding the chalk.

Key Terms

mandate-reimbursement
  requirements
accidental cities
shadow governments

regional government
city-county consolidation
substate districts

14

State and Local Finance

On June 6, 1991, Bridgeport, Connecticut, sailed into uncharted waters by declaring bankruptcy. The city of 142,000 people became the largest ever to seek protection under Chapter 9 of the federal bankruptcy code. Stunned residents and state officials anxiously grappled with important questions: Would police, fire, and other services be suspended? Would the city cease to exist as a legal entity? What would happen to creditors, given the massive debt left behind?

This once-prosperous manufacturing center had seen its industrial and tax base bled dry as firms moved to the suburbs or out of state, leaving behind a hollow core of vacant, decaying buildings. Years of accumulating deficits created serious cash-flow problems, made worse by the end of federal revenue sharing and cutbacks in state financial aid. But this threadbare city, situated, ironically, in the nation's wealthiest state, also suffered from years of political wheeling and dealing and mismanagement. Generous settlements with city labor unions escalated personnel costs even as city revenues declined. Expenditures were neither regularly monitored nor compared to revenues. No one, it seems, was minding the fiscal store.

Bridgeport faced a $16 million budget deficit for the fiscal year and a projected shortfall of $250 million over the next several years, according to Mayor Mary C. Moran. Because of Bridgeport's fiscal problems, the state in 1988 had created a Financial Review Board to monitor city finances. The state guaranteed $58.3 million in bonds to help the city get its budget back in balance. State Treasurer Francisco L. Borges claimed that Bridgeport was not insolvent—it had over $46 million in bank deposits and was paying its bills. He and the Financial Review Board insisted that the mayor and city council raise residential property tax rates by 18 percent to plug the deficit, or else cut expenditures by a similar amount. Mayor Moran refused and, without consulting city council members, declared bankruptcy instead.

The state contested the filing and won when a federal bankruptcy judge dismissed the case, ruling that Chapter 9 was not available simply because a city is financially distressed. The Republican mayor sought an appeal, but municipal elections intervened. She was soundly defeated by Democrat Joseph P. Ganim, who immediately abandoned the quest for bankruptcy.

Bridgeport is valiantly striving to address its problems largely on its own today, but the broader implications of its earlier actions and its plight did not go unnoticed. In the eyes of many, it has become a metaphor for the United States' financially ailing cities, and has sounded a wake-up call to the federal government and the states that the cities need help.[1]

But the national government, seemingly beached permanently on the shoals of its monumental budget deficit, is not likely to provide more than lip service and sympathy to the cities. The states, for their part, entered 1992 severely battered by a long and deep national recession and in the worst fiscal shape since the Great Depression. State revenues were being decimated by declining tax receipts while expenditures were rising for recession-related programs such as unemployment insurance, social services, welfare, and health care for the poor.

This chapter deals with state and local finance: the politics and policies of taxing and spending. It is a topic of continuing, visceral interest in state and local jurisdictions, and an activity characterized by much change and experimentation. From taxpayer revolts to rainy day funds, the fiscal landscape has profoundly changed during the past two decades.

....

The Principles of Finance

A major purpose of government is to provide services to citizens. This costs money: equipment must be purchased and employees must be paid. Governments raise needed funds through taxes and fees. In a democracy, the voters decide what range and quality of services they desire and register those opinions through elected representatives. Sometimes, when elected officials don't listen, voters revolt and take matters directly into their own hands.

Citizens in the eighteenth and nineteenth centuries expected few services from their state and local governments, and that is essentially what they received. The taxation of property was the major source of state and local revenue until the beginning of this century. Property taxes were augmented by business licenses, poll taxes, and a variety of miscellaneous sources. As the scope and level of services rose in response to citizen demands, states and localities developed a wider array of revenue-raising devices, including taxes on income, merchandise sales, auto license plates, alcohol, tobacco, gasoline, and certain services.

Two basic principles describe state and local financial systems as they have evolved: *interdependence* and *diversity*. State and local fiscal systems are closely interlinked and heavily influenced by national financial activities. Intergovernmental sharing of revenues is a pronounced feature of our interdependent federal fiscal system. Yet our state financial structures and processes are also highly diverse. Though affected by national activities, their own economic health, and competitive pressures from one another, the states enjoy substantial autonomy in designing individual revenue systems in response to citizens' policy preferences.

Interdependence

own-source revenue

Monies derived by a government from its own taxable resources.

intergovernmental transfers

The movement of money or other resources from one level of government to another.

The American governments raise huge amounts of money. In 1990, the national government took in over $1,109 billion, and the states and localities over $800 billion. That totals up to almost $2 trillion.[2] Most of this money is **own-source revenue,** garnered from taxes, charges, and fees applied to people, services, and products within the jurisdiction of each level of government. Nonnational governments also benefit from **intergovernmental transfers.** The national government in 1990 transferred some $127 billion to the states and localities. For their part, states passed on more than $172 billion to their cities, counties, and special-purpose governments.[3]

From 1902 (the first year such data were published) to the late 1970s, state and local governments gradually grew more and more dependent on federal revenue transfers. In 1980, 27.5 percent of total state revenues came from Washington, D.C., in the form of grants-in-aid and other sources; the corresponding percentage of intergovernmental (that is, national and state) contributions to local governments was 44.1 percent. During the 1980s, the importance of intergovernmental sources declined for both states and localities, primarily because of national aid reductions and the termination of the general revenue sharing program. By 1989, federal grants accounted for only 17.3 percent of state and local revenues.[4]

Figure 14.1 shows the rise and recent decline of national intergovernmental aid as a percentage of state and local spending. Actually, the impact of federal cutbacks is significantly understated here. Some 52 percent of all federal aid to nonnational governments goes to *individual* recipients (for example, people receiving Aid to Families with Dependent Children or Medicaid), not to state and local governments for general purposes. As a result, less than half of total grant dollars are available for the traditional functions of state and local governments, such as education, transportation, and public health.

Local governments rely heavily on the states, and to a lesser degree on the national government, for financial authority and assistance. Only the states can authorize localities to levy taxes and fees, incur debt, and spend money. State constitutions and laws place many conditions on local government taxing and

Figure 14.1

Federal Aid to State and Local Governments, 1955–1990

Federal aid as a percentage of total state and local government spending rose through 1978 and then declined rapidly.

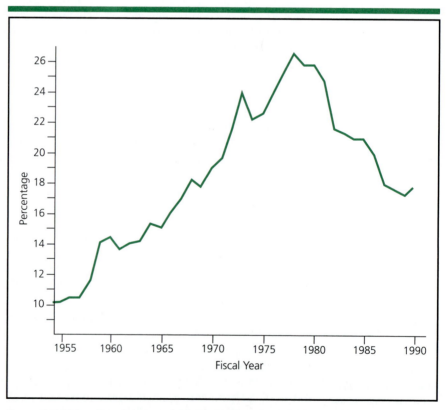

Source: U.S. Advisory Commission on Intergovernmental Relations, *Significant Features of Fiscal Federalism,* Vol. 2 (Washington, D.C.: ACIR, 1991), p. 50.

spending.[5] During the 1980s, states increased their monetary support of local governments through state grants-in-aid and revenue sharing and by assuming financial responsibility for activities previously paid for by localities—in particular, school and social welfare costs. The emergence of the states as "senior financial partners" in state-local finance[6] was jeopardized in some states during the 1990–1992 recession, as state aid to local governments was cut drastically. However, the national government was ill-prepared to step forward with significant new assistance of its own.

Although federal grants to local governments have dropped (in constant dollars) since 1978, state-local finances continue to be linked very closely to activities of the national government. When national monetary and fiscal policies lead the nation into a recession, it is state and local governments that suffer most. This fact was officially recognized until the early 1980s by Congress, which used to send substantial amounts of *countercyclical aid* to the states and localities to help them recover from the ravages of recession. During the severe recessions of 1982–1983 and 1990–1992, however, countercyclical aid was very limited.

Diversity

The second basic principle of state and local finance systems is diversity. Each level of government depends on one type of revenue device more than others. For the national government it is the income tax; for the states, the sales tax; and for local governments, the property tax. But diversity triumphs among the states. Differences in tax capacity (wealth), tax effort, and tax choices are obvious even to the casual observer. Most states tax personal income and merchandise sales, but a handful do not. A growing number of states operate lotteries and pari-mutuel betting facilities. And at least twenty-one states have found a novel way to raise revenue: by requiring dealers in illegal drugs to purchase tax stamps. Someone caught selling drugs can be prosecuted for tax evasion as well as for drug dealing. Minnesota's rates are $3.50 a gram for marijuana and $200 per gram for harder drugs. Dealers caught without stamps must pay the state double and face up to five years in prison as well as an additional $10,000 fine. Minnesota has managed to collect some tax-stamp dollars from apprehended dealers, along with automobiles and other property seized in lieu of taxes.[7]

There are high-tax states and low-tax states. Most fall somewhere in the middle. If the basic objective of taxing is to pluck the maximum number of feathers from the goose with the minimum amount of squawking, the wealthy states hold a great advantage, since they can reap high tax revenues with much less effort than poor states, which must tax at high rates just to pull in enough money to pay for the basics. Per capita state and local tax and fee revenues vary from $9,555 in resource-rich, sparsely populated Alaska to $1,688 in poverty-stricken Arkansas. The U.S. average in 1990 was $2,659. There is a fairly close relationship between state wealth (as measured by personal income) and tax revenues. Table 14.1 shows how the states compare in state and local tax revenues, controlling for personal income. Joining Alaska as high-tax states are New Mexico and Hawaii. At

Table 14.1

State and Local Tax
Revenues Per $1,000
of Personal Income,
1990

	Revenues Per $1,000
U.S. Average	$ 69.02
Alabama	68.07
Alaska	135.57
Arizona	77.88
Arkansas	72.85
California	74.97
Colorado	52.72
Connecticut	65.90
Delaware	90.82
Florida	59.43
Georgia	68.51
Hawaii	113.65
Idaho	81.94
Illinois	58.74
Indiana	69.14
Iowa	75.34
Kansas	64.38
Kentucky	83.19
Louisiana	72.18
Maine	78.59
Maryland	65.40
Massachusetts	71.46
Michigan	70.12
Minnesota	88.72
Mississippi	77.96
Missouri	58.76

the low-tax end of the scale are New Hampshire, South Dakota, and several southern states. Most of the low scorers are resource-poor, rural, or both. Tax levels can also reflect such factors as citizen attitudes, population characteristics and trends, climate, and the quality as well as quantity of services.

The U.S. Advisory Commission on Intergovernmental Relations (ACIR), a federal agency composed of elected officials from national, state, and local government, in addition to a professional staff, has devised an index to measure states' **fiscal capacity,** or potential ability to raise revenues from taxes. It is calculated by applying identical rates to each state for twenty-seven commonly used taxes. The national average for fiscal capacity is set at 100. States with scores above 100 have more than average capacity (in effect, greater wealth), while those below 100 have less than average. State fiscal capacity scores are found in Table 14.2, in the left-hand column. Note that there are regional dimensions to revenue capacity.

fiscal capacity

The taxable resources of a government jurisdiction.

Table 14.1 (cont.)

	Revenues Per $1,000
Montana	$ 75.62
Nebraska	60.80
Nevada	73.97
New Hampshire	26.53
New Jersey	56.72
New Mexico	100.30
New York	75.65
North Carolina	78.76
North Dakota	75.63
Ohio	64.04
Oklahoma	76.18
Oregon	62.06
Pennsylvania	63.58
Rhode Island	68.83
South Carolina	82.17
South Dakota	51.11
Tennessee	58.48
Texas	55.16
Utah	79.19
Vermont	71.72
Virginia	57.19
Washington	88.36
West Virginia	97.28
Wisconsin	81.92
Wyoming	88.85

Source: U.S. Department of Commerce, *State Government Finances in 1990* (Washington, D.C.: U.S. Government Printing Office, 1991), p. 47.

In addition, high-tax capacity is associated with high levels of urbanization, per capita income, industrialization, and natural resources.

Simply because a state has high revenue-raising capacity does not necessarily mean that it will maximize its tax-collecting possibilities. Indeed, many states with high revenue potential actually tax at relatively low rates. The degree to which a state exploits its fiscal potential, or tax capacity, is called *tax effort* by the ACIR. Tax effort depends on the scope and level of services desired by the people. Scope and level of services, in turn, are related to historical factors, political culture, and other state-specific variables. In the right-hand column of Table 14.2 are state scores on tax effort, as calculated by the ACIR. Comparison of capacity with effort shows some interesting deviations, as in Nevada and New Hampshire. These two states have the fiscal capacity to generate about twice as much tax revenue as they presently take in. How fully does your state exploit its tax capacity?

Table 14.2

Comparison of the States in Tax System Capacity and Effort

	Fiscal Capacity	Fiscal Effort
U.S.	100	100
Alabama	76	84
Alaska	159	127
Arizona	99	96
Arkansas	74	84
California	116	94
Colorado	107	89
Connecticut	143	90
Delaware	124	84
District of Columbia	123	154
Florida	104	82
Georgia	94	89
Hawaii	114	112
Idaho	76	93
Illinois	99	102
Indiana	87	93
Iowa	83	113
Kansas	91	104
Kentucky	81	88
Louisiana	83	90
Maine	98	105
Maryland	109	108
Massachusetts	129	94
Michigan	95	112
Minnesota	104	112
Mississippi	65	94

Diversity in state and local finance is also evident in terms of what the non-national governments choose to do with their revenues. All of them are spending at a rapid pace. State and local spending rose nearly 2,000 percent from 1950 to 1985, almost twice as fast as the gross national product and much faster than the level of inflation. The functional distribution of spending varies from state to state. Elementary and secondary education consumes the largest portion of total state and local spending (24.3 percent), followed by public welfare (12.5 percent), higher education and health and hospitals (8.9 percent each), and highways (7.6 percent). Within each of these functional categories is a wide range of financial commitments. For instance, higher education expenditures run from 14.6 percent of total state and local spending in Utah to only 4.6

		Fiscal Capacity	Fiscal Effort
Table 14.2			
(cont.)			
	Missouri	90	86
	Montana	85	102
	Nebraska	90	98
	Nevada	135	69
	New Hampshire	126	66
	New Jersey	124	101
	New Mexico	83	99
	New York	109	152
	North Carolina	91	93
	North Dakota	86	91
	Ohio	91	97
	Oklahoma	89	89
	Oregon	91	99
	Pennsylvania	94	97
	Rhode Island	99	104
	South Carolina	79	96
	South Dakota	78	95
	Tennessee	84	83
	Texas	96	88
	Utah	78	106
	Vermont	105	100
	Virginia	104	91
	Washington	98	102
	West Virginia	78	88
	Wisconsin	90	119
	Wyoming	123	94

Source: U.S. Advisory Commission on Intergovernmental Relations, *Intergovernmental Perspective* 16 (Fall: 1990): 18.

percent in Alaska. Georgia dedicates 16.6 percent to health and hospitals, while North Dakota sets aside just 3.8 percent of its expenditures.[8] Such differences represent historical trends, local economic circumstances, citizens' willingness to incur debt to pay for services, and related factors.

The largest expenditure gains in recent years have been registered in corrections. Swelling prison populations, court-ordered changes in corrections practices, and tougher sentencing policies have propelled corrections spending upward at a rate twice that of other functional categories (see Chapter 17). Medical costs are also accelerating rapidly. The Medicaid program alone now consumes 15 percent of the average state budget, and it is expected to account for around 17 percent by 1995.

....

Revenues

Although the fifty state and local finance systems have their own strengths, weaknesses, and peculiarities, certain trends are found in all of them. The property tax is increasingly unpopular. It is no longer a significant source of state revenue; its contribution to total own-source local coffers is still strong, but declining. User fees and other miscellaneous charges are gradually substituting for the property tax. States continue to depend heavily on the sales tax, but alternatives are being used more widely. Tax diversification is in fact an important trend in all state and local tax systems.

Criteria for Evaluating Taxes

Numerous criteria can be used to evaluate taxes. Moreover, what one person likes about a tax may be what another dislikes. Political scientists and economists agree that among the most important criteria are equity, yield, elasticity, ease of administration, political accountability, and acceptability.

Equity   If citizens or firms are expected to pay a tax, they should view it as fair. In the context of taxation, equity usually refers to distributing the burden of the tax in accordance with ability to pay: High income means greater ability to pay and, therefore, a larger tax burden. Equity has other dimensions as well, such as the relative tax burden on individuals versus firms and the impact of various types of taxes on income, age, and social class.

regressive tax

A tax in which the rate falls as the base or taxable income rises.

Taxes may be regressive, progressive, or proportional. A **regressive tax** places a greater burden on low-income citizens than on high-income citizens. This violates the ability-to-pay principle, with the result that upper-income groups contribute a smaller portion of their incomes than lower-income groups do. Most state and local levies, including property and sales taxes, are regressive. For example, both low-income and high-income people would pay a 5 percent sales tax. The latter will likely make more purchases and contribute more total dollars in sales tax, but at a lower percentage of their total income than the low-income individuals.

progressive tax

A tax in which the rate rises as the base or taxable income rises.

A **progressive tax** increases as a percentage of a person's income as that income rises. The more you make, the greater proportion of your income is extracted by the progressive tax. Thus, those better able to pay carry a heavier tax burden than the poor. The national income tax is the best example of a progressive tax. The more you earn, the higher your *income tax bracket*.

proportional tax

A tax in which people pay an identical rate regardless of income or economic transaction.

A **proportional tax** burdens everyone equally, at least in theory. For instance, a tax on income of, say, 10 percent that is applied across the board is a proportional tax. Whether you earn $100,000 or $10,000, you pay a flat 10 percent of the total in taxes. Of course, it can be argued that a low-income person is more burdened by a proportional tax than a high-income person (as in the case of the sales tax).

benefit principle

The principle that taxes should be levied on those who benefit directly from a government service.

In place of ability to pay, some people advocate the **benefit principle.** Under this principle, those who reap more benefits from government services should shoulder more of the tax burden than people who do not avail themselves of service opportunities to the same degree. For example, parents whose children attend public schools should pay higher taxes for education than should senior citizens, childless couples, or single people without children. The benefit principle is the theoretical underpinning for user fees, which charge a taxpayer directly for services received. Examples include water and sewer fees and trash collection fees.

Yield   Taxes can also be evaluated on the basis of efficiency, or how much money they contribute to government coffers compared to the effort expended to collect them. The administrative and other costs of applying a tax must be taken into consideration when determining yield. Taxes that return substantial sums of money at minimal costs are preferred to taxes that require large outlays for moderate revenues. Income and sales taxes have high yields because of the low costs of administering them. Property taxes have lower yields because they are more expensive to assess and collect. The broader the tax base, the higher the yield. For example, a sales tax applied to all purchases yields much more than a sales tax on cigarette purchases.

Elasticity   This criterion is related to yield. Tax yields should be automatically responsive to changes in economic conditions, and revenue devices should expand or contract their yields as government expenditure needs change. Specifically, as per capita income grows within the state and its localities, revenues should keep pace without increases in the tax rate. Tax reductions should accompany economic recession and declines in per capita income, so that citizens' tax burdens are not increased during hard times. The national income tax is considered to be elastic, because revenues increase as individuals earn more money and move into higher tax brackets and decline as income falls. Most state and local taxes, including sales, property, and user fees, generally do not move in tandem with economic conditions and are therefore considered to be inelastic.

Ease of Administration   Taxes should be simple to understand and compute. They should also be easy to apply in a nonarbitrary fashion and difficult to evade. Under the so-called tax simplification of the 1986 Tax Reform Act, the national income tax was rendered much more complex and confusing than it had been. However, it remains fairly easy to collect, because most people voluntarily compute and remit their tax to the national government. Local property taxes are difficult to administer, because of the time and expense involved in regularly appraising property values and the inherent subjectivity of placing a dollar value on buildings and land. The sales tax is easy to administer at the time and place of sale, and nearly impossible to evade (exception to this rule: out-of-state catalog sales). Problem Solving 14.1 illustrates a new approach to collecting taxes and fees.

Political Accountability   Tax increases should not be hidden. Instead, state and local legislative bodies should have to approve them deliberately—and publicly. Citizens should know how much they owe and when it must be paid. For

Problem Solving 14.1

Local Governments as Collection Agencies

The Problem: Financially stressed cities and counties need to collect all outstanding taxes, fees, and fines owed them as quickly as possible in order to pay their own bills.

The Solution: Adopt hard-nosed business techniques to encourage prompt payment of taxpayer debt and to collect delinquent accounts. Dallas County, Texas, for instance, arranges for property tax payments to be deposited directly in the county's bank account, thereby making a couple of days' interest on the money and saving staff time. And Groton, Connecticut, permits property tax payments by credit card, allowing taxpayers to make installment payments without any loss of revenue to the city.

A growing number of local governments use computers to centralize collection activities for everything from water and sewer bills to parking tickets, and to follow miscreants who move to another city or state. Debtors may be embarrassed to find their names, and tax bills, listed in the local newspaper. Roanoke County, Virginia, has even arranged for the state to deduct outstanding bills from state income tax refunds and remit them to the county. In fact, many cities and counties assess harsh penalties for late payments. When all else fails, debts may be turned over to a collection agency and reported to the credit bureau.

Some local governments try a more benign approach. Elderly citizens who tend to forget their property taxes are regularly reminded. And if taxes are not being paid because of a layoff or other temporary personal emergency, many jurisdictions will adjust payments or make other arrangements to help the homeowner avoid bank foreclosure on the mortgage loan.

Source: Adapted from Penelope Lemov, "How to Collect Every Last Dime," *Governing* 5 (January 1992): 24–25. Used by permission.

example, many state income taxes are silently hiked as wages rise in response to cost-of-living increases. After accounting for inflation, taxpayers make the same income as they did before, but they are driven into a higher income bracket for tax purposes. This phenomenon, known as bracket creep, can be eliminated by indexing income tax rates to changes in the cost of living.

Acceptability   The type and mix of taxes imposed should be congruent with citizen preferences. No tax commands wild enthusiasm, but some are less disagreeable than others. Tax acceptability varies from place to place depending on numerous factors, including the perceived pain of paying and equity implications. Large, direct payments, such as the annual property tax, inflict greater pain than small, indirect sales taxes. And a tax on someone else is always preferable. As Senator Russell Long of Louisiana put it many years ago, "Don't tax me, don't tax thee; tax that man behind the tree."

Major State and Local Taxes

The principal types of taxes are on property, sales, and income. User fees are also important revenue devices.

Property Tax   In 1942, taxes on personal and corporate property accounted for 53 percent of all state and local tax revenues. In 1989, they represented only 30.4 percent. States hardly utilize the property tax at all today—it accounts for less than 2 percent of their total revenues—but local governments continue to depend on it for three-quarters of all their own-source revenues. Interestingly, average property tax rates have not decreased. Instead, other revenue sources have augmented the property tax, so that its proportionate contribution has diminished. As always, there is considerable state-by-state variation. New Hampshire, which has no sales or income taxes, depends on property taxes for 65.7 percent of its total tax revenues. The state least committed to this particular tax is New Mexico, which derives 11.6 percent of state and local tax revenues from property taxes.[9]

The best thing about the property tax is that it is certain; owners of property must pay it or the government will seize and sell their land, buildings, or other taxable possessions. But it has lost acceptability in recent years because it tends to be regressive, lacks political accountability, and is hard to administer. At first thought, it seems that property taxes cannot be truly regressive, because only those people who own property pay taxes on it directly; however, renters pay property taxes indirectly through their monthly checks to the landlord. When property tax assessments climb, so do rental charges. Property taxes can also violate the ability-to-pay principle, when housing values spiral upward. Homeowners on fixed incomes, such as retired people, discover with alarm that their annual property tax bills are rising sharply as housing prices escalate.

Just this sort of situation helped precipitate Proposition 13 in California, which was credited with kicking off a taxpayer revolt across the United States. In the Los Angeles and San Francisco Bay areas during the 1970s, property taxes doubled and then tripled in only a few years. Some senior citizens were forced to sell their homes in order to pay their property tax. Proposition 13 reduced property tax bills by approximately $7 billion in the first year, and it imposed strict limitations on the ability of local governments to raise property and other taxes in the future. California dropped from the eighth highest property tax state to the twenty-eighth. This illustrates the problem of political accountability: When property values rise to lofty heights, taxpayers' bills keep pace, even though elected officials do not explicitly vote to hike property taxes.

Property taxes are difficult to administer and somewhat arbitrary. The process of levying an annual fee on "real property" (land and buildings) begins with a government assessor making a formal appraisal of the market value of the land and the buildings on it. Then property values are "equalized" so that similarly valued real estate is taxed at the same level. Time is set aside to make corrections and to review appeals on appraisals that the owner believes to be too high. Next, an assessment ratio is applied to the property. For instance, houses might be assessed for tax purposes at 80 percent of market value. A rate is placed on the assessed value to calculate the annual tax amount. This might strike you as fairly straightforward, but ultimately the appraised market value depends on the findings of the assessor, who may or may not be properly trained for the job or fully aware of conditions in the local housing market. Property can thus be under-appraised or overappraised. For the sake of equity, property should be appraised regularly (for example, every five years).

Property tax systems are further criticized for exempting certain types of real estate and buildings. Government buildings such as hospitals and state offices are not taxed, even though they utilize police and fire protection and other local government services. Churches and church-owned property used for religious purposes are also exempted in the vast majority of jurisdictions.

circuit breaker

A limit on taxes applied to certain categories of people, such as the poor or elderly.

In an effort to make property taxation more equitable and more in keeping with ability to pay, thirty-three states have enacted some form of **circuit breaker.** For instance, the property of low-income individuals is excluded from taxation in some states; others assign lower assessment ratios to the homes of senior citizens or set a top limit on the tax according to the owner's income (for example, 4 percent of net income). At least ten states have promoted political accountability by enacting provisions for rolling back property tax rates as appraised values rise rapidly. Most also offer homestead exemptions, in which owner-occupied homes are taxed at lower rates than rental homes or business property.[10]

Despite such attempts to make property taxes fairer, differences in property values among cities, counties, and school districts still have important implications for the quality and distribution of services. Jurisdictions with many wealthy families or capital-intensive industries can provide high levels of services with low tax rates, while areas with weak property tax bases must tax at high rates just to yield enough revenues to maintain minimal services. To alter the unequal distribution of property values is essentially beyond the control of local governments. As a result, "wealthy suburbs remain wealthy, poor communities remain poor, and services remain unequal."[11]

Sales Tax   Mississippi was the first state to adopt this form of taxation, in 1932. Others followed suit very rapidly, and states collect more of their revenues today from the general sales tax than from any other source. It accounted for 38 percent of own-source revenue in 1989, well ahead of the state income tax (24 percent).[12] Only five states do not levy a general sales tax: Alaska, Delaware, Montana, New Hampshire, and Oregon. State sales tax rates vary from 7 percent in New Jersey and Rhode Island to 3 percent in Wyoming and Colorado. The national median is 5 percent. Some states, particularly those that do not have personal income taxes, are exceptionally dependent on the sales tax: Florida derives approximately 50 percent of its own-source revenues from the sales tax, and Tennessee raises about 43 percent of its revenues from it.

The sales tax has remained in favor for two major reasons. First, citizen surveys by the ACIR have shown consistently that when a tax must be raised, voters prefer the sales tax. Although the reasons are not entirely clear, this tax is perceived to be fairer than other forms of taxation (see Table 14.3). Second, there is an abiding (though empirically unsubstantiated) belief that high state income taxes depress economic development.[13] Some states have lowered taxes on income and increased taxes on sales. Between 1985 and 1992, at least twenty-two states raised their sales tax rate, most by at least a penny. In its 1991

	1985	1986	1987	1988	1989
Federal income tax	38%	37%	30%	33%	27%
State income tax	10	8	12	10	10
State sales tax	16	17	21	18	18
Local property tax	24	28	24	28	32
Don't know	12	10	13	11	13

Source: Unpublished report by U.S. Advisory Commission on Intergovernmental Relations.

tax reform, Connecticut finally—and with extreme controversy—enacted a state income tax, while cutting the sales tax from 8 percent to 6 percent.

Thirty-two states authorize at least some of their municipalities and counties to levy local sales taxes.[14] When state and local sales taxes are combined, the total tax bite can be substantial. In Huntsville and Mobile, Alabama, the purchase of a $1 item requires 9.5 cents in sales tax, the highest in the country in 1991. The rate on the dollar is 9 cents in New Orleans and Shreveport, Louisiana. Sales taxes are almost always optional for the local jurisdiction, requiring majority approval by the city or county legislative body. Typically, states impose ceilings on how many pennies the localities can attach to the state sales tax; states also specify which sizes and types of local governments are permitted to exercise this option.

When applied to all merchandise, the sales tax is clearly regressive. Poor folks must spend a larger portion of their incomes than rich people on basics, such as food and clothing. Therefore, the sales tax places a much heavier burden on low-income people. Most of the forty-five states with a sales tax alleviate its regressivity by excluding certain "necessities." Twenty-seven states do not tax food, forty-three do not tax prescription drugs, twenty-seven exempt consumer electric and gas utilities, and six exclude clothing.[15] New Jersey excludes paper products. When the sales tax was extended to paper products in 1990, enraged Jerseyites mailed wads of toilet paper—some of it used—to legislators, who quickly rescinded the tax.

States can improve the yield of the sales tax by broadening the base to include services. In this way, more of the burden is passed on to upper-income individuals, who are heavier users of services. More than half of the states tax services such as household, automobile, and appliance repairs, barber and beauty shops, printing, rentals, dry cleaning, and interior decorating. Hawaii, New Mexico, and South Dakota tax virtually all professional and personal services. However, two states moved too far and too fast with taxes on services. Florida's 1987 move to broaden the base of its sales tax to services was repealed, following intense lobbying efforts by the business community. Florida businesses found the taxation of advertising and other services sold in Florida by firms in other states to be especially offen-

The Connecticut State Capitol grounds overflowed with anti–income tax protesters on October 6, 1991. Crowd estimates ranged from 40,000 to more than 70,000.

sive. Similarly, Massachusetts' broad service tax enacted in 1990 was repealed the next year by newly elected Governor William F. Weld.

These setbacks are likely to be temporary. Services are the largest and fastest-growing segment of the U.S. economy. Eighty-five percent of new jobs are in services. As political journalist Neil Peirce asked, "How can one rationalize taxing autos, videocassettes, and toothpaste, but not piped-in music, cable TV, parking lot services, or $100 beauty salon treatments?"[16] Pet grooming services, legal and financial services, and many others from landscaping to septic tank cleaning are likely to lose their tax-favored status in years to come.

Elasticity is not a strong point of the sales tax—its productivity falls when consumer purchases slow—but broadening the base helps. A few states have attempted to make the sales tax more responsive to short-term economic conditions by increasing it on a temporary basis. For example, Idaho raised its general sales tax by a penny in order to make up for lower-than-anticipated revenues in 1986, then reduced it when needed monies had been collected.[17] A problem with this tactic is that consumers tend to postpone major purchases until the tax rate falls.

The sales tax is relatively simple for governments to administer. Sellers of merchandise and services are required to collect it and remit it to the state on a regular basis. Political accountability is also an advantage, since legislative bodies must enact laws or ordinances to increase the sales tax rate. And, as we have observed, the sales tax is the least unpopular of the major taxes.

Income Tax   Most states tax personal and corporate income. Wisconsin was the first, in 1911, long before the national government enacted its own personal income tax. Forty-one states have broad-based taxes on personal income, while two (Tennessee and New Hampshire) limit theirs to capital gains, interest, and dividends. Only Alaska, Florida, Nevada, South Dakota, Texas, Washington, and Wyoming leave all personal income untaxed. The last five of these also refuse to tax corporate income. Personal income taxes garnered 24 percent of all state own-source revenues in 1989, and the corporate tax brought in 6 percent.[18] Fourteen states permit designated cities, counties, or school districts to levy taxes on personal income.[19]

State and local income taxes are equitable when they are progressive. This contingency normally entails a sliding scale, such that high-income filers pay a greater percentage of their income in taxes than low-income filers do. Almost half of the states do not levy a personal income tax on people whose earnings fall below a certain floor—say, $5,000. Overall, personal income taxes in the states are moderately progressive and are gradually becoming more so.

Personal and corporate income taxes are superior to other taxes on the criteria of yield and elasticity. By tapping virtually all sources of income, they draw in large sums of money and respond fairly well to short-term economic conditions. Through payroll withholding, income taxes are fairly simple to collect. Also, many states periodically manipulate income tax rates in response to annual revenue needs. In 1987 alone, thirty of the then forty states with broad-based income taxes made some rate adjustments.[20]

Problem Solving 14.2

Private Toll Roads

The Problem: State and local governments confront increasing traffic congestion and deteriorating roads and bridges, yet do not have the revenues necessary for new construction and maintenance.

The Solution: Toll roads and bridges can be financed, constructed, operated, and maintained by private firms, or through public-private cooperation. California is an innovator in soliciting proposals for transportation projects from construction firms. Altogether, some seventeen states are considering 976 miles of private tollways, adding to 5,000 existing miles of toll roads in the United States.

Yet private road and bridge construction paid for over time by user fees is not a panacea for the nation's deteriorating transportation infrastructure. State highway officials and labor unions resist privatization. Financing is difficult to obtain without state assistance, and collection costs account for only 15 to 30 percent of toll revenues. Corporations do not have the power of eminent domain, so they cannot take road rights-of-way unless landowners are willing to sell. The constant stopping and starting at toll booths pollutes the air and wastes gasoline. And, finally, drivers complain of inconvenience and delays.

On the positive side, private toll roads can be built faster and maintained as well as if not better than public roads. And problems of pollution, excess fuel consumption, and driver inconvenience can be eased by technology. For instance, laser toll collectors are being used in a growing number of locations. Bar-coded stickers on vehicle windows are scanned in specified toll lanes at up to 40 miles per hour, and bank accounts are automatically debited. Drivers without appropriate window stickers, however, still must drop their tolls into baskets or toll collectors' hands.

Sources: Stephen C. Fehr, ''Governments Look to Private Toll Roads,'' _Governing_ 3 (June 1990): 63–64; Kathleen Sylvester, ''Laser Toll Collectors Are Speeding Up Traffic,'' _Governing_ 3 (November 1990): 19.

As mentioned earlier, political accountability can be a problem with income taxes during periods of rising prices. Unless income tax rates are indexed to inflation, cost-of-living increases push salaries and corporate earnings into higher tax brackets. At least eight states have adopted indexing since 1978.

Three of the states without a personal income tax actively considered adopting one in 1991: Florida, Tennessee, and Texas. The income tax idea is not popular. In Texas, according to Lieutenant Governor Bob Bullock, "talking about the income tax is equated with devil worship."[21] But it appears to be a _fait accompli_ in several of the remaining holdouts.

User Fees Setting specific prices on goods and services provided by state and local governments is one method that clearly pursues the benefit principle: those who use the goods and services should pay. User fees have been in existence for many years. Examples include college tuition, water and sewer charges, and garbage-collection assessments. Toll roads and bridges are coming back in fashion as well (see Problem Solving 14.2). Today user fees are being applied broadly as state and especially local officials attempt to tie services to their true costs. Such fees are increasingly being levied on "nonessential" local govern-

Tax	Equity*	Yield	Elasticity	Ease of Adminis-tration	Political Account-ability	Accept-ability
Property	C	B	C	D	D	D
Sales	D	B	C	B	A	B
Personal and corporate income	B	A	B	B	C	C
User charges	C	B	A	C	C	B

A = Excellent
B = Good
C = Fair
D = Poor

 * Ability-to-pay principle.

ment services, such as parks and recreation, libraries, airports, and public transit. In 1990, the average American paid $450 a year in user fees, which accounted for 16.2 percent of own-source state-local revenue.[22]

User fees offer several advantages. If they are priced accurately, they are perfectly fair under the benefit principle and they enjoy a relatively high level of political acceptability. (But those who do not have enough money to purchase these goods and services may have to do without—a circumstance that violates the ability-to-pay principle. A good case in point is higher education, which is shifting increasingly from state funding to tuition funding.) User fees are structured to yield whatever is needed to finance a particular service. An added benefit is that service users who do not live in the taxing jurisdiction must also pay the price, say, for a day in the state park. Elasticity may be achieved by varying the amount of the charge so that it always covers service costs.

Because service users must be identified and charged, user fees can be difficult to administer. Political accountability is low, because the charges can be increased without legislative action. However, a special advantage of user fees is that they can be employed to ration certain goods or services. For instance, entrance charges can be increased to reduce attendance at an overcrowded public facility, or varied according to the day of the week in order to encourage more efficient utilization. If the municipal zoo has few visitors on Mondays, it can cut the entrance fee on that day of the week by one-half. Table 14.4 rates the four major taxes based on the six criteria discussed above.

Miscellaneous Taxes   A wide variety of miscellaneous taxes are assessed by state and local governments. "Sin taxes" raise about 5.5 percent of all state revenues.[23] All states tax cigarettes; the median tax per pack is 21 cents.

Connecticut discourages smokers with a 45-cent tax; Kentucky and North Carolina, tobacco states, charge only 3 cents and 5 cents per pack, respectively. Alcoholic beverages are also taxed in all fifty states, although rates vary according to classification: beer, wine, or spirits. Beer drinkers steer clear of Hawaii, where the tax per gallon of nondraft beer is 89 cents; draft beer is tapped at 50 cents per gallon. Frequent imbibers are invited to visit California, where the tax is only 4 cents per gallon. (The eighteen states that hold monopolies on wholesale distribution of alcoholic beverages or that have their own state-run liquor stores are not accounted for in these figures.) Ironically, as drinking and smoking have declined during the past few years, so have their tax-based revenues. Quite likely, rising alcohol and tobacco taxes have helped curtail these "sins." It has been suggested that marijuana and other "recreational" drugs be legalized so that they, too, can be taxed.[24] In the twenty-one states taxing illegal drugs, persons possessing such drugs who cannot show evidence of having paid the required tax on them are charged with felony tax evasion. Minnesota, which originated the "grass tax," collected nearly $1.2 million within the first four years from voluntary tax payments and seized assets.

Though not a "sin," gasoline falls under the taxman's shadow as well. The highest tax on driving is in Hawaii (32.5 cents per gallon), followed by Nebraska (24 cents), Connecticut and Washington (23 cents). The lowest is in Florida (4 cents).[25] All states further profit from personal transportation by taxing vehicles and vehicle licenses.

Most states tax death in one form or another. Estate taxes must be paid on the money and property of a deceased person before the remainder is disbursed to the survivors. Nineteen states tax those who inherit the assets of the deceased. Rates are generally staggered according to the value of the estate. Other miscellaneous sources of revenue include hunting and fishing licenses, business licenses, auto license fees, and restaurant, meal, and lodging taxes. States are also lobbying Congress to overturn 1967 and 1992 Supreme Court rulings that prohibit them from applying their sales tax to out-of-state mail order houses. At least ten cities tax the wages earned by professional athletes while playing within their jurisdictional limits. California cities, trying to cope with a decade-long fiscal crisis, even apply fees to scuba tank fillups, noise pollution, and solar heating. One Maryland county taxes parking spaces.

Two Revenue Devices

In the continuous search for new ways to pluck the tax goose, two old devices have received renewed interest and attention during the past two decades.

Severance Tax   States blessed with petroleum, coal, natural gas, and minerals have for many years taxed these natural resources as they are taken from the land and sold. A fortunate few are able to "export" a substantial portion of their tax bite to people living in other states. However, in-staters must pay the same tax rate as out-of-staters.[26] A large majority of states (thirty-eight) place a severance tax on some form of natural resource, but just ten states collect 90 percent of all severance tax revenues. Taxes on oil and natural gas account for almost 85 percent of total state revenues in Alaska. Wyoming brings in almost 60 percent of its revenues from severance taxes on coal, oil, and gas. Other states leaning heavily on this form of taxation are Texas, Louisiana, Oklahoma, Montana, New Mexico, and North Dakota. Several states are rather creative in applying the severance tax. Virginia levies the tax on pilings and poles; and Washington, on salmon and other game fish.[27]

Severance taxes are popular in states rich in natural resources, because they help keep income, property, and sales taxes relatively low. Severance tax revenues also help to pay for environmental damage resulting from resource extraction operations, such as strip mining. The major disadvantage is that a state too dependent on severance taxes can be hurt badly if the price of its natural resources declines. During the late 1970s, oil and coal prices skyrocketed, enriching the bank accounts of Texas, Oklahoma, Louisiana, and Alaska. For several consecutive years, every man, woman, and child resident of Alaska received a rebate from the state's permanent fund. Checks totaled $556.26 per person in 1986. But the share-the-wealth program was threatened with termination because of a dramatic decline in oil prices in the late 1980s. Every $1 drop in the price of a barrel of oil costs millions in forgone revenues for oil-dependent states like Alaska and Texas.

Lotteries   As of 1992, thirty-four states and the District of Columbia operated lotteries; others are expected to follow suit in the next few years. The lottery is an old American tradition; initially established in the 1600s, it was popular from the colonial days until the late 1800s. Lotteries flourished throughout the country as a means to raise money for such good causes as new schools, highways, canals, and bridges. But scandals and mismanagement led every state and the national government to ban "looteries." From 1895 to 1963, no legal lotteries were operated. Then New Hampshire established a new one, followed in 1967 by New York. Since then, a growing number of states have created lotteries.[28] Total profits in 1990 came to over $10 billion. The record jackpot was $118.8 million in California.

Several factors account for the rebirth of "bettor government." First, they bring in large sums of money. Second, they are popular and entertaining—in only one state, North Dakota, have voters disapproved a lottery during the past two decades. And they are voluntary—you do not have to participate. Third, lotteries help relieve pressure on major taxes. In some states, net lottery earnings take the place of a one-cent increase in the sales tax. Many states earmark lottery proceeds for special purposes (public education in California, senior citizens' programs in Pennsylvania). Fourth, state ownership of a game of chance offers a legal and fair alternative to illegal gambling operations such as neighborhood numbers games or betting (parlay) cards.

But there are disadvantages as well. First of all, lotteries are costly to administer and have low yields. Prize awards must be great enough to encourage future ticket sales. New games must be created to retain enthusiasm. Ticket vendors must be paid commissions. And tight (as well as expensive) security precautions are required to guarantee the game's integrity. As a result, lotteries generate only a small percentage of total state revenue, usually less than 3 percent of own-source income. The average yield for players is low as well: About 50 percent of the total revenues is returned to players in prize money. This is far below the returns of other games of chance, such as slot machines, roulette, or craps.[29]

Lotteries can also be attacked on the grounds of equity and elasticity. Although the purchase of a ticket is voluntary and thus seemingly fair, studies indicate that low-income individuals are more likely to play.[30] The lottery, then, is a regressive way to raise revenues. Furthermore, lotteries tend to encourage compulsive gambling. In recognition of this problem, some states earmark a portion of lottery proceeds for treatment programs. Lotteries are said to be inelastic because earnings are cyclical and generally unstable. Sales depend on such factors as the legalized gambling activities in neighboring states, the size of jackpots, and the effectiveness of marketing efforts.[31]

If the present trend continues, virtually every state will operate a lottery by 1995. And especially as interstate lottery competition depresses profits, states will increasingly adopt other forms of legalized gambling, such as pari-mutuel betting on horse and dog races, as well as gambling in casinos, on river boats, on Indian reservations, and at historical sites from the Old West like mining towns. Video poker will bring legalized gambling to the neighborhood tavern and convenience store. Interactive systems may even permit couch potatoes to place bets at home with their telephone or TV remote controls.[32] Revenues will definitely increase, but the net human costs are yet to be determined.

The Political Economy of Taxation

One of the most difficult decisions for an elected official is to go on record in favor of raising taxes. The political heat can scorch even the coolest incumbent. But when revenues do not equal service costs and citizens do not want to cut services, raising taxes may be the only answer. Unfortunately, most people do not want higher taxes. This is the familiar "tax-service paradox": People demand new, improved, or at least the same level of government services but do not want to pay for them through higher taxes. Is it any wonder that user charges have become a popular option? The **political economy**—the political choices that frame economic policy—has become enormously perplexing for state and local officials. There are three major reasons: the tax revolt, fiscal stress, and limited discretion in raising new revenues.

political economy

Political choices that have economic outcomes.

Tax Revolt

Taxpayer resentment of property taxes, and the general perception that government was too big, too costly, and too wasteful, first took on a tangible form in 1978 with passage of Proposition 13 in California. Between 1977 and 1980, eighteen states enacted statutory or constitutional limitations on taxing and spending. Thirty-six states slashed personal or corporate income taxes, nine indexed their income taxes to the cost of living, and twenty-two cut the sales tax. In some instances citizens took tax matters into their own hands through the initiative process. In other cases state legislators jumped in front of the parade and cut taxes and spending themselves. The taxpayer revolt continued at a much slower pace during the early 1980s and, today, has lost most of its force. Tax-revolt measures have failed in recent years in Colorado, Nebraska, Massachusetts, and other states. Its legacy, however, remains enormously important (for instance, an Oregon property tax limitation was passed by referendum in November 1990). Public officials must work hard to justify tax increases or risk a citizen uprising and perhaps political death. They are wise to view the taxpayer revolt as a smoldering but not quite dead prairie fire.

Most state and local jurisdictions managed the fallout of the tax revolt reasonably well. Many of them held large budget surpluses that they utilized to ameliorate the immediate effects of *taxation and expenditure limitations* (TELS). For example, California had a $3 billion surplus with which it temporarily replaced property tax revenues forgone by local governments. Only a handful of states followed California's stringent TELS, which cut property taxes by 60 percent. Massachusetts was one of them; approved on the general election ballot in 1980, Proposition 2½ limited local property tax revenues to 2½ percent of the total value of taxable property. Tax bills for Massachusetts homeowners soon dropped by $1.3 billion.[33] Thirty-seven states had some sort of property tax restriction in effect as of 1990, and many placed limitations on other forms of taxation as well.[34] Raising taxes now requires a constitutional amendment, voter approval, or an extraordinary legislative majority in quite a few states. States and localities have resisted reducing service levels, opting instead to shift tax burdens or to find new sources of revenues, such as user charges.[35] However, the recession of 1990–1992 pushed many into service cutbacks, under the rubric of "downsizing" or "rightsizing."[36] Hundreds of thousands of state and local jobs were cut, including 25,000 in New York and 4,700 in New Jersey. In several states, such as Rhode Island and Connecticut, a series of one-day state government shutdowns and mandatory employee furloughs helped balance the budget. Overall, state and local spending as a percentage of the gross national product declined from 14.7 percent in 1975 to 12.87 percent in 1985 (it had returned to 14 percent in 1990).[37]

Political and economic consequences of the tax revolt have been much studied in its birthplace, California. Local governments in the Golden State have experienced serious impacts. Counties, special districts, and school districts have fewer revenue-raising opportunities than states, apart from the now highly constricted property tax. As a result, they are dependent on the state for funding. Since California's huge budget surplus was depleted, cities have creatively tapped a variety of available revenue sources to replace lost property tax income. User fees have increased substantially, as have franchise fees, lodging taxes, and other miscellaneous revenues. Cities have maintained expenditure levels for essential services like police and fire protection but have made cuts in other areas, such as

A budget crisis in 1991 caused the temporary shutdown of numerous state-provided services in Connecticut, prompting this cartoon.

libraries, parks and recreation, and public works.[38] The financial pinch was finally eased somewhat in 1990, when California voters passed referenda doubling the gasoline tax and easing the caps on state spending.

Fiscal Stress

Following on the heels of the tax revolt was a serious economic downturn. As the Reagan administration strangled the national economy in order to control inflation, state and local revenues plummeted. Adding to the mounting woes of the nonnational governments were substantial reductions in federal aid, even while additional programmatic responsibilities were being turned over to the states. Grants-in-aid were eliminated or significantly pared back; revenue sharing contracted and finally ended entirely. Unlike the case in earlier recessions, little special countercyclical aid was forthcoming to help the states and localities. Although budgets improved greatly during the "Roaring 80s," they ran smack up against the recession of 1990–1992—the worst since the Great Depression. Before the Reagan presidency, federal aid to cities constituted 25.8 percent of total state and local revenues; by 1989, that figure had dropped to 17.3 percent.

As in the early 1980s, many state and local jurisdictions today are experiencing severe **fiscal stress:** They are unable to pay for programs and provide services

fiscal stress

Financial pressure on a government from such factors as revenue shortfalls and taxing and spending limitations.

that citizens want and need without taxing the citizens at unacceptably high levels. Many factors contribute to fiscal stress. Typically, adverse social and economic conditions, mostly beyond state and local government control, establish an environment conducive to these problems. Older industrial cities are particularly vulnerable. Many jobs and manufacturing industries have been lost because of the gradual but compelling shift to a service-based economy and to the Sunbelt. In cities such as Detroit, Philadelphia, and New York, the exodus of jobs and firms has eroded the value of taxable resources (mostly property); yet citizens left behind have growing service demands.

Concentration of the poor and minorities in deteriorating housing, the shortage of jobs, high levels of crime, the illegal drug trade, homelessness, and related factors have produced crisis-level situations. Declining infrastructure also plagues older cities: water and sewer lines, treatment plants, streets, sidewalks, and other components of the urban physical landscape are in dire need of restoration or replacement. Most of these problems, it should be noted, will require national government attention if they are to be addressed effectively. Special factors contributing to state fiscal stress in 1990–1992 included the national recession, collapsing real estate markets in the Northeast and West Coast regions, the downsizing of defense spending in response to the end of the Cold War, and court- and congressionally mandated spending increases in corrections, education, and other areas.[39]

Political sources of fiscal stress typically compound the economic problems of older cities. Mismanagement of resources and inefficient procedures and activities are common complaints. Pressures from city workers and their unions have also driven up service provision costs.[40] Thus, service demands and the costs of providing services grow while taxes and intergovernmental revenues decline. This is a well-tested recipe for fiscal stress, evoking fears of bond defaults and even bankruptcy, as the case of Bridgeport illustrates.

New York City offers another oft-cited case study of fiscal stress. People, jobs, and industry fled the city for the suburbs and the Sunbelt in the early 1970s, thereby reducing fiscal capacity. Yet public employees' pay and pensions grew to some of the highest levels in the United States, and welfare payments to the poor and a growing number of unemployed were generous. The tuition-free City University of New York (CUNY) had an enrollment of 265,000 students.

As revenues increasingly lagged behind expenditures, the city government played fiscal roulette with the budget and borrowed huge sums through municipal notes and bonds. Eventually it was poised on the brink of bankruptcy. Defaults on the city's bonds, notes, and other debt instruments seemed imminent. City officials cried out to the national government and New York State for help, but some people had little sympathy for a city that had lived beyond its means for too long.[41]

Aided by national guarantees of new long-term loans, New York State and other large holders of New York City debt finally agreed to a bail-out.[42] Had this immense urban financial edifice collapsed, the fiscal shocks would have threatened New York State's economic stability and even resulted in serious fiscal repercussions for other states and localities throughout the United States.

Unfortunately, the Big Apple in 1992 once again risked being reduced to a seedy core. It faced a budget deficit of $3.5 billion, a mass exodus of jobs (100,000 within just three years), and the enormous cost of thousands of AIDS and crack babies. Seventy percent of the city's more than 2,000 bridges desperately needed expensive repairs, and water and sewer lines were rupturing regularly. Mayor David Dinkins responded with a variety of actions, including massive city employee layoffs, closing libraries and clinics, and turning off 25 percent of the city's street lights.

Still another case of severe fiscal stress is Philadelphia, a city with a 35 percent poverty rate and a rapidly declining population and work force. Its debt has sunk to junk bond levels. Typically, there is plenty of blame to go around: administrative mismanagement; political infighting; intransigent unions; the lack of financial help from Washington, D.C., and the state legislature; and huge social service costs attributed to the contemporary urban problems noted in the case of New York.[43]

Most jurisdictions have not yet experienced the misfortune faced by New York City and Philadelphia. The taxpayer revolt and fiscal stress notwithstanding, budgets have been balanced, payrolls met, and most services maintained. For their part, state officials have increasingly swallowed hard, held their noses, and raised taxes. In 1992, thirty states hiked taxes and most others were seriously considering it.

Limited Discretion

TELS have placed ceilings on rates and amounts of taxation and spending, thus limiting the discretion of the nonnational governments. Other constraining factors, too, keep state and local governments from the temptation of taxing and spending orgies. An important one is interstate competition for jobs and economic development.[44] High-tax states run a serious risk of having jobs, firms, and investments "stolen" by low-tax states. It was just such a concern that convinced New York, Massachusetts, and other states to lower tax rates in the late 1980s, just before the recession wreaked financial havoc.

Earmarking taxes for popular programs also limits state and local taxing and spending discretion. Earmarking is well established: Gasoline taxes have been set aside for road and highway programs since automobiles first left ruts in muddy cow pastures. What differs today are the levels of specificity and creativity in earmarking. Nearly 25 percent of state tax revenues are earmarked today, much less than thirty years ago; but the number of dedicated purposes has grown markedly. Some fear "boutique government," in which taxpaying "shoppers" willingly pay only for programs that benefit them directly and personally.[45] Surpluses may accumulate in some dedicated funds, such as highways, while other important needs such as education or law enforcement are not sufficiently met. The hands of government officials are tied, however, because they cannot move the funds around.[46] Cigarette buyers in Washington cough up millions of dollars each year to help clean up Puget Sound. Earnings from the Illinois state lottery are designated for public schools. Several states earmark penny increases in the sales tax for public education. And tax revenues from New Jersey casinos go to aid senior citizens and the disabled.

Financial discretion is partly determined by one's position on the fiscal food chain. The national government can essentially tax and spend as it wishes, subject only to its underdeveloped capacity for self-discipline. States must meet federal spending mandates for Medicaid, corrections, and other functions while somehow balancing their budgets. Local governments, in this game of "shift and shaft federalism,"[47] must comply with an increasing number of state spending mandates even though their legal authority to raise revenues remains severely circumscribed in most states.

Borrowing and Debt

Sometimes state or local government expenditures substantially outstrip revenues, because either revenue has been underestimated or too much money has been spent. A more pleasing development occurs when revenues exceed expenditures. Because the nonnational governments must balance their operating budgets each fiscal year, the reliability of revenue estimates is very important.

Estimating Revenues

Until fairly recently, state and local governments estimated their annual revenues simply by extrapolating from past trends. This approach works well during periods of steady economic growth, but it fails miserably during years of boom or bust. The states and most larger cities and counties are much more sophisticated today. Using computer technology, they employ econometric modeling to derive mathematical estimates of future revenues.

This method places key variables in equations to predict the fiscal year yield of each major tax. A wide variety of variables are used, including employment levels, food prices, housing costs, oil and gas prices, consumer savings levels, interest rates, and state and local debt obligations. Because state and local economies are increasingly linked to national and international factors, estimates often include measures for the value of the dollar, international trade and investment, and national fiscal policy.

Two critical factors determine the accuracy of revenue estimates: the quality of the data and the validity of the economic assumptions. Econometric modeling of state and local economies can be a voyage into the unknown. Data problems include difficulty in measuring key variables, periodic revisions of historical economic data, which require new calculations, and modifications in tax laws or fee schedules. But the major source of error is the economic assumptions built into the models. Examples are legion: The national economy may not perform as expected; oil prices may plummet or soar; natural disasters can disrupt state or local economic growth. Sometimes taxpayers foul up revenue estimates by making errors on tax returns, failing to comply fully with laws, or remitting payments later than usual.[48] Recessions are particularly damaging to fiscal stability, since state and local taxes are highly sensitive to economic downturns. Sometimes the miscalculations are enormous. In fiscal year 1988 and again in 1989, California misjudged its revenues by approximately $1 billion. And during 1990–1992, wildly inaccurate national government economic data and forecasts wreaked havoc on state and local government budget projections.[49]

Politics can also intrude in the revenue projection process. For instance, politicians can purposely overestimate revenues in order to fund a popular new program. When projected revenues do not appear, implementation of the program may be delayed, but it now has official standing. Overestimates can also defer cuts in politically sensitive programs or levels of public employment and help incumbents survive the next election. When the revenue shortfall reaches serious proportions, cutbacks are much more palatable than they are when the shortfall is a mere projection, and elections are over for at least two years.[50] Actually, jurisdictions often err conservatively by underestimating revenues, because midyear cutbacks are painful and embarrassing for government officials,[51] and also because a year-end budget surplus may be chalked up to "good management."

Rainy Day Funds

Because a balanced budget is mandatory but estimation errors are inevitable, many states and localities establish contingency or budget stabilization funds. Popularly known as "rainy day funds," these savings accounts help insulate budgets from fiscal distortions caused by inaccurate data or faulty economic assumptions; they are also available for emergencies. Thirty-one states maintain some form of rainy day fund, many of which were put in place following the severe recession of 1981–1982. In years of economic health, the funds accumulate principal and interest. When the economy falls ill, governments can tap them to balance the budget, as they did in 1990–1992.

Deposits to rainy day accounts come through monies appropriated by the legislature or through a formula that links contributions to a general fund surplus or to the growth rate of the economy. During recessions, such funds may be depleted, and replenishment may be delayed until better days return. This occurred in many states during 1990–1992. As one commentator put it, "When you're in the midst of a hurricane, its too late to build up a rainy day fund."[52]

While rainy day funds have been widely adopted at the state level, they are rarely used by cities and counties. The task of balancing the budget is especially daunting in local governments, because of their lack of economic diversity, dependency on state taxes and financial aid, and sensitivity to economic dislocations. The departure of a single large employer can disrupt a local economy for years. Yet only a few of the nation's largest cities use rainy day accounts. A survey of the fifty-five largest cities identified only six with a rainy day fund: Houston, Milwaukee, Omaha, St. Paul, San Antonio, and Virginia Beach, Virginia.[53] Nonetheless, the potential advantages of such a fund are numerous.

Other Cash and Investment Management Practices

State and local governments, of necessity, are becoming more knowledgeable about how to manage cash and investments. Cash reserves that once sat idly in non–interest-bearing accounts or a desk drawer are now invested in short-term notes, treasury bills, certificates of deposit, and other financial instruments in order to maximize interest earnings. The process of spending and collecting monies is also manipulated to advantage. For example, large checks are deposited on the day they are received and payable checks are drawn on the latest date possible. In general, state and local financial management today resembles that of a large corporation instead of the "mom-and-pop" approach of years ago. After all, the nonnational governments spend nearly a trillion dollars annually, and invest around $70 billion.

State and local cooperation in investment management is found in such programs as bond banks. First established in Vermont in 1970 and now operating in eleven states, bond banks offer small localities the opportunity to sell bonds at competitive interest rates. Typically, the state gathers together a number of bonds from several small local jurisdictions and issues the total debt in a single state bond. This measure not only results in lower borrowing costs (interest rates); it also saves in expenses involved in marketing the bonds to investors. For a very small or newly incorporated municipality, the bond bank may be the only way to borrow a substantial amount of money. In the future, bond banks could also help meet capital requirements for the nation's growing problems with infrastructure (roads, bridges, and so forth). Several states are now implementing infrastructure bond funds.[54]

The most important state or local investment is usually the public employee pension fund. These retirement funds hold more than $800 billion in assets. In the past, they were conservatively managed and politically untouchable. Today, however, they represent a tempting honeypot for financially suffering governments. In 1991, California Governor Pete Wilson dipped his hand in the state pension fund and pulled out $1.6 billion to balance the budget; Governor Jim Edgar of Illinois scooped out $21 million from his state pension system. Some two-thirds of the states deferred or reduced state pension fund contributions in 1990–1992. New York omitted its entire 1991 contribution.[55] Public employees there fervently hoped that an improving economy would permit their employers to repay principal and interest obligations soon.

State and Local Debt

Every state except Vermont is constitutionally or statutorily mandated to balance its budget each fiscal year. In turn, the states require their local governments to balance *their* budgets. However, these requirements apply only to **operating budgets,** which are used for daily financial receipts and disbursements. Capital budgets, used for big purchases that must be paid for over time, such as a new bridge or school building, typically run substantial deficits. Operating budgets may also go into deficit during the fiscal year, so long as expenditures equal revenues at the end of the year.

In order to deal with temporary revenue shortfalls and to finance expensive items that cannot be absorbed in the operating budget, governments borrow money, just as individuals use credit cards to make relatively small purchases that they will pay for when they receive next month's salary, or as they finance the purchase of an automobile or a house over a longer period of time. Borrowing is a major state and local government activity, amounting to around $124 billion in 1989 alone.

Temporary cash-flow deficits in the operating budget are alleviated through tax anticipation or revenue anticipation notes. Investors such as banks lend money to a government on a short-term basis (typically thirty to ninety days). The loan is backed up by anticipated revenues from income, sales, and property taxes or other specified sources and is paid off as soon as the funds become available.

Long-Term Borrowing   Long-term debt obligations (typically five to twenty-five years) are financed through bonds. There are three conventional types: general obligation bonds, revenue bonds, and industrial development bonds.

The principal and interest payments on **general obligation bonds** are secured by the "full faith, credit, and taxing power" of the state or local jurisdiction issuing them. General obligation bonds are used to finance public projects such as highways, schools, and hospitals. Lenders are guaranteed repayment so long as the bond-issuing government is solvent; defaults are nearly nonexistent.

Revenue bonds are backed up by expected income from a specific project or service; examples include a toll bridge, municipal sewer system, mortgage loans, or student loans. Revenue bonds are payable only from the revenues derived from the specified source, not from general tax revenues. They are generally a riskier investment than general obligation bonds and therefore command a higher rate of interest.

Industrial development bonds (IDBs) are a type of revenue bond, inasmuch as the full faith, credit, and taxing power of the issuer are not pledged as security. The payment of principal and interest on IDBs depends solely on the ability of the user of the facilities financed by the bond (the industry) to meet its financial obligation. If the user fails to make payments, creditors can seize and sell any real or personal property associated with the facility. Private interests, such as shopping malls or firms, are the primary beneficiaries of IDBs. Conventionally, these private-purpose bonds are issued by local governments to attract economic activity and investments. IDBs are frequently used to furnish loans at highly favorable interest rates to small or medium-sized firms. This form of debt received a great deal of criticism in the early 1980s because many local governments were using IDBs to finance low-wage commercial and retail operations like McDonald's and K-mart, which were fully capable of obtaining private financing. The abuse of IDBs led Congress to prohibit their use for food establishments, entertainment facilities (such as cinemas), and related purposes, and to place an annual cap on total IDB activity in each state.

Two New Debt Instruments: COPs and SWAPs   *COPs—Certificates of Participation*—are tax-exempt instruments used primarily by local governments to finance construction of a new facility such as a convention center or to acquire costly capital equipment such as new fire trucks. Unlike most municipal bonds, COPs do not require voter approval. They involve lease-back financing, whereby the issuing government, instead of owning the new facility or equipment, leases it from a third party (usually a private firm or a nonprofit organization). Annual leasing fees are paid out of annual operating expenses and thus are not treated as debt. COPs first became popular in the 1980s and represent a $5 billion market today. They are used in all but a handful of states.[56]

SWAPs are a device used by governments to hedge against volatility in interest rates. Issuers "swap" interest rates, but not principal, on previously issued bonds. Usually, variable (floating) rate debt is exchanged for a fixed-rate bond (or vice versa), with a third-party holder such as a bank or investment company. This complicated public finance technique helps protect government debt against rapidly rising or declining interest rates; it also reduces total interest costs for the government. Nine states have legislation permitting SWAPs.[57]

Limits on Borrowing   As of 1990, the states owed $318 billion to various creditors and local governments had incurred debts of more than $510 billion. The total state and local debt came to $3,312 per man, woman, and child in the United States. Yet these gigantic sums pale in comparison to the national debt, which has reached a tidy sum of $3.0 *trillion*—almost $9,000 per person. State and local debt has remained at about 15.5 percent of the gross national product since the mid-1980s. The national debt leaped from 33 percent of the GNP in 1979 to more than 55 percent in 1989.[58]

Almost all states place constitutional or statutory restrictions on their own and local government borrowing. Some have set maximum levels of indebtedness; others require popular referenda to create debt or to exceed specified debt limits. They tightly restrict local government debt, especially general obligation bonds. (State-imposed constraints normally do not apply to revenue bonds.) The impetus for these restrictions came from a series of bond defaults in the 1860s and 1870s, and again during the Great Depression. COPs, described above, are one means of avoiding debt restrictions.

The bond market places its own informal limitations on debt by assessing the quality of bonds, notes, and other debt instruments. Investors in government bonds rely on Moodys Investors Service, Standard and Poor's Corporation, and other investment services for ratings of a jurisdiction's capacity to repay its obligations. Criteria taken into consideration in bond ratings include existing debt levels, rainy day funds, market value of real estate, population growth, per capita income, employment levels, and other measures of overall financial health and solvency. Highly rated bond issues receive ratings of Aaa, Aa, and A. Variations of B indicate medium to high risk. A rating of C is reserved for bonds in danger of default. The average interest rate on low-rated bonds usually exceeds that of top-rated ones by one and a half to two percentage points; this translates into a considerable difference in interest payments. Bond ratings can fall rapidly, as they did during the 1990–1992 recession when an unusually high number of credit rating downgrades occurred. The debt instruments of New York, Louisiana, and Massachusetts were assigned very low ratings because of growing state debt and near political paralysis. Four New England states, Illinois, Pennsylvania, and several others were placed on a "credit watch list" indicating that a rating downgrade was being considered.

State and Local Financial Relationships

The most critical aspect of state and local relations has to do with dollars and cents. Increasingly, local governments are fixing their sights on the states rather than on Washington, D.C., as the most available financial benefactor.

An Uneasy Relationship

An uneasy relationship exists between states and local governments when it comes to money. The status of localities is not unlike that of an eighteen-year-old with a part-time job. Since he still lives and eats at home, he remains dependent on his parents. He fervently wants to assert his independence; yet when he does, his parents often rein him in. As long as he dwells in his parents' house, he must bend to their authority.

Cities, counties, and other local governments will always live within the constitutional house of their parents, the states. They enjoy their own sources of revenue—property taxes, user fees, and business license fees—but depend on the states for the bulk of their income. They suffer the frustration of having to cope with rising expenditure demands from their residents while their authority to raise new monies is highly circumscribed by state law. No wonder they turned to their "grandparent"—the national government—in the 1960s and 1970s, to seek direct financial aid that "bypassed" the states. They returned again in 1992, hoping that the Los Angeles riots would turn Washington's attention to the problems of the cities.

The historical insensitivity of states to the economic problems of their cities and counties began slowly changing in the 1970s, largely because reapportionment brought urban interests greater standing in state legislatures. In the 1980s, the states had to assume an even more attentive posture. National aid to localities declined substantially during the eight years of the Reagan administration. Today, only about 14.5 percent of all federal grant-in-aid dollars go directly to cities and counties.[59]

The single largest source of local revenues is the state. More than one-third of all state expenditures ($172 billion in 1990) goes to local governments. But like federal grants-in-aid, state grants come with lots of strings attached. Most state dollars ($3 out of every $4) are earmarked for public education and social welfare; state aid accounts for more than 50 percent of total local education expenditures and 80 percent of public welfare spending. Other state assistance is earmarked for roads, hospitals, and public health. The result is that local governments have very little spending discretion.

Naturally, there is a great amount of diversity in levels of encumbered and un-encumbered state assistance to local jurisdictions, much of which is related to the distribution of functions between a state and its localities. Highly centralized states such as Hawaii, South Carolina, and West Virginia fund and administer many programs at the state level that are funded and administered locally in de-centralized states such as Maryland, New York, and Wisconsin. In states where taxation and expenditure limitations have hampered the ability of local jurisdictions to raise and spend revenues, the trend has been toward centralization. Once again, California offers the prototype. Since Proposition 13, public education and several other functions formerly dominated by local governments have been brought under state control. Greater fiscal centralization has also resulted from state efforts to reduce service disparities between wealthy and poor jurisdictions and to lessen the dependence of local governments on the property tax.

Table 14.5 shows the diversity in state aid to counties, municipalities, and townships, which varies from $1,369 per capita in Alaska to $8 in Maine; the average is $275. This surprisingly large variation has been explored in empirical research by political scientists. It appears that the most important predictors of state aid to localities are centralization of functions (for example, more than 50 percent of Alaska's total aid is for education), state wealth (rich states provide more money than poor states), fiscal need (fiscally stressed localities need greater state aid), and legislative professionalism (professional legislatures are willing to spend more on education, social welfare, and other local programs).[60]

What Local Governments Want from the States

What local governments want from their states and what they actually get may be a cosmos apart. Today states and their local jurisdictions conduct a lot of dialogue over financial matters. Increasingly, the states are willing to recognize and want to respond to local financial problems—subject, of course, to their own fiscal circumstances.

Simply put, local governments want *more money*. The tax revolt, terminations and reductions in federal grants-in-aid, the death rattle of revenue sharing, and the 1990–1992 recession have left local jurisdictions in a financial bind. State governments must provide help, and in general they have done so. The $165

Table 14.5

State Expenditures to Local Governments, Per Capita, Fiscal Year 1989

	Per Capita Payments to Counties, Municipalities, and Townships
U.S. Average	$275
New England	**401**
Connecticut	460
Maine	8
Massachusetts	541
New Hampshire	87
Rhode Island	380
Vermont	89
Mideast	**448**
Delaware	68
Maryland	486
New Jersey	289
New York	705
Pennsylvania	174
Great Lakes	**198**
Illinois	116
Indiana	123
Michigan	302
Ohio	165
Wisconsin	357
Plains	**165**
Iowa	166
Kansas	79
Minnesota	391
Missouri	41
Nebraska	101
North Dakota	181
South Dakota	106

billion in state aid for all local governments in 1989 was up from $82.8 billion in 1980—an increase that substantially outstrips inflation over that period. State aid also increased in 1990 and 1991, even though at least twelve states cut aid to local governments in fiscal year 1991.

Most increases in state aid are devoted to education and social services. Recently, however, states have been more willing to share revenues that cities or counties may spend as they desire. Many states distribute a portion of their tax revenues based on local fiscal need, thus tending to equalize or level economic disparities between local jurisdictions.

The specific means for sharing revenues takes many forms. Twenty-four states

Table 14.5
(cont.)

	Per Capita Payments to Counties, Municipalities, and Townships
Southeast	**$ 234**
Alabama	100
Arkansas	93
Florida	120
Georgia	58
Kentucky	80
Louisiana	81
Mississippi	153
North Carolina	710
South Carolina	91
Tennessee	420
Virginia	526
West Virginia	11
Southwest	**74**
Arizona	264
New Mexico	277
Oklahoma	67
Texas	17
Rocky Mountain	**139**
Colorado	162
Idaho	83
Montana	76
Utah	64
Wyoming	485
Far West*	**386**
California	453
Nevada	299
Oregon	181
Washington	120
Alaska	1,369
Hawaii	42

* Alaska and Hawaii are excluded from the Far West regional average but are included in the U.S. average.

Source: U.S. Advisory Commission on Intergovernmental Relations, *Significant Features of Fiscal Federalism,* Vol. 2 (Washington, D.C.: ACIR, 1991), pp. 64–65.

make special payments to local governments that host state buildings or other facilities, which are exempt from property tax but cause a drain on local services.[61] This is a particularly relevant concern for capital cities, in which large plots of prime downtown property are occupied by state office buildings.

In addition, local governments want the *legal capacity to raise additional revenues themselves,* especially through local option sales and income taxes (although a slice of gasoline, tobacco, and other tax benefits is greatly appreciated). The key is local option, in which jurisdictions decide for themselves which, if any, taxes they will exact. More than two-thirds of the states have authorized an optional sales or income tax for various local governments, and some permit localities to adopt optional earmarked taxes. (Nineteen states handed local governments some type of new taxing authority in 1991 alone.) For example, Florida empowers its counties to place an accommodations tax on local hotel and motel rooms. Revenues are dedicated to tourism development projects. Local option taxes are attractive because they provide local jurisdictions with the flexibility to take action as they see fit in response to local needs.[62] What protects citizens against "taxaholic" local legislative bodies in the aftermath of the taxpayer revolt is the state requirement that local tax hikes must be approved by the voters in a referendum.

Local governments also want *reimbursements for state mandates* that require them to spend money. Through constitutional provisions, statutes, and administrative regulations, all states require localities to undertake certain activities and operate programs in accordance with state standards and rules. These mandates are similar to the strings attached to federal grants-in-aid (which also affect local governments), and they are just as distasteful to local governments as federal mandates are to states. Many state mandates are associated with local personnel policies, such as minimum wages, pensions, and safe working conditions. Others entail special education programs, environmental protection standards, and access for the handicapped. Most are designed to achieve uniformity in levels and quality of local government services throughout the state. Sometimes, however, state mandates appear to be nitpicking. Examples include requirements that public libraries carry a certain number of books per resident or that school buses be refueled daily, whether their tanks are empty or not.

Local governments believe that they should not have to both obey *and* pay, and that states should reimburse them for expenses incurred in carrying out such mandates. Many states have responded to this request. Forty states now attach "fiscal notes" to any proposed legislation that involves local governments; these notes estimate the local costs of implementing the legislation. An increasing number of states are required by law to go one step further and fully reimburse local governments for mandated expenditures.[63] A constitutional amendment enacted in 1990 in Florida prohibits mandates without money unless two-thirds of both houses of the legislature approve.

State and Local Finance in the 1990s

The bankruptcy of Bridgeport was abnormal in certain respects, but overall it reflects common miseries afflicting the great majority of large American cities during the bad economic times that ushered in the decade of the 1990s. In the past, the federal and state governments would have ridden to the fiscal rescue with economic assistance. But today their own financial travails rival those of the local governments. The national government cuts aid to the states, which, in turn, contribute less to city and county coffers. The severe national recession of 1990–1992 threatened to bring down the fiscal foundation of the nonnational governments like an imploded high-rise building in the increasingly vacant central cities.

The keys to surviving financial crisis are intergovernmental cooperation, burden-sharing, and citizen comprehension of the basic tax-service relationship. The national and state economies will recover, but serious financial dislocations are likely to continue during the next several years. California, for example, had a combined 1991 and 1992 budget deficit of more than $14 billion, an amount greater than the total general fund of forty-five states. Governor Pete Wilson claimed that the budget would not be balanced even if he laid off all state employees and closed every prison and university.[64]

Long-term taxing and spending trends are being reconsidered by states and localities. They hope that the national government will join them in facing up to the spiraling costs of Medicaid, corrections, and public education—burdens that should not be laid on the back of a single level of government. Mandates without money should be abolished in most instances. When mandates and program responsibilities are pushed to a different rung of the federal ladder, funds should follow. Local governments, particularly, need more revenue-raising authority and a broader tax base to pay for the services they deliver. They also need more authority to consolidate services on a regional basis. Most states have been receptive to these principles; the federal government requires further education.

Education is also needed for taxpayers, who seldom grasp the relationship between taxes paid and services rendered. Resistance to new or existing taxes is fine, but citizens must be made to understand that the result may be fewer services. Elected officials have the primary responsibility for taxpayer education, but often politics intrudes.

The state and local governments remain laboratories of democracy, but "their laboratories are coming up with fiscal formulations far likelier to impart pain than pleasure."[65] Hard times mean hard solutions about what governments should and should not do, and how it all should be paid for. All things considered, the actions of the state and local government officials stand in stark contrast to the inactivity and fiscal irresponsibility in Washington, D.C.

....

Summary

State and local finance is characterized by interdependence and diversity. Major state and local taxes have been joined by severance taxes and user fees. All taxes can be evaluated using the criteria of equity, yield, elasticity, ease of administration, political accountability, and acceptability. State and local governments have been buffeted by a series of financial blows, including the taxpayer revolt, severe economic recessions, and painful reductions in national aid. All are likely to continue to affect nonnational governments during the 1990s.

State and local governments are doing a better job than they used to in managing their money. Revenue and expenditure estimates are becoming more accurate in the face of growing economic complexity. Rainy day funds are used to set aside monies for hard times and the next economic downturn. Bonded indebtedness is being kept at reasonable levels. And, of course, operating budgets are balanced each fiscal year.

Key Terms

own-source revenue
intergovernmental transfers
fiscal capacity
regressive tax
progressive tax
proportional tax
benefit principle
circuit breaker

political economy
fiscal stress
operating budget
general obligation bond
revenue bond
industrial development bond

15

Education Policy

Milwaukee's schools epitomize the failure of American public education in the cities. The average grade point average for the 97,000 students is 1.62 (D+), and only 1.35 for the 70 percent of the students who are black. Nearly half of all students drop out and never graduate. Teachers credit themselves with a successful day if a modicum of order is maintained in the classroom. According to a University of Wisconsin survey, 62 percent of them do not want their own children to attend the same school at which they teach.[1] Desperate conditions often produce radical measures. The Wisconsin legislature recently enacted a law to permit up to 1,000 children from low-income Milwaukee families to attend private, nonreligious schools at state expense—the first such experiment in the nation.

In the opinion of many Americans, education is the most important function performed by state and local government. The facts support this point of view. Education consumes more of state and local budgets than any other service. In 1990, more than $183 billion was spent on elementary and secondary schooling in the United States.[2] That comes to around $4,890 per pupil. The importance of education is also demonstrated by the sheer number of people involved in it. Fifty-five percent of the U.S. population is either enrolled in an educational institution or employed in the system that delivers educational services. Citizens have high expectations for their schools, assuming that they will teach everything from patriotism and good citizenship to driver and sex education. Schools have served at the front lines in the battle against racial segregation. And, to a great extent, the future of this country and its economy is linked to the quality of free public education. Milwaukee's school problems are not unusual for public education in the United States. These increasingly glaring educational shortcomings have been the subject of numerous studies and reports.

Indeed, in 1983, a prestigious national commission officially declared a crisis in the schools. In its much-cited report, *A Nation at Risk,* the National Commission on Excellence in Education lamented the erosion of the educational foundations of society "by a rising tide of mediocrity that threatens our very future." According to the authors, "If an unfriendly foreign power had attempted to impose on America the mediocre educational performance that exists today, we might well have viewed it as an act of war. . . . We have, in effect, been committing an act of unthinking, unilateral educational disarmament."[3]

This shocking statement is supported by studies documenting the dismal performance of American students in comparison with students in other countries. Scores in mathematics and science by American thirteen-year-olds are far below scores from South Korea, Ireland, Spain, the United Kingdom, and four Canadian provinces; American students typically rank last in math and close to the bottom in science.[4] National surveys in 1991 discovered that the majority of American adults cannot interpret a bus schedule or follow the major argument of a newspaper column. American firms provide corroborating horror stories. Recently, New York Telephone tested 60,000 applicants before they found 3,000 capable of filling entry-level jobs.

....

The Crisis in Education

Education policy has always been controversial. For more than a hundred years policymakers, parents, teachers, and others have debated how educational institutions should be organized and financed, what should be taught, and who should receive the greatest benefit from public schooling. The most recent crisis is in many respects simply an extension of what has happened before. "Crises" in American education have been solemnly declared every thirty years or so. (Periodic public alarm followed by neglect characterizes other policies as well.[5]) Before the most recent crisis, one was provoked in 1957 by the Soviet launching of Sputnik, the first orbiting space satellite. This momentous event led to a far-reaching effort to improve American education in science and mathematics, and eventually to American success in landing the first man on the moon.

The education crisis that began in the 1980s, however, is more profound in three respects. First, the rapidity of world economic and social change means that education policy must be constantly reformulated and altered if schooling is to be relevant and the United States is to remain a dominant player in the international sphere. Second, improved analysis and data collection have provided a clearer picture of our specific shortcomings in education and generated greater public awareness of them. Third, in spite of billions of additional dollars in state and local government spending in recent years, and a spate of institutional and classroom reforms, this education crisis appears to be worsening.

Public opinion reflects the education crisis. Each year since 1977, the Gallup Poll has asked Americans their opinions of community schools. One question requires respondents to grade their local school on a scale of A to F. In the first year of the poll, 37 percent awarded the schools an A or a B, but by 1991 the proportion of A's and B's had dropped to 21 percent. A growing number assign a grade of D or F.

One convincing piece of evidence of deterioration in the quality of schooling makes headlines in newspapers throughout the country each year: student performance on standardized college entrance exams. Scholastic Aptitude Test (SAT) and American College Test (ACT) scores on verbal and math sections dropped almost annually from 1963 to 1982, below the levels existing at the time of the last declared crisis in education (see Figure 15.1). Following a brief rally during the mid-1980s, scores again began eroding slowly and continue to do so today. Declining student performance is particularly disturbing when American students are compared to their peers in other countries, as we have noted.

What's wrong with the American education system? The widely recognized policy problems can be reduced to three major variables: standards, students, and teachers.[6]

Figure 15.1

Average SAT Verbal and Mathematics Scores, 1963–1991

Average SAT verbal and math scores began a prolonged period of decline in the early 1960s but turned upward in 1982. Although the current trend is not entirely clear, scores seem to be moving downward again.

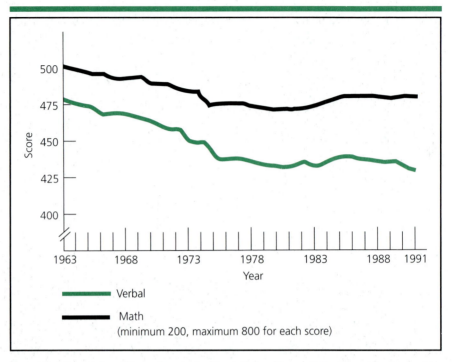

Verbal

Math

(minimum 200, maximum 800 for each score)

Source: Data from College Entrance Examination Board, *National Report: College-Bound Seniors,* as cited in U.S. Department of Education, Center for Statistics, *Digest of Education Statistics, 1991* (Washington, D.C.: U.S. Government Printing Office, 1991).

Standards

American schools have suffered from a malady that might be called curriculum drift. Especially from the 1960s to the early 1980s, courses designed to teach basic verbal and mathematical skills were de-emphasized while numerous non-essential topics became popular. For example, courses on the secondary school menu included Self-Awareness, Who Am I, Skiing, Sailing, Love and Marriage, and Bachelor Living. Most such ludicrous subjects have since disappeared, only to be replaced by courses on racial or cultural heritage—worthy topics, perhaps, but no substitute for the "basics." To many critics, education sometimes seems to be aimed at helping students feel comfortable with themselves and have a good time rather than at teaching them basic skills and the ability to think analytically. Business, military, and university leaders complain about having to invest millions of dollars in remedial education before ill-prepared high school graduates are ready to work, serve in the armed forces, or study.

Even more disturbing, some 25 million Americans are functionally illiterate—unable to perform simple tasks of reading, writing, and comprehension. About two-thirds of all students lack the ability to solve a math problem involving several steps, 80 percent cannot write a persuasive essay, and 40 percent are unable to "draw inferences from written material."[7] As a result, many students graduate from high school prepared for neither college nor the job market. Because it is virtually impossible to argue that the native intelligence of American youth has declined, considerable blame has been placed on vacillating educational standards for curricula and courses.

Students

Students themselves have not escaped criticism. They choose to soften up their curriculum with easy "lifestyle" courses rather than basic English, math, science, and social studies. Today's students are said to be poorly motivated and lazy in comparison to their predecessors. They are faulted for seeking instant gratification through television, video games, drugs, alcohol, and sex instead of seriously applying themselves to coursework. In a typical year, nearly one million students give up school altogether by dropping out.

Clearly, however, the legal and moral responsibility for providing direction to a young person's life rests with his or her parents. This responsibility includes encouraging the child to complete homework assignments and regulating television time. The potential contribution of parental involvement in the educational process was revealed by a six-year study of students in Japan, Taiwan, and the United States, in which researchers found that American children registered the lowest scores on math and reading tests principally because they started the first grade with fewer academic skills than their Asian counterparts. Japanese and Taiwanese parents gave their youngsters a head start by regularly working with them at home before they entered school. Coaching after school helped the Japanese and Taiwanese children maintain their early advantage.[8] But American parents tend to abdicate to the schools the responsibility for educating their children. Often parents have little choice; as a result of the dramatic jump in the number of single-parent and two-worker households in recent years, parents have less time, and energy, to spend helping their children. The shortage and expense of professional day care and after-school opportunities compounds the problem. Today almost 60 percent of married women with children under age six work outside the home, as do nearly 75 percent of those with school-age children. About 12 percent of all families are headed by a single parent. Eighteen percent of white babies and an astonishing 64 percent of black babies are born to unwed mothers.[9] The traditional American family depicted by old 1950s TV shows like "Ozzie and Harriet" is now the rare exception.

Teachers

Teachers are the linchpins between students and the learning process. Effective teaching can bestow lifelong learning skills on fortunate students, and poor teaching can result in indifference among good students and dropping out by marginal students. The problem with teaching is twofold. First, for many years the teaching profession declined in terms of the quality of individuals who chose to enter it. Second, teachers believed that their status and conditions of work had dropped substantially. Clearly, one part of the problem is closely related to the other.

The gradual decline in the quality of teachers is partly due to changes in the nature of the work force. Until about twenty-five years ago, most women had few job opportunities besides teaching, nursing, and clerical work. But in the mid-1960s, women began moving into traditionally male-dominated jobs in growing numbers. Even today, however, 70 percent of public school teachers are women.

In recent years, academically gifted women who once would have chosen the teaching profession have been more likely to seek out higher-paying, more prestigious positions in government and the private sector. This means that less able college graduates elect to become teachers, resulting in a severe shortage of qualified teachers in some states. SAT scores bear this out. Prospective teachers in 1982 earned average scores of 394 on the verbal section and 419 on the math; the national averages were 426 and 467. The fall in teacher quality was cruelly but honestly stated by Albert Shanker, president of the second-largest teachers union (the American Federation of Teachers): "For the most part you are getting illiterate, incompetent people who cannot go into any other field."[10] In some situations, school districts have little choice but to hire substandard teachers. For example, Dallas gave a basic competency test over a six-year period to 13,700 applicants for teaching jobs. Only 3,700 passed, but Dallas had to fill 5,000 vacancies. The result was that hundreds of unqualified individuals entered the classrooms.[11]

Part of the blame must also be placed on university and college education curricula that emphasize "educational methodology" courses, which aim to teach prospective instructors how to teach rather than giving them substantive knowledge of their subject matter. Another reason it has been difficult to find good teachers is that teaching has until recently been a low-wage occupation. The average starting salary was only slightly more than $12,000 in 1982; this compared very unfavorably with other fields for college graduates. Before the salary gains of the mid- to late 1980s, teacher compensation did not keep pace with the cost of living. Between 1973 and 1983, the average teacher lost over 11 percent of his or her purchasing power.[12]

In an effort to improve their pay and working conditions, most teachers have joined unions such as the American Federation of Teachers and the National Education Association. According to some critics, teacher unions, by furthering the narrow self-interest of teachers instead of more effective schools, have become part of the problem with public education.

The frustration of teaching is perhaps best illustrated by the responses of teachers when asked to identify the biggest problems facing public schools in their community. The lack of parents' interest and support comes in first by a wide margin. Drug and alcohol use and teenage pregnancies are other frequently noted problems. Another concern is discipline. Disruptive behavior by students, which is most likely in large schools in urban areas, spoils the learning environment. More than 100,000 assaults on teachers have been reported for a single year.[13] Enormous stress on teachers is created by disruptive classroom situations.

Because of these and other dissatisfactions, severe shortages of teachers, especially in the fields of mathematics, science, and foreign languages, developed in the late 1970s and 1980s. Meanwhile, the number of schoolchildren began increasing in 1986, following ten years of decline, and this trend is expected to continue until the "baby-boom echo" leaves the classroom in ten to twenty years. Teacher resignations and retirements have exacerbated the shortage. By 1994, the United States will require nearly one million new teachers, but many fewer will be available if current trends continue.[14]

Before reviewing the responses of the national, state, and local governments to these critical problems in American public education, we now look at how intergovernmental relationships have evolved.

······································

Intergovernmental Roles in Education

The responsibility for establishing, supporting, and overseeing public schools is reserved to the states under the Tenth Amendment and specifically provided for in the state constitutions. Day-to-day operating authority is delegated to local governments by all states except Hawaii, which has established a unitary, state-run system. Ninety percent of American primary and secondary school systems are operated by independent school districts, but cities, counties, towns, or townships run the schools in some states. Although "local control" is the tradition, the states have always been the dominant policymakers, deciding such important issues as the duration of the school year, curriculum requirements, textbook selection, teacher certification and compensation, minimum graduation requirements, and pupil-teacher ratios. The selection and dismissal of teachers, certain budget decisions, and management and operating details are carried out locally.

State involvement is growing substantially and is stronger than ever before, largely because of forceful actions taken to address the current education crisis. Centralization of state authority in education policy has always been greatest in the South, where poverty and race relations have called for high levels of state intervention. The tradition of local autonomy is strongest in New England. However, it is difficult to identify a single important school policy issue today that is not subject to state, rather than local, determination.

State and Local Roles

Since around 1965 there has been a steady trend of more state involvement in the public schools, as citizens and policymakers have lost confidence in the schools' ability to provide a quality education. In several states, local school systems have essentially lost their independence as the states have assumed full operational responsibilities. Such centralization is happening primarily because local school districts are unable to cope successfully with political and financial pressures.

Political Pressures   Political pressures rose to new heights in the 1960s as teachers, minority groups, and parents made new and controversial demands on their schools. Teachers formed unions and sought to bargain collectively over salaries and working conditions. Minority groups wanted to desegregate all-white schools. Bilingual education became an issue in states with large Hispanic populations. Religious groups fought to keep prayer in the classroom. Many local school boards wilted under the crescendo of demands, and teachers, minority groups, parents, and other parties interested in education policy have more and more often taken their demands to the next highest political level—to the governor, the state legislature, the courts, and the state board of education. In this way, school politics, once the province of local school boards and professional educators, has evolved into interest group politics at the state level.

Financial Pressures   The second factor behind state centralization has to do with increased financial pressures on the schools. Historically, schools have been funded largely through revenues derived from a tax on property. A school district can assess taxes only on property within its local boundaries, so wealthy districts with a lot of highly valued residential and/or commercial property can afford to finance public schools at high levels, whereas poor districts (even though they often tax their property at much higher rates than wealthy districts) tend to raise fewer dollars because of their lower property values. The consequence of financial inequities is that some children receive a more expensive, and possibly better, education than others, even though their parents may contribute fewer tax dollars. Frequently, it is the children of the poor and racial minorities who fare the worst.[15]

There is an important constitutional component of the states' assumption of financial responsibility for public schools. In the landmark case of *Serrano* v. *Priest* (1971), the California Supreme Court declared that inequalities in school district spending resulting from variations in taxable wealth were unconstitutional. The court observed that local control is a "cruel illusion"; poor districts simply cannot achieve excellence in education because of a low tax base, no matter how highly property is taxed.[16] Therefore, education must be considered a fundamental interest of the state; that is, the state must ensure that expenditures on education are not determined primarily by the tax wealth of the school district.

Following *Serrano,* lawsuits were filed in other states by plaintiffs who sought to have their own property tax–based systems declared unconstitutional. One of these cases, *San Antonio Independent School District* v. *Rodriguez* (1973), made its way to the U.S. Supreme Court. A federal district court had found the Texas school finance system to be unconstitutional under the equal protection clause

Problem Solving 15.1

Kentucky Reinvents Public Education

The Problem: On June 8, 1989, the Kentucky Supreme Court ruled on a suit alleging inequitable funding of public schools. The court not only found school financing to be unfair; it also declared the entire state education system to be unconstitutional and ordered the legislature to devise a new system.

The Solution: Governor Wallace Wilkinson and the Kentucky legislature appointed a 22-member task force to draft reform legislation. Ten months later, the governor signed the 906-page Kentucky Education Reform Act (KERA) and raised the state sales and income taxes to pay $1.3 billion for the first two years of implementation.

The pacesetting KERA is the most far-reaching state education reform ever, with the goal of reinventing elementary and secondary education in pursuit of equity and excellence. To ensure "substantially uniform" school spending, a new foundation level of $2,900 per pupil has been set. Incentives are provided to encourage school districts to raise their own education contributions above the minimum.

Excellence is being pursued through a five-year plan to expand preschool programs and after-school tutorial sessions, offer extensive teacher training, establish tougher curriculum standards, develop an assessment program with bonuses and/or sanctions for individual schools, and experiment with innovations such as ungraded kindergarten through third-grade classes. Local innovations are encouraged through school-based decision-making committees composed of teachers, principals, and parents.

Although it is too soon to evaluate the results of KERA, the nation's entire education community is watching with great interest.

Sources: Rochelle L. Stanfield, "Equity and Excellence," _National Journal_ (November 23, 1991): 2860–64. William Celis III, "Locally Running Kentucky Schools Leads to Rewards, and Some Stress," _New York Times_ (July 3, 1991): B5.

of the Fourteenth Amendment. However, the Burger Court reversed the lower court, holding that education is not a fundamental right under the Constitution (it is not even mentioned). Although the finance system in Texas resulted in unequal school expenditures, the Court did not find "that such disparities are the products of a system that is so irrational as to be invidiously discriminatory."[17] The issue was thus placed exclusively in the constitutional domain of the states, which would have to rely on their own constitutions to prevent arbitrary circumstances from predetermining the quality of a child's education.

A total of twenty-five state supreme courts have heard cases on educational financing, and suits are pending in at least eight others. Twelve states have determined that existing funding schemes were unconstitutional and have ordered equal funding for poor districts; Texas, Montana, New Jersey, and Kentucky are the most recent. (Problem Solving 15.1 describes the Kentucky case.) A recent study of these cases found that courts declaring unconstitutional spending disparities tend to have more liberal, active justices than courts that uphold school finance systems. Courts are also more likely to strike down as unconstitutional weak school systems and those with the most extreme disparities.[18]

All states have made efforts to equalize funding among school districts, usually by applying distribution formulas (the equalization formulas noted in Chap-

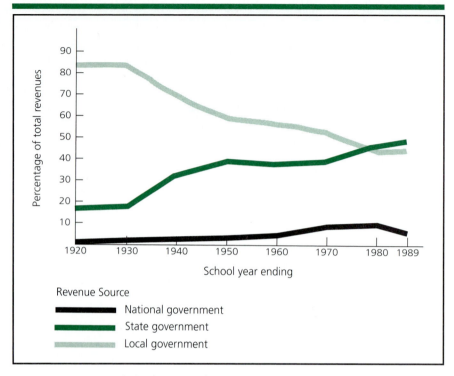

Source: U.S. Department of Education, Center for Statistics, *Digest of Education Statistics, 1990* (Washington, D.C.: U.S. Government Printing Office, 1990).

Figure 15.2

Trends in Revenue Sources for Public Elementary and Secondary Education, 1920–1989

Elementary and secondary education have received the greatest portion of revenues from state government since 1979. The national contribution declined markedly during the Reagan years.

ter 11) for state aid that take into account property values and property tax effort in individual districts. Most increased state financing has been targeted to districts with low property values through "foundation programs," which seek to provide all school districts with a minimum level of funding per pupil while furnishing extra financing to poor districts. From 1969 to 1979, state aid to the schools grew by 44.5 percent in real (noninflated) dollars, substantially surpassing new local and national allocations,[19] and the percentage of total state aid to education exceeded local government contributions for the first time in 1979. Figure 15.2 displays the increasing state revenue contributions for public schools since 1920. Note that local governments' share has plummeted since data were first collected in 1919, and that the federal portion has been declining for the last decade.

The Impact of Property Tax Cuts   Additional impetus to state assumption of school costs was provided by Proposition 13 in California and by similar state legacies of the taxpayer revolt of the late 1970s and early 1980s. Statutory and state constitutional limitations on taxing were typically aimed at the increasingly unpopular property tax. If public schools were to avoid closing their doors or other draconian measures to adjust to revenue shortfalls, the states had to increase their education contributions. In California, for example, Proposition

13 followed *Serrano* v. *Priest* by seven years. The consequence was a severe erosion of local property tax dollars for public education, in spite of the state supreme court order for more funds for poor districts. The local share of school funding dropped from 70 percent in 1970 to 20 percent in 1982,[20] and the state picked up the difference.

The California case also illustrates an important principle of education policy in the 1990s: State centralization and control follow financial responsibility. A long tradition of local control of schools was displaced as California state government became the prime education-policy decision maker. Local school districts in California and some other states have become mere administrative appendages of the state government.[21]

Remaining Inequities Although centralization of state control of education and efforts to equalize funding for poor districts have proceeded in all states, inequities continue to exist. A recent study indicates that nine out of ten state aid dollars are distributed on the basis of the number of pupils in a district rather than according to need.[22] Anyone who compares a wealthy suburban school with one in a poor rural district or in an urban ghetto cannot fail to be impressed by the differences in facilities and resources.

Although a great deal of progress has been made and the worst disparities have been eliminated, comparisons of state education spending reveal some abiding inequities. The reason is simple: Wealthy states can afford to allocate more money to schools than poor states can. Table 15.1 shows average state expenditures and national rankings for 1990.

Common sense tells us that money is related to the quality of schooling. Modern, well-designed buildings, up-to-date equipment, the latest learning materials, and an adequate heating and cooling system should enhance the quality of education. And schools that can afford to hire the best teachers and maintain low pupil-teacher ratios should be more effective than those with large classrooms and inexperienced or poorly prepared teaching staff. But research has revealed an astonishing paradox: There is no significant statistical relationship between school resources and student performance.

The first research to reach this conclusion was the so-called Coleman Report in 1966.[23] Sociologist James S. Coleman examined thousands of school situations and discovered that curricula, facilities, class size, expenditures, and other resource factors were not associated with achievement. He *did* find that the family and socioeconomic backgrounds of students influenced performance. For example, black students performed better in predominantly white schools than in predominantly black schools—a finding that later served as the grounds for busing to put an end to school segregation. Coleman's staggering conclusions have been followed by more than 150 related studies. An extensive review of 120 of these determined that only 18 found a statistically significant positive relationship between school expenditures and student performance. The conclusion is that no strong or systematic relationship exists between them.[24]

Thus, equity in school financing does not necessarily translate into equal effectiveness among schools. Controlling for the effects of inflation, total national spending on K–12 education grew nearly 80 percent from 1970 to 1990;

| State | Average Expenditures per Pupil* | |
	Amount	Rank
U.S. Average	$4,890	
Alabama	3,314	46
Alaska	7,252	5
Arizona	3,853	39
Arkansas	3,272	48
California	4,598	24
Colorado	4,580	26
Connecticut	7,934	3
Delaware	5,848	9
District of Columbia	7,407	4
Florida	5,051	19
Georgia	4,456	28
Hawaii	4,504	27
Idaho	3,037	50
Illinois	4,853	21
Indiana	4,126	36
Iowa	4,590	25
Kansas	4,706	22
Kentucky	3,824	40
Louisiana	3,457	45
Maine	5,577	12
Maryland	5,887	8
Massachusetts	6,170	7
Michigan	5,073	18
Minnesota	5,114	16
Mississippi	3,151	49

* Based on average daily attendance.

yet measurable quality improvements have been only marginal, as shown by SAT scores and other indicators. Something approaching equitable spending at the national and state levels is probably a prerequisite of education excellence, but money alone is not the answer. During the recession of 1990–1992, where to get the money for equalization and the pursuit of excellence became a salient question for many states and school districts. From Washington came exhortations, pronouncements, and plans—but little new money.

The National Role

The United States government has traditionally played a minimal role in primary and secondary education, especially when compared with most other countries,

Table 15.1
(cont.)

State	Average Expenditures per Pupil*	
	Amount	Rank
Missouri	$4,226	32
Montana	4,147	34
Nebraska	3,874	38
Nevada	4,387	30
New Hampshire	5,149	15
New Jersey	8,439	1
New Mexico	4,180	33
New York	8,094	2
North Carolina	4,386	31
North Dakota	3,581	42
Ohio	4,394	29
Oklahoma	3,484	44
Oregon	5,085	17
Pennsylvania	5,670	11
Rhode Island	6,523	6
South Carolina	3,731	41
South Dakota	3,312	47
Tennessee	3,503	43
Texas	4,056	37
Utah	2,733	51
Vermont	5,418	13
Virginia	5,000	20
Washington	4,638	23
West Virginia	4,146	35
Wisconsin	5,703	10
Wyoming	5,281	14

Source: National Education Association, as reported in U.S. Department of Education, Center for Statistics, Digest of Education Statistics, 1991 (Washington, D.C.: U.S. Government Printing Office, 1991), p. 149.

where public education is treated as a national responsibility. For instance, the first grant of money for education came only in 1917, when the Smith-Hughes Act financed vocational education in secondary schools. Much later, the National Defense Education Act provided funds to improve math, science, and foreign-language education following the humiliation of the Soviet Sputnik launching.

The national role was substantially enlarged during the 1960s and 1970s, primarily through the Elementary and Secondary Education Act of 1965 (ESEA), which emerged after years of negotiations among groups interested in public education. The ESEA established a direct national subsidy for education, providing funds to virtually every school district in the United States. Amounts were allocated for library acquisitions, audiovisual materials, teachers' aides, and compensatory programs for children of poor families and for the mentally and physically handicapped. ESEA monies were originally distributed in accordance with a formula that favored wealthy states, even though the program was considered to be an important component in the Johnson administration's War on Poverty.[25] Later, the formula was amended to the advantage of poor states. Parochial (religious) schools also benefited from ESEA funding, although no funds were provided for religious materials or courses or for teacher salaries.

During this period the national government assumed policy leadership in education. The Head Start program helped prepare poor children for school and provided many of them with their first medical, dental, and nutritional care. Matching grants encouraged states and localities to experiment with other programs, and research findings, statistics, and new policy information were disseminated by the National Institute of Education and the National Center for Education Statistics. Other national entities furnished consulting and technical aid to local schools and state education departments. The national commitment to public schools received a symbolic boost in 1979, when the Carter administration created the U.S. Department of Education. (Education previously held "office" status as part of the Department of Health, Education, and Welfare.)

These new commitments brought the national share of total school expenditures from 4.4 percent in 1960 to 9 percent in 1980. Ronald Reagan unsuccessfully sought to abolish the U.S. Department of Education but did succeed in drastically cutting national aid to education. By 1990, the federal government's proportion of education expenditures had declined to 6.0 percent, the lowest level in more than twenty-five years (see Figure 15.2).

George Bush's self-anointment as the "education president" has meant little in terms of direct federal financial aid for schooling. He did, however, eventually appoint as secretary of the U.S. Department of Education a highly respected former governor and education reform leader, Lamar Alexander of Tennessee. In 1991, three years into his first term, President Bush joined Alexander in announcing a much-publicized education initiative—America 2000. Included were a national network of 535 "new American schools" (one for each congressional district) to experiment with new teaching methods, technologies, and organizational arrangements; a proposal for a national achievement test for fourth-, eighth-, and twelfth-graders; and a controversial call for parental choice in selecting their children's schools. The president planned to raise $200 million from the business community for research on his proposal to "invent the school of the future."[26] By mid-1992, however, Bush's education policy initiative was disabled by Congress and dead-at-sea.

···

Actors in Education Policy

The proliferation of independent school districts in the latter part of the nineteenth century was accompanied by intensive politicization. School districts in big cities and rural areas alike were as likely to hire teachers and principals on the basis of patronage as for professional competence. Reformers (mostly professional educators) struggled to remove partisan politics from the public schools by electing school boards on a nonpartisan, at-large basis, and by giving the primary responsibility for running school systems to professionals.[27] These efforts were successful, but a new type of politics arose as teachers, school administrators, and state-level education actors began to dominate policy decisions.

Let us now consider the "education establishment": the teachers, the local school boards, the chief state school officers, the state board of education, and the state department of education. After that we will turn to the new power-wielders in school policy: the governors, legislators, judges, and the business sector.

The Education Establishment

In the past, the members of the education establishment tried to dominate school policymaking by resolving issues among themselves, then presenting a united front before legislative bodies and the governor. They constituted a very powerful political coalition that managed to win substantial financial commitments to the schools. Because of the political pressures we have already mentioned, however, the education establishment is fractured today in most (if not all) states.

Teachers   Teachers had little power or influence outside the classroom until they began to organize into professional associations and unions. Before the 1960s, teacher organizations, particularly the National Education Association (NEA), focused their attention on school improvement rather than on the economic well-being of teachers themselves. Teachers and administrators maintained a common front before the state legislature. Gradually, however, a newer teacher organization challenged the dominance and docility of the NEA, especially in large cities. This rival organization, the American Federation of Teachers (AFT), openly referred to itself as a labor union and struggled to win collective bargaining rights for teachers. When the AFT was elected in 1961 as the bargaining agent for teachers in New York City, the handwriting was on the blackboard. Both the NEA and the AFT lobbied for state legislation permitting collective bargaining in the late 1960s and 1970s and concentrated their efforts on winning better pay and working conditions for teachers. Today more than two-thirds of the nation's schoolteachers belong to one of these groups. However, many NEA locals, primarily in the southern and western states, still do not engage in collective bargaining, either because they choose not to or because their state does not permit it.

Teacher militancy accompanied unionization. Strikes and other job actions disrupted many local school districts as teachers battled for higher pay, fewer nonteaching duties, and related demands. The explosion of teacher unions forever fragmented the education lobby in most states, as teachers sought to look out for their own interests rather than the interests of school administrators. Teachers are the most influential of education interest groups at the state level.[28]

Oklahoma offers a recent example of teacher union strength. An eight-month special session of the Oklahoma legislature produced an education improvement package in 1990 to raise teacher pay, equalize funding between counties, and raise school accreditation standards. When the Senate balked at hiking the state sales and corporate and personal income taxes to pay for it, Oklahoma teachers went out on strike; 5,000 marched on the capitol. The Senate reconsidered its decision and enacted the bill into law.[29]

Local School Boards Another member of the education establishment, the local school board (LSB), is a legislative body responsible for administering public education at the local level. There are approximately 16,000 of these local bodies in the United States. Local school boards are made up of laypeople, not representatives of the professional education community. Board members are elected by voters in independent school districts in most states, although some or all of them are appointed by local legislative delegations in several southern states. The average board size is five to seven members.

The original American ideal of local control of public schools lodged its faith in local school boards, which were popularly elected and therefore responsive to citizens' opinions and points of view. In fact, their true authority has never equaled the myth of local control. Recently, the influence of LSBs has reached very low levels indeed. In one case, the management of a public school system has been turned over to a private university. In 1989, Boston University contracted to run the schools of Chelsea, Massachusetts, after the Chelsea school board failed to deal successfully with the system's problems. Recently, some school boards (for example, the board of Duluth, Minnesota) have contracted with private firms to run their schools.

School boards still determine school taxes and levy them on real estate in the district. They also continue to hire district superintendents of education and school administrators, approve teacher appointments, determine building and facility needs, set salary levels for certain personnel, and debate program needs. However, such issues are increasingly influenced by state standards and regulations. Moreover, LSBs often rely on their appointed superintendents to make such decisions.

The decline of school board power is also due to teacher collective bargaining, which often determines such matters as teacher compensation, working conditions, and even curriculum questions. In addition, local school boards suffer from "deep public apathy and indifference," "abysmally low" turnouts for board elections, and widespread ignorance of what LSBs are supposed to be doing.[30] About the only event that focuses citizen attention on LSBs is the occasional bond or tax referendum that threatens to raise property taxes in the school district.

Other Policy Actors Also known as the state education agency, the state board of education (SBE) exists in all states except Wisconsin. It exercises general supervision over all primary and secondary schools. The SBE members, ranging from six in Oklahoma to twenty-three in Ohio, are appointed by the governor (thirty-two states), popularly elected (ten), elected by the legislature (two), elected by local school boards (one), or selected through some combination of processes.[31]

SBEs are administrative boards, but most of them also make policy and budget recommendations to the governor and legislature. With few exceptions, however, they are not significant policy actors. They tend to lack political clout, policy expertise, and public visibility.[32] Like local school boards, state boards of education defer to the authority and expertise of another policy actor, in this case the chief state school officer (CSSO).

This person, known as the state superintendent of schools or the commissioner of education in some states, establishes and enforces standards for local school curricula, teacher certification, and certain other matters and provides technical and other assistance to the schools. She or he is appointed by the state board of education in twenty-nine states, popularly elected on a statewide ballot in fifteen,

Boston University faculty conduct a computer training program at Chelsea High School. The local school board contracted with the university to manage the Chelsea schools.

and appointed by the governor in six.[33] Although the formal relationship between the CSSO and the state board of education varies, nearly all CSSOs serve as executive officers and professional advisers to their state boards of education. Recently, however, as governors and state legislatures have increasingly provided policy leadership for the schools, their influence has declined.[34]

The state department of education (SDE) is responsible for furnishing administrative and technical support to the CSSO and the SBE. It also administers national and state aid programs for public schools. The state department of education is almost exclusively the habitat of education professionals.

Until the national government entered the school policy arena with ESEA and other programs in the 1960s, the SDEs were understaffed and underutilized. National and state financial support in the 1980s resulted in SDEs that are larger, much more competent and sophisticated, and more powerful. They have taken on the difficult job of monitoring the recent state education reforms, and they have significantly increased their capacities for program evaluation, data collection, and research.

The New Policy Leaders

Financial and political pressures on the education establishment, coinciding with a loss of public and business confidence in the schools, fragmented the coalition of actors described above. Simultaneously, state-level education actors and business organizations increased their interest in school issues and their capacity to respond to them, and governors and legislatures added staff and augmented their ability to collect data and conduct research. The strengthened state departments of education have now become handmaidens of the governors and legislatures. Education policymaking today orbits around state government rather than local education professionals, although the demand for, and tradition of, local control remains important.

Governors In the past, governors were weak participants in school policymaking. They rarely exercised leadership on education issues, leaving such matters in the hands of the education establishment. As school politics became energized in the 1960s, however, so did the governors. The American people usually turn to their chief executives in times of crisis.

Recent gubernatorial attention to education began with school finance reform. Changing the means of funding the schools demanded major alterations in tax policy—a highly charged issue in any state, given an extra jolt by the fact that education makes up the largest portion of state and local spending.

Today, state chief executives are deeply involved in all major aspects of education policymaking. Education issues often receive a lot of attention during campaigns, in state-of-the-state addresses, and throughout a governor's term of office. During the 1980s, education completely dominated governors' policy agendas in quite a few states, particularly in the South: The bulk of governors' legislative efforts in Tennessee, Texas, Mississippi, Georgia, Arkansas, and South

Carolina were directed toward education reform programs, and other pressing issues were placed on the back burner. This consuming passion has cooled somewhat in recent years, but education policy remains the most important "perennial issue" in most states.

In formulating, lobbying for, and implementing education policy, the governors rely heavily on their staff. Many governors have special divisions of education. Staff members facilitate the flow of information to and from the governor's office and the desks of other key education policymakers. They analyze information from all levels of government, in and out of state, and from national organizations. They also draft proposed legislation, lobby legislators and education groups, and attempt to influence public opinion on education issues. The most successful governors have managed to weave delicate coalitions among all significant education policy actors in order to enact substantial reform programs. They are assisted in these efforts by several interstate organizations, including the National Governor's Association and the Education Commission of the States.

State Legislatures   Legislatures have always had the final responsibility for enacting broad educational policy and for state funding of public schools. They were the leading state policy actors until governors upstaged them, and it is still on legislative turf where the critical policy battles are fought. In a few states, such as Florida and California, legislatures continue to dominate education policy.

Lobbyists for the education establishment are quite active in the statehouse, but their influence has diminished as issue conflicts have precluded a united front. Numerous other interests, including minority groups, the handicapped, and the economically disadvantaged, also receive a hearing from legislators. As national funding tapered off during the 1980s, such groups increasingly turned their sights on state legislatures. One writer has suggested that these groups participate in an education shopping mall, with "sophisticated specialty shops each catering to a small segment of the populace," including female students, the gifted, blacks, Hispanics, native Americans, and more.[35] Sometimes the mall becomes rather boisterous and crowded, as competing shoppers fight for limited public education goods.

Although governors are the education policy leaders in most states, legislatures have been rapidly developing their capabilities. They have added education staff specialists, enhanced their research capabilities, and extended oversight efforts. An important legislative contribution is ensuring that reform laws are fully implemented.

Courts   Federal courts, especially the U.S. Supreme Court, are important factors in public education. They have issued rulings on a variety of issues affecting students, such as censorship of school newspapers, personal grooming standards, female participation in sports programs, student discipline, and school prayer. Federal courts imposed desegregation policies on public schools through a series of decisions beginning with *Brown* v. *Board of Education of Topeka* (1954), which declared that racial segregation violated the Fourteenth Amendment's equal protection clause.[36] Court-ordered busing to achieve school desegregation was mandated in *Swann* v. *Charlotte–Mecklenberg County Schools* (in North Carolina) in 1971 and in other decisions involving districts that had practiced government-approved racial segregation.[37] These decisions, and the subsequent busing, were highly controversial and, in many places, contributed to "white flight" to the suburbs. In some cities, such as Boston, court-ordered busing led to violent protests. In 1991 and 1992, the Supreme Court handed down two decisions that loosened the legal requirements on school systems. A case involving Oklahoma City approved the concept of neighborhood schools (*Board of Education of Oklahoma City* v. *Dowell*), while a case concerning DeKalb County, Georgia, schools absolved school districts from the duty to remedy imbalances caused by demographic (housing segregation) patterns (*Freeman* v. *Pitts*).[38]

Yet in 1990, the U.S. Supreme Court, with a scant 5-to-4 majority, passed down a desegregation ruling with profoundly negative implications for American federalism. *Missouri* v. *Jenkins* concerned a 1977 suit against Missouri by a Kansas City school district and a group of minority students, claiming that the state was illegally maintaining segregated schools. The Supreme Court affirmed a lower court ruling ordering Kansas City school district officials to raise property taxes to fund a far-reaching and expensive desegregation plan, even though local citizens had rejected the plan six times in referendums. Civil rights groups heralded the decision, but local and state officials and various defenders of federalism assailed it as a tyrannical court pre-emption of local taxing power and "taxation without representation."[39]

State courts, too, have stimulated and even ordered changes in education policy. As we have noted, a number of state supreme courts have mandated school finance reform to attain more equity in funding public education. State courts are also being asked to resolve numerous legal disagreements spawned by education reforms. It is likely that the role of these courts as education policy-makers will continue to grow during the 1990s, since it is often only through the legal system that individuals and groups representing minority positions can capture the attention of top policymakers.

The Business Community Of necessity, businesses are becoming more involved in the public schools. It is increasingly obvious that high school graduates lack the basic skills and knowledge to tackle the demands of the contemporary workplace. As a consequence, some firms develop their own training and education programs, often incorporating fundamental reading and writing skills. For instance, Motorola spends $5 million annually on basic skills instruction.[40] As work becomes even more complex in the future, corporate education activities will grow apace.

To some members of the education establishment, business leaders are partly to blame for the sad state of the schools. Some industries based primarily on manual labor and unsophisticated skills historically opposed education reform as an unnecessary expense. As recently as 1983, for example, two dominant industries—textiles and retail trade—adamantly lobbied against an education improvement package in South Carolina. Firms are also criticized for negotiating local property tax breaks that deprive school districts of much-needed revenues, then castigating the poor quality of education in those very districts they are starving.

Today, however, most corporate leaders are vocal proponents of education improvement at all levels, from preschool to college. In a second round of South Carolina education reforms in 1990, the textile and retail trade industries strongly supported school improvements, largely because their work is becoming technologically more demanding.

voucher plan

An education reform in which parents are given a voucher, or check, to spend each year on primary or secondary schooling for their children, in either public or private schools.

Corporate involvement encompasses a broad range of activities, from purchasing computers and supplies for a local school and "adopt-a-school" programs to sponsoring "academies" in which students may concentrate on a specially designed curriculum in areas such as finance, tourism, or manufacturing, and then work in paid summer internships. In Chicago, a coalition of seventy corporations has created its own school for disadvantaged children.[41] Business leaders also try to influence the overall direction of public education by advocating performance-based accountability for school activities, decentralized school management systems, and market-based schemes such as **voucher plans.**

Educational Innovation in the States

In the short time since *A Nation at Risk* called national attention to the acute need for educational reforms, the states have responded on a large scale. Some three hundred task forces have thoroughly studied school problems and issued recommendations for resolving them. Many of these recommendations have been enacted into law.

First of all, the state share of school funding has risen dramatically. Many states have raised taxes specifically for aid to education. State support for schools jumped by more than 49 percent ($22 billion) from 1978 to 1983, and by another 32 percent from 1983 to 1987.[42] A broad and powerful coalition of state and local elected officials, professional educators, parents, and business interests has been important in the reform drive. Improvement in education is a bipartisan issue; Democrats and Republicans agree that the economic future of the United States depends on the quality of schooling.

A remarkable turnabout in the attitude of the American taxpayer has also been observed. After beating down school funding referenda all over the country during the 1970s, and having voted for the enactment of taxation and expenditure limitations that further deprived public education of needed resources, taxpayers became much more willing to support spending for the schools in the 1980s. In some states, such as South Carolina, they enthusiastically endorsed substantial tax increases for education. At the same time, taxpayers remained very concerned about how this money was being spent. One opinion researcher called the 1980s the "era of educational accountability."[43]

The states continue to move forward in the 1990s with innovations in the three critical areas of standards, students, and teachers. Every state has recorded remarkable program achievements in at least one of these categories, and a

Problem Solving 15.2

Radical Restructuring of Public Education

The Problem: In the view of a growing number of critics, the traditional American public education system is a failure. Even the recent reforms and increased school spending have failed to address the fundamental problem: a rigid, unyielding education establishment that resists innovation and change.

The Solution: Create a revolutionary new system of public education governed by market competition, parental choice, and decentralized school-based decision making. Two of the leading advocates, John E. Chubb and Terry M. Moe, believe states should withdraw authority from teachers and from state and local education bureaucracies (such as local school boards, or SBEs) and vest it directly in parents, students, and their local schools. Each student would be free to attend any public school in the state, paid for by a "scholarship" funded by federal, state, and local contributions. Schools would set their own tuitions and admissions standards (illegal discrimination would not be allowed). And teachers could be easily dismissed for poor performance. Schools not adjusting to market demands would "go out of business" because too few parents would choose to send their children there.

Opponents of "choice" are not convinced that parents are able to make the best school decisions for their children. They also wonder how the new schools will be held accountable to the broader interests of the community and the public interest. Opponents observe that no other advanced nation has experimented with choice, so there is no track record to speak of. And the few experiments done in the United States have yielded disturbing indications that choice perpetuates or even worsens discrimination against minority and poor children.

Choice efforts are currently under way in New York City's East Harlem, in Chicago, and in the state of Minnesota. East Harlem's students can select among a large number of specialized programs and schools in sports, science, health services, the performing arts, and other fields. Hundreds of white students cross district lines to attend predominantly Hispanic and black East Harlem schools. In Chicago, control of public schools is delegated by state law to local, elected councils, each consisting of six parents, two teachers, and two community representatives who approve budgets, make curriculum recommendations, and hire and fire principals. (Supporters herald the Chicago decentralization plan; opponents say it's like turning hospitals over to the patients.) Minnesota implemented a statewide school choice program in 1988, in which any public school student may enroll in any school in the state, paid for by a voucher system. Other such "choice" experiments are being planned by school systems elsewhere.

Sources: John E. Chubb and Terry M. Moe, *Politics, Markets, and America's Schools* (Washington, D.C.: Brookings, 1990); Joe Reed, "Grass Roots School Governance in Chicago," *National Civic Review* 80 (Winter 1991): 41–50; Kathleen Sylvester, "Schools of Choice," *Governing* 2 (July 1989): 50–54.

majority have implemented reforms in all three areas. States have also begun experimenting with a radical restructuring of public education (see Problem Solving 15.2).

Standards

Standards have been raised in virtually every state. Curriculum and graduation requirements have been strengthened, instructional time and the length of the school day have been increased, steps have been taken to minimize overcrowding, minimum competency tests in the basic skills have been introduced, and special programs have been developed to encourage gifted students.

For example, crowded school districts in a growing number of locales are experimenting with year-round schools. Los Angeles, Houston, Las Vegas, and two hundred other cities have adopted this idea, less to improve the quality of schooling than to ease overcrowding and save money. Typically, students are organized into four groups; they attend classes for forty-five, sixty, or ninety days at a time, then go on break for two or three weeks. Class schedules within grades overlap during a calendar year. Up to one-third more students can attend a school under such a plan. Teachers seem to like the concept because classes are smaller and they do not have to reteach as much after the shorter vacation periods. An important point is that students, too, appear to respond well to year-round schooling, inasmuch as they learn more material at a faster rate. However, the plan does cause certain difficulties: Air-conditioning may be needed, teachers have to give up summer jobs, and maintenance on buildings and equipment becomes difficult to schedule. Staggered vacations also can interfere with sports, extracurricular activities, and family vacations.[44] Nonetheless, expect to see additional districts adopt year-round schools in the 1990s.

Minimum competency testing for basic skills has been another widely adopted reform. More than forty states test students at several grade levels in order to monitor progress in the basics, and at least twenty-five now require students to pass a competency test before graduating from high school. The tests can also be used to identify outstanding student achievement, as in California and New York, or to diagnose students who need remedial instruction, as in South Carolina and Texas.[45] A movement is well under way to develop national achievement tests for fourth-, eighth-, and twelfth-graders in order to facilitate comparisons between states, monitor the progress of various reforms, and move the country toward a national curriculum. Most industrialized countries, including Japan and Germany, require all students to take national exams.[46]

Gifted students are singled out for special opportunities in several states. The North Carolina School of Science and Mathematics, established in 1980, places around 475 talented high school juniors and seniors in a college campus setting. The state pays all operating costs for the school (over $10,000 per student). Students are expected to balance high levels of academic work with weekly chores and community service.[47] Similar state schools for promising high school students have been established in Louisiana, Illinois, South Carolina, Texas, and elsewhere.[48]

Students

Students, of course, are the intended beneficiaries of the improvements and strengthening of standards. In general, expectations for student academic performance and classroom behavior have been raised, and preliminary results indicated that the reforms were having their intended effect. SAT scores in 1985 showed the biggest nationwide gain since 1963, with verbal scores rising five points and math scores up by four. This came in spite of the fact that the number of test-takers has increased—a trend that should depress average scores somewhat, as more marginal students participate. However, since 1985 SAT math scores have leveled out and verbal scores have declined by nine points. (Again, see Figure 15.1.)

Student classroom behavior has been a target of reformers in many states. Strict discipline codes are being enforced, as are stronger attendance policies. In especially difficult school settings, police officers, closed-circuit television monitors, and other devices help maintain order. Most of the states that have adopted more stringent discipline policies in the past few years have made it easier to remove troublemakers from the classroom and to expel them.

Incentives for regular, punctual attendance are being offered in many locales. For example, Boston, Baltimore, and Los Angeles reduce truancy and dropout rates by guaranteeing a job or admission to college to all graduating seniors with a minimum grade point average and regular attendance (Los Angeles specifies a 2.5 average and 95 percent attendance). Similar programs are being experimented with elsewhere in an effort to keep in school some of the 700,000 students who drop out each year, at an estimated annual cost of $77 billion in lost tax revenues and increased expenditures associated with welfare, unemployment, and crime. The participation of business makes this kind of program possible. Firms can set aside jobs for new graduates, offer placement services, and even teach students how to dress and act in the world of work.[49] West Virginia and several other states have chosen a punitive approach to encourage regular attendance by denying or suspending the drivers' licenses of high school dropouts.[50]

Teachers

Teachers have been the beneficiaries (or victims, depending on one's standpoint) of the most extensive and far-reaching educational reforms. They have universally welcomed higher pay, improved fringe benefits, and more opportunities for professional improvement. But they have been less pleased with competency testing and teacher merit pay schemes.

After falling behind in real dollar terms during the 1970s, teacher salaries caught up with the cost of living in most states in the late 1980s. Controlling for inflation, teacher pay increased by 21 percent from 1980 to 1990. Variations among the states continue to be rather pronounced, in response to differences in the cost of living, labor market conditions, and other factors (see Table 15.2). In 1989, teachers in Alaska earned an average salary of $43,746; those in South Dakota averaged $21,510. During the 1990–1992 recession, education spending cuts caused teacher pay increases to trail the cost of living in many locations.

Table 15.2

Estimated Average Annual Salary of Teachers in Public Elementary and Secondary Schools, by State, 1988–1989

State	Salary	State	Salary
Alabama	$26,392	Montana	$25,586
Alaska	43,746	Nebraska	24,983
Arizona	29,859	Nevada	30,216
Arkansas	22,416	New Hampshire	27,976
California	36,339	New Jersey	34,613
Colorado	30,968	New Mexico	25,037
Connecticut	39,125	New York	38,403
Delaware	33,092	North Carolina	26,966
District of Columbia	38,022	North Dakota	23,311
Florida	28,261	Ohio	31,087
Georgia	28,205	Oklahoma	23,437
Hawaii	32,247	Oregon	30,792
Idaho	23,819	Pennsylvania	32,739
Illinois	32,631	Rhode Island	35,867
Indiana	30,731	South Carolina	26,846
Iowa	27,008	South Dakota	21,510
Kansas	28,666	Tennessee	26,841
Kentucky	26,120	Texas	27,793
Louisiana	23,542	Utah	23,942
Maine	26,128	Vermont	28,385
Maryland	35,512	Virginia	30,169
Massachusetts	33,721	Washington	30,593
Michigan	36,061	West Virginia	22,949
Minnesota	32,123	Wisconsin	32,248
Mississippi	23,655	Wyoming	29,006
Missouri	27,247		
U.S. Average	$30,957		

Source: U.S. Department of Education, Center for Statistics, *Digest of Education Statistics, 1990* (Washington, D.C.: U.S. Government Printing Office, 1990), p. 84.

Teacher Shortages   Unfortunately, critical shortages of qualified teachers for math and science courses continue to exist in virtually all states, and projections of the total need for classroom teachers in the 1990s indicate even worse problems in teacher supply. Vacancies were expected to exceed greatly the supply of new teachers in states such as Florida, which needs 11,500 more teachers by the year 2000 but expects to graduate only 1,000 from its higher-education institutions. Moreover, teachers continue to quit the profession because of student discipline problems and other reasons.

The states are experimenting with several strategies to relieve teacher shortfalls. Most are taking steps to entice former teachers and education majors who are working in other fields back into the classroom. Others are setting up streamlined systems to certify noneducation majors. Several states (including Connecticut, Maine, New Jersey, and Oregon) no longer require teachers to be education majors, accepting regular academic majors instead. One particularly promising pool of new teachers consists of people who have retired early from military service, business, or government. Some school districts cast their recruiting nets amazingly far: Atlanta recruits math and science teachers from Belgium, and New York City fills teacher vacancies by hiring in Spain and Puerto Rico.

Not only the quantity but the quality of teachers needs improvement. Average SAT scores of prospective teachers still lag behind those of other college students by 21 points on the verbal portion and 36 points in math. Empirical evidence indicates that states offering high teacher salaries attract a larger number of bright college students into education careers than do states with low salaries.[51]

Other material incentives can be helpful as well. More than thirty-eight states offer special scholarships and loans to attract college students into the teaching profession. Kentucky, for example, instituted a program in 1982 that provides loans for room, board, tuition, and fees for students who commit to teaching math or science in Kentucky schools. For each year they teach, the state pays back one year's loan and interest.

Merit Plans A controversial approach to keeping good teachers on the job is to reward them with higher pay and professional status through various merit plans. **Merit pay plans** assess teacher performance in the classroom and grant larger salary increases to the best performers. **Career ladders** provide several promotional steps for teachers. Those who are promoted up the ladder receive higher professional status and substantial pay increases. Tennessee, Texas, and several other states are experimenting with this approach.

Merit pay plans and career ladders are criticized by teachers when they feel that the evaluation procedure that determines promotions and pay hikes is not fair. If principals do the ratings, they might unduly reward their personal favorites and sycophants. Where teachers are included on evaluation committees, however, acceptance of career ladder and merit pay plans is much more likely. In Arizona's career ladder plan, introduced in fifteen school districts in 1988, teachers are evaluated by principals and fellow teachers. Student test scores are also taken into account. Evaluating teacher performance is not an exact science, but multiple measures and teacher participation help make the process more equitable.

merit pay plan

A merit plan that seeks to reward high-performing teachers with special pay increases.

career ladder

A merit plan in which high-performing teachers are promoted up several career steps, each involving an increase in status and pay.

The Continuing Challenge of Public Education

The states have linked their plans for economic development to excellence in education, and they are providing the sort of national direction and leadership once thought to be possible only through efforts of the national government. Nowhere is the vitality, innovation, and capability of the states in better evidence than in education policy.

But we should not be overly generous in our praise. A wide gap separates policy enactment from policy implementation. More time must pass before we can accurately gauge the consequences of new state programs. It will take a tremendous act of political will and much hard work to bring to fruition the educational improvement goals represented in state legislation. We cannot pass well-meaning laws and then smugly walk away from them, expecting automatic implementation.

The continuing problems in public education are manifold and extremely complex. For example, the concern of state and local governments for accountability in the schools has spawned new problems, such as bloated school bureaucracies in large cities. Most experts agree that school resources would be better used in the classroom, yet mandates and other legal requirements force administrators to complete hundreds of reports and other paperwork each year. As education reform seemingly plods along, many frustrated parents have opted for alternative arrangements. During the 1980s, the number of private schools grew by almost 30 percent, and the number of children instructed at home has increased to more than 30,000.[52]

Putting state education reforms into practice requires the enthusiastic cooperation of teachers, school administrators, superintendents, students, and parents. The unfinished portrait for educational excellence has been framed by governors, legislatures, and the state education community. The local schools must now fill in the details. The states must encourage innovation and creative thinking at the local level while maintaining standards and accountability.

There is an important role for the national government as well. For the first time in history, at a 1989 education summit, the nation's fifty governors met with the president to establish joint education objectives for the year 2000. No one could claim that the objectives were unambitious. They include the following:

1. All children will receive sufficient health care and preschool training to prepare them for first grade.
2. The high school graduation rate will be raised from the current 71 percent to 90 percent.
3. Competency will be demonstrated in English, geography, history, math, and science for students in fourth, eighth, and twelfth grades.
4. U.S. students will be first in the world in math and science achievement.
5. All schools will be free of violence and drugs.
6. All adults will be literate and will possess the skills to compete in a global economy.

If the various education reforms of the 1980s fail to move us toward these objectives, radical rethinking and restructuring of American public education may well be in order.

Summary

In spite of a crisis in public education, for the past twenty years the national government has played a diminished role in public education finance and policymaking, while the state role has grown. Education is the single most important, and most costly, function performed by state and local government.

The activities of the education lobby and of intergovernmental actors in this important policy field largely determine policy outcomes. A wave of reform in the 1980s swept all state education systems into a richness of innovation and change unequaled in any other policy area. The basic characteristics of the reforms pertain to standards, students, and teachers. The results are anxiously awaited.

Key Terms

voucher plan   career ladder
merit pay plan

16

Economic Development

W hen United Airlines announced plans for a new $1 billion mainte-
nance center, cities and states around the country began to assemble
packages of incentives in hopes of luring United to their midst.
Florida, always anxious to diversify its economic base beyond tourism, offered
United from $60 million to $98.5 million in assorted tax breaks in an attempt
to bring United to Orlando or Miami. Oklahoma City put a $200 million
incentive proposal on the table. Denver topped that with a deal worth $323
million.[1] Meanwhile, Indiana and its capital city, Indianapolis, were quietly
putting together a $294.5 million joint-incentive package that proved to be the
winning entry. The United facility is expected to employ between 6,300 and
7,000 people with an additional 12,000 jobs in spinoff development. Estimates
indicate that it will take the city and state twelve to sixteen years to recover the
incentives.[2] The Indiana arrangement includes an innovative "giveback" clause
that requires United to return the incentive money if it does not meet its job
creation and investment projections.

**economic
development**

*A process by which a
community, state, or
nation increases its
level of per capita
income and capital
investment.*

The competition for the United Airlines facility is what **economic development** is all about in the country's states and localities these days. Capital investment, employment, income, tax base, and public services—all are linked to
economic development.

Regional Differences in Economic Prosperity

The United States continues to be a nation of diverse regional economies.[3]
When the headline in *USA Today* trumpets "Country gripped in recession," be
assured that the grip is a stranglehold in some places and a feathery touch in
others. Even within regions, economies can vary. Detroit and Columbus are
both in the Midwest; but, economically, the largest city in Michigan and the
largest city in Ohio are worlds apart. Different economic mixes of manufacturing, services, and retail employment mean different economic conditions.
Caught in the throes of a larger, global economic restructuring, states and
communities are doing their best to ride it out. Some will even flourish. There
may have been a recession in 1991, but you could not tell from looking at
Nevada or Hawaii. Meanwhile, back in the Northeast, the city of Bridgeport,
Connecticut, filed for bankruptcy and the state of Massachusetts put the Boston
suburb of Chelsea in receivership. Different economies, different situations.

Table 16.1 captures the varying economic fortunes of the states. The index in
this table is constructed from three equally weighted measures of economic
growth over a twelve-month period: percentage changes in population, employment, and personal income. The index is standardized by using the national
averages of these measures. Thus a state with a +1.00 index value has 1 percent
higher growth than the national average on all three indicators. From Table
16.1, it is evident that, in 1991, Western states fared substantially better than the
rest of the nation during the recession. With a couple of Midwestern exceptions,
the bottom ranks are dominated by Northeastern states.

Rank	State	Index	Rank	State	Index	Rank	State	Index
1	Nevada	4.79	18	Arkansas	0.45	34	North Dakota	−0.62
2	Alaska	2.99	19	Maryland	0.20	35	Wyoming	−0.62
3	Utah	2.82	20	Kentucky	0.14	36	Pennsylvania	−0.63
4	Washington	1.96	21	Ohio	0.05	37	Alabama	−0.64
5	Arizona	1.95	22	Montana	0.03	38	Indiana	−0.66
6	Hawaii	1.68		United States	0.00	39	New York	−0.66
7	Colorado	1.23	23	Louisiana	−0.03	40	Michigan	−0.76
8	Idaho	1.14	24	South Dakota	−0.04	41	Missouri	−0.82
9	Texas	1.11	25	Illinois	0.21	42	New Jersey	−0.89
10	Oregon	1.09	26	Virginia	−0.26	43	Iowa	−0.95
11	New Mexico	1.04	27	Mississippi	−0.29	44	West Virginia	−1.29
12	California	0.82	28	Connecticut	−0.32	45	Delaware	−1.43
13	South Carolina	0.74	29	Georgia	−0.36	46	Rhode Island	−2.02
14	Minnesota	0.51	30	North Carolina	−0.42	47	Massachusetts	−2.08
15	Nebraska	0.48	31	Kansas	−0.46	48	Maine	−2.19
16	Wisconsin	0.47	32	Tennessee	−0.59	49	Vermont	−2.31
17	Florida	0.47	33	Oklahoma	−0.59	50	New Hampshire	−3.08

Table 16.1   Index of State Economic Momentum, September 1991

Source: "State Economic Performance," *State Policy Reports* 9 (September 19, 1991): 3. Used with permission.

A similar chart several years ago would have produced quite a different ranking of the states. The Northeastern states would have topped the charts. The Western states would have been in the middle, along with the South, and the Midwestern states would have been clustered at the bottom. Therein lies an important point: Economies are dynamic. As one commentator puts it, "Extraordinary growth tends to lead to overheating and an eventual correction. . . . Local recession encourages people to move out and certain kinds of business to expand, eventually paving the way for growth from a downsized and transformed economic base."[4]

Good illustrations of that point can be found in Buffalo, New York, and in Houston, Texas. In both places, the local economies are experiencing dramatic turn-arounds after years of stagnation. And in Kenosha, Wisconsin, where pessimists had administered the last rites after its Chrysler plant shut down, the community regrouped, redesigned its economic development strategies, and is now actually enjoying a growth spurt. For state and local government officials, the challenge is to take the kinds of actions that will have positive economic results. The problem is, no one's exactly sure just what those actions are.

Approaches to Economic Development

Governments devise elaborate strategies *and spend a lot of money* to promote economic development within their boundaries. Although community efforts to spur economic development have a long history, it was not until the Great Depression that the first statewide program of industrial recruitment was created. Mississippi, with its Balance Agriculture with Industry plan, made it possible for local governments to issue bonds to finance the construction or purchase of facilities for relocating industry. Other southern states followed suit, luring businesses from elsewhere with tax breaks, public **subsidies**, and low wages.[5] Called "smokestack chasing," aggressive industrial recruitment had spread beyond the South by the 1970s. By the end of that decade, as states "raided" other states for industry, statistics showed that between 80 and 90 percent of new jobs came from existing firm expansions and start-up businesses, not from relocating businesses. About the same time, pressure from foreign competition intensified. Policymakers feverishly cast about for strategies that would spawn new businesses and keep state economies strong. These efforts began a new era or "second wave" in economic development. States established venture capital pools, created small-business incubators, and initiated work-force training programs in an attempt to support "homegrown" enterprise. Yet even with these new initiatives, states continued to chase out-of-state smokestacks.

Recently, some observers of the economic waters have argued that the second wave has crested and that a third wave is upon us.[6] This newest wave represents "a rethinking of what government can do and cannot do, and how it can do it more effectively."[7] Second-wave programs, well-intentioned perhaps, simply did not have sufficient scale or focus to transform state economies. An **enterprise zone**, for example, may revitalize a neighborhood, but unless there is an extensive network of zones throughout the state, the impact is marginal. Third-wave efforts seek to correct the deficiencies of second-wave programs. One of the keys to the third wave is getting economic development programs out of state agencies and into private organizations. Rather than directly supplying the program or the service as government has done in the first and second waves, government would provide seed capital. Some states already have third-wave programs in action. North Carolina's Rural Economic Development Center, a private nonprofit organization, receives $2 million annually in legislative appro-

subsidy

Financial assistance given by government to a firm or enterprise.

enterprise zone

Areas of a community that offer special government incentives aimed at stimulating investment.

priations. The center has raised $2.5 million from the private sector and offers information, technical assistance, and capital in needy rural communities. In Michigan, six Business and Industrial Corporations (BIDCOs) created by the state use small amounts of public money to leverage private investment. The combined funds are invested in moderately risky ventures that commercial banks will not touch. As part of the investment, the BIDCOs acquire some of the equity in the enterprise. When a BIDCO-assisted firm is successful, BIDCO shares in the profits, thus providing even more money to invest.[8]

Whether the third wave will be the one to rescue foundering states is as yet uncertain. Even as the third wave rolls in, states continue to use first- and second-wave approaches, as the bidding for the United Airlines maintenance facility demonstrates. How to "do" economic development remains a hotly debated subject.

Issues in Economic Development

An economy that is robust provides jobs for residents and revenues for governments. Therefore, economic health is a central public policy concern. Government actions intended to spark economic development are typically considered in the public interest.[9] Still, several questions are associated with government involvement in the economy. These include the impact, the extent, and the fairness of government action.

Do State and Local Government Initiatives Make Much Difference?

There are divergent views on the impact of government actions on the economy. Some studies suggest that many of the important factors that affect an economy are beyond the control of state and local governments.[10] Others contend that government action can greatly influence the fate of a local economy.[11] Both views contain a kernel of truth. One widely cited study of the location decisions of large firms found that a favorable labor climate and proximity to suppliers and consumers were important criteria to most firms.[12] Governments can affect the first factor but not the second. Also, states vary in the degree to which their economies are influenced by external forces.[13]

The debatable effect of government actions on the economy contributed to Rhode Island voters' rejection of the Greenhouse Compact in 1984.[14] Under the compact, the state would have created research "greenhouses" to generate high-technology products; it also would have provided subsidies to promising industries.[15] Of the total project costs (estimated to be $250 million), $40 million were to be generated by new taxes. The overwhelming defeat of the project at the polls was linked to persistent doubts about the actual economic benefits that the state would derive from the compact.

Questions about impact and return on investment continue to haunt state and local development officials. Can the actions of states and localities affect employment levels, income, and investment? Statistical tests suggest that the outcomes are mixed and marginal. Research by political scientists Margery Ambrosius and Paul Brace has shown that, in some places, at some times, some economic development tools produce the intended outcomes.[16] However, regardless of the modest results, governments continue to intervene in their economies. This behavior may rest in the political benefits of successful development projects to elected officials. Or, it may be an outgrowth of business influence in public policymaking. Whatever the explanation, the behavior continues, even into the third wave.

Does Government Spend Too Much?

Some observers claim that government gives away too much in its pursuit of economic health.[17] This concern develops out of the fundamental relationship between a federal system of government and a capitalistic economic system. Governmental jurisdictions cover specific territories, but capital is mobile, so business firms can move from one location to another. Because these firms are so important to a local economy, governments offer incentives to influence their location decisions. The impact of these incentives on firms' decisions is not clear, but most jurisdictions believe that they cannot afford *not* to offer them.[18] However, there is increasing concern that competition among jurisdictions to attract business may be counterproductive and costly to government. As a consequence, citizens are beginning to look more closely at the **incentive packages**—tax breaks, low-interest loans, and infrastructure development—that their governments offer to business.

incentive packages

The enticements that state and local governments offer to retain or attract business and industry.

These incentive packages can be extensive. For example, to lure Volkswagen (VW) during the 1970s, the state of Pennsylvania agreed to buy and refurbish an old Chrysler plant (at a cost of $40 million) and lease it to VW at a negligible interest rate.[19] Under a deal negotiated by the state, 95 percent of VW's local taxes were forgiven for the first two years, and 50 percent were forgiven for the following three years. In addition, Pennsylvania provided infrastructure support for VW in the form of a railway spur and highway construction. All told, the incentive package came to $71 million. To the state, the VW plant meant jobs and a boost to the area's sagging economy. Supporters hoped that the plant would have a ripple effect and spark additional investment. In 1988, however, VW closed the Pennsylvania plant, which had been operating at less than half its capacity for five years. In 1990, when the Sony Corporation of America approached the state about occupying the abandoned plant, Pennsylvania offered a "learn from experience" incentive package worth a modest $23.5 million.[20]

Examples of government concessions to the automobile industry abound—the Honda plant in Ohio, the Mazda facility in Michigan, the General Motors Saturn operation in Tennessee, and, most recently, the BMW plant in South

Carolina. The fundamental question is how extensive these incentives should be. An examination of one recent case helps shed light on the answer.

In 1987, Kentucky taxpayers provided an incentive package worth an estimated $325 million for a new Toyota assembly plant in the community of Georgetown.[21] Half of the state's costs ($167 million) were in the form of interest payments to purchasers of economic development bonds (the primary source of capital for the project). Land and site preparation expenses were estimated at close to $33 million. Local highway construction absorbed $47 million in state funds. Another $65 million was spent for employee training. Opposition to the incentive package came from local small businesses, unionized labor, and environmental protection advocates,[22] but their opposition was blunted by a study predicting that the state would reap $632 million in taxes from Toyota and the industrial and commercial development that would follow.[23] The package was presented to taxpayers as a wise business decision. (Of course, the ten Toyota Camrys that the company gave to the community did not hurt, either.) A 1991 study of the impact of the Toyota plant on Georgetown and Kentucky concluded that it was "a success story."[24]

Does Government Spend Fairly?

Traditionally, government involvement in economic development has taken the form of efforts to reduce costs to business. According to economic development professionals, the central business district, local developers, the local labor force, and existing business firms derive the greatest benefit from city-sponsored economic development activity.[25] However, as citizens began to ask *who* benefits, some state governments refocused their efforts toward direct investments in human resources. An outstanding illustration of this reorientation can be found in Arizona—a model of successful economic revitalization. At the top of the Arizona agenda for economic development are the goals of strengthening education, improving health care, and increasing skills training.[26]

Local governments have been especially active in expanding the concept of economic development beyond a narrow concern with business investment. Led by the pioneering efforts of San Francisco and Boston, some local governments are tying economic development initiatives to the achievement of social objectives, an approach called **linkaging.** A growing number of U.S. cities are linking large-scale commercial development (office and retail buildings and hotels) to such concerns as housing and employment. This movement grew out of frustration over the disappearance of older low-income neighborhoods from revitalized, commercially oriented downtown areas.[27] With linkaging, developers are required to provide low- or moderate-income housing or employment to targeted groups or to contribute funding to programs that support these objectives. In return for the opportunity to enter a lucrative local market, a developer pays a price. This process has been called "the cities' attempt to share the profits of their prospering sectors with their poor."[28]

Linkaging works best in cities with booming economies. But even in cities with more stable economies, local government can negotiate with developers for

linkaging

A means by which local governments use large-scale commercial development projects to accomplish social objectives.

social concessions. In Richmond, Virginia, for example, city officials convinced developers to provide substantial minority participation in a major retail project in the downtown area. In return for city approval of a massive redevelopment project in Jersey City, New Jersey, developers agreed to reserve a certain percentage of dwelling units for low- and moderate-income individuals.

Concern over the relative fairness of government actions is spreading. Court cases challenging a city's right to use linkaging have not met with success. However, as neighborhood groups throughout the country pushed for the enactment of linkage policies, the recession of 1990–1992 has cooled local economies and, with it, governmental enthusiasm for linkaging.

Competition and Cooperation

The characteristic that distinguishes state and local economic development activity is competitiveness.[29] Nonnational governments are awash in competition for economic development, primarily for a structural reason: A fragmented federal system fosters interjurisdictional competition.[30] After Connecticut raised taxes in 1991 to solve the state's financial woes, other states began to prey on Connecticut's businesses. Kansas, for example, offered free trips to Connecticut business owners so that they could check out the Sunflower State and, perhaps, move their businesses. It is no wonder, then, that among influential local development officials, 82 percent described the environment as "very competitive."[31] An example of competition (in this case, on an international level) can be found in Profile 16.1.

Economic competition is most apparent when the stakes are high—that is, when the location decision will mean a substantial number of jobs. In 1991, the McDonnell Douglas corporation announced that it was seeking a site for its new aircraft plant that would employ five thousand workers (and generate another five thousand jobs in spin-off enterprises). In an apparent slap at California—the company builds its commercial jetliners in Long Beach—McDonnell Douglas indicated that it would entertain bids only from communities with "business-friendly" attitudes. More specifically, the company wanted hundreds of million dollars in incentives, including a below-market price on six hundred acres adjacent to an airport, tax breaks, infrastructure improvements, and worker training programs.[32] Ultimately, nine cities submitted bids for the plant. Figure 16.1 shows the location of the competing cities and evaluates their comparative advantages.

The McDonnell Douglas case calls to mind one of the issues raised in the preceding section: Is the economic payoff worth the investment of taxpayer money? Voters in Kansas City, Missouri, apparently did not think so. They rejected a proposed property tax increase to help pay for improvements at the proposed McDonnell Douglas site. As one analyst noted, "Cities and states have been burned before. . . . They have to think harder about whether it's worth

Profile 16.1

Atlanta a World-Class City?

The International Olympics Committee Says Yes. Atlanta, Georgia, was on a roll in the early 1990s. The bumper stickers frequently seen on area cars ("Go Braves and Take the Falcons with You") had disappeared as both professional teams made it into post-season play in 1991. *Fortune* magazine named Atlanta the best city in the country for business in 1991, ahead of Dallas. United Parcel Service and its ubiquitous brown trucks were leaving suburban New York City and heading to Hot-lanta. Delta Airlines had bought Pan Am, people were drinking Coca-Cola products, and the Cable News Network had scored big with its coverage of the war in the Persian Gulf. Residents swelled with pride as the prizes mounted. Atlanta was picked to host the 1994 Super Bowl. But the biggest event of them all occurred when the International Olympic Committee (IOC) selected Atlanta to hold the 1996 Summer Olympic Games. As Mayor Maynard Jackson gushed:

"I felt like an exclamation point has just been laid down in the life of our city."[1]

Winning the right to hold the Olympic Games was no small feat. The city spent $7 million on its bid, designing computerized graphics, producing elaborate videos, entertaining IOC members on their visits to Atlanta, and sending a delegation of three hundred people to the IOC meeting in Tokyo. And although Athens, Greece, had a sentimental appeal—having been the site of the ancient games as well as the first modern Olympics in 1896—Atlanta won handily on the fifth ballot.

The Olympics is important to Atlanta in two respects. First, it yields substantial direct economic payoffs. Local officials estimate that the Games will generate more than $3.4 billion in spending in the Atlanta area over their sixteen days.[2] Second, hosting the Games affects Atlanta's image. It gives the city an international stage on which to present itself as a racially tolerant, economically progressive place. In short, it makes Atlanta a world-class city.

1. Steven B. Weisman, "Atlanta Selected over Athens for 1996 Olympics," *New York Times,* September 19, 1990, p. A1.
2. Ronald Smothers, "Jubilant Atlanta Basks in Success of Its Olympic Feat," *New York Times,* September 19, 1990, p. D27.

it."[33] In today's climate of economic instability, the competition for economic development is fraught with risk.

The debate over the impact of interjurisdictional competition continues. As we noted earlier, incentives and concessions amount to a giveaway to business. Critics claim that competition for economic development is nothing more than the relocation of a given amount of economic activity from one community to another, with no overall increase in national productivity.[34] The solution, they argue, is increased cooperation. However, this objective has been elusive at both the state and local levels. For example, governors of the Great Lakes states have been unsuccessful in establishing a "no pirating" pact within the region.[35] Counties, too, have found cooperation challenging. A National Association of Counties study of urban counties reported that only 5 percent frequently coordinated their economic development activities with other counties.[36] Only

Figure 16.1

Vying for a New Plan
Landing the new Mc-
Donnell Douglas plant
would be an economic
coup. Each of the com-
peting communities
thinks that it has the
"right stuff" to attract
the firm.

Vying for a New Plant

Nine cities are competing for a new McDonnell Douglas plant. The company is based in St. Louis and it has major aircraft operations in Long Beach, Calif.

1 **Salt Lake City:** The company already has a commercial aircraft parts plant near International Airport. The state recently redrew the boundary of a Congressional district so the proposed site of the new plant would not be represented by a foe of McDonnell Douglas.

2 **Mesa:** The Arizona city is already home to McDonnell Douglas Helicopter Company and would be convenient to commercial aircraft division's executives who are based in southern California.

3 **Fort Worth:** The city's bid is backed by H. Ross Perot, who owns land that could be the plant site. The region has thousands of trained aerospace workers laid off from General Dynamics.

4 **Houston:** The company has small plant in area to work on space station program for NASA, but the city is considered a long shot.

5 **Kansas City:** Voters in Missouri rejected a $90 million property-tax increase to fund site improvements, but city and state governments say their proposal is competitive.

6 **Tulsa:** The area already is an aerospace center, with more than 350 companies located in the area, including a large McDonnell Douglas facility.

7 **Belleville:** A trained pool of labor, including many workers laid off from company's military programs, live in this Illinois town, 20 miles east of St. Louis, the company's corporate headquarters.

8 **Shreveport:** Economically depressed Louisiana is pushing hard for the plant. Economic development officials have received 80,000 pieces of mail from residents in support of efforts to woo the company.

9 **Mobile:** The Alabama city has a port to bring in large aircraft parts and a burgeoning aerospace industry.

slightly more (19 percent) indicated frequent coordination with cities located within their boundaries. Economic development has tended to be a singular proposition, with each jurisdiction pursuing its own destiny.

Economic conditions may ultimately serve as the catalyst for greater cooperation among jurisdictions—exactly what has occurred in the Monongahela River Valley area. This 7,400-square-mile section of southwestern Pennsylvania, northern West Virginia, and western Maryland has found that the markets for its products and traditional sources of investment are drying up. Individual jurisdictions have realized that the economic problems are too big for them to solve alone, that the troubled economies of the cities and counties are symptoms of a regionwide malaise. After a series of false starts, local leaders have journeyed across county and state boundaries to develop a coordinated agenda for economic revival. Organizers of the first Monongahela River Valley economic summit conference put it bluntly: "Our theme is unity. We have no other choice."[37]

There are other examples as well. Those same Great Lakes states, where governors could not agree on industrial pirating, formed a Great Lakes protection fund and launched a $750,000 international marketing campaign to promote "North America's Fresh Coast."[38] And there is the Mid-South Trade Council, a loose confederation of six states centered in Memphis. Each member state leads an overseas visit or coordinates an initiative (such as a foreign buying trip) for the other states. If Tennessee firms do not produce the equipment that a Taiwanese environmental technology company is seeking, perhaps there is an Arkansas or Kentucky firm that does. Member states are finding that a joint effort is more productive than a single-state endeavor. These illustrations underscore the new, but modest, trend toward multistate and regional cooperation.

The coexistence of competition and cooperation is not as puzzling as one might think. A survey of state development officials showed an absence of consensus on appropriate models of government behavior.[39] Although a higher proportion of respondents favored a "state-local cooperative" model as a way to pursue economic development, a significant minority believed that a more competitive model was preferable. Interjurisdictional competition is not necessarily an evil, they argued. In their assessment, competition enhances the generation of effective solutions to economic problems.

The Politics of Economic Development

Economic development occupies a central role in campaigns for state and local elective office. Like reducing crime and improving education, it is a consensus issue: Everybody is in favor of it. Each candidate, then, tries to convince the voters that his or her approach to economic development will be the most effective. At both the state and local levels, the campaign rhetoric typically emphasizes jobs and employment.

Most states have created a variety of mechanisms to aid in implementing economic development strategies.[40] Ideally, a state government should be internally united for its economic development effort, but several natural cleavages—partisan politics, legislative-executive disputes, and agency turf battles—make cohesion hard to come by. And because economic development is a central issue, a lot of political posturing goes on around it. In the end, a state government with a unified, cohesive approach to economic development is likely to be more successful than a state without one.

As a state's top elected official and chief executive, the governor commonly takes the lead in economic development, creating task forces and blue-ribbon panels.[41] In the 1980s, these approaches were quite popular. Arkansas governor Bill Clinton set up a staff task force, for instance, by asking the directors of five state agencies to design an economic development program for the state. The task force considered the availability of capital for investment, the skill level of the work force, the retention and expansion of existing business, and local-level promotion of economic development. Its recommendations, as modified by the governor, served as the basis for legislative proposals, some of which eventually became law.

The blue-ribbon panel approach was used by Iowa governor Terry Branstad, who appointed a group of citizens and officials to the Committee on Iowa's Future Growth and charged it with several tasks. The committee reviewed economic conditions in the state and recommended corrective public and private actions. One of its recommendations led to the creation of the Iowa Partnership for Economic Progress, a policy planning and coordinating organization that advises state government.

Most states use advisory boards to refine and adjust their economic strategies as changing conditions dictate. These committees vary in responsibility and authority. Their primary function is to provide input from a variety of perspectives. The composition of Washington's Economic Development Board is typical of a comprehensive board; it is composed of the governor, four legislators, directors of four development-related state agencies, five citizens, one economic development professional, and one representative each from different-sized manufacturing firms, organized labor, financial institutions, agriculture, education, tourism, forest products, female-owned businesses, and minority-owned businesses. Other advisory committees are less comprehensive and deal with specific subjects, such as small business, science and technology, international trade, or tourism.

Once an economic development strategy is in place, the next challenge is implementation. During what we earlier referred to as the "first wave" of economic development strategies, the responsibility for implementation belonged to state agencies. Adherents to the "third wave," however, argue that state agencies have not responded creatively and effectively to the challenges confronting them. Third wavers advocate getting government agencies out of the economic development business and replacing them with more flexible, public-private hybrids or private-sector organizations. The legislatures of Illinois, Iowa, Kansas, and North Carolina seemed to be riding the third wave in 1991 when they cut the budgets of their economic development agencies. Hardest hit was the Illinois Department of Commerce and Community Affairs, which was cut by 40 percent—from $90 million to $51 million.[42]

Greater involvement by nongovernment organizations in providing economic development programs and services is risky. State governments have always had a complex relationship with the private sector. They must contend with demands from a variety of interests, of which business is only one (albeit a powerful one). Nevertheless, state policymakers have generally tried to accommodate the demands of the business community. In fact, one persistent criticism of state legislatures is that they have been *too* receptive to the entreaties of business. Business leaders believe that because their success is central to a state's economy, they ought to be treated as a public interest rather than as a special interest group.[43] So a state may feel that it is less a partner than a captive. In response to the question "Who runs Massachusetts?" one state legislator responded: "The businesses that threaten to move out of the state. They have a chokehold on us."[44] This statement may be extreme in tone, but it conveys the frustration that some state officials feel about their government's relationship with business. It also highlights the skepticism with which many state policymakers greet calls for less government involvement in economic development.

One successful partnership that has emerged in some states is that between industries and universities. The Committee for Economic Development, a national group of prominent business executives and educators, identifies five ways in which states can facilitate these partnerships: state-established centers, state grants to university research centers, research incubators, small-business development centers, and research parks.[45]

One means of channeling state funds into university research is through "centers of excellence," a designation that makes the specific research activity eligible for special grants from the state. For example, at Arizona State University's Center for Excellence in Engineering, the legislature provides matching funds for research in solid-state electronics and thermosciences, among other topics. (The genesis of Arizona's actions is interesting: The center was created after the state lost out to Texas in the battle for a microelectronics computer consortium.)

Government involvement in economic development is extensive. Whether the third wave will carry most states with it into a new era of innovative organizational arrangements remains to be seen. It may, as waves typically do, crash upon the shore only to be quickly followed by another.

Current Initiatives

State governments, aware that their economic development activities have appeared incoherent and even counterproductive to the outside world, have attempted to clarify their role. In doing so, many states have engaged in strategic planning.

Strategic Planning

strategic planning

An approach to economic development that emphasizes adaptation to changing conditions and anticipation of future events.

Strategic planning can be useful for several reasons, according to the National Association of State Development Agencies.[46] First, it produces an understanding of the state's economic bedrock. Second, it provides a venue in which public- and private-sector leaders can exchange perspectives and develop a consensus about the state's economic future. In addition, strategic planning moves the economic development issue from goal setting to implementation. Finally, it provides a mechanism for adjusting and correcting the state's actions in reaction to emerging economic trends.

By 1988, sixteen states were using strategic economic development plans. Wisconsin's approach is similar to actions taken in the other states. Its twenty-three-member Strategic Development Commission was established by the governor in 1984, during a time of economic turmoil in the state, caused in large part by the loss of industrial jobs. The commission's assignment was to analyze the Wisconsin economy and identify avenues for government action.

The commission's analysis revealed an interesting combination of strengths and weaknesses compared to other states. On the "strengths" side were a diverse economy, a skilled labor force imbued with a strong work ethic, a sound infrastructure, and a world-class university system, among others. On the "weaknesses" side, Wisconsin was considered to have relatively high personal taxes, an expensive government, a lack of entrepreneurial characteristics, and fairly high wage rates in certain industries.[47] Armed with this understanding of the economic context, the commission commenced an exhaustive study of the job-creation process. Eighteen months and $500,000 later, it produced its strategic plan. (One-half the cost of the report was paid for by state government; the remainder was picked up by major corporations in Wisconsin.)[48]

The Wisconsin plan differed from some in that it set out three specific objectives for the year 1990: to create 150,000 new jobs in Wisconsin, to lower the unemployment rate to 5 percent, and to increase per capita disposable income by 18 percent. These objectives were to be achieved by preserving the existing job base, fostering new jobs, and adopting the ethos that "Wisconsin is first in quality." More than one hundred specific recommendations were included in the plan. Some of them were aimed at improving government performance through the creation of a business-labor council, the establishment of an office of industrial economics in the Department of Natural Resources, and the strengthening of the Department of Development's economic adjustment team. Other recommendations were more financial in nature, such as the creation of different funds for seed capital, start-up capital, and growth capital for Wisconsin firms. Still others sought to expand markets by promoting international trade and establishing a product development corporation to invest in specific products. Ideally, these actions would increase demand for Wisconsin-produced goods.

The commission's strategic plan became the subject of a special legislative session on economic development and the focus of a series of public hearings throughout the state. Its task completed, the commission dissolved and was replaced by the Wisconsin Strategic Planning Council, a public-private partnership. For the most part, the state has been successful in achieving its targeted objectives, and the council continues its work.

Many states have a less strategic economic development plan and use a more incremental, eclectic approach. The actual programs and tools that state and local governments use to accomplish their economic development objectives are many and varied. Four that are being used as promotional tools in the early 1990s are travel and tourism, the arts, sports, and international trade.

Travel and Tourism

Travel and tourism are big business. How big? According to National Conference of State Legislatures figures, spending by travelers accounts for 6.7 percent of the gross national product and finances 6 million jobs, thus making travel and tourism the country's third largest retail industry.[49] States are actively marketing the virtues of their coasts, their mountains, their Revolutionary War battlefields, their national parks, their cuisine—whatever might attract a mobile dollar. Problem Solving 16.1 highlights an innovative strategy undertaken by Iowa. In 1990, total state spending on tourism promotion amounted to $340 million, led by Hawaii's $22.5 million. At the local level, convention and visitors' bureaus, frequently a joint venture of the chamber of commerce and city government, have been created to promote individual communities and their assets.

Some states are going after the foreign tourist. Hawaii and California actively court the Japanese; Florida and New York pursue Latin American travelers. And among the states just beginning to tap the foreign travel market is South Carolina, whose new tourism promotion plan is aimed at the British and Germans.

Travel and tourism are especially appealing because of the tax yield. Most states levy an accommodations tax (commonly referred to as a "bed tax"), and the spending that travelers and tourists do is also subject to state (as well as local) sales taxes. All in all, nonresidents contribute a significant sum to the tax base of tourism-rich localities. In fact, there is much debate about the "tax sensitivity" of tourists. At what point does tax burden drive tourists away?

One thing is certain: Jurisdictions are vulnerable to threats of boycotts by conventioneering groups. When the state of Utah enacted a restrictive abortion law in January 1991, the National Organization for Women asked its members to boycott the state. And, in 1990, after Arizona voters rejected the creation of a state holiday in honor of slain civil rights leader Dr. Martin Luther King, Jr., sixty-eight groups canceled their Phoenix conventions in protest. An estimate put the economic impact of the cancellations at $39 million. But the biggest plum lost by Arizona in the aftermath was the scheduled 1993 National Football League's Super Bowl—a $200 million extravaganza.[50] During the heated 1991 Louisiana gubernatorial race between former governor Edwin Edwards and state senator (and former Ku Klux Klan grand dragon) David Duke, several groups threatened to pull their conventions out of New Orleans if Duke won.

Riverboat Gambling: A Safer Bet than Farming?

The Problem: To localities along the upper Mississippi River, the 1980s were not kind economically. Factory closings, population loss, and the accompanying tax-base erosion cast a gloomy pall over these once-bustling places.

The Solution: Some Iowa communities came up with an innovative solution: riverboat gambling. Now, paddle wheelers make their way out of docks in Dubuque, Davenport, and Bettendorf carrying farmers and factory workers on gambling excursions. It took the approval of the state legislature and the voters in the affected counties to get the nonprofit, family-oriented riverboats afloat. It was not smooth sailing initially. Some rural conservatives feared that the floating casinos would transform the communities into seedy gambling dens. Others believed that the area would become a mini–Las Vegas on the Mississippi or a junior–Atlantic City without a boardwalk. To mollify these concerns, the state imposed limits on wagers ($5 a bet) and losses ($200 per trip). And the boats began cruising the Mississippi River on April 1, 1991.[1]

Casino profits are shared by the cities and local charities. Riverboat gambling is not expected to solve all of Iowa's nagging economic problems, but the hope is that it will generate substantial spin-offs. Tourism in the area was expected to reach the 2-million-visitor mark in the first year that the riverboats were in operation.[2] In Davenport and Bettendorf, preliminary estimates of riverboat-related development (such as shops, restaurants, hotels, and parking facilities) totaled $61 million and $57 million, respectively.

As is typical with problem solving in a federal system, a successful experiment in one jurisdiction spreads to others. Nearby states are emulating Iowa's solution. The Illinois legislature approved a riverboat gambling bill in 1990 and by 1991 seven licenses had been granted, including three for the Mississippi River. Gambling operations began in Illinois in 1992. In contrast to the Iowa approach, Illinois's riverboats are operated as for-profit ventures, with no limits on wagers or losses. In fact, high-stakes gambling and the glitter of Las Vegas would suit these operations just fine.

Riverboat gambling is not an economic cure-all, but it may keep afloat the economies of these depressed communities along the Mississippi.

---

1. Joseph R. Marbach, "State Influence on Local Economic Development: Quad Cities," a paper presented at the annual meeting of the American Political Science Association, Washington, D.C., August 1991.
2. Isabel Wilkerson, "Gambling Boats Return to the Mississippi," *New York Times,* April 2, 1991, pp. B1, B8.

The Arts

Throughout the country, in medium-sized to large cities, performing arts lovers (patrons of dance, opera, theater, and orchestra) are joining with business leaders to forge a coalition. Their intent is to use the arts as a development strategy. Promoting the arts as a development tool may not be as farfetched as one might initially think.[51] Cities hope that, by sponsoring world-class concerts in acoustically perfect arenas, they can bring audiences of white-collar workers back to the city's center. Such events would also generate secondary spending by the audience (and participants) at restaurants, retail shops, parking garages, and hotels. And just as important, a new sense of liveliness and vitality would pervade

amenities

Comforts and conveniences that contribute to quality of life.

the nighttime quiet. In fact, the accessibility of community **amenities** such as the arts is a factor that frequently contributes to business-relocation decisions. Members of arts coalitions argue that company officials might look more favorably at their city if it regularly attracts Broadway shows and the Bolshoi ballet. And they point out that a successful performing arts center could stimulate additional physical development in the downtown area. Indeed, there are many reasons why a community might invest in an arts strategy.

One city that has taken this argument to heart is Louisville, Kentucky. When the city opened its $33.5 million Kentucky Center for the Arts, some considered it a way of revitalizing downtown Louisville and of countering the state's "Li'l Abner" image.[52] Louisville is not alone in its embrace of the arts as a development tool. In cities as large as Los Angeles and Dallas, and as small as Eugene, Oregon, and Charleston, South Carolina, the performing arts are seen as a key development tool.

The emphasis on arts as a development tool is not confined to those that can be performed. Beaumont, Texas, a city of 119,000 residents located 85 miles east of Houston, is seeking to diversify its economic base (long dominated by petroleum and shipping) through the arts. The city has created its own version of an arts mega-block with the construction of both an art museum and an energy museum and the restoration of a historic library on adjacent properties. These arts projects are expected to stimulate not only economic diversification but also additional development in the downtown area.

Sports

Professional sports and big-league cities go hand in hand. Hosting a professional sports franchise is evidence that a city has arrived—that it is not simply a large city but a major-league city. Only fifty cities in the country host a top-level professional baseball, basketball, football, or hockey team.

Acquiring or retaining professional sports teams has become an important element in local economic development plans.[53] Just ask Baltimore and Indianapolis. In 1984, the National Football League's Baltimore Colts relocated to Indianapolis, and neither city has been the same since. Two cities new to the big-league ranks are Charlotte, North Carolina, and Orlando, Florida. In 1987, they were named as sites for expansion teams in the National Basketball Association. Subsequently, in 1991, Denver and Miami had their multiple major-league status confirmed when Major League Baseball selected them for new franchises. These two cities beat out four other finalists—St. Petersburg and Orlando in Florida as well as Washington, D.C., and Buffalo. Denver and Miami had several factors in their favor including geography, strong local support, and, in the case of Denver, secure stadium financing. (The Miami team will play in an existing NFL stadium.) Meanwhile, St. Petersburg's Suncoast Dome sits eerily quiet, hosting the Kids 'n Kubs (a local softball league made up of septuagenarians) and an occasional tractor pull. And Buffalo, with its comparatively small television market, wonders whether it will ever land a major-league baseball team.

Although the debate over the amount of public investment continues, Baltimore's new ballpark in the heart of the city attracted sell-out crowds to many of its games during the 1992 season.

Cities want professional sports franchises, but such things do not come easily. In fact, cities have to bid for franchises, typically through some sort of public subsidy. This usually comes in the form of below-market-rate leases and tax breaks for the stadium (depending on whether the facility is publicly or privately owned). City leaders defend these subsidies, arguing that the return, both economically and symbolically, is worth it. They point to Cincinnati and Seattle, where the construction of sports stadiums in their downtown areas stimulated additional development activity.

A recent study on the impact of sports stadiums on nine local economies challenges these assumptions.[54] It found that the stadiums had negligible effects on jobs and development; instead, they diverted economic development from manufacturing to the service sector. And a cost-benefit analysis of minor-league stadiums turned up negative.[55] Yet in Baltimore, still smarting from the departure of the Colts, a new $105.4 million ballpark opened in 1992, to keep the Orioles from flying away. After paying for business relocations and demolition in the area, the public costs will total slightly over $200 million.[56] Meanwhile, baseball's Cleveland Indians, Texas Rangers, Milwaukee Brewers, Atlanta Braves, and Detroit Tigers are looking forward to being in new stadiums before the end of the decade.

International Trade

States are no longer content to concentrate on domestic markets for the goods and services produced in their jurisdictions—they are venturing abroad. With the sounds of Patriot missiles still echoing through Kuwait, Governor William

Donald Schaefer was in the country offering medical and engineering aid *and* urging Kuwaiti officials to use Maryland ports and companies as the country began its postwar recovery.[57]

States pursue international trade for two reasons. First, foreign markets can be important consumers of state goods. Second, foreign investors may have capital to commit to projects in a state. International trade promotion, then, is a two-way street: State products are exported and investment capital is imported.

One highly visible means by which state governments pursue international markets and investments is through trade missions, in which the governor, top business leaders, and economic development agency officials make formal visits, most often to Europe and the Far East. The state delegation exchanges information with representatives of the country's public and private sectors and establishes ties that members hope will lead to exports and investments.

State governments perform three important roles in export promotion: brokering information, offering technical support, and providing export financing.[58] As information brokers, states conduct seminars and conferences, sponsor trade shows, publish export handbooks, and offer individual counseling to American businesses. Oklahoma, for instance, has set up an international division in its economic development department to encourage export activity. One of its key functions is to identify export opportunities for Oklahoma's business firms. Once an opportunity has been identified, the division provides technical support to help the relevant firm become more knowledgeable about the exporting process.

Technical support is critical, because U.S. firms may not be aware of the details involved in exporting: working with international banks, complying with another country's laws and regulations, securing the necessary licensing agreements, designing appropriate packaging for products, and the like. The move toward a unified European economic market (commonly referred to as EC 1992)* has resulted in new rules for trading with Europe. In anticipation, thirty states have set up offices in EC 1992's unofficial capital in Brussels.[59] Export finance is also important because, without it, a state's information brokerage and technical support functions are weakened. The first state to tackle the export finance issue was Minnesota, in 1983; it provides a firm with operating capital for the period between the signing of a sales agreement and the delivery of a product. In addition to working capital, some states offer insurance and export credit. The availability of financing converts the fantasy of exporting into reality.

State government is also involved in promoting the state as a place for foreign investment, although public sensitivity about foreign influences on the domestic economy necessitates a cautious approach. According to the U.S. Bureau of the Census, more than 4.4 million jobs are a direct result of foreign investment (10 percent of them are in California).[60] The value of foreign-owned property, plants, and equipment was close to $500 billion in 1989, with one-quarter of this investment located in two states: Texas and California. One trend likely to continue is the establishment of joint ventures, whereby domestic firms join with foreign ones to produce goods and services in the United States.

---

* "EC" stands for European Community.

In a bid for German investment, South Carolina has designed a series of appealing advertisements. With the 1992 announcement that BMW would locate its new automobile factory in the state, South Carolina leaders felt that their efforts had paid off.

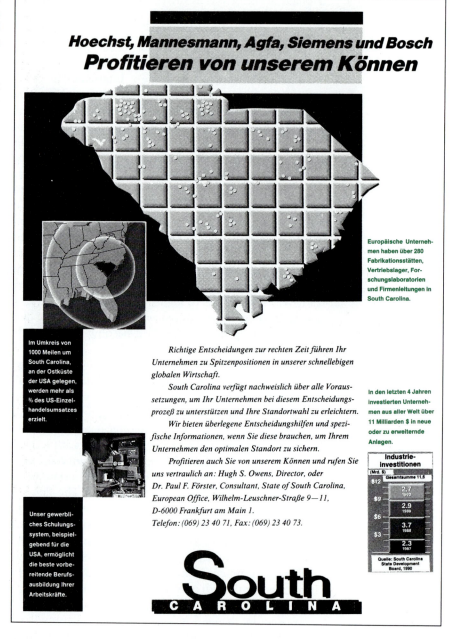

Hoechst, Mannesmann, Agfa, Siemens und Bosch
Profitieren von unserem Können

Europäische Unterneh-men haben über 280 Fabrikationsstätten, Vertriebslager, For-schungslaboratorien und Firmenleitungen in South Carolina.

Im Umkreis von 1000 Meilen um South Carolina, an der Ostküste der USA gelegen, werden mehr als ⅔ des US-Einzel-handelsumsatzes erzielt.

Richtige Entscheidungen zur rechten Zeit führen Ihr Unternehmen zu Spitzenpositionen in unserer schnellebigen globalen Wirtschaft.

South Carolina verfügt nachweislich über alle Voraus-setzungen, um Ihr Unternehmen bei diesem Entscheidungs-prozeß zu unterstützen und Ihre Standortwahl zu erleichtern.

Wir bieten überlegene Entscheidungshilfen und spezi-fische Informationen, wenn Sie diese brauchen, um Ihrem Unternehmen den optimalen Standort zu sichern.

Profitieren auch Sie von unserem Können und rufen Sie uns vertraulich an: Hugh S. Owens, Director, oder Dr. Paul F. Förster, Consultant, State of South Carolina, European Office, Wilhelm-Leuschner-Straße 9—11, D-6000 Frankfurt am Main 1.
Telefon: (069) 23 40 71, Fax: (069) 23 40 73.

In den letzten 4 Jahren investierten Unterneh-men aus aller Welt über 11 Milliarden $ in neue oder zu erweiternde Anlagen.

Unser gewerbli-ches Schulungs-system, beispiel-gebend für die USA, ermöglicht die beste vorbe-reitende Berufs-ausbildung Ihrer Arbeitskräfte.

Industrie-investitionen		
(Mrd. $)	Gesamtsumme 11,6	
$12	2,7 1990	
$9	2,9 1989	
$6	3,7 1988	
$3	2,3 1987	

Quelle: South Carolina State Development Board, 1990

South
C A R O L I N A

....

The Implications of Economic Development Policy

A healthy economy is central to the functioning of government. State and local officials know this and act accordingly. The slogan for Rhode Island's 1989 economic development campaign sums up the attitude: "Every state says they'll move mountains to get your business. We're moving rivers."[61] The ad did not exaggerate: Rhode Island is redirecting two rivers as part of a $200 million redevelopment project in its capital city of Providence.

Yet when an observer steps back and ponders such strategies and deals, a degree of skepticism is inevitable. Could New York City have better spent the millions it committed to Chase Manhattan Bank to keep the financial institution from moving 4,600 office workers to New Jersey? The deal involved $235 million worth of tax abatements, discounted utilities, site improvements, and job training tax credits over the next twenty years.[62] And which state really won when a division of Eastman Kodak turned down Maryland's $4.5 million package of subsidized land, tax breaks, and employee training in favor of Pennsylvania's $14 million deal? Some might conclude that corporations are staging raids on public treasuries. But many state and local government officials would argue that concessions for business serve an important function by creating jobs and generating economic activity, thus improving the local tax base, which in turn funds public services. It may be that economic development's "third wave" will be characterized by more creative and productive endeavors for achieving this outcome.

State and localities continue to experiment with an array of economic development programs, with varying results. A recent evaluation ranked the economic development approaches of Connecticut and Maryland at the top, followed closely by those of California, Minnesota, and New Jersey.[63] Scoring low with their programs were Louisiana and West Virginia. And at the local level, the economically "hot" metropolitan areas in 1991, according to *Inc.* magazine, were Burlington (Vermont) in the Northeast, Orlando in the Southeast, Indianapolis in the Midwest, Dallas–Ft. Worth in the Southwest, and Seattle on the West Coast.[64] As one might expect, states and localities scoring high on these rankings place far more value on them than their low-scoring counterparts do—at least publicly.

....

Summary

State and local governments are immersed in economic development policy. They engage in a wide range of activities intended to improve their economies, yet there is tremendous uncertainty about the impact of government action, its relative cost, and its focus.

The importance of economic development to state and local governments is such that, despite the uncertainty, jurisdictions must press on. Moreover, economic development continues to be a highly competitive endeavor. A combination of approaches, heavy on first and second waves, light on the third, characterizes most jurisdictions. Strategic planning, travel and tourism, the arts, sports, and international trade are popular tools in the effort to stimulate economies.

Key Terms

economic development   linkaging
subsidy   strategic planning
enterprise zone   amenities
incentive packages

17

Criminal Justice

When Americans are asked what they believe to be the most important problems facing the nation, they often mention crime first. Nearly 35 million crimes were committed in 1990, one for every six men, women, and children. In large sections of the United States' cities, many people are afraid to leave their homes after dark. Inside homes there are more firearms than ever before, more dogs, and more electronic burglar devices. An estimated 23,700 Americans lost their lives to violence in 1991, with a murder committed every 25 minutes. The fear in many cities is palpable.

Washington, D.C., "the capital of the free world," has become the murder capital of the United States, displacing Detroit. In 1990, 472 homicides took place in Washington—exactly 100 more than the year before. Many of these killings occur within blocks of the Capitol and the White House. Washington's escalating murder rate has been attributed to the influx of cheap drugs, especially crack, and the ready availability of handguns.

How Much Crime Is There?

Crime data are available from two major sources: the FBI's *Uniform Crime Reports* and victimization surveys. The FBI's annual crime index covers four kinds of violent crime (assault, murder, rape, robbery) and four categories of property crime (arson, burglary, larceny, motor vehicle theft). It tracked a sharp increase in criminal behavior between 1960 and 1980, during which time the rate of violent crime tripled and that of property crime more than doubled. But beginning in 1981, the rates of both types of crime began to drop. Seven percent fewer offenses were reported to the FBI in 1985 than in 1981. However, the crime index for 1986 showed a 5 percent increase over the previous year, fueled by a jump in figures from the Sunbelt. And 1990 figures indicated that a record number of residents were victims of violent crime.

Is a new "crime wave" under way? One cannot judge by the *Uniform Crime Reports.* The FBI's statistics are suspect for three reasons. First, they reflect only those crimes reported to local police departments. It is estimated that only one out of every three crimes is officially known to the police. If a greater proportion of criminal acts are discovered by the police through their data-collection efforts or from citizen contacts, then the crime rate will show an increase, even when the true extent of criminal activity stays the same or actually declines. Second, some types of crime are more likely to be reported than others. Murders and auto thefts are almost always reported, whereas larceny and rape victims, out of embarrassment or fear, may remain silent. Third, the FBI's crime data include only eight types of criminal behavior. Most white-collar crimes are excluded, in spite of the fact that their number may be growing faster than any other type of crime. Thus, the index provides only a partial picture of actual criminal activity.

Because of these disadvantages, a second, more accurate approach to measuring crime is used. *Victimization surveys* scientifically poll residents of certain jurisdictions, asking them whether they or members of their household have been victims of crime during a specified recent time period. Long utilized by larger metropolitan areas and some states, victimization surveys have been conducted on a nationwide basis by the U.S. Bureau of the Census since 1973. According to the National Crime Survey, the true rate of crime is much higher than that reported by the *Uniform Crime Reports,* nearly two and one-half times higher in 1990.

Studies predicting criminal activity in the 1990s tend to be contradictory. Some say that crime will drop because the proportion of fifteen- to twenty-nine-year-old males—the segment of the population that commits most crimes—will decline until the year 2000 and perhaps beyond. Others project that drug-related crimes and the growing black and Hispanic "underclass" will drive up the crime rate.

Prediction is problematic, because we do not really know what *causes* crime. We can state authoritatively, however, that it is associated with certain factors. As noted above, crime is most likely to be committed by young males. Approximately half of the arrests for FBI index crimes in any given year are of men under the age of twenty.[1] Crime rates are higher in densely populated cities and states than in rural areas. Urban areas present more targets of opportunity, a better chance of escape for criminals, and a haven for gangs. Additionally, crime appears to be related to poverty, unemployment, drug abuse, and race.

But the issue is more complex than that. Businesspeople are convicted of insider trading and other white-collar abuses on Wall Street that cost their victims millions of dollars. Some wealthy contractors rig bids on government construction projects and Pentagon defense contracts; some bankers embezzle money; some judges accept bribes; the occasional priest or minister sodomizes a child. The underlying causes of these and other sad cases cannot be attributed to economic deprivation, age, neighborhood, or race. Greed certainly contributes to many crimes; the origins of others remain unknown.

Although reasonable people disagree about the causes of crime, virtually everyone with even a passing familiarity with the criminal justice system in the United States agrees that it is not effective in apprehending and deterring criminals. Fewer than 20 percent of all property crimes reported to police are "cleared" by an arrest. For violent crimes the record is better: About 75 percent of murders are cleared, along with 60 percent of assaults, 50 percent of rapes, and 25 percent of robberies.[2] Probably two-thirds of the arrests, however, do not result in a conviction or in any sort of punishment for the offender. Extrapolation from these somewhat rough estimates indicates that a criminal has only a slight chance of being arrested and punished for a crime—maybe one chance in a hundred.

Throwing money at the problem does not seem to do much good; research has been unable to find a link between higher police expenditures on personnel and materials and a subsequent reduction in crime.[3] Most criminal activities cannot be prevented by law enforcement officials, and unreported crimes are very difficult to investigate. The only factors that appear to be associated with higher arrest rates, and perhaps lower crime rates as well, are related to the attitude and tactical deployment of police officers. Aggressive and active police

Problem Solving 17.1

Community Policing

The Problem: Four white Los Angeles police officers brutally beat a black man, with the scene caught on video camera, and are acquitted by a jury of using excessive force. A riot ensues. A Washington, D.C., policewoman shoots a Latino whom she alleges pulled a knife—provoking a riot. Across the nation, accusations of police misconduct are registered; citizens feel alienated from those whose job is to protect them; violent crime soars; police officers become increasingly frustrated in their efforts to balance citizen demands for law and order with respect for civil rights.

The Solution: Community policing. Police officers build personal links to neighborhoods by regularly walking a beat, interacting with residents, and developing a deeper understanding of community concerns. By returning to foot patrols, police officers become more aware of personalities and problems in their immediate jurisdiction, and can more easily be held accountable for halting criminal activities there. At the same time, community residents' fear of crime is lessened by a reliable police presence.

Community policing has become official policy in New York City, Houston, Los Angeles, and many other cities. The greatest success story is Charleston, S.C., which has used the system since 1989. According to Police Chief Reuben Greenberg, Charleston's burglary, auto theft, and larceny rates and dangerous drug arrests have plummeted to levels last recorded more than twenty years ago.

Critics of community policing include recalcitrant police officers who don't want to become uniformed social workers. And in some cities, researchers have been unable to measure improvements in police effectiveness. Moreover, some fear that community policing simply pushes criminal activity into other neighborhoods. In spite of these concerns, a growing number of cities are adopting community policing systems.

Sources: Neal R. Peirce, "The Case for Community Policing," *National Journal* (December 7, 1991): 2982; W. John Moore, "Crime Pays," *National Journal* (May 25, 1991): 1218–1221.

work in responding to calls from citizens and in investigating criminal events seems to help, as does the use of one-officer instead of two-officer patrol units for a more widespread police presence.[4] One promising new strategy is community policing, in which officers are assigned specific territorial areas of responsibility and encouraged to use their imagination and experience in fighting crime (see Problem Solving 17.1).

Intergovernmental Roles in Criminal Justice

The failure of the American system of criminal justice cannot be attributed to a lack of human and material resources. In 1990, there were 1.6 million full-time employees in national, state, and local police and corrections agencies. Total state and local expenditures exceeded $47 billion.[5]

New York City's Housing Authority is experimenting with bike patrols to curtail crime in public housing areas.

Responsibility for confronting crime rests primarily with the states and localities. Municipal police departments carry much of the load of law enforcement, employing approximately 60 percent of all sworn police employees; counties employ 30 percent, and the state law enforcement organizations (highway patrol and special agencies), just over 9 percent.[6] These state and local entities enforce state laws and local ordinances. Federal crimes such as treason, kidnapping, and counterfeiting are dealt with by the FBI and processed through the federal courts and correctional system. The two systems are separate, but some cooperation occurs. For instance, the FBI and state law enforcement agencies exchange such information as fingerprints and details of the movements of fugitives and drug smugglers, and sometimes work together in criminal investigations.

Nine out of every ten dollars spent on police protection and corrections come from the coffers of state and local government—an illustration of the decentralized nature of criminal justice spending in the United States. The national government's resources are concentrated on its own enforcement and corrections agencies. However, Washington has provided certain forms of direct financial assistance to the states and localities.

One of the biggest federal programs was the Law Enforcement Assistance Administration (LEAA). Created through the Omnibus Crime Control and Safe Street Act of 1968, LEAA transferred hundreds of millions of dollars to state and local police agencies during the 1970s to meet equipment, manpower, and training needs. One of the first block grants, the LEAA program was downgraded into a formula grant with greatly reduced funding in 1979. Other national efforts to assist states and localities, such as the 1968 Juvenile Delinquency Prevention and Control Act and the 1970 Organized Crime Control Act, were also folded into other programs or drastically cut back. Among the few contributions during the Reagan years was the 1984 Comprehensive Crime Control Act, which provided limited funding for law enforcement projects, prison construction, and state victim-compensation programs.

Greater national involvement in state and local law enforcement appears to be called for, given the rise in new types of computer-aided white-collar crime, the growing economic and political dimensions of organized crime and drug trafficking, and the fact that criminal activities do not respect national, state, or local jurisdictional boundaries. Unfortunately, more financial aid for fighting crime is unlikely. President Bush, for example, has called for reducing restrictions on prosecutors, making sentences more severe, limiting appeals, and increasing victim compensation, but has not coughed up any federal dollars.

Actors in Criminal Justice Policy

There is a large cast of actors in state and local criminal justice systems. Policy leadership is exercised by the governor, who also has the job of replacing county sheriffs, city police chiefs, and other law enforcement officials who are accused or convicted of wrongdoing. Normally, the governor sets the tone for the pursuit of law and order through state-of-the-state addresses, proposed legislation, and public presentations. His role in the appointment of judges is also important, as pointed out in Chapter 10.

Besides being involved in judicial selection in several states, legislative bodies establish the structure of the legal system and decide which behaviors constitute a violation of law. Legislatures tend to be responsive to citizen pressures on law enforcement issues, as demonstrated by recent legislative activity in such areas as victimless crimes, gun control, the death penalty, and sentencing reform.

Law Enforcement Officials

The state attorney general formally heads the law enforcement function in most states; county and city attorneys and district attorneys generally follow the attorney general's lead. These positions call for a great deal of discretion in deciding whom to prosecute for what alleged crimes or civil violations. The prosecution of offenses is a politically charged endeavor, particularly when it is within the authority of people who are aiming for higher political office.

The state highway patrol, special state law enforcement divisions modeled on the FBI, sheriffs, police chiefs, and local line and staff officers are also important. All are responsible for enforcing the policies decided on by elected officials and for carrying out the basic day-to-day activities connected with enforcing the law.

The Courts

State and local courts decide the innocence or guilt of defendants brought before them, based on the evidence submitted. Courts also can influence the procedural aspects of criminal justice through rulings that specify correct policy procedures in criminal cases. A number of U.S. Supreme Court decisions, in particular, have shaped the criminal justice process. The federal courts have the final word on cases in which the defendant claims that his or her federal civil rights have been violated by state or local law enforcement personnel. State courts handle alleged violations of state constitutional rights.

Critics have asserted that the Supreme Court under Chief Justice Earl Warren made it more difficult to convict criminals through decisions that expanded the rights of the accused. The first of these famous cases was *Gideon* v. *Wainwright* (1963), in which the Warren Court said that all accused persons have a constitutional right to be defended by counsel. If they cannot afford to pay an attorney, the state or locality must provide one free of charge.[7] The second ruling, *Escobedo* v. *Illinois* (1964), required that the accused be informed of the right to remain silent at the time of his or her arrest.[8]

The often-cited case of *Miranda* v. *Arizona* (1966) further expanded the rights of the accused by requiring police officers to inform anyone suspected of a crime of the right to remain silent, the fact that anything said can and will be used against him in a court of law, and the right to be represented by counsel, paid for by the state if necessary.[9] Evidence obtained when the accused has not clearly indicated his understanding of these "Miranda warnings" nor explicitly waived his rights is not legally admissible in the courtroom, as it is considered a violation of the Fifth Amendment right not to incriminate oneself.

The Supreme Court cited evidence showing that before the *Miranda* decision, it was not uncommon for police to extract confessions from suspects by wearing them down through physical or psychological abuse or misrepresenting or lying to them about their rights regarding self-incrimination and counsel. Many believed that *Miranda* would severely disrupt police efforts to obtain confessions and thereby result in some criminals getting off scot-free. Post-*Miranda* research seems to confirm that confessions are now less likely to serve as the basis for convictions.[10] However, many accused criminals decline to exercise their *Miranda* rights and spill the beans anyway, whether because of a strong sense of guilt or because they fail to comprehend the full implications of the warnings. And in the vast majority of cases there is sufficient material evidence or testimony from witnesses to convict without a confession; law enforcement officers must simply work a bit harder to obtain it. In fact, although the Supreme Court threw out Mr. Miranda's confession, he was later found guilty because of the overwhelming physical evidence against him.

Under Chief Justice Warren Burger, the Supreme Court issued a series of decisions that narrowed the scope of *Miranda*. Further limitations have recently come from the Rehnquist Court. For example, a confession that is shown to have been coerced does not automatically compel a new trial if other evidence is sufficient to convict the accused,[11] and an undercover agent posing as a fellow inmate need not give *Miranda* warnings to a suspect in jail awaiting trial for an unrelated charge.[12] In spite of these rulings, the basic principles of *Miranda* have not been overturned.

The U.S. Supreme Court also influenced state and local criminal procedure in the case of *Mapp* v. *Ohio* (1961). Basing its decision on the due process clause of the Fourteenth Amendment, the Warren Court ruled that evidence obtained illegally by the police cannot be introduced in court.[13] This "exclusionary rule" extended the constitutional protection from illegal search and seizure. The police must have a search warrant specifying what person or place will be searched and what will be seized. However, the Supreme Court later eased this requirement, particularly in circumstances in which the police were acting in good faith. A recent case concerned a raid of an apartment by Baltimore police officers, which turned up heroin and drug paraphernalia. By mistake the officers searched the apartment next to the one for which they had a warrant, but they were permitted to use the seized materials as evidence to convict the unlucky defendant.[14] Other recent Supreme Court decisions permit police to ask to search the belongings of bus passengers without suspicion of wrongdoing, and to search all closed containers in a vehicle even when they have neither a search warrant nor probable cause to suspect that a particular container contains contraband.[15]

The Public's Involvement

Another participant in justice policy is the voting public. Citizens make demands on officials (the governor, legislators, judges, police, and so on) to conform to public opinion on crime and criminals. Generally, the pressure is for more law and order, and it results in criminal codes and correctional policies aimed toward that end.[16] Citizens also participate directly in the criminal justice system by serving on juries, which are selected from driver's license lists, tax returns, or registered-voter rolls. Most citizens consider it their public duty to serve on a jury from time to time, and such service does tend to be an interesting (if not always edifying) experience. Occasionally, a jury trial will drag out over a lengthy period; the longest was concluded in October 1987, in Belleville, Illinois, after a forty-four-month marathon concerning liability for a toxic chemical spill. Attorneys for the losing party then announced that they would appeal.[17]

grand jury

A group of citizens appointed to examine evidence in order to determine whether there is enough evidence to bring a person to trial.

Citizens also participate in criminal justice by serving on grand juries. A **grand jury** (which is composed of up to twenty-three members, but averages twelve) serves as a check on the power of the state or local prosecutor by considering evidence in a case, then deciding whether to indict the accused. Twenty states require a grand jury indictment for serious crime; in other states it is optional, or a preliminary hearing before a judge is used instead. Grand juries are usually organized on a county or district basis. In practice, they are inclined to rubber-stamp whatever course of action is recommended by the prosecutor. Rarely does one question the professional legal opinion of the district attorney or attorney general.

An additional function of the grand jury is to act as an investigatory body for certain types of crimes, especially vice, political corruption, and organized crime. In this capacity it is empowered to issue subpoenas for suspects and evidence that it wishes to examine. A statewide grand jury is most appropriate for criminal investigations, because it can deal with activities that cross county or district boundaries. Among the states that provide for statewide grand juries are Arizona, Colorado, Florida, New Jersey, South Carolina, and Virginia.

The Victim

The last influence on criminal justice policy is the one most frequently ignored in the past—the victim. Many victims are left psychologically, physically, and/or financially injured for lengthy periods after the crime. Since 1965, some forty states have responded to this sad fact by developing victim compensation programs. These are typically administered by a board, which assesses the validity of victims' claims and determines a monetary award to help compensate for hospital and doctor bills, loss of property, and other financial needs resulting from the crime. Maximum benefits usually vary from $1,500 to $45,000, depending on the state. Rarely is a victim "made whole" by these limited payments, but at least some assistance is provided to help the person deal with the various traumas of the crime.

....

Two Policy Areas

The nature of any state's approach to crime is determined by the interactions of the various participants in the system. The states' handling of victimless crimes and capital punishment illuminates this important point.

Victimless Crime

victimless crime

An illegal act that, in theory, does no one harm.

Statutes enacted by legislative bodies define what constitutes criminal behavior, and public opinion usually influences what activities the legislatures treat as criminal. **Victimless crimes** are voluntary acts that violate the law but are perceived by some to present little or no threat to society. Examples are the production, consumption, and sale of illegal drugs; gambling; pornography; and prostitution and other prohibited sexual behavior. It is estimated that 50 percent of all arrests in urban areas are for victimless crimes.[18]

Some people argue that such crimes should be wiped off the books, because those who engage in these activities suffer "willingly." A strong case can be made for legalizing, regulating, and taxing gambling, prostitution, and drugs. People are going to do these things anyhow, so why criminalize a large portion of the population unnecessarily? Instead, why not get a little piece of the action for the public purse? Moreover, state regulation of gambling could help diminish the role of organized crime, and regulation of prostitution could help prevent the spread of sexually transmitted diseases by requiring regular medical checkups for the prostitutes. Almost every state permits some form of gambling, such as lotteries, bingo, and betting on horse or dog racing, but only Nevada has legalized and regulated prostitution. Finally, legalizing drugs promises to take the profits out of the drug trade and to reduce drug-related crime and corruption.

Opponents claim that *victimless* is the wrong word to describe these actions. For example, gambling can become an addictive social disease that can destroy individuals and their families. Studies have shown that gamblers tend to come from lower socioeconomic groups—those who can least afford to lose their money. As for selling sex, prostitutes and their clients can become infected with the HIV virus and other communicable diseases. Legalization of drugs such as heroin or crack cocaine might lead to a significant rise in addiction rates and require higher taxes for treatment and health care. And if legalization were selective—say, only cocaine and heroin were made available legally—new, more powerful "designer drugs" would likely debut on the market.

In states where legislative bodies define the scope of criminal behavior broadly, to include victimless crimes, an extra burden is placed on other actors in the criminal justice system. Prosecutors and law enforcement authorities find much of their time consumed by these relatively minor and nonthreatening activities when they could be concentrating on more serious crimes, such as murder, rape, and robbery. The courts, too, must spend a great deal of time on processing these cases. The legalization of victimless crimes would not only immediately shorten the dockets of prosecutors, police, and judges but also render the process more manageable and reduce the burgeoning prison and jail population as well. A less radical strategy is *decriminalization*—the prescribing of a minor penalty (usually a small fine) for certain crimes. For example, Oregon and a handful of other states and localities have decriminalized possession of small amounts of marijuana.

In practice, hard-pressed prosecutors often drop charges against perpetrators of victimless crimes, judges dismiss the least offensive cases or administer a small fine or a suspended sentence, and law enforcement personnel tend to look the other way when passing near a streetwalker or a pot smoker. De facto decriminalization is the norm for many victimless crimes in much of the United States. This is especially true in the case of prohibited sexual behavior between consenting adults, including sodomy, adultery, and the ever-popular fornication.

Capital Punishment

Capital punishment offers a second example of how a state's approach to crime is affected by the interaction of various participants. Public opinion helps determine a legislature's propensity to enact a death penalty statute. Prosecutors must decide under what circumstances to seek the death penalty. Only juries can find a defendant guilty or innocent in a capital case. Judges must enforce the penalty of death, subject to lengthy appellate review. And the federal courts have played an important role in determining the conditions under which a state can legally put a person to death for a crime.

Before the 1960s, criminal executions were commonplace in the United States, and the appeals process was much shorter than it is today. A total of 717 people were legally executed during the 1950s. States took the lives of 199 human beings in 1935 alone. But public opinion began to turn against capital punishment (only two individuals were executed in 1967), and so did the U.S. Supreme Court. In the 1972 case of *Furman* v. *Georgia,* a 5-to-4 majority held that in principle the death penalty did not represent cruel and unusual punishment, in violation of the Eighth Amendment, but that in practice it had been applied in a cruel and unusual manner by the states.[19]

The Supreme Court expressly declared unconstitutional the capital punishment statutes in Louisiana and North Carolina and implicitly invalidated similar laws in many other states. It held that death penalty laws could be valid only if used in accordance with correct procedures and standards, and could be invoked solely for lethal crimes. This position was confirmed in a later case, *Gregg* v. *Georgia* (1976), in which the court struck down a law permitting imposition of the death penalty for rape of an adult female.[20]

However, the Rehnquist Court has taken a different, less restrictive direction on capital punishment. In a 1987 case again involving Georgia (*McCleskey* v. *Kemp*), the Court dismissed an allegation that the new death penalty statute was being utilized in a discriminatory way.[21] And in 1989 the Court ruled that the use of the death penalty for the mentally retarded (*Penry* v. *Lynaugh*) and those who committed crimes while juveniles (*Stanford* v. *Kentucky*) is not unconstitutional.[22]

Several states voluntarily abolished capital punishment in the 1960s and 1970s. The majority, however, rewrote their statutes to conform with the Supreme Court's guidelines. Thirty-six states have death penalty laws in place today (see Figure 17.1). In early 1991, 2,356 inmates were languishing on death row. Texas had 320 inmates awaiting execution, more than any other state. Florida (299), California (280), Illinois (128), and Pennsylvania (121) enjoyed the dubious distinction of following.[23] While statutes were being rewritten and clarified between 1968 and 1976, no executions were carried out. Since January 1977, however, more than 143 people have made the long walk from death row to the death chamber, mostly in the South. Texas is still the leading executioner, killing 37 people between 1976 and early 1991 (see Table 17.1).

Despite the increased popularity of capital punishment (recent public opinion polls indicate that more than 70 percent of the people favor it), it remains a rather tedious endeavor. Willie Darden waited thirteen years after his murder conviction before being executed in Florida's electric chair in March 1988. The appeals process presents numerous opportunities for delay, and it is not unusual for an inmate to spend four or five years on death row before he escapes the death penalty through the legal process. Even though a recent Supreme Court

Figure 17.1 States with Capital Punishment
Most states permit capital punishment, although some have not actually carried out the death penalty for many years.

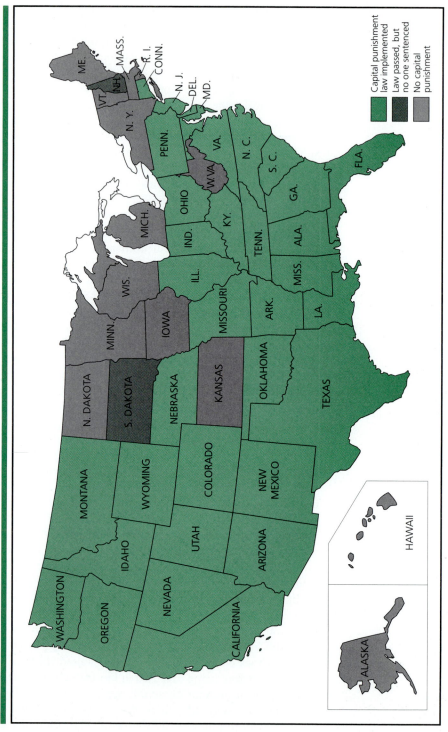

Table 17.1

Executions, by State and Method, 1977–1990

State	Number Executed	Lethal Injec-tion	Elec-trocu-tion	Lethal Gas	Firing Squad	Hang-ing*
Texas	37	37				
Florida	25		25			
Louisiana	19		19			
Georgia	14		14			
Virginia	11		11			
Alabama	8		8			
Missouri	5	5				
Nevada	5	4		1		
Mississippi	4			4		
North Carolina	3	3				
South Carolina	3		3			
Utah	3	2			1	
Arkansas	2	1	1			
Indiana	2		2			
Illinois	1	1				
Oklahoma	1	1				
Total	143	54	83	5	1	0

* Hanging permitted in Delaware, Montana, and Washington, but not applied during this time period.

Source: Bureau of Justice Statistics, Capital Punishment in 1990 (Washington, D.C.: U.S. Department of Justice, 1991).

ruling limited the ability of death row inmates to seek court review of their cases, the process remains lengthy.[24]

One troublesome aspect of the death penalty is that blacks receive it well out of proportion to their numbers. Although black people make up less than 12 percent of the U.S. population, 39 percent of those executed have been black, as were 40 percent of those on death row in 1991.[25] Homicide is the leading cause of death among fifteen- to twenty-four-year-old African-American men.

A great deal of controversy continues to surround the issue of executing criminals. Researchers generally agree that if punishment is to discourage future criminal behavior, it must be swift and certain. Neither of these conditions is met by the death penalty in the United States. And few reasonable and informed people today argue that capital punishment acts as a deterrent, except in the specific case of the unfortunate individual who is executed. Studies comparing homicide rates between states with and without death penalties either find no significant differences or disclose that states with capital punishment actually have higher rates of homicide.[26] For example, Virginia, which imposes the death penalty, has a higher homicide rate than Oregon, Maine, and West Virginia, which do not.

On the other side is the argument for the legitimacy of *lex talionis,* the ancient principle that punishment should fit the crime. In contemporary terminology this is known as retribution. According to this view, some crimes are so heinous that only the death of the perpetrator can balance the scales of justice and relieve the moral outrage of society. The argument for justice as retribution cannot be validated on empirical grounds; it is an ethical question that each individual must personally resolve. As mentioned earlier, public opinion polls tell us that the majority of Americans do believe in this justification for executing convicted murderers.

Correctional Policy

A person convicted of a crime in a court of law becomes the object of correctional policy, which, as its name implies, aims to "correct" behavior that society finds unacceptable. It proposes to accomplish this daunting task in several ways. First, an offender should be punished, both for retribution and to deter future criminal behavior by the offender and by other potential criminals. Second, convicted lawbreakers should be rehabilitated, so that they can become productive, law-abiding citizens after fulfilling the terms of their punishment. Third, criminals who represent a danger to society should be physically separated from the general public.

If correcting criminal behavior is the overarching goal of correctional policy in the states, we have a terrible policy failure on our hands. As we have already noted, most crimes do not result in an arrest. Even when an offender is detained by the police, she stands a good chance of avoiding conviction or incarceration. Thus, deterrence is a fallacy. Remember that the best way to prevent undesirable behavior is through swift and certain punishment. Those of us who quizzically stuck a tiny finger into an electrical outlet in childhood received the shock of swift punishment. If we were foolish enough to try it a second time, we discovered that the punishment was certain. Only idiots and masochists subject themselves to such abuse a third time. That is how our correctional policy would have to work if deterrence is to be achieved. But for a variety of reasons, swift and certain punishment is improbable as long as we live in a humane, democratic society.

Rehabilitation was a correctional fad of the 1960s and 1970s that was largely ignored in the 1980s. The U.S. Justice Department estimates that more than 60 percent of all felonies are committed by previous felons, many of them recently released from prison.[27] It appears that prisons actually increase the likelihood that an individual will commit additional crimes when he is freed. Our state prisons have been called breeding pens for criminals. Instead of being rehabilitated, the first-time offender is likely to receive expert schooling in various criminal professions. Overcrowding, understaffing, physical and sexual brutality, and rampant drug abuse also make it unlikely that an offender will become a law-abiding citizen. Many schemes have been tried—counseling, vocational training, basic education, and others—but nothing has consistently been able to overcome the criminalizing environment of state prison systems.

Without doubt, most incarcerated offenders do see deprivation of their freedom as punishment, and so retribution does occur. Just as surely, prison effectively removes undesirable characters from our midst. These objectives of correctional policy are achieved to some degree, although cynics point out that sentencing tends to be rather inconsistent and few criminals serve even half of their sentences before release.

Sentencing

Sentencing reform has recently received a great deal of attention in the states. The inconsistency of criminal sentencing is obvious if we examine incarceration rates. In January 1991, they varied from 451 inmates per 100,000 population in South Carolina to 67 in North Dakota (see Table 17.2). Southern states tend to be toughest on crime: they are more than twice as likely as other states to convict people arrested on felony charges, and their sentences are more severe than those in other regions. It is interesting to note that crime rates and incarceration rates are not closely related. States with relatively high rates of crime may lock up fewer people than do states with lower crime rates.

indeterminate sentencing

Sentencing in which a judge sentences an offender to a variable number of years.

Historically, state courts have imposed **indeterminate sentencing,** whereby judges have great discretion in deciding the number of years for which an offender should be sentenced to prison. The offender then becomes eligible for parole after a minimum period is served. For instance, a ten- to twenty-year sentence for armed robbery will require the inmate to serve at least ten years. After that time he becomes eligible for parole, subject to the judgment of a parole board (usually appointed by the governor), which reviews his case and behavior in prison.

determinate sentencing

Sentencing that requires an offender, by law, to serve a fixed period in jail or prison without possibility of parole.

The trend of the 1980s was toward **determinate sentencing,** in which offenders are given mandatory terms that they must serve without possibility of parole. Twenty-one states now provide for the chilling sentence of "life without possibility of parole." Determinate sentencing is designed to reduce sentencing disparity among judges. It also eliminates the need for parole. Inmates who stay out of trouble can be awarded "good time," which will deduct a limited amount of time from their terms.

Naturally, determinate sentencing keeps prisoners incarcerated for longer periods than indeterminate sentencing does. In conjunction with the generally punitive public attitude toward criminals in the 1970s and 1980s, which helped stiffen the sentences awarded by judges as well as the judgments of parole boards, determinate sentencing has contributed to a dramatic rise in the number of prisoners across the United States, making it one of the highest in the world. Prison populations have tripled from 100 inmates per 100,000 persons in 1970 to 300 per 100,000 today. The increasing crime rate of the 1960s and 1970s did its part as well. The result is prison overcrowding—the nation's greatest crisis in corrections policy.

Table 17.2

Prisoners in State
and Federal Correc-
tional Institutions by
Region and State,
December 31, 1990.

Region and State	Number	Incarceration Rate
U.S. total	739,763	299
Federal	52,208	21
State	687,555	272
Northeast	119,062	232
Connecticut	7,771	238
Maine	1,480	118
Massachusetts	7,899	132
New Hampshire	1,342	117
New Jersey	21,128	271
New York	54,895	304
Pennsylvania	22,281	183
Rhode Island	1,585	157
Vermont	681	117
Midwest	145,493	239
Illinois	27,516	234
Indiana	12,615	223
Iowa	3,967	139
Kansas	5,777	227
Michigan	34,267	366
Minnesota	3,176	72
Missouri	14,919	287
Nebraska	2,286	140
North Dakota	435	67
Ohio	31,855	289
South Dakota	1,345	187
Wisconsin	7,335	149
South	274,813	315
Alabama	15,365	370
Arkansas	6,718	277
Delaware	2,231	321
District of Columbia	6,660	1,125
Florida	44,387	336
Georgia	21,605	327
Kentucky	9,023	241
Louisiana	18,599	427
Maryland	16,684	347
Mississippi	8,179	311
North Carolina	17,713	264
Oklahoma	12,322	383
South Carolina	16,208	451
Tennessee	10,388	207
Texas	50,042	290
Virginia	17,124	274
West Virginia	1,565	85

Table 17.2
(cont.)

Region and State	Number	Incarceration Rate
West	148,187	276
Alaska	1,851	348
Arizona	13,781	375
California	94,122	311
Colorado	7,018	209
Hawaii	1,708	150
Idaho	2,074	201
Montana	1,409	174
Nevada	5,322	444
New Mexico	2,879	184
Oregon	6,436	221
Utah	2,482	143
Washington	7,995	162
Wyoming	1,110	237

Source: Bureau of Justice Statistics, *Prisoners in 1990* (Washington, D.C.: U.S. Department of Justice, 1991), p. 2.

Prison Conditions

More than 739,000 people were confined to state and federal prisons in the United States in 1990. It is estimated that another 200,000 reside in local jails. Because criminals today are more likely to receive prison sentences (as well as longer sentences), and because probation and parole have fallen into disfavor with the advent of determinate sentencing, the number of prisoners literally increases each day, which means overcrowding. At the end of 1990, for instance, 690,157 inmates were incarcerated in state institutions designed to hold fewer than 598,495.[28]

The Role of the Federal Courts   In the past, exceeding maximum intended inmate capacity was not a serious problem for the state correctional systems. The courts assumed a hands-off policy toward offenders once they were behind prison walls. The administration of state correctional systems was the sole responsibility of corrections officials. But the prime mover of correctional policy during the past twenty-five years has been the federal courts.

In a series of decisions, the federal courts applied the Eighth Amendment prohibition on cruel and unusual punishment and the Fourteenth Amendment provision for due process and equal protection of the laws to prison inmates. In addition, the Supreme Court permitted inmates of state and local facilities to bypass less sympathetic state courts and file suits alleging violations of their civil rights in federal courts. As a consequence of these various federal court rulings, the nature of correctional policy has been vastly changed.

Much of the litigation has been concerned with overcrowding. As more and more people were sentenced to prison, corrections officials responded by doubling, tripling, and even quadrupling cell arrangements. It was not unusual for inmates to be crowded together at the rate of one per ten square feet of floor space.

Drastic improvements were long overdue in Arkansas and Alabama, for instance. At Arkansas's maximum security institution, Cumming Farms, inmates were worked in the fields like slaves, ten hours a day, six days a week, in all types of weather. At night they slept in one-hundred-man barracks. Homosexual rapes and other forms of physical violence occurred regularly. A 1970 federal court suit led to a finding that Arkansas's entire penal system was in violation of the Eighth Amendment. Similarly, in 1976, a federal judge ordered the Alabama state prison system to surrender to federal authority. Federal officials assumed the responsibility for day-to-day management decisions, including cell size, the placement of urinals, water temperature in the showers, and the number of inmates permitted in various institutions.[29]

The entire prison systems of nine states are being overseen by the national government under federal court orders. Another twenty-eight states are subject to a more limited type of federal court order, and four others are involved in litigation in federal courts (see Table 17.3). State officials face the disturbing choice of balancing the stringent law-and-order approach sought by the public and elected representatives with court orders that seem to require them to turn convicted criminals onto the streets to relieve overcrowding. Some have taken what seemed to be the easiest path out of the dilemma by seeking to acquire or construct additional space for incarceration. Unfortunately, this option requires states to raise new revenues for prison construction and operation or to divert money from more popular programs such as education and health care.

The intrusion of the federal courts into state correctional policy is quite controversial, particularly when they have taken over full operating responsibility or ordered increased state and local expenditures for prisons. Important questions concerning the proper division of power between the national government and the states have been raised, as have questions about the competence of federal court officials to run state prison systems. Still, there is no denying that some states have operated prisons under less than humane conditions.

State Response to Federal Orders   However these important issues in federalism are ultimately resolved, the immediate problem for most states is producing more space for their growing prison populations (and finding the money to pay for it). The only short-term alternatives are to release inmates, to sentence all newly convicted offenders to something other than incarceration, or to find new space for lockup. Following a federal judge's ruling in late 1985 that Tennessee prisons could not accept any additional inmates without special permission, prison officials locked up inmates in school gyms, public libraries, and prison reception centers. They also transferred state inmates to overpopulated and understaffed local jails. At one point in the crisis the sheriff

Table 17.3

States Under Court
Order or Facing Liti-
gation Because of
Prison Conditions,
1990

Entire prison system under court order:	Alabama*	Rhode Island
	Florida	South Carolina
	Hawaii	Tennessee
	Mississippi	Texas
	Oklahoma*	

One or more facilities under court order:	Arizona	Michigan
	California	Missouri
	Colorado	Nevada
	Connecticut	New Hampshire
	Delaware	New Mexico
	Georgia	North Carolina
	Idaho	Ohio
	Illinois	South Dakota
	Indiana	Utah
	Iowa	Virginia
	Kansas	Washington
	Kentucky	West Virginia
	Louisiana	Wisconsin
	Maryland	Wyoming

| One or more facilities in litigation: | Alaska | Massachusetts |
| | Arkansas | Pennsylvania |

No litigation pending:	Maine	New York
	Minnesota	North Dakota
	Montana	Oregon
	Nebraska	Vermont
	New Jersey	

* In these states, the federal court no longer maintains a compliance mechanism but the court order is still in effect.

of Shelby County, Tennessee, removed twelve state prisoners from the overcrowded county jail and defiantly chained them to a fence at the state penitentiary.

Court orders to relieve prison overcrowding have brought some states to the point of fiscal disaster. In the 1980 case of *Ruiz* v. *Estelle*, a U.S. District Court judge ordered the Texas Department of Corrections to make sweeping changes in its prison system. Prison officials were instructed to halt triple and quadruple celling, reduce the use of force by prison employees, hire more guards, eliminate internal inmate control of prison activities, upgrade inmate health care, improve inmate disciplinary practices, and correct problems concerning fire and safety standards. In January 1987, U.S. District Court Judge William Wayne Justice ruled that these requirements had not been met and that the state of Texas was therefore in contempt of court, even though it had spent millions of dollars. The aptly-named Judge Justice stated that if the problems were not remedied by April 1987, he would fine the state approximately $800,000 per day.

Texas, hurt critically by a huge drop in the price of oil, already faced a $56 million budget shortfall for the 1988 fiscal year. Governor William P. Clements halted new prison admissions on at least ten occasions during 1987 until inmate releases opened up new space. An admissions procedure was set up so that prisoners could be transferred to state institutions on Tuesdays and Wednesdays only. When capacity was reached, admissions were stopped. Local jails took up the slack.

Corrections officials proposed that $1.37 billion be allocated for the construction of two new maximum security prisons and five minimum security camps for trustees. Even though these expenditures would add some 9,950 beds to the system, projections indicated that another 10,000 beds would be necessary to meet the terms of the court order.[30] Meanwhile, federally ordered prison reforms were playing havoc with inmate discipline and safety.

For other states, prisons are becoming "budget rat holes," diverting state expenditures from education, highways, and social services. California, for example, plans to add 51,000 prison beds by 1995, at a cost of $5 billion for construction and $1 billion per year for operations. State and local spending on prisons and jails has been rising at the startling rate of 15 to 20 percent annually since the late 1980s. Room, board, and care for a state prison inmate averages $25,000 per year. And each new prison bed space for the growing ranks of confined criminals exacts a total cost of $50,000 to $100,000.[31] There seems to be no end in sight for prison spending, because of "Murphy's Law of Incarceration": The number of inmates expands to fill all available space, or "if you build them, you'll fill them."[32]

Local jails have entered the litigation battlefield in increasing numbers. Almost every county and good-sized municipality has a jail, and many have been the target of prisoners' rights lawsuits.[33] The overcrowding and legal vulnerability of local jails, and their increasingly intimate links to state prison systems, have prompted states to mandate operational standards and conduct inspections to enforce those standards. Alabama, Connecticut, Delaware, Hawaii, Rhode Island, and Vermont now have state-run systems. Other states, such as Kentucky, have dedicated large sums of money to rehabilitating local corrections facilities.

Policy Alternatives for States and Localities

In addition to the immediate responses made necessary by federal court actions, states and localities are attempting to devise a more comprehensive approach to coping with the problem of overcrowding. Whatever their past failings, today they are demonstrating an increasing propensity for experimentation and innovation. Three basic strategies are being employed to bring and keep inmate populations in line with institutional capacity: back-door strategies, front-door strategies, and capacity enhancement.

Back-Door Strategies

Back-door strategies include several methods for releasing offenders from prisons before they have served their full sentences. This is the most conventional of the three strategies, but some interesting innovations are being tested.

An unimaginative but nonetheless quite effective way to deal with prison overcrowding is to grant early release to enough inmates such that new admissions do not push the institutional population beyond capacity. Most states have early release programs in place, but the method of implementation varies. In some states the governor or parole board simply lops off the last few months or weeks of sentences that are nearly completed, until the necessary number of inmates have left the prison. Other states apply a formula that predicts the likelihood that certain inmates, if released, will commit another serious offense. For example, nonviolent offenders are freed before violent offenders, larcenists before burglars, drunk drivers before heroin dealers, and so on. An inmate's personal characteristics, prison behavior, and work history may also be taken into consideration.

Early release reduces inmate population quickly, but human behavior is not entirely predictable. Public outcries are certain to follow when an offender released before expiration of his sentence commits a highly publicized violent crime. Presidential fortunes may even turn on such events, as the Willie Horton case demonstrated in 1988, to the detriment of Democratic candidate Michael Dukakis.

Conventional parole is not a very effective program today, although it is still widely used. In most states that utilize this technique, the parole officers, whose duty it is to keep up with the progress of parolees, are terribly overworked. It is not unusual for a parole officer to be responsible for 100 to 150 offenders—a nearly impossible task. Often, parolees can escape supervision by moving to a different state.[34]

Electronic House Detention An interesting new approach to parole that is being tested by several state and local governments takes advantage of fairly sophisticated technology to monitor parolees' whereabouts. Sometimes called *electronic house detention,* this technique requires released inmates to wear a transmitter (usually on their ankle) that steadily emits signals to a receiver in their home. Failure to detect a signal causes the receiver to dial a central computer automatically. The computer is programmed to know when the inmate is permitted to be away from home (usually during work hours). If an unusual signal appears, the computer prints out the anomaly for review by law enforcement officers. Removal of the transmitter also triggers an alarm at the central computer.

Electronic monitoring has been tried successfully in New Jersey, New Mexico, Oklahoma, and several other states, as well as in numerous counties. Not only cheaper than jail or prison, it also enables a working prisoner to pay her own share of the program and, in some cases, to repay the victim of the crime as well. The electronic house arrest program of Palm Beach County, Florida, which has been in effect since December 1984, requires each inmate to pay a rental fee for the electronic equipment, helping to save $42.50 per day by keeping the inmate out of the county jail.[35]

Vocational Programs   Another back-door strategy reduces the sentences of prisoners who participate in educational and vocational programs. These programs are intended to teach convicts skills that can help them obtain jobs once they are out of prison, and they have the added benefit of keeping inmates involved in productive, rather than destructive, activities while behind prison walls.

The idea of "factories with fences" has considerable appeal.[36] In addition to using their time productively and learning marketable skills, inmates earn wages that can help defray the cost of their room and board, provide monetary restitution to victims, and fund savings accounts for the inmates to have when they are released. Several experiments have had encouraging results. One example is Best Western International's reservations center in the minimum security Arizona Center for Women: More than thirty inmates have accepted jobs with Best Western after their release.[37] Another is Trans World Airlines' use of California inmates to handle flight reservation calls; more than twenty parolees have secured a permanent job with TWA upon their release.[38]

Prison industry experiments in other states are now being planned. The major source of opposition to this idea is private business, which feels threatened by the low cost of prison labor. Many states have laws restricting production in prison industries or prohibiting the sale of prison-made goods. These laws will have to be repealed if factories with fences are to proliferate.

Front-Door Strategies

The second basic strategy being used to balance the number of prisoners with the supply of beds is the front-door approach, which aims to keep minor offenders out of prison in the first place by directing them into alternative programs.

creative sentencing

Sentencing in which a judge is able to fit the punishment to the crime and to the characteristics of the convicted person.

Creative Sentencing   One method is to grant judges more flexibility in determining sentences. **Creative sentencing** permits judges to match the punishment with the crime while keeping the nonviolent offender in society. One option that has gained increasing acceptance is community service—sentencing the offender to put in a specified number of hours cleaning up parks or streets, working in a public hospital, painting public buildings, or performing specialized tasks related to her professional expertise, such as dentistry or accounting. At least eight states allow their judges to assign community service in lieu of incarceration. Another option is to link the sentence to available prison space. This about-face from determinate sentencing is being tried in Minnesota, Oregon, and Washington, and is being actively considered by other states. In addition, judges can assess fines in lieu of prison for relatively serious nonviolent crimes. A substantial fine, some argue, is just as strong a deterrent as a short stay in jail.

A municipal court judge in Los Angeles provided an especially edifying example for any renter who has ever lived in a substandard building ignored by the landlord. A Beverly Hills neurosurgeon who had earned the nickname "Ratlord" because of numerous city citations for health, fire, and building code violations in his four apartment buildings was sentenced to move into one of his own apartments for a term of thirty days. The apartment contained mounds of rodent droppings, an army of cockroaches, inadequate plumbing, faulty wiring, and other problems. Ratlord was fitted with an electronic anklet to ensure that he remained in his "cell" from 5:30 P.M. to 8:30 A.M. Permanent residents soon noted improvements in the building's conditions.[39]

Regional Restitution Centers   Another front-door strategy used in Florida, Arizona, Georgia, and other states is the *regional restitution center,* a variation on the standard work-release center. Nonviolent offenders are housed in restitution centers near their homes and work in the community during the day; they receive regular supervision. Their paychecks are turned over to center staff, who subtract expenses for food and housing and distribute the remainder to the offenders' victims as restitution, to the court for payment of fines, and to the offenders' spouses and children for support. Anything left over belongs to the inmates.

Intensive Probation Supervision   A third front-door strategy is *intensive probation supervision* (IPS), which was pioneered by Georgia in 1982. (Southern states are in the forefront of corrections policy innovation, largely because they have the biggest problems with prison overcrowding.) More than twelve states are now experimenting with IPS

IPS is somewhat like house arrest in that it is designed to keep first-time offenders guilty of a serious but usually nonviolent crime (for example, drunk driving or drug dealing) out of state institutions. Those who qualify for the program face intense, highly intrusive supervision and surveillance for a prescribed period. IPS requires at least five face-to-face contacts between offenders and the IPS staff each week in the office, on the job, or in the home; random alcohol and drug testing; weekly employment verification; an early nightly curfew (usually 8:00 P.M.); weekly monitoring for any lawbreaking encounters with state or local law enforcement personnel; and at least eight hours per week of unpaid community service for employed probationers and up to forty hours for those who are not working.[40] Those without a high school diploma may be required to study for the GED.

IPS officers usually work in a team consisting of a professional probation officer and a surveillance officer, who generally has law enforcement experience. Caseload is limited to twenty-five. In addition to surveillance, the team helps probationers locate a place to live and a job. People who progress without problems are gradually eased into regular probation status; violations result in imprisonment.

Problem Solving 17.2

Boot Camps

The Problem: State prisons are massively over-crowded and the construction costs of new cell space are prohibitive, yet judges continue to sentence offenders to "do time."

The Solution: An increasingly popular front-door approach to easing prison overcrowding is boot camps, or *shock incarceration*. Louisiana, Georgia, Maryland, Mississippi, Florida, Oklahoma, and South Carolina are among the seventeen states experimenting with this method. Young (seventeen- to twenty-five-year-old) first-time felony offenders are given the option of serving their prison term or undergoing three to four months in a shock incarceration center, which resembles boot camp in the U.S. Marine Corps. In fact, former Marine drill instructors are often in charge. Inmates arise by 4:00 or 5:00 A.M. to begin a rigid schedule of manual labor, physical training, and discipline. They clean their barracks, march, do calisthenics, perform work details, and undergo inspections. Psychological, drug, and alcohol counseling are required. Lights are out by 9:00 or 9:30 P.M. Those who successfully complete the three- to six-month program win early release. Those who fall short the first time can try again. A second failure results in assignment to the regular prison population. (Several states operate women's boot camps as well.)

Shock incarceration is aimed at more than just re-lief of prison overcrowding: It is also intended to teach self-control and self-discipline to young people who come from broken homes or from selfish, undisciplined personal backgrounds. On a daily basis, shock incarceration costs about the same as prison, but it can save a state millions of dollars from the early release of those who compete the program. Florida reports annual savings of $1.1 million; and New York, more than $5.1 million. Other states claim similar savings. If shock incarceration has the long-term impact its advocates claim, it will keep thousands of young offenders from becoming recidivists (ex-inmates who commit further crimes). Preliminary evidence from several states indicates that boot-camp graduates are less likely to return to prison than regular prisoners are.

Critics, however, say shock incarceration is simply a public-relations fad with no lasting effect on young felons' lives. They claim that cost savings are illusory, and that the boot camps have not reduced recidivism. Some judges apparently assign young felons to boot camp instead of probation, thus effectively canceling out savings. And inmate deaths have resulted from physical training in Louisiana and Mississippi.

While empirical evaluation results are still awaited to assess the costs and benefits, boot camps are catching on in additional states and in some local jurisdictions as well.

Sources: Richard L. Berke, "For Criminals, Camp Is No Vacation," *New York Times,* May 30, 1989, p. A14; Charles Mahtesian, "The March of Boot Camps," *Governing* 4 (June, 1991): 21–22.

The track record for IPS in Georgia is impressive. IPS probationers have been much less likely to commit subsequent crimes than conventional probationers or other former inmates. The program is basically self-supporting, since probationers pay from $10 to $50 per month to the program, as well as provide restitution to their victims. The program has given Georgia prisons much-needed breathing space and saved a substantial sum of money for each offender diverted from prison.[41] Annually, some 13,000 criminals are sentenced to do time in Georgia; the total prison capacity is less than 16,000. Problem Solving 17.2 describes another controversial front-door approach initiated in Georgia: boot camps.

Capacity Enhancement

Capacity enhancement is the third major strategy for matching available prison beds with the number of inmates. Usually it entails construction of new prison facilities, which cost the states billions of dollars in the 1980s. A five-hundred-bed prison in 1991 cost around $30 million to build. Building new prisons is costly, but operating them is even more expensive. During the recession of 1990–1992, Alabama, Connecticut, and other states completed new facilities but could not afford to staff and run them at approximately $25,000 a year per prisoner. As we have noted, this money could be allocated instead to education, health care, or a tax reduction. Many taxpayers resent spending it on the care and feeding of criminals—although, ironically, they want convicted criminals to be locked up.

When capacity enhancement is the selected strategy, states have few alternatives to new construction. There have been some rather interesting types of construction, however. The New York City Department of Correction built a floating jail five stories high and the length of two football fields and moored it off the Bronx in 1990. It holds eight hundred beds. Four old barges and ferries have been brought into service also, housing altogether almost one thousand prisoners.[42] Floating jails have been discussed in Texas as well. They offer the advantage of being quickly sited and less expensive than conventional prisons.

Private Prisons   One long-term capacity enhancement innovation worthy of serious consideration is private prisons or "prisons for profit," a new idea spawned from the near hopelessness of many overcrowded state correctional systems. The private sector has for many years provided limited services and programs to prisons, including health care, food services, alcohol and drug treatment, education and training, counseling, and construction. But the actual management of a correctional facility by a private firm is a recent innovation.

Adults and juveniles are held in privately run correctional institutions in at least twelve states. These include a delinquent treatment unit in Pennsylvania, the Okeechobee School for Boys in Florida, a 250-bed adult medium security prison in Tennessee, and several county jails in Texas and Wyoming. Many additional projects are under construction or being planned, including a 998-bed medium security facility near Clifton, Tennessee.[43]

Prison privatization is a controversial idea. Those who support it claim that prisons built and operated by the private sector will save the taxpayers money. Because of less red tape, facilities can be constructed relatively quickly and cheaply. Because personnel policies are more flexible in the absence of civil service protections, operations will be more economical. Most important, they claim, private prisons will reduce overcrowding. Opponents of privatization, however, question whether firms can in fact build and operate correctional facilities significantly less expensively than state or local governments can. They believe that the profit motive is misplaced in a prison setting. A company whose business is prisons benefits from filling up cell space as soon as it is built, and might even run advertisements encouraging fear of crime to foster a "lock 'em up and throw away the key" approach. Such a firm might also lobby legislators for stricter sentencing requirements and additional prisons.

Preliminary evidence on the economics of prison privatization is mixed. Most of the experimentation has been with juveniles, illegal aliens, and minimum security offenders. Cost savings have been marginal (at Pennsylvania's juvenile facility in Weaversville, for example) or nonexistent (as is the case at Kentucky's adult facility at Marion), according to most studies.[44] Overcrowded conditions may be relieved more promptly, but the burden on the taxpayers appears to be about the same.

Who Should Be Responsible for Prisons? Although economic considerations are obviously important, constitutional and legal issues may ultimately be the undoing of prisons for profit. One of the basic questions is whether the delegation of the corrections function to a private firm is constitutionally permissible. Under the necessary and proper clause, Congress can "delegate authority . . . sufficient to effect its purpose." The U.S. Supreme Court and state courts will have to determine whether incarceration, punishment, deterrence, and rehabilitation can properly be delegated, and who is legally liable for running a private facility.[45]

Another set of legal considerations concerns practical accountability for the day-to-day operation of jails and prisons. Who is responsible for developing operational rules, procedures, and standards and for ensuring that they are carried out? Who is responsible for maintaining security at the institutions and using force against a prisoner? Who will implement disciplinary actions against inmates? What happens if prison employees go out on strike? (Strikes by state correctional employees are illegal, but those by their private-sector counterparts are not.) What if the corporation hikes its fees substantially. Or declares bankruptcy?

Economic and legal issues aside, perhaps the most important question is who *should* operate our jails and prisons. Legal scholar Ira Robbins suggests that we should remember the words of the novelist Dostoevsky: "The degree of civilization in a society can be judged by entering its prisons." Robbins adds:

> . . . just as the prisoner should perhaps be obliged to know—day by day, minute by minute—that he is in the custody of the state, perhaps too the state should be obliged to know—also day by day, minute by minute—that it alone is its brother's keeper, even with all of its flaws. To expect any less of the criminal-justice system may simply be misguided.[46]

The state, after all, administers justice in the courtroom. Should it not also be responsible for carrying out justice in the correctional facilities?

Does Prison Pay? The construction and operation of prisons is the fastest-growing budget item in most states, even faster than the growth of Medicaid. Forty-three states are adding prison bed space today. Every dollar sunk into correctional facilities is one less to pay for highways, social services, higher education, and, unfortunately, the needs of children. Our priorities seem skewed indeed when we invest only $4,000–5,000 each year for a child's education while prisoners command over $25,000 apiece.

Does prison pay by keeping repeat offenders out of action? Benefit-cost analyses comparing the costs of incarceration with estimated savings to society from forgone burglaries, larcenies, murders, and rapes do indicate a net benefit to society. A 1987 study published by the National Institute of Justice assumed an average cost of confinement of $25,000; an average cost per crime of $2,300 in property losses, physical harm, or human suffering; and an estimated 187 crimes per year by a typical offender. Its conclusion: Incarceration enjoys a benefit-cost ratio of 17:1. However, this study was attacked on the grounds of flawed analysis and faulty assumptions. A more accurate benefit-cost ratio, based on a study on corrections in Wisconsin, may be 2:1.[47] Attaching dollar signs to criminal acts is problematic at best: What cost should be assigned to the personal indignity of rape, or the tragic loss of a human life?

Perhaps the most rational approach is to confine for life violent criminals who are judged likely to be repeat offenders, along with habitual or hard-core criminals who are beyond redemption. Reserve other forms of punishment such as probation, parole, intensive supervision, and half-way houses for the others. Such an approach would contain correctional costs while locking up the most troublesome and difficult cases.

The Continuing Crisis in Crime and Corrections

The idea of placing people in prisons in order to punish them with deprivation of their freedom was devised only two hundred years ago. Until recently, brutality was the operating norm. Deliberately painful executions, maiming, flogging, branding, and other harsh punishments were applied to both serious and minor offenders. Misbehavior in prison was likely to be met with beatings, or with more elaborate tortures such as "stretching" from ropes attached to a pulley in the ceiling or long confinement in an unventilated "sweat box." Troublemakers in some prisons were shackled naked to a wall, then "cooled down" with a high-pressure hose targeted for maximum discomfort. By contrast, prison conditions in the states today seem almost luxurious. Inmates typically enjoy recreational activities, training and educational opportunities, the use of televisions, stereos, and VCRs in their cells, and other amenities. Rules enforcement, too, is much more civilized and respectful of inmates' human rights.

But many prisons are very overcrowded, and they still don't do a very good job of preparing inmates for a productive, law-abiding life outside institutional walls. There appears to be very little that police can do to fight crime, short of apprehending criminals and sending them through the overloaded criminal justice system.

Crime and corrections present major challenges to state and local governments. How they meet these challenges will go far in determining their future role in American federalism. Certainly any long-term success will have to come from the recognition that all major criminal justice system components are interrelated to some extent. Thus, a broad approach to fighting court, crime, and corrections challenges is called for. A recent U.S. Justice Department report illustrates the need for a comprehensive treatment.[48] The report found that 50 to 75 percent of men arrested for serious crimes in various U.S. cities tested positive for illegal drug use. The purported link among drug use, criminal activity, and prison overcrowding was empirically verified. Add to this toxic equation homelessness, AIDS, and gang-related violence. Before the states can successfully cope with the challenges described in this chapter, we must understand such complex relationships more fully.

Summary

Dealing with crime today is almost entirely the responsibility of the states and localities. The national government offers much moralizing but little financial support, though the federal courts were the most influential policy instigators of the 1970s and 1980s in the field of corrections. Concern for prison overcrowding and harsh conditions resulted in a series of federal court rulings that forced state corrections systems to increase spending and significantly modify long-standing policies.

As the 1990s proceed, the states are valiantly attempting to cope with crime, prison overcrowding, and related difficulties. They are experimenting and innovating at a dizzying pace, exploring new approaches to deterring criminal behavior and using back-door, front-door, and capacity enhancement strategies to redefine corrections policy and the handling of criminals. We may anticipate continued innovation in this important policy field.

Key Terms

grand jury
victimless crime
indeterminate sentencing

determinate sentencing
creative sentencing

Environmental Policy

On March 22, 1987, a 230-foot garbage barge named *Mobro 4000* put out to sea from a dock in Queens, New York. It was loaded with 3,186 tons of commercial trash from New York City, the town of Islip, and Nassau County. After an odyssey of 6,000 miles and four and a half months, the barge returned to anchor in New York harbor, its load still intact.

The owner had originally intended to unload the trash at a garbage-to-methane-gas plant in North Carolina, but the *Mobro* was turned away because it lacked the necessary permits. In succession, the trash was refused by Alabama, Mississippi, Louisiana, Texas, Florida, Mexico, Belize, and the Bahamas. Public officials feared that it contained lead, cadmium, and other dangerous heavy metals.

After *Mobro 4000* spent some two and a half months at anchorage, state and local officials in New York agreed to burn the cargo in a Brooklyn incinerator and to bury the ash in a landfill in Islip, where the bulk of the trash had originated. Following court battles to block first the incineration and then the burial of the ashes, the infamous garbage was finally disposed of.

The incident of the *Mobro 4000* graphically illustrates an increasingly critical environmental policy problem in the United States: what to do with the huge quantities of solid waste produced by individuals, households, and industries. Similar dilemmas confront national, state, and local governments with regard to toxic wastes and nuclear wastes. Across the United States the **NIMBY** (Not in My Back Yard) syndrome runs rampant. Yet, as environmental author Barry Commoner observed more than twenty years ago, "Everything must go somewhere."

NIMBY

Public sentiment to keep an unwanted facility out of a neighborhood.

One can almost hear the earth screaming. Garbage barges sailing around aimlessly are the least of our global problems. Consider the following environmental crises.

The ozone layer that protects people and other living things from dangerous ultraviolet radiation is thinning. An "ozone hole" twice the size of the continental United States has been discovered over Antarctica. The incidence of skin cancer, eye damage, and related conditions is growing significantly.

The "greenhouse effect" refers to suggestions of a global warming trend caused by the buildup of atmospheric gases that permit heat from the sun to penetrate but prevent this heat from escaping. The possible impacts are of tremendous—and frightening—magnitude. They include marked changes in weather patterns, with severe implications for world agriculture, and rising ocean levels as the polar ice caps melt.[1] Coastal areas in the southern and eastern states may be inundated with seawater.

Acid rain and air pollution, principally from the burning of fossil fuels, menace the world's forests, lakes, streams, and people. Huge sectors of forests have been damaged in Europe, Canada, and other countries. Thousands of lakes have been "killed" by high acidity in the United States and elsewhere.[2]

Tropical rain forests are being cut at astonishingly high rates as population growth and hunger drive Third World farmers onto marginal land and greed compels firms to harvest tropical hardwoods at unsustainable rates. Soil erosion and the accumulation of carbon dioxide in the atmosphere have resulted. Related to the devastation of the rain forests is the extinction of thousands of plant and animal species annually.

Surface and underground water supplies are being depleted by intensive use and poisoned by chemicals, pesticides, fertilizers, and other toxic substances. "Industrial disease" jeopardizes the lives of millions of people around the world. Life expectancies have actually declined in some countries. In Poland, 25 percent of the soil is so contaminated with chemicals that it is unfit for growing food.[3]

The 1986 nuclear disaster at Chernobyl in the Soviet Union irradiated much of Europe. In the United States, nuclear energy and weapons plants periodically spew and leak radioactive materials into the air, onto the land, and into the water.

The U.S. Environmental Protection Agency estimates that 8 million homes have dangerous levels of radon gas.[4] Up to 20,000 deaths from lung cancer per year are attributed to this colorless, odorless gas.

Syringes, vials, and other medical waste contaminate the beaches. Massive oil spills pollute the oceans, rivers, and harbors. High lead levels endanger children who live near heavily used roads and highways. And as world population grows, environmental degradation intensifies.

The horror stories could go on and on. It is crystal clear that our environment has become dangerously polluted. As the Worldwatch Institute put it, "Without a dramatic reordering of priorities, our grandchildren will inherit a less healthy, biologically impoverished planet, one lacking in aesthetic pleasures as well as economic opportunities."[5]

At first thought, there seems to be very little that state and local governments can do about such problems as acid rain, the greenhouse effect, or deforestation. Global problems require global solutions. Within the United States, environmental protection would seem to be a function properly assigned to the national government. Polluted air and water certainly do not respect state boundaries. But in the face of national government indecisiveness and serious obstacles, the states and localities have become increasingly important environmental protectors.

....

The Political Economy of Environmental Protection

Environmental policy choices are made especially difficult by their economic implications. Controlling pollution is a significant economic cost for many firms today. In the essentially nonregulatory era prior to the 1960s, this expense was either quite low or nonexistent. Increasing government regulatory intervention in industrial processes and outputs reflects the indisputable fact that market forces by themselves will not guarantee the protection of health and environment. Polluters have little economic incentive to stop polluting, but clean air and water are public goods that should be available to all of us.

Left unregulated, most firms tend to maximize profits by minimizing costs—including the costs of environmental protection. Determining exactly what constitutes pollution or environmental degradation and deciding how stringently to regulate polluting activities have tremendous economic implications for firms and governments. Too much regulation could depress economic growth at national, state, and local levels, reduce employment, and even force some companies into bankruptcy.

The tradeoffs between economic growth and environmental protection spawn conflict, and are evident wherever these important objectives clash. The 1990 Clean Air Act amendments, it is estimated, will eliminate 15,000 jobs in the coal mines and cost U.S. industry $21.5 billion per year. In Oregon, powerful timber interests have to harvest trees in order to preserve the 68,000 jobs they contribute to that state's economy, yet environmentalists have fought for federal court prohibitions on logging where the endangered spotted owl is threatened. (Loggers responded with T-shirt logos such as "Save a Logger—Eat an Owl.")[6]

All of us are potential or actual victims of environmental problems (hence, environmentalists argue, we should at least be more environmentally aware in terms of what we choose to buy). Polluted air, water, and land offend us aesthetically; but, more important, they threaten the health and safety of ourselves, our children, and our grandchildren. People who drink contaminated water and breathe polluted air experience the costs very directly. From a differ-

ent perspective, all citizens must help pay the price of a safe and clean environment. We do this through the portion of our taxes that goes to government pollution-control efforts and through the prices we pay for goods, which include the cost of pollution control. The costs to consumers are especially heavy where the products of chemical companies, the auto industry, and coal-burning power plants are concerned. Not surprisingly, these industries have lobbied heavily against what they perceive to be excessive regulation.

Government's role is to balance economic growth with environmental protection by regulating polluters. The political economy of environmental protection argues strongly for national domination of policymaking. Because states and local governments compete for industry, a nonnational jurisdiction might be tempted to relax environmental protection standards in order to influence a firm's decision as to where to construct or expand a new manufacturing facility. Only national policies and standards can prevent the sacrifice of environmental quality in jurisdictions that seek growth and development at virtually any cost.

Intergovernmental Relationships in Environmental Policy

The first government forays into the now-tangled jungle of environmental protection policy began in the early 1800s with local ordinances aimed at garbage, human and animal waste, contaminated drinking water, and other unsanitary, health-endangering conditions in American cities. Local failures to contain and control such problems were punctuated by cholera and typhoid epidemics throughout the nineteenth century. In 1878, a yellow-fever epidemic caused 5,000 deaths and the exodus of another 25,000 fearful residents from Memphis, Tennessee. The population of that city dropped by more than half over a period of just two months.[7]

Such episodes prompted the states to begin regulating conditions causing waterborne diseases, thereby redefining what had been a private problem into a problem for state government. By 1948, states had taken over responsibility for water pollution control. Their early regulatory efforts were rather weak, however.[8]

The issue of water pollution control shows the evolving centralization of national government authority in environmental decision making. The national government paid little attention to environmental problems until after World War II, when urbanization and industrial production began to draw attention to the national dimensions of environmental dangers. The initial federal statutory step into the policy field was the Water Pollution Control Act of 1948. Under the original version of this act, the national government assumed limited enforcement authority for water pollution. Since then, seven other major federal statutes or amendments have been enacted to address the problem. Under this overall statutory framework, the national government pre-empted existing state and local water-quality standards and substituted national standards.

The reasons for this are not difficult to fathom. We have already noted the cross-boundary dimensions. Polluted water, like contaminated air, cannot be

Table 18.1
Major Congressional
Environmental Leg-
islation

Date	Legislation	Major Provisions
1948	Water Pollution Control Act	Provided loans for construction of treatment plants
1956	Amendments to Water Pollution Control Act	Provided grants for construction of treatment plants
1963	Clean Air Act	Provided grants to state and local programs
1965	Water Quality Act	Provided grants for research and development of sewers
1965	Motor Vehicle Air Pollution Control Act	Established national standards on auto emissions
1967	Air Quality Act	Set deadlines for state air pollution standards
1969	National Environmental Policy Act	Required environmental-impact statements
1970	Amendments to Water Pollution Control Act	Set national water quality goals; established national pollution discharge permit
1972	Environmental Pesticide Control Act	Required registration of all pesticides
1972	Coastal Zone Management Act	Provided federal grants for state development of coastal management
1973	Endangered Species Act	Required protection of all "threatened" and "endangered" species

contained within state or local boundaries. It does little good for a downstream state to regulate water quality strictly if an upstream state is cavalier about dumping. A classic example of border-crossing water pollution is the Pigeon River in the southeastern United States. A Champion International paper plant turns the pristine Pigeon into an ugly, malodorous mess before the river crosses the North Carolina border into Tennessee.[9]

Increasingly strong federal statutes also addressed the problems of air pollution, pesticides, and hazardous waste. By the late 1970s, the national government had extended its authority to endangered species, strip mining, coastal zones, and many other areas (see Table 18.1). Thus, environmental protection was redefined as a national problem requiring national solutions. However, the

Table 18.1 (cont.)

Date	Legislation	Major Provisions
1974	Safe Water Drinking Act	Set national standards for quality of public drinking water supplies
1976	Toxic Substances Control Act	Allowed EPA to ban chemicals that threaten health or the environment; prohibited PCBs
1976	Resource Conservation and Recovery Act	Set standards for hazardous waste treatment, storage, transportation, and disposal
1977	Surface Mining Control and Reclamation Act	Set controls on strip mining and required land restoration
1980	Comprehensive Environmental Response, Compensation, and Liability Act	Created "Superfund"
1980	Low-Level Radioactive Waste Policy Act	Required interstate compacts for LLW disposal
1984	Asbestos School Hazard Policy Act	Provided funds to remove asbestos from schools
1986	Superfund Reauthorization Act	Increased Superfund to $9 billion
1990	Amendments to Clean Air Act	Imposed stronger vehicular emissions and other air pollution standards; mandated alternative fuel vehicles

national government does not operate alone; it has many state and local traveling companions.

States and localities speak with an important policy voice even in fields that appear to be outside their proper sphere of influence. Take public lands as an example. Governed by Congress and managed by eight federal agencies, including the Bureau of Land Management, Forest Service, and National Park Service, the nation's 732 million acres of public lands make up almost one-third of the continental United States and more than one-half of the land area of six western states. These lands contain vast timber, petroleum, coal, and mineral resources. The states have an enormous economic stake in the ways in which these resources and their environmental implications are managed. The western states, principally, have consistently sought a greater role in deciding how these resources are used, even insisting that much of the land be deeded over to the respective states.[10]

The Recent National Role

The lead agency in national environmental policy is the Environmental Protection Agency (EPA), which was created in 1970 as an independent regulatory body for pollution control. Its director appointed by the president, the EPA is faced with the task of coordinating and enforcing the broad array of environmental protection programs established by Congress. The scope of the EPA's responsibility can be overwhelming, involving regular interaction and conflict with other national agencies, powerful private interests, and state and local governments. Its job is complicated by the tendency of Congress to pass environmental legislation that sets unattainable program goals and implementation dates. Most deadlines for compliance with federal laws have been missed by the EPA, which lends ammunition to its critics on all sides.[11] Litigation brought by regulated industries and environmental groups has further ensnarled the agency, and a shortage of money and staff has plagued the EPA since the Reagan years.

An example of the scope of the EPA's responsibilities is water pollution control. Every private and public facility that discharges wastes directly into waters must obtain a permit from the EPA or, in some instances, from its state counterpart. The national government, through the EPA, establishes specific discharge standards. Day-to-day oversight and implementation, however, are performed by the states. In effect, the national government makes the rules and lets the states enforce them according to their own circumstances. (This is known as "**partial pre-emption**.") The national government also disburses grants to state and local governments for the treatment and monitoring of water resources. Over $30 billion was transferred to the nonnational governments for the construction of waste-water treatment plants in the 1970s and 1980s.[12] Millions more went for technical assistance and research and development.[13]

partial pre-emption

An approach common to federal environmental laws that requires states to apply national standards.

Several factors have led to the expansion of state and local environmental protection roles since the 1980s. One is the increased capability of the states and localities to assume more control over their environmental destinies. Another is the growing propensity of the national government to turn over program responsibilities to the states. But the most important immediate factor in greater state involvement is the legacy of the environmental policy decisions of the Reagan administration, which resulted in severe financial aid reductions and a general de-emphasis of national activities.

Ronald Reagan was openly hostile to environmental causes.[14] During the 1980 presidential campaign he repeatedly attacked the Clean Air Act and "excessive" environmental regulations, and during his eight years in office he sought to disembowel or terminate most existing antipollution programs. Reagan's attitude toward the environment was exemplified by his first appointees to direct the EPA (Anne Gorsuch) and the Department of the Interior (James Watt), both of whom were openly biased in favor of industry and against environmentalists. Watt appointed many former employees of industries regulated by the

Interior Department; when environmental groups criticized his decisions, Watt called them members of "a left-wing cult."[15] Gorsuch was soon accused of mismanagement, intentional delays, conflicts of interest, and using political criteria to determine which states would receive grants for the cleanup of hazardous waste sites. Congress soon had enough of her and cited her for contempt, among other things. After little more than two years in office, Gorsuch was forced to resign. Watt, too, eventually resigned under fire.[16]

Although national funding of environmental programs was cut by 50 percent during the first few years of Reagan's administration, few programs were actually terminated. Instead, the severe cutback in funding and qualified, experienced personnel seriously hindered the EPA's effectiveness. Even more drastic cuts sought by Reagan in later years were not granted by Congress. By that time there was a broad realization that environmental policy had become highly institutionalized and enjoyed widespread support across the political spectrum. Large and influential interest groups such as the Sierra Club and the National Wildlife Federation rallied their troops to fight further cutbacks and to sabotage Reagan's policy efforts.[17] In the end, Reagan's budget cuts, staff reductions, and hostile political appointments seriously damaged environmental protection policy at the national level but could not deal it a death blow.

George Bush entered the White House in 1989 with a much more benign attitude toward the environment. Proclaiming himself to be the "environmental president," Bush appointed William K. Reilly, former president of the World Wildlife Fund and the Conservation Foundation, as director of the EPA. During his first term, President Bush cooperated with the Congress in significantly strengthening the Clean Air Act. However, behind-the-scene operations to undercut administrative rules implementing the Clean Air Act and other environmental protection laws cast serious doubt on his true commitment to the environment.

Environmental Policy Today in the States and Localities

As the resolve of the national government weakened during the 1980s, the determination of the state and local governments grew. Increasingly, the nonnational governments are taking on greater responsibility for financing and operating environmental protection programs and are once again becoming policy initiators. For example, Congress was stalled on acid rain legislation for years, but several states took unilateral actions to cut sulfur dioxide emissions within their borders (New Hampshire and New York were the first). Several states, including New Jersey and Ohio, have passed legislation requiring firms to clean up hazardous wastes from industrial property before they can sell it. Such legislation helps prevent companies from abandoning polluted sites that present health risks and leaving them for the states to clean up. California's far-reaching policies to improve the nation's worst air quality have become a model for other states and the national government.

States continue to operate their pollution control programs under the auspices of national legislation and the EPA. They must develop and implement plans and standards under the host of laws listed in Table 18.1. If a state does not enforce national regulations properly, the EPA will take over and operate the program itself. However, most states have willingly taken on the task of environmental protection. State officials chafe at the funding reductions that seem to accompany each new transfer of program authority, and they deeply resent the laborious paperwork and other strings attached to national grants-in-aid. But, ultimately, state and local governments are closer to pollution problems and, hence, are best situated to address them on a day-to-day basis—subject to national laws and standards. Of course, states vary in their commitment to environmental protection. One rating system, based on programs in air pollution reduction, soil conservation, hazardous waste management, solid waste management and recycling, and renewable energy and conservation, identified the "greenest" states to be Oregon, Maine, and Vermont, and the "least green" to be Alabama, Louisiana, and Arkansas.[18]

Resolving Environmental Conflict: The Role of the Courts

Three types of legal conflicts arise in environmental law. First, the government may bring enforcement actions against industrial polluters who do not comply with national or state law. Second, the government may be sued by firms or by environmental organizations. Finally, one government may take legal action against another government. Often the EPA or its state counterpart—an agency such as Michigan's Department of Natural Resources or California's Department of Health Services—is party to a suit, largely because of the broad discretionary authority given to it by legislation. Industries, environmental groups, and state and local governments test the boundaries of this authority by appealing decisions of the EPA and its state partners.

Typically, the principal effect of litigation is simply to delay mandated actions. In the majority of cases involving a government, the courts side with the government, and the result is often a decision to send the case back to the enforcement agency for action.[19] Interestingly enough, state courts are just as likely as federal courts to rule against polluters,[20] contrary to the beliefs of those who still do not trust the states to police their environments aggressively.

The large number, broad scope, and deliberate ambiguity of environmental laws, as well as the increasing legal expertise of environmental policy actors, ensure that the courts will remain deeply involved in environmental affairs. This involvement can be controversial: The competence of judges to make technical decisions on environmental issues may be called into question, and the courtroom is unlikely to produce any sort of coherent policy through case-by-case adjudication. It is more desirable to determine policy through the legislative process. Also, litigation is very time-consuming and expensive.[21] In some instances more resources are expended *litigating* environmental laws than *imple-*

menting them. Hence the increased reliance on "environmental mediation" to resolve disputes and reconcile differences. In environmental mediation, a non-biased, third-party mediator promotes a voluntary settlement between litigants. This technique is faster, cheaper, and usually more satisfying to everyone involved, but it is not appropriate in all disputes.[22]

Solid Waste Management: Garbage and What to Do with It

The tragicomic saga of the *Mobro 4000* is a metaphor for the problem of what to do with the vast quantities of household and industrial trash generated in the United States. On a per capita basis, Americans produce five and a half pounds of garbage each day. Of the 500 billion pounds of solid waste generated in a year, about 9 percent is recycled or composted and another 8 percent is incinerated. That leaves 83 percent destined for landfills.[23] And landfills are filling up fast. Since 1980, more than three-quarters of these disposal facilities have closed; and of the remaining 7,300 operative landfills, 2,000 are expected to exhaust their capacity within the next five years.[24] To make matters even worse, the still-functioning garbage dumps, along with those that have been shut down, pose serious hazards to surface and underground water supplies.

Like nuclear and hazardous waste, solid waste involves the NIMBY syndrome. Everyone generates garbage, and lots of it, but no one wants to have it smelling over the back fence or threatening the well water. The shortage of sites has naturally driven up the price of land disposal in the dumps that still operate, and disposal fees have tripled in many localities during the past few years. Many cities must ship their waste hundreds of miles and across state lines to find an open dump site. For example, household garbage from suburban New York City communities may be transported to a dump in central Illinois or rural Virginia. New York and New Jersey account for 53 percent of the trash that crosses state lines.[25] And in the picturesque Pacific Northwest, a train carries Seattle's trash to a landfill in north-central Oregon. As dump space becomes scarce, the average "tipping fee" charged by landfill operators (most of which are local governments) leaped from $5 per ton in 1980 to $25 per ton by 1987.[26] By 1990, the cost of dumping exceeded $100 per ton in parts of the Northeast.

Solid waste management is primarily a local government responsibility. Garbage collection and disposal was one of the first local government services in American cities. In the 1800s, most of the trash was piled up on vacant land outside urban areas; some of it was hauled out to sea, a practice that persisted for decades off the New Jersey shore. A 1988 national law that was intended to halt ocean dumping by 1992 offers at least some reassurance that medical waste and other garbage will not continue to wash up on East Coast beaches.

Although the national government has largely left the states and localities to their own devices in dealing with the solid waste dilemma, the EPA enters the scene when water quality is threatened or when burning of trash pollutes the air, and some national grants are available to assist with alternative approaches. Essentially, however, state and local governments hold the policy mantle for solid wastes. They face the questions of how to dispose of existing garbage and how to reduce the quantity of solid waste generated in the future.

Concerned with the garbage disposal problem, Oregon enacted a law in 1983 that permits state officials to override local opposition to new landfills. Wisconsin uses a more cooperative approach, whereby state officials negotiate with local officials and citizens to guarantee the value of nearby property or to provide cash grants to local areas and residents willing to host a landfill. Both approaches have shown signs of success.[27] For most states, though, incineration and recycling are the leading alternatives for reducing the quantity of garbage.

Incineration

Burning has for many centuries served as an alternative to burying or stacking up trash. In rural areas across the United States, homeowners and industries burn leaves, paper, and other organic wastes. Because burning presents a fire hazard to nearby land and buildings and pollutes the air, it is prohibited in most urban areas. Yet it remains the most common alternative to landfilling. States like New York and Florida burn nearly 10,000 tons of trash daily. Incineration reduces waste volume by approximately 90 percent, and, depending on the extent of pollution controls and the size of the operation, it can be inexpensive. The remaining ash is usually buried in a landfill, although some of it must be treated as hazardous waste because it contains heavy metals and other toxic materials. Most of the large incineration operations in the United States utilize the principle of *cogeneration,* through which the heat from burning garbage is used to produce steam or electricity.

There is no disputing the fact that incineration drastically reduces the volume of solid waste. However, serious reservations about large-scale burning have been raised. First, incinerators are expensive. A 1,500-ton-per-day plant costs more than $150 million—quite a chunk of money for a local government to raise. The second big drawback to incineration is the environmental cost. The Sierra Club, the Environmental Defense Fund, and other environmental groups oppose burning because of its danger to public health. The process releases quantities of toxic substances, such as heavy metals, into the air around the site. Firms that build and sell the facilities claim that proper filtering of smoke and proper disposal of the contaminated ash make incineration a safe technology, but doubts seem to be growing. Many proposed incinerator projects were canceled during the late 1980s. Further difficulties arise in siting incinerators in local communities, where they are rarely welcome. And, of course, that which is incinerated cannot be recycled.

Recycling

With landfill space diminishing, disposal fees climbing, and health concerns increasing, recycling has been presented as a better option. It does not pollute, is relatively inexpensive, and is ecologically sound, since waste materials are utilized productively. Recycling programs are now in various stages of implementation in most states. Like other solid waste management activities, recycling is primarily a local government responsibility. States typically provide technical and financial assistance to the municipalities, which operate the programs.

Recycling is a promising technology that makes good sense. Although the estimates vary, approximately 37 percent of municipal solid waste is paper, 18 percent is yard waste, 10 percent is metals, and 7 percent is plastics.[28] Much of this can be recycled. The late 1980s saw states aggressively tackling the mounting garbage problem, and by 1991 thirty-four states had passed some form of statewide recycling law.[29] New Jersey's Source Separation and Recycling Act, which required all 567 local communities to implement programs for sorting and recycling household garbage, has produced a recycling rate of 38.9 percent. A growing number of cities and counties have begun their own recycling efforts. One of the most unusual is the "cash for trash" program of St. Cloud, Minnesota. Residents who bag newspapers, glass, aluminum cans, and other reusable materials and place them on the curb for monthly pickup become eligible for a special cash award.[30]

Many states and localities recycle yard waste as well. Leaves, grass cuttings, shrub prunings, and similar materials take up a large volume of precious landfill space.[31] This debris is biodegradable and valuable as a soil builder and fertilizer when composted. And even in communities with no apparent use or market for the compost, the process drastically shrinks the original amount of trash at little or no cost.

Recycling is not a panacea for the solid waste problem, however. It requires citizen cooperation if it is to be affordable, and some people simply will not cooperate. Cities with mandatory recycling laws report that 74 percent of their households participate; those with voluntary policies average 40 percent participation rates.[32] A city cannot refuse to collect nonparticipants' garbage without creating a public health problem. Another problem is the shortage of markets for recycled paper, aluminum cans, plastics, and other materials. As the director of environmental management in Rhode Island warned, "This is no garden club collecting a few bottles and cans. We are going to have to restructure fairly large pieces of the national and international economy to digest what we're going to feed it."[33] For states new to recycling, such as Ohio, glutted markets and low prices for recyclables make it difficult to reach their 25 percent recycling goals.[34]

Even if recycling were carried out to the fullest extent possible, substantial quantities of solid waste, particularly styrofoam and plastics, would remain. One idea is to ban nonrecyclable beverage and fast-food containers. Suffolk County, New York, home of the long-suffering garbage barge, is the innovator. In 1981 it prohibited the sale of nonreturnable bottles, and in 1988 it banned plastic packages that are not biodegradable.[35] Suffolk County's action, emulated by other communities, is generally credited with pressuring the plastics industry to develop environmentlier friendlier products and prodding the McDonald's Corporation into abandoning the styrofoam burger box.[36] (In fact, McDonald's, in an effort to stay a step ahead of the environmentalists hot on its heels, announced optimistic plans in 1991 to reduce by 80 percent its daily generation of 2 million pounds of garbage.)[37]

All three techniques—landfilling, incineration, and recycling—will be needed in the future to manage the vast quantity of solid waste generated in our mass-consumption, throw-away society. Recycling, the most appealing option, is likely to flourish in the 1990s. Simply recycling the Sunday editions of the *New York Times* would spare an estimated 4 million trees annually.[38] But we cannot recycle everything. Some of the garbage must therefore be incinerated or landfilled. Every new waste technology has its own difficult issues, and the states and localities, with virtually no assistance from Washington, D.C., are striving to deal effectively with the huge task of managing the country's garbage.

Hazardous Waste: The Politics of Confusion

The image of garbage mountains rising above the horizon is disconcerting, to say the least. When New York City completes its Fresh Kills Landfill on Staten Island in 2005, the mammoth garbage mound is expected to rival the great pyramids of Egypt in size.[39] But solid waste is just one of several contributors to environmental destruction. A more insidious public health threat comes from hazardous waste—the poisonous by-products of industry. If these by-products possess toxic, corrosive, flammable, or reactive properties, they are considered hazardous. The industries that generate 90 percent of the hazardous waste in the United States are chemical and allied products, primary metals, petroleum and coal products, fabricated metal products, and rubber and plastic products.[40]

Hazardous waste is even more ubiquitous than most people realize. Pesticide residues, used motor oil, discarded cadmium batteries, used refrigerants, and paint sludge are hazardous leftovers that are frequently found in households and in so-called nonpolluting industries.[41] It is no exaggeration to say that hazardous waste is all around us. Limited data provided by industry to the EPA indicate that more than 5.7 billion pounds of toxic substances were emitted into the environment (air, water, land, and underground) in 1989. Table 18.2 lists the ten states responsible for more than half of these emissions. And as huge a quantity as 5.7 billion pounds may seem, Congress's Office of Technology Assessment argues that the EPA figures vastly underestimate the amount of toxic emissions.[42]

The primary dilemma concerning hazardous waste is what to do with it. The discovery that wastes were not being properly or safely disposed of triggered government involvement; as hazardous liquids began seeping into people's basements from long-buried barrels, as children playing in fields uncovered rotting drums of toxic waste, as motorists developed unusual skin rashes from pesticides sprayed along the roadway, government was called in. Some states feared that imposing tough new hazardous waste regulations would make them less attractive to industry. Others were concerned that tightening the laws for waste

Table 18.2

The Toxic Ten

State	Millions of Pounds of Toxic Pollutants Released into the Environment, 1989
Texas	792.8
Louisiana	493.5
Ohio	358.7
Tennessee	264.3
Indiana	255.0
Illinois	248.0
Michigan	220.1
Pennsylvania	194.2
Florida	192.0
Kansas	185.1

Source: U.S. Environmental Protection Agency, "Toxic Release Inventory," May 1991 (pamphlet).

disposal would actually increase the incidence of illegal dumping. A national policy initiative seemed preferable to state attempts at solving the problems.

The national government responded to the mounting crisis with two pieces of legislation: the Resource Conservation and Recovery Act of 1976 (RCRA) and the Comprehensive Environmental Response, Compensation and Liability Act of 1980 (known as Superfund). RCRA provides for "cradle-to-grave" tracking of waste and establishes standards for its treatment, storage, and disposal. The Superfund program cleans up existing abandoned waste sites. If RCRA is successful, it should lessen the need for programs like Superfund in the future.

RCRA: An Effort to Manage Hazardous Waste

RCRA is considered partially pre-emptive in that states have a degree of discretion and flexibility in implementing it. Under RCRA, the EPA establishes minimum standards that state programs must meet and may exceed. Once the EPA is satisfied that a state program meets its standards and possesses adequate enforcement mechanisms, it authorizes the state to operate its own hazardous waste management program. If subsequent state regulatory behavior is insufficient or if a state chooses not to start its own program (as Wyoming has), the EPA steps in and operates the program. By 1992, most states had received authorization to run their own hazardous waste control systems.

Figure 18.1   Number of National Priority List (Superfund) Sites by State, 1990
The discovery of new hazardous waste sites outpaces the cleanup of existing sites.

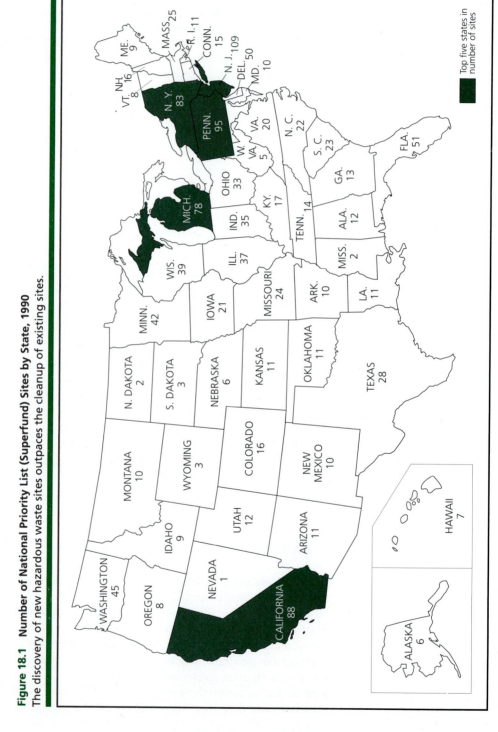

Source: U.S. Environmental Protection Agency, "National Priorities List" (August 1990).

State officials are not completely happy with the hazardous waste management system. Many use phrases like "too time-consuming," "burdensome," and "resource-intensive" to describe their state's experience with RCRA implementation.[43] Generally, they have difficulty adapting RCRA to the specific conditions and problems in their state. Ironically, while state officials lament the lack of flexibility in RCRA, some members of Congress believe that too much discretion is left to the states. EPA officials often hear from Congress because of inadequacies in state programs.

hammer provisions

Automatic penalties if an agency or jurisdiction fails to meet deadlines specified in a statute.

In its 1984 reauthorization of RCRA, Congress included specific deadlines as well as **hammer provisions,** which penalize a state for failure to act. Although progress has been made, the complexity of hazardous waste regulation slows the process. For example, as of early 1988, the EPA and the states had issued operating permits to fewer than 15 percent of the nation's four thousand active hazardous waste management facilities.[44] Congressional review and reauthorization of RCRA was underway in 1992.

Superfund: Cleaning Up Hazardous Waste

Superfund was passed in 1980 in recognition of the fact that no matter how comprehensive and cautious hazardous waste management is in the future, the pollution of the past remains with us. Under Superfund, the national government can intervene to clean up a threatening hazardous waste site.

One of the first actions taken under Superfund was the identification of particularly dangerous sites that were in need of immediate cleanup. These sites formed what is known as the National Priorities List (NPL). In its first phase, the NPL listed 110 sites, and New Jersey contained more than any other state. By 1990, the list had grown to 1,197; New Jersey, with 109 sites, continued to have the dubious honor of first place. (The number of NPL sites in each state is shown in Figure 18.1.) Despite its early promise, most analysts have concluded that Superfund has fallen far short of its goals. At only about 20 percent of the NPL sites is cleanup under way or completed.[45]

One factor confounding the Superfund program (aside from the EPA's uncertain interest in it in the early 1980s) is the number of government and private interests that are inevitably involved in cleanups. Research on early cleanups found them hopelessly entangled in a web involving national, state, and local technicians, administrators, and politicians. Not surprisingly, very little was accomplished. Cleanup work bogged down over issues of responsibility and definition ("How clean is clean?"). As tensions escalated among local officials, environmental activists, nearby residents, state bureaucrats, EPA administrators, and the cleanup contractors, the hazardous waste sites remained. Profile 18.1 recounts the story of the Vertac Chemical Corporation pesticide plant in Arkansas, number 18 on the NPL list.

As with RCRA, congressional concern over the slow pace of implementation spurred legislative action. In renewing Superfund, Congress increased the funding level rather generously, from $1.6 billion (1980–1985) to $9 billion (1986–

Profile 18.1

Incinerating Hazardous Waste in Arkansas, or "What's That Smell?"

Amid the mountain laurels and magnolias of Arkansas lurks a dangerous threat: the Vertac Chemical Corporation's abandoned pesticide plant. In the late 1960s, residents of Jacksonville welcomed the new plant as a source of jobs and tax base. Over time, however, persistent reports of health problems linked to the facility's operation turned public support into citizen protests and class-action lawsuits. The Vertac Chemical Corporation filed for bankruptcy in 1986, closed the plant, paid a $10.7 million fine—and, in a heartbeat, they were out of there. Not so the 28,300 barrels of toxic chemicals and 140 vats of heavy chemicals accumulated over fifteen years of herbicide and pesticide production. Most deadly is the dioxin—a cancer-causing substance that has contaminated the soil near the plant site.

Vertac ranks eighteenth on the Superfund National Priorities List, with conditions serious enough to attract attention but so problematic as to elude easy solution. After lengthy deliberations, the disposal remedy favored by the U.S. Environmental Protection Agency and the Arkansas Department of Pollution Control and Ecology is on-site incineration. The barrels, the tanks, the buildings, and even the dirt are to be burned over a seven- to ten-month period. In fact, Vertac is a test case. If the burn there is successful, that is, if EPA clean-air standards can be met—on-site incineration will occur at nineteen other Superfund sites. The EPA defends on-site incineration, claiming that a properly operated, carefully monitored burn is completely safe. After all, more than 99.99 percent of the waste would burn, leaving minuscule amounts of toxic ash. Nearby residents are not quite so sanguine about the technology. The Environmental Congress of Arkansas (ECA), a coalition of grassroots environmental organizations from across the state, has filed a lawsuit to block the Vertac incineration. As of late 1991, the courts had allowed preliminary test-burns to proceed. If the assurances of government agencies and the cleanup contractors are proven correct, even the ECA will be pleased. But if they are not . . .

Source: Donovan Webster, "They Stood Up," Outside 17 (January 1992): 34–38, 86–90.

1991). The new law contained several key provisions affecting state governments, which now play a greater role in selecting remedies but have a lessened obligation to pay for long-term cleanup. To address the problem of a lack of disposal facilities, Superfund now requires states to ensure that they have adequate disposal capacity either within state boundaries or in other states, or risk losing their federal funding allocations.[46]

What Can States Do?

Some states have actively pursued their own hazardous waste control agendas. More than half have enacted mini-Superfund statutes that authorize them to conduct site assessments and initiate remedial cleanup actions or force a responsible party to do so.[47] Twenty states have enacted "community right to know" statutes, and many have conducted household hazardous waste collection drives.

The issue that has caused the greatest trouble in the states is disposal. Hazardous waste disposal is a *locally unwanted land use* (LULU). Which level of government should make decisions about LULUs—state or local? Some states have been aggressive in siting waste facilities, opting for an approach known as **state pre-emption.** Under this approach, state governments take the lead in evaluating the disposal potential of possible sites, conducting hearings, and approving construction and operation. New Jersey and Arizona are among the more than twenty states that have chosen to go with pre-emption.[48] Other states, primarily in the South and West, have taken a different tack, allowing local governments to veto construction of a facility within their borders. An approach that falls between these extremes is a joint state/local decision-making process like the ones that Illinois, Maine, and Minnesota use. Another, which is being explored in Massachusetts and Wisconsin, is the use of negotiation and third-party arbiters in the site-selection process.

There is no single best way to make such decisions; since 1984, only Colorado has sited a new disposal facility.[49] It was ten years and many lawsuits before the landfill in the ironically named town of Last Chance began operating in 1991. And Arizona's fourteen-year effort to site a landfill/incinerator facility in a rural area thirty miles from Phoenix culminated in a shoot-out, both literally and figuratively, in 1991.[50] Sheriff's deputies fired stun guns at environmentalists and others who were protesting the dump's construction. Politicians, scrambling to get on the "right" side of the issue, devised a way of buying Arizona out of the contract with the waste firm, to the tune of $44 million. Meanwhile, in Texas, a proposal to bury toxic waste in a mammoth underground salt dome near Houston is drawing a curious collection of advocates and opponents.

As efforts to site new facilities drag on, hazardous waste generated in one state is frequently shipped to another state for disposal. Thirty-five states are net exporters of hazardous waste; fifteen are net importers.[51] Feeling abused by their neighbors, waste-importing states, especially Alabama, Louisiana, Ohio, and South Carolina, began to just say no in the late 1980s. When Alabama's ban on hazardous waste importation from twenty-two states was struck down by the federal courts, lawmakers responded·with a tough, two-tiered tipping fee that taxed out-of-state waste at three times the rate of in-state-generated waste. The effect was dramatic: The quantity of out-of-state waste dropped by one-half and still generated $30 million for the state treasury. Unfortunately for Alabama, in 1992 the U.S. Supreme Court ruled that the surcharge on out-of-state waste violated the interstate commerce clause. Regardless, efforts to block out-of-state waste will continue until the hazardous waste disposal burden is more equitably shared among states.

One eminently plausible, if partial, solution to waste disposal dilemmas is to reduce the amount of waste generated. If less waste is produced, there will be less waste to dispose of. Yet this sensible solution is surprisingly difficult to impose. Reducing waste often means redesigning the production process, which in turn entails costs that industry has proven unwilling to absorb. New York developed the first waste reduction program in 1981; North Carolina (1983)

state pre-emption

State government assumption of the authority to take action, thereby precluding local government action.

and Minnesota (1984) followed suit. By 1991, twenty states had enacted waste reduction laws; Massachusetts's legislation is considered the model.[52] One of the key features of the programs is the use of economic incentives to promote waste reduction.

....

Nuclear Waste: The Lingering Horror

Nuclear events have a particularly horrifying drama. The near meltdown of Pennsylvania's Three Mile Island nuclear reactor in 1979 continues to haunt the public and the industry; no new nuclear power plants have been ordered in the ensuing years, and many that were on the drawing boards have been canceled. Adequate safety has been the primary concern of the general public; increased costs, especially those dictated for safety reasons, have troubled investors. Additional fears have been triggered by revelations from defense-related nuclear facilities. The news that uranium was regularly released into the environment at the Fernald nuclear weapons production facility in Ohio, and that serious safety violations have occurred at the Savannah River Site in South Carolina, has raised troubling questions about contamination of air, soil, and water.

Types of Nuclear Trash

Nuclear power carries a heavy price: waste. As with solid and hazardous wastes, the key question is what to do with it. Nuclear waste is divided into three types—high level, transuranic, and low level—based on the persistence of toxicity. High-level wastes maintain their extreme toxicity for hundreds of thousands of years. Transuranic wastes are dangerous for very long periods but are not as persistent as the high-level variety. Low-level wastes are much less toxic, in a relative sense, and break down to safe levels of radioactivity in anywhere from a few days or months to three hundred years.

The case of low-level radioactive waste (LLW) demonstrates the difficulties of the problem. LLW is produced by commercial nuclear power installations (54 percent), nuclear-related industries (11 percent), and medical and research institutions (35 percent). The waste, much of it stored in fifty-five-gallon steel drums, includes items such as contaminated laboratory clothes, tools, equipment, and leftover bomb materials as well as bulk wastes.

As several early burial sites exhausted their capacity or began to leak radioactive materials and were closed, the nation came to rely on three sites—Barnwell, South Carolina; Beatty, Nevada; and Hanford, Washington—for the disposal of LLW. Some citizens in these states began to question their role as "nuclear toilets." They reasoned that since the waste was being produced in all fifty states, its disposal ought to be dispersed as well. The governors of the three states met to develop a strategy for a national LLW policy. They provoked action by increasing disposal fees, reducing the volume of waste they would accept, and periodically shutting down the LLW dumps. Washingtonians went so far as to pass an initiative that banned the disposal at Hanford of waste from states that were not developing their own burial sites.

The resulting clamor from the nuclear industry and from medical and research facilities precipitated congressional action, leading to the Low-Level Radioactive Waste Policy Act of 1980. Quite simply, the act made each state responsible for the disposal of the waste generated within its borders. Although a 1992 U.S. Supreme Court decision weakened the law by invalidating the provision forcing a state to assume ownership of its waste, other sections of the act remain in force. States have the choice of managing LLW within their own jurisdictions (that is, developing their own disposal sites) or entering into an interstate compact for out-of-state disposal. As expected, some states have opted to handle the problem alone, but most have joined with their neighbors to forge a regional answer to the disposal question.

Low-Level Waste and Interstate Compacts

interstate compacts

Formal agreements among a subset of states, usually to solve a problem that affects each of the member states.

The use of **interstate compacts** to address the LLW problem was particularly inventive, since nuclear waste disposal has historically been considered a national responsibility. Under the act, states can venture into the arena of regulating interstate commerce, a territory typically off limits to them. Interstate LLW compacts are unique in another way: Usually interstate compacts distribute costs and benefits across a unified area. The "goods" (water systems or transportation networks) are to be enjoyed by all members; the "bads" (pollution or crime) are to be borne by all. Low-level waste compacting, however, actually concentrates public bads (the location of a nuclear waste disposal site) in one or two states while the benefits (the ability to use the site) are enjoyed by all member states.[53]

When successful, interstate compacts are a shining example of what the states, left to their own devices, can accomplish. The process can be somewhat tortuous, however, as initial enthusiasm encounters the hard realities of self-interested behavior. Interstate compacting begins with the negotiation of a draft document by delegates representing interested states. The draft must be ratified by the legislatures of potential member states, and the compact must receive congressional consent. It is then ready for implementation. In a typical case, a compact commission composed of representatives of member states serves as the implementing agency.

Much attention has been focused on the Southeast Compact, wherein member states wrestled over which state would replace South Carolina as a host site in 1993.[54] No state volunteered for the role, and so decision makers developed a weighting system whereby they could evaluate the disposal potential of member states according to waste volume, population density, land suitability, transportation systems, and meteorological conditions. The process led to the designation of North Carolina as the successor to South Carolina. Many in the Tar Heel State contended that the designation process was biased, and some state legislators called for North Carolina to pull out of the Southeast Compact

Figure 18.2 Low-Level Waste Compacts, through January 1992

By January 1, 1996, states are to have met their LLW disposal needs either through compacts with other states or by developing their own facilities.

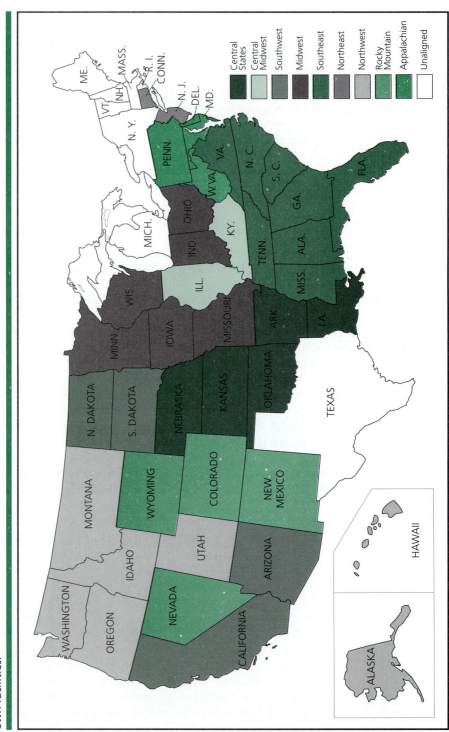

Source: Southeast Compact Commission for Low-Level Radioactive Waste Management, Raleigh, N.C.

and develop a disposal facility exclusively for its own use. The secession talk died down, however, and it appears that North Carolina will assume its regional nuclear responsibility by 1996. South Carolina legislators agreed to keep Barnwell open until the North Carolina site is operational.

Independent action could have been a costly course for North Carolina. Because it takes four or five years to identify, construct, and license a facility, North Carolina would have been forced to use out-of-state disposal facilities during that period. South Carolina probably would not have been very receptive to truckloads of toxins from its northern neighbor, and other states with disposal capacity might have used North Carolina's predicament to impose heavy surcharges on incoming waste. Moreover, Congress might have forced North Carolina to accept waste from other states once its facility was operating.

Although a lot of time and negotiation was involved, nine interstate LLW compacts have been formed. Eight states remained unaligned, including three major LLW generators: Texas, Massachusetts, and New York. The compacts and member states are illustrated in Figure 18.2. The lack of guarantees about the future makes nuclear waste disposal a prospect both fascinating and not a little bit frightening. And, of course, the NIMBY syndrome comes to full bloom when facility siting is discussed.

Environmental Tradeoffs

Research tells us that Americans generally support the goals of environmental protection. Public opinion polls indicate that most people are in favor of increased government spending for environmental protection and oppose efforts to weaken environmental standards.[55] This resounding endorsement weakens, however, when environmental protection is pitted against goals such as economic growth and adequate energy. When members of Earth First square off against loggers in the forests of the Pacific Northwest, environmentalism becomes more than an abstraction. Environmental protection does not occur in a vacuum; achieving its goals comes at the expense of other valued objectives.

Economics Versus the Environment

The proposed development of a cargo port on Sears Island along the central coast of Maine illustrates the economics/environment issue.[56] Supporters of the new port include business leaders and state and local officials. Lined up on the opposing side are the Sierra Club and the EPA. The dispute boils down to jobs versus coastline preservation. Proponents claim that the port will provide jobs, reduce shipping costs for local businesses, and stimulate additional development—a powerful lure to the economically depressed area. Opponents counter that the economic potential of the port does not justify the environmental damage that its construction and operation will cause. There are a multitude of side issues, such as whether an existing port might be modernized and how much profit will accrue to the railroad company whose real-estate subsidiary owns most of the island. The chance of a compromise acceptable to both sides appears remote.

Slightly different themes emerged during the battle to clean up smog-shrouded southern California. A government-approved plan developed in 1989 aims to reduce the amount of harmful emissions released into the atmosphere by establishing tough new standards to be phased in over a twenty-year period. Already the key issue has become improving air quality without causing economic harm.[57] But achieving the goals of the plan is quite likely to disrupt the normal flow of business, especially in the transportation industry.

According to the plan, by 1998, 40 percent of all automobiles, 70 percent of trucks, and all buses are to use methanol or other "clean" fuels. By 2008, the plan envisions car dealers selling vehicles that run on electricity or other alternative fuels. Other industries are affected as well. The plan calls for reformulation of paints, solvents, and aerosol sprays, installation of filters at breweries and emission control devices at bakeries and dry cleaners, and a ban on gasoline-powered lawnmowers, bias-ply tires, and certain types of barbeque grills. Vast technological development and widespread public acceptance must occur for the plan to have a reasonable chance of success. Its announcement unleashed a flurry of discussion about relative benefits and substantial costs.[58]

Energy Versus the Environment

The demand for energy raises a series of environmental questions. First and probably foremost is the question of just how much environmental degradation can be justified on behalf of energy production. Another is the degree to which those who enjoy the benefits of abundant energy should bear the costs of energy production. The seriousness of the issue was illustrated rather dramatically by the Alaskan oil spill that occurred in the spring of 1989.

Alaska owes much of its newfound prosperity to its plentiful supply of oil. In fiscal year 1988–1989, oil sales and taxes collected from oil companies provided 85 percent of the state's budget.[59] At the same time that Alaska was basking in the glow of excess revenues, it allowed the oil industry to relax its preparations for environmental emergencies. But the state was shocked out of its complacency when the *Exxon Valdez* ran aground, spilling 240,000 barrels of oil and turning Prince William Sound into a marine graveyard. After much hand-wringing and finger-pointing, Alaska, the EPA, and Exxon sought to contain the damage.

Just how much this tragedy will affect future energy exploration remains unclear. What is clear is that issues like this will not disappear. The waters of the Atlantic off the coast of North Carolina offer another venue for a clash between environmental concerns and energy needs. Mobil Oil has applied to the U.S. Interior Department for a lease to drill for natural gas in a limestone reef off Cape Hatteras.[60] Opponents to the lease charge that drilling could irreparably damage the ecosystem of the Outer Banks area. Proponents argue that in the fifty-two existing drilling sites off the East Coast, there has never been a well blowout or an oil spill. The risk is low, they argue, and certainly preferable to greater reliance on foreign sources of energy. But environmentalists counter that the "drain America first" strategy overlooks conservation and alternative energy sources.

. . . .

Environmental Challenges for State and Local Governments

These examples—the development of Maine's new port, southern California's smog-reduction plan, the Alaskan oil spill, and energy exploration off the North Carolina coast—raise fundamental questions about environmental quality in the future. The actions of state and local governments, as well as those of the national government, will chart the course.(See Problem Solving 18.1)

Admittedly, the challenges posed by the environment will sorely test the capacities of state and local governments. Recognizing that there is a problem is the first step; designing workable solutions is the much tougher second step. Most state and local governments are aware of the problem, but their willingness and ability to do anything about it are another matter. The modernization and overall improvement of state and local governments during the past two

Beachfront communities solve two problems (erosion and Christmas tree disposal) when they build tree fences along the shoreline. It doesn't take long for wind-blown sand to transform the row of trees into mini-dunes.

Problem Solving 18.1

The Federal System in Its Finest Flowering: Decentralized Solutions to Environmental Problems

The Problem: Reducing pollution and gaining greater industry compliance with environmental laws.
Louisiana's Solution: Adopt a tax policy that establishes a link between the amount of property taxes a company pays and its environmental record.

The Problem: Agricultural runoff, especially phosphorus, polluting Everglades National Park.
Florida's Solution: Take 35,000 acres of farmland out of production and covert it into artificial marshlands to renourish the Everglades.

The Problem: Four million plastic foam cups discarded after the state fair.
Minnesota's Solution: Recycle the cups for use as building insulation.

The Problem: Glutted markets for recycling of tires and plastics.
North Carolina's Solution: Widen existing roads, using finely ground tires in asphalt paving; use shredded tire-and-soil mix for embankments; and construct protective fencing out of recycled plastic posts.

The Problem: Industries' use of Native American land that is not subject to state environmental regulations for solid and hazardous waste landfills.
California's Solution: Require tribes to negotiate with the state regarding the design of appropriate regulatory plans.

The Problem: Unused capacity at in-state solid waste landfills because of less expensive out-of-state alternatives.
Rhode Island's Solution: Assess a $1,000 fine on firms caught shipping solid waste out of state.

The Problem: Unhealthy levels of smog in the air.
Colorado's Solution: Require the use of oxygenated fuels such as ethanol to improve air quality in smog-laden metropolitan areas.

The Problem: The increasing number of unsubstantiated "green" marketing claims.
Wisconsin's Solution: Enact "truth-in-labeling" standards for products advertised as recycled, recyclable, or degradable.

The Problem: Discarded Christmas trees at the end of the holiday season.
The Solution in some Connecticut, North Carolina, and Texas Communities: Chip the trees into mulch that can be used in gardens, or build a tree fence along the shoreline to capture wind-blown sand to form mini-dunes.

decades are promising signs. But the history of environmental policy in this country indicates that the national government will always play a major role in encouraging, and in some instances forcing, them to act. And even national action may be insufficient for problems that are global in scope.

One approach popular with some economists is the use of "market-based" environmental policies. Under this system, government would set an allowable total pollution level and allocate this amount among polluting firms. Firms emitting less pollution than their permitted levels could sell their surplus "pollution capacity" to firms that exceed their allotted limits.[61] Proponents argue that market-based policies are more cost-effective than traditional regulatory mechanisms. This approach is getting a trial run in the 1990 Clean Air Act Amendments. Another promising approach for state and local governments involves rethinking the entire issue. Rather than regarding environmental protection as pollution control, governments can think of it as pollution *prevention*. For example, waste that is not produced in the first place is waste that does not have to be treated, transported, and disposed. This fundamental reorientation toward environmental protection will not happen overnight, but some of the examples cited in this chapter suggest that it can occur gradually, in one community after another, as citizens think globally and act locally. What's more, there will be lessons to be learned from the ultimate in environmental experiments, Biosphere 2. In 1991, eight people entered a glass-enclosed miniature world in the Arizona desert, intent on a two-year stay.[62] Along with 3,800 species of plants and animals, the Biospherians plan to live in ecological harmony, recycling and reusing virtually everything.

Summary

Environmental protection policymaking is primarily a national government responsibility, but policy implementation is increasingly up to the states and localities. Funding cutbacks during the Reagan years weakened the EPA but also opened the door to greater activity by the nonnational governments.

The United States produces substantial quantities of solid, hazardous, and nuclear waste. State and local governments for the most part have followed the lead of the national government in attempting to address the environmental problems spawned by waste. Rather than relying solely on old technologies such as landfilling, governments are beginning to experiment with newer approaches, such as incineration and recycling. The economic costs of environmental protection make it a complex policy area.

Key Terms

NIMBY   state pre-emption
partial pre-emption   interstate compacts
hammer provisions

References

1 New Directions for State and Local Government pp. 1–19

1. "From Kansas to New York, the Cry of Secession Goes Up," *The State,* May 3, 1992, p. 6D.

2. "What's in a Name? Ask North Dakotans," *New York Times,* March 23, 1989, p. 11.

3. Bill Richards, "North Dakotans Find Themselves in a State of Flux," *Wall Street Journal,* March 17, 1989, pp. A1, A6.

4. U.S. Bureau of the Census, *Statistical Abstract of the United States: 1991* (Washington, D.C.: U.S. Government Printing Office, 1991).

5. U.S. Bureau of the Census, *Projections of the Population of States, by Age, Sex, and Race: 1988–2010* (Washington, D.C.: U.S. Government Printing Office, 1988).

6. "Estimating State Population," *State Policy Reports* 7 (January 1989): 2–5.

7. Daniel J. Elazar, *American Federalism: A View from the States,* 3d ed. (New York: Harper & Row, 1984).

8. Joel Lieske, "Political Subcultures of the United States," a paper presented at the annual meeting of the American Political Science Association, Washington, D.C., 1991.

9. Eric B. Herzik, "The Legal-Formal Structuring of State Politics: A Cultural Explanation," *Western Political Quarterly* 38 (September 1985): 413–23.

10. Jody L. Fitzpatrick and Rodney E. Hero, "Political Culture and Political Characteristics of the American States: A Consideration of Some Old and New Questions," *Western Political Quarterly* 41 (March 1988): 145–53.

11. Frederick M. Wirt, " 'Soft' Concepts and 'Hard' Data: A Research Review of Elazar's Political Culture," *Publius* 21 (Spring 1991): 1–13.

12. Bruce Wallin, "State and Local Governments Are American, Too," *The Political Science Teacher* 1 (Fall 1988): 1–3.

13. Governor Mike Sullivan, as quoted in "Wyoming's Governor Signs Law to Restructure State Government," *Denver Post,* March 5, 1989, p. 8B.

14. "Innovations in State and Local Government 1991," Report of the Ford Foundation, September 1991.

15. Beth Walter Honadle, "Defining and Doing Capacity Building: Perspective and Experiences," in Beth Walter Honadle and Arnold M. Howitt, eds., *Perspectives on Management Capacity Building* (Albany, N.Y.: SUNY Press, 1986), pp. 9–23.

16. John Herbers, "The New Federalism: Unplanned, Innovative, and Here to Stay," *Governing* 1 (October 1987): 28–37.

17. Ibid., p. 28.

18. Ann O'M. Bowman and Richard C. Kearney, *The Resurgence of the States* (Englewood Cliffs, N.J.: Prentice-Hall, 1986).

19. Ibid., p. 12.

20. Terry Sanford, *Storm Over the States* (New York: McGraw-Hill, 1967).

21. Ann O'M. Bowman and Richard C. Kearney, "Dimensions of State Government Capability," *Western Political Quarterly* 41 (June 1988): 341–62.

22. Larry Sabato, *Goodbye to Goodtime Charlie: The American Governor Transformed,* 2d. ed. (Washington, D.C.: Congressional Quarterly Press, 1983).

23. Deil S. Wright, *Understanding Intergovernmental Relations,* 3d ed. (Pacific Grove, Calif.: Brooks-Cole, 1988).

24. James L. Garnett, *Reorganizing State Government: The Executive Branch* (Boulder, Colo.: Westview, 1981).

25. Alan Rosenthal, *Legislative Life: People, Process, and Performance in the States* (New York: Harper & Row, 1981).

26. Robert A. Kagan et al., "The Evolution of State Supreme Courts," *Michigan Law Review* 76 (1978): 961–1005.

27. Jacqueline Calmes, "444 North Capitol Street: Where State Lobbyists Are Learning Coalition Politics," *Governing* 1 (February 1988): 17–21.

28. Eben Shapiro, "Nintendo and Minnesota Set a Living-Room Lottery Test," *New York Times,* September 27, 1991, pp. A1, C6.

29. Dabney T. Waring, Jr., "Deregulation Puts Trucking Safety in the Back Seat," *State Government News* 30 (April 1987): 12–13.

30. Tamar Lewin, "Battle for Family Leave Will Be Fought in States," *New York Times,* July 27, 1991, p. A6.

31. Gary Enos, "States Take Lead on Health," *City & State,* 9 (April 20, 1992): 1, 23.

32. Raymond E. Glazier, Jr., "State Remedies for the AIDS Epidemic," *State Government News* 30 (February 1987): 27–30.

33. Lisa W. Foderaro, "Teachers as Social Workers: Experiment Finds Resistance," *New York Times,* April 14, 1989, pp. 1, 24.

34. William Celis III, "Unusual Public School Aiming to Turn a Profit," *New York Times,* November 6, 1991, p. B8.

35. James Edwin Kee and William Kiehl, *Assessing the Costs of Federal Mandates on State and Local Government* (Washington, D.C.: Academy for State and Local Government, 1988).

36. Kathy Kiely, "Washington Has a Big Beef over Texas 'Foreign Policy,'" *Houston Post,* February 6, 1989, pp. A1, A10.

37. Gary Enos, "Court-Ordered Tax Hikes Upheld," *City & State,* 7 (April 23, 1990): 49.

38. Lyle J. Denniston, "O'Connor, Rehnquist and Uncertainty: The States and the Supreme Court," *State Legislatures* 9 (April 1983): 10–13.

39. Stuart Taylor, Jr., "Congress Can Tax Municipal Bonds, High Court Rules," *New York Times,* April 21, 1988, p. 1.

40. *Webster* v. *Reproductive Health Services,* 109 S.Ct. 3040 (1989); *Planned Parenthood* v. *Casey,* 60 USLW 4795 (1992).

41. *Perpich* v. *Defense,* 58 USLW 4750 (1990).

42. Michael A. Pagano, Ann O'M. Bowman, and John Kincaid, "The State of American Federalism— 1990–1991," *Publius* 21 (Summer 1991): 1–26.

43. Richard Nathan as quoted in Mary B. W. Tabor, "State Worker's Fiscal Coup: Windfall for Massachusetts," *New York Times,* June 8, 1991, p. 5.

44. Todd Sloane, "Governors Face Mounting Deficits," *City & State,* 8 (November 4, 1991): 1, 20.

45. Penelope Lemov, "Climbing Out of the Medicaid Trap," *Governing* 5 (October 1991): 49–53.

46. Neal R. Peirce, "Cities Must Learn When to Say No," *Houston Chronicle,* February 13, 1989, p. 12A.

47. John Shannon, "The Return to Fend-for-Yourself Federalism: The Reagan Mark," *Intergovernmental Perspective* 13 (Summer/Fall 1987): 34–37.

48. U.S. Advisory Commission on Intergovernmental Relations Staff Report, "Public Assistance in the Federal System," *Intergovernmental Perspective* 14 (Spring 1988): 5–10.

49. Alan D. Monroe, George C. Kiser, and Anthony J. Walesby, "Comparing the State of the States," paper presented at the annual meeting of the Midwest Political Science Association, Chicago, 1991.

50. "Downsizing State Government: The Revolution of the 90s?" *State Legislatures* 17 (May 1991): 5–6.

51. David Osborne and Ted Gaebler, *Reinventing Government* (Reading, Mass.: Addison-Wesley, 1992).

2 The Evolution of Federalism pp. 21–48

1. Richard Hofstadter, *The American Political Tradition* (New York: Vintage Books, 1948), p. 5.

2. Ibid., p. 9.

3. Ibid., pp. 9–10.

4. Richard H. Leach, *American Federalism* (New York: W. W. Norton, 1970), p. 1.

5. David B. Walker, *Toward a Functioning Federalism* (Cambridge, Mass.: Winthrop, 1981), p. 25.

6. James Madison, *The Federalist,* No. 45, 1788.

7. Walter Berns, "The Meaning of the Tenth Amendment," in Robert A. Goldwin, ed., *A Nation of States* (Chicago: Rand McNally, 1961), p. 130.

8. Walker, *Functioning Federalism,* pp. 47–48.

9. Hofstadter, *American Political Tradition,* p. 72.

10. *McCulloch* v. *Maryland,* 4 Wheaton 316 (1819).

11. *Gibbons* v. *Ogden,* 9 Wheaton 1 (1824).

12. Franklin Pierce, *Congressional Globe,* 33rd Congress, 1st Session, May 3, 1854, p. 1062.

13. *Brown* v. *Board of Education,* 347 U.S. 487 (1954).

14. The Civil Rights Act of 1964 prohibited racial discrimination in public accommodations and in employment. Relying on the commerce clause, the Supreme Court has turned down all challenges to the act.

15. Berns, "Meaning of the Tenth Amendment," p. 130.

16. *United States* v. *Darby,* 312 U.S. 100 (1941) at 124.

17. *National League of Cities* v. *Usery,* 426 U.S. 833 (1976).

18. *Garcia* v. *San Antonio Metropolitan Transit Authority,* 105 S.Ct. 1007, 1011 (1985).

19. Ibid. (O'Connor, dissenting).

20. William H. Stewart, "Metaphors, Models and the Development of Federal Theory," *Publius* 12 (Spring 1982): 5–24.

21. Morton Grodzins, *The American System: A New View of Government in the United States* (Chicago: Rand McNally, 1966), pp. 42–53.

22. Deil S. Wright, *Understanding Intergovernmental Relations,* 2d ed. (Monterey, Calif.: Brooks/Cole, 1982), pp. 40–42.

23. Walker, *Functioning Federalism,* pp. 46–65.

24. Ibid., p. 52.

25. Morton Grodzins, "Centralization and Decentralization in the American Federal System," in Robert A. Goldwin, ed., *A Nation of States* (Chicago: Rand McNally, 1961), pp. 1–3.

26. Wright, *Understanding Intergovernmental Relations,* pp. 38–41.

27. Walker, *Functioning Federalism,* p. 101.

28. Terry Sanford, *Storm Over the States* (New York: McGraw-Hill, 1967), p. 80.

29. Wright, *Understanding Intergovernmental Relations,* p. 63.
30. James Madison, *The Federalist,* No. 10, 1788.
31. Michael Kinsley, "The Withering Away of the States," *The New Republic* (March 1981), pp. 3–7.
32. *Merriam* v. *Moody's Executors,* 25 Iowa 163, 170 (1868). Dillon's Rule was first written in the case of *City of Clinton* v. *Cedar Rapids and Missouri Railroad Co.* (1868).
33. Daniel J. Elazar, *American Federalism: A View from the States,* 3d ed. (New York: Harper & Row, 1984), p. 203.
34. *Community Communications Company, Inc.* v. *City of Boulder,* 102 S.Ct. 835 (1982).
35. See *Hallie* v. *Eau Claire,* 85L Ed 2d 24 (1985), and *Columbia* v. *Omni Outdoor Advertising* (1991).
36. Wright, *Understanding Intergovernmental Relations,* pp. 333–34.
37. Samuel H. Beer, "The Future of the States in the Federal System," in Peter Woll, ed., *American Government: Readings and Cases* (Boston: Little, Brown, 1981), p. 92.

3 Federalism and Public Policy pp. 49–83

1. John Shannon, "The Return to Fend-for-Yourself Federalism: The Reagan Mark," *Intergovernmental Perspective* 13 (Summer/Fall 1987): 34–37.
2. Michael D. Reagan and John G. Sanzone, *The New Federalism* (New York: Oxford University Press, 1981).
3. U.S. Advisory Commission on Intergovernmental Relations, *A Catalog of Federal Grant-in-Aid Programs to State and Local Governments: Grants Funded FY 1989* (Washington, D.C.: U.S. Government Printing Office, 1987).
4. Deil S. Wright, *Understanding Intergovernmental Relations,* 3d ed. (Pacific Grove, Calif.: Brooks Cole, 1988).

5. ACIR, *A Catalog of Federal Grant-in-Aid Programs,* pp. 15–35.
6. U.S. Office of Management and Budget, *Budget of the United States Government, Fiscal Year 1989, Special Analysis H* (Washington, D.C.: U.S. Government Printing Office, 1988), p. H-23.
7. Richard P. Nathan and Fred C. Doolittle, eds., *Reagan and the States* (Princeton, N.J.: Princeton University Press, 1987).
8. Michael A. Pagano, *The Effects of the 1986 Tax Reform Act on City Finances* (Washington, D.C.: National League of Cities, 1987).
9. Quoted in *The New York Times,* January 27, 1982, p. 16.
10. Ronald Reagan, "National Conference of State Legislatures," *Weekly Compilation of Presidential Documents* 17 (August 3, 1981), p. 834.
11. Robert D. Reischauer, "Fiscal Federalism in the 1980s: Dismantling or Rationalizing the Great Society," in Marshall Kaplan and Peggy L. Cuciti, eds., *The Great Society and Its Legacy* (Durham, N.C.: Duke University Press, 1986), pp. 179–97.
12. Richard S. Williamson, "A New Federalism: Proposals and Achievements of President Reagan's First Three Years," *Publius* 16 (Winter 1986): 11–28; and Richard L. Cole and Delbert A. Taebel, "The New Federalism: Promises, Programs, and Performance," *Publius* 16 (Winter 1986): 3–10.
13. Timothy J. Conlan, "Federalism and Competing Values in the Reagan Administration," *Publius* 16 (Winter 1986): 29–47.
14. "The Test of Vital National Interest: Necessary and Sufficient Conditions for Activity by the National Government" *Intergovernmental Perspective* 12 (Summer 1986): 13
15. Demetrios Caraley and Yvette R. Schlussel, "Congress and Reagan's New Federalism," *Publius* 16 (Winter 1986): 79.
16. Paul E. Peterson, Barry G. Rabe, and Kenneth K. Wong, *When Federalism Works* (Washington, D.C.:

Brookings Institution, 1986), pp. 219–29.
17. Ibid., p. 3.
18. Ann O'M. Bowman and Michael A. Pagano, "The State of American Federalism 1989–1990," *Publius* 20 (Summer 1990): 1–25.
19. Michael A. Pagano, Ann O'M. Bowman, and John Kincaid, "The State of American Federalism 1990–1991," *Publius* 21 (Summer 1991): 7.
20. Timothy A. Conlan, "And the Beat Goes On: Intergovernmental Mandates and Preemption in an Era of Deregulation," *Publius* 21 (Summer 1991): 43–57.
21. Joseph F. Zimmerman, "Federal Preemption Under Reagan's New Federalism," *Publius* 21 (Winter 1991): 7–28.
22. Conlan, "And the Beat Goes On," p. 43.
23. John Kincaid, "From Cooperative to Coercive Federalism," *Annals of the American Academy of Political and Social Science* 509 (May 1990): 139–52.
24. Cheryl Arvidson, "As the Reagan Era Fades, Its Discretion vs. Earmarking in the Struggle Over Funds," *Governing* 3 (March 1990): 21–27.
25. Eileen Shanahan, "The Other Side of the Recession," *Governing* 4 (March 1991): 50.
26. Pagano et al., "The State of American Federalism," p. 2.
27. U.S. Bureau of the Census, *Statistical Abstract of the United States, 1991* (Washington, D.C.: U.S. Government Printing Office, 1991), p. 430.
28. Fred Block, Richard A. Cloward, Barbara Ehrenreich, and Francis Fox Piven, *The Mean Season: The Attack on the Welfare States* (New York: Pantheon Books, 1987), p. 92.
29. Charles A. Murray, *Losing Ground: American Social Policy, 1950–1980* (New York: Basic Books, 1984).
30. John E. Schwarz, *American's Hidden Success,* rev. ed. (New York:

W. W. Norton, 1988); Block et al., *The Mean Season.*

31. *Statistical Abstract of the United States, 1991,* Tables 43 and 745.

32. Michael Novack, ed., *The New Consensus on Family and Welfare* (Milwaukee: American Enterprise Institute for Public Policy Research, 1987).

33. Ibid., pp. 4–5; see also Harry J. Holzer, ed., *The Black Youth Employment Crisis* (Chicago: University of Chicago Press, 1986); and Ken Auletta, *The Underclass* (New York: Random House, 1982).

34. Novack, *The New Consensus,* p. 5.

35. *Statistical Abstract of the United States, 1991,* Table 615.

36. U.S. House of Representatives, Committee on Ways and Means, *Background Material and Data on Programs Within the Jurisdiction of the Committee on Ways and Means* (Washington, D.C.: U.S. Government Printing Office, 1978), p. 388.

37. Daniel Patrick Moynihan, "Our Poorest Citizens — Children," *Focus* 11 (Spring 1988): 5.

38. Irwin Garfinkel, "The Evolution of Child Support Policy," *Focus* 11 (Spring 1988): 12–13.

39. Neal R. Peirce, "Children's Agenda Makes Headway," *P.A. Times* (December 1, 1986): 2; *State Government News* 30 (November 1987): 27.

40. See Charles Garvin, Audrey Smith, and William Reid, eds., *The Work Incentive Experience* (Montclair, N.J.: Allenheld, Osman, 1978).

41. John Herbers, "Governors Ask Work Plan for Welfare Recipients," *The New York Times,* February 22, 1987, p. 30; Julie Rovner, "Welfare Reform: The Issue That Bubbled Up from the States to Capitol Hill," *Governing* 1 (December 1988): 17–21.

42. Joel F. Handler, "Consensus on Redirection — Which Direction?" *Focus* 11 (Spring 1988): 31–32.

43. See Judith M. Gueron, *Reforming Welfare with Work* (New York: Ford Foundation, 1987).

44. See Candace L. Romig, "Welfare Reform: How Well Is It Working?" *Intergovernmental Perspective* 17 (Spring 1991): 20–23.

45. Jeff Worsham and Evan J. Ringquist, "State Policy Innovation and Intergovernmental Agenda Setting: The Case of Learnfare," paper presented at the 1991 annual meeting of the American Political Science Association, Washington, D.C. Also see Kitty Dumas, "States Bypassing Congress in Reforming Welfare," *Congressional Quarterly* (April 11, 1992): 950–53.

46. U.S. General Accounting Office, *Medicaid Expansions,* GAO/HRD 91-78. Washington, D.C.: U.S. General Accounting Office, June 1991.

47. In Julie Rovner, "Governors Ask Congress for Relief from Burdensome Medicaid Mandates," *Congressional Quarterly* (February 16, 1991): 416.

48. David Rapp, "The Medicaid Shell Game: Too Good to Last," *Governing* (January 1992): 62.

49. Penelope Lemov, "Health Insurance for All: A Possible Dream?" *Governing* 4 (November 1990): 56–59.

50. Robert B. Albritton and Robert D. Brown, "Intergovernmental Impacts on Policy Variation Within States: Effects of Local Discretion on General Assistance Programs," *Policy Studies Review* 5 (February 1986): 529–35.

51. Kathleen Sylvester, "Welfare: The Hope and the Frustration," *Governing* 5 (November 1991): 50–55.

52. Bryan D. Jones and Arnold Vedlitz, "Higher Education Policies and Economic Growth in the American States," paper presented at the annual meeting of the Midwest Political Science Association, April 9–11, 1987.

53. U.S. Department of Education, National Center for Education Statistics, *Digest of Education Statistics, 1990* (Washington, D.C.: National Center for Education Statistics, 1990).

54. Three states — namely, —combine coordination of higher education with primary and secondary education under a single state administrative agency.

55. Carnegie Foundation for the Advancement of Teaching, *The State and Higher Education* (San Francisco: Jossey-Bass, 1976), p. 19.

56. See Samuel K. Gove, "Governors and Higher Education, 1983," *Publius* 14 (Summer 1984): 111–19.

57. Frank Newman, "Building a Partnership," *State Government News* 30 (October 1987): 10.

58. U.S. Department of Education, *Fall Enrollment in Higher Education, 1984.*

59. Newman, "Building a Partnership," pp. 10–11.

60. See Anthony DePalma, "With Latest Rise in Tuition, State College Bargains End," *The New York Times* (October 16, 1991), pp. A1, B8; and Kathleen Sylvester, "The College of Hard Times," *Governing* 4 (September 1991): 28-33.

61. Richard H. Leach, *American Federalism* (New York: W. W. Norton and Co., 1979), p. ix.

62. Ibid., p. 45.

63. Timothy Conlan, *New Federalism: Intergovernmental Reform from Nixon to Reagan* (Washington, D.C.: Brookings Institution, 1988).

64. Michael A. Pagano and Ann O'M. Bowman, "The State of American Federalism — 1988–89," *Publius* 20 (Summer 1989): 1–17.

4 State Constitutions pp. 85–111

1. *Lloyd Corp.* v. *Tanner,* 407 U.S. 551 (1972); *Hudgens* v. *NLRB,* 424 U.S. 507 (1976).

2. *Robins* v. *Prune Yard Shopping Center,* 23 Cal.3d 899, 592 P.2d 341 (1979).

3. U.S. Advisory Commission on Intergovernmental Relations, *State Constitutions in the Federal System,* A-113 (Washington, D.C.: ACIR, 1989), p. 2.

4. Donald S. Lutz, "The United States Constitution as an Incomplete Text," *Annals of the American Acad-*

emy of Political and Social Science 496
(March 1989: 23–32).

5. G. Alan Tarr and Mary Cornelia
Porter, "Introduction: State Constitutionalism and State Constitutional Law," *Publius* 17 (Winter
1987): 5.

6. Daniel J. Elazar, "The Principles
and Traditions Underlying State Constitutions," *Publius* 12 (Winter
1982): 11.

7. Albert L. Sturm, "The Development of American State Constitutions," *Publius* 12 (Winter 1982):
61.

8. Ibid., pp. 62–63.

9. Paul G. Reardon, "The Massachusetts Constitution Makes a Mile-
stone," *Publius* 12 (Winter 1982):
45–55.

10. James Bryce, "Nature of the
American State," in Bruce Stinebrick-
ner, ed., *State and Local Government,*
3d ed. (Guilford, Conn.: Dushkin,
1987), pp. 20–23.

11. Thomas Parrish, "Kentucky's
Fourth Constitution a Product of Its
1980 Times," in Thad L. Beyle, ed.,
*State Government: CQ's Guide to
Current Issues and Activities 1991–92*
(Washington, D.C.: CQ Press,
1991), p. 46.

12. U.S. Advisory Commission on
Intergovernmental Relations, *The
Question of State Government Capability* (Washington, D.C.: ACIR,
1985), p. 36.

13. David Fellman, "What Should a
State Constitution Contain?" in
W. Brooke Graves, ed., *Major Prob-
lems in State Constitutional Revision*
(Chicago: Public Administration Ser-
vice, 1960), p. 146.

14. Sturm, "American State Constitutions," p. 64.

15. Lewis A. Froman, Jr., "Some
Effects of Interest Group Strength in
State Politics," *American Political
Science Review* 60 (December 1966):
956.

16. David C. Nice, "Interest Groups
and State Constitutions: Another
Look," *State and Local Government Review* 20 (Winter 1988): 21–
27.

17. Ibid., p. 22.

18. U.S. Advisory Commission on
Intergovernmental Relations, *A
Report to the President for Transmit-
tal to the Congress* (Washington,
D.C.: U.S. Government Printing
Office, 1955).

19. National Municipal League,
Model State Constitution, 6th ed., rev.
(New York: National Municipal
League, 1968).

20. Council of State Governments,
*Modernizing State Constitutions
1966–1972* (Lexington, Ky.:
Council of State Governments,
1973), p. 4.

21. Thomas C. Marks, Jr., and John
F. Cooper, *State Constitutional Law*
(St. Paul: West, 1988).

22. Ibid., p. 38.

23. Ibid., pp. 38–42.

24. Ibid., p. 46.

25. Ibid.

26. Sue Davis and Taunya Lovell
Banks, "State Constitutions, Freedom
of Expression, and Search and Seizure: Prospects for State Court Re-
incarnation," *Publius* 17 (Winter
1987): 13–31.

27. Paulette Thomas, "Mississippi's
Quirky Constitution Regulates Duels
and Prevents Governors from
Governing Too Much," *Wall Street
Journal,* August 19, 1986,
p. 56.

28. Marks and Cooper, *State Constitutional Law,* p. 47.

29. Tarr and Porter, "Introduction,"
p. 9.

30. Stanley H. Friedelbaum, "The
Complementary Role of Federal and
State Courts," *Publius* 17 (Winter
1987): 48.

31. Susan P. Fino, "Judicial Federalism and Equality Guarantees in State
Supreme Courts," *Publius* 17 (Winter
1987): 66–67.

32. Janice C. May, "State Constitutions and Constitutional Revision:
1988–89 and the 1980s," *The Book of
the States 1990–91* (Council of State
Governments, Washington, D.C.,
1991), p. 21.

33. Albert L. Sturm, *Thirty Years of
State Constitution-Making: 1938–*

1968 (New York: National Municipal
League, 1970), pp. 27–28.

34. Elmer E. Cornwell, Jr., Jay S.
Goodman, and Wayne R. Swanson,
*State Constitutional Conventions:
The Politics of the Revision Process in
Seven States* (New York: Praeger,
1975),
p. 72.

35. Ibid., p. 62.

36. Sturm, *Thirty Years,* p. 69.

37. Jay S. Goodman et al., "Public
Responses to State Constitutional Re-
vision," *American Journal of Political
Science* 17 (August 1973): 571–96.

38. Wayne R. Swanson, Sean Kelle-
her, and Arthur English, "Socializa-
tion of Constitution-Makers:
Experience, Role Conflict, and Attitude Change," *Journal of Politics* 34
(February 1972): 183–98.

39. Ibid.

40. Cornwell, Goodman, and Swanson, *State Constitutional Conventions,*
p. 81.

41. Janice C. May, "Texas Constitutional Revision: Lessons and La-
ments," *National Civic Review* 66
(February 1977): 64–69.

42. Sturm, "American State Constitutions," p. 85.

43. Ibid., p. 84.

44. May, "State Constitutions and
Constitutional Revision," p. 25.

45. Quoted in U.S. Advisory Commission on Intergovernmental Relations, *State Constitutions in the
Federal System* (Washington, D.C.:
ACIR, 1989), p. 37.

46. Sturm, "American State Constitutions," p. 104.

47. W. Brooke Graves, "State Con-
stitutional Law: A Twenty-five Year
Summary," *William and Mary Law
Review* 8 (Fall 1966): 12.

48. ACIR, *State Government Capability,* p. 60.

49. Richard H. Leach, "A Quiet
Revolution: 1933–1976," *The Book of
the States, 1975–76* (Lexington, Ky.:
Council of State Governments,
1976), p. 25.

50. Terry Sanford, *Storm Over the
States* (New York: McGraw-Hill,
1967), p. 189.

5 Participation and Interest Groups pp. 113–143

1. John Stuart Hall and Louis F. Weschler, "The Phoenix Futures Forum: Creating Visions, Implanting Community," *National Civic Review* 80 (Spring 1991): 135–57.

2. William J. McCoy, "Building Coalitions for the Future in Charlotte-Mecklenburg," *National Civic Review* 80 (Spring 1991): 120–34.

3. William E. Lyons and David Lowery, "Citizen Responses to Dissatisfaction in Urban Communities: A Test of a General Model," paper presented at the annual meeting of the Southern Political Science Association, Charlotte, N.C., 1987.

4. Sidney Verba and Norman H. Nie, *Participation in America* (New York: Harper & Row, 1972).

5. Ibid. See also Richard Murray and Arnold Vedlitz, "Race, Socioeconomic Status, and Voting Participation in Large Southern Cities," *Journal of Politics* 39 (November 1977): 1064–72.

6. Virginia Sapiro, *The Political Integration of Women* (Urbana: University of Illinois Press, 1983).

7. Earl Black and Merle Black, *Politics and Society in the South* (Cambridge, Mass.: Harvard University Press, 1987).

8. U.S. Bureau of the Census, *Statistical Abstract of the United States, 1988* (Washington, D.C.: U.S. Government Printing Office, 1987).

9. Richard Smolka, "Election Legislation: 1990–91," in *The Book of the States, 1992–93* (Lexington, Ky.: Council of State Governments, 1992), pp. 258–64.

10. "Outlook: Data Base," *U.S. News and World Report*, June 29, 1992, p. 10.

11. "Voter Registration Information," in *The Book of the States, 1992–93,* p. 279.

12. Ibid.

13. Paul E. Parker and James T. Przybylski, "Electoral Reform and Voter Participation: The Case of the Mail Ballot Election," paper presented at the annual meeting of the Southern Political Science Association, Tampa, November 1991.

14. E. J. Dionne, Jr., "If Nonvoters Had Voted: Same Winner, But Bigger," *New York Times,* November 21, 1988, p. 10.

15. Stephen Earl Bennett and David Resnick, "The Implications of Nonvoting for Democracy in the United States," *American Journal of Political Science* 34 (August 1990): 771–802.

16. David B. Magleby, "Taking the Initiative: Direct Legislation and Direct Democracy in the 1980s," *PS: Political Science and Politics* 21 (Summer 1988): 600–11.

17. Ibid., p. 600.

18. Ibid., p. 602.

19. David D. Schmidt, "Initiative Pendulum Begins Leftward Swing," *P.A. Times* 5 (September 15, 1982): 1, 10.

20. Robert Pear, "Voters Spurn Array of Plans for Protecting Environment," *New York Times,* November 8, 1990, pp. A13, A23.

21. Timothy Egan, "Washington Voters Weigh If There Is a Right to Die," *New York Times,* October 14, 1991, pp. A1, A9.

22. Joann S. Lublin, "Rising Use of Ballot Initiatives Threatens Legislatures' Powers," *Wall Street Journal,* October 30, 1984, p. 33.

23. W. John Moore, "Election Day Lawmaking," *National Journal* (September 17, 1988): 2296.

24. F. Christopher Arterton, "Political Participation and 'Teledemocracy,'" *PS: Political Science and Politics* 21 (Summer 1988): 620–27.

25. Ibid., p. 521.

26. George B. Merry, "Citizen-Initiated Legislation May Be on the Ballot in 19 States," *Christian Science Monitor,* May 15, 1984, p. 7.

27. Paula D. McClain, "Arizona 'High Noon': The Recall and Impeachment of Evan Mecham," *PS: Political Science and Politics* 21 (Summer 1988): 628–38.

28. Judge Archie Simonson, as quoted in Laura R. Woliver, "Feminism at the Grassroots: The Recall of Judge Archie Simonson," *Frontiers* 11 (Fall/Winter 1990): 111.

29. McClain, "Arizona 'High Noon,'" p. 629.

30. Joseph F. Zimmerman, *Participatory Democracy: Populism Revived* (New York: Praeger, 1986).

31. Jim Cleary, as quoted in "Fighting City Hall — and Winning," *The State* (Columbia, S.C.), May 26, 1987, p. 7A.

32. Thomas E. Cronin, "Public Opinion and Direct Democracy," *PS: Political Science and Politics* 21 (Summer 1988): 612–19.

33. L. Harmon Zeigler, "Interest Groups in the States," in Virginia Gray, Herbert Jacob, and Kenneth N. Vines, eds., *Politics in the American States,* 4th ed. (Boston: Little, Brown, 1983), pp. 97–131.

34. Clyde Brown, "Explanations of Interest Group Membership Over Time: The Farm Bureau in Five Midwestern States," *American Politics Quarterly* 17 (January 1989): 32–53.

35. Mitzi Mahoney, "Interest Group Use of the Legislative Rule Review Process in Three States," paper presented at the annual meeting of the Southern Political Science Association, Charlotte, N.C., 1987.

36. Clive S. Thomas and Ronald J. Hrebenar, "Interest Groups in the States," in Virginia Gray, Herbert Jacob, and Robert B. Albritton, eds., *Politics in the American States,* 5th ed. (Glenview, Il.: Scott, Foresman/Little, Brown, 1990), pp. 144–45.

37. Ibid., pp. 147–48.

38. Zeigler, "Interest Groups in the States," pp. 111–19.

39. Sarah McCally Morehouse, *State Politics, Parties and Policy* (New York: Holt, Rinehart and Winston, 1981).

40. Zeigler, "Interest Groups in the States," p. 117.

41. Clive S. Thomas and Ronald J. Hrebenar, "Comparative Interest Group Politics in the American West," *State Government* 59 (September/October 1986): 124–36.

42. Allan J. Cigler and Dwight Kiel, "Special Interests in Kansas: Representation in Transition," paper presented at the annual meeting of the Midwest Political Science Association, Chicago, 1987.

43. Ibid., p. 28.

44. Thomas and Hrebenar, "Interest Groups in the States," p. 143.

45. "Lobbyists: As Defined in State Statutes," *The Book of the States, 1992–93,* p. 205.

46. Ellen Perlman, "The Art of Persuasion," *City & State* 9 (May 18, 1992): 3, 29.

47. "Lobbyists: Registration and Reporting," *The Book of the States, 1992–93,* pp. 207–208.

48. Theodore B. Pedeliski, "Interest Groups in North Dakota: Constituency Coupling in a Moralistic Political Culture," paper presented at the annual meeting of the Midwest Political Science Association, Chicago, 1987.

49. William P. Browne and Delbert J. Ringquist, "Michigan Interests: The Politics of Diversification," paper presented at the annual meeting of the Midwest Political Science Association, Chicago, 1987, p. 15.

50. Thomas and Hrebenar, "Comparative Interest Group Politics in the American West," p. 130.

51. William P. Browne, "Variations in the Behavior and Style of State Lobbyists and Interest Groups," *Journal of Politics* 47 (May 1985): 450–68; and Charles W. Wiggins, Keith E. Hamm, and Charles G. Bell, "Interest Group and Party Influence Agents in the Legislative Process: A Comparative State Analysis," *Journal of Politics* 54 (February 1992): 82–100.

52. Charles W. Wiggins and Keith E. Hamm, "Iowa: Interest Group Politics in an Undistinguished Place," paper presented at the annual meeting of the Midwest Political Science Association, Chicago, 1987.

53. Ibid., p. 8.

54. Browne and Ringquist, "Michigan Interests: The Politics of Diversification," p. 24.

55. Howard A. Faye, Allan Cigler, and Paul Schumaker, "The Municipal Group Universe: Changes in Agency Penetration by Political Groups," paper presented at the annual meeting of the American Political Science Association, Washington, D.C., 1986.

56. Glenn Abney and Thomas P. Lauth, *The Politics of State and City Administration* (Albany: State University of New York Press, 1986).

57. Steven H. Haeberle, "Good Neighbors and Good Neighborhoods: Comparing Demographic and Environmental Influences on Neighborhood Activism," *State and Local Government Review* 18 (Fall 1986): 109–116.

58. U.S. Advisory Commission on Intergovernmental Relations, *Citizen Participation in the American Federal System* (Washington, D.C.: ACIR, 1979).

59. Ibid.

60. Neil Peirce, "Oregon's Rx for Mistrusted Government," *National Journal* 24 (February 29, 1992): 529.

61. Zimmerman, *Participatory Democracy,* pp. 145–54.

62. Thomas I. Miller, "How to Really Get in Touch with Your Constituents," *Governing* 5 (June 1992): 12–13.

63. Bruce H. Kirschner, "Electronic Democracy in the 21st Century," *National Civic Review* 80 (Fall 1991): 406–412.

64. Michael D. Reagan and John G. Sanzone, *The New Federalism,* 2d ed. (New York: Oxford University Press, 1981).

65. Steve Millard, "Voluntary Action and the States: The Other Alternative," *National Civic Review* 72 (May 1983): 262–69.

66. Harry P. Hatry and Carl F. Valente, "Alternative Service Delivery Approaches Involving Increased Use of the Private Sector," in International City Management Association, *The Municipal Year Book 1983* (Washington, D.C.: ICMA, 1983), pp. 199–216.

67. Mary A. Culp, "Volunteering as Helping," *National Civic Review* 77 (May/June 1988): 224–230.

68. Neal R. Peirce, "Denver Campaigns for Generous Giving," *P.A. Times,* April 15, 1987, p. 2.

69. Ronald K. Vogel and Bert E. Swanson, "Setting Agendas for Community Change: The Community Goal-Setting Strategy," *Journal of Urban Affairs* 10, no. 1 (1988): 41–61.

70. McCoy, "Building Coalitions for the Future in Charlotte-Mecklenburg," pp. 120–134; Hall and Weschler, "The Phoenix Futures Forum: Creating Visions, Implanting Community," pp. 135–157.

6 Political Parties, Elections, and Campaigns pp. 145–173

1. Timothy Egan, "The Comedian Politician Heads Back to His Roots," *New York Times,* February 14, 1992, p. A9.

2. Larry J. Sabato, *The Party's Just Begun* (Glenview, Ill.: Scott, Foresman, 1987).

3. Kenneth Janda, Jeffrey M. Berry, and Jerry Goldman, *The Challenge of Democracy: Government in America,* 2d ed. (Boston: Houghton Mifflin, 1989), p. 304.

4. Coleman L. Blease, as quoted in George Brown Tindall, *The Disruption of the Solid South* (Athens: University of Georgia Press, 1972), p. 47.

5. Denise L. Baer, "Interest Intermediation and Political Party Reform: A Comparative Study of State Party Charters," paper presented at the annual meeting of the American Political Science Association, Washington, D.C., 1988.

6. Malcolm E. Jewell and David M. Olson, *Political Parties and Elections in American States,* 3d ed. (Chicago: Dorsey Press, 1988).

7. James L. Gibson et al., "Whither the Local Parties?: A Cross-Sectional and Longitudinal Analysis of the Strength of Party Organizations,"

American Journal of Political Science 29 (February 1985): 139–60.

8. Dwaine Marvick, "Stability and Change in the Views of Los Angeles Party Activists," in William Crotty, ed., *Political Parties in Local Areas* (Knoxville: University of Tennessee Press, 1986), p. 124.

9. William Crotty, "The Machine in Transition," in William Crotty, ed., *Political Parties in Local Areas* (Knoxville: University of Tennessee Press, 1986), p. 190.

10. Ibid., p. 54.

11. "County GOP Sundered by Evangelicals," *Governing* 1 (July 1988): 64–65.

12. Frank J. Sorauf and Paul Allen Beck, *Party Politics in America,* 6th ed. (Glenview, Ill.: Scott, Foresman, 1988).

13. Ibid., p. 47.

14. Euel Elliott, Gerard S. Gryski, and Bruce Reed, "Alternative Models of Non-Major Party Support in State Legislative Elections, 1976–1984," paper presented at the annual meeting of the American Political Science Association, Washington, D.C., 1988.

15. Ibid., p. 11.

16. Jewell and Olson, *Political Parties and Elections,* p. 29.

17. "Something Is Gaining on State's Democrats," *Atlanta Journal and Constitution,* November 10, 1988, p. 22.

18. Ibid.

19. Stephen C. Craig, "The Decay of Mass Partisanship," *Polity* 20 (Summer 1988): 705–13.

20. Cornelius P. Cotter et al., *Party Organizations in American Politics* (New York: Praeger, 1984).

21. Paul S. Hernnson, "The Importance of Party Campaigning," *Polity* 20 (Summer 1988): 714–19.

22. *Campaigns and Elections* 9 (May/June 1988): 1.

23. Jerry Hagstrom and Robert Guskind, "Selling the Candidate," *National Journal* 18 (November 1, 1986): 2619–26.

24. Karl Struble, as quoted in ibid., p. 2626.

25. Ibid.

26. Robert G. Berger, "The Home-made Home Video," *Campaigns and Elections* 12 (October/November 1991): 44–46.

27. Thad Beyle, "Costs of the 1990 Gubernatorial Campaigns," *Comparative State Politics* 12 (October 1991): 3–7.

28. Ibid., p. 5.

29. Micheal W. Giles and Anita Pritchard, "Campaign Expenditures and Legislative Elections in Florida," *Legislative Studies Quarterly* 10 (February 1985): 71–88.

30. Stephen A. Salmore and Barbara G. Salmore, "Determinants of State Legislative Elections: The Case of New Jersey," paper presented at the annual meeting of the American Political Science Association, Chicago, 1987.

31. Ibid., pp. 3–4.

32. Sarah M. Morehouse, "Money Versus Party Effort: Nominating for Governor," paper presented at the annual meeting of the American Political Science Association, Chicago, 1987.

33. Common Cause, "Should State Elections Be Publicly Financed?" in Herbert M. Levine, ed., *The Politics of State and Local Government Debated* (Englewood Cliffs, N.J.: Prentice-Hall, 1985), pp. 84–85.

34. Robert J. Huckshorn, "Who Gave It? Who Got It?: The Enforcement of Campaign Finance Laws in the States," *Journal of Politics* 47 (August 1985): 773.

35. "Campaign Finance Laws: Limitations on Contributions by Organizations, by Individuals," *The Book of the States, 1992–1993* (Lexington, Ky.: Council of State Governments, 1992), pp. 304–16.

36. Ibid., pp. 283–93.

37. Joel A. Thompson, William Cassie, and Malcolm E. Jewell, "A Sacred Cow or Just a Lot of Bull?: The Impact of Money in Competitive State Legislative Campaigns," paper presented at the annual meeting of the American Political Science Association, Washington, D.C., 1991.

38. "Funding of State Elections: Tax Provisions and Public Financing," *The Book of the States, 1992–1993,* pp. 326–28.

39. Ruth S. Jones, "State Public Financing and the State Parties," in Michael J. Malbin, ed., *Parties, Interest Groups, and Campaign Finance Laws* (Washington, D.C.: American Enterprise Institute, 1980), pp. 283–303.

40. Elizabeth G. King and David G. Wegge, "The Rules Are Never Neutral: Public Funds in Minnesota and Wisconsin Legislative Elections," paper presented at the annual meeting of the Midwest Political Science Association, Chicago, 1984.

41. James M. Penning and Corwin E. Smidt, "Views of American State Legislators on Public Funding of Legislative Elections," *Legislative Studies Quarterly* 8 (February 1983): 97–109.

42. Ruth S. Jones, "State Public Campaign Finance: Implications for Partisan Politics," *American Journal of Political Science* 25 (May 1981): 342–61.

43. Jones, "State Public Financing and the State Parties."

44. "Methods of Nominating Candidates for State Offices," *The Book of the States, 1992–1993,* pp. 273–74.

45. William J. Keefe, *Parties, Politics, and Public Policy in America,* 5th ed. (Washington, D.C.: Congressional Quarterly, 1988).

46. Jewell and Olson, *Political Parties and Elections.*

47. Priscilla L. Southwell, "Open Versus Closed Primaries and Candidate Fortunes, 1972–1984," *American Politics Quarterly* 16 (July 1988): 280–95.

48. Charles S. Bullock III and Loch K. Johnson, "Runoff Elections in Georgia," *Journal of Politics* 47 (August 1985): 937–46.

49. Ibid., p. 940.

50. Steven H. Haeberle, "Rundown on the Runoff: Party Runway Run Amok," paper presented at the annual meeting of the Southern Political Science Association, Charlotte, N.C., 1987.

51. Barbara G. Salmore and Stephen A. Salmore, "The Transformation of State Electoral Politics," in Carl E. Van Horn, ed., *The State of the States* (Washington, D.C.: Congressional Quarterly, 1989), pp. 175–208.

52. Ibid.

53. Tari Renner, "Municipal Election Processes: The Impact on Minority Representation," in International City Management Association, *The Municipal Year Book 1988* (Washington, D.C.: ICMA, 1988), pp. 13–21.

54. Carol A. Cassel, "The Nonpartisan Ballot in the United States," in Bernard Grofman and Arend Lijphart, eds., *Electoral Laws and Their Consequences* (New York: Agathon, 1986), pp. 226–41.

55. Ibid.

56. Lana Stein and Arnold Fleischmann, "Newspaper and Business Endorsements in Municipal Elections: A Test of Conventional Wisdom," *Journal of Urban Affairs* 9, no. 4 (1987): 325–36.

57. Ibid., p. 331.

58. "For Mayor: Sandy Freedman," *Tampa Tribune*, February 25, 1987, p. 8A.

59. Charles S. Bullock III and Susan A. MacManus, "Endorsements, Spending, and Minority Group Success in Municipal Elections," paper presented at the annual meeting of the American Political Science Association, Washington, D.C., 1986.

60. Ibid., p. 14.

61. Michael A. Pagano, Ann O'M. Bowman, and John Kincaid, "The State of American Federalism, 1990–1991," *Publius* 22 (Summer 1991): 1–26.

7 **Governors pp. 175–213**

1. Neil R. Peirce, "Lesson from a Political Pariah," *National Journal* (March 16, 1991): 659.

2. Ann O'M. Bowman and Richard C. Kearney, *The Resurgence of the States* (Englewood Cliffs, N.J.: Prentice-Hall, 1986), p. 52.

3. For a more detailed discussion of the processes and results of the state government reform movement, see Bowman and Kearney, *Resurgence*, pp. 47–54.

4. Eric B. Herzik, "Governors and Issues: A Typology of Concerns," paper presented at the annual meeting of the Southern Political Science Association, Memphis, Tenn., November 1981.

5. Ibid.

6. Coleman B. Ransome, Jr., *The American Governorship* (Westport, Conn.: Greenwood Press, 1982), p. 125.

7. Thad L. Beyle, "The Governor as Chief Legislator," *State Government* 51 (Winter 1978): 2–10.

8. Alan Rosenthal, *Governors and Legislators: Contending Powers* (Washington, D.C.: Congressional Quarterly Press, 1990), pp. 52–54.

9. Sharon Sherman, "Powersplit: When Legislatures and Governors Are of Opposing Parties," *State Legislatures* 10 (May/June 1984): 9–12.

10. Sarah McCally Morehouse, "The Governor and His Legislative Party," *American Political Science Review* 60 (December 1966): 933–41.

11. Wayne L. Francis, *Legislative Issues in the Fifty States: A Comparative Analysis* (Chicago: Rand McNally, 1967), p. 35.

12. Thad L. Beyle and Lynn R. Muchmore, *Reflections on Being Governor* (Washington, D.C.: National Governors' Association, 1978), p. 45.

13. Beyle, "Governor as Chief Legislator," p. 8.

14. Rosenthal, *Governors and Legislators*, pp. 87–89.

15. Ibid., p. 70; see also Martha W. Weinberg, *Managing the State* (Cambridge, Mass.: MIT Press, 1977), p. 7.

16. Lynn Muchmore, "The Governor as Manager," *State Government* 54 (March 1981): 72.

17. H. Edward Flentje, "Governor as Manager: A Political Assessment," *State Government* 54 (Summer 1981): 76–81.

18. Chase Riveland, "Gubernatorial Styles: Is There a Right One?" *Journal of State Government* 62 (July/August 1989): 136–39.

19. Beyle, "Governor as Chief Legislator."

20. Thad L. Beyle and Lynn R. Muchmore, "The Governor and the Public," in Beyle and Muchmore, eds., *Reflections on Being Governor*, p. 24.

21. Thad L. Beyle and Lynn R. Muchmore, "Governors and Intergovernmental Relations: Middleman in the Federal System," in Beyle and Muchmore, eds., *Being Governor*, p. 193.

22. Susan E. Howell and James M. Vanderleeuw, "Economic Effects on State Governors," *American Politics Quarterly* 18 (April, 1990): 158–68.

23. Cited in Rosenthal, *Governors and Legislators*, p. 18.

24. Thad L. Beyle and Lynn R. Muchmore, "The Governor as Party Leader," in Beyle and Muchmore, eds., *Being Governor*, pp. 44–51.

25. Larry Sabato, *Goodbye to Goodtime Charlie: The American Governorship Transformed* (Lexington, Mass.: Lexington Books, 1978), p. 13.

26. Ibid.

27. Ibid., p. xi.

28. Ibid., pp. 27–31.

29. Thad L. Beyle, "Introduction," *State Government: CQ's Guide to Current Issues and Activities 1991–92* (Washington, D.C.: CQ Press, 1991), pp. 131–32.

30. Ibid., p. 133.

31. Thad L. Beyle, "Introduction," *State Government: CQ's Guide to Current Issues and Activities, 1987–88* (Washington, D.C.: CQ Press, 1987), pp. 95–101.

32. Thad L. Beyle, "The Governors, 1988–89," *The Book of the States, 1990–91* (Lexington, Ky.: The Council of State Governments, 1990), pp. 51–52.

33. Ibid., p. 95.

34. Ibid., p. 96.

35. Quoted in George Weeks,

"Statehouse Hall of Fame, Ten Outstanding Governors of the 20th Century," paper presented at the annual meeting of the Southern Political Science Association, Memphis, Tenn., November 1981.

36. Charles N. Wheeler III, "Gov. James R. Thompson, 1977–1991: The Complete Campaigner, The Pragmatic Centrist," *Illinois Issues* 16 (December 1990): 12–16.

37. Tom McCall, quoted in Samuel R. Soloman, "Governors: 1960–1970," *National Civic Review* (March 1971): 126–46.

38. Thad L. Beyle and Robert Dalton, "Appointment Power: Does It Belong to the Governor?" *State Government* 54 (Winter 1981): 4.

39. Ibid., p. 8.

40. Diane Kincaid Blair, "The Gubernatorial Appointment Power: Too Much of a Good Thing?" in Beyle and Muchmore, eds., *Being Governor,* p. 117.

41. Ransome, *American Governorship,* p. 121.

42. Beyle and Dalton, "Appointment Power."

43. *Rutan et al.* v. *Republican Party of Illinois,* 1110 S.Ct. 2229, 1990.

44. Gerald Benjamin, "The Diffusion of the Governor's Veto Power," *State Government* 55 (March 1982): 99–105.

45. Charles W. Wiggins, "Executive Vetoes and Legislative Overrides in the American States," *Journal of Politics* 42 (November 1980): 1110–17.

46. Rosenthal, *Governors and Legislators,* pp. 11–12.

47. See, for example, *The Book of the States, 1980–81* (Lexington, Ky.: Council of State Governments, 1980), pp.110–11.

48. Beyle, "Governor as Chief Legislator."

49. David Osborne, *Laboratories of Democracy* (Boston: Harvard Business School Press, 1988): 138–39.

50. Glenn Abney and Thomas P. Lauth, "The Governor of Chief Administrator," *Public Administration Review* 43 (January/February 1983): 40–49.

51. Ibid., p. 46.

52. Thad L. Beyle, "The Governor's Formal Powers: A View from the Governor and Chair," *Public Administration Review* 28 (November/December 1968): 540–45.

53. E. Lee Bernick and Charles W. Wiggins, "The Governor's Executive Order: An Unknown Power," *State and Local Government Review* 16 (Winter 1984): 3–10.

54. See U.S. Advisory Commission on Intergovernmental Relations, *The Question of State Government Capability,* A-98 (Washington, D.C.: ACIR, 1985), pp. 143–55. See also James L. Garnett, *Reorganizing State Government: The Executive Branch* (Boulder, Colo.: Westview Press, 1980).

55. James D. Carney, "Downsizing Government: Iowa's Challenge," *State Government* 60 (July/August 1987): 183–90.

56. James K. Conant, "In the Shadow of Wilson and Brownlow: Executive Branch Reorganization in the States, 1965 to 1987," *Public Administration Review* 47 (September/October 1988): 892.

57. Chase Riveland, "Gubernatorial Styles: Is There a Right One?" *Journal of State Government* 62 (July/August 1989): 136–39.

58. James Conant, "State Reorganization: A New Model?" *State Government* 58 (April 1985): 130–38. For further discussion of the New Jersey reorganization, see also Conant, "Reorganization and the Bottom Line," *Public Administration Review,* 46 (January/February 1986): 48–56.

59. Garnett, *Reorganizing State Government,* pp. 124–25.

60. Robert F. Bennett, quoted in Flentje, "Governor as Manager," p. 70. For a description of failure in reorganization in Florida, see also Less Garner, "Managing Change Through Organization Structure," *State Government* 60 (July/August 1987): 191–95.

61. James K. Conant, "Executive Branch Reorganization: Can It Be an Antidote for Fiscal Stress in the States?" *State and Local Government Review* 24 (Winter 1992): 3–11.

62. Donald P. Sprengel, "Trends in Staffing the Governor's Office," *Comparative State Politics Newsletter* 9 (June 1988): 11.

63. Thad L. Beyle, "Governors' Offices: Variation on Common Themes," in Beyle and Muchmore, eds., *Being Governor,* pp. 158–73.

64. H. Edward Flentje, "Clarifying Purpose and Achieving Balance in Gubernatorial Administration," *Journal of State Government* 62 (July/August 1989): 161–67.

65. Richard C. Kearney, "How a 'Weak' Governor Can Be Strong: Dick Riley and Education Reform in South Carolina," *State Government* 60 (July/August 1987): 150–56.

66. Dan Durning, "Change Masters for the States," *State Government* 60 (July/August 1987): 145–49.

67. Rosenthal, *Governors and Legislators,* p. 27.

68. Ransome, *American Governorship,* p. 156.

69. Lee Sigelman and Roland Smith, "Personal, Office, and State Characteristics as Predictors of Gubernatorial Performance," *Journal of Politics* 43 (February 1981): 169–80.

70. Scott M. Matheson, with James Edwin Kee, *Out of Balance* (Salt Lake City: Peregrine Smith Books, 1986), p. 186.

71. See Paul West, "They're Everywhere! For Today's Governors, Life Is a Never-Ending Campaign," *Governing* 3 (March 1990): 51–55.

72. W. John Moore, "New Cops on the Beat," *National Journal* 19 (May 23, 1987): 1338–42.

73. Alice Chasan Edelman, "Is There Room at the Top?" in Beyle and Muchmore, eds., *Being Governor,* p. 107.

74. Thad L. Beyle, "The Governors, 1988–89," *The Book of the States, 1990–91* (Lexington, Ky.: Council of State Governments, 1990), 56.

8 The Bureaucracy pp. 215–247

1. Beverly A. Cigler and Heidi L. Neiswender, " 'Bureaucracy' in the Introductory American Government Textbook," *Public Administration Review* 51 (September/October 1991): 442–50.

2. J. Norman Baldwin, "Public Versus Private Employees: Debunking Stereotypes," *Review of Public Personnel Administration* 11 (Fall 1990–Spring 1991): 1–27.

3. U.S. Bureau of the Census, *Statistical Abstract of the United States, 1991* (Washington, D.C.: U.S. Government Printing Office, 1991).

4. Jay Shafritz, "The Cancer Eroding Public Personnel Professionalism," *Public Personnel Management* 3 (November/December 1974): 486–92.

5. U.S. Advisory Commission on Intergovernmental Relations, *The Question of State Government Capability,* A-98 (Washington, D.C.: ACIR, 1985), pp. 168–69.

6. See, for example, Kenneth J. Meier, "Representative Bureaucracy: An Empirical Analysis," *American Political Science Review* 69 (June 1975): 526–42; and Samuel Krislov and David H. Rosenbloom, *Representative Bureaucracy and the American Political System* (New York: Praeger, 1981), pp. 31–73, 75–107.

7. U.S. Equal Employment Opportunity Commission, *Affirmative Action and Equal Employment: A Guidebook for Employers* (Washington, D.C.: U.S. Government Printing Office, 1974).

8. *Ward's Cove Packing Co.* v. *Atonio,* 109 S.Ct. 2115 (1989).

9. *Richmond* v. *Croson,* 1989, 57 Law Week 4.32.

10. *Memphis* v. *Stotts,* 467 U.S. 561 (1984).

11. See, for example, James D. Slack, "Affirmative Action and City Managers: Attitudes Toward Recruitment of Women," *Public Administration Review* 47 (March/April 1987): 199–

206; William G. Lewis, "Toward Representative Bureaucracy: Blacks in City Police Organizations, 1975–1985," *Public Administration Review* 49 (May/June 1989): 257–267; Lois R. Wise, "Social Equity in Civil Service Systems," *Public Administration Review* 50 (September/October 1990): 567–75.

12. Deil S. Wright, Jae-Won Yoo, and Jennifer Cohen, "The Evolving Profile of State Administrators," *Journal of State Government* 64 (January-March 1991): 30–38.

13. See Karen Torry, "Comparable Worth: A Developing Issue or One Losing Steam?" in Thad L. Beyle, ed., *State Government: CQ's Guide to Current Issues and Activities, 1986–87* (Washington, D.C.: Congressional Quarterly, 1986), pp. 116–21.

14. Keon S. Chi, "Comparable Worth in State Governments," *State Government News* 27 (November 1984): 4–6.

15. *Meritor Savings Bank* v. *Vinson,* 1986, 477 U. S. 57.

16. See M. Dawn McCaghy, *Sexual Harassment: A Guide to Resources* (Boston: G. K. Hall, 1985); Dail Ann Neugarten, "Sexual Harassment in Public Employment," in Steven W. Hays and Richard C. Kearney, eds., *Public Personnel Administration: Problems and Prospects,* 2d ed. (Englewood Cliffs, N.J.: Prentice-Hall, 1990): pp. 205–14.

17. Cynthia S. Ross and Robert E. England, "State Governments' Sexual Harassment Policy Initiatives," *Public Administration Review* 47 (May/June 1987): 259–62.

18. U.S. Bureau of the Census, *Labor-Management Relations,* Vol. 13: *Public Employment* (3) (Washington, D.C.: U.S. Government Printing Office, 1987).

19. Jay F. Atwood, "Collective Bargaining's Challenge: Five Imperatives for Public Managers," *Public Personnel Management* 5 (January/February 1976): 24–32.

20. See Richard C. Kearney, "Mone-

tary Impacts," in *Labor Relations in the Public Sector,* 2d ed. (New York: Marcel Dekker Co., 1992).

21. Joel M. Douglas, "State Civil Service Systems and Collective Bargaining: Systems in Conflict," *Public Administration Review* 52 (January/February 1992): 162–71.

22. See Raymond D. Horton, David Levin, and James W. Kuhn, "Some Impacts of Collective Bargaining on Local Government: A Diversity Thesis," *Administration and Society* 7 (February 1976): 497–516.

23. Glenn Abney and Thomas P. Lauth, *The Politics of State and City Administration* (Albany: SUNY Press, 1986), pp. 76–78, 178–81.

24. Kenneth J. Meier, Joseph Stewart, Jr., and Robert E. England, "The Politics of Bureaucratic Discretion: Educational Access as an Urban Service," *American Journal of Political Science* 35 (February 1991): 155–177.

25. John T. Scholz and Feng Heng Wei, "Regulatory Enforcement in a Federalist System," *American Political Science Review* 8 (December 1986): 1249–70; see also Abney and Lauth, *Politics of State and City Administration.*

26. Abney and Lauth, *Politics of State and City Administration,* pp. 132–53.

27. See Richard C. Kearney and Chandan Sinha, "Professionalism and Bureaucratic Responsiveness: Conflict or Compatibility?" *Public Administration Review* 48 (January/February 1988): 571–79.

28. See Frederick C. Mosher, *Democracy and the Public Service,* 2d ed. (New York: Oxford University Press, 1982).

29. Robert Bell, "Professional Values and Organizational Decision Making," *Administration and Society* 17 (May 1985): 21–60.

30. Kearney and Sinha, "Professionalism and Bureaucratic Responsiveness," pp. 571–79.

31. Ibid.

32. Charles T. Goodsell, *The Case for Bureaucracy: A Public Administration*

Polemic (Chatham, N.J.: Chatham House, 1983), pp. 44–48; also see Abney and Lauth, *Politics of State and City Administration*, pp. 209–10.

33. Kearney and Sinha, "Professionalism and Bureaucratic Responsiveness."

34. Ibid.

35. Jonathan Walters, "The Shrink-Proof Bureaucracy," *Governing* 5 (March 1992): 33–38.

36. Gregory R. Weiher and Jon Lorence, "Growth in State Government Employment: A Time Series Analysis," *Western Political Quarterly* 44 (June, 1991): 373–88.

37. John Rehfuss, "Contracting Out and Accountability in State and Local Governments — The Importance of Contract Monitoring," *State and Local Government Review* 22 (Winter 1990): 44–48.

38. David Osborne, *Reinventing Government: How the Entrepreneurial Spirit Is Transforming the Public Sector* (New York: Addison-Wesley, 1992).

39. M. J. Richter, "The Real Advantages of Putting Government on Line," *Governing* 4 (May 1991): 60.

40. Harold D. Lasswell, *Politics: Who Gets What, When, Where, How?* (Cleveland: World, 1958).

41. See Irene S. Rubin, *The Politics of Public Budgeting* (Chatham, N.J.: Chatham House Publishers, 1990): 167–80.

42. Aaron Wildavsky, "Toward a Radical Incrementalism," in Alfred De Grazia, ed., *Congress: The First Branch of Government* (Washington, D.C.: American Enterprise Institute, 1966).

43. Aaron Wildavsky, *The Politics of the Budgetary Process* (Boston: Little, Brown, 1964), pp. 1–13.

44. Abney and Lauth, *Politics of State and City Administration*, pp. 110–11, 115, 142–43.

45. Charles E. Lindblom, "The Science of Muddling Through," *Public Administrative Review* 19 (Spring 1959): 79–88.

46. James Ramsey and Merlin H. Backbart, *Innovations in State Budgeting: Process, Impact* (Lexington, Ky.: Center for Public Affairs, 1980), p. 7.

47. U.S. Advisory Commission on Intergovernmental Relations, *The Question of State Government Capability*, p. 179.

48. Stanley B. Botner, "The Use of Budgeting/Management Tools by State Governments," *Public Administration Review* 45 (September/October 1985): 130–32.

49. Charles Barrileaux, Richard Feiock, and Robert E. Crew, Jr., "Measuring and Comparing American States' Administrative Characteristics," *State and Local Government Review* 24 (Winter 1992): 12–18.

9 State Legislatures pp. 249–280

1. Ronald M. Peters, Jr., and Elizabeth Himmerich, "Policy Shift and Leadership Coalition: The Revolt Against Speaker Barker in Oklahoma," paper presented at the annual meeting of the American Political Science Association, San Francisco, August 1990.

2. James N. Miller, "Hamstrung Legislatures," *National Civic Review* 54 (June 1989): 28–33.

3. Ibid.

4. "Legislative Sessions: Legal Provisions," *The Book of the States, 1990-91* (Lexington, Ky.: Council of State Governments, 1990).

5. Elizabeth Kolbert, "As Workload Grows, Number of Part-Time Legislators Falls," *New York Times,* June 4, 1989, p. 13.

6. National Municipal League, *Apportionment in the 1960s,* rev. ed. (New York: National Municipal League, 1970).

7. *Baker* v. *Carr,* 369 U.S. 186, 82 S.Ct. 691 (1962).

8. *Reynolds* v. *Sims,* 84 S.Ct. 1362 (1964).

9. Timothy G. O'Rourke, *The Impact of Reapportionment* (New Brunswick, N.J.: Transaction Books, 1980).

10. David C. Saffell, "Reapportionment and Public Policy: State Legislators' Perspectives," in Bernard Gronfman et al., eds. *Representation and Redistricting Issues* (Lexington, Mass.: D.C. Heath, 1982), pp. 203–19.

11. Tim Storey, "Dickering Over the Districts," *State Legislatures* 18 (February 1992): 22–23.

12. *Davis* v. *Bandemer,* 106 S.Ct. 2797 (1986).

13. Sam Roberts, "Where Will Mappers of New Districts Draw the Line?" *New York Times,* March 23, 1992, p. B12.

14. Robert Pear, "Citing Racial Bias, U.S. Rejects Plans for Redistricting," *New York Times,* July 3, 1991, pp. A1, A7.

15. Kimball Brace, Bernard Grofman, and Lisa Handley, "Does Redistricting Aimed to Help Blacks Necessarily Help Republicans?" *Journal of Politics* 49 (February 1987): 169–85.

16. Roberto Suro, "Texas Republicans Win Battle on Redistricting," *New York Times,* January 17, 1992, p. A11.

17. William T. Pound, "The State Legislatures," in Council of State Governments, *The Book of the States, 1992–93* (Lexington, Ky.: Council of State Governments, 1992), pp. 124–35.

18. "Legislative Compensation: Regular and Special Sessions," *The Book of the States, 1992–1993*, pp. 151–52.

19. Peverill Squire, "Member Career Opportunities and the Internal Organization of Legislatures," *Journal of Politics* 50 (August 1988): 726–44.

20. Robert Harmel and Keith E. Hamm, "Political Party Development in State Legislatures: The Case of Texas," paper presented at the annual meeting of the Midwest Political Science Association, Chicago, April 1991.

21. Joel A. Thompson, "Bringing Home the Bacon: The Politics of Pork Barrel in the North Carolina

Legislature," *Legislative Studies Quarterly* 11 (February 1986): 91–108.

22. Keith E. Hamm, "The Role of 'Subgovernments' in U.S. State Policy Making: An Exploratory Analysis," *Legislative Studies Quarterly* 11 (August 1986): 321–51.

23. Alan Rosenthal, *Legislative Life: People, Processes, and Performance in the States* (New York: Harper & Row, 1981).

24. "Bill and Resolution Introduction and Enactment," *The Book of the States, 1992–1993,* pp. 183–85.

25. Harvey J. Tucker, "Legislative Logjams: A Comparative State Analysis," *Western Political Quarterly* 38 (September 1985): 432–446.

26. E. Lee Bernick and Charles W. Wiggins, "Legislative Norms in Eleven States," *Legislative Studies Quarterly* 8 (May 1983): 191–200.

27. Roy Brasfield Herron, "Diary of a Legislator," *Southern Magazine* 2 (May 1988): 31.

28. Squire, "Member Career Opportunities."

29. Peverill Squire, "Career Opportunities and Membership Stability in Legislatures," *Legislative Studies Quarterly* 13 (February 1988): 65–77.

30. Herron, "Diary of a Legislator," p. 31.

31. Eric M. Uslaner and Ronald E. Weber, "U.S. State Legislators' Opinions and Perceptions of Constituency Attitudes," *Legislative Studies Quarterly* 4 (November 1979): 563–85.

32. Donald R. Songer et al., "The Influence of Issues on Choice of Voting Cues Utilized by State Legislators," *Western Political Quarterly* 39 (March 1986): 118–25.

33. Jon Hurwitz, "Determinants of Legislative Cue Selection," *Social Science Quarterly* 69 (March 1988): 212–23.

34. Citizens' Conference on State Legislatures, *The Sometimes Governments: A Critical Study of the 50 American Legislatures,* 2d ed. (Kansas City, Mo.: CCSL, 1973), pp. 41–42.

35. The Council of State Governments, "Stated Briefly," *State Government News* 31 (June 1988): 30.

36. Pound, "The State Legislatures," p. 79.

37. Ibid., p. 82.

38. John Grumm, "The Effects of Legislative Structure on Legislative Performance," in Richard Hofferbert and Ira Sharkansky, eds., *State and Urban Politics: Readings in Comparative Public Policy* (Boston: Little, Brown, 1971), pp. 298–322.

39. Albert K. Karning and Lee Sigelman, "State Legislative Reform and Public Policy: Another Look," *Western Political Quarterly* 28 (September 1975): 548–52.

40. Philip W. Roeder, "State Legislative Reform: Determinants and Policy Consequences," *American Politics Quarterly* 7 (January 1979): 51–70.

41. Ann O'M. Bowman and Richard C. Kearney, "Dimensions of State Government Capability," *Western Political Quarterly* 41 (June 1988): 341–62.

42. Alan Rosenthal, "The New Legislature: Better or Worse and for Whom?" *State Legislatures* 12 (July 1986): 5.

43. Andrea Paterson, "Is the Citizen Legislator Becoming Extinct?" *State Legislatures* 12 (July 1986): 22–25.

44. Charles W. Wiggins, as quoted in Paterson, "Is the Citizen Legislator Becoming Extinct?" p. 24.

45. Representative Vic Krouse, as quoted in Paterson, "Is the Citizen Legislator Becoming Extinct?" p. 24.

46. Alan Rosenthal, "The State Legislature," paper presented at the Vanderbilt Institute for Public Policy Studies, November 1987.

47. Michael A. Pagano, Ann O'M. Bowman, and John Kincaid, "The State of American Federalism, 1990–1991," *Publius* 21 (Summer 1991): 17.

48. Stuart Rothenberg, "How Term Limits Became a National Phenomenon," *State Legislatures* 18 (January 1992): 35–39.

49. Karl T. Kurtz, "Limiting Terms—What's in Store?" *State Legislatures* 18 (January 1992): 32–34.

50. Lucinda Simon, "Legislatures and Governors: The Wrestling Match," *State Government* 59 (Spring 1986): 1.

51. Ted Strickland, as quoted in Simon, "Legislatures and Governors," p. 5.

52. Sharon Randall, "From Big Shot to Boss," *State Legislatures* 14 (June 1988): 34–38.

53. Governor Tommy Thompson, as quoted in Randall, "From Big Shot to Boss," p. 36.

54. Tom Loftus, as quoted in Randall, "From Big Shot to Boss," p. 36.

55. Madeleine Kunin, as quoted in Randall, "From Big Shot to Boss," p. 34.

56. Simon, "Legislatures and Governors."

57. Samuel K. Gove, "State Management and Legislative-Executive Relations," *State Government* 54, no. 3 (1981): 99–101.

58. Rosenthal, *Legislative Life.*

59. Richard E. Brown, "Legislative Performance Auditing: Its Goals and Pitfalls," *State Government* 52 (Winter 1979): 31–34.

60. William M. Pearson and Van A. Wigginton, "Effectiveness of Administrative Controls: Some Perceptions of State Legislators," *Public Administrations Review* 46 (July/August 1986): 328–31.

61. Rosenthal, "The New Legislature," p. 5.

62. Alan Ehrenhalt, "An Embattled Institution," *Governing* 5 (January 1992): 28–33.

10 The Judiciary pp. 281–308

1. W. John Moore, "In Whose Court?" *National Journal* (October 15, 1991): 2396.

2. Henry Robert Glick and Kenneth N. Vines, *State Court Systems* (Englewood Cliffs, N.J.: Prentice-Hall, 1973), p. 19.

3. Ibid., p. 21.

4. See, for example, Robert A. Kagan et al., "The Evolution of State

Supreme Courts," *Michigan Law Review* 76 (May 1978): 961–1005.

5. See Larry Berkson and Susan Carbon, *Court Unification: History, Politics and Implementation* (Washington, D.C.: U.S. Department of Justice, National Institute for Law Enforcement and Criminal Justice, 1978).

6. U.S. Advisory Commission on Intergovernmental Relations, "State Court Systems," in *The Question of State Government Capability* (Washington, D.C.: ACIR, 1985), p. 191.

7. American Bar Association, *Standards Relating to Court Organization* (New York: ABA, 1974), pp. 43–44.

8. *The Book of the States 1985–86* (Lexington, Ky.: Council of State Governments, 1985), p. 159.

9. Herbert Jacob, "The Effect of Institutional Differences in the Recruitment Process: The Case of State Judges," *Journal of Public Law* 33, no. 113 (1964): 104–19.

10. Francis Graham Lee, "Party Representation of State Supreme Courts: 'Unequal Representation' Revisited," *State and Local Government Review* 11 (May 1979): 48–52. See also Herbert Jacob, *Justice in America* (Boston: Little, Brown, 1965), p. 98.

11. "Is Texas Justice for Sale?" *Time*, January 11, 1988, p. 45.

12. Sheila Kaplan, "Justice for Sale," *State Government: CQ's Guide to Current Issues and Activities 1986–87* (Washington, D.C.: CQ Press, 1987), pp. 151–57.

13. Ibid., p. 152.

14. Tom Watson, "The Run for the Robes," *Governing* 4 (July 1991): 49–52.

15. John H. Culver, "Politics and the California Plan for Choosing Appellate Judges: A Lesson at Large on Judicial Selection," *Judicature* 66 (September/October 1982): 152–53.

16. See, for example, Richard A. Watson and Ronald C. Downing, *The Politics of the Bench and Bar* (New York: John Wiley and Sons, 1969), pp. 43–48, 136–38.

17. Ibid.

18. Susan Carbon, "Judicial Reten-

tion Elections: Are They Serving Their Intended Purpose?" *Judicature* 64 (November 1980): 210–33.

19. Ibid., p. 221.

20. John Culver, "California Supreme Court Election: 'Rose Bird and the Supremes,'" *Comparative State Politics Newsletter*, February 1987, p. 13.

21. Bradley C. Canon, "The Impact of Formal Selection Processes on the Characteristics of Judges — Reconsidered," *Law and Society Review* 6 (1972): 575–93; Burton M. Atkins and Henry R. Glick, "Formal Judicial Recruitment and State Supreme Court Decisions," *American Politics Quarterly* 2 (October 1974): 427–49.

22. John Paul Ryan et al., *American Trial Judges* (New York: Free Press, 1980), pp. 125–30.

23. Philip L. Dubois, *From Ballot to Bench: Judicial Elections and the Quest for Accountability* (Austin: University of Texas Press, 1980), Chapter 4.

24. Philip L. Dubois, "State Trial Court Appointments: Does the Governor Make a Difference?" *Judicature* 69 (June/July 1985): 22; Bradley C. Canon, "Characteristics and Career Patterns of State Supreme Court Justices," *State Government* 45 (Winter 1972): 34–41.

25. Glick and Vines, *State Court Systems*, p. 44.

26. Ibid.

27. Dubois, "State Trial Court Appointments."

28. Ibid., pp. 24–25.

29. N. Alozie, "Black Representation on State Judiciaries," *Social Science Quarterly* 69 (1988): 979–86; Barbara Luck Graham, "Do Judicial Systems Matter?" *American Politics Quarterly* 18 (July 1990): 316–36.

30. U.S. Advisory Commission on Intergovernmental Relations, *State Government Capability*, p. 190.

31. *Gregory* v. *Ashcroft* (1991) 111 S.Ct. 2395.

32. U.S. Advisory Commission on Intergovernmental Relations, *State Government Capability*, p. 190.

33. Harry Kalven, Jr., and Hans Zeisel, *The American Jury* (Boston: Little, Brown, 1966), pp. 502–503.

34. Glick and Vines, *State Court Systems*, p. 78; Kenyon D. Bunch and Gregory Casey, "Political Controversy on Missouri's Supreme Court: The Case of Merit Versus Politics," *State and Local Government Review* 22 (Winter 1990): 5–16.

35. Glick and Vines, *State Court Systems*, pp. 81–82.

36. Bunch and Casey, "Political Controversy," p. 12.

37. Melinda Gann Hall, "Electoral Politics and Strategic Voting in State Supreme Courts," *Journal of Politics* (forthcoming, 1992).

38. Gregory A. Caldeira, "The Transmission of Legal Precedent: A Study of State Supreme Courts," *American Political Science Review* 79 (March 1985): 178–93.

39. Gregory A. Caldeira, "Legal Precedent: Structures of Communication Between State Supreme Courts," *Social Network* 10 (1988): 29–55.

40. Paul Brace and Melinda Gann Hall, "Neo-Institutionalism and Dissent in State Supreme Courts," *Journal of Politics* 51 (1990): 54–70.

41. Stuart Nagel, "Political Party Affiliation and Judges' Decisions," *American Political Science Review* 55 (December 1961): 843–60.

42. See Beverly Cook, "Women Judges and Public Policy in Sex Integration," in Debra Stewart, ed., *Women in Local Politics* (London: Scarecrow Press, 1980); Gerald S. Gryski, Eleanor C. Main, and William J. Dixon, "Models of State High Court Decision Making in Sex Discrimination Cases," *Journal of Politics* 48 (February 1986): 143–55; Diane E. Wall and David W. Allen, "Elite Female Justices' Decision Making Within the South," paper presented at the annual meeting of the Southern Political Science Association, Charlotte, N.C., November 1987.

43. Richard C. Kearney and Reginal Sheehan, "Supreme Court Decision Making: The Impact of Court Composition on State and Local Government Litigation," *Journal of Politics* (November/December 1992) (forthcoming).

44. Bradley C. Canon, "Defining the Dimensions of Judicial Activism," *Judicature* 66 (December/January 1983): 236–47.

45. John J. Scheb, III, Terry Bowen, and Gary Anderson, "Ideology, Role Orientations, and Behavior in the State Courts of Last Resort," *American Politics Quarterly* 19 (July 1991): 324–35.

46. Canon, "Defining the Dimensions," pp. 238–39.

47. Quoted in Stanley M. Mosk, "The Emerging Agenda in State Constitutional Law," *Intergovernmental Perspective* 13 (Spring 1987): 21.

48. Mark L. Glasser and John Kincaid, "Selected Rights Enumerated in State Constitutions," *Intergovernmental Perspective* 17 (Fall 1991): 35–44.

49. Mosk, "The Emerging Agenda," p. 22.

50. See John Patrick Hagan, "Patterns of Activism on State Supreme Courts," *Publius* 18 (Winter 1988): 97–115.

51. Canon, "Defining the Dimensions," pp. 246–47.

52. American Bar Association, *Standards,* pp. 97–104.

53. Charles G. Douglas III, "Innovative Appellate Court Processing: New Hampshire's Experience with Summary Affirmance," *Judicature* 69 (October/November 1985): 147–52.

54. Ibid., p. 148.

55. Jef Feeley, "Appellate Arbitration Set in South Carolina," *National Law Journal* (January 14, 1985): 11, 38.

56. Dixie K. Knoebel, "The State of the Judiciary," *The Book of the States 1990–1991* (Lexington, Ky.: Council of State Governments, 1990), pp. 194–212.

57. Marcia J. Lim, "State of the Judiciary," in *The Book of the States 1985–1986* (Lexington, Ky.: Council of State Governments, 1985).

58. "The Cameras Are Rolling in Kentucky Courts," *Governing* 2 (October 1988): 32–34.

59. Knoebel, "The State of the Judiciary," pp. 194–96.

60. Thomas B. Marvell, "Judicial Salaries: Doing More Work for Less Pay," *Judges Journal* 24 (Winter 1985): 34–37, 46–47.

61. Edward B. McConnell, "State Judicial Salaries: A National Perspective," *State Government* 61 (September/October 1988): 179–82.

62. Knoebel, "The State of the Judiciary," pp. 201–202.

11 **The Structure of Local Government   pp. 309–336**

1. Steve Lohr, "Forget Peoria. It's Now: 'Will It Play in Tulsa?'" *New York Times*, June 1, 1992, pp. A1, C5.

2. "Local Government in Metropolitan Areas," *1982 Census of Governments* (Washington, D.C.: U.S. Department of Commerce, 1985).

3. John Kincaid, "Municipal Perspectives on Federalism," unpublished manuscript, 1987.

4. Dennis Hale, "The City as Polity and Economy," *Polity* 17 (Winter 1984): 205–24.

5. Kincaid, "Municipal Perspectives," p. 56.

6. Oliver P. Williams and Charles R. Adrian, *Four Cities: A Study in Comparative Policy Making* (Philadelphia: University of Pennsylvania Press, 1963).

7. Herbert Sydney Duncombe, *Modern County Government* (Washington, D.C.: National Association of Counties, 1977).

8. Carolyn B. Lawrence and John M. DeGrove, "County Government Services," in National Association of Counties and International City Management Association, *The County Year Book 1976* (Washington, D.C.: NACO and ICMA, 1976), pp. 91–129.

9. U.S. Advisory Commission on Intergovernmental Relations, *State and Local Roles in the Federal System* (Washington, D.C.: ACIR, 1982).

10. Tanis J. Salant, "County Governments: An Overview," *Intergovernmental Perspective* 17 (Winter 1991): 5–9.

11. Barbara P. Greene, "Counties and the Fiscal Challenges of the 1980s," *Intergovernmental Perspective* 13 (Winter 1987): 14–19.

12. John Herbers, "Seventeenth-Century Counties Struggle to Cope with Twentieth-Century Problems," *Governing* 2 (May 1989): 42–48.

13. "Counties Out of Date," *State Legislatures* 17 (March 1991): 17.

14. Douglas Yates, *The Ungovernable City* (Cambridge, Mass.: MIT Press, 1977).

15. Edward C. Banfield, *The Unheavenly City* (Boston: Little, Brown, 1968).

16. Data from John Marinucci, Project Manager, Boundary and Annexation Survey, U.S. Department of Commerce, Bureau of the Census, June 1992.

17. Robert Bradley Rice, *Progressive Cities* (Austin: University of Texas Press, 1977).

18. Heywood T. Sanders, "The Government of American Cities: Continuity and Change in Structure," *The Municipal Year Book 1982* (Washington, D.C.: International City Management Association, 1982), pp. 178–86.

19. David R. Morgan, *Managing Urban America*, 2d ed. (Belmont, Calif.: Wadsworth, 1984).

20. James H. Svara, *Official Leadership in the City* (New York: Oxford University Press, 1990).

21. Robert D. Thomas, "Metropolitan Structural Development: The Territorial Imperative," *Publius* 14 (Spring 1984): 83–115.

22. Melville C. Branch, *Comprehensive City Planning* (Chicago: American Planning Association, 1985).

23. Brian M. Green and Yda Schreuder, "Growth, Zoning and Neighborhood Organizations," *Journal of Urban Affairs* 13, no.1 1991): 97–110.

24. Arnold Fleischmann and Carol A. Pierannunzi, "Citizens, Development Interests, and Local Land-Use Regulation," *Journal of Politics* 52 (August 1990): 838–53.

25. Barry J. Kaplan, "Houston: The Golden Buckle of the Sunbelt," in Richard M. Bernard and Bradley R. Rice, eds., *Sunbelt Cities: Politics and Growth Since World War II* (Austin: University of Texas Press, 1983), pp. 196–212.

26. "Rankings of 75 Largest Cities for Selected Subjects," *County and City Data Book 1983* (Washington, D.C.: U.S. Government Printing Office, 1983).

27. Platon N. Rigos and Charles J. Spindler, "Municipal Incorporations and State Statutes: A State-Level Analysis," *State and Local Government Review* 23 (Spring 1991): 76–81.

28. Michael A. Pagano, *City Fiscal Conditions in 1991* (Washington, D.C.: National League of Cities, 1991).

29. Michael deCourcy Hinds, "Short of Cash, Scranton Is Reorganizing," *New York Times,* December 26, 1991, p. A13.

30. Tari Renner, "Municipal Election Processes: The Impact on Minority Representation," in *The Municipal Year Book 1988,* pp. 13–21.

31. Susan Welch and Timothy Bledsoe, *Urban Reform and Its Consequences: A Study in Representation* (Chicago: University of Chicago Press, 1988).

32. Peggy Heilig and Robert J. Mundt, "The Effect of Adopting Districts on Representational Equity," *Social Science Quarterly* 64 (June 1983): 393–97.

33. Renner, "Municipal Election Processes."

34. Alva W. Stewart and Phung Nguyen, "Electing the City Council: Historic Change in Greensboro," *National Civic Review* 72 (July/August 1983): 377–81.

35. Peggy Heilig and Robert J. Mundt, *Your Voice at City Hall* (Albany: State University of New York Press, 1984).

36. Welch and Bledsoe, *Urban Reform and Its Consequences.*

37. Dave Drury, "Town Meetings: An Enduring Image Changes," *Hartford Courant*, September 22, 1991, pp. A1, A10–A11.

38. Gary A. Mattson, "Municipal Services and Economic Policy Priorities Among Florida's Smaller Cities," *National Civic Review* 79 (September/October 1990): 436–45.

39. U.S. Advisory Commission on Intergovernmental Relations, *State and Local Roles in the Federal System,* p. 243.

40. Thomas L. Daniels, "Rationing Government Resources Calls for 'Small-Town Triage,' " *Governing* (March 1988): 74.

41. Frank Bryan and John McClaughry, *The Vermont Papers* (Post Mills, Vt.: Chelsea Green, 1989).

42. U.S. Advisory Commission on Intergovernmental Relations, *State and Local Roles in the Federal System,* p. 154.

43. John C. Bollens, *Special District Governments in the United States* (Berkeley: University of California Press, 1957).

44. Charlie B. Tyer, "The Special Purpose District in South Carolina," in Charlie B. Tyer and Cole Blease Graham, Jr., eds., *Local Government in South Carolina* (Columbia, S.C.: Bureau of Governmental Research and Series, 1984), pp. 75–89.

45. Robert S. Lorch, *State and Local Politics* (Englewood Cliffs, N.J.: Prentice-Hall, 1983), p. 280.

46. Robert D. Thomans, Suphapong Boonyapratuang, and Renee Gilliam, "Local Government Complexity: Consequences for Counties," paper presented at the annual meeting of the American Political Science Association, Washington, August 1991.

47. Scott Bollens, "Examining the Link Between State Policy and
the Creation of Local Special Districts," *State and Local Government Review* 18 (Fall 1986): 117–24.

48. Ibid.

49. Harvey Tucker and L. Harmon Zeigler, *The Politics of Educational Governance: An Overview* (Eugene: ERIC Clearinghouse on Education Management, University of Oregon, 1980).

50. Chester E. Finn, as quoted in Edward B. Fiske, "Parental Choice in Public Schools Gains," *New York Times,* July 11, 1988, p. 1.

51. Michael A. Pagano, Ann O'M. Bowman, and John Kincaid, "The State of American Federalism, 1990–1991," *Publius* 21 (Summer 1991): 20.

52. William Celis III, "In Effort to Improve Schools, Pupils to Be Assigned on Basis of Income," *New York Times,* January 22, 1992, p. A13.

53. Terry Minger and Parry Burnap, "A Metropolitan Crisis: The Mile High View," paper presented at the National Urban Policy Conference, Denver, 1986, p. 16.

54. William R. Dodge, "The Emergence of Intercommunity Partnerships in the 1980s," *Public Management* 70 (July 1988): 2–7.

55. Ibid., p. 7.

56. Stephen Forman and Walt Crowley, "The Cultivation of Strategic Consensus: A New Mission for the Regional Citizen," paper presented at the Roundtable of Governments, Lincoln Institute of Land Policy, Denver, 1986.

57. Ibid., p. 6.

58. National Municipal League, "All-America Cities 1985–1986 Continue a Heritage of Achievement," *National Civic Review* 75 (May/June 1986): 130–37.

59. Harry P. Hatry, "Would We Know a Well-Governed City If We Saw One? *National Civic Review* 75 (May/June 1986): 142–46.

12 Local Leadership pp. 337–362

1. Thomas Farragher and Maline Hazle, "Playing Politics," *San Jose Mercury News,* September 2, 1990, pp. 1A, 22A.

2. Jameson W. Doig and Erwin C. Hargrove, eds., *Leadership and Innovation* (Baltimore: Johns Hopkins University Press, 1987).

3. Thomas J. Peters and Robert H. Waterman, Jr., *In Search of Excellence* (New York: Harper & Row, 1982).

4. Thomas J. Peters and Nancy Austin, *A Passion for Excellence: The Leadership Difference* (New York: Random House, 1985), p. 5.

5. Warren Bennis and Burt Nanus, *Leaders: The Strategies for Taking Charge* (New York: Harper & Row, 1985).

6. Wayne F. Anderson, Chester A. Newland, and Richard J. Stillman II, *The Effective Local Government Manager* (Washington, D.C.: International City Management Association, 1983).

7. George P. Barbour, Jr., and George A. Sipel, "Excellence in Leadership: Public Sector Model," *Public Management* (August 1986): 3–5.

8. Gaetano Mosca, *The Ruling Class* (New York: McGraw-Hill, 1939).

9. Robert Michels, *Political Parties* (New York: Free Press, 1962).

10. Robert S. Lynd and Helen M. Lynd, *Middletown* (New York: Harcourt Brace and World, 1929); Robert S. Lynd and Helen M. Lynd, *Middletown in Transition* (New York: Harcourt Brace and World, 1937).

11. Floyd Hunter, *Community Power Structure* (Chapel Hill: University of North Carolina Press, 1953); Floyd Hunter, *Community Power Succession* (Chapel Hill: University of North Carolina Press, 1980).

12. Hunter, *Community Power Succession,* p. 16.

13. Harvey Molotch, "Strategies and Constraints of Growth Elites," in Scott Cummings, ed., *Business Elites*

and Urban Development (Albany: State University of New York Press, 1988), pp. 25–47.

14. Robert Dahl, *Who Governs?* (New Haven, Conn.: Yale University Press, 1961).

15. Nelson Polsby, *Community Power and Political Theory* (New Haven, Conn.: Yale University Press, 1963).

16. Charles M. Bonjean and David M. Olson, "Community Leadership: Directions of Research," *Administrative Science Quarterly* 9 (December 1964): 278–300.

17. Peter Bachrach and Morton S. Baratz, "Two Faces of Power," *American Political Science Review* 56 (December 1962): 947–53.

18. G. William Domhoff, *Who Really Rules?* (Santa Monica, Calif.: Goodyear, 1978).

19. Bonjean and Olson, "Community Leadership," p. 288.

20. Robert Agger, Daniel Goldrich, and Bert Swanson, *The Rulers and the Ruled,* rev. ed. (Belmont, Calif.: Wadsworth, 1972).

21. Anne B. Shlay and Robert P. Giloth, "The Social Organization of a Land-Based Elite: The Case of the Failed Chicago 1992 World's Fair," *Journal of Urban Affairs* 9, no. 4 (1987): 305–24.

22. Ibid., p. 320.

23. Ann O'M. Bowman, "Elite Organization and the Growth Machine," in G. William Domhoff and Thomas R. Dye, eds., *Power Elites and Organizations* (Newbury Park, Calif.: Sage, 1987), pp. 116–25.

24. Clarence N. Stone, "Systemic Power in Community Decision Making," *American Political Science Review* 74 (December 1980): 978–90.

25. Ibid., p. 989.

26. Clarence N. Stone, "The Study of the Politics of Urban Development," in Clarence N. Stone and Heywood T. Sanders, eds., *The Politics of Urban Development* (Lawrence: University of Kansas Press, 1987), pp. 3–22.

27. H. V. Savitch and John Clayton Thomas, "Conclusion: End of the

Millennium Big City Politics," in H. V. Savitch and John Clayton Thomas, eds., *Big City Politics in Transition* (Newbury Park, Calif.: Sage, 1991), pp. 235–51.

28. George J. Gordon, *Public Administration in America,* 3d ed. (New York: St. Martin's, 1986).

29. Glen Sparrow, "The Emerging Chief Executive: The San Diego Experience," *National Civic Review* 74 (November 1985): 542.

30. Ibid., p. 545.

31. Douglas Yates, *The Ungovernable City* (Cambridge, Mass.: MIT Press, 1977).

32. John P. Kotter and Paul R. Lawrence, *Mayors in Action* (New York: Wiley, 1974).

33. W. John Moore, "From Dreamers to Doers," *National Journal* (February 13, 1988): 372–77.

34. Ibid., p. 373.

35. Ibid., p. 375.

36. Huey L. Perry, "Deracialization as an Analytical Construct in American Urban Politics," *Urban Affairs Quarterly* 27 (December 1991): 181–91.

37. Mary E. Summers and Philip A. Klinkner, "The Daniels Election in New Haven and the Failure of the Deracialization Hypothesis," *Urban Affairs Quarterly* 27 (December 1991): 202–15.

38. Timothy Hagan, as quoted in Gary Enos, "Development Is Gateway to Mayor's Success," *City & State* 8 (June 3–16, 1991): 19.

39. E. J. Dionne, Jr., "Blacks Study Politics of Polarization," *New York Times,* April 11, 1989, p. 7.

40. As quoted in Martin J. Schiesl, *The Politics of Efficiency* (Berkeley: University of California Press, 1977).

41. Clifford J. Wirth and Michael L. Vasu, "Ideology and Decision Making for American City Managers," *Urban Affairs Quarterly* 22 (March 1987): 454–74.

42. Alan Ehrenhalt, "The City Manager Myth," *Governing* 3 (September 1990): 40–48.

43. This subject is debated in H. George Frederickson, *Ideal & Prac-*

tice in Council-Manager Government (Washington, D.C.: International City Management Association, 1989).

44. Anderson, Newland, and Stillman, *The Effective Local Government Manager,* pp. 45–73.

45. Ibid., p. 48.

46. Sparrow, "The Emerging Chief Executive," p. 545.

47. Anderson, Newland, and Stillman, *The Effective Local Government Manager,* pp. 18–21.

48. Larry Azevedo, as quoted in Alan Ehrenhalt, "How a Liberal Government Came to Power in a Conservative Suburb," *Governing* 1 (March 1988): 51–56.

49. Kenneth Prewitt, *The Recruitment of Political Leaders: A Study of Citizen-Politicians* (Indianapolis: Bobbs-Merrill, 1970).

50. Susan Welch and Timothy Bledsoe, *Urban Reform and Its Consequences* (Chicago: University of Chicago Press, 1988).

51. James Svara, "Council Profile: More Diversity, Demands, Frustration," *Nation's Cities Weekly* 14 (November 18, 1991): 4.

52. Robert D. Thomas, "The Search for Legitimacy and Competency in Mayor-Council Relations: The Case of Houston," paper presented at the annual meeting of the Southern Political Science Association, Charlotte, N.C., 1987.

53. Ibid., p. 6.

54. John Williams, "Saenz's Victory Changes Council's Racial Balance," *Houston Chronicle,* December 8, 1991, pp. 1A, 25A.

55. Susan A. MacManus and Rayme Suarez, "Female Representation on School Boards: Supportive Constituency Characteristics," paper presented at the Annual Meeting of the Southern Political Science Association, Tampa, November 1991.

56. R. Darcy and Charles D. Hadley, "Black Women in Politics: The Puzzle of Success," *Social Science Quarterly* 69 (September 1988): 629–45.

57. Susan A. MacManus and Charles S. Bullock III, "Women on Southern

City Councils: A Decade of Change," *Journal of Political Science* 17 (Spring 1989): 32–49.

58. Svara, "Council Profile," p. 4.

59. Rita Mae Kelly, Michelle A. Saint-Germain, and Jody D. Horn, "Female Public Officials: A Different Voice?" *The Annals of the American Academy of Political and Social Science* 515 (May 1991): 77–87.

60. James H. Svara, "Dichotomy and Duality: Reconceptualizing the Relationship between Policy and Administration in Council-Manager Cities," *Public Administration Review* 45 (January/February 1985): 221–32.

61. James H. Svara, "The Complementary Roles of Officials in Council-Manager Government," in International City Management Association, *The Municipal Year Book 1988* (Washington, D.C.: ICMA, 1988), pp. 23–33.

62. Ibid., pp. 25–26.

63. Thomas P. Ryan, Jr., as quoted in Jane Mobley, "Politician or Professional? The Debate Over Who Should Run Our Cities Continues," *Governing* 1 (February 1988): 42–48.

64. Ronald Reagan, as quoted in Peter A. Harkness, "Publisher's Desk," *Governing* 1 (March 1988): 6.

65. Doig and Hargrove, *Leadership and Innovation,* pp. 7–8.

66. Richard W. Stevenson, "Challenging the Billboard Industry," *New York Times,* August 30, 1988, pp. 25, 38.

67. "Those Plastic Packages Aren't Welcome in Suffolk County, N.Y. Anymore," *Governing* 1 (July 1988): 14.

68. "A Guarantee for Graduates," *New York Times,* January 15, 1991, p. A14.

69. Eric Pace, "New York City Moves Against Cigarette Machines," *New York Times,* October 15, 1990, pp. A1, A17.

70. Robert Reinhold, "Rail Pact Sets Off Anti-Japan Furor," *New York Times,* January 22, 1992, pp. A1, A8; Robert Reinhold, "Los Angeles Can-

cels Huge Contract with a Japanese Maker of Rail Cars," *New York Times,* January 23, 1992, pp. A8.

71. Andrew Pollack, "San Francisco's Computer Bill Becomes Law," *New York Times,* December 28, 1990, p. B9; Andrew Pollack, "San Francisco Law on V.D.T.s Is Struck Down," *New York Times,* February 14, 1992, p. A9.

72. Lurton Blassingame, "Frostbelt Success Story: Oshkosh, Wisconsin," *Journal of Urban Affairs* 9, no. 1 (1987): 37–46.

73. Josh Barbanel, "New Yorkers Doubt Any Mayor Can Solve City's Worst Problems," *New York Times,* June 22, 1989, pp. 1, 22.

13 State-Local Relations pp. 363–385

1. Gary Enos, "Counties Escape Prisoner Dilemma," *City & State* 8 (June 3–16, 1991): 1, 23.

2. Steven D. Gold, "NCSL State-Local Task Force: The First Year," *Intergovernmental Perspective* 13 (Winter 1987): 11.

3. U.S. Advisory Commission on Intergovernmental Relations, *The Organization of Local Public Economies* (Washington, D.C.: ACIR, December 1987), p. 54.

4. Joseph R. Marbach, "State Influence on Local Economic Development: Quad Cities," paper presented at the annual meeting of the American Political Science Association, Washington, D.C., August 1991.

5. Joseph F. Zimmerman, *State-Local Relations* (New York: Praeger, 1983).

6. Alan Ehrenhalt, "Power Shifts in a Southern City as Groups That Took Orders Learn How to Give Them," *Governing* 1 (September 1988): 48–53.

7. U.S. Advisory Commission on Intergovernmental Relations, *State and Local Roles in the Federal System* (Washington, D.C.: ACIR, 1982).

8. David R. Berman and Lawrence

L. Martin, "State-Local Relations: An Examination of Local Discretion," *Public Administration Review* 48 (March/April 1988): 637–41.

9. William L. Waugh, Jr., and Ronald John Hy, "Fiscal Stress and Local Autonomy: State-County Relations in a Changing Intergovernmental System," paper presented at the annual meeting of the American Political Science Association, Washington, D.C., August 1986.

10. U.S. Advisory Commission on Intergovernmental Relations, *Local Perspectives on State-Local Highway Consultation and Cooperation* (Washington, D.C.: ACIR, July 1987).

11. R. G. Downing, "Urban County Fiscal Stress," *Urban Affairs Quarterly* 27 (December 1991): 314–25.

12. Paul D. Moore and Karen A. Scheer, "The 'State' of State-Local Relations: How Officials See It," *Intergovernmental Perspective* 14 (Winter 1988): 19–21.

13. Ibid., p. 20.

14. Jane Massey and Edwin Thomas, *State Mandated Local Government Expenditures and Revenue Limitations in South Carolina, Part Four* (Columbia: Bureau of Governmental Research and Service, University of South Carolina, March 1988).

15. Susan A. MacManus, " 'Mad' About Mandates: The Issue of Who Should Pay Resurfaces in the 1990s," *Publius* 21 (Summer 1991): 59–75.

16. Jonathan Walters, "Set Us Free," *Governing* 5 (January 1992): 40–43.

17. Gold, "NCSL State-Local Task Force," p. 12.

18. Ibid.

19. Andree E. Reeves, "State ACIRs: Elements of Success," *Intergovernmental Perspective* 17 (Summer 1991): 13.

20. Corina Eckl, "Spotlight on Colorado's Advisory Committee on Intergovernmental Relations," *Intergovernmental Perspective* 17 (Spring 1991): 6.

21. U.S. Advisory Commission on Intergovernmental Relations, *State-Local Relations Bodies: State ACIRs and Other Approaches* (Washington, D.C.: ACIR, 1981).

22. Ibid., pp. 38–40.

23. Anthony Downs, as cited in Joel Garreau, "From Suburbs, Cities Are Springing Up in Our Back Yards," *Washington Post,* March 8, 1987, p. A26.

24. Jack Meltzner, *Metropolis to Metroplex* (Baltimore: Johns Hopkins University Press, 1984), p. 17.

25. Todd K. Buchta, "Will We Live in Accidental Cities or Successful Communities?" *Conservation Foundation Letter* 6 (1987).

26. Joel Garreau, *Edge City* (New York: Doubleday, 1991).

27. Joel Garreau, "Solving the Equation for Success," *Washington Post,* June 20, 1988, p. A8; Garreau, *Edge City,* p. 434.

28. Arthur T. Johnson, *Intergovernmental Influences on Local Land Use Decision Making* (Washington, D.C.: National League of Cities, 1989).

29. Robert Lindsey, "The Crush on Waikiki Gives Birth to 2d City," *New York Times,* March 22, 1988, p. 8.

30. Joel Garreau, "The Shadow Governments," *Washington Post,* June 14, 1987, p. A14.

31. Debra L. Dean, "Residential Community Associations: Partners in Local Governance or Headaches for Local Government?" *Intergovernmental Perspective* 15 (Winter 1989): 36–39.

32. Robert Jay Dilger, "Residential Community Associations: Issues, Impacts, and Relevance for Local Government," *State and Local Government Review* 23 (Winter 1991): 17–23.

33. Christopher Leinberger, as quoted in Libby Howland, "Back to Basics," *Urban Land* 46 (May 1987): 7.

34. J. Edwin Benton and Darwin Gamble, "City/County Consolidation and Economies of Scale: Evidence from a Time-Series Analysis in Jacksonville, Florida," *Social Science Quarterly* 65 (March 1984): 190–98.

35. Howard W. Hallman, *Small and Large Together: Governing the Metropolis* (Beverly Hills, Calif.: Sage, 1977).

36. U.S. Advisory Commission on Intergovernmental Relations, *State and Local Roles in the Federal System* (Washington, D.C.: ACIR, 1982).

37. Cole Blease Graham, Jr., "State Consultation Processes After Federal A-95 Overhaul," *State and Local Government Review* 17 (Spring 1985): 207–12.

38. Ann O'M. Bowman and James L. Franke, "The Decline of Substate Regionalism," *Journal of Urban Affairs* 6 (Fall 1984): 51–63.

39. Eileen Shanahan, "Going It Jointly," *Governing* 4 (August 1991): 70–76.

40. Marvin McGraw, "Congress Kills UDAG for Space Dreams," *Nation's Cities Weekly* 11 (June 27, 1988): 1, 13–14.

41. Langley Keyes, lecture on "Rebuilding a Sense of Community," at the Urban Policy Roundtable, Boston, June 1988.

42. Byron Katsuyama, "State Actions Affecting Local Governments," in International City Management Association, *The Municipal Year Book* (Washington, D.C.: ICMA, 1988), pp. 85–99.

43. Robert Kuttner, "Bad Housekeeping: The Housing Crisis and What to Do About It," *The New Republic* (April 25, 1988): 22–25.

44. Pat Choate and Susan Walter, *America in Ruins: Beyond the Public Works Pork Barrel* (Washington, D.C.: Council of State Planning Agencies, 1981).

45. Terry Busson and Judith Hackett, *State Assistance for Local Public Works* (Lexington, Ky.: Council of State Governments, 1987).

46. Ibid., p. 32.

47. Thomas C. Hayes, "Texas Fast-Train Franchise Given to French-U.S. Group," *New York Times,* May 29, 1991, pp. A1, C4.

48. Kirk Victor, "Paying for the Roads," *National Journal,* February 16, 1991, pp. 374–79.

49. DeWitt John, as quoted in William K. Stevens, "Struggle for Re-

covery Altering Rural America," *New York Times,* February 5, 1988, p. 8.

50. Jim Seroka, "Community Growth and Administrative Capacity," *National Civic Review* 77 (January/February 1988): 42–46.

51. Ibid., p. 43.

52. Stevens, "Struggle for Recovery Altering Rural America."

53. Seroka, "Community Growth and Administrative Capacity," p. 45.

54. Beryl A. Radin, "Rural Development Councils: An Intergovernmental Coordination Experiment," *Publius* 23 (Summer 1992).

55. John Herbers, "Seattle: Defeated by the Sprawl," *Governing* 2 (April 1989): 34–35.

56. William Fulton, "In Land-Use Planning, A Second Revolution Shifts Control to the States," *Governing* 2 (March 1989): 40–45.

57. Kathleen Sylvester, "The Tobacco Industry Will Walk a Mile to Stop an Anti-Smoking Law," *Governing* 2 (May 1989): 34–40.

58. Carl H. Neu, Jr., and Jack Ethredge, "Community-Sensible Governance: The Emerging Political Reality of the 21st Century," *National Civic Review* 80 (Fall 1991): 381–92.

14 **State and Local Finance   pp. 387–424**

1. The details of the Bridgeport case have been compiled from articles and editorials in *The Hartford Courant.*

2. U.S. Advisory Commission on Intergovernmental Relations, *Significant Features of Fiscal Federalism 1991,* Vol. 2 (Washington, D.C.: ACIR, 1991), pp. 41, 46.

3. U.S. Department of Commerce, *State Court Finances in 1990* (Washington, D.C.: U.S. G.P.O., 1991), p. 30.

4. U.S. Advisory Commission on Intergovernmental Relations, *Significant Features of Fiscal Federalism 1991,* Vol. 2, p. 6.

5. Susan A. MacManus, "State

Government: The Overseer of Municipal Finance," in Alberta M. Sbragia, ed., *The Municipal Money Chase: The Politics of Local Government Finance* (Boulder, Colo.: Westview, 1983), pp. 145–83.

6. U.S. Advisory Commission on Intergovernmental Relations, *The Question of State Government Capability* (Washington, D.C.: ACIR, 1985), p. 308.

7. "Tax Report," *Wall Street Journal,* December 10, 1986, p. 1; *Wall Street Journal,* August 30, 1989, p. 1.

8. U.S. Advisory Commission on Intergovernmental Relations, *Significant Features of Fiscal Federalism,* Vol. 2, pp. 192–93.

9. Ibid., p. 185.

10. U.S. Advisory Commission on Intergovernmental Relations, *Significant Features of Fiscal Federalism 1991,* Vol. 1, pp. 132–38.

11. Mark Schneider, "Local Budgets and the Maximization of Local Property Wealth in the System of Suburban Government," *Journal of Politics* 49 (November 1987): 1114.

12. Calculated from U.S. Advisory Commission on Intergovernmental Relations, *Significant Features of Fiscal Federalism 1991,* Vol. 2, p. 134.

13. Stephen D. Gold, "Developments in State Finances, 1983–1986," *Public Budgeting and Finance* 7 (Spring 1987): 16.

14. U.S. Advisory Commission on Intergovernmental Relations, *Significant Features of Fiscal Federalism 1991,* Vol. 1, pp. 94–95.

15. Ibid., pp. 88–89.

16. Neil R. Peirce, "Service Tax May Rise Again," *Public Administration Times* 11 (August 12, 1988): 2.

17. Thomas M. Fullerton, Jr., "Rational Reactions to Temporary Sales Tax Legislation: An Idaho Case Study," *Public Budgeting and Finance* 7 (Summer 1987).

18. Steven D. Gold, "The Blizzard of 1987: A Year of Tax Reform Activity in the States," *Publius* 18 (Summer 1988): 18.

19. U.S. Advisory Commission on Intergovernmental Relations,

Significant Features of Fiscal Federalism 1991, Vol. 1, pp. 46, 48–49.

20. Donald Axelrod, *Budgeting for Modern Government* (New York: St. Martin's, 1988), p. 218.

21. "Bob Bullock: Trading in the Open," *Governing* 4 (July 1991): 20.

22. U.S. Advisory Commission on Intergovernmental Relations, "State and Local Governments Increase Reliance on User Charges," *Intergovernmental Relations* 18 (Spring 1992): 21; see also Robert Cervero, Paying for Off-Site Road Improvements Through Fees, Assessments, and Negotiations: Lessons from California," *Public Administration Review* 48 (January/February 1988): 534–41.

23. On "sin taxes," see Cathy M. Johnson and Kenneth J. Meier, "The Wages of Sin: Taxing America's Legal Vices," *Western Political Quarterly* 43 (September 1990): 577–96.

24. Lester Grinspoon, "A Harmful Tax: Legalize and Tax Drugs," *Journal of State Government* 63 (April–June 1991): 46–49.

25. "Thirty States Will Raise $17 Billion in New FY '92 Taxes," Tax Features (September 1991): 8.

26. Michael J. Wolkoff, "Exploring the State Choice of Financing Options," *State and Local Government Review* 19 (Spring 1987): 73.

27. U.S. Advisory Commission on Intergovernmental Relations, *Significant Features of Fiscal Federalism 1991,* Vol. 1, pp. 118–119.

28. Elder Witt, "States Place Their Bets on a Game of Diminishing Returns," *Governing* 1 (November 1987): 52–57.

29. John L. Mikesell and Kurt Zorn, "State Lotteries for Public Revenue," *Public Budgeting and Finance* 8 (Spring 1988): 43.

30. See, for example, Charles R. Clotfelter, "On the Regressivity of State-Operated 'Number' Games," *National Tax Journal* 32 (December 1979): 543–48.

31. Mikesell and Zorn, "State Lotteries for Public Revenue," pp. 40–41.

32. "State-Sponsored Gambling: A

Growth Industry," *National Journal* (September 14, 1991): 2207; Jeffrey L. Katz, "Lottery Fatigue," *Governing* 4 (September 1991): 62–66.

33. See Sherry Tvedt, "Enough Is Enough! Proposition 2 1/2 in Massachusetts," *National Civic Review* 70 (November 1981): 527–33.

34. U.S. Advisory Commission on Intergovernmental Relations, *Significant Features of Fiscal Federalism 1991*, Vol. 2, pp. 102–103.

35. Elaine B. Sharp and David Elkins, "The Impact of Fiscal Limitation: A Tale of Seven Cities," *Public Administration Review* 47 (September/October 1987): 385–92.

36. See Cal Clark and B. Oliver Walter, "Urban Political Culture, Financial Stress, and City Fiscal Austerity Strategies," *Western Political Quarterly* 44 (Spring 1991): 676–97.

37. U.S. Advisory Commission on Intergovernmental Relations, *Significant Features of Fiscal Federalism 1991*, Vol. 2, p. 47.

38. Gary J. Reid, "How Cities in California Have Responded to Fiscal Pressure Since Proposition 13," *Public Budgeting and Finance* 8 (Spring 1988): 20–37.

39. Susan B. Hansen, "State Fiscal Strategies for the 1990s: Balancing Budgets in a Recession," *Publius* 21 (Summer 1991): 155–68.

40. P. Nivola, "Apocalypse Now? Whither the Urban Fiscal Crisis," *Policy* 14 (Spring 1981): 371–94.

41. Terry Nichols Clark and London Crowley Ferguson, *City Money* (New York: Columbia University Press, 1983), p. 2.

42. See Patricia Giles Leeds, "City Politics and the Market: The Case of New York City's Financing Crisis," in Sbragia, *The Municipal Money Chase*, pp. 113–44.

43. Dick Kirschten, "Philadelphia Squeeze," *National Journal* (December 22, 1990): 3080–85; Neal R. Peirce, "Philadelphia: A 1990s Omen for Cities," *National Journal* (September 22, 1990): 2287.

44. John Shannon, "The Return to Fend-for-Yourself Federalism: The Reagan Mark," *Intergovernmental Perspective* 13 (Summer/Fall 1987): 34–37.

45. Allen Schick, *The Capacity to Budget* (Washington, D.C.: Urban Institute Press, 1990), p. 150.

46. Hansen, "State Fiscal Strategies for the 1990s," pp. 166–67.

47. Neal R. Peirce, "State Budget Disasters: Any Way Out?" *National Journal* (April 27, 1991): 1008.

48. See Jon David Vasche and Brad Williams, "Optimal Governmental Budgeting Contingency Reserve Funds," *Public Budgeting and Finance* 7 (Spring 1987): 66–82.

49. Eileen Shanahan, "Cracks in the Crystal Ball," *Governing* 5 (December, 1991): 29–32.

50. Ibid.

51. Irene S. Rubin, "Estimated and Actual Urban Revenues: Exploring the Gap," *Public Budgeting and Finance* 7 (Winter 1987): 83–93; Steven D. Gold, "Are States Playing Budget Roulette?" *State Legislatures* 14 (March 1988): 29.

52. Michael Wolkoff, "An Evaluation of Municipal Rainy Day Funds," *Public Budgeting and Finance* 7 (Summer 1987): 52–62.

53. Gold, "Are States Playing Budget Roulette?" p. 30.

54. Nancy P. Humphrey and Diane Rausa Maurice, "Infrastructure Bond Bank Initiatives: Policy Implications and Credit Concerns," *Public Budgeting and Finance* 6 (Autumn 1986): 38–40.

55. Jonathan Walters, "The Pension Fund Grab of '91," *Governing* 5 (February 1992): 18.

56. Penelope Lemov, "The Brave New World of Public Finance," *Governing* 5 (February 1992): 27–28.

57. Ibid.

58. Alberta M. Sbragia, "Politics, Local Government, and the Municipal Bond Market," in Sbragia, *The Municipal Money Chase*, pp. 90–93.

59. David B. Walker, *Bypassing: A Unique Feature of the American Political System*, Occasional Paper (Washington, D.C.: National Academy of Public Administration, October 1990).

60. See David R. Morgan and Robert E. England, "State Aid to Cities: A Casual Inquiry," *Publius* 14 (Spring 1984): 67–82; and Keith J. Mueller, "Explaining Variation in State Assistance Programs to Local Communities: What to Expect and Why," *State and Local Government Review* 19 (Fall 1987): 101–107.

61. U.S. Advisory Commission on Intergovernmental Relations, *Significant Features of Fiscal Federalism 1991*, Vol. 1, p. 143.

62. Ann O'M. Bowman and Richard C. Kearney, *The Resurgence of the States* (Englewood Cliffs, N.J.: Prentice-Hall, 1986), p. 174.

63. See Susan A. MacManus, " 'Mad' About Mandates: The Issue of Who Should Pay for What Resurfaces in the 1990s," *Publius* 21 (Summer 1991): 59–75.

64. Neal R. Peirce, "State Budget Disasters: Any Way Out?" *National Journal* (April 27, 1991): 1008.

65. Lawrence J. Haas, "Just Saying No," *National Journal* (January 4, 1992): 18–21.

15 Education Policy pp. 425–452

1. John H. Fund, "Milwaukee's Schools Open—to Competition," *The Wall Street Journal* (September 4, 1990): A14.

2. National Education Association, *Estimate of School Statistics* (Washington, D.C.: NEA, 1990), Table No. 244.

3. National Commission on Excellence in Education, *A Nation at Risk: The Imperative for Educational Reform* (Washington, D.C.: U.S. Government Printing Office, 1983), p. 1.

4. Gary Putka, "U.S. Students' Skills in Math and Science Are Below Average," *Wall Street Journal*, February 1, 1989, p. B4.

5. See Anthony Downs, "Up and Down with Ecology — The 'Issue-

Attention Cycle,' " *Public Interest* (Summer 1972): 38–50.

6. This discussion draws on Ann O'M. Bowman and Richard C. Kearney, *The Resurgence of the States* (Englewood Cliffs, N.J.: Prentice-Hall, 1986), pp. 206–12.

7. National Commission on Excellence in Education, *A Nation at Risk,* pp. 4–5.

8. Bowman and Kearney, *The Resurgence of the States,* p. 208.

9. U.S. Bureau of the Census, *Statistical Abstract of the United States, 1991* (Washington, D.C.: U.S. Government Printing Office, 1991).

10. Albert Shanker, quoted in David Savage, "Teaching: The Heart of the Problem," *State Legislatures* 9 (October 1983): 212–24.

11. Ann Cooper, "In the Real World of Educational Reform, Vigilance May Be the Key to Success," *National Journal* 17 (March 2, 1985): 460–66.

12. National Education Association, *Estimates of School Statistics* (Washington, D.C.: NEA, 1982).

13. "The Gallup Poll of Teachers' Attitudes Toward the Public Schools," *Phi Delta Kappan* (October 1984).

14. William E. Blundell, "A Certified Need: Teachers," *Wall Street Journal,* May 19, 1989, p. 1. See also U.S. Department of Education, National Center for Education Statistics, *Projections of Education Statistics to 1992–93* (January 1985).

15. Jonathan Kozol, *Savage Inequalities: Children in America's Schools* (New York: Crown Publishers, 1991).

16. *Serrano* v. *Priest,* 5 Cal.3d 584 (1971).

17. *San Antonio Independent School District* v. *Rodriguez,* 411 U.S. 1 (1973).

18. Bill Swingford, "A Predictive Model of Decision Making in State Supreme Courts: The School Financing Cases," *American Politics Quarterly* 19 (July, 1991): 336–52.

19. Frederick M. Wirt and Michael W. Kirst, *Schools in Conflict* (Berke-

ley, Calif.: McCutchan, 1982), p. 236.

20. Robert B. Hawkins, Jr., "Education Reform California Style," *Publius* 14 (Summer 1984): 100.

21. Ibid., pp. 99–109.

22. John P. Pelissero and David R. Morgan, "State Aid to Public Schools: An Analysis of State Responsiveness to School District Needs," *Social Science Quarterly* 68 (September 1987): 466–77.

23. James S. Coleman, *Equality of Educational Opportunity* (Washington, D.C.: U.S. Government Printing Office, 1966).

24. Eric A. Hanushek, "Throwing Money at Schools," *Journal of Policy Analysis and Management* (Fall 1981): 19–41; "The Economics of Schooling: Production and Efficiency in Public Schools," *Journal of Economic Literature* 24 (September 1986): 1141–77.

25. See B. Guy Peters, "Educational Policy in the United States," in B. Guy Peters, ed., *American Public Policy* (New York: Franklin Watts, 1982), pp. 253–55.

26. Rochelle L. Stanfield, "School Business," *National Journal* (July 27, 1991): 1862–67.

27. Elisabeth Hanost and David Tyack, "A Usable Past: Using History in Education Policy," in Ann Lieberman and W. McLaughlin, eds., *Policy Making in Education* (Chicago: University of Chicago Press, 1982), pp. 1–10.

28. See J. Alan Aufderheide, "Educational Interest Groups and the State Legislature," in Roald F. Campbell and Tim L. Mazzoni, Jr., eds., *State Policy Making for the Public Schools* (Berkeley, Calif.: McCutchan, 1976), pp. 176–216.

29. Jeffrey L. Katz, "State Tax Politics, 1990: No Place to Hide." *Governing* 3 (June, 1990): 31.

30. See Neal R. Peirce, "Can School Boards Survive Reapproval?" *P.A. Times* 9 (November 15, 1986): 2.

31. William S. Lee, "PRO: North Carolina Needs an Appointed Superintendent of Public Education,"

North Carolina Insight 12 (September 1990): 9.

32. Campbell and Mazzoni, eds., *State Policy Making for the Public Schools,* pp. 28–80.

33. Lee, p. 8.

34. Wirt and Kirst, *Schools in Conflict,* pp. 20–21.

35. Jerome T. Murphy, "Programs and Problems: The Paradox of State Reform," in Lieberman and McLaughlin, eds., *Policy Making in Education,* p. 207.

36. *Brown* v. *Board of Education of Topeka,* 347 U.S. 483 (1954).

37. *Swann* v. *Charlotte–Mecklenburg County Schools,* 402 U.S. 1 (1971).

38. *Board of Education of Oklahoma City* v. *Dowell,* 498 U.S. (1991); *Freeman* v. *Pitts,* 503 U.S. (1992).

39. John Clayton Thomas and Dan H. Hoxworth, "The Limits of Judicial Desegregation Remedies after *Missouri* v. *Jenkins,*" *Publius* 21 (Summer 1991): 93–108.

40. Stanfield, "School Business," p. 1863.

41. Kathleen Sylvester, "The Strange Romance of Business and the Schools." *Governing* 4 (April 1991): 64–69.

42. U.S. Department of Education, Center for Statistics, *Digest of Education Statistics 1990* (Washington, D.C.: U.S. Government Printing Office, 1991).

43. See Patricia Lines, "First Reading," *State Legislatures* 9 (October 1983): 5–7.

44. Earl C. Gottshalk, Jr., "Cities Turn to Year-Round Schools as Answer to Crowded Conditions," *Wall Street Journal,* January 8, 1986, pp. 1, 3; Joseph Anthony, "Schools Cope with the New Baby Boom," *Governing* 2 (October 1988): 70–72.

45. Education Commission of the States, "State Activity—Minimum Competency Testing," *Clearinghouse Notes* (November 1985).

46. Kris Kurtenbach, "As Reform Fever Rises, Officials Reach for National Test Thermometer." *Congressional Quarterly* (April 20, 1991): 984–85; Mary Jordan, "Nationwide

Test Urged for Schools." *Washington Post*, January 25, 1992, pp. A1, A4.

47. See Elaine S. Knapp, "North Carolina School for Excellence," *State Government News* 26 (September 1983): 3–5.

48. "Maryland Wants a New Whiz-Kid School," *Governing* 1 (November 1987): 11.

49. Jay Mathews, "Guarantees for Inner-City Graduates," *Washington Post*, June 15, 1987, p. 89.

50. "West Virginia Law Returns Dropouts to Class," *Governing* 2 (March 1989): 18.

51. Harvey J. Tucker and David B. Hill, "Teacher Quality and Expenditures for Public Education," *State Government* 58 (Fall 1985): 105–107.

52. John Kincaid, "Is Education Too Intergovernmental?" *Intergovernmental Perspective* 18 (Winter 1992): 28.

16 **Economic Development pp. 453–474**

1. Jennifer Gavin, "Fla. Officials Dealing for United," *Denver Post,* July 22, 1991, pp. 1A, 5A.

2. Gary Enos, "Incentives Dogfits Rev Up," *City & State* 8 (November 4, 1991): 1, 23.

3. R. Scott Fosler, "The State Economic Role in Perspective," in R. Scott Fosler, ed., *The New Economic Role of American States* (New York: Oxford University Press, 1988), pp. 8–18.

4. "State Economic Performance," *State Policy Reports* 9 (September 19, 1991): 3.

5. John Herbers, "A Third Wave of Economic Development," *Governing* 3 (June 1990): 43–50.

6. Doug Ross and Robert E. Friedman, "The Emerging New Wave: New Economic Development Strategies," in R. Scott Fosler, ed., *Local Economic Development* (Washington, D.C.: International City Management Association, 1991), pp. 125–37.

7. R. Scott Fosler, as quoted in Dan Pilcher, "The Third Wave of Economic Development," *State Legislatures* 17 (November 1991): 34.

8. Herbers, "A Third Wave of Economic Development."

9. Institute for Public Policy Studies, *Economic Revitalization in the City: A Sourcebook* (Philadelphia: Temple University, 1985).

10. Richard S. Krannich and Craig R. Humphrey, "Local Mobilization and Community Growth: Toward an Assessment of the 'Growth Machine' Hypothesis," *Rural Sociology* 48 (Spring 1983): 60–81.

11. John M. Levy, *Urban and Metropolitan Economics* (New York: McGraw-Hill, 1985).

12. Roger Schmenner, "Location Decisions of Large Firms: Implications for Public Policy," *Commentary* 5 (January 1981): 307.

13. Paul Brace, "Isolating the Economies of States," *American Politics Quarterly* 17 (July 1989): 256–76.

14. Peter W. Bernstein, "States Are Going Down the Industrial Policy Lane," *Wall Street Journal,* June 13, 1984, p. 1.

15. Mark S. Hyde, William E. Hudson, and John J. Carroll, "Business and State Economic Development," *Western Political Quarterly* 41 (March 1988): 181–91.

16. Margery Marzahn Ambrosius, "Are Political Benefits the Only Benefits of State Economic Development Policies?" a paper presented at the annual meeting of the American Political Science Association, San Francisco, September 1990; Paul Brace, "The Changing Context of State Political Economy," *Journal of Politics* 53 (May 1991): 297–316.

17. Terry F. Buss and F. Stevens Redburn, "The Politics of Revitalization: Public Subsidies and Private Interests," in Gary Gappert, ed., *The Future of Winter Cities* (Beverly Hills: Sage, 1986), pp. 285–96.

18. Larry C. Ledebur and William W. Hamilton, *Tax Concessions in State and Local Economic Develop-*

ment (Washington, D.C.: Aslan Press, 1986).

19. Neal R. Peirce, Jerry Hagstrom, and Carol Steinbach, *Economic Development: The Challenge of the 1980s* (Washington, D.C.: Council of State Planning Agencies, 1979).

20. William Fulton, "Will Sony Succeed Where VW Failed?" *Governing* 3 (July 1990): 58–59.

21. Eugene Carlson, "What's a Toyota Plant Worth to Kentucky? Possibly Plenty," *Wall Street Journal,* June 9, 1987, p. 37.

22. Ernest J. Yanarella and Herbert G. Reid, "Labor, Environmentalist, and Small Business Opposition to the Georgetown/Toyota Project: A Fragmented Challenge to State Economic Development and Multinational Capital," a paper presented at the annual meeting of the Southern Political Science Association, Charlotte, N.C., November 1987.

23. Ibid.

24. Michelle Hoyman, "The Impact of Economic Development on Small Communities: The Case of the Automobile Industry," a paper presented at the annual meeting of the American Political Science Association, Washington, D.C., August 1991.

25. Ann O'M. Bowman, *The Visible Hand: Major Issues in City Economic Policy* (Washington, D.C.: National League of Cities, 1987).

26. David Osborne, *Laboratories of Democracy* (Boston: Harvard Business School Press, 1988).

27. Peter Waldman, "Cities Are Pressured to Make Developers Share Their Wealth," *Wall Street Journal,* March 10, 1987, p. 1.

28. Carol Steinbach, "Tapping Private Resources," *National Journal,* April 26, 1986, p. 993.

29. Enid F. Beaumont and Harold A. Hovey, "State, Local, and Federal Economic Development Policies: New Federal Patterns, Chaos, or What?" *Public Administration Review* 45 (March/April 1985): 327–32.

30. Susan E. Clarke, "Urban America, Inc. — Corporatist Convergence of Power in American Cities?" in Ed-

ward M. Bergman, ed., *Local Economies in Transition* (Durham, N.C.: Duke University Press, 1986), pp. 37–58.

31. Ann O'M. Bowman, "Competition for Economic Development among Southeastern Cities," *Urban Affairs Quarterly* 24 (June 1988): 511–27.

32. Richard W. Stevenson, "9 Towns Spare No Effort to Snare New Plant," *New York Times,* December 18, 1991, pp. A1, C4.

33. Virginia Mayer, as quoted ibid., p. C4.

34. Robert Goodman, *The Last Entrepreneurs: America's Regional Wars for Jobs and Dollars* (Boston: South End Press, 1979).

35. Eugene Carlson, "Great Lakes Governors Split over Truce on Industry Raids," *Wall Street Journal,* July 12, 1983, p. 41.

36. National Association of Counties, "Economic Development Survey: Urban Counties," unpublished report, no date.

37. The Monongahela River Valley Steering Group, "An Interstate River Valley in Economic Transition," unpublished paper, October 1986, p. 3.

38. Harry Bacas, "Allies for Growth," *Nation's Business* 78 (November 1990): 40–43.

39. Margery Marzahn Ambrosius and Steven Maynard-Moody, "Normative Models of Federalism in Economic Development," a paper presented at the annual meeting of the American Political Science Association, Washington, D.C., August 1991.

40. Committee for Economic Development, *Leadership for Dynamic State Economies,* pp. 56–67.

41. Marianne K. Clarke, *Revitalizing State Economies* (Washington, D.C.: National Governors' Association, 1986).

42. Pilcher, "The Third Wave of Economic Development," p. 34.

43. Charles E. Lindblom, *Politics and Markets* (New York: Basic Books, 1977).

44. Richard Reeves, *American Jour-*

ney (New York: Simon and Schuster, 1982), p. 46.

45. Committee for Economic Development, *Leadership for Dynamic State Economies,* pp. 73–77.

46. National Association of State Development Agencies, *The NASDAA Newsletter,* January 21, 1987, pp. 1–7.

47. Keon S. Chi, "Strategic Planning for Economic Development: The Wisconsin Experience," in *Innovations* (Lexington, Ky.: Council of State Governments, 1986).

48. National Association of State Development Agencies, *The NASDAA Newsletter,* p. 5.

49. National Conference on State Legislatures, *Travel and Tourism: A Legislator's Guide* (Denver, Colo.: National Conference of State Legislatures, 1991).

50. Ellen Perlman, "Boycotts Burden Tourist Economies," *City & State* 8 (May 6–19, 1991): 1, 31.

51. J. Allen Whitt, "The Arts Coalition in Strategies of Urban Development," in Clarence N. Stone and Heywood T. Sanders, eds., *The Politics of Urban Development* (Lawrence, Kan.: University Press of Kansas, 1987), pp. 144–56.

52. J. Allen Whitt, "The Role of the Performing Arts in Urban Competition and Growth," in Scott Cummings, ed., *Business Elites and Urban Development* (Albany, N.Y.: State University of New York Press, 1988), pp. 49–69.

53. Arthur T. Johnson, "Economic and Policy Implications of Hosting Sports Franchises: Lessons from Baltimore," *Urban Affairs Quarterly* 21 (March 1986): 411–33.

54. Rodd Zolkos, "Cities Blast Stadium Study," *City & State* 4 (April 1987): 3, 53.

55. Gary Enos and Rodd Zolkos, "Stadiums Ding Home Runs," *City & State* 8 (September 23–October 6, 1991): 1, 24.

56. Mark Rosentraub and David Swindell, "Just Say No? The Economic and Political Realities of a Small City's Investment in Minor

League Baseball," *Economic Development Quarterly* 5 (May 1991).

57. B. Drummond Ayres, Jr., "Businesses in Maryland Gain Priority on Kuwait Contracts," *New York Times,* May 4, 1991, p. 6.

58. John Larkin, "States Spark Foreign Relations of their Own," *PA Times,* June 1, 1992, pp. 1, 20.

59. Andreas van Agt, "Trading with the New Europe," *State Government News* 34 (December 1991): 20–23.

60. U.S. Department of Commerce, Bureau of Economic Analysis, *Foreign Direct Investment in the United States: Operations of U.S. Affiliates of Foreign Companies,* 1989 Preliminary Estimates (Washington, D.C.: U.S. Government Printing Office, August 1991).

61. "Taking Care of Business," *The Economist* (February 18, 1989): 28.

62. Neal Peirce, "Cities Must Learn When to Say No," *Houston Chronicle,* February 13, 1989, p. A12.

63. The Corporation for Enterprise Development, *The 1991 Development Report Card for the States* (Washington, D.C.: Corporation for Enterprise Development, 1991).

64. "Editor's Choice: America's Best Cities for Growing a Business," *Inc.* (June 1991): 78–79.

17 Criminal Justice pp. 475–502

1. See Federal Bureau of Investigation, *Crime in the United States* (Washington, D.C.: U.S. Department of Justice, various years). Also see Travis Hirschi and Michael Gottfredson, "Age and the Explanation of Crime," *American Journal of Sociology* 89 (November 1983): 552–84.

2. Federal Bureau of Investigation, *Crime in the United States* (1988).

3. See James Q. Wilson and Barbara Boland, *The Effect of Police on Crime* (Washington, D.C.: U.S. Department of Justice, 1979).

4. Ibid., pp. 12–17.

5. Bureau of Justice Statistics, *Sourcebook of Criminal Justice Statis-*

tics, 1990 (Washington, D.C.: U.S. Department of Justice, 1991), Tables 1–1, 1–13.

6. Federal Bureau of Investigation, *Crime in the United States* (1988).

7. *Gideon* v. *Wainwright,* 372 U.S. 335 (1963).

8. *Escobedo* v. *Illinois,* 378 U.S. 478 (1964).

9. *Miranda* v. *Arizona,* 384 U.S. 486 (1966).

10. Richard Seeburger and Stanley Wetlick, "Miranda in Pittsburgh: A Statistical Study," in Theodore Becker and Malcolm Freely, eds., *The Impact of Supreme Court Decisions,* 2d ed. (New York: Oxford University Press, 1973).

11. *Colorado* v. *Connelly,* 497 U.S. 157, 1075 S. Ct. 513 (1986).

12. *Illinois* v. *Perkins,* 496 U.S. 110 S. Ct. 2394 (1990).

13. *Mapp* v. *Ohio,* 307 U.S. 643 (1961).

14. *Maryland* v. *Garrison,* 480 U.S. 79 S. Ct. 1013 (1987).

15. *Florida* v. *Bostick,* 115 L.Ed. 2d 389, 111 S. Ct. 2382 (1991); *California* v. *Acevedo,* 114 L.Ed. 2d 619, 111 S. Ct. 1982 (1991).

16. Samuel Walker, *Popular Justice: A History of American Criminal Justice* (New York: Oxford University Press, 1980); Susan L. Rhodes, "Democratic Justice: The Responsiveness of Prison Population Size to Public Policy Preferences," *American Politics Quarterly* 18 (July, 1990): 337–375.

17. "Free at Last, Free at Last," *Time* 44 (November 2, 1987): 55.

18. See Edwin M. Schur and Hugo Adam Bedan, *Victimless Crimes: Two Sides of a Controversy* (Englewood Cliffs, N.J.: Prentice-Hall, 1974).

19. *Furman* v. *Georgia,* 408 U.S. 238 (1972).

20. *Gregg* v. *Georgia,* 428 U.S. 153 (1976).

21. *McCleskey* v. *Kemp,* 481 U.S. 279 (1987).

22. *Penry* v. *Lynaugh,* U.S. Law Week 4958; *Stanford* v. *Kentucky,* 57 U.S. Law Week 4973.

23. Bureau of Justice Statistics, *Capital Punishment in 1990* (Washington, D.C.: U.S. Department of Justice, 1991), p. 6.

24. *McCleskey* v. *Zant,* 113 L.Ed. 2d 517, 111 S. Ct. (1991).

25. Bureau of Justice Statistics, *Capital Punishment in 1990,* p. 8.

26. See Thorsten Sellin, *The Penalty of Death* (Beverly Hills, Calif.: Sage, 1980).

27. *Wall Street Journal,* April 4, 1989, p. A1.

28. Bureau of Justice Statistics, *Prisoners in 1990* (Washington, D.C.: U.S. Department of Justice, 1991), p. 7.

29. Tinsley Yarbrough, "The Alabama Prison Litigation," *Justice System Journal* 9, no. 3 (1984): 276.

30. "The Eyes of Justice Are on Texas," *Newsweek* (January 19, 1987): 55.

31. Richard B. Abell, "Beyond Willie Horton: The Battle of the Prison Bulge," *Policy Review* (Winter 1989): 32–35.

32. See William Nagel, "On Behalf of a Moratorium on Prison Construction," *Crime and Delinquency* (April 1977): 154–172; and Michael Sherman and Gordon Hawkins, *Imprisonment in America: Choosing the Future* (Chicago: University of Chicago Press, 1981).

33. Jim Thomas, Devin Keller, and Kathy Harris, "Issues and Misconceptions in Prison Litigation: A Critical View," *Criminology* 24 (November 1986): 775–97.

34. Deborah Hansen, "State Efforts Toward National Crime Control," *Journal of State Government* 63 (July/September 1990): 72–79.

35. "Electronic Detention Proves Successful," *P.A. Times* (June 16, 1987): 1, 3.

36. Warren E. Burger, "Prison Industries: Turning Warehouses into Factories with Fences," *Public Administration Review* 45 (November 1985): 754–57.

37. Ibid., p. 757 (fn. 7).

38. Brenda L. Wilson, "Captive

Work Force," *Governing* 4 (September 1991): 27.

39. Judy Farah, " 'Ratlord' Sent to Live in Own Dump," *The State* (July 14, 1987): 1.

40. John P. Conrad, "The Penal Dilemma and Its Emerging Solution," *Crime and Delinquency* (July 1985): 411–22.

41. Alan L. Otten, "Georgia Lets Some Offenders Do Time at Home Under Close Watch to Ease Crowding in Prisons," *Wall Street Journal,* July 23, 1987, p. 64.

42. "Take a Cruise? Not on These Boats," *Governing* 3 (June 1990): 15.

43. Charles H. Logan and Sharla P. Rausch, "Punish and Profit: The Emergence of Private Enterprise Prisons," *Justice Quarterly* (September 1985): 303–18; Samuel Jan Brakel, "Give Private Firms a Greater Role," *Wall Street Journal,* March 21, 1989, p. A19.

44. See Logan and Rausch, "Punish and Profit," p. 231; and John D. Donahue, *Prisons for Profit: Public Justice, Private Interests* (Washington, D.C.: Economic Policy Institute, 1988); and U.S. General Accounting Office, *Private Prisons: Cost Savings and DOP's Statutory Authority Need To Be Resolved.* Washington, D.C.: US-GAO; 1991.

45. For a helpful discussion of this issue, see Ira P. Robbins, "Privatization of Corrections: Defining the Issues," *Judicature* 69 (April/May 1986): 325–31.

46. Ibid., p. 33.

47. John J. DiIulio, Jr., and Anne Morrison Piehl, "Does Prison Pay?" *Brookings Review* 9 (Fall 1991): 28–35.

48. Peter Kerr, "Drug-Crime Link Underlined," *International Herald Tribune,* January 23–24, 1988, p. A3.

18 Environmental Policy pp. 503–529

1. See Lester R. Brown and Christopher Flavin, "The Earth's Vital

Signs," in Lester R. Brown, ed., *State of the World* (New York: W. W. Norton, 1988), pp. 4–5.

2. Ibid., p. 6.

3. Ibid., p. 7.

4. Joseph A. Davis, "Radon Answers Are Surfacing in the States," *Governing* 2 (February 1988): 54–56; Dag Ryen, "The Earth's Natural Waste," *State Government News* 30 (September 1987): 4.

5. Brown and Flavin, "The Earth's Vital Signs," p. 8.

6. "Still at Loggerheads: Oregon's Lumberjacks vs. Tree Huggers," *Time,* July 10, 1989, p. 24.

7. John J. Harrigan, *Political Change in the Metropolis,* 4th ed. (Glenview, Ill.: Scott, Foresman, 1989), pp. 22, 24.

8. J. Clarence Davies III, *The Politics of Pollution* (Indianapolis: Pegasus, 1970), p. 121.

9. Frank Trippett, "A Big Stink on the Pigeon," *Time,* June 6, 1988, p. 37; Orville E. Bach, Jr., "Battle over a Big, Two-Hearted River," *Southern,* (June 1988): 16.

10. Walter A. Rosenbaum, *Environmental Politics and Policy,* 2d ed. (Washington, DC: Congressional Quarterly Press, 1991), pp. 277–79.

11. Norman J. Vig and Michael E. Kraft, "Environmental Policy from the Seventies to the Eighties," in Norman J. Vig and Michael E. Kraft, eds., *Environmental Policy in the 1980s* (Washington, D.C.: Congressional Quarterly, 1984), p. 17.

12. Helen M. Ingram and Dean E. Mann, "Preserving the Clean Water Act: The Appearance of Environmental Victory," in Vig and Kraft, *Environmental Policy in the 1980s,* pp. 251–71.

13. James L. Regens and Margaret A. Reams, "The State Strategies for Regulating Groundwater Quality," *Social Science Quarterly* 69 (March 1988): 53–69.

14. Henry C. Kenski and Helen M. Ingram, "The Reagan Administration and Environmental Regulation: The Constraint of the Political Market," in Sheldon Kamieniecki, Robert O'Brien, and Michael Clark, eds., *Controversies in Environmental Policy* (Albany: SUNY Press, 1986), p. 278.

15. Robert Cameron Mitchell, "Public Opinion and Environmental Politics in the 1970s and 1980s," in Vig and Kraft, *Environmental Policy in the 1980s,* p. 61.

16. J. Clarence Davies, "Environmental Institutions and the Reagan Administration," in Vig and Kraft, *Environmental Policy in the 1980s,* pp. 143–60.

17. Mitchell, "Public Opinion and Environmental Politics," p. 61.

18. Bob Hall and Mary Lee Kerr, *1991–1992 Green Index* (Washington, D.C.: Island Press, 1991), p. 3.

19. Lettie Wenner, *The Environmental Decade in Court* (Bloomington: Indiana University Press, 1982).

20. Werner F. Grunbaum and Lettie M. Wenner, "Comparing Environmental Litigation in State and Federal Courts," *Publius* 10 (Summer 1980): 129–42.

21. See Barry G. Rabe, "The Politics of Environmental Dispute Resolution," *Policy Studies Journal* 16 (Spring 1988): 585–601.

22. Gail Bingham, *Resolving Environmental Disputes* (Washington, D.C.: Conservation Foundation, 1986).

23. Hall and Kerr, *1991–1992 Green Index,* p. 70.

24. Ibid.

25. Don Phillips, "Garbage on the Rail: Out of Sight, Out of Mind," *Washington Post,* December 22, 1991, p. A21.

26. Paul Doyle, "The Garbage Crisis," *State Legislatures* 13 (October 1987): 24.

27. Ibid., p. 25.

28. Zachary A. Smith, *The Environmental Policy Paradox* (Englewood Cliffs, N.J.: Prentice-Hall, 1991).

29. Todd Sloane, "Recycling Laws Proliferate," *City & State* 8 (November 4, 1991): 15.

30. "St. Cloud Gives Cash for Trash," *Governing* (April 1988): 16.

31. Susan Fine, "Composting Nature's 'Garbage,'" *World Watch* 2 (January/February 1989): 5.

32. David H. Folz and Joseph M. Hazlett, "A National Survey of Municipal Strategies for Marketing Recyclables," a paper presented at the annual meeting of the Southern Political Science Association, Tampa, November 1991.

33. Ibid.

34. Sloane, "Recycling Laws Proliferate," p. 18.

35. "Those Plastic Packages Aren't Welcome in Suffolk County, N.Y., Anymore," *Governing* (July 1988): 14.

36. Josh Barbanel, "Plastic's Image Up on Eve of Long Island Ban," *New York Times,* December 31, 1991, pp. A1.

37. Eric N. Berg, "McDonald's Planning to Cut Its Garbage," *New York Times,* April 17, 1991, p. A8.

38. Neal R. Peirce, "Hats Off to the Pariah Barge," *The State,* May 5, 1987, p. 14.

39. Richard Severo, "Monument to Modern Man: 'Alp' of Trash Is Rising," *New York Times,* April 13, 1989, p. 13.

40. Congressional Budget Office, *Hazardous Waste Management: Recent Changes and Policy Alternatives* (Washington, D.C.: U.S. Government Printing Office, 1985).

41. Clifford S. Russell, "Economic Incentives in the Management of Hazardous Wastes," paper presented at the Colloquium on New Directions in Environmental Policy, Columbia University Law School, October 1987.

42. Hall and Kerr, *1991–1992 Green Index,* p. 63.

43. Ann O'M. Bowman and James P. Lester, "Implementing Intergovernmental Policy: The Resource Conservation and Recovery Act of 1976," paper presented at the annual meeting of the Southern Political Science Association, November 1987.

44. James E. McCarthy, "Hazardous Waste Management: RCRA Oversight in the 100th Congress" (Washington, D.C.: Congressional Research Service, March 4, 1988).

45. U.S. Environmental Protection Agency, "Superfund Progress Report," May 1990.

46. James P. Lester, "Superfund Implementation: Exploring the Conditions of Environmental Gridlock," *Environmental Impact Assessment Review* (1988): 63–70.

47. Scott Ridley, *The State of the States 1987* (Washington, D.C.: Fund for Renewable Energy and the Environment, 1987).

48. R. Steven Brown, "Siting Hazardous Waste Facilities," *State Government News* 30 (September 1987): 10–11, 17.

49. Jonathan Walters, "The Poisonous War over Hazardous Waste," *Governing* 5 (November 1991): 32–35.

50. Don Harris, "Winning and Losing — A Hazardous Waste Standoff," *State Legislatures* 18 (January 1992): 28.

51. Walters, "The Poisonous War over Hazardous Waste."

52. Susan Biemesderfer, "Stopping Pollution Before It Starts," *State Legislatures* 17 (August 1991): 36–37.

53. Richard C. Kearney and John J. Stucker, "Interstate Compacts and the Management of Low-Level Radioactive Wastes," *Public Administration Review* 42 (January/February 1985): 14–24.

54. Ibid.

55. Riley E. Dunlap, "Public Opinion on the Environment in the Reagan Era," *Environment* 29 (July/August 1987): 6–11, 32–37.

56. Allan R. Gold, "Fight for Maine Coast Intensifies over Port Plan," *New York Times,* July 20, 1988, p. 8.

57. Richard W. Stevenson, "Facing Up to a Clean-Air Plan," *New York Times,* April 3, 1989, p. 28.

58. Gina Kolata, "How Much Is Too Much to Pay to Meet Standards for Smog?" *New York Times,* April 3, 1989, pp. 1, 11.

59. Keith Schneider, "Under Oil's Powerful Spell, Alaska Was Off Guard," *New York Times,* April 2, 1989, pp. 1, 11.

60. Peter Applebome, "Energy Vs. Environment on Carolina Beaches," *New York Times,* January 30, 1989, pp. 1, 7.

61. "Economic Incentives and Environmental Policy," *Public's Capital* 2 (Spring 1991): 1.

62. Seth Mydans, "8 Seek Better Work in 2-Year Ecology Project," *New York Times,* September 27, 1991.

Index